Praise for Robert Lowell and *Collected Poems*

"[Lowell] transformed American poetry."

—Charles McGrath, *The New York Times Magazine*

"Thanks to the *Collected Poems*, we have the rare pleasure of rediscovering that place where once our own spirits led the highest life."

—Eric Ormsby, *The New York Sun*

"Long awaited and much anticipated, [*Collected Poems*] is a show-stopping assertion of Lowell's ambition, industry and art."

—Carmine Starnino, *The Globe and Mail* (Toronto)

"[Lowell's poems are] endlessly approachable, wonderfully communicative and perfectly inexhaustible: stately, supple, personal and resourceful."

—Michael Hofmann, *London Review of Books*

"*Collected Poems* liberates the poetry from the poet we think we know. It allows us to see Lowell as more than one person at the same time. As a result Lowell emerges as a poet who loves language in the way that a painter loves the feeling of paint . . . Bidart's visceral relationship to language violates the decorum of textual editing so passionately that the work of editing Lowell's poems feels like a continuation of the process by which the poems were made, a dialogue between two people that by its nature cannot end conclusively . . . Bidart has given Lowell life after death."

—James Longenbach, *Boston Review*

Robert Lowell
Collected Poems

ROBERT LOWELL was born in Boston in 1917. He attended Harvard University and Kenyon College, where he received his B.A. in 1940. Lowell was the dominant poetic voice of his era, the renowned and controversial author of many books of poems, plays, and translations, famously a conscientious objector during World War II, and a forceful opponent of America's involvement in Vietnam. His ongoing interrogation of his familial legacy, his personal struggle with manic depression, and his mastery of the traditions of English poetry formed the foundation for the groundbreaking, autobiographical *Life Studies* (1959) and the books that followed it, including *For the Union Dead* (1964), *Near the Ocean* (1967), *History* (1973), and *Day by Day* (1977).

Robert Lowell died in New York City in 1977. His *Collected Prose* was published in 1987, and *The Letters of Robert Lowell* in 2005.

FRANK BIDART is the author of several works of poetry, including *In the Western Night: Collected Poems 1965–90* (1990), *Desire* (1997), and *Star Dust* (2005). He teaches at Wellesley College.

DAVID GEWANTER is the author of two books of poems, *In the Belly* (1997) and *The Sleep of Reason* (2003). He teaches at Georgetown University.

ALSO BY ROBERT LOWELL

Land of Unlikeness (1944)

Lord Weary's Castle (1946)

The Mills of the Kavanaughs (1951)

Life Studies (1959)

Phaedra (translation) (1961)

Imitations (1961)

For the Union Dead (1964)

The Old Glory (plays) (1965)

Near the Ocean (1967)

The Voyage & other versions of poems by Baudelaire (1969)

Prometheus Bound (translation) (1969)

Notebook 1967–68 (1969) (revised and expanded edition, *Notebook*, 1970)

History (1973)

For Lizzie and Harriet (1973)

The Dolphin (1973)

Selected Poems (1976) (revised edition, 1977)

Day by Day (1977)

The Oresteia of Aeschylus (translation) (1978)

Collected Prose (1987)

The Letters of Robert Lowell (2005)

Selected Poems (2007)

Collected Poems

Robert Lowell

Collected Poems

Edited by Frank Bidart and David Gewanter
with the editorial assistance of DeSales Harrison

Farrar, Straus and Giroux
New York

Farrar, Straus and Giroux
19 Union Square West, New York 10003

Grateful acknowledgment is made to Frank Parker to reproduce his original frontispiece illustrations, and to the following to reproduce copyrighted material: *Lord Weary's Castle*, copyright © 1946 and renewed 1974 by Robert Lowell, reprinted by permission of Harcourt, Inc.; *The Mills of the Kavanaughs*, copyright © 1951, 1950, 1948, 1947, 1946 by Robert Lowell, renewed 1979, 1978 by Harriet W. Lowell, renewed 1976, 1975, 1974 by Robert Lowell, reprinted by permission of Harcourt, Inc.; manuscript poems reprinted by permission of the Houghton Library, Harvard University, and the Harry Ransom Humanities Research Center, the University of Texas at Austin; "After Enjoying Six or Seven Essays On Me" by Robert Lowell, copyright © 1977 by Robert Lowell, reprinted by permission of *Salmagundi Magazine*; "Chronology" from *The Critical Response to Robert Lowell* edited by Steven Gould Axelrod, copyright © 1999 by Steven Gould Axelrod, reprinted by permission of the Greenwood Publishing Group Inc., Westport, CT. Previously uncollected poems first appeared in *A New Anthology of Modern Poetry* (The Modern Library/Random House), *The Atlantic Monthly*, *Botteghe Oscure*, *Common Sense*, *Hika*, *The Kenyon Review*, *The New Republic*, *The New Review*, *The New York Review of Books*, *Lincoln and the Gettysburg Address* (University of Illinois Press), *Partisan Review*, *Perspectives U.S.A.*, *Ploughshares*, and *Western Review*. *Land of Unlikeness* in its entirety was first published by Cummington Press.

The Library of Congress has cataloged the hardcover edition as follows:
Lowell, Robert, 1917–1977.
    [Poems]
    Collected poems / Robert Lowell ; edited by Frank Bidart and David Gewanter ;
with the editorial assistance of DeSales Harrison.— 1st ed.
        p.   cm.
    Includes bibliographical references (p.   ) and index.
    ISBN-13: 978-0-374-12617-9 (alk. paper)
    ISBN-10: 0-374-12617-8 (alk. paper)
    I. Title.

PS3523.O89 A17 2003
811'.52—dc20

96017254

Paperback ISBN-13: 978-0-374-53032-7
Paperback ISBN-10: 0-374-53032-7

www.fsgbooks.com

10 9 8 7 6 5 4 3 2 1

Contents

Introduction

"You Didn't Write, You *Rewrote*"

Robert Lowell was above all an audacious *maker*—in poetry, one of the great makers of the twentieth century. He became famous as a "confessional" writer, but he scorned the term. His audacity, his resourcefulness and boldness lie not in his candor but his art. Therefore the present edition: by laying before the reader materials often buried since first publication, the present edition hopes to bring into focus Lowell's practice as an artist, his nature as a maker.

When he published in 1973 three sonnet books—*The Dolphin*, *History* and *For Lizzie and Harriet*—many reviewers were bewildered: two of these volumes came out of his previous book called *Notebook*. *The Times Literary Supplement*, in what we may characterize as an unsympathetic view of revision, with its review ran a drawing of a meat grinder chewing up books, turned by a man who stares out at us fixedly, demonically, with a half-smile. The man is, of course, Robert Lowell. Yet look at his work with any closeness and you discover that rethinking work, reimagining it, rewriting it was fundamental to him from the very beginning, and pervasive until the end. This was not a new swerve, an odd idiosyncrasy on his part; it proceeded very deeply from the nature of what he was doing as a writer, what he imagined his work as a writer to be.

In *History*, in a sonnet titled "Randall Jarrell," the ghost of Jarrell appears to Lowell.

> The dream went like a rake of sliced bamboo,
> slats of dust distracted by a downdraw;
> I woke and knew I held a cigarette;
> I looked, there was none, could have been none;
> I slept off years before I woke again,
> palming the floor, shaking the sheets. I saw

nothing was burning. I awoke, I saw
I was holding two lighted cigarettes. . . .
They come this path, old friends, old buffs of death.
Tonight it's Randall, his spark still fire though humble,
his gnawed wrist still cradled like *Kitten*. "What kept you so long,
racing the cooling grindstone of your ambition?
You didn't write, you *re*wrote. . . . But tell me,
Cal, why did we live? Why do we die?"

The dreampath the dead take to reach us is inseparable from confusion, truth and untruth without cease shifting places. Jarrell's assertion that "You didn't write, you *re*wrote" breaks in with an air of fact, accuracy, ironic summary. Because it so jaggedly punctuates the word "ambition," to my ear there is also muted but unmistakable accusation. (Jarrell was, of course, a crucial figure for Lowell. In the 1961 *Paris Review* interview with Frederick Seidel, he says that "Jarrell's a great man of letters, a very informed man, and the best critic of my generation, the best professional poet." I once said to Lowell that I thought the revisions that he had made in the text of *Life Studies* between the English and American editions—the English appeared first—were great improvements, especially the punctuation. He smiled with pleasure, and said that Randall Jarrell had helped him with them.)

There is a long dialogue, an argument running through Lowell's poetry and prose about his own practice as a writer. In the *Paris Review* interview, he tells a story that could seem simply to be about the merits of using rhyme. He says that in his early work, he usually began by writing a poem out in blank verse, and then put in rhymes. "The most I could hope for at first was that the rhymed version wouldn't be much inferior to the blank verse." But he discovered that, by much labor, he could make the rhymed version *better*, much better than the unrhymed version. This is a story about what the difficulties of rhyme, in his early work, allowed him to do, but it is also a story about revision itself. This early experience sets the pattern for his writing life. It suggests the reason that he was again and again willing to perform an act of self-criticism that at some moments he thought of as humiliating. I spent a great deal of time with him when he was working on the poems of his last ten years; more than once he said at the end of the day, to the amusement of whoever happened to be present, "Well, it's been another day of humiliations."

"Waking Early Sunday Morning" crystallizes his nature as a maker, his seriousness, his willingness radically to rethink his work. Generally considered one of Lowell's greatest poems, it is the poem by Lowell that Elizabeth Bishop perhaps most admired. The book version is startlingly different from the first version, published in *The New York Review of Books*. The book version not only reorders the stanzas in the second half of the poem, but two of the most eloquent stanzas are (in effect) cut. This is the original opening:

> Oh to break loose, like the chinook
> salmon jumping and falling back,
> nosing up to the impossible
> stone and bone-crushing waterfall—
> raw-jawed, weak fleshed there, stopped by ten
> steps of the roaring ladder, and then
> to clear the top on the last try,
> alive enough to spawn and die.
>
> Stop, back off. The salmon breaks
> water, and now my body wakes
> to feel the unpolluted joy
> and criminal leisure of a boy—
> no rainbow smashing a dry fly
> in the white run is free as I,
> here squatting like a dragon on
> time's hoard before the day's begun!
>
> Time to grub up and junk the year's
> output, a dead wood of dry verse:
> dim confession, coy revelation,
> liftings, listless self-imitation,
> whole days when I could hardly speak,
> came pluming home unshaven, weak
> and willing to read anyone
> things done before and better done.
>
> Fierce, fireless mind, running down hill . . .

The poem then shifts restlessly among the things that the eye sees (the harbor, a glass of water), that the mind overhears and broods upon (the church's "new electric bells," the Bible) seeking to "break loose." The "dregs and dreck" of the woodshed lead him to St. Paul and Christianity, "the wordless sign, the tinkling cymbal." Then these lines:

> Empty, irresolute, ashamed,
> when the sacred texts are named,
> I lie here on my bed apart,
> and when I look into my heart,
> I discover none of the great
> subjects: death, friendship, love and hate—
> only old china doorknobs, sad,
> slight, useless things to calm the mad.
>
> Oh to break loose now. All life's grandeur
> is something with a girl in summer . . .

The intimacy, the "nakedness" of the two stanzas beginning "Time to grub up and junk . . ." and "Empty, irresolute, ashamed" (nakedness intensified in the second) is important. The poem as a whole dramatizes the spirit's oscillations as it moves among the things of its world, what is left of the cultural, religious, political past, until at last it projects (in the final stanza) a future based on that past:

> Pity the planet, all joy gone
> from this sweet volcanic cone;
> peace to our children when they fall
> in small war on the heels of small
> war—until the end of time
> to police the earth, a ghost
> orbiting forever lost
> in our monotonous sublime.

The inwardness of the two earlier stanzas becomes a recurring pole, a recurring "drop" into the uncertain self-accusing self, that is part of this landscape.

For the volume *Near the Ocean*, Lowell radically rewrote both "naked" stanzas, as well as reordered the second half of the poem. The two recast stanzas become much cooler in revision, more "impersonal." This is the first:

Vermin run for their unstopped holes;
in some dark nook a fieldmouse rolls
a marble, hours on end, then stops;
the termite in the woodwork sleeps—
listen, the creatures of the night
obsessive, casual, sure of foot,
go on grinding, while the sun's
daily remorseful blackout dawns.

Fierce, fireless mind, running downhill . . .

This has grandeur, substituting a vision of the world's processes ("the creatures of the night . . . go on grinding") for frustration with the writing self. Nonetheless, after the slightly-on-stilts formality of the tetrameter couplets of the poem's opening, the sudden intimacy of tone in the original disarms; I miss it. This is even more true of the second rewritten stanza. Supplanting "Empty, irresolute, ashamed, / when the sacred texts are named," the new version reads:

When will we see Him face to face?
Each day, He shines through darker glass.
In this small town where everything
is known, I see His vanishing
emblems, His white spire and flag-
pole sticking out above the fog,
like old white china doorknobs, sad,
slight, useless things to calm the mad.

In the original, Lowell follows the famous injunction heard by Sidney, "Look in thy heart, and write"; but what he finds there is useless, bric-a-brac, sad "things to calm the mad." In one sense this act is merely "personal" (perhaps most human beings feel that all too often they find there "death, friendship, love and hate"), but it is "impersonal" insofar as it discovers, for this consciousness on this Sunday morning, the bewildering uselessness of a great inherited injunction. The simplicity of diction and delicacy of rhythm in the original version contrast touchingly with the more allusive, rhythmically relentless stanza that precedes it. The contrast is lost in revision.

But the order of stanzas as revised is *much* better. Lowell's dilemma was that the original "naked" stanzas cannot simply be plugged into the new order. In the revised order, the noose tightens more compellingly as options get closed off and the spirit is forced to conclude "Pity the planet. . . ." "No weekends for the gods now" is far more powerful as the penultimate stanza; "Sing softer!" (originally penultimate) in retrospect seems thin. This new order depends upon the rewriting of the second "naked" stanza. If "Empty, irresolute, ashamed" is put into its old position, replacing "When will we see Him face to face," the stanza that then follows ("Hammering military splendor") is overemphatic and awkward; and the next "Sing softer!" lines, with their shift back to self-accusation, seem to come too quickly.

The two versions refuse to be joined. I think that the poem as a whole is greater in the revised version; but I can't escape the haunting memory of the first.

Well, at some point I said something like this to Lowell. To my amazement he said that he felt the same way. I had fiddled with and fiddled with the lines, trying to join the two versions, and failed. He had done the same. I bemoaned this state of affairs.

His reply is something that I have never forgotten, something that resonates throughout his work: "But they both exist."

The tradition of thinking about poetry in which I grew up does not for the most part imagine this statement as a satisfactory answer to the problem. Many great works of art exist in versions that partly are incompatible: *Messiah, Don Giovanni*. But we perceive these (if we think of them at all) as exceptions, oddities resulting from the vagaries of available performance resources. The usual cultural assumption is that there can be a perfect version that contains all the virtues of a given work of art. This is one reason why many editions of *Hamlet*, for example, say little to the reader about the fact that the text they offer is a conflation of shorter, quite distinct texts (in a handful of lines, the editor must choose which version to print).

Lowell was willing to live with the idea that they both exist, that there is no perfect version of "Waking Early Sunday Morning." *That we need not choose*. He often said that something is lost in revision even if something is gained. Each version is a journey: each occasion that he inhabited the material, slightly different. On the actual physical page, because of what James calls "the thrilling ups and downs of the compositional problem," the marvelous inwardness of the magazine version of "Waking Early Sunday Morning" eludes connection to the more powerful movement between cultural issues, political issues, visionary passages in the second.

For most readers, of course, they don't both exist; the magazine version has been invisible. One aim of the present edition is to allow both to exist. In an appendix the poem as first printed appears in its entirety; the reader can experience the original stanzas in their original order. This is true for several poems. In the volume as a whole, the reader will find the much longer magazine version of "Beyond the Alps" (prolix, and I think not a success, but fascinating as a seedbed for other poems); the well-known version at the beginning of *Life Studies*; the version Lowell printed in *For the Union Dead*, with a stanza restored at the suggestion of John Berryman; Lowell's final, isolated, perhaps best version of the restored stanza, in *History*. My co-editor, David Gewanter, and I, along with our research assistant, DeSales Harrison, have attempted to look at every published version of every Lowell poem. If there is a set of lines that seems particularly interesting or important that did not survive into the final version, it is included in the notes. This has constantly involved, of course, judgment on our part: another set of readers would have chosen different passages. But from the very beginning of this project, I had no wish to do a variorum, which tends to leave every variant at the same level of importance. In general, I think, Lowell revised, rethought his poems very well. *Land of Unlikeness* appears, for the first time since its only publication, in an appendix. (Lowell never allowed it to be reprinted. What most people think of as his first book, *Lord Weary's Castle*, is not a "revision" of *Land of Unlikeness*—less than a quarter of it transforms material from the earlier book—but it is, I think, the book that *Land of Unlikeness* wanted to be.)

•

In a handful of cases, the main text is not Lowell's final version. A single example: "Night Sweat" is made up of two stanzas, the first a Shakespearean sonnet (i.e., three four-line sections followed by a rhymed couplet), the second a Petrarchan sonnet (i.e., a unit of eight lines followed by a unit of six lines, the six lines usually rhyming *abcabc*). The first stanza ends:

> one universe, one body . . . in this urn
> the animal night sweats of the spirit burn.

The heavy sense of closure embodied by this final rhymed couplet reflects a closed system. In an earlier line, "always inside me is the child who died." The spirit cannot escape the body which, one with the universe, is an urn in which the sweating spirit is encased and burns. The poet glimpses a partial, qualified release from this, in the poem's final seven lines:

> my wife . . . your lightness alters everything,
> and tears the black web from the spider's sack,
> as your heart hops and flutters like a hare.
> Poor turtle, tortoise, if I cannot clear
> the surface of these troubled waters here,
> absolve me, help me, Dear Heart, as you bear
> this world's dead weight and cycle on your back.

The poet's optimism ("your lightness alters everything") is partly reinforced but partly denied by the cyclical final rhymes (*abccba*). Transformation is not decisively closed off by a rhymed final couplet, but the agent of transformation still must bear "this world's dead weight," the cycle that will return, that cannot be shaken off.

Lowell and I had talked about the poem; it's a poem I particularly love. The second stanza (especially the first half) is weaker than the first; Lowell said that he had been frustrated by this and tried rewriting it, but never had been able to make it as good.

Then, in 1976, twelve years after the poem appeared in *For the Union Dead*, the galleys for *Selected Poems* arrived. The poem was printed as one stanza, in twenty-eight continuous lines, without a space. (The sonnets originally appeared on separate facing pages, so the printer had to guess.) I said something offhand like, "Well, that has to be fixed," and he said, "Oh no no no." He liked what he had read. He thought the difference in quality dissolved if there was no stanza break. We argued. In *Selected Poems* (revised and unrevised editions) it appears without a stanza break.

I cannot read the poem without the break. Literally, it's physically painful for me. The eye needs rest, physical space, after the "urn/burn" couplet; there is a large shift in feeling before the next phrases, "Behind me! You!" The reader must sense that the poem is made up of two balanced units of equal length—that the ending of each is different, formally.

That was not Lowell's judgment. The gain, for him, was greater than the loss. In the present edition the stanza break appears, with a note making clear that this was not Lowell's final decision. There are only a handful of such cases, and none other about which I feel so passionately.

•

There is a disputed territory at the heart of Lowell's work which has to do with the relation between the personal and impersonal. Many of his revisions (as in the case of "Waking Early Sunday Morning") reflect it as a kind of fault-line. He takes up the subject at some length in the *Paris Review* interview. He worried the subject the whole of his writing life. The question that hung over his work was, what does this have to do with other people? In what sense is the subject matter of this poem merely personal?

Elizabeth Bishop wrote a statement printed as flap copy for the American edition of *Life Studies*, a brilliant introduction to the book. She asserts that in these poems the question of impersonality is unproblematic: "A poem like 'My Last Afternoon with Uncle Devereux Winslow,' or 'Skunk Hour,' can tell us as much about the state of society as a volume of Henry James at his best." This reflects a confidence that one can untangle the relation between what is personal, specific, idiosyncratic and what is emblematic, public, general, societal, that I don't think Lowell himself felt. (Or do I read Bishop's "as much as" too naively, less hedged than it is?)

I think that Lowell was right not to feel confidence. This territory possessed him, and each new act of making offered new mysteries. In conclusion, two instances.

When I first read *Life Studies*, it did not end with "Skunk Hour." (I was an undergraduate at the University of California, Riverside, and I remember where I was standing when I plucked the Vintage paperback edition off the college bookstore shelf. I was quite overwhelmed. Standing up I read "Man and Wife," thought the poem was too much, and of course bought the book.)

The first paperback edition of *Life Studies* ended (following "Skunk Hour") with a poem called "Colonel Shaw and the Massachusetts 54th." It's the poem that we now know as "For the Union Dead," with little changed except the title. What happened was that Lowell, after he finished *Life Studies*, wrote something much more obviously "public" in range. For a short time, he thought that the real ending of *Life Studies*—this great sequence, his own favorite of his books—was a poem that openly contemplates the state of the nation, what the inherited past has come to. Quite quickly he decided that this was the wrong decision. But the fact that he tested it, tried it out by printing it in the first paperback edition, suggests how little the issue of the relation between the private and public was settled for him. And "For the Union Dead," of course, would not be the poem that it is if it had continued to be titled "Colonel Shaw and the Massachusetts 54th." The present title not only places the poem in relation to Allen Tate's "Ode to the Confederate Dead," but confidently lays claim to the territory of large public speech before a common history. As the title of a book, it promises the public aspect that is present in many of the book's poems.

I have just come across a letter by Lowell that startled me. It suggests how at least once for Lowell beneath revision lay the fulfillment of a project long desired, but even to himself perhaps only half-admitted. In 1959, he wrote to Bishop:

> In the hospital I spent a mad month or more rewriting *everything* in my three books [*Lord Weary's Castle*, *The Mills of the Kavanaughs*, *Life Studies*]. I arranged the poems chronologically, starting in Greek and Roman times and finally rose to air and the present with *Life Studies*. I felt that I had hit the skies, that all cohered. I[t] was mostly waste.

What is eerie about this is that it describes *History*—poems arranged chronologically, starting in Greek and Roman times, finally rising to include Lowell's present life. The thrill associated with madness, unreachable when sane, is the sensation that all "coheres." Thirteen years later I watched Lowell carve *History* out of *Notebook*, first as a long sequence called "Heroes," then the book it became. For two years he had carried around a copy of *Notebook* with dozens of penciled corrections on every page; he seemed incapable of resting with anything as provisional in feeling and texture as *Notebook*. But he never suggested that the project of *History* had lain in his mind for many years. Perhaps he had forgotten. I was both amanuensis and sounding board. How strange that the sounds coming across the room had begun so long before.

FRANK BIDART

A Note on the Text

The most radical editorial decision was the earliest made—to print *History* rather than *Notebook*. For a one-volume *Collected Poems* a choice had to be made. *Notebook* is less "well-written," perhaps—but, in its free-wheeling catch-as-catch-can improvisations, compelling in an entirely different way from *History*. Lowell in the end didn't think of either book as replacing the other, and hoped both would remain in print. When, in his *Selected Poems* the year before his death, he had to choose which to excerpt, he chose *History*.

•

No attempt has been made to regularize punctuation or spelling. "After-dinner" and "after dinner" and "afterdinner" are each different rhythmically (as are "blood-red" and "blood red" or "girl-friend" and "girlfriend" or "goldfinch-nest" and "goldfinchnest"). Subtleties of rhythm are the life of a poem; to make Lowell's lines conform to present-day practice would be to rub away some of his music.

Only obvious spelling errors have been corrected (e.g., "sun-guilded"). In a very small number of cases, commas have been deleted or added when their presence or absence confused the sense; such changes are given in the notes.

F.B.

Collected Poems

Lord Weary's Castle

(1946)

NOTE

My title comes from an old ballad:

> "It's Lambkin was a mason good
> As ever built wi' stane:
> He built Lord Wearie's castle
> But payment gat he nane . . ."

When I use the word *after* below the title of a poem, what follows is not a translation but an imitation which should be read as though it were an original English poem. The last line of "The Shako" is taken literally from a translation by C. F. McIntyre. "Our Lady of Walsingham" is an adaptation of several paragraphs from E. I. Watkin's *Catholic Art and Culture*. I hope that the source of "After the Surprising Conversions" will be recognized.

R.L.

Suscipe, Domine, munera pro tuorum commemoratione Sanctorum: ut, sicut illos passio gloriosos effecit; ita nos devotio reddat innocuos.

The Exile's Return

There mounts in squalls a sort of rusty mire,
Not ice, not snow, to leaguer the Hôtel
De Ville, where braced pig-iron dragons grip
The blizzard to their rigor mortis. A bell
Grumbles when the reverberations strip
The thatching from its spire,
The search-guns click and spit and split up timber
And nick the slate roofs on the Holstenwall
Where torn-up tilestones crown the victor. Fall
And winter, spring and summer, guns unlimber
And lumber down the narrow gabled street
Past your gray, sorry and ancestral house
Where the dynamited walnut tree
Shadows a squat, old, wind-torn gate and cows
The Yankee commandant. You will not see
Strutting children or meet
The peg-leg and reproachful chancellor
With a forget-me-not in his button-hole
When the unseasoned liberators roll
Into the Market Square, ground arms before
The Rathaus; but already lily-stands
Burgeon the risen Rhineland, and a rough
Cathedral lifts its eye. Pleasant enough,
Voi ch'entrate, and your life is in your hands.

The Holy Innocents

Listen, the hay-bells tinkle as the cart
Wavers on rubber tires along the tar
And cindered ice below the burlap mill
And ale-wife run. The oxen drool and start
In wonder at the fenders of a car,
And blunder hugely up St. Peter's hill.
These are the undefiled by woman—their
Sorrow is not the sorrow of this world:
King Herod shrieking vengeance at the curled
Up knees of Jesus choking in the air,

A king of speechless clods and infants. Still
The world out-Herods Herod; and the year,
The nineteen-hundred forty-fifth of grace,
Lumbers with losses up the clinkered hill
Of our purgation; and the oxen near
The worn foundations of their resting-place,
The holy manger where their bed is corn
And holly torn for Christmas. If they die,
As Jesus, in the harness, who will mourn?
Lamb of the shepherds, Child, how still you lie.

Colloquy in Black Rock

Here the jack-hammer jabs into the ocean;
My heart, you race and stagger and demand
More blood-gangs for your nigger-brass percussions,
Till I, the stunned machine of your devotion,
Clanging upon this cymbal of a hand,
Am rattled screw and footloose. All discussions

End in the mud-flat detritus of death.
My heart, beat faster, faster. In Black Mud
Hungarian workmen give their blood
For the martyre Stephen, who was stoned to death.

Black Mud, a name to conjure with: O mud
For watermelons gutted to the crust,
Mud for the mole-tide harbor, mud for mouse,
Mud for the armored Diesel fishing tubs that thud
A year and a day to wind and tide; the dust
Is on this skipping heart that shakes my house,

House of our Savior who was hanged till death.
My heart, beat faster, faster. In Black Mud
Stephen the martyre was broken down to blood:
Our ransom is the rubble of his death.

Christ walks on the black water. In Black Mud
Darts the kingfisher. On Corpus Christi, heart,
Over the drum-beat of St. Stephen's choir
I hear him, *Stupor Mundi*, and the mud
Flies from his hunching wings and beak—my heart,
The blue kingfisher dives on you in fire.

Christmas in Black Rock

Christ God's red shadow hangs upon the wall
The dead leaf's echo on these hours
Whose burden spindles to no breath at all;
Hard at our heels the huntress moonlight towers
And the green needles bristle at the glass
Tiers of defense-plants where the treadmill night
Churns up Long Island Sound with piston-fist.
Tonight, my child, the lifeless leaves will mass,
Heaving and heaping, as the swivelled light
Burns on the bell-spar in the fruitless mist.

Christ Child, your lips are lean and evergreen
Tonight in Black Rock, and the moon
Sidles outside into the needle-screen
And strikes the hand that feeds you with a spoon
Tonight, as drunken Polish night-shifts walk
Over the causeway and their juke-box booms
Hosannah in excelsis Domino.
Tonight, my child, the foot-loose hallows stalk
Us down in the blind alleys of our rooms;
By the mined root the leaves will overflow.

December, old leech, has leafed through Autumn's store
Where Poland has unleashed its dogs
To bay the moon upon the Black Rock shore:
Under our windows, on the rotten logs
The moonbeam, bobbing like an apple, snags
The undertow. O Christ, the spiralling years
Slither with child and manger to a ball
Of ice; and what is man? We tear our rags
To hang the Furies by their itching ears,
And the green needles nail us to the wall.

New Year's Day

Again and then again . . . the year is born
To ice and death, and it will never do
To skulk behind storm-windows by the stove
To hear the postgirl sounding her French horn
When the thin tidal ice is wearing through.
Here is the understanding not to love
Our neighbor, or tomorrow that will sieve
Our resolutions. While we live, we live

To snuff the smoke of victims. In the snow
The kitten heaved its hindlegs, as if fouled,
And died. We bent it in a Christmas box
And scattered blazing weeds to scare the crow
Until the snake-tailed sea-winds coughed and howled
For alms outside the church whose double locks
Wait for St. Peter, the distorted key.
Under St. Peter's bell the parish sea

Swells with its smelt into the burlap shack
Where Joseph plucks his hand-lines like a harp,
And hears the fearful *Puer natus est*
Of Circumcision, and relives the wrack
And howls of Jesus whom he holds. How sharp
The burden of the Law before the beast:
Time and the grindstone and the knife of God.
The Child is born in blood, O child of blood.

The Quaker Graveyard in Nantucket

(FOR WARREN WINSLOW, DEAD AT SEA)

Let man have dominion over the fishes of the sea and the fowls of the air and the beasts and the whole earth, and every creeping creature that moveth upon the earth.

I.
A brackish reach of shoal off Madaket,—
The sea was still breaking violently and night
Had steamed into our North Atlantic Fleet,
When the drowned sailor clutched the drag-net. Light
Flashed from his matted head and marble feet,
He grappled at the net
With the coiled, hurdling muscles of his thighs:
The corpse was bloodless, a botch of reds and whites,
Its open, staring eyes
Were lustreless dead-lights
Or cabin-windows on a stranded hulk
Heavy with sand. We weight the body, close
Its eyes and heave it seaward whence it came,
Where the heel-headed dogfish barks its nose
On Ahab's void and forehead; and the name
Is blocked in yellow chalk.
Sailors, who pitch this portent at the sea
Where dreadnaughts shall confess
Its hell-bent deity,
When you are powerless
To sand-bag this Atlantic bulwark, faced
By the earth-shaker, green, unwearied, chaste
In his steel scales: ask for no Orphean lute
To pluck life back. The guns of the steeled fleet
Recoil and then repeat
The hoarse salute.

II.

Whenever winds are moving and their breath
Heaves at the roped-in bulwarks of this pier,
The terns and sea-gulls tremble at your death
In these home waters. Sailor, can you hear
The Pequod's sea wings, beating landward, fall
Headlong and break on our Atlantic wall
Off 'Sconset, where the yawing S-boats splash
The bellbuoy, with ballooning spinnakers,
As the entangled, screeching mainsheet clears
The blocks: off Madaket, where lubbers lash
The heavy surf and throw their long lead squids
For blue-fish? Sea-gulls blink their heavy lids
Seaward. The winds' wings beat upon the stones,
Cousin, and scream for you and the claws rush
At the sea's throat and wring it in the slush
Of this old Quaker graveyard where the bones
Cry out in the long night for the hurt beast
Bobbing by Ahab's whaleboats in the East.

III.

All you recovered from Poseidon died
With you, my cousin, and the harrowed brine
Is fruitless on the blue beard of the god,
Stretching beyond us to the castles in Spain,
Nantucket's westward haven. To Cape Cod
Guns, cradled on the tide,
Blast the eelgrass about a waterclock
Of bilge and backwash, roil the salt and sand
Lashing earth's scaffold, rock
Our warships in the hand
Of the great God, where time's contrition blues
Whatever it was these Quaker sailors lost
In the mad scramble of their lives. They died
When time was open-eyed,
Wooden and childish; only bones abide
There, in the nowhere, where their boats were tossed
Sky-high, where mariners had fabled news

Of IS, the whited monster. What it cost
Them is their secret. In the sperm-whale's slick
I see the Quakers drown and hear their cry:
"If God himself had not been on our side,
If God himself had not been on our side,
When the Atlantic rose against us, why,
Then it had swallowed us up quick."

IV.
This is the end of the whaleroad and the whale
Who spewed Nantucket bones on the thrashed swell
And stirred the troubled waters to whirlpools
To send the Pequod packing off to hell:
This is the end of them, three-quarters fools,
Snatching at straws to sail
Seaward and seaward on the turntail whale,
Spouting out blood and water as it rolls,
Sick as a dog to these Atlantic shoals:
Clamavimus, O depths. Let the sea-gulls wail

For water, for the deep where the high tide
Mutters to its hurt self, mutters and ebbs.
Waves wallow in their wash, go out and out,
Leave only the death-rattle of the crabs,
The beach increasing, its enormous snout
Sucking the ocean's side.
This is the end of running on the waves;
We are poured out like water. Who will dance
The mast-lashed master of Leviathans
Up from this field of Quakers in their unstoned graves?

V.
When the whale's viscera go and the roll
Of its corruption overruns this world
Beyond tree-swept Nantucket and Woods Hole
And Martha's Vineyard, Sailor, will your sword
Whistle and fall and sink into the fat?

In the great ash-pit of Jehoshaphat
The bones cry for the blood of the white whale,
The fat flukes arch and whack about its ears,
The death-lance churns into the sanctuary, tears
The gun-blue swingle, heaving like a flail,
And hacks the coiling life out: it works and drags
And rips the sperm-whale's midriff into rags,
Gobbets of blubber spill to wind and weather,
Sailor, and gulls go round the stoven timbers
Where the morning stars sing out together
And thunder shakes the white surf and dismembers
The red flag hammered in the mast-head. Hide
Our steel, Jonas Messias, in Thy side.

VI.

OUR LADY OF WALSINGHAM

There once the penitents took off their shoes
And then walked barefoot the remaining mile;
And the small trees, a stream and hedgerows file
Slowly along the munching English lane,
Like cows to the old shrine, until you lose
Track of your dragging pain.
The stream flows down under the druid tree,
Shiloah's whirlpools gurgle and make glad
The castle of God. Sailor, you were glad
And whistled Sion by that stream. But see:

Our Lady, too small for her canopy,
Sits near the altar. There's no comeliness
At all or charm in that expressionless
Face with its heavy eyelids. As before,
This face, for centuries a memory,
Non est species, neque decor,
Expressionless, expresses God: it goes
Past castled Sion. She knows what God knows,
Not Calvary's Cross nor crib at Bethlehem
Now, and the world shall come to Walsingham.

VII.

The empty winds are creaking and the oak
Splatters and splatters on the cenotaph,
The boughs are trembling and a gaff
Bobs on the untimely stroke
Of the greased wash exploding on a shoal-bell
In the old mouth of the Atlantic. It's well;
Atlantic, you are fouled with the blue sailors,
Sea-monsters, upward angel, downward fish:
Unmarried and corroding, spare of flesh
Mart once of supercilious, wing'd clippers,
Atlantic, where your bell-trap guts its spoil
You could cut the brackish winds with a knife
Here in Nantucket, and cast up the time
When the Lord God formed man from the sea's slime
And breathed into his face the breath of life,
And blue-lung'd combers lumbered to the kill.
The Lord survives the rainbow of His will.

The First Sunday in Lent

I.

IN THE ATTIC

The crooked family chestnut sighs, for March,
Time's fool, is storming up and down the town;
The gray snow squelches and the well-born stamp
From sermons in a scolded, sober mob
That wears away the Sabbath with a frown,
A world below my window. What will clamp
The weak-kneed roots together when the damp
Aches like a conscience, and they grope to rob
The hero under his triumphal arch?

This is the fifth floor attic where I hid
My stolen agates and the cannister
Preserved from Bunker Hill—feathers and guns,
Matchlock and flintlock and percussion-cap;
Gettysburg etched upon the cylinder
Of Father's Colt. A Lüger of a Hun,
Once blue as Satan, breaks Napoleon,
My china pitcher. Cartridge boxes trap
A chipmunk on the saber where they slid.

On Troy's last day, alas, the populous
Shrines held carnival, and girls and boys
Flung garlands to the wooden horse; so we
Burrow into the lion's mouth to die.
Lord, from the lust and dust thy will destroys
Raise an unblemished Adam who will see
The limbs of the tormented chestnut tree
Tingle, and hear the March-winds lift and cry:
"The Lord of Hosts will overshadow us."

II.

THE FERRIS WHEEL

This world, this ferris wheel, is tired and strains
Its townsman's humorous and bulging eye,
As he ascends and lurches from his seat
And dangles by a shoe-string overhead
To tell the racing world that it must die.
Who can remember what his father said?
The little wheel is turning on the great
In the white water of Christ's blood. The red
Eagle of Ares swings along the lanes

Of camp-stools where the many watch the sky:
The townsman hangs, the eagle swings. It stoops
And lifts the ferris wheel into the tent
Pitched for the devil. But the man works loose,
He drags and zigzags through the circus hoops,
And lion-taming Satan bows and loops
His cracking tail into a hangman's noose;
He is the only happy man in Lent.
He laughs into my face until I cry.

Christmas Eve Under Hooker's Statue

Tonight a blackout. Twenty years ago
I hung my stocking on the tree, and hell's
Serpent entwined the apple in the toe
To sting the child with knowledge. Hooker's heels
Kicking at nothing in the shifting snow,
A cannon and a cairn of cannon balls
Rusting before the blackened Statehouse, know
How the long horn of plenty broke like glass
In Hooker's gauntlets. Once I came from Mass;

Now storm-clouds shelter Christmas, once again
Mars meets his fruitless star with open arms,
His heavy saber flashes with the rime,
The war-god's bronzed and empty forehead forms
Anonymous machinery from raw men;
The cannon on the Common cannot stun
The blundering butcher as he rides on Time—
The barrel clinks with holly. I am cold:
I ask for bread, my father gives me mould;

His stocking is full of stones. Santa in red
Is crowned with wizened berries. Man of war,
Where is the summer's garden? In its bed
The ancient speckled serpent will appear,
And black-eyed susan with her frizzled head.
When Chancellorsville mowed down the volunteer,
"All wars are boyish," Herman Melville said;
But we are old, our fields are running wild:
Till Christ again turn wanderer and child.

Buttercups

When we were children our papas were stout
And colorless as seaweed or the floats
At anchor off New Bedford. We were shut
In gardens where our brassy sailor coats
Made us like black-eyed susans bending out
Into the ocean. Then my teeth were cut:
A levelled broom-pole butt
Was pushed into my thin
And up-turned chin—
There were shod hoofs behind the horseplay. But
I played Napoleon in my attic cell
Until my shouldered broom
Bobbed down the room
With horse and neighing shell.

Recall the shadows the doll-curtains veined
On Ancrem Winslow's ponderous plate from blue
China, the breaking of time's haggard tide
On the huge cobwebbed print of Waterloo,
With a cracked smile across the glass. I cried
To see the Emperor's sabered eagle slide
From the clutching grenadier
Staff-officer
With the gold leaf cascading down his side—
A red dragoon, his plough-horse rearing, swayed
Back on his reins to crop
The buttercup
Bursting upon the braid.

In Memory of Arthur Winslow

I.

DEATH FROM CANCER

This Easter, Arthur Winslow, less than dead,
Your people set you up in Phillips House
To settle off your wrestling with the crab—
The claws drop flesh upon your yachting blouse
Until longshoreman Charon come and stab
Through your adjusted bed
And crush the crab. On Boston Basin, shells
Hit water by the Union Boat Club wharf:
You ponder why the coxes' squeakings dwarf
The *resurrexit dominus* of all the bells.

Grandfather Winslow, look, the swanboats coast
That island in the Public Gardens, where
The bread-stuffed ducks are brooding, where with tub
And strainer the mid-Sunday Irish scare
The sun-struck shallows for the dusky chub
This Easter, and the ghost
Of risen Jesus walks the waves to run
Arthur upon a trumpeting black swan
Beyond Charles River to the Acheron
Where the wide waters and their voyager are one.

II.

DUNBARTON

The stones are yellow and the grass is gray
Past Concord by the rotten lake and hill
Where crutch and trumpet meet the limousine
And half-forgotten Starks and Winslows fill
The granite plot and the dwarf pines are green
From watching for the day
When the great year of the little yeomen come
Bringing its landed Promise and the faith
That made the Pilgrim Makers take a lathe
And point their wooden steeples lest the Word be dumb.

O fearful witnesses, your day is done:
The minister from Boston waves your shades,
Like children, out of sight and out of mind.
The first selectman of Dunbarton spreads
Wreaths of New Hampshire pine cones on the lined
Casket where the cold sun
Is melting. But, at last, the end is reached;
We start our cars. The preacher's mouthings still
Deafen my poor relations on the hill:
Their sunken landmarks echo what our fathers preached.

III.

FIVE YEARS LATER

This Easter, Arthur Winslow, five years gone
I came to mourn you, not to praise the craft
That netted you a million dollars, late
Hosing out gold in Colorado's waste,
Then lost it all in Boston real estate.
Now from the train, at dawn
Leaving Columbus in Ohio, shell
On shell of our stark culture strikes the sun
To fill my head with all our fathers won
When Cotton Mather wrestled with the fiends from hell.

You must have hankered for our family's craft:
The block-house Edward made, the Governor,
At Marshfield, and the slight coin-silver spoons
The Sheriff beat to shame the gaunt Revere,
And General Stark's coarse bas-relief in bronze
Set on your granite shaft
In rough Dunbarton; for what else could bring
You, Arthur, to the veined and alien West
But devil's notions that your gold at least
Could give back life to men who whipped or backed the King?

IV.

A PRAYER FOR MY GRANDFATHER TO OUR LADY

Mother, for these three hundred years or more
Neither our clippers nor our slavers reached
The haven of your peace in this Bay State:
Neither my father nor his father. Beached
On these dry flats of fishy real estate,
O Mother, I implore
Your scorched, blue thunderbreasts of love to pour
Buckets of blessings on my burning head
Until I rise like Lazarus from the dead:
Lavabis nos et super nivem dealbabor.

"On Copley Square, I saw you hold the door
To Trinity, the costly Church, and saw
The painted Paradise of harps and lutes
Sink like Atlantis in the Devil's jaw
And knock the Devil's teeth out by the roots;
But when I strike for shore
I find no painted idols to adore:
Hell is burned out, heaven's harp-strings are slack.
Mother, run to the chalice, and bring back
Blood on your finger-tips for Lazarus who was poor."

Winter in Dunbarton

Time smiling on this sundial of a world
Sweltered about the snowman and the worm,
Sacker of painted idols and the peers
Of Europe; but my cat is cold, is curled
Tight as a boulder: she no longer smears
Her catnip mouse from Christmas, for the germ—
Mindless and ice, a world against our world—
Has tamped her round of brains into her ears.

This winter all the snowmen turn to stone,
Or, sick of the long hurly-burly, rise
Like butterflies into Jehovah's eyes
And shift until their crystals must atone

In water. Belle, the cat that used to rat
About my father's books, is dead. All day
The wastes of snow about my house stare in
Through idle windows at the brainless cat;
The coke-barrel in the corner whimpers. May
The snow recede and red clay furrows set
In the grim grin of their erosion, in
The caterpillar tents and roadslides, fat

With muck and winter dropsy, where the tall
Snow-monster wipes the coke-fumes from his eyes
And scatters his corruption and it lies
Gaping until the fungus-eyeballs fall

Into this eldest of the seasons. Cold
Snaps the bronze toes and fingers of the Christ
My father fetched from Florence, and the dead
Chatters to nothing in the thankless ground
His father screwed from Charlie Stark and sold

To the selectmen. Cold has cramped his head
Against his heart: my father's stone is crowned
With snowflakes and the bronze-age shards of Christ.

Mary Winslow

Her Irish maids could never spoon out mush
Or orange-juice enough; the body cools
And smiles as a sick child
Who adds up figures, and a hush
Grips at the poised relations sipping sherry
And tracking up the carpets of her four
Room kingdom. On the rigid Charles, in snow,
Charon, the Lubber, clambers from his wherry,
And stops her hideous baby-squawks and yells,
Wit's clownish afterthought. Nothing will go
Again. Even the gelded picador
Baiting the twinned runt bulls
With walrus horns before the Spanish Belles
Is veiled with all the childish bibelots.

Mary Winslow is dead. Out on the Charles
The shells hold water and their oarblades drag,
Littered with captivated ducks, and now
The bell-rope in King's Chapel Tower unsnarls
And bells the bestial cow
From Boston Common; she is dead. But stop,
Neighbor, these pillows prop
Her that her terrified and child's cold eyes
Glass what they're not: our Copley ancestress,
Grandiloquent, square-jowled and worldly-wise,
A Cleopatra in her housewife's dress;
Nothing will go again. The bells cry: "Come,
Come home," the babbling Chapel belfry cries:
"Come, Mary Winslow, come; I bell thee home."

Salem

In Salem seasick spindrift drifts or skips
To the canvas flapping on the seaward panes
Until the knitting sailor stabs at ships
Nosing like sheep of Morpheus through his brain's
Asylum. Seaman, seaman, how the draft
Lashes the oily slick about your head,
Beating up whitecaps! Seaman, Charon's raft
Dumps its damned goods into the harbor-bed,—
There sewage sickens the rebellious seas.
Remember, seaman, Salem fishermen
Once hung their nimble fleets on the Great Banks.
Where was it that New England bred the men
Who quartered the Leviathan's fat flanks
And fought the British Lion to his knees?

Concord

Ten thousand Fords are idle here in search
Of a tradition. Over these dry sticks—
The Minute Man, the Irish Catholics,
The ruined bridge and Walden's fished-out perch—
The belfry of the Unitarian Church
Rings out the hanging Jesus. Crucifix,
How can your whited spindling arms transfix
Mammon's unbridled industry, the lurch
For forms to harness Heraclitus' stream!
This Church is Concord—Concord where Thoreau
Named all the birds without a gun to probe
Through darkness to the painted man and bow:
The death-dance of King Philip and his scream
Whose echo girdled this imperfect globe.

Children of Light

Our fathers wrung their bread from stocks and stones
And fenced their gardens with the Redman's bones;
Embarking from the Nether Land of Holland,
Pilgrims unhouseled by Geneva's night,
They planted here the Serpent's seeds of light;
And here the pivoting searchlights probe to shock
The riotous glass houses built on rock,
And candles gutter by an empty altar,
And light is where the landless blood of Cain
Is burning, burning the unburied grain.

Rebellion

There was rebellion, father, when the mock
French windows slammed and you hove backward, rammed
Into your heirlooms, screens, a glass-cased clock,
The highboy quaking to its toes. You damned
My arm that cast your house upon your head
And broke the chimney flintlock on your skull.
Last night the moon was full:
I dreamed the dead
Caught at my knees and fell:
And it was well
With me, my father. Then
Behemoth and Leviathan
Devoured our mighty merchants. None could arm
Or put to sea. O father, on my farm
I added field to field
And I have sealed
An everlasting pact
With Dives to contract
The world that spreads in pain;
But the world spread
When the clubbed flintlock broke my father's brain.

At a Bible House

At a Bible House
Where smoking is forbidden
By the Prophet's law,
I saw you wiry, bed-ridden,
Gone in the kidneys; raw
Onions and a louse
Twitched on the sheet before
The palsy of your white
Stubble—a Mennonite
Or die-hard Doukabor,
God-rooted, hard. You spoke
Whistling gristle-words
Half inaudible
To us: of raw-boned birds
Migrating from the smoke
Of cities, of a gull
Perched on the redwood
Thrusting short awl-shaped leaves:
Three hundred feet of love
Where the Pacific heaves
The tap-root—wise above
Man's wisdom with the food
Squeezed from three thousand years'
Standing. It is all
A moment. The trees
Grow earthward: neither good
Nor evil, hopes nor fears,
Repulsion nor desire,
Earth, water, air or fire
Will serve to stay the fall.

The Drunken Fisherman

Wallowing in this bloody sty,
I cast for fish that pleased my eye
(Truly Jehovah's bow suspends
No pots of gold to weight its ends);
Only the blood-mouthed rainbow trout
Rose to my bait. They flopped about
My canvas creel until the moth
Corrupted its unstable cloth.

A calendar to tell the day;
A handkerchief to wave away
The gnats; a couch unstuffed with storm
Pouching a bottle in one arm;
A whiskey bottle full of worms;
And bedroom slacks: are these fit terms
To mete the worm whose molten rage
Boils in the belly of old age?

Once fishing was a rabbit's foot—
O wind blow cold, O wind blow hot,
Let suns stay in or suns step out:
Life danced a jig on the sperm-whale's spout—
The fisher's fluent and obscene
Catches kept his conscience clean.
Children, the raging memory drools
Over the glory of past pools.

Now the hot river, ebbing, hauls
Its bloody waters into holes;
A grain of sand inside my shoe
Mimics the moon that might undo
Man and Creation too; remorse,
Stinking, has puddled up its source;

Here tantrums thrash to a whale's rage.
This is the pot-hole of old age.

Is there no way to cast my hook
Out of this dynamited brook?
The Fisher's sons must cast about
When shallow waters peter out.
I will catch Christ with a greased worm,
And when the Prince of Darkness stalks
My bloodstream to its Stygian term . . .
On water the Man-Fisher walks.

The North Sea Undertaker's Complaint

Now south and south and south the mallard heads,
His green-blue bony hood echoes the green
Flats of the Weser, and the mussel beds
Are sluggish where the webbed feet spanked the lean
Eel grass to tinder in the take-off. South
Is what I think of. It seems yesterday
I slid my hearse across the river mouth
And pitched the first iced mouse into the hay.
Thirty below it is. I hear our dumb
Club-footed orphan ring the Angelus
And clank the bell-chain for St. Gertrude's choir
To wail with the dead bell the martyrdom
Of one more blue-lipped priest; the phosphorous
Melted the hammer of his heart to fire.

Napoleon Crosses the Berezina

"There will the eagles be gathered together"

Here Charlemagne's stunted shadow plays charades
With pawns and bishops whose play-canister
Shivers the Snowman's bones, and the Great Bear
Shuffles away to his ancestral shades,
For here Napoleon Bonaparte parades;
Hussar and cuirassier and grenadier
Ascend the tombstone steppes to Russia. Here
The eagles gather as the West invades
The Holy Land of Russia. Lord and glory
Of dragonish, unfathomed waters, rise!
Although your Berezina cannot gnaw
These soldier-plumed pontoons to matchwood, ice
Is tuning them to tumbrils, and the snow
Blazes its carrion-miles to Purgatory.

The Soldier

In time of war you could not save your skin.
Where is that Ghibelline whom Dante met
On Purgatory's doorstep, without kin
To set up chantries for his God-held debt?
So far from Campaldino, no one knows
Where he is buried by the Archiano
Whose source is Camaldoli, through the snows,
Fuggendo a piedi e sanguinando il piano,
The soldier drowned face downward in his blood.
Until the thaw he waited, then the flood
Roared like a wounded dragon over shoal
And reef and snatched away his crucifix
And rolled his body like a log to Styx;
Two angels fought with bill-hooks for his soul.

War

(After Rimbaud)

Where basilisk and mortar lob their lead
Whistling against the cloud sheep overhead,
Scarlet or green, before their black-tongued Sire,
The massed battalions flounder into fire
Until the furnace of affliction turns
A hundred thousand men to stone and burns
The poor dead in the summer grass. Their friend,
The earth, was low and thrifty to this end:
It is a god untouched by papal bulls,
The great gold chalice and the thuribles:
Cradled on its hosannahs, it will rock,
Dead to the world, until their mother, fat
With weeping underneath her cracked black hat,
Hands it her penny knotted in a sock.

Charles the Fifth and the Peasant

(After Valéry)

Elected Kaiser, burgher and a knight,
Clamped in his black and burly harness, Charles
Canters on Titian's sunset to his night;
A wounded wolfhound bites his spurs and snarls:
So middle-aged and common, it's absurd
To picture him as Caesar, the first cause
Behind whose leg-of-mutton beard, the jaws
Grate on the flesh and gristle of the Word.

The fir trees in the background buzz and lurch
To the disgruntled sing-song of their fears:
"How can we stop it, stop it, stop it?" sing
The needles; and the peasant, braining perch
Against a bucket, rocks and never hears
His Ark drown in the deluge of the King.

The Shako
(After Rilke)

Night and its muffled creakings, as the wheels
Of Blücher's caissons circle with the clock;
He lifts his eyes and drums until he feels
The clavier shudder and allows the rock
And Scylla of her eyes to fix his face:
It is as though he looks into a glass
Reflecting on this guilty breathing-space
His terror and the salvos of the brass
From Brandenburg. She moves away. Instead,
Wearily by the broken altar, Abel
Remembers how the brothers fell apart
And hears the friendless hacking of his heart,
And strangely foreign on the mirror-table
Leans the black shako with its white death's-head.

France

(From the Gibbet)

My human brothers who live after me,
See how I hang. My bones eat through the skin
And flesh they carried here upon the chin
And lipping clutch of their cupidity;
Now here, now there, the starling and the sea
Gull splinter the groined eyeballs of my sin,
Brothers, more beaks of birds than needles in
The fathoms of the Bayeux Tapestry:
"God wills it, wills it, wills it: it is blood."
My brothers, if I call you brothers, see:
The blood of Abel crying from the dead
Sticks to my blackened skull and eyes. What good
Are *lebensraum* and bread to Abel dead
And rotten on the cross-beams of the tree?

1790

(From the Memoirs of General Thiebault)

On Maundy Thursday when the King and Queen
Had washed and wiped the chosen poor and fed
Them from a boisterous wooden platter; here
We stood in forage-caps upon the green:
Green guardsmen of the Nation and its head.
The King walked out into the biting air,
Two gentlemen went with him; as they neared
Our middle gate, we stood aside for welcome;
A stone's throw lay between us when they cleared
Two horse-shoe flights of steps and crossed the Place Vendome.

"What a dog's life it is to be a king,"
I grumbled and unslung my gun; the chaff
And cinders whipped me and began to sting.
I heard our Monarch's Breughel-peasant laugh
Exploding, as a spaniel mucked with tar
Cut by his Highness' ankles on the double-quick
To fetch its stamping mistress. Louis smashed
Its backbone with a backstroke of his stick:
Slouching a little more than usual, he splashed
As boyish as a stallion to the Champ de Mars.

Between the Porch and the Altar

I.

MOTHER AND SON

Meeting his mother makes him lose ten years,
Or is it twenty? Time, no doubt, has ears
That listen to the swallowed serpent, wound
Into its bowels, but he thinks no sound
Is possible before her, he thinks the past
Is settled. It is honest to hold fast
Merely to what one sees with one's own eyes
When the red velvet curves and haunches rise
To blot him from the pretty driftwood fire's
Façade of welcome. Then the son retires
Into the sack and selfhood of the boy
Who clawed through fallen houses of his Troy,
Homely and human only when the flames
Crackle in recollection. Nothing shames
Him more than this uncoiling, counterfeit
Body presented as an idol. It
Is something in a circus, big as life,
The painted dragon, a mother and a wife
With flat glass eyes pushed at him on a stick;
The human mover crawls to make them click.
The forehead of her father's portrait peels
With rosy dryness, and the schoolboy kneels
To ask the benediction of the hand,
Lifted as though to motion him to stand,
Dangling its watch-chain on the Holy Book—
A little golden snake that mouths a hook.

II.

ADAM AND EVE

The Farmer sizzles on his shaft all day.
He is content and centuries away
From white-hot Concord, and he stands on guard.
Or is he melting down like sculptured lard?
His hand is crisp and steady on the plough.
I quarrelled with you, but am happy now
To while away my life for your unrest
Of terror. Never to have lived is best;
Man tasted Eve with death. I taste my wife
And children while I hold your hands. I knife
Their names into this elm. What is exempt?
I eye the statue with an awed contempt
And see the puritanical façade
Of the white church that Irish exiles made
For Patrick—that Colonial from Rome
Had magicked the charmed serpents from their home,
As though he were the Piper. Will his breath
Scorch the red dragon of my nerves to death?
By sundown we are on a shore. You walk
A little way before me and I talk,
Half to myself and half aloud. They lied,
My cold-eyed seedy fathers when they died,
Or rather threw their lives away, to fix
Sterile, forbidding nameplates on the bricks
Above a kettle. Jesus rest their souls!
You cry for help. Your market-basket rolls
With all its baking apples in the lake.
You watch the whorish slither of a snake
That chokes a duckling. When we try to kiss,
Our eyes are slits and cringing, and we hiss;
Scales glitter on our bodies as we fall.
The Farmer melts upon his pedestal.

III.

KATHERINE'S DREAM

It must have been a Friday. I could hear
The top-floor typist's thunder and the beer
That you had brought in cases hurt my head;
I'd sent the pillows flying from my bed,
I hugged my knees together and I gasped.
The dangling telephone receiver rasped
Like someone in a dream who cannot stop
For breath or logic till his victim drop
To darkness and the sheets. I must have slept,
But still could hear my father who had kept
Your guilty presents but cut off my hair.
He whispers that he really doesn't care
If I am your kept woman all my life,
Or ruin your two children and your wife;
But my dishonor makes him drink. Of course
I'll tell the court the truth for his divorce.
I walk through snow into St. Patrick's yard.
Black nuns with glasses smile and stand on guard
Before a bulkhead in a bank of snow,
Whose charred doors open, as good people go
Inside by twos to the confessor. One
Must have a friend to enter there, but none
Is friendless in this crowd, and the nuns smile.
I stand aside and marvel; for a while
The winter sun is pleasant and it warms
My heart with love for others, but the swarms
Of penitents have dwindled. I begin
To cry and ask God's pardon of our sin.
Where are you? You were with me and are gone.
All the forgiven couples hurry on
To dinner and their nights, and none will stop.
I run about in circles till I drop
Against a padlocked bulkhead in a yard
Where faces redden and the snow is hard.

IV.
AT THE ALTAR

I sit at a gold table with my girl
Whose eyelids burn with brandy. What a whirl
Of Easter eggs is colored by the lights,
As the Norwegian dancer's crystalled tights
Flash with her naked leg's high-booted skate,
Like Northern Lights upon my watching plate.
The twinkling steel above me is a star;
I am a fallen Christmas tree. Our car
Races through seven red-lights—then the road
Is unpatrolled and empty, and a load
Of ply-wood with a tail-light makes us slow.
I turn and whisper in her ear. You know
I want to leave my mother and my wife,
You wouldn't have me tied to them for life . . .
Time runs, the windshield runs with stars. The past
Is cities from a train, until at last
Its escalating and black-windowed blocks
Recoil against a Gothic church. The clocks
Are tolling. I am dying. The shocked stones
Are falling like a ton of bricks and bones
That snap and splinter and descend in glass
Before a priest who mumbles through his Mass
And sprinkles holy water; and the Day
Breaks with its lightning on the man of clay,
Dies amara valde. Here the Lord
Is Lucifer in harness: hand on sword,
He watches me for Mother, and will turn
The bier and baby-carriage where I burn.

To Peter Taylor on the Feast of the Epiphany

Peter, the war has taught me to revere
The rulers of this darkness, for I fear
That only Armageddon will suffice
To turn the hero skating on thin ice
When Whore and Beast and Dragon rise for air
From allegoric waters. Fear is where
We hunger: where the Irishmen recall
How wisdom trailed a star into a stall
And knelt in sacred terror to confer
Its fabulous gold and frankincense and myrrh:
And where the lantern-noses scrimmage down
The highway to the sea below this town
And the sharp barker rigs his pre-war planes
To lift old Adam's dollars for his pains;
There on the thawing ice, in red and white
And blue, the bugs are buzzing for the flight.
December's daylight hours have gone their round
Of sorrows with the sun into the sound,
And still the grandsires battle through the slush
To storm the landing biplanes with a rush—
Until their cash and somersaulting snare
Fear with its fingered stop-watch in mid-air.

As a Plane Tree by the Water

Darkness has called to darkness, and disgrace
Elbows about our windows in this planned
Babel of Boston where our money talks
And multiplies the darkness of a land
Of preparation where the Virgin walks
And roses spiral her enamelled face
Or fall to splinters on unwatered streets.
Our Lady of Babylon, go by, go by,
I was once the apple of your eye;
Flies, flies are on the plane tree, on the streets.

The flies, the flies, the flies of Babylon
Buzz in my ear-drums while the devil's long
Dirge of the people detonates the hour
For floating cities where his golden tongue
Enchants the masons of the Babel Tower
To raise tomorrow's city to the sun
That never sets upon these hell-fire streets
Of Boston, where the sunlight is a sword
Striking at the withholder of the Lord:
Flies, flies are on the plane tree, on the streets.

Flies strike the miraculous waters of the iced
Atlantic and the eyes of Bernadette
Who saw Our Lady standing in the cave
At Massabieille, saw her so squarely that
Her vision put out reason's eyes. The grave
Is open-mouthed and swallowed up in Christ.
O walls of Jericho! And all the streets
To our Atlantic wall are singing: "Sing,
Sing for the resurrection of the King."
Flies, flies are on the plane tree, on the streets.

The Crucifix

How dry time screaks in its fat axle-grease,
As spare November strikes us through the ice
And the Leviathan breaks water in the rice
Fields, at the poles, at the hot gates to Greece;
It's time: the old unmastered lion roars
And ramps like a mad dog outside the doors,
Snapping at gobbets in my thumbless hand.
The seaways lurch through Sodom's knees of sand
Tomorrow. We are sinking. "Run, rat, run,"
The prophets thunder, and I run upon
My father, Adam. Adam, if our land
Become the desolation of a hand
That shakes the Temple back to clay, how can
War ever change my old into new man?
Get out from under my feet, old man. Let me pass;
On Ninth Street, through the Hallowe'en's soaped glass,
I picked at an old bone on two crossed sticks
And found, to *Via et Vita et Veritas*
A stray dog's signpost is a crucifix.

Dea Roma

Augustus mended you. He hung the tongue
Of Tullius upon your rostrum, lashed
The money-lenders from your Senate-house;
And Brutus bled his forty-six per cent
For *Pax Romana*. Quiet as a mouse
Blood licks the king's cosmetics with its tongue.

Some years, your legions soldiered through this world
Under the eagles of Lord Lucifer;
But human torches lit the captains home
Where victims warped the royal crucifix:
How many roads and sewers led to Rome.
Satan is pacing up and down the world

These sixteen centuries, Eternal City,
That we have squandered since Maxentius fell
Under the Milvian Bridge; from the dry dome
Of Michelangelo, your fisherman
Walks on the waters of a draining Rome
To bank his catch in the Celestial City.

The Ghost

(After Sextus Propertius)

A ghost is someone: death has left a hole
For the lead-colored soul to beat the fire:
    Cynthia leaves her dirty pyre
    And seems to coil herself and roll
        Under my canopy,
Love's stale and public playground, where I lie
And fill the run-down empire of my bed.
I see the street, her potter's field, is red
And lively with the ashes of the dead;

But she no longer sparkles off in smoke:
It is the body carted to the gate
    Last Friday, when the sizzling grate
    Left its charred furrows on her smock
        And ate into her hip.
A black nail dangles from a finger-tip
And Lethe oozes from her nether lip.
Her thumb-bones rattle on her brittle hands,
As Cynthia stamps and hisses and demands:

"Sextus, has sleep already washed away
Your manhood? You forget the window-sill
    My sliding wore to slivers? Day
    Would break before the Seven Hills
        Saw Cynthia retreat
And climb your shoulders to the knotted sheet.
You shouldered me and galloped on bare feet
To lay me by the crossroads. Have no fear:
Notus, who snatched your promise, has no ear.

"But why did no one call in my deaf ear?
Your calling would have gained me one more day.
    Sextus, although you ran away
    You might have called and stopped my bier

A second by your door.
No tears drenched a black toga for your whore
When broken tilestones bruised her face before
The Capitol. Would it have strained your purse
To scatter ten cheap roses on my hearse?

"The State will make Pompilia's Chloris burn:
I knew her secret when I kissed the skull
    Of Pluto in the tainted bowl.
    Let Nomas burn her books and turn
        Her poisons into gold;
The finger-prints upon the potsherd told
Her love. You let a slut, whose body sold
To Thracians, liquefy my golden bust
In the coarse flame that crinkled me to dust.

"If Chloris' bed has left you with your head,
Lover, I think you'll answer my arrears:
    My nurse is getting on in years,
    See that she gets a little bread—
        She never clutched your purse;
See that my little humpback hears no curse
From her close-fisted friend. But burn the verse
You bellowed half a lifetime in my name:
Why should you feed me to the fires of fame?

"I will not hound you, much as you have earned
It, Sextus: I shall reign in your four books—
    I swear this by the Hag who looks
    Into my heart where it was burned:
        Propertius, I kept faith;
If not, may serpents suck my ghost to death
And spit it with their forked and killing breath
Into the Styx where Agamemnon's wife
Founders in the green circles of her life.

"Beat the sycophant ivy from my urn,
That twists its binding shoots about my bones
    Where apple-sweetened Anio drones

Through orchards that will never burn
　　While honest Herakles,
My patron, watches. Anio, you will please
Me if you whisper upon sliding knees:
'Propertius, Cynthia is here:
She shakes her blossoms when my waters clear.'

"You cannot turn your back upon a dream,
For phantoms have their reasons when they come:
　　We wander midnights: then the numb
　　Ghost wades from the Lethean stream;
　　　Even the foolish dog
Stops its hell-raising mouths and casts its clog;
At cock-crow Charon checks us in his log.
Others can have you, Sextus; I alone
Hold: and I grind your manhood bone on bone."

In the Cage

The lifers file into the hall,
According to their houses—twos
Of laundered denim. On the wall
A colored fairy tinkles blues
And titters by the balustrade;
Canaries beat their bars and scream.
We come from tunnels where the spade
Pick-axe and hod for plaster steam
In mud and insulation. Here
The Bible-twisting Israelite
Fasts for his Harlem. It is night,
And it is vanity, and age
Blackens the heart of Adam. Fear,
The yellow chirper, beaks its cage.

At the Indian Killer's Grave

"Here, also, are the veterans of King Philip's War, who burned villages and slaughtered young and old, with pious fierceness, while the godly souls throughout the land were helping them with prayer."   —HAWTHORNE.

Behind King's Chapel what the earth has kept
Whole from the jerking noose of time extends
Its dark enigma to Jehoshaphat;
Or will King Philip plait
The just man's scalp in the wailing valley! Friends,
Blacker than these black stones the subway bends
About the dirty elm roots and the well
For the unchristened infants in the waste
Of the great garden rotten to its root;
Death, the engraver, puts forward his bone foot
And Grace-with-wings and Time-on-wings compel
All this antique abandon of the disgraced
To face Jehovah's buffets and his ends.

The dusty leaves and frizzled lilacs gear
This garden of the elders with baroque
And prodigal embellishments but smoke,
Settling upon the pilgrims and their grounds,
Espouses and confounds
Their dust with the off-scourings of the town;
The libertarian crown
Of England built their mausoleum. Here
A clutter of Bible and weeping willows guards
The stern Colonial magistrates and wards
Of Charles the Second, and the clouds
Weep on the just and unjust as they will,—
For the poor dead cannot see Easter crowds
On Boston Common or the Beacon Hill
Where strangers hold the golden Statehouse dome
For good and always. Where they live is home:
A common with an iron railing: here
Frayed cables wreathe the spreading cenotaph

Of John and Mary Winslow and the laugh
Of Death is hacked in sandstone, in their year.

A green train grinds along its buried tracks
And screeches. When the great mutation racks
The Pilgrim Fathers' relics, will these placques
Harness the spare-ribbed persons of the dead
To battle with the dragon? Philip's head
Grins on the platter, fouls in pantomime
The fingers of kept time:
"Surely, this people is but grass,"
He whispers, "this will pass;
But, Sirs, the trollop dances on your skulls
And breaks the hollow noddle like an egg
That thought the world an eggshell. Sirs, the gulls
Scream from the squelching wharf-piles, beg a leg
To crack their crops. The Judgment is at hand;
Only the dead are poorer in this world
Where State and elders thundered *raca*, hurled
Anathemas at nature and the land
That fed the hunter's gashed and green perfection—
Its settled mass concedes no outlets for your puns
And verbal Paradises. Your election,
Hawking above this slime
For souls as single as their skeletons,
Flutters and claws in the dead hand of time."

When you go down this man-hole to the drains,
The doorman barricades you in and out;
You wait upon his pleasure. All about
The pale, sand-colored, treeless chains
Of T-squared buildings strain
To curb the spreading of the braced terrain;
When you go down this hole, perhaps your pains
Will be rewarded well; no rough-cast house
Will bed and board you in King's Chapel. Here
A public servant putters with a knife
And paints the railing red
Forever, as a mouse

Cracks walnuts by the headstones of the dead
Whose chiselled angels peer
At you, as if their art were long as life.

I ponder on the railing at this park:
Who was the man who sowed the dragon's teeth,
That fabulous or fancied patriarch
Who sowed so ill for his descent, beneath
King's Chapel in this underworld and dark?
John, Matthew, Luke and Mark,
Gospel me to the Garden, let me come
Where Mary twists the warlock with her flowers—
Her soul a bridal chamber fresh with flowers
And her whole body an ecstatic womb,
As through the trellis peers the sudden Bridegroom.

Mr. Edwards and the Spider

I saw the spiders marching through the air,
Swimming from tree to tree that mildewed day
    In latter August when the hay
    Came creaking to the barn. But where
      The wind is westerly,
Where gnarled November makes the spiders fly
Into the apparitions of the sky,
They purpose nothing but their ease and die
Urgently beating east to sunrise and the sea;

What are we in the hands of the great God?
It was in vain you set up thorn and briar
    In battle array against the fire
    And treason crackling in your blood;
      For the wild thorns grow tame
And will do nothing to oppose the flame;
Your lacerations tell the losing game
You play against a sickness past your cure.
How will the hands be strong? How will the heart endure?

A very little thing, a little worm,
Or hourglass-blazoned spider, it is said,
    Can kill a tiger. Will the dead
    Hold up his mirror and affirm
      To the four winds the smell
And flash of his authority? It's well
If God who holds you to the pit of hell,
Much as one holds a spider, will destroy,
Baffle and dissipate your soul. As a small boy

On Windsor Marsh, I saw the spider die
When thrown into the bowels of fierce fire:
    There's no long struggle, no desire
    To get up on its feet and fly—

It stretches out its feet
And dies. This is the sinner's last retreat;
Yes, and no strength exerted on the heat
Then sinews the abolished will, when sick
And full of burning, it will whistle on a brick.

But who can plumb the sinking of that soul?
Josiah Hawley, picture yourself cast
    Into a brick-kiln where the blast
    Fans your quick vitals to a coal—
        If measured by a glass,
How long would it seem burning! Let there pass
A minute, ten, ten trillion; but the blaze
Is infinite, eternal: this is death,
To die and know it. This is the Black Widow, death.

After the Surprising Conversions

September twenty-second, Sir: today
I answer. In the latter part of May,
Hard on our Lord's Ascension, it began
To be more sensible. A gentleman
Of more than common understanding, strict
In morals, pious in behavior, kicked
Against our goad. A man of some renown,
An useful, honored person in the town,
He came of melancholy parents; prone
To secret spells, for years they kept alone—
His uncle, I believe, was killed of it:
Good people, but of too much or little wit.
I preached one Sabbath on a text from Kings;
He showed concernment for his soul. Some things
In his experience were hopeful. He
Would sit and watch the wind knocking a tree
And praise this countryside our Lord has made.
Once when a poor man's heifer died, he laid
A shilling on the doorsill; though a thirst
For loving shook him like a snake, he durst
Not entertain much hope of his estate
In heaven. Once we saw him sitting late
Behind his attic window by a light
That guttered on his Bible; through that night
He meditated terror, and he seemed
Beyond advice or reason, for he dreamed
That he was called to trumpet Judgment Day
To Concord. In the latter part of May
He cut his throat. And though the coroner
Judged him delirious, soon a noisome stir
Palsied our village. At Jehovah's nod
Satan seemed more let loose amongst us: God
Abandoned us to Satan, and he pressed
Us hard, until we thought we could not rest

Till we had done with life. Content was gone.
All the good work was quashed. We were undone.
The breath of God had carried out a planned
And sensible withdrawal from this land;
The multitude, once unconcerned with doubt,
Once neither callous, curious nor devout,
Jumped at broad noon, as though some peddler groaned
At it in its familiar twang: "My friend,
Cut your own throat. Cut your own throat. Now! Now!"
September twenty-second, Sir, the bough
Cracks with the unpicked apples, and at dawn
The small-mouth bass breaks water, gorged with spawn.

The Slough of Despond

At sunset only swamp
Afforded pursey tufts of grass . . . these gave,
I sank. Each humus-sallowed pool
Rattled its cynic's lamp
And croaked: "We lay Apollo in his grave;
Narcissus is our fool."

My God, it was a slow
And brutal push! At last I struck the tree
Whose dead and purple arms, entwined
With sterile thorns, said: "Go!
Pluck me up by the roots and shoulder me;
The watchman's eyes are blind."

My arms swung like an axe.
And with my tingling sword I lopped the knot:
The labyrinthine East was mine
But for the asking. Lax
And limp, the creepers caught me by the foot,
And then I toed their line;

I walk upon the flood:
My way is wayward; there is no way out:
Now how the weary waters swell,—
The tree is down in blood!
All the bats of Babel flap about
The rising sun of hell.

The Blind Leading the Blind

Nothing will hustle: at his own sweet time
My father and his before him humanized
The seedy fields and heaped them on my house
Of straw; no flaring, hurtling thing surprised
Us out of season, and the corn-fed mouse
Reined in his bestial passions. Hildesheim
Survived the passing angel; who'd require
Our passion for the Easter? Satan snored
By the brass railing, while his back-log roared
And coiled its vapors on St. Gertrude's blue stone spire:

A land of mattocks; here the brothers strode,
Hulking as horses in their worsted hose
And cloaks and shin-guards—each had hooked his hoe
Upon his fellow's shoulder; by each nose
The aimless waterlines of eyeballs show
Their greenness. They are blind—blind to the road
And to its Maker. Here my father saw
The leadman trip against a pigpen, crash,
Legs spread, his codpiece split, his fiddle smash . . .
These mammoth vintners danced their blood out in the straw.

The Fens
(After Cobbett)

From Crowland to St. Edmund's to Ipswich
The fens are level as a drawing-board:
Great bowling greens divided by a ditch—
The grass as thick as grows on ground. The Lord
High Sheriff settles here, as on a sea,
When the parochial calm of sunset chills
The world to its four corners. And the hills
Are green with hops and harvest, and a bitch
Spuddles about a vineyard on a tree;

Here everything grows well. Here the fat land
Has no stone bigger than a ladybug,
No milkweed or wild onion can withstand
The sheriff's men, and sunlight sweats the slug.
Here the rack-renting system has its say:
At nightfall sheep as fat as hogs shall lie
Heaped on the mast and corncobs of the sty
And they will rise and take the landlord's hand;
The bailiff bears the Bell, the Bell, away.

The Death of the Sheriff

"forsitan et Priami fuerint quae fata, requiras?"

I.

NOLI ME TANGERE

We park and stare. A full sky of the stars
Wheels from the pumpkin setting of the moon
And sparks the windows of the yellow farm
Where the red-flannelled madmen look through bars
At windmills thrashing snowflakes by an arm
Of the Atlantic. Soon
The undertaker who collects antiques
Will let his motor idle at the door
And set his pine-box on the parlor floor.
Our homicidal sheriff howled for weeks;

We kiss. The State had reasons: on the whole,
It acted out of kindness when it locked
Its servant in this place and had him watched
Until an ordered darkness left his soul
A *tabula rasa*; when the Angel knocked
The sheriff laid his notched
Revolver on the table for the guest.
Night draws us closer in its bearskin wrap
And our loved sightless smother feels the tap
Of the blind stars descending to the west

To lay the Devil in the pit our hands
Are draining like a windmill. Who'll atone
For the unsearchable quicksilver heart
Where spiders stare their eyes out at their own
Spitting and knotted likeness? We must start:
Our aunt, his mother, stands
Singing *O Rock of Ages,* as the light
Wanderers show a man with a white cane

Who comes to take the coffin in his wain,
The thirsty Dipper on the arc of night.

The whiskey circulates, until I smash
The candelabrum from the mantel's top,
And scorch Poseidon on the panel where
He forks the blocks of Troy into the air.
A chipmunk shucks the strychnine in a cup;
The popping pine-cones flash
Like shore-bait on his face in oils. My bile
Rises, and beads of perspiration swell
To flies and splash the *Parmachenie Belle*
That I am scraping with my uncle's file.

I try the barb upon a pencilled line
Of Vergil. Nothing underneath the sun
Has bettered, Uncle, since the scaffolds flamed
On butchered Troy until Aeneas shamed
White Helen on her hams by Vesta's shrine . . .
All that the Greeks have won
I'll cancel with a sidestroke of my sword;
Now I can let my father, wife and son
Banquet Apollo for Laomedon:
Helen will satiate the fire, my Lord.

I search the starlight . . . Helen will appear,
Pura per noctem in luce . . . I am chilled,
I drop the barbless fly into my purse
Beside his nickel shield. It is God's curse,
God's, that has purpled Lucifer with fear
And burning. God has willed;
I lift the window. Digging has begun,
The hill road sparkles, and the mourners' cars
Wheel with the whited sepulchres of stars
To light the worldly dead-march of the sun.

The Dead in Europe

After the planes unloaded, we fell down
Buried together, unmarried men and women;
Not crown of thorns, not iron, not Lombard crown,
Not grilled and spindle spires pointing to heaven
Could save us. Raise us, Mother, we fell down
Here hugger-mugger in the jellied fire:
Our sacred earth in our day was our curse.

Our Mother, shall we rise on Mary's day
In Maryland, wherever corpses married
Under the rubble, bundled together? Pray
For us whom the blockbusters marred and buried;
When Satan scatters us on Rising-day,
O Mother, snatch our bodies from the fire:
Our sacred earth in our day was our curse.

Mother, my bones are trembling and I hear
The earth's reverberations and the trumpet
Bleating into my shambles. Shall I bear,
(O Mary!) unmarried man and powder-puppet,
Witness to the Devil? Mary, hear,
O Mary, marry earth, sea, air and fire;
Our sacred earth in our day is our curse.

Where the Rainbow Ends

I saw the sky descending, black and white,
Not blue, on Boston where the winters wore
The skulls to jack-o'-lanterns on the slates,
And Hunger's skin-and-bone retrievers tore
The chickadee and shrike. The thorn tree waits
Its victim and tonight
The worms will eat the deadwood to the foot
Of Ararat: the scythers, Time and Death,
Helmed locusts, move upon the tree of breath;
The wild ingrafted olive and the root

Are withered, and a winter drifts to where
The Pepperpot, ironic rainbow, spans
Charles River and its scales of scorched-earth miles.
I saw my city in the Scales, the pans
Of judgment rising and descending. Piles
Of dead leaves char the air—
And I am a red arrow on this graph
Of Revelations. Every dove is sold
The Chapel's sharp-shinned eagle shifts its hold
On serpent-Time, the rainbow's epitaph.

In Boston serpents whistle at the cold.
The victim climbs the altar steps and sings:
"Hosannah to the lion, lamb, and beast
Who fans the furnace-face of IS with wings:
I breathe the ether of my marriage feast."
At the high altar, gold
And a fair cloth. I kneel and the wings beat
My cheek. What can the dove of Jesus give
You now but wisdom, exile? Stand and live,
The dove has brought an olive branch to eat.

The Mills of the Kavanaughs

(1951)

The Mills of the Kavanaughs

"Ah, love let us be true
To one another! for the world, which seems
To lie before us like a land of dreams . . ."
                    —"DOVER BEACH"

"Morals are the memory of success that no longer succeeds."
                    —IN THE AMERICAN GRAIN

An afternoon in the fall of 1943; a village a little north of Bath, Maine. Anne Kavanaugh is sitting in her garden playing solitaire. She pretends that the Bible she has placed in the chair opposite her is her opponent. At one end of the garden is the grave of her husband, Harry Kavanaugh, a naval officer who was retired after Pearl Harbor. The Kavanaughs are a Catholic family that came to Maine in the 17th century. Their house is called Kavanaugh; *it is on a hill, and at its foot, there is a mill pond, and by it a marble statue of Persephone, the goddess who became a queen by becoming queen of the dead. The Abnakis, or Penobscots, are almost extinct Maine Indians, who were originally converted by the French. Anne comes of a poor family. She was adopted by the Kavanaughs many years before she married. Most of the poem is a revery of her childhood and marriage, and is addressed to her dead husband.*

The Douay Bible on the garden chair
Facing the lady playing solitaire
In blue-jeans and a sealskin toque from Bath
Is *Sol*, her dummy. There's a sort of path
Or rut of weeds that serpents down a hill
And graveyard to a ruined burlap mill;
There, a maternal nineteenth century
Italian statue of Persephone
Still beckons to a mob of Bacchanals
To plunge like dogs or athletes through the falls,
And fetch her the stone garland she will hurl.
The lady drops her cards. She kneels to furl
Her husband's flag, and thinks his mound and stone
Are like a buried bed. "This is the throne

They must have willed us. Harry, not a thing
Was missing: we were children of a king.

"Our people had kept up their herring weirs,
Their rum and logging grants two hundred years,
When Cousin Franklin Pierce was President—
Almost three hundred, Harry, when you sent
His signed engraving sailing on your kite
Above the gable, where your mother's light,
A daylight bulb in tortoise talons, pipped
The bull-mad june-bugs on the manuscript
That she was typing to redeem our mills
From Harding's taxes, and we lost our means
Of drawing pulp and water from those hills
Above the Saco, where our tenants drilled
Abnaki partisans for Charles the First,
And seated our Republicans, while Hearst
And yellow paper fed the moose that swilled
Our spawning ponds for weeds like spinach greens.

"Love, is it trespassing to call them ours?
They are now. Once I trespassed—picking flowers
For keepsakes of my journey, once I bent
Above your well, where lawn and battlement
Were trembling, yet without a flaw to mar
Their sweet surrender. Ripples seemed to star
My face, the rocks, the bottom of the well;
My heart, pursued by all its plunder, fell,
And I was tossing petals from my lair
Of copper leaves above your mother's chair.
Alone in that *verboten*, how I mocked
Her erudition, while she read and rocked.
And how I queened it, when she let me lop
At pigeons with my lilliputian crop,
And pester squirrels from that beech tree's bole
Colored with bunting like a barber's pole."

The lady sees the statues in the pool.
She dreams and thinks, "My husband was a fool

To run out from the Navy when disgrace
Still wanted zeal to look him in the face."
She wonders why her fancy makes her look
Across the table, where the open Book
Forgets the ease and honor of its shelf
To tell her that her gambling with herself
Is love of self. She pauses, drops the deck,
And feels her husband's fingers touch her neck.
She thinks of Daphne—Daphne could outrun
The birds, and saw her swiftness tire the sun,
And yet, perhaps, saw nothing to admire
Beneath Apollo, when his crackling fire
Stood rooted, half unwilling to undo
Her laurel branches dropping from the blue.

The leaves, sun's yellow, listen, Love, they fall.
She hears her husband, and she tries to call
Him, then remembers. Burning stubble roars
About the garden. Columns fill the life
Insurance calendar on which she scores.
The lady laughs. She shakes her parasol.
The table rattles, and she chews her pearled,
Once telescopic pencil, till its knife
Snaps open. "*Sol*," she whispers, laughing, "*Sol,*
If you will help me, I will win the world."
Her husband's thumbnail scratches on her comb.
A boy is pointing at the sun. He cries:
O dandelion, wish my wish, be true,
And blows the callow pollen in her eyes.
"Harry," she whispers, "we are far from home—
A boy and girl a-Maying in the blue

"Of March or April. We are tumbling through
The chalk-pits to our rural demigod,
Old skull-and-horns, the bullock Father slew,
There on the sky-line. Let the offal sod
Our fields with Ceres. Here is piety;
Ceres is here replenished to the full—
Green the clairvoyance of her deity,

Although the landscape's like a bullock's skull . . .
Things held together once," she thinks. "But where?
Not for the life of me! How can I see
Things as they are, my Love, while April steals
Through bog and chalk-pit, till these boulders bear
Persephone—illusory, perhaps,
Yet her renewal, no illusion, for this air
Is orgied, Harry, and your setter yaps
About the goddess, while it nips her heels."

The setter worries through the coils of brush
And steaming bramble, and the children rush
Hurrahing, where no marsh or scrubby field
Or sorry clump of virgin pine will yield
A moment's covert to the half-extinct
And pileated bird they trail with linked
Fingers and little burlap sacks of salt.
The bird, a wise old uncle, knows what fault
Or whimsy guides the children when they halt
For sling-stones. Too distinguished to exalt,
It drops and cruises, while the children vault
The trifling mill-stream, where it used to kill
The sandsnakes in the flotsam with its bill;
Its stoned red-tufted shadow skims the pond;
Now it is lifting, now it clears the mill,
And, tired with child's-play, sails beyond beyond.

The children splash and paddle. Then, hand in hand,
They duck for turtles. Where she cannot stand,
The whirlpool sucks her. She has set her teeth
Into his thumb. She wrestles underneath
The sea-green smother; stunned, unstrung and torn
Into a thousand globules by that horn
Or whorl of river, she has burst apart
Like churning water on her husband's heart—
A horny thumbnail! Then they lie beside
The marble goddess. "Look, the stony-eyed
Persephone has mouldered like a leaf!"
The children whisper. Old and pedestalled,

Where rock-pools used to echo when she called
Demeter—sheathed in Lincoln green, a sheaf—
The statue of Persephone regards
The river, while it moils a hundred yards

Below her garland. Here, they used to build
A fire to broil their trout. A beer can filled
With fishskins marks the dingle where they died.
They whisper, "Touch her. If her foot should slide
A little earthward, Styx will hold her down
Nella miseria, smashed to plaster, balled
Into the whirlpool's boil." Here bubbles filled
Their basin, and the children splashed. They died
In Adam, while the grass snake slid appalled
To summer, while Jehovah's grass-green lyre
Was rustling all about them in the leaves
That gurgled by them turning upside down;
The time of marriage!—worming on all fours
Up slag and deadfall, while the torrent pours
Down, down, down, down—and she, a crested bird,
Or rainbow, hovers, lest the thunder-word

Deluge her playmate in Jehovah's beard
Of waterfalls. She listens to his feared
Footsteps, no longer muffled by the green
Torrent, that serpents up and down between
Them, while she sprints along the shelf.
Her toes curl. "I am married to myself,"
She hears him shout, and answers, "All for us."
And *ah, ah, ah* echoes the cavernous
Cascading froth's crescendo: *Stammerer,*
You cannot answer, Child, you cannot answer.
She wades. The boy, too small to follow her,
Calls out in anger, and three times her answer
Struggles to tell him, but her bubbles star
The cheerful surface idly. She is part
Of the down-under beating like her heart.
Although the voice is near her, it sounds far.

"The world hushed. Dying in your arms, I heard
The mowers moving through that golden-eared
Avernal ambush, and I seemed to hear
The harvesters, who rose to volunteer
As escorts for Persephone's deferred
Renewal of the earth, so vainly feared;
And all their voices, light as feathers, sighed
Unwelcome to that violated bride,
Uncertain even of her hold on hell,
Who curbed her horses, as if serpent-stung,
While shadows massed in earnest to rebel.
Weary and glorious, once, when time was young,
She ran from Hades. All Avernus burned.
Black horse and chariot thundered at her heel.
She, fleeting earthward, nothing seemed to steal,
But the fruition that her hell had earned.

"On days of Obligation, if our farm
Stockaded by wild cherries, and the spruce
My father hacked like weeds to keep us warm
Through summer, if it crossed your path; what use
Was it? His thirteen children and his goat,
Those cook-stove heated clapboards, where we slept
In relays, beaver dams of cans, a moat
Our cesspool drained on—if on that, he kept
A second woman twenty farms up road;
What use was it? The air we breathed he owed
The poor-box. Is it throwing money down
A well to help the poor? They die. They glitter
Like a cathedral—whiskey, tears and tapers.
He died. Your mother came and signed my papers.
She plucked me like a kitten from that litter,
And charged my board and lodging to the town.

"Your house, can you forget it? Or its *school*,
Where Bowdoin students taught us cowboy pool—
Brother and sister! How Abnakis, screened
In bleeding sumac, scared us, when they leaned
Against us—pocked and warlocked—to pursue

Their weaponed shadows raiding through the dew
Of twilight after crickets? How we spiked
Our bows with pears for flinging? When we hiked
Homeward, you winged our falcon with a rock—
Fumbling for the tail-feathers of a cock,
Blue-blooded, gluttonous, it swallowed blood,
While mother fetched its parrot perch and hood,
And set it by the daub of Kavanaugh,
Sheriff for Lincoln County and the King,
Whose old two-handed eighteenth century saw
Hung like a whale's jaw lashed with bits of string.

"The blazings of the woodsman left a track
Straight as an arrow to the blacksmith's shack
Where I was born. There, just a month before
Our marriage, I can see you: we had dressed
Ourselves in holly, and you cut your crest,
A stump and green shoots, on my father's door,
And swore our marriage would renew the cleft
Forests and skulls of the Abnakis left
Like saurian footprints by the lumber lord,
Who broke their virgin greenness cord by cord
To build his clearing. Once his axe was law
And culture, but this house in its decline
Forgets how tender green shoots used to spring
From the decaying stump—Red Kavanaugh
Who built it, and inscribed its Latin line:
Cut down we flourish, on his signet ring.

"And there was greenwood spitting on the fire-dogs,
That looked like Hessians. It was June, and Maine
Smouldered to greenness, and the perching frogs
Chirred to the greener sizzle of a rain
That freshened juniper and Wilson's thrush
Before the Revolution. We were hot,
And climbed the Portland wagon-road to push
Past vineyards to the *praying niggers'* lot.
There, the Abnakis, christened by the French,
Chanted our *Miserere*. Love, how wild,

Their fragrance! Grouse were pecking on their trench—
Red Kavanaugh's, who burned and buried child
And squaw and elder in their river bed,
A pine-tree shilling a scalp; yes, scalped their king
In the dead drop—and both already dead,
Drowned in the dazzling staidness of our spring.

"Marriage by drowning! Soon enough our own,"
She whispers, laughing. "Though they left no stone
Unturned to stop us, soon the maids in red
Were singing Cinderella at our mass;
They called me Cinderella, but I said:
'Prince Charming is my shadow in the glass.' "
The lady stacks her cards. She laughs and scores.
She dreams. Her husband holds his mansion doors
Open. He helps the bridesmaids, stoops to tie
Her roses. "Anne," he teases, "Anne, my whole
House is your serf. The squirrel in its hole
Who hears your patter, Anne, and sinks its eye-
Teeth, bigger than a human's, in its treasure
Of rotten shells, is wiser far than I
Who have forsaken all my learning's leisure
To be your man and husband—God knows why!"

"God knows," she wonders, "when I watched you sail
From Boston Harbor on the *Arkansas*
For the Pacific, I was glad. No mail
Until December. You returned. I saw
Your horses pulling up the hill, and heard
You crying like a white, bewildered bird
The sea rejected. You were on the floor,
And clowning like a boy. You grimaced, bared
Your chest, and bellowed, 'Listen, undeclared
War seems to . . . static . . . the United States
And Honolulu are at war. War, War!
Pearl Harbor's burning!' But I knew you cared
Little, and that was why you turned to creak
The rusty hinges of the oven door.

You creaked and puttered, till I thought our plates
Of numbered birds would smash their frames, and shriek.

"The horses stumbled, and we had to stop.
The mountain soared. Its top, the Widow's Walk,
A mile above us, balanced on a drop,
Where dryfall after dryfall crashed to chalk.
The roots were charcoal. Standing shells of stocks
At each meander marched to block our climb
Along a snake-trail weighted down with rocks.
This was Avernus. There, about this time,
Demeter's daughter first reviewed the dead—
Most doomed and pompous, while the maples shed
Their martyr's rubric, and a torrent stood
Stock-still, reflecting; and she heard the bell,
Then lifted on a crossing wind, alarm
The river parish by her mother's farm—
There, hearing how she'd come to little good,
She took a husband to dispirit hell."

She thinks of how she watched her husband drive
To meetings with Macaulay's life of Clive
Tucked in a pocket—there, unshaven, white,
And mumbling to himself, he would recite
The verses on Lucretia from the *Lay
Of Ancient Rome*, and ape her Roman way
Of falling from dishonor on a sword;
And yet she'd thought her kindness had restored
Pearl Harbor's shell-shock, thought he would enjoy . . .
As if God's touch, as if Jehovah's joy,
Allowed him to resume the wearisome
Renown of merely living, when he'd come,
Like Atlas with the world about his ears,
To tell her nothing. Once again she hears
Her husband's stubborn laugh. A pair of boulder
Gray squirrels romp like kittens on his shoulder.

Then it was Christmas. "Harry's mine for good,"
She'd shouted, running down the stairs to find

Him stumbling for his little strip of wood
To stir the bowl. She sees the flurries blind
The barren Christmas greens, as winter dusks
The double window, and she hears the slow
Trek of the Magi hoofing cotton snow
Behind their snow-shoes on the golden husks
Of birdseed cast like breadcrumbs for their three
Gold-dusty camels by the Christmas tree,
A withered creeping hemlock in a cup;
Its star of hope and only ornament,
A silver dollar. He turned the burners up,
And stirred the stoup of glüg—a quart of grain,
Two quarts of claret, every condiment,
Berry and nut and rind and herb in Maine!

"You went to bed, Love, finished—through, through, through.
Hoping to find you useless, dead asleep,
I stole to bed beside you, after two
As usual. Had you drugged yourself to keep
Your peace? I think so. If our bodies met,
You'd flinch, and flounder on your face. I heard
The snowplow banging; its eye-headlights set
On mine—a clowning dragon—so absurd,
Its thirty gangling feet of angled lights,
Red, blue and orange. Having broken loose
From Ringling Brothers, it had lost the use
Of sense, Love, and was worming days and nights
To hole up *some*where. Then I slept. I found
That I was stalking in my moccasins
Below the mill-fall, where our cave begins
To shake its head, a green Medusa, crowned

"With juniper. A dragon writhed around
A knob above you, and its triple tails
Fanned at your face. Furlongs of glaucous scales
Wallowed to splatter the reproachful hound
Eyes of the gorgon on the monstrous targe,
Plated with hammered-down tobacco tins,
You pushed and parried at the water's charge.

Your blue and orange broadsword lopped its fins
And roaring . . . I was back in bed. The day
Was graying on us. So that you could keep
An eye upon them, Harry, sword and shield
Loomed from your shoebag. 'I will have to yield
You to the dragon, if you fall asleep.'
You pulled my nightgown. 'Maiden, they have belled
The dragon's tail. The dragon's on its way
To woo you.' Then I slept. Your fingers held. . . .

"You *held* me! 'Please, Love, let your elbows . . . quick,
Quick it!' I shook you, 'can't you see how sick
This playing . . . take me; Harry's driving back.
Take me!' 'Who am I?' 'You are you; not black
Like Harry; you're a boy. Look out, his car's
White eyes are at the window. Boy, your chin
Is bristling. You have gored me black and blue.
I am all prickle-tickle like the stars;
I am a sleepy-foot, a dogfish skin
Rubbed backwards, wrongways; you have made my hide
Split snakey, Bad one—*one!*' Then I was wide
Awake, and turning over. 'Who, who, who?'
You asked me, 'tell me who.' Then everything
Was roaring, Harry. Harry, I could feel
Nothing—it was so black—except your seal,
The stump with green shoots on your signet ring.

"I couldn't tell you; but you shook the bed,
And struck me, Harry. 'I will shake you dead
As earth,' you chattered, 'you, you, you, you, you. . . .
Who are you keeping, Anne?' you mocked me, 'Anne,
You want yourself.' I gagged, and then I ran.
My maid was knocking. Snow was chasing through
The open window. 'Harry, I am glad
You tried to kill me; it is out, you know;
I'll shout it from the housetops of the Mills;
I'll tell you, so remember, you are mad;
I'll tell them, listen Harry: husband kills
His wife for dreaming. You must help. No, no!

I've always loved you; I am just a girl;
You mustn't choke me!' Then I thought the beams
Were falling on us. Things began to whirl.
'Harry, we're not accountable for dreams.'

"Spread-eagled backward on your backless chair,
Inhaling the regardless, whirling air,
Rustling about you from the oven jets,
Sparkling and crackling on the cigarettes
Still burning in the saucer, where you'd tossed
Almost a carton, Love, before you lost
All sense of caring, and I saw your eyes
Looking in wonder at your bloody hand—
And like an angler wading out from land,
Who feels the bottom shelving, while he sees
His nibbled bobber twitch the dragonflies:
You watched your hand withdrawing by degrees—
Enthralled and fearful—till it stopped beneath
Your collar, and you felt your being drip
Blue-purple with a joy that made your teeth
Grin all to-whichways through your lower lip.

"I must have fainted. Harry, where I sank,
The gulls were yelping and a river stank,
And I was seated in a wicker chair
Beside a tub of crabs. And you were there
Above me and I held a jelly-roll
And read the comics, while you stood to pole
Our dory with a pitchfork to the pier.
You shout directions, but I cannot steer
Because the boat stops, and the spilling tub
Bubbles with torment, as you trip and lance
Your finger at a crab. It strikes. You rub
It inch-meal to a bilge of shell. You dance
Child-crazy over tub and gunnel, grasping
Your pitchfork like a trident, poised to stab
The greasy eel-grass clasping and unclasping
The jellied iridescence of the crab.

"Then yellow water, and the summer's drought
Boiled on its surface underneath our grounds'
Disordered tousle. *Wish my, wish my, wish*,
Said the dry-flies snapping past my ears to whip
Those dead-horse waters, faster than a fish
Could follow—longer too. I gasped. My mouth
Was open, and I seemed to mime your hound's
Terrified panting; and our trimming ship
Was shipping water . . . I was staring at
Our drifting oars. The moon was floating—flat
As the old world of maps. I thought, 'I'll stay.
Harry,' I whispered, 'hurry, I will pray
So truly; hurry! God, you must, you must
Hurry, for Death, carousing like a king
On nothing but his lands, will take your ring
To bind me, and possess me to the dust.'

"Then life went on; you lived, or lived at least
To baby-smile into the brutal gray
Daylight each morning, and your sofa lay
Beside the window, and you watched the east
Wind romping, till it swept the sullen blue
Bluster of April in the mouth of May,
The month of mating. Yellow warblers flew
About the ivied window, calling you.
You smiled. Then your eyes wandered to alight
As aliens on your charts of black and white
New England birds: the kinds, once memorized
By number, now no longer recognized,
Were numbers, numbers! 'What's the twenty-eight,
The twenty-eight, the twenty-eight—O wait:
A cardinal bird, a scarlet tanager,
The redbird that I used to whittle her.'

"You lived. Your rocker creaked, as you declined.
To the ungarnished ruin of your mind
Came the persona of the murderous Saul
In dirty armor, followed by a boy,

Who twanged a jew's-harp. Stumbling on one leg,
You speared our quaking shadows to the wall.
'Where is my harper? Music! Must I beg
For music?' Then you sucked your thumb for joy,
And baby-smiled through strings of orange juice.
'Where are you, Anne? A harper for the King.'
When the phantasmagoria left, you wept
For their return. Ah Harry, what's the use
Of lying? I called the doctor while you slept.
'Now it's as if he'd never lived,' I thought;
'As if I'd never, never anything.'
I felt the stump and green shoots at my throat.

" 'Sleep, sleep,' I hushed you. 'Sleep. You must abide
The lamentations of the nuptial mass—
Then you are rising. Then you are alive;
The bridesmaids scatter daisies, and the bride,
A daisy choired by daisies, sings: "My life
Is like a horn of plenty gone to grass,
Or like the yellow bee-queen in her hive."
She whispers, "Who is this, and who is this?
His eyes are coals. His breath is myrrh; his kiss,
The consummation of the silvered glass.
His lightning slivers through me like a knife." '
The door is open, but I hope to pass
Unheard. Your male-attendant tries to feed
You. I can hear him talking (O for keeps!)
'Mother of Jesus, had her while she sleeps;
She took him for the other guy, she'd . . .' *She'd*!"

Then summer followed: children rollerskate
And fight with hockey sticks about a crate
Of cannon crackers. They have mined the road.
Someone is shouting. Tufts of grass explode.
Somewhere a child is dancing in his grease
And war-paint. "Mees," he shouts, "town ring! Mees, Mees,
Town ring. Lieutenant Kavanaugh eeth dead."
She sees the body sitting up in bed
Before the window. "You must bury me

As if you gloried in my liberty.
I died," it seems to tell her, "while July,
The month of freedom, tigerstriped the sky
With bombs and rockets." How will she disown
The leisured condescension of his frown
That still refuses, while she moves about
The body, saying, "Blow the candle out."

"But it's so dull," she whispers, "it's so dull,
This autumn, Harry, from the line-storm lull
Through Hallows', playing Patience to defeat
Poor *Sol*. Pearl Harbor's whole Pacific fleet
Has sea-room in my mind. Here, Peace, the Pearl
Hawaiians dive for . . . I am just a girl,
Just one man's not the fleet's." She stands, then sits
And makes a card-house; it's as if her wits
Were overseas. The cards are Kavanaughs,
Or sinister, bewildered effigies
Of kings and queens. Another game begins;
Shuffling so badly that she always wins,
She dreams her luck has brought her husband home.
"Harry," she whispers, "listen, the applause
Is rising for you. Gods of ancient Rome
Rise from the mill-pond on their marble knees.

"They watch like water-polo players—their eyes,
Stars of a recognition, no disguise
Or veil will hinder, now that they have found
Me their Persephone, gone underground
Into myself to supplicate the throne
And horn of Hades to restore that stone,
Imperial garland, once the living flower,
Now stone—Harvest, my mother's, only dower
To the dark monarch, and the futile dead
In Hades, where I lost my maidenhead.
Horns of the moon, they chant, *our Goddess*." Then
She wakes. She stacks her cards, and once again
She rambles down the weedy path, past hill
And graveyard to the ruined burlap mill.

She lifts a pail. She pushes on an oar.
Her metal boat is moving from the shore.

The heron warps its neck, a broken pick,
To study its reflection on the scales,
Or knife-bright shards of water lilies, quick
In the dead autumn water with their snails
And water lice. Her ballet glasses hold
Him twisted by a fist of spruce, as dry
As flint and steel. She thinks: "The bird is old,
A cousin to all scholars; that is why
He will abet my thoughts of Kavanaugh,
Who gave the Mills its lumberyard and weir
In eighteen hundred, when our farmers saw
John Adams bring their Romish church a bell,
Cast—so the records claim—by Paul Revere.
The sticks of *Kavanaugh* are buried here—
Many of them, too many, Love, to tell—
Faithful to where their virgin forest fell."

And now the mussed blue-bottles bead her float:
Bringers of luck. Of luck? At worst, a rest
From counting blisters on her metal boat,
That spins and staggers. North and south and west:
A scene, perhaps, of Fragonard—her park,
Whose planted poplars scatter penny-leaves,
White underneath, like mussels to the dark
Chop of the shallows. Extirpation grieves
The sunken martyred laughter of the loon,
Where Harry's mother bathed in navy-blue
Stockings and skirts. But now, the afternoon
Is sullen, it is all that she can do
To lift the anchor. She can hardly row
Against these whitecaps—surely never lulled
For man and woman. Washing to and fro,
The floorboards bruise the lilies that she pulled.

"Even in August it was autumn—all
A pond could harbor." Now her matches fall

In dozens by her bobber to expire
As target-circles on the mirrored fire-
Escapes of *Kavanaugh*. She sees they hold
Her mirror to her—just a little cold;
A ground hog's looking glass. "The day is sharp
And short, Love, and its sun is like this carp,
Or goldfish, almost twenty inches long,
Panting, a weak old dog, below a prong
Of deadwood fallen from my copper beech;
The settling leaves embower its warmth. They reach
For my reflection, but it glides through shoal
Aground, to where the squirrel held its roots
And freehold, Love, unsliding, when our boots
Pattered—a life ago once—on its hole.

"I think we row together, for the stern
Jumps from my weaker stroke, and down the cove
Our house is floating, and the windows burn,
As if its underpinnings fed the stove.
Her window's open; look, she waits for us,
And types, until the clattering tin bell
Upon her room-large table tolls for us.
Listen, your mother's asking, *is it well?*
Yes, very well. He died outside the church
Like Harry Tudor. Now we near the sluice
And burial ground above the burlap mill;
I see you swing a string of yellow perch
About your head to fan off gnats that mill
And wail, as your disheartened shadow tries
The buried bedstead, where your body lies—
Time out of mind—a failing stand of spruce.

"God knows!" she marvels. "Harry, *Kavanaugh*
Was lightly given. Soon enough we saw
Death like the Bourbon after Waterloo,
Who learning and forgetting nothing, knew
Nothing but ruin. Why must we mistrust
Ourselves with Death who takes the world on trust?
Although God's brother, and himself a god,

Death whipped his horses through the startled sod;
For neither conscience nor omniscience warned
Him from his folly, when the virgin scorned
His courtship, and the quaking earth revealed
Death's desperation to the Thracian field.
And yet we think the virgin took no harm:
She gave herself because her blood was warm—
And for no other reason, Love, I gave
Whatever brought me gladness to the grave."

Falling Asleep over the Aeneid

An old man in Concord forgets to go to morning service. He falls asleep, while reading Vergil, and dreams that he is Aeneas at the funeral of Pallas, an Italian prince.

The sun is blue and scarlet on my page,
And *yuck-a, yuck-a, yuck-a, yuck-a,* rage
The yellowhammers mating. Yellow fire
Blankets the captives dancing on their pyre,
And the scorched lictor screams and drops his rod.
Trojans are singing to their drunken God,
Ares. Their helmets catch on fire. Their files
Clank by the body of my comrade—miles
Of filings! Now the scythe-wheeled chariot rolls
Before their lances long as vaulting poles,
And I stand up and heil the thousand men,
Who carry Pallas to the bird-priest. Then
The bird-priest groans, and as his birds foretold,
I greet the body, lip to lip. I hold
The sword that Dido used. It tries to speak,
A bird with Dido's sworded breast. Its beak
Clangs and ejaculates the Punic word
I hear the bird-priest chirping like a bird.
I groan a little. "Who am I, and why?"
It asks, a boy's face, though its arrow-eye
Is working from its socket. "Brother, try,
O Child of Aphrodite, try to die:
To die is life." His harlots hang his bed
With feathers of his long-tailed birds. His head
Is yawning like a person. The plumes blow;
The beard and eyebrows ruffle. Face of snow,
You are the flower that country girls have caught,
A wild bee-pillaged honey-suckle brought

To the returning bridegroom—the design
Has not yet left it, and the petals shine;
The earth, its mother, has, at last, no help:
It is itself. The broken-winded yelp
Of my Phoenician hounds, that fills the brush
With snapping twigs and flying, cannot flush
The ghost of Pallas. But I take his pall,
Stiff with its gold and purple, and recall
How Dido hugged it to her, while she toiled,
Laughing—her golden threads, a serpent coiled
In cypress. Now I lay it like a sheet;
It clinks and settles down upon his feet,
The careless yellow hair that seemed to burn
Beforehand. Left foot, right foot—as they turn,
More pyres are rising: armored horses, bronze,
And gagged Italians, who must file by ones
Across the bitter river, when my thumb
Tightens into their wind-pipes. The beaks drum;
Their headman's cow-horned death's-head bites its tongue,
And stiffens, as it eyes the hero slung
Inside his feathered hammock on the crossed
Staves of the eagles that we winged. Our cost
Is nothing to the lovers, whoring Mars
And Venus, father's lover. Now his car's
Plumage is ready, and my marshals fetch
His squire, Acoetes, white with age, to hitch
Aethon, the hero's charger, and its ears
Prick, and it steps and steps, and stately tears
Lather its teeth; and then the harlots bring
The hero's charms and baton—but the King,
Vain-glorious Turnus, carried off the rest.
"I was myself, but Ares thought it best
The way it happened." At the end of time,
He sets his spear, as my descendants climb
The knees of Father Time, his beard of scalps,
His scythe, the arc of steel that crowns the Alps.
The elephants of Carthage hold those snows,
Turms of Numidian horse unsling their bows,
The flaming turkey-feathered arrows swarm

Beyond the Alps. "Pallas," I raise my arm
And shout, "Brother, eternal health. Farewell
Forever." Church is over, and its bell
Frightens the yellowhammers, as I wake
And watch the whitecaps wrinkle up the lake.
Mother's great-aunt, who died when I was eight,
Stands by our parlor sabre. "Boy, it's late.
Vergil must keep the Sabbath." Eighty years!
It all comes back. My Uncle Charles appears.
Blue-capped and bird-like. Phillips Brooks and Grant
Are frowning at his coffin, and my aunt,
Hearing his colored volunteers parade
Through Concord, laughs, and tells her English maid
To clip his yellow nostril hairs, and fold
His colors on him. . . . It is I. I hold
His sword to keep from falling, for the dust
On the stuffed birds is breathless, for the bust
Of young Augustus weighs on Vergil's shelf:
It scowls into my glasses at itself.

Her Dead Brother

I.
The Lion of St. Mark's upon the glass
Shield in my window reddens, as the night
Enchants the swinging dories to its terrors,
And dulls your distant wind-stung eyes; alas,
Your portrait, coiled in German-silver hawsers, mirrors
The sunset as a dragon. Enough light
Remains to see you through your varnish. Giving
Your life has brought you closer to your friends;
Yes, it has brought you home. All's well that ends:
Achilles dead is greater than the living;

My mind holds you as I would have you live,
A wintering dragon. Summer was too short
When we went picnicking with telescopes
And crocking leather handbooks to that fort
Above the lank and heroned Sheepscot, where its slopes
Are clutched by hemlocks—spotting birds. I give
You back that idyll, Brother. Was it more?
Remember riding, scotching with your spur
That four-foot milk-snake in a juniper?
Father shellacked it to the ice-house door.

Then you were grown; I left you on your own.
We will forget that August twenty-third,
When Mother motored with the maids to Stowe,
And the pale summer shades were drawn—so low
No one could see us; no, nor catch your hissing word,
As false as Cressid! Let our deaths atone:
The fingers on your sword-knot are alive,
And Hope, that fouls my brightness with its grace,
Will anchor in the narrows of your face.
My husband's Packard crunches up the drive.

II.

The ice is out: the tidal current swims
Its blocks against the launches as they pitch
Under the cruisers of my Brother's fleet.
The gas, uncoiling from my oven burners, dims
The face above this bottled *Water Witch*,
The knockabout my Brother fouled and left to eat
Its heart out by the Boston Light. My Brother,
I've saved you in the ice-house of my mind—
The ice is out. . . . Our fingers lock behind
The tiller. We are heeling in the smother,

Our sails, balloon and leg-o'mutton, tell
The colors of the rainbow; but they flap,
As the wind fails, and cannot fetch the bell. . . .
His stick is tapping on the millwheel-step,
He lights a match, another and another—
The Lord is dark, and holy is His name;
By my own hands, into His hands! My burners
Sing like a kettle, and its nickel mirrors
Your squadron by the Stygian Landing. Brother,
The harbor! The torpedoed cruisers flame,

The motor-launches with their searchlights bristle
About the targets. You are black. You shout,
And cup your broken sword-hand. Yes, your whistle
Across the crackling water: *Quick, the ice is out.* . . .
The wind dies in our canvas; we were running dead
Before the wind, but now our sail is part
Of death. O Brother, a New England town is death
And incest—and I saw it whole. I said,
Life is a thing I own. Brother, my heart
Races for sea-room—we are out of breath.

Mother Marie Therese

(Drowned in 1912)

The speaker is a Canadian nun stationed in New Brunswick.

Old sisters at our Maris Stella House
Remember how the Mother's strangled grouse
And snow-shoe rabbits matched the royal glint
Of Pio Nono's vestments in the print
That used to face us, while our aching ring
Of stationary rockers saw her bring
Our cake. Often, when sunset hurt the rocks
Off Carthage, and surprised us knitting socks
For victims of the Franco-Prussian War,
Our scandal'd set her frowning at the floor;
And vespers struck like lightning through the gloom
And oaken ennui of her sitting room.
It strikes us now, but cannot re-inspire;
False, false and false, I mutter to my fire.
The good old times, ah yes! But good, that all's
Forgotten like our Province's cabals;
And Jesus, smiling earthward, finds it good;
For we were friends of Cato, not of God.
This sixtieth Christmas, I'm content to pray
For what life's shrinkage leaves from day to day;
And it's a sorrow to recall our young
Raptures for Mother, when her trophies hung,
Fresh in their blood and color, to convince
Even Probationers that Heaven's Prince,
Befriending, whispered: "Is it then so hard?
Tarry a little while, O disregard
Time's wings and armor, when it flutters down
Papal tiaras and the Bourbon crown;
For quickly, priest and prince will stand, their shields
Before each other's faces, in the fields,

Where, as I promised, virtue will compel
Michael and all his angels to repel
Satan's advances, till his forces lie
Beside the Lamb in blissful fealty."
Our Indian summer! Then, our skies could lift,
God willing; but an Indian brought the gift.
"A sword," said Father Turbot, "not a saint";
Yet He who made the Virgin without taint
Chastised our Mother to the Rule's restraint.
Was it not fated that the sweat of Christ
Would wash the worldly serpent? Christ enticed
Her heart that fluttered, while she whipped her hounds
Into the quicksands of her manor grounds,
A lordly child, her habit fleur-de-lys'd—
There she dismounted, sick; with little heed,
Surrendered. Like Proserpina, who fell
Six months a year from earth to flower in hell;
She half-renounced by Candle, Book and Bell
Her flowers and fowling pieces for the Church.
She never spared the child and spoiled the birch;
And how she'd chide her novices, and pluck
Them by the ears for gabbling in Canuck,
While she was reading Rabelais from her chaise,
Or parroting the *Action Française*.
Her letter from the soi-disant French King,
And the less treasured golden wedding ring
Of her shy Bridegroom, yellow; and the regal
Damascus shot-guns, pegged upon her eagle
Emblems from Hohenzollern standards, rust.
Our world is passing; even she, whose trust
Was in its princes, fed the gluttonous gulls,
That whiten our Atlantic, when like skulls
They drift for sewage with the emerald tide.
Perpetual novenas cannot tide
Us past that drowning. After Mother died,
"An émigrée in this world and the next,"
Said Father Turbot, playing with his text.
Where is he? Surely, he is one of those,
Whom Christ and Satan spew! But no one knows

What's happened to that porpoise-bellied priest.
He lodged with us on Louis Neuvième's Feast,
And celebrated her memorial mass.
His bald spot tapestried by colored glass,
Our angels, Prussian blue and flaking red,
He squeaked and stuttered: "N-n-nothing is so d-dead
As a dead s-s-sister." Off Saint Denis' Head,
Our Mother, drowned on an excursion, sleeps.
Her billy goat, or its descendant, keeps
Watch on a headland, and I hear it bawl
Into this sixty-knot Atlantic squall,
"Mamamma's Baby," past Queen Mary's Neck,
The ledge at Carthage—almost to Quebec,
Where Monsieur de Montcalm, on Abraham's
Bosom, asleep, perceives our world that shams
His New World, lost—however it atones
For Wolfe, the Englishman, and Huron bones
And priests'. O Mother, here our snuffling crones
And cretins feared you, but I owe you flowers:
The dead, the sea's dead, has her sorrows, hours
On end to lie tossing to the east, cold,
Without bed-fellows, washed and bored and old,
Bilged by her thoughts, and worked on by the worms,
Until her fossil convent come to terms
With the Atlantic. Mother, there is room
Beyond our harbor. Past its wooden Boom
Now weak and waterlogged, that Frontenac
Once diagrammed, she welters on her back.
The bell-buoy, whom she called the Cardinal,
Dances upon her. If she hears at all,
She only hears it tolling to this shore,
Where our frost-bitten sisters know the roar
Of water, inching, always on the move
For virgins, when they wish the times were love,
And their hysterical hosannahs rouse
The loveless harems of the buck ruffed grouse,
Who drums, untroubled now, beside the sea—
As if he found our stern virginity
Contra naturam. We are ruinous;

God's Providence through time has mastered us:
Now all the bells are tongueless, now we freeze,
A later Advent, pruner of warped trees,
Whistles about our nunnery slabs, and yells,
And water oozes from us into wells;
A new year swells and stirs. Our narrow Bay
Freezes itself and us. We cannot say
Christ even sees us, when the ice floes toss
His statue, made by Hurons, on the cross,
That Father Turbot sank on Mother's mound—
A whirligig! Mother, we must give ground,
Little by little; but it does no good.
Tonight, while I am piling on more driftwood,
And stooping with the poker, you are here,
Telling your beads; and breathing in my ear,
You watch your orphan swording at her fears.
I feel you twitch my shoulder. No one hears
Us mock the sisters, as we used to, years
And years behind us, when we heard the spheres
Whirring *venite*; and we held our ears.
My mother's hollow sockets fill with tears.

David and Bathsheba in the Public Garden

I.

DAVID TO BATHSHEBA

"Worn out of virtue, as the time of year,
The burning City and its bells surround
The Public Garden. What is sound
Past agony is fall:
The children crowding home from school at five,
Punting a football in the bricky air—
You mourn Uriah? If he were alive,
O Love, my age were nothing but the ball
Of leaves inside this lion-fountain, left
For witch and winter." "Yet the leaves' complaint
Is the King's fall . . . whatever suffers theft."
"The Latin labels on the foreign trees are quaint.

The trees, for decades, shook their discontent
On strangers; rustling, rustling the Levant."
"Uriah might have found the want
Of what was never his
A moment, found the falling colors welcome."
"But he was dead before Jehovah sent
Our shadows to the lion's cave. What's come
Is dancing like a leaf for nothing. Kiss:
The leaves are dark and harp." "My Lord, observe
The shedding, park-bound mallards, how they keep
Circling and diving for Uriah's sleep;
Driven, derided, David, and my will a curve.

The fountain's falling waters ring around
The garden." "Love, if you had stayed my hand
Uriah would not understand
The lion's rush, or why
This stone-mouthed fountain laps us like a cat."

"And he is nothing after death but ground,
Anger and anguish, David? When we sat
The nights of summer out, the gravity
Of reaching for the moon. . . . Perhaps it took
Of fall, the Fall?" "Perhaps, I live. I lie
Drinking our likeness from the water. Look:
The Lion's mane and age! Surely, I will not die."

II.

BATHSHEBA'S LAMENT IN THE GARDEN

Baring the mares'-nests that the squirrels set
To tangle with the wood-winds of the North,
October blows to wood . . . the fourth
Since David broke our vows
And married Abishag to warm him. Cold!
The pigeons bluer with it, since we met
Beside the lion-fountain, and unrolled
The tackle of our model boats. Our prows
Were sworded as the marlin, and they locked,
Clearing the mallards' grotto, half a mile
Up pond—and foundered; and our splashing mocked
The lion's wrinkled brow. My Love, a little while,

The lion frothed into the basin . . . all,
Water to water—water that begets
A child from water. And the jets
That washed our bodies drowned
The curses of Uriah when he died
For David; still a stranger! *Not-at-all*,
We called him, after the withdrawing tide
Of Joab's armor-bearers slew him, and he found
Jehovah, the whale's belly of the pit.
He is the childless, the unreconciled
Master of darkness. Will Uriah sit
And judge? You nod and babble. But, you are a child;

At last, a child—what we were playing, when
We blew our bubbles at the moon, and fought
Like brothers, and the lion caught
The moonbeams in its jaws.
The harvest moon, earth's friend, that cared so much
For us and cared so little, comes again;
Always a stranger! Farther from my touch,
The mountains of the moon . . . whatever claws
The harp-strings chalks the harper's fingers. Cold
The eyelid drooping on the lion's eye
Of David, child of fortune. I am old;
God is ungirded; open! I must surely die.

The Fat Man in the Mirror
(After Werfel)

What's filling up the mirror? O, it is not I;
Hair-belly like a beaver's house? An old dog's eye?
    The forenoon was blue
    In the mad King's zoo
Nurse was swinging me so high, so high!

The bullies wrestled on the royal bowling green;
Hammers and sickles on their hoods of black sateen. . . .
    Sulking on my swing
    The tobacco King
Sliced apples with a pen-knife for the Queen.

This *I*, who used to mouse about the paraffined preserves,
And jammed a finger in the coffee-grinder, serves
    Time before the mirror.
    But this pursey terror . . .
Nurse, it is a person. *It is nerves.*

Where's the Queen-Mother waltzing like a top to staunch
The blood of Lewis, King of Faerie? Hip and haunch
    Lard the royal grotto;
    Straddling Lewis' motto,
Time, the Turk, its sickle on its paunch.

Nurse, Nurse, it rises on me . . . O, it starts to roll,
My apples, O, are ashes in the meerschaum bowl. . . .
    If you'd only come,
    If you'd only come,
Darling, if . . . The apples that I stole,

While Nurse and I were swinging in the Old One's eye . . .
Only a fat man with his beaver on his eye
    Only a fat man,
    Only a fat man
Bursts the mirror. O, it is not I!

Thanksgiving's Over

Thanksgiving night, 1942: a room on Third Avenue. Michael dreams of his wife, a German-American Catholic, who leapt from a window before she died in a sanatorium. The church referred to in the first and last stanzas is the Franciscan church on 31st Street.

Thanksgiving night: Third Avenue was dead;
My fowl was soupbones. Fathoms overhead,
Snow warred on the El's world in the blank snow.
"Michael," she whispered, "just a year ago,
Even the shoreleave from the *Normandie*
Were weary of Thanksgiving; but they'd stop
And lift their hats. I watched their arctics drop
Below the birdstoup of the Anthony
And Child who guarded our sodality
For lay-Franciscans, Michael, till I heard
The birds inside me, and I knew the Third
Person possessed me, for I was the bird
Of Paradise, the parrot whose absurd
Garblings are glory. *Cherry ripe, ripe, ripe:*
I shrilled to Christ the Sailor's silver pipe
And cherry-tasselled tam. Now Michael sleeps,
Thanksgiving's over, nothing is for keeps:
New earth, new sky, new life: I hear the word
Of Brother Francis, child and bird, descend,
Calling the war of Michael a pretend;
The Lord is Brother Parrot, and a friend."

"Whose friend?" I answered. I was dreaming. Cars
Trampled the Elevated's scaffolding,
And jerked the fire-proofed pumpkins on the line
Her Aunt had fixed with Christophers and stars
To make her joyful; and the bars

Still caged her window—half a foot from mine,
It mirrored mine:
My window's window. On its cushioned ring,
Her celluloid and bargain cockatoo,
Yellow and blue,
Grew restive from her fingering—
Poor numskull, he had beebees in his tail.
"The birds inside me choir to Christ the Healer;
Thanksgiving's over." She was laughing. Bars
Shielded her vigil-candle, while it burned
Pin-beaded, indigo:
A bluebird in a tumbler. "Let me go!
Michael," she whispered, "all I want to do
Is kill you." Then the bars
Crashed with her, and I saw her vanishing
Into the neon of the restaurant—
Clawing and screaming . . . "If you're worth the burying
And burning, Michael, God will let you know
Your merits for the love I felt the want
Of, when your mercy shipped me to Vermont

To the asylum. Michael, was there warrant
For killing love? As if the birds that range
The bestiary-garden by my cell,
Like angels in the needle-point my Aunt
Bequeathed our altar guild, could want
To hurt a fly! . . . But Michael, I was well;
My mind was well;
I wanted to be loved—to thaw, to change,
To *April*! Now our mountains, seventeen
Bald Brothers, green
Below the timberline, must change
Their skullcaps for the green of Sherwood Forest;
Mount Leather-Jacket leads the season. Outlaws,
We enter a world of children, perched on gaunt
Crows-nests in hemlocks over flat-iron torrents;
And freely serve our term
In prison. I will serve you, Love. Affirm
The promise, move the mountains, while they lean,

As dry as dust for want
Of trusting. Michael, look, the lordly range
Over our brooks' chorale of broken rocks,
Lifting a bowshot's distance, clouds and suffers change—
Blue cloud! There, ruin toils not, though infirm:
Our water-shed! Our golden weathercocks
Are creaking: Fall is here, and starlings. Flocks
Scavenge for El Dorado in the hemlocks.

O Michael, hurry up and ring my bell.
Ring, ring for me! . . . Why do you make us kneel?
Why are we praying? Michael, Venus locks
My lattice, lest a chatterbox
Archangel—O so jealous—spoil and steal
Her commonweal,
My bedroom. Is it just another cell,
This *Primavera*, where the Graces wear
Only the air:
Unmarried April! It is hell!
A lying-in house where the Virtues wither.
I promise, Michael. Michael, I will promise.
I promise on my kneeler—in these stocks!
Your Virtues, owls or parrots, bend my ear
And babble: *Chatterer,*
Our owlet, once in a blue moon we stir;
Our elbows almost touch you. How we care
And worry, Goldilocks;
Thanksgiving's Goose, poor loveless Venus: life's a sell:
Our loveless fingers crook to crunch your sage
And parsley through your wishbone—you! I'll tell
You, Michael Darling: an adulterer,
My Husband, shows me in a parrot's cage
And feeds me like a lion. While I age,

Virtues and elders eye me. Love, the outrage
Would have undone me, if my mind had held
Together, half a moment. Altar boys
Lit candles with my diary. Page by page,
Its refuse, sparkling through my cage,

Branded me, Michael!" Then a popping noise:
It was her toy's
Fragments: her cockatoo. She yelled.
The whisky tumbler in her hand
Became a brand.
Her pigtails that her Aunt had belled
To tell us she was coming, flashed and tinkled.
"Husband, you used to call me Tomcat-kitten;
While we were playing Hamlet on our stage
With curtain rods for foils, my eyes were bleeding;
I was your valentine.
You are a bastard, Michael, aren't you! *Nein*,
Michael. It's no more valentines." Her hand
Covered her eyes to cage
Their burning from the daylight. Sleep dispelled
The burden of her spirit. But the cars
Rattled my window. *Where am I to go?* She yelled:
"Let go my apron!" And I saw them shine,
Her eyeballs—like a lion at the bars
Across my open window—like the stars!

Winter had come on horseback, and the snow,
Hostile and unattended, wrapped my feet
In sheepskins. Where I'd stumbled from the street,
A red cement Saint Francis fed a row
Of toga'd boys with birds beneath a Child.
His candles flamed in tumblers, and He smiled.
"Romans!" she whispered, "look, these overblown
And bootless Brothers tell us we must go
Barefooted through the snow where birds recite:
Come unto us, our burden's light—light, light,
This burden that our marriage turned to stone!
O Michael, must we join this deaf and dumb
Breadline for children? Sit and listen." So
I sat. I counted to ten thousand, wound
My cowhorn beads from Dublin on my thumb,
And ground them. *Miserere?* Not a sound.

Life Studies

(1959)

FOR ELIZABETH

Part One

Beyond the Alps

(On the train from Rome to Paris. 1950, the year Pius XII defined the dogma of Mary's bodily assumption.)

Reading how even the Swiss had thrown the sponge
in once again and Everest was still
unscaled, I watched our Paris pullman lunge
mooning across the fallow Alpine snow.
O bella Roma! I saw our stewards go
forward on tiptoe banging on their gongs.
Life changed to landscape. Much against my will
I left the City of God where it belongs.
There the skirt-mad Mussolini unfurled
the eagle of Caesar. He was one of us
only, pure prose. I envy the conspicuous
waste of our grandparents on their grand tours—
long-haired Victorian sages accepted the universe,
while breezing on their trust funds through the world.

When the Vatican made Mary's Assumption dogma,
the crowds at San Pietro screamed *Papa.*
The Holy Father dropped his shaving glass,
and listened. His electric razor purred,
his pet canary chirped on his left hand.
The lights of science couldn't hold a candle
to Mary risen—at one miraculous stroke,
angel-wing'd, gorgeous as a jungle bird!
But who believed this? Who could understand?
Pilgrims still kissed Saint Peter's brazen sandal.
The Duce's lynched, bare, booted skull still spoke.
God herded his people to the *coup de grâce*—
the costumed Switzers sloped their pikes to push,
O Pius, through the monstrous human crush. . . .

Our mountain-climbing train had come to earth.
Tired of the querulous hush-hush of the wheels,
the blear-eyed ego kicking in my berth
lay still, and saw Apollo plant his heels
on terra firma through the morning's thigh . . .
each backward, wasted Alp, a Parthenon,
fire-branded socket of the Cyclops' eye.
There were no tickets for that altitude
once held by Hellas, when the Goddess stood,
prince, pope, philosopher and golden bough,
pure mind and murder at the scything prow—
Minerva, the miscarriage of the brain.

Now Paris, our black classic, breaking up
like killer kings on an Etruscan cup.

The Banker's Daughter

*(Marie de Medici, shortly after the assassination of her husband, Henri IV.
Later, she was exiled by her son and lived in a house lent to her by Rubens.)*

Once this poor country egg from Florence lay
at her accouchement, such a virtuous ton
of woman only women thought her one.
King Henry pirouetted on his heel
and jested, "Look, my cow's producing veal."

O cozy scuffles, soft obscenities,
wardrobes that dragged the exchequer to its knees,
cables of pearl and crazy lutes strung tight—
O tension, groin and backbone! Every night
I kicked the pillows and embroidered lies
to rob my husband's purse. I said his eyes
flew kiting to my dormer from the blue.
I was a sparrow. He was fifty-two.

Alas, my brutal girlish mood-swings drove
my husband, wrenched and giddy, from the Louvre,
to sleep in single lodgings on the town.

He feared the fate of kings who died in sport. . . .
Murder cut him short—
a kitchen-knife honed on a carriage-wheel.

Your great nerve gone, Sire, sleep without a care.
No Hapsburg galleon coasts off Finisterre
with bars of bullion now to subsidize
the pilfering, pillaging democracies,
the pin-head priest, the nihilist grandee.
Sleep, sleep, my husband. There at Saint Denis,
the chiselled bolster and Carrara hound

show no emotion when we kiss the ground.
Now seasons cycle to the laughing ring
of scything children; king must follow king
and walk the plank to his immortal leap.
Ring, ring, tired bells, the King of France is dead;
who'll give the lover of the land a bed?
My son is adding inches in his sleep.
I see his dimpled fingers clutch Versailles.
Sing lullaby, my son, sing lullaby.
I rock my nightmare son, and hear him cry
for ball and sceptre; he asks the queen to die. . . .
And so I press my lover's palm to mine;
I am his vintage, and his living vine
entangles me, and oozes mortal wine
moment to moment. By repeated crime,
even a queen survives her little time.
You too, my husband. How you used to look
for blood and pastime! If you ever took
unfair advantages by right of birth,
pardon the easy virtues of the earth.

Inauguration Day: January 1953

The snow had buried Stuyvesant.
The subways drummed the vaults. I heard
the El's green girders charge on Third,
Manhattan's truss of adamant,
that groaned in ermine, slummed on want. . . .
Cyclonic zero of the word,
God of our armies, who interred
Cold Harbor's blue immortals, Grant!
Horseman, your sword is in the groove!

Ice, ice. Our wheels no longer move.
Look, the fixed stars, all just alike
as lack-land atoms, split apart,
and the Republic summons Ike,
the mausoleum in her heart.

A Mad Negro Soldier Confined at Munich

"We're all Americans, except the Doc,
a Kraut DP, who kneels and bathes my eye.
The boys who floored me, two black maniacs, try
to pat my hands. Rounds, rounds! Why punch the clock?

In Munich the zoo's rubble fumes with cats;
hoydens with air-guns prowl the Koenigsplatz,
and pink the pigeons on the mustard spire.
Who but my girl-friend set the town on fire?

Cat-houses talk cold turkey to my guards;
I found my *Fräulein* stitching outing shirts
in the black forest of the colored wards—
lieutenants squawked like chickens in her skirts.

Her German language made my arteries harden—
I've no annuity from the pay we blew.
I chartered an aluminum canoe,
I had her six times in the English Garden.

Oh mama, mama, like a trolley-pole
sparking at contact, her electric shock—
the power-house! . . . The doctor calls our roll—
no knives, no forks. We file before the clock,

and fancy minnows, slaves of habit, shoot
like starlight through their air-conditioned bowl.
It's time for feeding. Each subnormal boot-
black heart is pulsing to its ant-egg dole."

Part Two

91 Revere Street

The account of him is platitudinous, worldly and fond, but he has no Christian name and is entitled merely Major *M*. Myers in my Cousin Cassie Mason Myers Julian-James's privately printed *Biographical Sketches: A Key to a Cabinet of Heirlooms in the Smithsonian Museum*. The name-plate under his portrait used to spell out his name bravely enough: he was Mordecai Myers. The artist painted Major Myers in his sanguine War of 1812 uniform with epaulets, white breeches, and a scarlet frogged waistcoat. His right hand played with the sword "now to be seen in the Smithsonian cabinet of heirlooms." The pose was routine and gallant. The full-lipped smile was good-humoredly pompous and embarrassed.

Mordecai's father, given neither name nor initial, is described with an air of hurried self-congratulation by Cousin Cassie as "a friend of the Reverend Ezra Styles, afterward President of Yale College." As a very young man the son, Mordecai, studied military tactics under a French émigré, "the Bourbons' celebrated Colonel De la Croix." Later he was "matured" by six years' practical experience in a New York militia regiment organized by Colonel Martin Van Buren. After "the successful engagement against the British at Chrysler's Field, thirty shrapnel splinters were extracted from his shoulder." During convalescence, he wooed and won Miss Charlotte Bailey, "thus proving himself a better man than his rivals, the united forces of Plattsburg." He fathered ten children, sponsored an enlightened law exempting Quakers from military service in New York State, and died in 1870 at the age of ninety-four, "a Grand Old Man, who impressed strangers with the poise of his old-time manners."

Undoubtedly Major Mordecai had lived in a more ritualistic, gaudy, and animal world than twentieth-century Boston. There was something undecided, Mediterranean, versatile, almost double-faced about his bearing which suggested that, even to his contemporaries, he must have seemed gratuitously both *ci-devant* and *parvenu*. He was a dark man, a German Jew—no downright Yankee, but maybe such a fellow as Napoleon's mad, pomaded son-of-an-innkeeper general, Junot, Duc D'Abrantes; a man like mad George III's pomaded, disreputable son, "Prinny," the Prince Regent. Or he was one of those Moorish-looking dons painted by his contemporary, Goya—some leader of Spanish guerrillas against Bonaparte's occupation, who fled to South America. Our Major's suffering almond eye rested on his luxurious dawn-colored fingers ruffling an off-white glove.

Bailey-Mason-Myers! Easy-going, Empire State patricians, these relatives of my Grandmother Lowell seemed to have given my father his character. For he likewise lacked that granite *back-countriness* which Grandfather Arthur Winslow attributed to his own ancestors, the iconoclastic, mulish Dunbarton New Hampshire Starks. On the joint Mason-Myers bookplate, there are two merry and naked mermaids—lovely marshmallowy, boneless, Rubensesque butterballs, all burlesque-show bosoms and Flemish smiles. Their motto, *malo frangere quam flectere*, reads "I prefer to bend than to break."

Mordecai Myers was my Grandmother Lowell's grandfather. His life was tame and honorable. He was a leisured squire and merchant, a member of the state legislature, a mayor of Schenectady, a "president" of Kinderhook village. Disappointingly, his famous "blazing brown eye" seems in all things to have shunned the outrageous. After his death he was remembered soberly as a New York State gentleman, the friend and host of worldly men and politicians with Dutch names: De Witt Clinton, Vanderpoel, Hoes, and Schuyler. My mother was roused to warmth by the Major's scarlet vest and exotic eye. She always insisted that he was the one properly dressed and dieted ancestor in the lot we had inherited from my father's Cousin Cassie. Great-great-Grandfather Mordecai! Poor sheepdog in wolf's clothing! In the anarchy of my adolescent war on my parents, I tried to make him a true wolf, the wandering Jew! *Homo lupus homini!*

Major Mordecai Myer's portrait has been mislaid past finding, but out of my memories I often come on it in the setting of our Revere Street house, a setting now fixed in the mind, where it survives all the distortions of fantasy, all the blank befogging of forgetfulness. There, the vast number of remembered *things* remains rocklike. Each is in its place, each has its function, its history, its drama. There, all is preserved by that motherly care that one either ignored or resented in his youth. The things and their owners come back urgent with life and meaning—because finished, they are endurable and perfect.

Cousin Cassie only became a close relation in 1922. In that year she died. After some unpleasantness between Mother and a co-heiress, Helen Bailey, the estate was divided. Mother used to return frozen and thrilled from her property disputes, and I, knowing nothing of the rights and wrongs, would half-perversely confuse Helen Bailey with Helen of Troy and harden my mind against the monotonous *parti pris* of Mother's voice. Shortly after our move to Boston in 1924, a score of unwanted Myers portraits was delivered to our new house on Revere Street. These were later followed by "their dowry"—four moving vans groaning with heavy Edwardian furniture. My father began to receive his first quarterly payments from the Mason-Myers Julian-James Trust Fund, sums "not grand enough to corrupt us," Mother explained, "but sufficient to prevent Daddy from being entirely at the mercy of his salary." The Trust sufficed: our lives became tantalized with possibilities, and my father felt encouraged to take the risk—a small one in those boom years—of resigning from the Navy on the gamble of doubling his income in business.

I was in the third grade and for the first time becoming a little more popular at school. I was afraid Father's leaving the Navy would destroy my standing. I was a churlish, disloyal, romantic boy, and quite without hero worship for my father, whose actuality seemed so inferior to the photographs in uniform he once mailed to us from the Golden Gate. My real *love*, as Mother used to insist to all new visitors, was toy soldiers. For a few months at the flood tide of this infatuation, people were ciphers to me—valueless except as chances for increasing my armies of soldiers. Roger Crosby, a child in the second grade of my Brimmer Street School, had thousands—not mass-produced American stereotypes, but hand-painted solid lead soldiers made to order in Dijon, France. Roger's father had a still more artistic and adult collection; its ranks—each man at least six inches tall—marched in glass cases under the eyes of recognizable replicas of mounted Napoleonic captains: Kléber, Marshal Ney, Murat, King of Naples. One delirious afternoon Mr. Crosby showed me his toys and was perhaps the first grownup to talk to me not as a child but as an equal when he discovered how feverishly I followed his anecdotes on uniforms and the evolution of tactical surprise. Afterwards, full of high thoughts, I ran up to Roger's play room and hoodwinked him into believing that his own soldiers were "ballast turned out by central European sweatshops." He agreed I was being sweetly generous when I traded twenty-four worthless Jordan Marsh papier-mâché doughboys for whole companies of his gorgeous, imported Old Guards, Second Empire "redlegs," and modern *chasseurs d'Alpine* with sky-blue berets. The haul was so huge that I had to take a child's wheelbarrow to Roger's house at the top of Pinckney Street. When I reached home with my last load, Mr. Crosby was talking with my father on our front steps. Roger's soldiers were all returned; I had only the presence of mind to hide a single soldier, a peely-nosed black sepoy wearing a Shriner's fez.

Nothing consoled me for my loss, but I enjoyed being allowed to draw Father's blunt dress sword, and I was proud of our Major Mordecai. I used to stand dangerously out in the middle of Revere Street in order to see through our windows and gloat on this portrait's scarlet waistcoat blazing in the bare, Spartan whiteness of our den-parlor. Mordecai Myers lost his glory when I learned from my father that he was only a "major *pro tem*." On a civilian, even a civilian soldier, the flamboyant waistcoat was stuffy and no more martial than officers' costumes in our elementary school musicals.

In 1924 people still lived in cities. Late that summer, we bought the 91 Revere Street house, looking out on an unbuttoned part of Beacon Hill bounded by the North End slums, though reassuringly only four blocks away from my Grandfather Winslow's brown pillared house at 18 Chestnut Street. In the decades preceding and following the First World War, old Yankee families had upset expectation by regaining this section of the Hill from the vanguards of the lace-curtain Irish. This was bracing news for my parents in that topsy-turvy era when the Republican Party and what were called "people of the right sort" were no longer dominant in city elections. Still, even in the palmy, laissez-faire '20s, Revere Street refused to be a straightforward, immutable residential fact. From one end to the other, houses kept being sanded down, repainted, or abandoned to the flaking of decay. Houses, changing hands, changed their language and nationality. A few doors to our south the householders spoke "Beacon Hill British" or the flat *nay nay* of the Boston Brahmin. The parents of the children a few doors north spoke mostly in Italian.

My mother felt a horrified giddiness about the adventure of our address. She once said, "We are barely perched on the outer rim of the hub of decency." We were less than fifty yards from Louisburg Square, the cynosure of old historic Boston's plain-spoken, cold roast elite—the Hub of the Hub of the Universe. Fifty yards!

As a naval ensign, Father had done postgraduate work at Harvard. He had also done postgraduate work at M.I.T., preferred the purely scientific college, and condescended to both. In 1924, however, his tone began to change; he now began to speak warmly of Harvard as his second alma mater. We went to football games at the Harvard Stadium, and one had the feeling that our lives were now being lived in the brutal, fashionable expectancy of the stadium: we had so many downs, so many minutes, and so many yards to go for a winning touchdown. It was just such a winning financial and social advance that my parents promised themselves would follow Father's resignation from the Navy and his acceptance of a sensible job offered him at the Cambridge branch of Lever Brothers' Soap.

The advance was never to come. Father resigned from the service in 1927, but he never had a civilian *career*; he instead had merely twenty-two years of the civilian *life*. Almost immediately he bought a larger and more stylish house; he sold his ascetic, stove-black Hudson and bought a plump brown Buick; later the Buick was exchanged for a high-toned, as-good-as-new Packard with a custom-designed royal blue and mahogany body. Without drama, his earnings more or less decreased from year to year.

But so long as we were on Revere Street, Father tried to come to terms with it and must have often wondered whether he on the whole liked or disliked the neighborhood's lack of side. He was still at this time rather truculently democratic in what might be described as an upper middle-class, naval, and Masonic fashion. He was a mumbler. His opinions were almost morbidly hesitant, but he considered himself a matter-of-fact man of science and had an unspoiled faith in the superior efficiency of northern nations. He modeled his allegiances and humor on the cockney imperialism of Rudyard Kipling's swearing Tommies, who did their job. Autochthonous Boston snobs, such as the Winslows or members of Mother's reading club, were alarmed by the brassy callousness of our naval visitors, who labeled the Italians they met on Revere Street as "grade-A" and "grade-B wops." The Revere Street "grade-B's" were Sicilian Catholics and peddled crummy second-hand furniture on Cambridge Street, not far from the site of Great-great-Grandfather Charles Lowell's disused West Church, praised in an old family folder as "a haven from the Sodom and Gomorrah of Trinitarian orthodoxy and the tyranny of the letter." Revere Street "grade-A's," good North Italians, sold fancy groceries and Colonial heirlooms in their shops near the Public Garden. Still other Italians were Father's familiars; they sold him bootleg Scotch and *vino rosso* in teacups.

The outside of our Revere Street house was a flat red brick surface unvaried by the slightest suggestion of purple panes, delicate bay, or triangular window-cornice—a sheer wall formed by the seamless conjunction of four inseparable façades, all of the same commercial and purgatorial design. Though placed in the heart of Old Boston, it was ageless and artless, an epitome of those "leveler" qualities Mother found most grueling about the naval service. 91 Revere Street was mass-produced, *regulation-issue*, and yet struck Boston society as stupidly out of the ordinary, like those white elephants—a mother-of-pearl scout knife or a tea-kettle barometer—which my father used to pick up on sale at an Army-Navy store.

The walls of Father's minute Revere Street den-parlor were bare and white. His bookshelves were bare and white. The den's one adornment was a ten-tube home-assembled battery radio set, whose loudspeaker had the shape and color of a Mexican sombrero. The radio's specialty was getting programs from Australia and New Zealand in the early hours of the morning.

My father's favorite piece of den furniture was his oak and "rhinoceros hide" armchair. It was ostentatiously a masculine, or rather a bachelor's, chair. It had a notched, adjustable back; it was black, cracked, hacked, scratched, splintered, gouged, initialed, gunpowder-charred and tumbler-ringed. It looked like pale tobacco leaves laid on dark tobacco leaves. I doubt if Father, a considerate man, was responsible for any of the marring. The chair dated from his plebe days at the Naval Academy, and had been bought from a shady, shadowy, roaring character, midshipman "Beauty" Burford. Father loved each disfigured inch.

My father had been born two months after his own father's death. At each stage of his life, he was to be forlornly fatherless. He was a deep boy brought up entirely by a mild widowed mother and an intense widowed grandmother. When he was fourteen and a half, he became a deep young midshipman. By the time he graduated from Annapolis, he had a high sense of abstract form, which he beclouded with his humor. He had reached, perhaps, his final mental possibilities. He was deep—not with profundity, but with the dumb depth of one who trusted in statistics and was dubious of personal experience. In his forties, Father's soul went underground: as a civilian he kept his high sense of form, his humor, his accuracy, but this accuracy was henceforth unimportant, recreational, *hors de combat*. His debunking grew myopic; his shyness grew evasive; he argued with a fumbling languor. In the twenty-two years Father lived after he resigned from the Navy, he never again deserted Boston and never became Bostonian. He survived to drift from job to job, to be displaced, to be grimly and literally that old cliché, a fish out of water. He gasped and wheezed with impotent optimism, took on new ideals with each new job, never ingeniously enjoyed his leisure, never even hid his head in the sand.

Mother hated the Navy, hated naval society, naval pay, and the trip-hammer rote of settling and unsettling a house every other year when Father was transferred to a new station or ship. She had been married nine or ten years and still suspected that her husband was savorless, unmasterful, merely considerate. Unmasterful—Father's specialized efficiency lacked utterly the flattering bossiness she so counted on from her father, my Grandfather Winslow. It was not Father's absence on sea-duty that mattered; it was the eroding necessity of moving *with* him, of keeping in step. When he was far away on the Pacific, she had her friends, her parents, a house to herself— Boston! Fully conscious of her uniqueness and normality she basked in the refreshing stimulation of dreams in which she imagined Father as suitably sublimed. She used to describe such a sublime man to me over tea and English muffins. He was Siegfried carried lifeless through the shining air by Brunnhilde to Valhalla, and accompanied by the throb of my Great Aunt Sarah playing his leitmotif in the released manner taught her by the Abbé Liszt. Or Mother's hero dove through the grottoes of the Rhine and slaughtered the homicidal and vulgar dragon coiled about the golden hoard. Mother seemed almost light-headed when she retold the romance of Sarah Bernhardt in *L'Aiglon*, the Eaglet, the weakling! She would speak the word *weakling* with such amused vehemence that I formed a grandiose and false image of L'Aiglon's Father, the *big* Napoleon: he was a strong man who scratched under his paunchy little white vest a torso all hair, muscle, and manliness. Instead of the dreams, Mother now had the insipid fatigue of keeping house. Instead of the *Eagle*, she had a twentieth-century naval commander interested in steam, radio, and "the fellows." To avoid naval yards, steam, and "the fellows," Mother had impulsively bought the squalid, impractical Revere Street house. Her marriage daily forced her to squander her subconsciously hoarded energies.

"Weelawaugh, we-ee-eeelawaugh, weelawaugh," shrilled Mother's high voice. *"But-and, but-and, but-and!"* Father's low mumble would drone in answer. Though I couldn't be sure that I had caught the meaning of the words, I followed the sounds as though they were a movie. I felt drenched in my parents' passions.

91 Revere Street was the setting for those arthritic spiritual pains that troubled us for the two years my mother spent in trying to argue my father into resigning from the Navy. When the majestic, hollow boredom of the second year's autumn dwindled to the mean boredom of a second winter, I grew less willing to open my mouth. I bored my parents, they bored me.

"Weelawaugh, we-ee-eelawaugh, weelawaugh!" "But-and, but-and, but-and!"

During the week ends I was at home much of the time. All day I used to look forward to the nights when my bedroom walls would once again vibrate, when I would awake with rapture to the rhythm of my parents arguing, arguing one another to exhaustion. Sometimes, without bathrobe or slippers, I would wriggle out into the cold hall on my belly and ambuscade myself behind the banister. I could often hear actual words. "Yes, yes, yes," Father would mumble. He was "backsliding" and "living in the fool's paradise of habitual retarding and retarded do-nothing inertia." Mother had violently set her heart on the resignation. She was hysterical even in her calm, but like a patient and forbearing strategist, she tried to pretend her neutrality. One night she said with murderous coolness, "Bobby and I are leaving for Papá's." This was an ultimatum to force Father to sign a deed placing the Revere Street house in Mother's name.

I writhed with disappointment on the nights when Mother and Father only lowed harmoniously together like cows, as they criticized Helen Bailey or Admiral De Stahl. Once I heard my mother say, "A *man* must make up his *own* mind. Oh Bob, if you are going to resign, do it *now* so I can at least plan for your son's *survival* and education on a single continent."

About this time I was being sent for my *survival* to Dr. Dane, a Quaker chiropractor with an office on Marlborough Street. Dr. Dane wore an old-fashioned light tan druggist's smock; he smelled like a healthy old-fashioned drugstore. His laboratory was free of intimidating technical equipment, and had only the conservative lay roughness and toughness that was so familiar and disarming to us in my Grandfather Winslow's country study or bedroom. Dr. Dane's rosy hands wrenched my shoulders with tremendous éclat and made me feel a hero; I felt unspeakable joy whenever an awry muscle fell back into serenity. My mother, who had no curiosity or imagination for cranky occultism, trusted Dr. Dane's clean, undrugged manliness—so like home. She believed that chiropractic had cured me of my undiagnosed asthma, which had defeated the expensive specialists.

"A penny for your thoughts, Schopenhauer," my mother would say.

"I am thinking about pennies," I'd answer.

"When *I* was a child I used to love telling Mamá everything I had done," Mother would say.

"But you're not a child," I would answer.

I used to enjoy dawdling and humming "Anchors Aweigh" up Revere Street after a day at school. "Anchors Aweigh," the official Navy song, had originally been the song composed for my father's class. And yet my mind always blanked and seemed to fill with a clammy hollowness when Mother asked prying questions. Like other tongue-tied, difficult children, I dreamed I was a master of cool, stoical repartee. "What have you been doing, Bobby?" Mother would ask. "I haven't," I'd answer. At home I thus saved myself from emotional exhaustion.

At school, however, I was extreme only in my conventional mediocrity, my colorless, distracted manner, which came from restless dreams of being admired. My closest friend was Eric Burckhard, the son of a professor of architecture at Harvard. The Burckhards came from Zurich and were very German, not like Ludendorff, but in the kindly, comical, nineteenth-century manner of Jo's German husband in *Little Men*, or in the manner of the crusading *sturm und drang* liberal scholars in second year German novels. "Eric's mother and father are *both* called Dr. Burckhard," my mother once said, and indeed there was something endearingly repellent about Mrs. Burckhard with her doctor's degree, her long, unstylish skirts, and her dramatic, dulling blond braids. Strangely the Burckhards' sober continental bourgeois house was without golden mean—everything was either hilariously old Swiss or madly modern. The Frau Doctor Burckhard used to serve mid-morning hot chocolate with rosettes of whipped cream, and receive her friends in a long, uncarpeted hall-drawing room with lethal ferns and a yellow beeswaxed hardwood floor shining under a central skylight. On the wall there were large expert photographs of what at a distance appeared to be Mont Blanc—they were in reality views of Frank Lloyd Wright's Japanese hotel.

I admired the Burckhards and felt at home in their house, and these feelings were only intensified when I discovered that my mother was always ill at ease with them. The heartiness, the enlightenment, and the bright, ferny greenhouse atmosphere were too much for her.

Eric and I were too young to care for books or athletics. Neither of our houses had absorbing toys or an elevator to go up and down in. We were inseparable, but I cannot imagine what we talked about. I loved Eric because he was more popular than I and yet absolutely *sui generis* at the Brimmer School. He had a chalk-white face and limp, fine, white-blond hair. He was frail, elbowy, started talking with an enthusiastic Mont Blanc chirp and would flush with bewilderment if interrupted. All the other boys at Brimmer wore little tweed golf suits with knickerbockers, but Eric always arrived in a black suit coat, a Byronic collar, and cuffless gray flannel trousers that almost hid his shoes. The long trousers were replaced on warm days by gray flannel shorts, such as were worn by children still in kindergarten. Eric's unenviable and freakish costumes were too old or too young. He accepted the whims of his parents with a buoyant tranquillity that I found unnatural.

My first and terminating quarrel with Eric was my fault. Eventually almost our whole class at Brimmer had whooping cough, but Eric's seizure was like his long trousers—untimely: he was sick a month too early. For a whole month he was in quarantine and forced to play by himself in a removed corner of the Public Garden. He was certainly conspicuous as he skiproped with his Swiss nurse under the out-of-the-way Ether Memorial Fountain far from the pond and the swan boats. His parents had decided that this was an excellent opportunity for Eric to brush up on his German, and so the absoluteness of his quarantine was monstrously exaggerated by the fact that child and nurse spoke no English but only a guttural, British-sounding, Swiss German. Round and round and round the Fountain, he played intensely, fraily, obediently, until I began to tease him. Though motioned away by him, I came close. I had attracted some of the most popular Brimmer School boys. For the first time I had gotten favorable attention from several little girls. I came close. I shouted. Was Eric afraid of girls? I imitated his German. *Ein, zwei, drei, BEER*. I imitated Eric's coughing. "He is afraid he will give you whooping cough if he talks or lets you come nearer," the nurse said in her musical Swiss-English voice. I came nearer. Eric flushed, grew white, bent double with coughing. He began to cry, and had to be led away from the Public Garden. For a whole week I routed Eric from the Garden daily, and for two or three days I was a center of interest. "Come see the Lake Geneva spider monkey!" I would shout. I don't know why I couldn't stop. Eric never told his father, I think, but when he recovered we no longer spoke. The breach was so unspoken and intense that our classmates were actually horrified. They even devised a solemn ritual for our reconciliation. We crossed our hearts, mixed spit, mixed blood. The reconciliation was hollow.

My parents' confidences and quarrels stopped each night at ten or eleven o'clock, when my father would hang up his tuxedo, put on his commander's uniform, and take a trolley back to the naval yard at Charlestown. He had just broken in a new car. Like a chauffeur, he watched this car, a Hudson, with an informed vigilance, always giving its engine hair-trigger little tinkerings of adjustment or friendship, always fearful lest the black body, unbeautiful as his boiled shirts, should lose its outline and gloss. He drove with flawless, almost instrumental, monotony. Mother, nevertheless, was forever encouraging him to walk or take taxis. She would tell him that his legs were growing vestigial from disuse and remind him of the time a jack had slipped and he had broken his leg while shifting a tire. "Alone and at night," she would say, "an amateur driver is unsafe in a car." Father sighed and obeyed—only, putting on a martyred and penny-saving face, he would keep his self-respect by taking the trolley rather than a taxi. Each night he shifted back into his uniform, but his departures from Revere Street were so furtive that several months passed before I realized what was happening—we had *two* houses! Our second house was the residence in the Naval Yard assigned to the third in command. It was large, had its own flagpole, and screen porches on three levels—yet it was something to be ashamed of. Whatever pomp or distinction its possession might have had for us was destroyed by an eccentric humiliation inflicted on Father by his superior, Admiral De Stahl, the commandant at Charlestown. De Stahl had not been consulted about our buying the 91 Revere Street house. He was outraged, stormed about "flaunting private fortunes in the face of naval tradition," and ordered my father to sleep on bounds at the Yard in the house provided for that purpose.

On our first Revere Street Christmas Eve, the telephone rang in the middle of dinner; it was Admiral De Stahl demanding Father's instant return to the Navy Yard. Soon Father was back in his uniform. In taking leave of my mother and grandparents he was, as was usual with him under pressure, a little evasive and magniloquent. "A woman works from sun to sun," he said, "but a sailor's watch is never done." He compared a naval officer's hours with a doctor's, hinted at surprise maneuvers, and explained away the uncommunicative arrogance of Admiral De Stahl: "The Old Man has to be hush-hush." Later that night, I lay in bed and tried to imagine that my father was leading his engineering force on a surprise maneuver through arctic wastes. A forlorn hope! "Hush-hush, hush-hush," whispered the snowflakes as big as street lamps as they broke on Father—broke and buried. Outside, I heard real people singing carols, shuffling snow off their shoes, opening and shutting doors. I worried at the meaning of a sentence I had heard quoted from the *Boston Evening Transcript*: "On this Christmas Eve, as usual, the whole of Beacon Hill can be expected to become a single old-fashioned open house—the names of mine host the Hill, and her guests will read like the contents of the Social Register." I imagined Beacon Hill changed to the snow queen's palace, as vast as the north pole. My father pressed a cold finger to his lip: "hush-hush," and led his surprise squad of sailors around an altar, but the altar was a tremendous cash register, whose roughened nickel surface was cheaply decorated with trowels, pyramids, and Arabic swirls. A great drawer helplessly chopped back and forth, unable to shut because choked with greenbacks. "Hush-hush!" My father's engineers wound about me with their eye-patches, orange sashes, and curtain-ring earrings, like the Gilbert and Sullivan pirates' chorus. . . . Outside on the streets of Beacon Hill, it was night, it was dismal, it was raining. Something disturbing had befallen the familiar and honorable Salvation Army band; its big drum and accordion were now accompanied by drunken voices howling: *The Old Gray Mare, she ain't what she used to be, when Mary went to milk the cow*. A sound of a bosun's whistle. Women laughing. Someone repeatedly rang our doorbell. I heard my mother talking on the telephone. "Your inebriated sailors have littered my doorstep with the dregs of Scollay Square." There was a gloating panic in her voice that showed she enjoyed the drama of talking to Admiral De Stahl. "Sir," she shrilled, "you have compelled my husband to leave me alone and defenseless on Christmas Eve!" She ran into my bedroom. She hugged me. She said, "Oh Bobby, it's such a comfort to have a man in the house." "I am not a man," I said, "I am a boy."

Boy—at that time this word had private associations for me; it meant weakness, outlawry, and yet was a status to be held onto. Boys were a sideline at my Brimmer School. The eight superior grades were limited to girls. In these grades, moreover, scholarship was made subservient to discipline, as if in contempt of the male's two idols: career and earning power. The school's tone, its *ton*, was a blend of the feminine and the military, a bulky reality governed in turn by stridency, smartness, and steadiness. The girls wore white jumpers, black skirts, stockings, and rectangular low-heeled shoes. An ex-West Pointer had been appointed to teach drill; and, at the moment of my enrollment in Brimmer, our principal, the hitherto staid Miss Manice, was rumored to be showing signs of age and of undermining her position with the school trustees by girlish, quite out of character, rhapsodies on the varsity basketball team, winner of two consecutive championships. The lower four grades, peaceful and lackadaisical, were, on the other hand, almost a separate establishment. Miss Manice regarded these "coeducated" classes with amused carelessness, allowed them to wear their ordinary clothes, and . . . carelessness, however, is incorrect—Miss Manice, in her administration of the lower school, showed the inconsistency and euphoria of a dual personality. Here she mysteriously shed all her Prussianism. She quoted Emerson and Mencken, disparaged the English, threatened to break with the past, and boldly coquetted with the non-military American genius by displaying movies illustrating the careers of Edison and Ford. Favored lower school teachers were permitted to use us as guinea pigs for mildly radical experiments. At Brimmer I *unlearned* writing. The script that I had mastered with much agony at my first school was denounced as illegible: I was taught to print according to the Dalton Plan—to this day, as a result, I have to print even my two middle names and can only really *write* two words: "Robert" and "Lowell." Our instruction was subject to bewildering leaps. The usual fall performance by the Venetian glass-blowers was followed by a tour of the Riverside Press. We heard Rudy Vallee, then heard spirituals sung by the Hampton Institute choir. We studied grammar from a formidable, unreconstructed textbook written by Miss Manice's father. There, I battled with figures of speech and Greek terminology: *Chiasmus*, the arrangement of corresponding words in opposite order; *Brachylogy*, the failure to repeat an element that is supplied in more or less modified form. Then all this pedantry was nullified by the introduction of a new textbook which proposed to lift the face of syntax by using game techniques and drawings.

Physical instruction in the lower school was irregular, spontaneous, and had nothing of that swept and garnished barrack-room cameraderie of the older girls' gymnasium exercises. On the roof of our school building, there was an ugly concrete area that looked as if it had been intended for the top floor of a garage. Here we played tag, drew lines with chalk, and chose up sides for a kind of kids' soccer. On bright spring days, Mr. Newell, a submerged young man from Boston University, took us on botanical hikes through the Arboretum. He had an eye for inessentials—read us Martha Washington's poems at the Old State House, pointed out the roof of Brimmer School from the top of the Customs House, made us count the steps of the Bunker Hill Monument, and one rainy afternoon broke all rules by herding us into the South Boston Aquarium in order to give an unhealthy, eager, little lecture on the sewage-consumption of the conger eel. At last Miss Manice seemed to have gotten wind of Mr. Newell's moods. For an afternoon or two she herself served as his substitute. We were walked briskly past the houses of Parkman and Dana, and assigned themes on the spunk of great persons who had overcome physical handicaps and risen to the top of the ladder. She talked about Elizabeth Barrett, Helen Keller; her pet theory, however, was that "women simply are not the equals of men." I can hear Miss Manice browbeating my white and sheepish father, "How can we stand up to you? Where are our Archimedeses, our Wagners, our Admiral Simses?" Miss Manice adored "Sir Walter Scott's *big bow-wow*," wished "Boston had banned the tubercular novels of the Brontës," and found nothing in the world "so simpatico" as the "strenuous life" lived by President Roosevelt. Yet the extravagant hysteria of Miss Manice's philanthropy meant nothing; Brimmer was entirely a woman's world—*dummkopf*, perhaps, but not in the least Quixotic, Brimmer was ruled by a woman's obvious aims and by her naive pragmatism. The quality of this regime, an extension of my mother's, shone out in full glory at general assemblies or when I sat with a handful of other boys on the bleachers of Brimmer's new Manice Hall. In unison our big girls sang "America"; back and forth our amazons tramped—their brows were wooden, their dress was black and white, and their columns followed standard-bearers holding up an American flag, the white flag of the Commonwealth of Massachusetts, and the green flag of Brimmer. At basketball games against Miss Lee's or Miss Winsor's, it was our upper-school champions who rushed onto the floor, as feline and fateful in their pace as lions. This was our own immediate and daily spectacle; in comparison such masculine displays as trips to battle cruisers commanded by comrades of my father seemed eyewash—the Navy moved in a realm as ghostlike and removed from my life as the elfin acrobatics of Douglas Fairbanks or Peter Pan. I wished I were an older girl. I wrote Santa Claus for a field hockey stick. To be a boy at Brimmer was to be small, denied, and weak.

I was promised an improved future and taken on Sunday afternoon drives through the suburbs to inspect the boys' schools: Rivers, Dexter, Country Day. These expeditions were stratagems designed to give me a chance to know my father; Mother noisily stayed behind and amazed me by pretending that I had forbidden her to embark on "men's work." Father, however, seldom insisted, as he should have, on seeing the headmasters in person, yet he made an astonishing number of friends; his trust begat trust, and something about his silences encouraged junior masters and even school janitors to pour out small talk that was detrimental to rival institutions. At each new school, however, all this gossip was easily refuted; worse still Mother was always ready to cross-examine Father in a manner that showed that she was asking questions for the purpose of giving, not of receiving, instruction; she expressed astonishment that a wishy-washy desire to be everything to everybody had robbed a naval man of any reliable concern for his son's welfare. Mother regarded the suburban schools as "gerrymandered" and middle-class; after Father had completed his round of inspections, she made her own follow-up visits and told Mr. Dexter and Mr. Rivers to their faces that she was looking for a "respectable stop-gap" for her son's "three years between Brimmer and Saint Mark's." Saint Mark's was the boarding school for which I had been enrolled at birth, and was due to enter in 1930. I distrusted change, knew each school since kindergarten had been more constraining and punitive than its predecessor, and believed the suburban country day schools were flimsily disguised fronts for reformatories. With the egotistic, slightly paranoid apprehensions of an only child, I wondered what became of boys graduating from Brimmer's fourth grade, feared the worst—we were darkly imperiled, like some annual bevy of Athenian youths destined for the Minotaur. And to judge from my father, men between the ages of six and sixty did nothing but meet new challenges, take on heavier responsibilities, and lose all freedom to explode. A ray of hope in the far future was my white-haired Grandfather Winslow, whose unchecked commands and demands were always upsetting people for their own good—he was all I could ever want to be: the bad boy, the problem child, the commodore of his household.

When I entered Brimmer I was eight and a half. I was distracted in my studies, assented to whatever I was told, picked my nose whenever no one was watching, and worried our third-grade teacher by organizing creepy little gangs of boys at recess. I was girl-shy. Thick-witted, narcissistic, thuggish, I had the conventional prepuberty character of my age; whenever a girl came near me, my whole person cringed like a sponge wrung dry by a clenching fist. I was less rather than more bookish than most children, but the girl I dreamed about continually had wheel-spoke black and gold eyelashes, double-length page-boy blond hair, a little apron, a bold, blunt face, a saucy, shivery way of talking, and . . . a paper body—she was the girl in John Tenniel's illustrations to *Alice in Wonderland*. The invigorating and symmetrical aplomb of my ideal Alice was soon enriched and nullified by a second face, when my father took me to the movies on the afternoon of one of Mother's headaches. An innocuous child's movie, the bloody, all-male *Beau Geste* had been chosen, but instead my father preferred a nostalgic tour of places he had enjoyed on shore leave. We went to the Majestic Theater where he had first seen Pola Negri—where we too saw Pola Negri, sloppy-haired, slack, yawning, ravaged, unwashed . . . an Anti-Alice.

Our class belles, the Norton twins, Elie and Lindy, fell far short of the Nordic Alice and the foreign Pola. Their prettiness, rather fluffy, freckled, bashful, might have escaped notice if they had been one instead of two, and if their manners had been less goodhumored, entertaining, and reliable. What mattered more than sex, athletics, or studies to us at Brimmer was our popularity; each child had an unwritten class-popularity poll inside his head. Everyone was ranked, and all day each of us mooned profoundly on his place, as it quivered like our blood or a compass needle with a thousand revisions. At nine character is, perhaps, too much *in ovo* for a child to be strongly disliked, but sitting next to Elie Norton, I glanced at her and gulped prestige from her popularity. We were not close at first; then nearness made us closer friends, for Elie had a gracious gift, the gift of gifts, I suppose, in a child: she forgot all about the popularity-rank of the classmate she was talking to. No moron could have seemed so uncritical as this airy, chatty, intelligent child, the belle of our grade. She noticed my habit of cocking my head on one side, shutting my eyes, and driving like a bull through opposition at soccer— wishing to amuse without wounding, she called me Buffalo Bull. At general assembly she would giggle with contented admiration at the upper-school girls in their penal black and white. "What bruisers, what beef-eaters! Dear girls," she would sigh, parroting her sophisticated mother, "we shall all become fodder for the governess classes before graduating from Brimmer." I felt that Elie Norton understood me better than anyone except my playful little Grandmother Winslow.

One morning there was a disaster. The boy behind me, no friend, had been tapping at my elbow for over a minute to catch my attention before I consented to look up and see a great golden puddle spreading toward me from under Elie's chair. I dared not speak, smile, or flicker an eyelash in her direction. She ran bawling from the classroom. Trying to catch every eye, yet avoid commitment, I gave sidelong and involuntary smirks at space. I began to feel manic with superiority to Elie Norton and struggled to swallow down a feeling of goaded hollowness—was I deserting her? Our teacher left us on our honor and ran down the hall. The class milled about in a hesitant hush. The girls blushed. The boys smirked. Miss Manice, the principal, appeared. She wore her whitish-brown dress with darker brown spots. Shimmering in the sunlight and chilling us, she stood mothlike in the middle of the classroom. We rushed to our seats. Miss Manice talked about how there was "nothing laughable about a malaise." She broke off. Her face took on an expression of invidious disgust. She was staring at me. . . . In the absent-mindedness of my guilt and excitement, I had taken the nearest chair, the chair that Elie Norton had just left. "Lowell," Miss Manice shrieked, "are you going to soak there all morning like a bump on a log?"

When Elie Norton came back, there was really no break in her friendliness toward me, but there was something caved in, something crippled in the way I stood up to her and tried to answer her disengaged chatter. I thought about her all the time; seldom meeting her eyes now, I felt rich and raw in her nearness. I wanted passionately to stay on at Brimmer, and told my mother a fib one afternoon late in May of my last year. "Miss Manice has begged me to stay on," I said, "and enter the fifth grade." Mother pointed out that there had never been a boy in the fifth grade. Contradicted, I grew excited. "If Miss Manice has begged me to stay," I said, "why can't I stay?" My voice rose, I beat on the floor with my open hands. Bored and bewildered, my mother went upstairs with a headache. "If you won't believe me," I shouted after her, "why don't you telephone Miss Manice or Mrs. Norton?"

Brimmer School was thrown open on sunny March and April afternoons and our teachers took us for strolls on the polite, landscaped walks of the Public Garden. There I'd loiter by the old iron fence and gape longingly across Charles Street at the historic Boston Common, a now largely wrong-side-of-the-tracks park. On the Common there were mossy bronze reliefs of Union soldiers, and a captured German tank filled with smelly wads of newspaper. Everywhere there were grit, litter, gangs of Irish, Negroes, Latins. On Sunday afternoons orators harangued about Sacco and Vanzetti, while others stood about heckling and blocking the sidewalks. Keen young policemen, looking for trouble, lolled on the benches. At nightfall a police lieutenant on horseback inspected the Common. In the Garden, however, there was only Officer Lever, a single white-haired and mustached dignitary, who had once been the doorman at the Union Club. He now looked more like a member of the club. "Lever's a man about town," my Grandfather Winslow would say. "Give him Harris tweeds and a glass of Scotch, and I'd take him for Cousin Herbert." Officer Lever was without thoughts or deeds, but Back Bay and Beacon Hill parents loved him just for being. No one asked this hollow and leonine King Log to be clairvoyant about children.

One day when the saucer magnolias were in bloom, I bloodied Bulldog Binney's nose against the pedestal of George Washington's statue in full view of Commonwealth Avenue; then I bloodied Dopey Dan Parker's nose; then I stood in the center of a sundial tulip bed and pelted a little enemy ring of third-graders with wet fertilizer. Officer Lever was telephoned. Officer Lever telephoned my mother. In the presence of my mother and some thirty nurses and children, I was expelled from the Public Garden. I was such a bad boy, I was told, "that *even* Officer Lever had been forced to put his foot down."

New England winters are long. Sunday mornings are long. Ours were often made tedious by preparations for dinner guests. Mother would start airing at nine. Whenever the air grew so cold that it hurt, she closed the den windows; then we were attacked by sour kitchen odors winding up a clumsily rebuilt dumb-waiter shaft. The windows were again thrown open. We sat in an atmosphere of glacial purity and sacrifice. Our breath puffed whitely. Father and I wore sleeveless cashmere jerseys Mother had bought at Filene's Basement. A do-it-yourself book containing diagrams for the correct carving of roasts lay on the arm of Father's chair. At hand were Big Bill Tilden on tennis, Capablanca on chess, newspaper clippings from Sidney Lenz's bridge column, and a magnificent tome with photographs and some American's nationalist sketch of Sir Thomas Lipton's errors in the Cup Defender races. Father made little progress in these diversions, and yet one of the authors assured him that mastery demanded only willing readers who understood the meaning of English words. Throughout the winter a gray-whiteness glared through the single den window. In the apoplectic brick alley, a fire escape stood out against our sooty plank fence. Father believed that churchgoing was undignified for a naval man; his Sunday mornings were given to useful acts such as lettering his three new galvanized garbage cans: R.T.S. LOWELL—U.S.N.

Our Sunday dinner guests were often naval officers. Naval officers were not Mother's sort; very few people *were* her sort in those days, and that was her trouble—a very authentic, human, and plausible difficulty, which made Mother's life one of much suffering. She did not have the self-assurance for wide human experience; she needed to feel liked, admired, surrounded by the approved and familiar. Her haughtiness and chilliness came from apprehension. She would start talking like a *grande dame* and then stand back rigid and faltering, as if she feared being crushed by her own massively intimidating offensive.

Father's old Annapolis roommate, Commander Billy "Battleship Bilge" Harkness, was a frequent guest at Revere Street and one that always threw Mother off balance. Billy was a rough diamond. He made jokes about his "all-American family tree," and insisted that his name, pronounced Harkness, should be spelled Herkness. He came from Louisville, Kentucky, drank whisky to "renew his Bourbon blood," and still spoke with an accent that sounded—so his colleagues said—"like a bran-fed stallion." Like my father, however, Commander Billy had entered the Naval Academy when he was a boy of fourteen; his Southernisms had been thoroughly rubbed away. He was teased for knowing nothing about race horses, mountaineers, folk ballads, hams, sour mash, tobacco . . . Kentucky Colonels. Though hardly an officer and a gentleman in the old Virginian style, he was an unusual combination of clashing virtues: he had led his class in the sciences and yet was what his superiors called "a *mathmaddition* with the habit of command." He and my father, the youngest men in their class, had often been shipmates. Bilge's executive genius had given color and direction to Father's submissive tenacity. He drank like a fish at parties, but was a total abstainer on duty. With reason Commander Harkness had been voted the man most likely to make a four-star admiral in the class of '07.

Billy called his wife *Jimmy* or *Jeems*, and had a rough friendly way of saying, "Oh, Jimmy's bright as a penny." Mrs. Harkness was an unpleasant rarity: she was the only naval officer's wife we knew who was also a college graduate. She had a flat flapper's figure, and hid her intelligence behind a nervous twitter of vulgarity and toadyism. "Charlotte," she would almost scream at Mother, "is this mirAGE, this MIRacle your *own* dining room!"

Then Mother might smile and answer in a distant, though cosy and amused, voice, "I usually manage to make myself pretty comfortable."

Mother's comfort was chic, romantic, impulsive. If her silver service shone, it shone with hectic perfection to rebuke the functional domesticity of naval wives. She had determined to make her *ambiance* beautiful and luxurious, but wanted neither her beauty nor her luxury unaccompanied. Beauty pursued too exclusively meant artistic fatuity of a kind made farcical by her Aunt Sarah Stark Winslow, a beauty too lofty and original ever to marry, a prima donna on the piano, too high-strung ever to give a public recital. Beauty alone meant the maudlin ignominy of having one's investments managed by interfering relatives. Luxury alone, on the other hand, meant for Mother the "paste and fool's-gold polish" that one met with in the foyer of the new Statler Hotel. She loathed the "undernourishment" of Professor Burckhard's Bauhaus modernism, yet in moments of pique she denounced our pompous Myers mahoganies as "suitable for politicians at the Bellevue Hotel." She kept a middle-of-the-road position, and much admired Italian pottery with its fresh peasant colors and puritanical, clean-cut lines. She was fond of saying, "The French *do* have taste," but spoke with a double-edged irony which implied the French, with no moral standards to support their finish, were really no better than naval yahoos. Mother's beautiful house was dignified by a rich veneer of the useful.

"I have always believed carving to be *the* gentlemanly talent," Mother used to proclaim. Father, faced with this opinion, pored over his book of instructions or read the section on table carving in the Encyclopædia Britannica.

Eventually he discovered among the innumerable small, specialized Boston "colleges" an establishment known as a carving school. Each Sunday from then on he would sit silent and erudite before his roast. He blinked, grew white, looked winded, and wiped beads of perspiration from his eyebrows. His purpose was to reproduce stroke by stroke his last carving lesson, and he worked with all the formal rightness and particular error of some shaky experiment in remote control. He enjoyed quiet witticisms at the expense of his carving master—"a philosopher who gave himself all the airs of a Mahan!" He liked to pretend that the carving master had stated that "No two cuts are identical," *ergo*: "each offers original problems for the *executioner*." Guests were appeased by Father's saying, "I am just a plebe at this guillotine. Have a hunk of my roast beef hash."

What angered Father was Mrs. Harkness's voice grown merciless with excitement, as she studied his hewing and hacking. She was sure to say something tactless about how Commander Billy was "a stingy artist at carving who could shave General Washington off the dollar bill."

Nothing could stop Commander Billy, that born carver, from reciting verses:

> *"By carving my way*
> *I lived on my pay;*
> *This* reeward, *though small,*
> *Beats none at all . . .*

> *My carving paper-thin*
> *Can make a guinea* hin,
> *All giblets, bones, and skin,*
> *Canteen a party of* tin."

And I, furious for no immediate reason, blurted out, "Mother, how much does Grandfather Winslow have to fork up to pay for Daddy's carving school?"

These Sunday dinners with the Harknesses were always woundingly boisterous affairs. Father, unnaturally outgoing, would lead me forward and say, "Bilge, I want you to meet my first coupon from the bond of matrimony."

Commander Billy would answer, "So this is the range-finder you are raising for future wars!" They would make me salute, stand at attention, stand at ease. "Angel-face," Billy would say to me, "you'll skipper a flivver."

"Jimmy" Harkness, of course, knew that Father was anxiously negotiating with Lever Brothers' Soap, and arranging for his resignation from the service, but nothing could prevent her from proposing time and again her "hens' toast to the drakes." Dragging Mother to her feet, Jimmy would scream, "To Bob and Bilgy's next battleship together!"

What Father and Commander Billy enjoyed talking about most was their class of '07. After dinner, the ladies would retire to the upstairs sitting room. As a special privilege I was allowed to remain at the table with the men. Over and over, they would talk about their ensigns' cruise around the world, escaping the "reeport," gunboating on the upper Yangtze during the Chinese Civil War, keeping sane and sanitary at Guantanamo, patroling the Golfo del Papayo during the two-bit Nicaraguan Revolution, when water to wash in cost a dollar a barrel and was mostly "alkali and wrigglers." There were the class casualties: Holden and Holcomb drowned in a foundered launch off Hampton Roads; "Count" Bowditch, killed by the Moros and famous for his dying words to Commander Harkness: "I'm all right. Get on the job, Bilge."

They would speak about the terrible 1918 influenza epidemic, which had killed more of their classmates than all the skirmishes or even the World War. It was an honor, however, to belong to a class which included "Chips" Carpender, whose destroyer, the *Fanning*, was the only British or American warship to force a German submarine to break water and surrender. It was a feather in their caps that three of their classmates, Bellinger, Reade, and another, should have made the first trans-Atlantic seaplane flight. They put their faith in teamwork, and Lindbergh's solo hop to Paris struck them as unprofessional, a newspaper trick. What made Father and Commander Billy mad as hornets was the mare's-nest made of naval administration by "deserving Democrats." Hadn't Secretary of State Bryan ordered their old battlewagon the *Idaho* to sail on a goodwill mission to Switzerland? "Bryan, Bryan, Bryan," Commander Billy would boom, "the pious swab had been told that Lake Geneva had annexed the Adriatic." Another "guy with false gills," Josephus Daniels, "ordained by Divine Providence Secretary of the Navy," had refused to send Father and Billy to the war zone. "You are looking," Billy would declaim, "at martyrs in the famous victory of red tape. Our names are rubric." A man they had to take their hats off to was Theodore Roosevelt; Billy had been one of the lucky ensigns who had helped "escort the redoubtable Teddy to Panama." Perhaps because of his viciously inappropriate nickname, "Bilge," Commander Harkness always spoke with brutal facetiousness against the class *bilgers*, officers whose "services were no longer required by the service." In more Epicurean moods,

Bilge would announce that he "meant to accumulate a lot of dough from complacent, well-meaning, although misguided West Point officers gullible enough to bet their shirts on the Army football team."

"Let's have a squint at your *figger* and waterline, Bob," Billy would say. He'd admire Father's trim girth and smile familiarly at his bald spot. "Bob," he'd say, "you've maintained your displacement and silhouette unmodified, except for somewhat thinner top chafing gear."

Commander Billy's drinking was a "pain in the neck." He would take possession of Father's sacred "rhino" armchair, sprawl legs astraddle, make the tried and true framework groan, and crucify Mother by roaring out verbose toasts in what he called "me boozy cockney-h'Irish." He would drink to our cocktail shaker. " 'Ere's to the 'older of the Lowelldom nectar," he would bellow. "Hip, hip, hooray for señor Martino, h'our h'old hipmate, 'elpmate, and hhonorary member of '07—h'always h'able to navigate and never says dry." We never got through a visit without one of Billy's "Bottoms up to the 'ead of the Nation. 'Ere's to herb-garden 'Erb." This was a swaggering dig at Herbert Hoover's notoriously correct, but insular, refusal to "imbibe anything more potent than Bromo-Seltzer" at a war-relief banquet in Brussels. Commander Billy's bulbous, water-on-the-brain forehead would glow and trickle with fury. Thinking on Herbert Hoover and Prohibition, he was unable to contain himself. "What a hick! We haven't been steered by a gentleman of parts since the redoubtable Teddy." He recited *wet* verses, such as the following inserted in Father's class book:

> "*I tread the bridge with measured pace;*
> *Proud, yet anguish marks my face—*
> *What worries me like crushing sin*
> *Is where on the sea can I buy dry gin?*"

In his cups, Commander Bilge acted as though he owned us. He looked like a human ash-heap. Cigar ashes buried the heraldic hedgehog on the ash tray beside him; cigar ashes spilled over and tarnished the golden stork embroidered on the table-cover; cigar ashes littered his own shiny blue-black uniform. Greedily Mother's eyes would brighten, drop and brighten. She would say darkly, "I was brought up by Papá to be like a naval officer, to be ruthlessly neat."

Once Commander Billy sprawled back so recklessly that the armchair began to come apart. "You see, Charlotte," he said to Mother, "at the height of my *climacteric* I am breaking Bob's chair."

Harkness went in for tiresome, tasteless harangues against Amy Lowell, which he seemed to believe necessary for the enjoyment of his after-dinner cigar. He would point a stinking baby stogie at Mother. " 'Ave a peteeto cigareeto, Charlotte," he would crow. "Puff on this whacking black cheroot, and you'll be a match for any reeking señorita *femme fatale* in the spiggotty republics, where blindness from Bob's bathtub hooch is still unknown. When you go up in smoke, Charlotte, remember the *Maine*. Remember Amy Lowell, that cigar-chawing, guffawing, senseless and meterless, multimillion-heiress, heavyweight mascot on a floating fortress. Damn the *Patterns*! Full speed ahead on a cigareeto!"

Amy Lowell was never a welcome subject in our household. Of course, no one spoke disrespectfully of Miss Lowell. She had been so plucky, so *formidable, so beautifully and unblushingly immense*, as Henry James might have said. And yet, though irreproachably decent herself apparently, like Mae West she seemed to provoke indecorum in others. There was an anecdote which I was too young to understand: it was about Amy's getting her migraine headaches from being kept awake by the exercises of honeymooners in an adjacent New York hotel room. Amy's relatives would have liked to have honored her as a *personage*, a personage a little *outrée* perhaps, but perfectly within the natural order, like Amy's girlhood idol, the Duse. Or at least she might have been unambiguously tragic, short-lived, and a classic, like her last idol, John Keats. My parents piously made out a case for Miss Lowell's *Life of Keats*, which had killed its author and was so much more manly and intelligible than her poetry. Her poetry! But was *poetry* what one could call Amy's loud, bossy, unladylike *chinoiserie*—her free verse! For those that could understand it, her matter was, no doubt, blameless, but the effrontery of her manner made my parents relish Robert Frost's remark that "writing free verse was like playing tennis without a net."

Whenever Amy Lowell was mentioned Mother bridled. Not distinguishing, not caring whether her relative were praised or criticized, she would say, "Amy had the courage of her convictions. She worked like a horse." Mother would conclude characteristically, "Amy did insist on doing everything the *hard* way. I think, perhaps, that her brother, the President of Harvard, did more for *other* people."

Often Father seemed to pay little attention to the conversation of his guests. He would smack his lips, and beam absentmindedly and sensuously, as if he were anticipating the comforts of civilian life—a perpetual shore leave in Hawaii. The Harknesses, however, cowed him. He would begin to feel out the subject of his resignation and observe in a wheedle obscurely loaded with significance that "certain *cits*, no brighter than you or I, pay income taxes as large as a captain's yearly salary."

Commander Harkness, unfortunately, was inclined to draw improper conclusions from such remarks. Disregarding the "romance of commerce," he would break out into ungentlemanly tirades against capital. "Yiss, old Bob," he would splutter, "when I consider the ungodly hoards garnered in by the insurance and broking gangs, it breaks my heart. Riches, reaches, overreaches! If Bob and I had half the swag that Harkness of Yale has just given Lowell of Harvard to build Georgian houses for Boston quee-eers with British accents!" He rumbled on morosely about retired naval officers "forced to live like coolies on their half-pay. Hurrah for the Bull Moose Party!" he'd shout. "Hurrah for Boss Curley! Hurrah for the Bolshies!"

Nothing prevented Commander Billy from telling about his diplomatic mission in 1918, when "his eyes had seen the Bolshie on his native heath." He had been in Budapest "during the brief sway of Béla Kun-Whon. Béla was giving those Hunkyland money-bags and educators the boot into the arms of American philanthropy!"

Then Mother would say, hopefully, "Mamá always said that the *old* Hungarians *did* have taste. Billy, your reference to Budapest makes me heartsick for Europe. I am dying for Bob and Bobby's permission to spend next summer at Etretat."

Commander Billy Harkness specialized in verses like "The Croix de Guerre":

> *"I toast the guy, who, crossing over,*
>   *Abode in London for a year,*
> *The guy who to his wife and lover*
>   *Returned with conscience clean and clear,*
> *Who nightly prowling Piccadilly*
>   *Gave icy stares to floozies wild,*
> *And when approached said, 'Bilgy Billy*
>   *Is mama's darling angel child—'*
> *Now he's the guy who rates the croy dee geer!"*

Mother, however, smiled mildly. "Billy," she would say, "my cousin, Admiral Ledyard Atkinson, always has a twinkle in his eye when he asks after your *vers de société*."

" 'Tommy' Atkins!" snorted Commander Billy. "I know Tommy better than my own mother. He's the first chapter in a book I'm secretly writing and leaving to the archives called *Wild Admirals I Have Known*. And now my bodily presence may no longer grace the inner sanctum of the Somerset Club, for fear Admiral Tommy'll assault me with five new chapters of his *Who Won the Battle of Jutland?*"

After the heat and push of Commander Billy, it was pleasant to sit in the shade of the Atkinsons. Cousin Ledyard wasn't exactly an admiral: he had been promoted to this rank during the World War and had soon reverted back to his old rank of captain. In 1926 he was approaching the retiring age and was still a captain. He was in charge of a big, stately, comfortable, but anomalous warship, which seldom sailed further than hailing distance from its Charlestown drydock. He was himself stately and anomalous. Serene, silver-maned, and Spanish-looking, Cousin Ledyard liked full-dress receptions and crowed like a rooster in his cabin crowded with liveried Filipinos, Cuban trophies, and racks of experimental firearms, such as pepper-box pistols and a machine gun worked by electric batteries. He rattled off Spanish phrases, told first-hand adventure stories about service with Admiral Schley, and reminded one of some landsman and diplomat commanding a galleon in Philip II's Armada. With his wife's money he had bought a motor launch which had a teak deck and a newfangled diesel engine. While his warship perpetually rode at anchor, Cousin Ledyard was forever hurrying about the harbor in his launch. "Oh, Led Atkinson has dash and his own speedboat!" This was about the best my father could bring himself to say for his relative. Commander Billy, himself a man of action, was more sympathetic: "Tommy's about a hundred horse and buggy power." Such a dinosaur, however, had little to offer an '07 Annapolis graduate. Billy's final judgment was that Cousin Ledyard knew less *trig* than a schoolgirl, had been promoted through mistaken identity or merely as "window-dressing," and "was really plotting to put airplane carriers in square sails to stem the tide of our declining Yankee seamanship." Mother lost her enthusiasm for Captain Atkinson's stately chatter—he was "unable to tell one woman from another."

Cousin Ledyard's wife, a Schenectady Hoes distantly related to my still living Great-Grandmother Myers, was twenty years younger than her husband. This made her a trying companion; with the energy of youth she demanded the homage due to age. Once while playing in the Mattapoisett tennis tournament, she had said to her opponent, a woman her own age but married to a young husband, "I believe I'll call you Ruth; you can call me Mrs. Atkinson." She was a radiant Christian Scientist, darted about in smart serge suits and blouses frothing with lace. She filled her purse with Science literature and boasted without irony of "Boston's greatest grand organ" in the Christian Science mother temple on Huntington Avenue. As a girl, she had grown up with our Myers furniture. We dreaded Mrs. Atkinson's descents on Revere Street. She pooh-poohed Mother's taste, snorted at our ignorance of Myers family history, treated us as mere custodians of the Myers furniture, resented alterations, and had the memory of a mastodon for Cousin Cassie's associations with each piece. She wouldn't hear of my mother's distress from neuralgia, dismissed my asthma as "growing-pains," and sought to rally us by gossiping about healers. She talked a prim, sprightly babble. Like many Christian Scientists, she had a bloodless, euphoric, inexhaustible interest in her own body. In a discourse which lasted from her first helping of roast beef through her second demitasse, Mrs. Atkinson held us spellbound by telling how her healer had "surprised and evaporated a cyst inside a sac" inside her "major intestine."

I can hear my father trying to explain his resignation from the Navy to Cousin Ledyard or Commander Billy. Talking with an unnatural and importunate jocularity, he would say, "Billy Boy, it's a darned shame, but this State of Massachusetts doesn't approve of the service using its franchise and voting by mail. I haven't had a chance to establish residence since our graduation in '07. I think I'll put my blues in mothballs and become a *cit* just to prove I still belong to the country. The directors of Lever Brothers' Soap in Cambridge . . . I guess for *cits*, Billy, they've really got something on the ball, because they tell me they want me on their team."

Or Father, Cousin Ledyard, Commander Billy, and I would be sitting on after dinner at the dining-room table and talking man to man. Father would say, "I'm afraid I'll grow dull and drab with all this goldbricking ashore. I am too old for tennis singles, but too young for that confirmed state of senility known as golf."

Cousin Ledyard and Commander Billy would puff silently on their cigars. Then Father would try again and say pitifully, "I don't think a naval man can ever on the *outside* replace the friends he made during his years of wearing the blue."

Then Cousin Ledyard would give Father a polite, funereal look and say, "Speaking of golf, Bob, you've hit me below the belt. I've been flubbing away at the game for thirty years without breaking ninety."

Commander Billy was blunter. He would chaff Father about becoming a "beachcomber" or "purser for the Republican junior chamber of commerce." He would pretend that Father was in danger of being jailed for evading taxes to support "Uncle Sam's circus." *Circus* was Commander Billy's slang for the Navy. The word reminded him of a comparison, and once he stood up from the table and bellowed solemnly: "Oyez, oyez! Bob Lowell, our bright boy, our class baby, is now on a par with 'Rattle-Ass Rats' Richardson, who resigned from us to become press agent for Sells-Floto Circus, and who writes me: 'Bilgy Dear—Beating the drum ahead of the elephants and the spangled folk, I often wonder why I run into so few of my classmates.' "

Those dinners, those apologies! Perhaps I exaggerate their embarassment because they hover so grayly in recollection and seem to anticipate ominously my father's downhill progress as a civilian and Bostonian. It was to be expected, I suppose, that Father should be in irons for a year or two, while becoming detached from his old comrades and interests, while waiting for the new life.

I used to sit through the Sunday dinners absorbing cold and anxiety from the table. I imagined myself hemmed in by our new, inherited Victorian Myers furniture. In the bleak Revere Street dining room, none of these pieces had at all that air of unhurried condescension that had been theirs behind the summery veils of tissue paper in Cousin Cassie Julian-James's memorial volume. Here, table, highboy, chairs, and screen—mahogany, cherry, teak— looked nervous and disproportioned. They seemed to wince, touch elbows, shift from foot to foot. High above the highboy, our gold National Eagle stooped forward, plastery and doddering. The Sheffield silver-plate urns, more precious than solid sterling, peeled; the bodies of the heraldic mermaids on the Mason-Myers crest blushed a metallic copper tan. In the harsh New England light, the bronze sphinxes supporting our sideboard looked as though manufactured in Grand Rapids. All too clearly no one had worried about synchronizing the grandfather clock's minutes, days, and months with its mellow old Dutch seascape-painted discs for showing the phases of the moon. The stricken, but still striking gong made sounds like steam banging through pipes. Colonel Myers' monumental Tibetan screen had been impiously shortened to fit it for a low Yankee ceiling. And now, rough and gawky, like some Hindu water buffalo killed in mid-rush but still alive with mad momentum, the screen hulked over us . . . and hid the pantry sink.

Our real blue-ribbon-winning *bête noire* was of course the portrait of Cousin Cassie's father, Mordecai Myers' fourth and most illustrious son: Colonel Theodorus Bailey Myers. The Colonel, like half of our new portraits, was merely a collateral relation; though really as close to us as James Russell Lowell, no one called the Colonel "Great Grand Uncle," and Mother playfully pretended that her mind was overstrained by having to remember his full name, rank, and connection. In the portrait, Colonel Theodorus wore a black coat and gray trousers, an obsequiously conservative costume which one associated with undertakers and the musicians at Symphony Hall. His spats were pearl gray plush with pearl buttons. His mustache might have been modeled on the mustache of a bartender in a Western. The majestic Tibetan screen enclosed him as though he were an ancestor-god from Lhasa, a blasphemous yet bogus attitude. Mr. Myers' colonel's tabs were crudely stitched to a civilian coat; his New York Yacht Club button glowed like a carnation; his vainglorious picture frame was a foot and a half wide. Forever, his right hand hovered over a glass dome that covered a model locomotive. He was vaguely Middle-Eastern and waiting. A lady in Mother's sewing circle had pertly interpreted this portrait as, "King Solomon about to receive the Queen of Sheba's shares in the Boston and Albany Railroad." Gone now was the Colonel's place of honor at Cousin Cassie's Washington mansion; gone was his charming satire on the belles of 1850, entitled, *Nothing to Wear*, which had once been quoted "throughout the length and breadth of the land as generally as was Bret Harte's *Heathen Chinee*"; gone was his priceless collection of autographed letters of *all* the Signers of the Declaration of Independence—he had said once, "my letters will be my tombstone." Colonel Theodorus Bailey Myers had never been a New Englander. His family tree reached to no obscure Somersetshire yeoman named Winslowe or Lowle. He had never even, like his father, Mordecai, gloried in a scarlet War of 1812 waistcoat. His portrait was an indifferent example from a dull, bad period. The Colonel's only son had sheepishly changed his name from Mason-Myers to Myers-Mason.

Waiting for dinner to end and for the guests to leave, I used to lean forward on my elbows, support each cheekbone with a thumb, and make my fingers meet in a clumsy Gothic arch across my forehead. I would stare through this arch and try to make life stop. Out in the alley the sun shone irreverently on our three garbage cans lettered: R.T.S. LOWELL—U.S.N. When I shut my eyes to stop the sun, I saw first an orange disc, then a red disc, then the portrait of Major Myers apotheosized, as it were, by the sunlight lighting the blood smear of his scarlet waistcoat. Still there was no *coup de théâtre* about the Major as he looked down on us with his portly young man's face of a comfortable upper New York State patroon and the friend of Robert Livingston and Martin Van Buren. Great-great-Grandfather Myers had never frowned down in judgment on a Salem witch. There was no allegory in his eyes, no *Mayflower*. Instead he looked peacefully at his sideboard, his cut-glass decanters, his cellaret—the worldly bosom of the Mason-Myers mermaid engraved on a silver-plated urn. If he could have spoken, Mordecai would have said, "My children, my blood, accept graciously the loot of your inheritance. We are all dealers in used furniture."

The man who seems in my memory to sit under old Mordecai's portrait is not my father, but Commander Billy—*the* Commander after Father had thrown in his commission. There Billy would sit glowing, perspiring, bragging. Despite his rowdiness, he even then breathed the power that would make him a vice-admiral and hero in World War II. I can hear him boasting in lofty language of how he had stood up for democracy in the day of Lenin and Béla Kun; of how he "practiced the sport of kings" (i.e., commanded a destroyer) and combed the Mediterranean, Adriatic, and Black Seas like gypsies—seldom knowing what admiral he served under or where his next meal or load of fuel oil was coming from.

It always vexed the Commander, however, to think of the strings that had been pulled to have Father transferred from Washington to Boston. He would ask Mother, "Why in God's name should a man with Bob's brilliant cerebellum go and mess up his record by actually *begging* for that impotent field nigger's job of second in command at the defunct Boston Yard!"

I would squirm. I dared not look up because I knew that the Commander abhorred Mother's dominion over my father, thought my asthma, supposedly brought on by the miasmal damp of Washington, a myth, and considered our final flight to Boston a scandal.

My mother, on the other hand, would talk back sharply and explain to Billy that there was nothing second-string about the Boston Yard except its commandant, Admiral De Stahl, who had gone into a frenzy when he learned that my parents, supposed to live at the naval yard, had set themselves up without his permission at 91 Revere Street. The Admiral had *commanded* Father to reside at the yard, but Mother had bravely and stubbornly held on at Revere Street.

"A really great person," she would say, "knows how to be courteous to his superiors."

Then Commander Harkness would throw up his hands in despair and make a long buffoonish speech. "Would you believe it?" he'd say. "De Stahl, the anile slob, would make Bob Lowell sleep seven nights a week and twice on Sundays in that venerable twenty-room pile provided for his third in command at the yard. 'Bobby me boy,' the Man says, 'henceforth I will that you sleep wifeless. You're to push your beauteous mug into me boudoir each night at ten-thirty and each morn at six. And don't mind me laying to alongside the Missus De Stahl,' the old boy squeaks; 'we're just two oldsters as weak as babies. But Robbie Boy,' he says, 'don't let me hear of you hanging on your telephone wire and bending off the ear of that forsaken frau of yours sojourning on Revere Street. I might have to phone you in a hurry, if I should happen to have me stroke.' "

Taking hold of the table with both hands, the Commander tilted his chair backwards and gaped down at me with sorrowing Gargantuan wonder: "I know why Young Bob is an only child."

Part Three

Ford Madox Ford

(1873–1939)

The lobbed ball plops, then dribbles to the cup. . . .
(a birdie Fordie!) But it nearly killed
the ministers. Lloyd George was holding up
the flag. He gabbled, "Hop-toad, hop-toad, hop-toad!
Hueffer has used a niblick on the green;
it's filthy art, Sir, filthy art!"
You answered, "What is art to me and thee?
Will a blacksmith teach a midwife how to bear?"
That cut the puffing statesman down to size,
Ford. You said, "Otherwise,
I would have been general of a division." Ah Ford!
Was it war, the sport of kings, that your *Good Soldier,*
the best French novel in the language, taught
those Georgian Whig magnificoes at Oxford,
at Oxford decimated on the Somme?
Ford, five times black-balled for promotion,
then mustard gassed voiceless some seven miles
behind the lines at Nancy or Belleau Wood:
you emerged in your "worn uniform,
gilt dragons on the revers of the tunic,"
a Jonah—O divorced, divorced
from the whale-fat of post-war London! Boomed,
cut, plucked and booted! In Provence, New York . . .
marrying, blowing . . . nearly dying
at Boulder, when the altitude
pressed the world on your heart,
and your audience, almost football-size,
shrank to a dozen, while you stood
mumbling, with fish-blue-eyes,
and mouth pushed out
fish-fashion, as if you gagged for air. . . .
Sandman! Your face, a childish *O.* The sun
is pernod-yellow and it gilds the heirs
of all the ages there on Washington

and Stuyvesant, your Lilliputian squares,
where writing turned your pockets inside out.
But master, mammoth mumbler, tell me why
the bales of your left-over novels buy
less than a bandage for your gouty foot.
Wheel-horse, O unforgetting elephant,
I hear you huffing at your old Brevoort,
Timon and Falstaff, while you heap the board
for publishers. Fiction! I'm selling short
your lies that made the great your equals. Ford,
you were a kind man and you died in want.

For George Santayana
(1863–1952)

In the heydays of 'forty-five,
bus-loads of souvenir-deranged
G.I.'s and officer-professors of philosophy
came crashing through your cell,
puzzled to find you still alive,
free-thinking Catholic infidel,
stray spirit, who'd found
the Church too good to be believed.
Later I used to dawdle
past Circus and Mithraic Temple
to *Santo Stefano* grown paper-thin
like you from waiting. . . .
There at the monastery hospital,
you wished those geese-girl sisters wouldn't bother
their heads and yours by praying for your soul:
"There is no God and Mary is His Mother."

Lying outside the consecrated ground
forever now, you smile
like Ser Brunetto running for the green
cloth at Verona—not like one
who loses, but like one who'd won . . .
as if your long pursuit of Socrates'
demon, man-slaying Alcibiades,
the demon of philosophy, at last had changed
those fleeting virgins into friendly laurel trees
at *Santo Stefano Rotondo*, when you died
near ninety,
still unbelieving, unconfessed and unreceived,
true to your boyish shyness of the Bride.
Old trooper, I see your child's red crayon pass,
bleeding deletions on the galleys you hold

under your throbbing magnifying glass,
that worn arena, where the whirling sand
and broken-hearted lions lick your hand
refined by bile as yellow as a lump of gold.

To Delmore Schwartz

(Cambridge 1946)

We couldn't even keep the furnace lit!
Even when we had disconnected it,
the antiquated
refrigerator gurgled mustard gas
through your mustard-yellow house,
and spoiled our long maneuvered visit
from T. S. Eliot's brother, Henry Ware. . . .

Your stuffed duck craned toward Harvard from my trunk:
its bill was a black whistle, and its brow
was high and thinner than a baby's thumb;
its webs were tough as toenails on its bough.
It was your first kill; you had rushed it home,
pickled in a tin wastebasket of rum—
it looked through us, as if it'd died dead drunk.
You must have propped its eyelids with a nail,
and yet it lived with us and met our stare,
Rabelaisian, lubricious, drugged. And there,
perched on my trunk and typing-table,
it cooled our universal
Angst a moment, Delmore. We drank and eyed
the chicken-hearted shadows of the world.
Underseas fellows, nobly mad,
we talked away our friends. "Let Joyce and Freud,
the Masters of Joy,
be our guests here," you said. The room was filled
with cigarette smoke circling the paranoid,
inert gaze of Coleridge, back
from Malta—his eyes lost in flesh, lips baked and black.
Your tiger kitten, *Oranges,*
cartwheeled for joy in a ball of snarls.
You said:
"We poets in our youth begin in sadness;
thereof in the end come despondency and madness;

Stalin has had two cerebral hemorrhages!"
The Charles
River was turning silver. In the ebb-
light of morning, we stuck
the duck
-'s web-
foot, like a candle, in a quart of gin we'd killed.

Words for Hart Crane

"When the Pulitzers showered on some dope
or screw who flushed our dry mouths out with soap,
few people would consider why I took
to stalking sailors, and scattered Uncle Sam's
phoney gold-plated laurels to the birds.
Because I knew my Whitman like a book,
stranger in America, tell my country: I,
Catullus redivivus, once the rage
of the Village and Paris, used to play my role
of homosexual, wolfing the stray lambs
who hungered by the Place de la Concorde.
My profit was a pocket with a hole.
Who asks for me, the Shelley of my age,
must lay his heart out for my bed and board."

Part Four

LIFE STUDIES

I

My Last Afternoon with Uncle Devereux Winslow

1922: the stone porch of my Grandfather's summer house

I.
"I won't go with you. I want to stay with Grandpa!"
That's how I threw cold water
on my Mother and Father's
watery martini pipe dreams at Sunday dinner.
. . . Fontainebleau, Mattapoisett, Puget Sound. . . .
Nowhere was anywhere after a summer
at my Grandfather's farm.
Diamond-pointed, athirst and Norman,
its alley of poplars
paraded from Grandmother's rose garden
to a scary stand of virgin pine,
scrub, and paths forever pioneering.

One afternoon in 1922,
I sat on the stone porch, looking through
screens as black-grained as drifting coal.
Tockytock, tockytock
clumped our Alpine, Edwardian cuckoo clock,
slung with strangled, wooden game.
Our farmer was cementing a root-house under the hill.
One of my hands was cool on a pile
of black earth, the other warm
on a pile of lime. All about me
were the works of my Grandfather's hands:
snapshots of his *Liberty Bell* silver mine;
his high school at *Stukkert am Neckar*;
stogie-brown beams; fools'-gold nuggets;
octagonal red tiles,
sweaty with a secret dank, crummy with ant-stale;
a Rocky Mountain chaise longue,

its legs, shellacked saplings.
A pastel-pale Huckleberry Finn
fished with a broom straw in a basin
hollowed out of a millstone.
Like my Grandfather, the décor
was manly, comfortable,
overbearing, disproportioned.

What were those sunflowers? Pumpkins floating shoulder-high?
It was sunset, Sadie and Nellie
bearing pitchers of ice-tea,
oranges, lemons, mint, and peppermints,
and the jug of shandygaff,
which Grandpa made by blending half and half
yeasty, wheezing homemade sarsaparilla with beer.
The farm, entitled *Char-de-sa*
in the Social Register,
was named for my Grandfather's children:
Charlotte, Devereux, and Sarah.
No one had died there in my lifetime . . .
Only Cinder, our Scottie puppy
paralyzed from gobbling toads.
I sat mixing black earth and lime.

II.
I was five and a half.
My formal pearl gray shorts
had been worn for three minutes.
My perfection was the Olympian
poise of my models in the imperishable autumn
display windows
of Rogers Peet's boys' store below the State House
in Boston. Distorting drops of water
pinpricked my face in the basin's mirror.
I was a stuffed toucan
with a bibulous, multicolored beak.

III.

Up in the air
by the lakeview window in the billiards-room,
lurid in the doldrums of the sunset hour,
my Great Aunt Sarah
was learning *Samson and Delilah.*
She thundered on the keyboard of her dummy piano,
with gauze curtains like a boudoir table,
accordionlike yet soundless.
It had been bought to spare the nerves
of my Grandmother,
tone-deaf, quick as a cricket,
now needing a fourth for "Auction,"
and casting a thirsty eye
on Aunt Sarah, risen like the phoenix
from her bed of troublesome snacks and Tauchnitz classics.

Forty years earlier,
twenty, auburn headed,
grasshopper notes of genius!
Family gossip says Aunt Sarah
tilted her archaic Athenian nose
and jilted an Astor.
Each morning she practiced
on the grand piano at Symphony Hall,
deathlike in the off-season summer—
its naked Greek statues draped with purple
like the saints in Holy Week. . . .
On the recital day, she failed to appear.

IV.

I picked with a clean finger nail at the blue anchor
on my sailor blouse washed white as a spinnaker.
What in the world was I wishing?
. . . A sail-colored horse browsing in the bulrushes . . .
A fluff of the west wind puffing
my blouse, kiting me over our seven chimneys,
troubling the waters. . . .

As small as sapphires were the ponds: *Quittacus, Snippituit,*
and *Assawompset*, halved by "the Island,"
where my Uncle's duck blind
floated in a barrage of smoke-clouds.
Double-barrelled shotguns
stuck out like bundles of baby crow-bars.
A single sculler in a camouflaged kayak
was quacking to the decoys. . . .

At the cabin between the waters,
the nearest windows were already boarded.
Uncle Devereux was closing camp for the winter.
As if posed for "the engagement photograph,"
he was wearing his severe
war-uniform of a volunteer Canadian officer.
Daylight from the doorway riddled his student posters,
tacked helter-skelter on walls as raw as a boardwalk.
Mr. Punch, a watermelon in hockey tights,
was tossing off a decanter of Scotch.
La Belle France in a red, white and blue toga
was accepting the arm of her "protector,"
the ingenu and porcine Edward VII.
The pre-war music hall belles
had goose necks, glorious signatures, beauty-moles,
and coils of hair like rooster tails.
The finest poster was two or three young men in khaki kilts
being bushwhacked on the veldt—
They were almost life-size. . . .

My Uncle was dying at twenty-nine.
"You are behaving like children,"
said my Grandfather,
when my Uncle and Aunt left their three baby daughters,
and sailed for Europe on a last honeymoon . . .
I cowered in terror.
I wasn't a child at all—
unseen and all-seeing, I was Agrippina
in the Golden House of Nero. . . .
Near me was the white measuring-door

my Grandfather had pencilled with my Uncle's heights.
In 1911, he had stopped growing at just six feet.
While I sat on the tiles,
and dug at the anchor on my sailor blouse,
Uncle Devereux stood behind me.
He was as brushed as Bayard, our riding horse.
His face was putty.
His blue coat and white trousers
grew sharper and straighter.
His coat was a blue jay's tail,
his trousers were solid cream from the top of the bottle.
He was animated, hierarchical,
like a gingersnap man in a clothes-press.
He was dying of the incurable Hodgkin's disease. . . .
My hands were warm, then cool, on the piles
of earth and lime,
a black pile and a white pile. . . .
Come winter,
Uncle Devereux would blend to the one color.

Dunbarton

My Grandfather found
his grandchild's fogbound solitudes
sweeter than human society.

When Uncle Devereux died,
Daddy was still on sea-duty in the Pacific;
it seemed spontaneous and proper
for Mr. MacDonald, the farmer,
Karl, the chauffeur, and even my Grandmother
to say, "your Father." They meant my Grandfather.

He was my Father. I was his son.
On our yearly autumn get-aways from Boston
to the family graveyard in Dunbarton,
he took the wheel himself—
like an admiral at the helm.
Freed from Karl and chuckling over the gas he was saving,
he let his motor roller-coaster
out of control down each hill.
We stopped at the *Priscilla* in Nashua
for brownies and root-beer,
and later "pumped ship" together in the Indian Summer. . . .

At the graveyard, a suave Venetian Christ
gave a sheepdog's nursing patience
to Grandfather's Aunt Lottie,
his Mother, the stone but not the bones
of his Father, Francis.
Failing as when Francis Winslow could count
them on his fingers,
the clump of virgin pine still stretched patchy ostrich necks
over the disused millpond's fragrantly woodstained water,
a reddish blur,
like the ever-blackening wine-dark coat

in our portrait of Edward Winslow
once sheriff for George the Second,
the sire of bankrupt Tories.

Grandfather and I
raked leaves from our dead forebears,
defied the dank weather
with "dragon" bonfires.

Our helper, Mr. Burroughs,
had stood with Sherman at Shiloh—
his thermos of shockless coffee
was milk and grounds;
his illegal home-made claret
was as sugary as grape jelly
in a tumbler capped with paraffin.

I borrowed Grandfather's cane
carved with the names and altitudes
of Norwegian mountains he had scaled—
more a weapon than a crutch.
I lanced it in the fauve ooze for newts.
In a tobacco tin after capture, the umber yellow mature newts
lost their leopard spots,
lay grounded as numb
as scrolls of candied grapefruit peel.
I saw myself as a young newt,
neurasthenic, scarlet
and wild in the wild coffee-colored water.

In the mornings I cuddled like a paramour
in my Grandfather's bed,
while he scouted about the chattering greenwood stove.

Grandparents

They're altogether otherworldly now,
those adults champing for their ritual Friday spin
to pharmacist and five-and-ten in Brockton.
Back in my throw-away and shaggy span
of adolescence, Grandpa still waves his stick
like a policeman;
Grandmother, like a Mohammedan, still wears her thick
lavender mourning and touring veil;
the Pierce Arrow clears its throat in a horse-stall.
Then the dry road dust rises to whiten
the fatigued elm leaves—
the nineteenth century, tired of children, is gone.
They're all gone into a world of light; the farm's my own.

The farm's my own!
Back there alone,
I keep indoors, and spoil another season.
I hear the rattley little country gramophone
racking its five foot horn:
"O Summer Time!"
Even at noon here the formidable
Ancien Régime still keeps nature at a distance. Five
green shaded light bulbs spider the billiards-table;
no field is greener than its cloth,
where Grandpa, dipping sugar for us both,
once spilled his demitasse.
His favorite ball, the number three,
still hides the coffee stain.

Never again
to walk there, chalk our cues,
insist on shooting for us both.
Grandpa! Have me, hold me, cherish me!
Tears smut my fingers. There

half my life-lease later,
I hold an *Illustrated London News*—;
disloyal still,
I doodle handlebar
mustaches on the last Russian Czar.

Commander Lowell

(1887–1950)

There were no undesirables or girls in my set,
when I was a boy at Mattapoisett—
only Mother, still her Father's daughter.
Her voice was still electric
with a hysterical, unmarried panic,
when she read to me from the Napoleon book.
Long-nosed Marie Louise
Hapsburg in the frontispiece
had a downright Boston bashfulness,
where she grovelled to Bonaparte, who scratched his navel,
and bolted his food—just my seven years tall!
And I, bristling and manic,
skulked in the attic,
and got two hundred French generals by name,
from *A* to *V*—from Augereau to Vandamme.
I used to dope myself asleep,
naming those unpronounceables like sheep.

Having a naval officer
for my Father was nothing to shout
about to the summer colony at "Matt."
He wasn't at all "serious,"
when he showed up on the golf course,
wearing a blue serge jacket and numbly cut
white ducks he'd bought
at a Pearl Harbor commissariat. . .
and took four shots with his putter to sink his putt.
"Bob," they said, "golf's a game you really ought to know how to play,
if you play at all."
They wrote him off as "naval,"
naturally supposed his sport was sailing.
Poor Father, his training was engineering!
Cheerful and cowed

among the seadogs at the Sunday yacht club,
he was never one of the crowd.

"Anchors aweigh," Daddy boomed in his bathtub,
"Anchors aweigh,"
when Lever Brothers offered to pay
him double what the Navy paid.
I nagged for his dress sword with gold braid,
and cringed because Mother, new
caps on all her teeth, was born anew
at forty. With seamanlike celerity,
Father left the Navy,
and deeded Mother his property.

He was soon fired. Year after year,
he still hummed "Anchors aweigh" in the tub—
whenever he left a job,
he bought a smarter car.
Father's last employer
was Scudder, Stevens and Clark, Investment Advisors,
himself his only client.
While Mother dragged to bed alone,
read Menninger,
and grew more and more suspicious,
he grew defiant.
Night after night,
à la clarté déserte de sa lampe,
he slid his ivory Annapolis slide rule
across a pad of graphs—
piker speculations! In three years
he squandered sixty thousand dollars.

Smiling on all,
Father was once successful enough to be lost
in the mob of ruling-class Bostonians.
As early as 1928,
he owned a house converted to oil,
and redecorated by the architect

of St. Mark's School. . . . Its main effect
was a drawing room, "longitudinal as Versailles,"
its ceiling, roughened with oatmeal, was blue as the sea.
And once
nineteen, the youngest ensign in his class,
he was "the old man" of a gunboat on the Yangtze.

Terminal Days at Beverly Farms

At Beverly Farms, a portly, uncomfortable boulder
bulked in the garden's center—
an irregular Japanese touch.
After his Bourbon "old fashioned," Father,
bronzed, breezy, a shade too ruddy,
swayed as if on deck-duty
under his six pointed star-lantern—
last July's birthday present.
He smiled his oval Lowell smile,
he wore his cream gabardine dinner-jacket,
and indigo cummerbund.
His head was efficient and hairless,
his newly dieted figure was vitally trim.

Father and Mother moved to Beverly Farms
to be a two minute walk from the station,
half an hour by train from the Boston doctors.
They had no sea-view,
but sky-blue tracks of the commuters' railroad shone
like a double-barrelled shotgun
through the scarlet late August sumac,
multiplying like cancer
at their garden's border.

Father had had two coronaries.
He still treasured underhand economies,
but his best friend was his little black *Chevie*,
garaged like a sacrificial steer
with gilded hooves,
yet sensationally sober,
and with less side than an old dancing pump.
The local dealer, a "buccaneer,"
had been bribed a "king's ransom"
to quickly deliver a car without chrome.

Each morning at eight-thirty,
inattentive and beaming,
loaded with his "calc" and "trig" books,
his clipper ship statistics,
and his ivory slide rule,
Father stole off with the *Chevie*
to loaf in the Maritime Museum at Salem.
He called the curator
"the commander of the Swiss Navy."

Father's death was abrupt and unprotesting.
His vision was still twenty-twenty.
After a morning of anxious, repetitive smiling,
his last words to Mother were:
"I feel awful."

Father's Bedroom

In my Father's bedroom:
blue threads as thin
as pen-writing on the bedspread,
blue dots on the curtains,
a blue kimono,
Chinese sandals with blue plush straps.
The broad-planked floor
had a sandpapered neatness.
The clear glass bed-lamp
with a white doily shade
was still raised a few
inches by resting on volume two
of Lafcadio Hearn's
Glimpses of Unfamiliar Japan.
Its warped olive cover
was punished like a rhinoceros hide.
In the flyleaf:
"Robbie from Mother."
Years later in the same hand:
"This book has had hard usage
on the Yangtze River, China.
It was left under an open
porthole in a storm."

For Sale

Poor sheepish plaything,
organized with prodigal animosity,
lived in just a year—
my Father's cottage at Beverly Farms
was on the market the month he died.
Empty, open, intimate,
its town-house furniture
had an on tiptoe air
of waiting for the mover
on the heels of the undertaker.
Ready, afraid
of living alone till eighty,
Mother mooned in a window,
as if she had stayed on a train
one stop past her destination.

Sailing Home from Rapallo

(February 1954)

Your nurse could only speak Italian,
but after twenty minutes I could imagine your final week,
and tears ran down my cheeks. . . .

When I embarked from Italy with my Mother's body,
the whole shoreline of the *Golfo di Genova*
was breaking into fiery flower.
The crazy yellow and azure sea-sleds
blasting like jack-hammers across
the *spumante*-bubbling wake of our liner,
recalled the clashing colors of my Ford.
Mother travelled first-class in the hold;
her *Risorgimento* black and gold casket
was like Napoleon's at the *Invalides*. . . .

While the passengers were tanning
on the Mediterranean in deck-chairs,
our family cemetery in Dunbarton
lay under the White Mountains
in the sub-zero weather.
The graveyard's soil was changing to stone—
so many of its deaths had been midwinter.
Dour and dark against the blinding snowdrifts,
its black brook and fir trunks were as smooth as masts.
A fence of iron spear-hafts
black-bordered its mostly Colonial grave-slates.
The only "unhistoric" soul to come here
was Father, now buried beneath his recent
unweathered pink-veined slice of marble.
Even the Latin of his Lowell motto:
Occasionem cognosce,
seemed too businesslike and pushing here,
where the burning cold illuminated
the hewn inscriptions of Mother's relatives:

twenty or thirty Winslows and Starks.
Frost had given their names a diamond edge. . . .

In the grandiloquent lettering on Mother's coffin,
Lowell had been misspelled *LOVEL*.
The corpse
was wrapped like *panettone* in Italian tinfoil.

During Fever

All night the crib creaks;
home from the healthy country to the sick city,
my daughter in fever
flounders in her chicken-colored sleeping bag.
"Sorry," she mumbles like her dim-bulb father, "sorry."

Mother, Mother!
as a gemlike undergraduate,
part criminal and yet a Phi Bete,
I used to barge home late.
Always by the bannister
my milk-tooth mug of milk
was waiting for me on a plate
of Triskets.
Often with unadulterated joy,
Mother, we bent by the fire
rehashing Father's character—
when he thought we were asleep,
he'd tiptoe down the stairs
and chain the door.

Mother, your master-bedroom
looked away from the ocean.
You had a window-seat,
an electric blanket,
a silver hot water bottle
monogrammed like a hip-flask,
Italian china fruity
with bunches and berries
and proper *putti*.
Gold, yellow and green,
the nuptial bed
was as big as a bathroom.

Born ten years and yet an aeon
too early for the twenties,
Mother, you smile
as if you saw your Father
inches away yet hidden, as when he groused behind a screen
over a National Geographic Magazine,
whenever young men came to court you
back in those settled years of World War One.
Terrible that old life of decency
without unseemly intimacy
or quarrels, when the unemancipated woman
still had her Freudian papá and maids!

Waking in the Blue

The night attendant, a B.U. sophomore,
rouses from the mare's-nest of his drowsy head
propped on *The Meaning of Meaning*.
He catwalks down our corridor.
Azure day
makes my agonized blue window bleaker.
Crows maunder on the petrified fairway.
Absence! My heart grows tense
as though a harpoon were sparring for the kill.
(This is the house for the "mentally ill.")

What use is my sense of humor?
I grin at Stanley, now sunk in his sixties,
once a Harvard all-American fullback,
(if such were possible!)
still hoarding the build of a boy in his twenties,
as he soaks, a ramrod
with the muscle of a seal
in his long tub,
vaguely urinous from the Victorian plumbing.
A kingly granite profile in a crimson golf-cap,
worn all day, all night,
he thinks only of his figure,
of slimming on sherbet and ginger ale—
more cut off from words than a seal.

This is the way day breaks in Bowditch Hall at McLean's;
the hooded night lights bring out "Bobbie,"
Porcellian '29,
a replica of Louis XVI
without the wig—
redolent and roly-poly as a sperm whale,
as he swashbuckles about in his birthday suit
and horses at chairs.

These victorious figures of bravado ossified young.

In between the limits of day,
hours and hours go by under the crew haircuts
and slightly too little nonsensical bachelor twinkle
of the Roman Catholic attendants.
(There are no Mayflower
screwballs in the Catholic Church.)

After a hearty New England breakfast,
I weigh two hundred pounds
this morning. Cock of the walk,
I strut in my turtle-necked French sailor's jersey
before the metal shaving mirrors,
and see the shaky future grow familiar
in the pinched, indigenous faces
of these thoroughbred mental cases,
twice my age and half my weight.
We are all old-timers,
each of us holds a locked razor.

Home After Three Months Away

Gone now the baby's nurse,
a lioness who ruled the roost
and made the Mother cry.
She used to tie
gobbets of porkrind in bowknots of gauze—
three months they hung like soggy toast
on our eight foot magnolia tree,
and helped the English sparrows
weather a Boston winter.

Three months, three months!
Is Richard now himself again?
Dimpled with exaltation,
my daughter holds her levee in the tub.
Our noses rub,
each of us pats a stringy lock of hair—
they tell me nothing's gone.
Though I am forty-one,
not forty now, the time I put away
was child's-play. After thirteen weeks
my child still dabs her cheeks
to start me shaving. When
we dress her in her sky-blue corduroy,
she changes to a boy,
and floats my shaving brush
and washcloth in the flush. . . .
Dearest, I cannot loiter here
in lather like a polar bear.

Recuperating, I neither spin nor toil.
Three stories down below,
a choreman tends our coffin's length of soil,
and seven horizontal tulips blow.
Just twelve months ago,

these flowers were pedigreed
imported Dutchmen; now no one need
distinguish them from weed.
Bushed by the late spring snow,
they cannot meet
another year's snowballing enervation.

I keep no rank nor station.
Cured, I am frizzled, stale and small.

II

Memories of West Street and Lepke

Only teaching on Tuesdays, book-worming
in pajamas fresh from the washer each morning,
I hog a whole house on Boston's
"hardly passionate Marlborough Street,"
where even the man
scavenging filth in the back alley trash cans,
has two children, a beach wagon, a helpmate,
and is a "young Republican."
I have a nine months' daughter,
young enough to be my granddaughter.
Like the sun she rises in her flame-flamingo infants' wear.

These are the tranquillized *Fifties*,
and I am forty. Ought I to regret my seedtime?
I was a fire-breathing Catholic C.O.,
and made my manic statement,
telling off the state and president, and then
sat waiting sentence in the bull pen
beside a Negro boy with curlicues
of marijuana in his hair.

Given a year,
I walked on the roof of the West Street Jail, a short
enclosure like my school soccer court,
and saw the Hudson River once a day
through sooty clothesline entanglements
and bleaching khaki tenements.
Strolling, I yammered metaphysics with Abramowitz,
a jaundice-yellow ("it's really tan")
and fly-weight pacifist,
so vegetarian,
he wore rope shoes and preferred fallen fruit.
He tried to convert Bioff and Brown,
the Hollywood pimps, to his diet.

Hairy, muscular, suburban,
wearing chocolate double-breasted suits,
they blew their tops and beat him black and blue.

I was so out of things, I'd never heard
of the Jehovah's Witnesses.
"Are you a C.O.?" I asked a fellow jailbird.
"No," he answered, "I'm a J.W."
He taught me the "hospital tuck,"
and pointed out the T-shirted back
of *Murder Incorporated's* Czar Lepke,
there piling towels on a rack,
or dawdling off to his little segregated cell full
of things forbidden the common man:
a portable radio, a dresser, two toy American
flags tied together with a ribbon of Easter palm.
Flabby, bald, lobotomized,
he drifted in a sheepish calm,
where no agonizing reappraisal
jarred his concentration on the electric chair—
hanging like an oasis in his air
of lost connections. . . .

Man and Wife

Tamed by *Miltown*, we lie on Mother's bed;
the rising sun in war paint dyes us red;
in broad daylight her gilded bed-posts shine,
abandoned, almost Dionysian.
At last the trees are green on Marlborough Street,
blossoms on our magnolia ignite
the morning with their murderous five days' white.
All night I've held your hand,
as if you had
a fourth time faced the kingdom of the mad—
its hackneyed speech, its homicidal eye—
and dragged me home alive. . . . Oh my *Petite*,
clearest of all God's creatures, still all air and nerve:
you were in your twenties, and I,
once hand on glass
and heart in mouth,
outdrank the Rahvs in the heat
of Greenwich Village, fainting at your feet—
too boiled and shy
and poker-faced to make a pass,
while the shrill verve
of your invective scorched the traditional South.

Now twelve years later, you turn your back.
Sleepless, you hold
your pillow to your hollows like a child;
your old-fashioned tirade—
loving, rapid, merciless—
breaks like the Atlantic Ocean on my head.

k of Woe That Is in Marriage"

...future generation that presses into being by means of these exuberant feelings and super-sensible soap bubbles of ours."
                                                                    SCHOPENHAUER

"The hot night makes us keep our bedroom windows open.
Our magnolia blossoms. Life begins to happen.
My hopped up husband drops his home disputes,
and hits the streets to cruise for prostitutes,
free-lancing out along the razor's edge.
This screwball might kill his wife, then take the pledge.
Oh the monotonous meanness of his lust. . . .
It's the injustice . . . he is so unjust—
whiskey-blind, swaggering home at five.
My only thought is how to keep alive.
What makes him tick? Each night now I tie
ten dollars and his car key to my thigh. . . .
Gored by the climacteric of his want,
he stalls above me like an elephant."

Skunk Hour

(FOR ELIZABETH BISHOP)

Nautilus Island's hermit
heiress still lives through winter in her Spartan cottage;
her sheep still graze above the sea.
Her son's a bishop. Her farmer
is first selectman in our village;
she's in her dotage.

Thirsting for
the hierarchic privacy
of Queen Victoria's century,
she buys up all
the eyesores facing her shore,
and lets them fall.

The season's ill—
we've lost our summer millionaire,
who seemed to leap from an L. L. Bean
catalogue. His nine-knot yawl
was auctioned off to lobstermen.
A red fox stain covers Blue Hill.

And now our fairy
decorator brightens his shop for fall;
his fishnet's filled with orange cork,
orange, his cobbler's bench and awl;
there is no money in his work,
he'd rather marry.

One dark night,
my Tudor Ford climbed the hill's skull;
I watched for love-cars. Lights turned down,
they lay together, hull to hull,
where the graveyard shelves on the town. . . .
My mind's not right.

A car radio bleats,
"Love, O careless Love. . . ." I hear
my ill-spirit sob in each blood cell,
as if my hand were at its throat. . . .
I myself am hell;
nobody's here—

only skunks, that search
in the moonlight for a bite to eat.
They march on their soles up Main Street:
white stripes, moonstruck eyes' red fire
under the chalk-dry and spar spire
of the Trinitarian Church.

I stand on top
of our back steps and breathe the rich air—
a mother skunk with her column of kittens swills the garbage pail.
She jabs her wedge-head in a cup
of sour cream, drops her ostrich tail,
and will not scare.

Imitations

(1961)

FOR ELIZABETH BISHOP

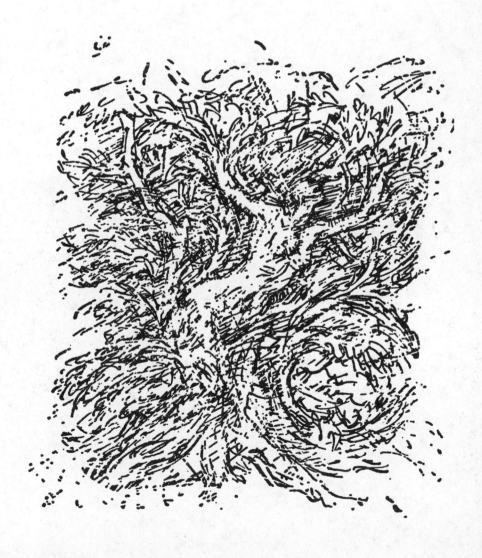

INTRODUCTION

This book is partly self-sufficient and separate from its sources, and should be first read as a sequence, one voice running through many personalities, contrasts and repetitions. I have hoped somehow for a whole, to make a single volume, a small anthology of European poetry. The dark and against the grain stand out, but there are other modifying strands. I have tried to keep something equivalent to the fire and finish of my originals. This has forced me to do considerable re-writing.

Boris Pasternak has said that the usual reliable translator gets the literal meaning but misses the tone, and that in poetry tone is of course everything. I have been reckless with literal meaning, and labored hard to get the tone. Most often this has been *a* tone, for *the* tone is something that will always more or less escape transference to another language and cultural moment. I have tried to write alive English and to do what my authors might have done if they were writing their poems now and in America.

Most poetic translations come to grief and are less enjoyable than modest photographic prose translations, such as George Kay has offered in his *Penguin Book of Italian Verse*. Strict metrical translators still exist. They seem to live in a pure world untouched by contemporary poetry. Their difficulties are bold and honest, but they are taxidermists, not poets, and their poems are likely to be stuffed birds. A better strategy would seem to be the now fashionable translations into free or irregular verse. Yet this method commonly turns out a sprawl of language, neither faithful nor distinguished, now on stilts, now low, as Dryden would say. It seems self-evident that no professor or amateur poet, or even good poet writing hastily, can by miracle transform himself into a fine metricist. I believe that poetic translation—I would call it an imitation—must be expert and inspired, and needs at least as much technique, luck and rightness of hand as an original poem.

My licenses have been many. My first two Sappho poems are really new poems based on hers. Villon has been somewhat stripped; Hebel is taken out of dialect; Hugo's "Gautier" is cut in half. Mallarmé has been unclotted, not because I disapprove of his dense medium but because I saw no way of giving it much power in English. The same has been done with Ungaretti and some of the more obscure Rimbaud. About a third of "The Drunken Boat" has been left out. Two stanzas have been added to Rilke's "Roman Sarcophagus," and one to his "Pigeons." "Pigeons" and Valéry's "Helen" are more idiomatic and informal in my English. Some lines from Villon's "Little Testament" have been shifted to introduce his "Great Testament." And so forth! I have dropped lines, moved lines, moved stanzas, changed images and altered meter and intent.

Pasternak has given me special problems. From reading his prose and many translations of his poetry, I have come to feel that he is a very great poet. But I know no Russian. I have rashly tried to improve on other translations, and have been helped by exact prose versions given me by Russian readers. This is an old practice; Pasternak himself, I think, worked this way with his Georgian poets. I hope I caught something worthy of his all-important tone.

This book was written from time to time when I was unable to do anything of my own. It began some ten years ago when I read a parallel French translation of Rilke's "Orpheus," and felt that a much better job might be done in English. I had long been amazed by Montale, but had no idea how he might be worked until I saw that unlike most good poets—Horace and Petrarch are extremes—he was strong in simple prose and could be made still stronger in free verse. My Baudelaires were begun as exercises in couplets and quatrains and to get away from the longer, less concentrated problems of translating Racine's *Phèdre*.

All my originals are important poems. Nothing like them exists in English, for the excellence of a poet depends on the unique opportunities of his native language. I have been almost as free as the authors themselves in finding ways to make them ring right for me.

—ROBERT LOWELL

The Killing of Lykaon

Sing for me, Muse, the mania of Achilles
that cast a thousand sorrows on the Greeks
and threw so many huge souls into hell,
heroes who spilled their lives as food for dogs
and darting birds. God's will was working out,
from that time when first fell apart fighting
Atrides, king of men, and that god, Achilles . . .

*   *   *

"Coward, do not speak to me of ransom!
Before the day of terror overtook Patroklos,
sparing Trojans was my heart's choice and rest—
thousands I seized alive and sold like sheep!
Now there's not one who'll run out with his life,
should the god throw him to me before Troy,
but none are more accursed than Priam's sons . . .
You too must die, my dear. Why do you care?
Patroklos, a much better man, has died.
Or look at me—how large and fine I am—
a goddess bore me, and my father reigned,
yet I too have my destiny and death:
either at sunrise, night, or at high noon,
some warrior will spear me down in the lines,
or stick me with an arrow through the heel."

He spoke so, and Lykaon lost his heart,
his spear dropped, and he fluttered his two hands
begging Achilles to hold back his sword.
The sword bit through his neck and collarbone,
and flashed blue sky. His face fell in the dust,
the black blood spouted out, and soaked the earth.

Achilles hurled Lykaon by his heel
in the Skamander, and spoke these wingéd words:

"Lie with the fish, they'll dress your wounds, and lick
away your blood, and have no care for you,
nor will your mother groan beside your pyre
by the Skamander, nor will women wail
as you swirl down the rapids to the sea,
but the dark shadows of the fish will shiver,
lunging to snap Lykaon's silver fat.
Die, Trojans—you must die till I reach Troy—
you'll run in front, I'll scythe you down behind,
nor will the azure Skamander save your lives,
whirling and silver, though you kill your bulls
and sheep, and throw a thousand one-hoofed horse,
still living, in the ripples. You must die,
and die and die and die, until the blood
of Hellas and Patroklos is avenged,
killed by the running ships when I was gone."

Homer: *Iliad*, from Bks. I and XXI.

Three Letters to Anaktoria

The man or hero loves Anaktoria, later Sappho; in the end, he withdraws or dies.

I.
I set that man above the gods and heroes—
all day, he sits before you face to face,
like a cardplayer. Your elbow brushes his elbow—
if you should speak, he hears.

The touched heart madly stirs,
your laughter is water hurrying over pebbles—
every gesture is a proclamation,
every sound is speech . . .

Refining fire purifies my flesh!
I hear you: a hollowness in my ears
thunders and stuns me. I cannot speak.
I cannot see.

I shiver. A dead whiteness spreads over
my body, trickling pinpricks of sweat.
I am greener than the greenest green grass—
I die!

II.
For some the fairest thing on the dark earth is Thermopylae
and the Spartan phalanx lowering lances to die—
Salamis and the half-moon of Athenian triremes
sprinting to pin down the Persian fleet;
nothing is as fair as my beloved.

I can easily make you understand this:
dwell on the gentleness of his footstep,
the shimmer of his shining face fairer than ten thousand
barbarous scythe-wheeled Persian chariots,
or the myriad hanging gardens in Persepolis.

Helen forgot her husband and dear children
to cherish Paris,
the loveliest of mortals,
the murderer of Troy—
she bestowed her heart far off.

How easily a woman is led astray!
She remembers nothing of what is nearest at hand:
her loom, her household, her helots . . .
Anaktoria, did you cherish my love,
when the Bridegroom was with you?

A woman seldom finds what is best—
no, never in this world,
Anaktoria! Pray
for his magnificence I once pined to share . . .
to have lived is better than to live!

III.
The moon slides west,
it is midnight,
the time is gone—
I lie alone!

Sappho.

Children

Years back here we were children
and at the stage of running
in gangs about the meadows—
here to this one, there to that one.
Where we picked up violets
on lucky days,
you can now see cattle gadding about.

I still remember hunching
ankle deep in violets,
squabbling over which bunches were fairest.
Our childishness was obvious—
we ran dancing rounds,
we wore new green wreaths.
So time passes.

Here we ran swilling strawberries
from oak to pine,
through hedges, through turnstiles—
as long as day was burning down.
Once a gardener
rushed from an arbor:
"O.K. now, children, run home."

We came out in spots
those yesterdays, when we stuffed on strawberries;
it was just a childish game to us.
Often we heard
the herdsman
hooing and warning us:
"Children, the woods are alive with snakes."

And one of the children breaking
through the sharp grass, grew white

and shouted, "Children, a snake
ran in there. He got our pony.
She'll never get well.
I wish that snake
would go to hell!"

"Well then, get out of the woods!
If you don't hurry away quickly,
I'll tell you what will happen—
if you don't leave the forest
behind you by daylight,
you'll lose yourselves;
your pleasure will end in bawling."

Do you know how five virgins
dawdled in the meadow,
till the king slammed his dining-room door?
Their shouting and shame were outrageous:
their jailer tore everything off them,
down to their skins
they stood like milk cows without any clothes.

Der Wilde Alexander: *Hie vor dô wir kinder wâren.*

The Great Testament

(FOR WILLIAM CARLOS WILLIAMS)

I am thirty this year,
near Christmas, the dead season,
when wolves live off the wind,
and the poor peasants fear
the icy firmament.
Sound in body and mind,
I write my Testament,
but the ink has frozen.

Where are those gallant men
I ran with in my youth?
They sang and spoke so well!
Ah nothing can survive
after the last amen;
some are perhaps in hell.
May they sleep in God's truth;
God save those still alive!

Some have risen—are grave
merchants, lords, divines;
some only see bread when
it's out of reach in windows;
others have taken vows:
Carthusians, Celestines,
wear boots like oyster men—
what different lives men have!

These mighty men—God grant
they do good works, increase,
and live in charity—
who will correct the great?
But the poor are like me,
they've nothing. They can wait—

the gods take what they want,
and eat their bread and cheese.

I have loved—all I could!—
when I try love again,
diseases ring like bells
through my liver and blood,
and warn me off this road.
Sell love to someone else,
who puts away more food—
dancing's for fatter men!

If I had studied, God,
in my youth's day of joy,
and lived by book and rule,
I would have slept in down;
but I ran off from school,
like a delinquent boy—
my heart swims in its blood,
when I must write this down!

I took the preacher's text
too much for Gospel truth:
"In the light of your eyes,
rejoice and have your wish!"
In the verse coming next,
he serves another dish:
"What are childhood and youth,
but vanity and vice?"

How quickly my youth went,
like ravellings of cloth
the weaver holds to cut
with wisps of burning straws!
Kinsmen, kinswomen, both—
I tell the truth—now cut
me when I pass, because
I have no goods or rent.

I think now of those skulls
piling up in the morgue—
all masters of the rolls,
or the king's treasurers,
or water-carriers,
or blacksmiths at the forge.
Who'll tell me which is which,
which poor, and which were rich?

And there are women here,
who used to bow and scrape,
and struggle for earth's joys;
some of them gave commands,
and others served in fear.
I see that none escape:
bishops, laymen, or boys!
They rot with folded hands.

They're dead, God rest their souls!
These poor corpses were once
kings, princes of the blood,
living on tender food,
puddings and creams and rice—
no one laughs out or cries;
the dust eats up their bones.
Jesus, absolve their souls! . . .

Ah God, the days I lost!
Youth and what I loved most
went when my back was turned!
Old age came limping on—
I was less ripe than black!
nothing left on horseback
or foot, alas! What then?
My life suddenly burned.

I descend from no name—
poor from my mother's womb,

poverty claws me down.
My father was poor; Horace,
his father, was the same—
on my ancestors' tomb,
God rest their souls! there is
neither scepter nor crown.

When I curse poverty,
often my heart tells me,
Villon, why do you give
poverty so much room?
Though you've less than Jacques Coeur,
men in cheap cloth still live—
why play the grand seigneur
to rot in a rich tomb?

Poor has-been lords, you die,
you are lords no more. Look,
King David's Psalter says,
"their place forgets their name."
I'll let the rest go by,
it's not my business—
teaching preachers the book
is not my trade and game.

What more have I to tell?
I'm no arch-angel's heir,
crowned with the stars and moon.
My father (God have mercy!)
is in the ground, and soon
my mother also must die—
poor soul, she knows it well,
her son must follow her.

I know that rich and base,
priests, laymen, clerks and sots,
lords, bishops, serfs and thieves,
beautiful, squat or tall,
ladies with ermined sleeves,

and men of every class,
in cone or horse-hair hats . . .
Who else? Death takes them all.

Helen has paid this debt—
no one who dies dies well:
breath goes, and your eyes too,
your spleen bursts through your life,
then sweat . . . God knows . . . you sweat!
No mother, child or wife
wishes to die for you,
and suffer your last hell.

Who cares then to die shriven?
Feet cramp, the nostrils curve,
eyes stare, the stretched veins hiss
and ache through joint and nerve—
Oh woman's body, poor,
supple, tender—is this
what you were waiting for?
Yes, or ascend to heaven.

Villon: *Le grand testament.*

Ballad for the Dead Ladies

Say in what land, or where
is Flora, the lovely Roman,
Andromeda, or Helen,
far lovelier,
or Echo, who would answer
across the brook or river—
her beauty was more than human!
Oh where is last year's snow?

Where is the wise Eloise,
and Peter Abelard
gelded at Saint Denis
for love of her?
That queen who threw Buridan
in a sack in the Seine—
who will love her again?
Oh where is last year's snow?

Queen Blanche, the fleur-de-lys,
who had a siren's voice,
Bertha Big Foot, Beatrice,
Arembourg, ruler of Maine,
or Jeanne d'Arc of Lorraine
the British burned at Rouen?
Where are they, where? Oh Virgin,
where is last year's snow?

Prince, do not ask this year
or next year, where they are;
or answer my refrain:
Oh where is last year's snow?

Villon: *Le grand testament.*

The Old Lady's Lament for Her Youth

I think I heard the belle
we called the Armoress
lamenting her lost youth;
this was her whore's language:
"Oh treacherous, fierce old age,
you've gnawed me with your tooth,
yet if I end this mess
and die, I go to hell.

"You've stolen the great power
my beauty had on squire,
clerk, monk and general;
once there was no man born
who wouldn't give up all
(whatever his desire)
to have me for an hour—
this body beggars scorn!

"Once I broke the crown's laws,
and fled priests with a curse,
because I kept a boy,
and taught him what I knew—
alas, I only threw
myself away, because
I wanted to enjoy
this pimp, who loved my purse.

"I loved him when he hid
money, or used to bring
home whores and smash my teeth—
Oh when I lay beneath,
I forgave everything—
my tongue stuck to his tongue!

Tell me what good I did?
What's left? Disease and dung.

"He's dead these thirty years,
and I live on, grow old,
and think of that good time,
what was, what I've become;
sometimes, when I behold
my naked flesh, so numb,
dry, poor and small with time,
I cannot stop my tears.

"Where's my large Norman brow,
arched lashes, yellow hair,
the wide-eyed looks I used
to trap the cleverest men?
Where is my clear, soft skin,
neither too brown or fair,
my pointed ears, my bruised
red lips? I want to know.

"Where's the long neck I bent
swanlike, when asking pardon?
My small breasts, and the lips
of my vagina that sat
inside a little garden
and overlooked my hips,
plump, firm and so well set
for love's great tournament?

"Now wrinkled cheeks, and thin
wild lashes; nets of red
string fill the eyes that used
to look and laugh men dead.
How nature has abused
me. Wrinkles plow across
the brow, the lips are skin,
my ears hang down like moss.

"This is how beauty dies:
humped shoulders, barrenness
of mind; I've lost my hips,
vagina, and my lips.
My breasts? They're a retreat!
Short breath—how I repeat
my silly list! My thighs
are blotched like sausages.

"This is how we discuss
ourselves, and nurse desire
here as we gab about
the past, boneless as wool
dolls by a greenwood fire—
soon lit, and soon put out.
Once I was beautiful . . .
That's how it goes with us."

*   *   *

Villon: *Le grand testament.*

Villon's Prayer for His Mother to Say to the Virgin

Lastly I give the poor
woman, my mother, who bore
much pain for me—God knows!
this prayer to our Mistress,
Mary, my house and fortress
against the ills and sorrows
of life. I have no other
patron, nor has my mother.

"Lady of heaven, queen of the world,
and ruler of the underworld,
receive your humble Christian child,
and let her live with those you save;
although my soul is not much worth
saving, my Mistress and my Queen,
your grace is greater than my sin—
without you no man may deserve,
or enter heaven. I do not lie:
in this faith let me live and die.

"Say to your Son that I am his;
Mary of Egypt was absolved,
also the clerk, Theophilus,
whom you consented to restore,
although he'd made a pact with hell.
Save me from ever doing such ill,
our bond with evil is dissolved,
Oh Virgin, undefiled, who bore
Christ whom we celebrate at Mass—
in this faith let me live and die.

"I am a woman—poor, absurd,
who never learned to read your word—

at Mass each Sunday, I have seen
a painted paradise with lutes
and harps, a hell that boils the damned:
one gives me joy, the other doubts.
Oh let me have your joy, my Queen,
bountiful, honest and serene,
by whom no sinner is condemned—
in this faith let me live and die.

"You bore, oh Virgin and Princess,
Jesus, whose Kingdom never ends—
Our Lord took on our littleness,
and walked the world to save his friends—
he gave his lovely youth to death,
that's why I say to my last breath
in this faith let me live and die."

Villon: *Le grand testament.*

Villon's Epitaph

"Oh brothers, you live after us,
because we shared your revenue.
God may have mercy upon you,
if you have mercy upon us.
Five, six—you see us tied up here,
the flesh we overfed hangs here,
our carrion rots through skin and shirt,
and we, the bones, have changed to dirt.
Do not laugh at our misery:
pray God to save your souls and ours!

We hang in chains to satisfy
your justice and your violence,
brother humans—surely, you see
that all men cannot have good sense!
Here no man may look down on us—
Oh Child of Mary, pity us,
forgive our crimes—if dying well
saved even the poor thief from hell,
the blood of Christ will not run dry:
pray God to save your souls and ours!

The rain has soaked and washed us bare,
the sun has burned us black. Magpies
and crows have chiselled out our eyes,
have jerked away our beards and hair.
Our bodies have no time to rest:
our chains clank north, south, east and west,
now here, now there, to the winds' dance—
more beaks of birds than knives in France!
Do not join our fraternity:
pray God to save your souls and ours!

Prince Jesus, king of earth and air,
preserve our bodies from hell's powers—
we have no debts or business there.
We were not hanged to make you laugh.
Villon, who wrote our epitaph,
prays God to save your souls and ours!"

Villon: *Ballade des pendus.*

Infinite

That hill pushed off by itself was always dear
to me and the hedges near
it that cut away so much of the final horizon.
When I would sit there lost in deliberation,
I reasoned most on the interminable spaces
beyond all hills, on their antediluvian resignation
and silence that passes
beyond man's possibility.
Here for a little while my heart is quiet inside me;
and when the wind lifts roughing through the trees,
I set about comparing my silence to those voices,
and I think about the eternal, the dead seasons,
things here at hand and alive,
and all their reasons and choices.
It's sweet to destroy my mind
and go down
and wreck in this sea where I drown.

Leopardi: *L'infinito*.

Saturday Night in the Village

The day
is ready to close;
the girl takes the downward
path homeward from the vineyard,
and jumps from crevice to crevice
like a goat, as she holds a swath
of violets and roses
to decorate her hair and bodice
tomorrow as usual for the Sabbath.

Her grandmother sits,
facing the sun going out,
and spins and starts to reason
with the neighbors, and renew the day,
when she used to dress herself for the holiday
and dance away
the nights—still quick and healthy,
with the boys, companions of her fairer season.

Once again the landscape is brown,
the sky drains to a pale blue,
shadows drop from mountain and thatch,
the young moon whitens.
As I catch
the clatter of small bells,
sounding in the holiday,
I can almost say
my heart takes comfort in the sound.
Children place their pickets
and sentinels,
and splash round and round
the village fountain.
They jump like crickets,
and make a happy sound.

The field-hand,
who lives on nothing,
marches home whistling,
and gorges on the day of idleness at hand.

Then all's at peace;
the lights are out;
I hear the rasp of shavings,
and the rapping hammer
of the carpenter, working all night
by lanternlight—
hurrying and straining himself
to increase his savings
before the whitening day.

This is the most kind
of the seven days; tomorrow, you will wait
and pray for Sunday's boredom and anguish
to be extinguished
in the workdays' grind
you anticipate.

Lively boy,
the only age you are alive
is like this day of joy,
a clear and breathless Saturday
that heralds life's holiday.
Rejoice, my child,
this is the untroubled instant.
Why should I undeceive you?
Let it not grieve you,
if the following day is slow to arrive.

Leopardi: *Il sabato del villaggio.*

Sylvia

Sylvia, do you remember the minutes
in this life overhung by death,
when beauty flamed
through your shy, serious meditations,
and you leapt beyond the limits
of girlhood?

Wild,
lightning-eyed child,
your incessant singing
shook the mirror-bright cobbles,
and even the parlor,
shuttered from summer,
where you sat at your sewing
and such girlish things—
happy enough to catch
at the future's blurred offer.
It was the great May,
and this is how you spent your day.

I could forget
the fascinating studies in my bolted room,
where my life was burning out,
and the heat
of my writings made the letters wriggle and melt
under drops of sweat.
Sometimes, I lolled on the railing of my father's house,
and pricked up my ears, and heard the noise
of your voice
and your hand run
to the hum of the monotonous loom.

I marvelled at the composed sky,
the little sun-gilded dust-paths,

and the gardens, running high
and half out of sight,
with the mountains on one side and the Adriatic
far off to the right.
How can human tongue
say what I felt?

What tremendous meaning, supposing,
and light-heartedness, my Sylvia!
What a Marie-Antoinette
stage-set
for life and its limits!
When I think of that great puff of pride,
sour constrictions choke me,
I turn aside to deride
my chances wrenched into misadventure.
Nature, harsh Nature,
why will you not pay
your promise today?
Why have you set
your children a bird-net?

Even before the Sirocco had sucked
the sap from the grass,
some undiagnosable disease
struck you and broke you—
you died, child,
and never saw your life flower,
or your flower plucked
by young men courting you
and arguing love
on the long Sunday walk—
their heads turned and lost
in your quick, shy talk.

Thus hope subsided
little by little;
fate decided
I was never to flower.

Hope, dear comrade of my shrinking summer,
how little you could keep
your color! You make me weep.
Is this your world?
These, its diversions, its infatuations,
its accomplishments, its sensations,
we used to unravel together?
You broke before the first
advance of truth;
the grave
was the final, shining milestone
you had always been pointing to
with such insistence
in the undistinguishable distance.

Leopardi: A Silvia.

Sic Transit

A conversation on the Basel road between Steinen and Bromback, at night.

THE BOY
Now nearly always, Father, when I see
Rötteln Castle stand out like that, I wonder
if our own house will go down that way too.
Just look at it, it hangs there as tattered
and black as Death in the Dance of Death at Basel.
The more I look at it, the worse I feel.
Our house sits on a hill; it's like a church;
its leaded windows glitter; it looks grand.
Father, will our house tumble like the castle?
Sometimes, I think it simply must not happen.

FATHER
God help us, of course it must; what do you think?
Things start out young and new, and then they slide
gently downhill. They age and ache to their end;
nothing stands still. You hear the water rush?
You see how the stars hang side by side up there?
Perhaps you think things in the world stand still? No,
all's on the move, everything grows, then goes.

That's how things are; you mustn't stare at me.
You're young still, I was just as young once, now
I'm changed, and age, old age, is coming on,
and everywhere I go, to Wies, to Basel,
to the fields, woods, or home, it's all the same,
I'm travelling to the churchyard—that's the story;
when you are bearded, grown, and old as I,
I shan't be watching; sheep and goats will graze
over my grave. Our house is growing dirty;
night after night, the rain will wash it blacker,

day by day, the sun will blister away its trim;
you'll feel the raindrops thudding through its loft,
you'll hear the black winds whistling through its cracks,
the beetles click and tick behind its wainscot,
and when you die, my Son, your children's children
will come and patch it up, but then the rot
will ooze away its frame and underpinnings,
and when the year 2000 comes around,
all will be gone, our village will have slumped
into its grave. In time, the plough will go
where the church stood, the mayor's house and the rector's.

BOY
How silly, Father!

FATHER
                No, stop staring at me;
that's how things are. Take Basel, it's a great
city with houses larger than most churches,
more churches than the houses in our village.
Basel! what is it? It's a crowd of people,
mountains of money, armies of gentlemen,
and there's another larger city, full
of men and women I knew once—they lie
behind the cloisters of the Munsterplatz,
and sleep. All's dead there, but the hour will strike,
when even Basel must fall down and die,
and only stick an arm up here and there:
a gable, a cellar, a tower, or a chimney,
an elm here, here a beech, or there a fir,
crab-grass and moss and ferns; herons will wade
through marshy basements—it is sad, my Son,
but there's no help, and ghosts will roister there,
if people are as silly then as now!
Frau Fast—she is already there, I think—
and Lippi Lappelli, God knows who besides . . .
Why do you push me with your elbow, Son?

BOY

Hush Father, wait until we've crossed the bridge,
and left that creepy wood and hill behind us.
A madman takes pot-shots at boys up there.
That clump there's where the girl who peddled eggs
died slashed and murdered, seven months ago.
Look how our Laubi* snorts and shies away!

FATHER

Son, don't be childish. Laubi has a cold.
The dead people hurt us much less than the living.
What was I saying? Oh yes, Basel. Basel
will go, and if some traveller passes by,
just half an hour or even an hour away,
he'll stare across its dust, if there's no mist,
and say to his companion, "That was Basel;
that hump of litter was St. Peter's Church.
It's sad it's finished!"

BOY

                    Father, you are teasing.
What do you mean?

FATHER

                    That's how things are, my son,
stop staring at me like a child. In time,
the world and all its growth will change to fire;
then in the middle of the night, a watchman,
some foreigner that no one knows, will come.
He'll glitter like Napoleon's star, and shout:
"Wake up, wake up! The Day has come!" The sky
will redden, there'll be thunder everywhere,
first soft, then loud, like the French Terrorists'
bombardment here in seventeen-ninety-six.
The earth will totter, and make the churches rock,
they'll toll their bells for service far and wide,
and everyone will pray. The Day will come;

*Laubi is one of the two oxen.

oh God preserve us, we won't need the sun then,
the heavens will be a waterfall of lightning,
and earth a hod of coals. Lots more will happen.
I have no time to tell you; everything
will catch and burn wherever there is land.
No one will be anywhere to put it out;
it'll have to put itself out in the end.
What do you think the earth will look like then?

BOY
Don't tell me, Father! What will happen to all
the people, when everything is burned and burning?

FATHER
When the fire comes, the people won't be there,
they'll be . . . where will they be? Live right, do good
whatever happens, keep a pure conscience.
Do you see how the sky streams with bright stars?
Each star might be a village; farther up,
perhaps, there is a capital. Go easy,
it can't be seen from here. Live right, do good,
and you will go to one of those bright stars;
I'll be there, if God's willing, and your mother,
my poor Elizabeth. Perhaps, you'll drive
a pair of oxen up the Milky Way,
and find the unknown city—looking down
from one side earthward then, what will you see?
Rötteln Castle! The Belchen will be charred,
and the Blauen . . . just like two old chimneys,
and everything between them will have burned
down to the ground. There won't be any water
then in the Wiese, everything will be
gritty and black and still as death itself,
as far as eye can reach. You'll see all that,
and say to your companion, "Take a look!
That's where the world was, that black mountain, that
was called the Belchen, over there is Wieslet—
I lived there once, and used to harness oxen
to carry mountain-loads of oak to Basel,

there's where I plowed and drained the bottom land,
scared rabbits through the brush, made splints for torches . . .
That's where I learned to drudge away my life.
All the king's horses cannot drag me back!"

Hebel: Die Vergänglichkeit.

Heine Dying in Paris

I.

DEATH AND MORPHINE

Yes, in the end they are much of a pair,
my twin gladiator beauties—thinner than a hair,
their bronze bell-heads hum with the void; one's more austere,
however, and much whiter; none dares cry down his character.
How confidingly the corrupt twin rocked me in his arms;
his poppy garland, nearing, hushed death's alarms
at sword-point for a moment.
Soon a pinpoint of infinite regression! And now that incident
is closed. There's no way out,
unless the other turn about
and, pale, distinguished, perfect, drop his torch.
He and I stand alerted for life's Doric, drilled, withdrawing march:
sleep is lovely, death is better still,
not to have been born is of course the miracle.

II.

Every idle desire has died in my breast;
even hatred of evil things, even my feeling
for my own and other men's distress.
What lives in me is death.
The curtain falls, the play is done;
my dear German public is goosestepping home, yawning.
They are no fools, these good people:
they are slurping their dinners quite happily,
bear-hugging beer-mugs—singing and laughing.

That fellow in Homer's book was quite right:
he said: the meanest little Philistine living
in Stukkert-am-Neckar is luckier
than I, the golden-haired Achilles, the dead lion,
glorious shadow-king of the underworld.

III.

My zenith was luckily happier than my night:
whenever I touched the lyre of inspiration, I smote
the Chosen People. Often—all sex and thunder—
I pierced those overblown and summer clouds . . .
But my summer has flowered. My sword is scabbarded
in the marrow of my spinal discs.
Soon I must lose all these half-gods
that made my world so agonizingly half-joyful.

The hand clangs to a close on the dominant;
the champagne glass of orange sherbet breaks
on my lips—all glass; straws in the wind?
Little Aristophanes? I give my sugared leasehold on life
to the great Aristophanes and author of life—
midsummer's frail and green-juice bird's-nest.

Heine: *Morphine; Der Scheidende; Mein Tag war heiter.*

Russia 1812

The snow fell, and its power was multiplied.
For the first time the Eagle bowed its head—
dark days! Slowly the Emperor returned—
behind him Moscow! Its onion domes still burned.
The snow rained down in blizzards—rained and froze.
Past each white waste a further white waste rose.
None recognized the captains or the flags.
Yesterday the Grand Army, today its dregs!
No one could tell the vanguard from the flanks.
The snow! The hurt men struggled from the ranks,
hid in the bellies of dead horse, in stacks
of shattered caissons. By the bivouacs,
one saw the picket dying at his post,
still standing in his saddle, white with frost,
the stone lips frozen to the bugle's mouth!
Bullets and grapeshot mingled with the snow,
that hailed . . . The Guard, surprised at shivering, march
in a dream now; ice rimes the gray mustache.
The snow falls, always snow! The driving mire
submerges; men, trapped in that white empire,
have no more bread and march on barefoot—gaps!
They were no longer living men and troops,
but a dream drifting in a fog, a mystery,
mourners parading under the black sky.
The solitude, vast, terrible to the eye,
was like a mute avenger everywhere,
as snowfall, floating through the quiet air,
buried the huge army in a huge shroud.
Could anyone leave this kingdom? A crowd—
each man, obsessed with dying, was alone.
Men slept—and died! The beaten mob sludged on,
ditching the guns to burn their carriages.
Two foes. The North, the Czar. The North was worse.
In hollows where the snow was piling up,

one saw whole regiments fallen asleep.
Attila's dawn, Cannaes of Hannibal!
The army marching to its funeral!
Litters, wounded, the dead, deserters—swarm,
crushing the bridges down to cross a stream.
They went to sleep ten thousand, woke up four.
Ney, bringing up the former army's rear,
hacked his horse loose from three disputing Cossacks . . .
All night, the *qui vive?* The alert! Attacks;
retreats! White ghosts would wrench away our guns,
or we would see dim, terrible squadrons,
circles of steel, whirlpools of savages,
rush sabering through the camp like dervishes.
And in this way, whole armies died at night.

The Emperor was there, standing—he saw.
This oak already trembling from the axe,
watched his glories drop from him branch by branch:
chiefs, soldiers. Each one had his turn and chance—
they died! Some lived. These still believed his star,
and kept their watch. They loved the man of war,
this small man with his hands behind his back,
whose shadow, moving to and fro, was black
behind the lighted tent. Still believing, they
accused their destiny of *lèse-majesté.*
His misfortune had mounted on their back.
The man of glory shook. Cold stupefied
him, then suddenly he felt terrified.
Being without belief, he turned to God:
"God of armies, is this the end?" he cried.
And then at last the expiation came,
as he heard some one call him by his name,
some one half-lost in shadow, who said, "No,
Napoleon." Napoleon understood,
restless, bareheaded, leaden, as he stood
before his butchered legions in the snow.

Victor Hugo: L'expiation.

At Gautier's Grave

Friend, poet, spirit—you have fled our night,
and leave its dark to voyage for the light;
here on the tomb's severe sill, I greet you:
you knew the beautiful, go, find the true!
Somewhere you shine, and I who knew you young
and gallant, I who loved you, I who hung
on your supporting shoulder, when I fled,
broken, from the great flights: I'm seventy, white
with the old years that snow down on my head,
I think of the bright times that changed to worse,
that young past, when we saw the rising day,
the fight, the tumult, the arena curse
and cheer our new art offered to the mob.

Yes, I listen: the great wind dies away,
I feel the summit's sinister cold breath,
I hurry. Do not close the gate of death,
for when my friends die, I start back and see
their fixed eyes draw me to infinity;
I have begun to die by being alone,
I banished here, I who must soon be gone;
my night is breaking vaguely into stars,
my too long thread thrills, quivers for the shears!

We die. That is the law. None holds it back,
all leans; and this great age with all its light
glides to the shadow, where we flee—pale, black!
The oaks felled for the pyre of Hercules,
what a harsh roar they make in the red night!
Death's horses throw their heads, neigh, roll their eyes—
they are joyful, for the shining day now dies,
our age that mastered the high wind and wave
expires . . . And you, their brother and their peer,
join Lamartine, Dumas, Musset—Gautier,

the ancient sea that made us young is dry,
youth has no fountain, age has no more Styx,
and Time moves forward with his heavy blade,
thoughtful, and step by step, to the last ear.
My turn comes round; night fills my troubled eye,
which prophesies the future from the past,
weeps over cribs, and smiles at this new grave.

Victor Hugo: *A Théophile Gautier.*

To the Reader

(FOR STANLEY KUNITZ)

Infatuation, sadism, lust, avarice
possess our souls and drain the body's force;
we spoonfeed our adorable remorse,
like whores or beggars nourishing their lice.

Our sins are mulish, our confessions lies;
we play to the grandstand with our promises,
we pray for tears to wash our filthiness,
importantly pissing hogwash through our sties.

The devil, watching by our sickbeds, hissed
old smut and folk-songs to our soul, until
the soft and precious metal of our will
boiled off in vapor for this scientist.

Each day his flattery makes us eat a toad,
and each step forward is a step to hell,
unmoved, though previous corpses and their smell
asphyxiate our progress on this road.

Like the poor lush who cannot satisfy,
we try to force our sex with counterfeits,
die drooling on the deliquescent tits,
mouthing the rotten orange we suck dry.

Gangs of demons are boozing in our brain—
ranked, swarming, like a million warrior-ants,
they drown and choke the cistern of our wants;
each time we breathe, we tear our lungs with pain.

If poison, arson, sex, narcotics, knives
have not yet ruined us and stitched their quick,
loud patterns on the canvas of our lives,
it is because our souls are still too sick.

Among the vermin, jackals, panthers, lice,
gorillas and tarantulas that suck
and snatch and scratch and defecate and fuck
in the disorderly circus of our vice,

there's one more ugly and abortive birth.
It makes no gestures, never beats its breast,
yet it would murder for a moment's rest,
and willingly annihilate the earth.

It's BOREDOM. Tears have glued its eyes together.
You know it well, my Reader. This obscene
beast chain-smokes yawning for the guillotine—
you—hypocrite Reader—my double—my brother!

Baudelaire: Au lecteur.

My Beatrice

While I was walking in a pitted place,
crying aloud against the human race,
letting thoughts ramble here and there apart—
knives singing on the whetstone of my heart—
I saw a cloud descending on my head
in the full noon, a cloud inhabited
by black devils, sharp, humped, inquisitive
as dwarfs. They knew where I was sensitive,
now idling there, and looked me up and down,
as cool delinquents watch a madman clown.
I heard them laugh and snicker blasphemies,
while swapping signs and blinking with their eyes.

"Let's stop and watch this creature at our leisure—
all sighs and sweaty hair. We'll take his measure.
It's a great pity that this mountebank
and ghost of Hamlet strutting on his plank
should think he's such an artist at his role
he has to rip the lining from his soul
and paralyze the butterflies and bees
with a peepshow of his indecencies—
and even we, who gave him his education,
must listen to his schoolboy declamation."

Wishing to play a part (my pride was high
above the mountains and the devil's cry)
like Hamlet now, I would have turned my back,
had I not seen among the filthy pack
(Oh crime that should have made the sun drop dead!)
my heart's queen and the mistress of my bed
there purring with the rest at my distress,
and sometimes tossing them a stale caress.

Baudelaire: *La Béatrice.*

Spleen

I'm like the king of a rain-country, rich
but sterile, young but with an old wolf's itch,
one who escapes Fénelon's apologues,
and kills the day in boredom with his dogs;
nothing cheers him, darts, tennis, falconry,
his people dying by the balcony;
the bawdry of the pet hermaphrodite
no longer gets him through a single night;
his bed of fleur-de-lys becomes a tomb;
even the ladies of the court, for whom
all kings are beautiful, cannot put on
shameful enough dresses for this skeleton;
the scholar who makes his gold cannot invent
washes to cleanse the poisoned element;
even in baths of blood, Rome's legacy,
our tyrants' solace in senility,
he cannot warm up his shot corpse, whose food
is syrup-green Lethean ooze, not blood.

Baudelaire: *Spleen*.

Autumn

Now colder shadows . . . Who'll turn back the clock?
Goodbye bright summer's brief too lively sport!
The squirrel drops its acorn with a shock,
cord-wood reverberates in my cobbled court.

Winter has entered in my citadel:
hate, anger, fear, forced work like splitting rock,
and like the sun borne to its northern hell,
my heart's no more than a red, frozen block.

Shaking, I listen for the wood to fall;
building a scaffold makes no deafer sound.
Each heart-beat knocks my body to the ground,
like a slow battering ram crumbling a wall.

I think this is the season's funeral,
some one is nailing a coffin hurriedly.
For whom? Yesterday summer, today fall—
the steady progress sounds like a goodbye.

Baudelaire: *Chant d'automne.*

The Ruined Garden

My childhood was only a menacing shower,
cut now and then by hours of brilliant heat.
All the top soil was killed by rain and sleet,
my garden hardly bore a standing flower.

From now on, my mind's autumn! I must take
the field and dress my beds with spade and rake
and restore order to my flooded grounds.
There the rain raised mountains like burial mounds.

I throw fresh seeds out. Who knows what survives?
What elements will give us life and food?
This soil is irrigated by the tides.

Time and nature sluice away our lives.
A virus eats the heart out of our sides,
digs in and multiplies on our lost blood.

Baudelaire: *L'ennemi.*

The Flawed Bell

Propped on my footstool by the popping log
and sitting out the winter night, I hear
my boyish falsetto crack and disappear
to the sound of the bells jangling through the fog.

Lucky the carrying and loud-tongued bell,
whose metal fights the wear and rust of time
piously to repeat its fractured chime,
like an old trooper playing sentinel!

My soul is flawed, and often when I try
to shrug away my early decrepitude,
and populate the night with my shrill cry,

I hear the death-cough of mortality
choked under corpses by a lake of blood—
my rocklike, unhinging effort to die.

Baudelaire: *La cloche fêlée.*

Meditation

Calm down, my Sorrow, we must move with care.
You called for evening; it descends; it's here.
The town is coffined in its atmosphere,
bringing relief to some, to others care.

Now while the common multitude strips bare,
feels pleasure's cat o' nine tails on its back,
and fights off anguish at the great bazaar,
give me your hand, my Sorrow. Let's stand back;

back from these people! Look, the dead years dressed
in old clothes crowd the balconies of the sky.
Regret emerges smiling from the sea,

the sick sun slumbers underneath an arch,
and like a shroud strung out from east to west,
listen, my Dearest, hear the sweet night march!

Baudelaire: *Recueillement.*

The Injured Moon

Oh Moon, discreetly worshipped by our sires,
still riding through your high blue countries, still
trailed by the shining harem of your stars,
old Cynthia, the lamp of our retreats . . .

the lovers sleep open-mouthed! When they breathe,
they show the white enamel of their teeth.
The writer breaks his teeth on his work-sheets,
the vipers couple under the hot hill.

Dressed in your yellow hood, do you pursue
your boy from night to dawn, till the sun climbs
skyward, where dim Endymion disappears?

"I see your mother, Child of these poor times,
crushed to her mirror by the heavy years.
She cunningly powders the breast that nourished you."

Baudelaire: *La lune offensée.*

The Abyss

Pascal's abyss went with him at his side,
closer than blood—alas, activity,
dreams, words, desire: all holes! On every side,
spaces, the bat-wing of insanity!
Above, below me, only depths and shoal,
the silence! And the Lord's right arm
traces his nightmare, truceless, multiform.
I cuddle the insensible blank air,
and fear to sleep as one fears a great hole.
My spirit, haunted by its vertigo,
sees the infinite at every window,
vague, horrible, and dropping God knows where . . .
Ah never to escape from numbers and form!

Baudelaire: *Le gouffre.*

The Swan

I.
Andromache, I think of you. Here men
move on, diminished, from those grander years,
when Racine's tirades scourged our greasy Seine,
this lying trickle swollen with your tears!

Some echo fertilized my magpie mind,
as I was crossing the new Carrousel.
Old Paris is done for. (Our cities find
new faces sooner than the heart.) Its shell

was all I noticed, when I strolled beneath
its barracks, heaps of roughed-out capitals,
stray apple carts, troughs, greening horses' teeth,
commercial gypsies clinking in their stalls.

A strolling circus had laid out its tent,
where I was dragging home through the dawn's red;
labor was rising, and a sprinkler spread
a hurricane to lay the sediment.

I saw a swan that had escaped its cage,
and struck its dry wings on the cobbled street,
and drenched the curbing with its fluffy plumage.
Beside a gritty gutter, it dabbed its feet,

and gobbled at the dust to stop its thirst.
Its heart was full of its blue lakes, and screamed:
"Water, when will you fall? When will you burst,
oh thunderclouds?" How often I have dreamed

I see this bird like Ovid exiled here
in Paris, its Black Sea—it spears and prods
its snake-head at our blue, ironic air,
as if it wanted to reproach the gods.

II.
Paris changes; nothing in my melancholy
stirs . . . new mansards, *arrondissements* razed *en bloc*,
glass, scaffolding, slum wards—all allegory!
My memories are heavier than rock!

Here by the Louvre my symbol oppresses me:
I think of the great swan hurled from the blue,
heroic, silly—like a refugee
dogged by its griping angst—also of you,

Andromache, fallen from your great bridegroom,
and now the concubine and baggage of Pyrrhus—
you loiter wailing by the empty tomb,
Hector's widow and the last wife of Helenus!

I think of you, tubercular and sick,
blindly stamping through puddles, Jeanne Duval,
peering into the Paris fog's thick wall
for the lost coco-palms of Mozambique.

I think of people who have lost the luck
they never find again, and waste their powers,
like wolf-nurses giving grief a tit to suck,
or public orphans drying up like flowers;

and in this forest, on my downward drag,
my old sorrow lets out its lion's roar.
I think of Paris raising the white flag,
drowned sailors, fallen girls . . . and many more!

Baudelaire: Le cygne.

Voyage to Cythera

My heart, a seagull rocketed and spun
about the rigging, dipping joyfully;
our slow prow rocking under cloudless sky
was like an angel drunk with the live sun.

What's that out there? Those leagues of hovering sand?
"It's Cythera famous in the songs,
the gay old dogs' El Dorado, it belongs
to legend. Look closely, it's a poor land."

Island of secret orgies none profess,
the august shade of Aphrodite plays
like clouds of incense over your blue bays,
and weights the heart with love and weariness.

Island whose myrtle esplanades arouse
our nerves, here heart-sighs and the adoration
of every land and age and generation
ramble like coal-red roses on a house

to the eternal cooing of the dove.
"No, Cythera crumbles, cakes and dries,
a rocky desert troubled by shrill cries . . ."
And yet I see one portent stretch above

us. Is it a temple where the pagan powers
hover in naked majesty to bless
the arbors, gold-fish ponds and terraces;
and the young priestess is in love with flowers?

No, nosing through these shoals, and coming near
enough to scare the birds with our white sails,
we saw a man spread-eagled on the nails
of a cross hanging like a cypress there.

Ferocious vultures choking down thick blood
gutted the hanging man, already foul;
each smacked its beak like the flat of a trowel
into the private places of their food.

His eyes were holes and his important paunch
oozed lazy, looping innards down his hips;
those scavengers, licking sweetmeats from their lips,
had hung his pouch and penis on a branch.

Under his foot-soles, shoals of quadrupeds
with lifted muzzles nosed him round and guzzled;
a huge antediluvian reptile muscled
through them like an executioner with his aides.

Native of Cythera, initiate,
how silently you hung and suffered insult
in retribution for your dirty cult
and orgasms only death could expiate.

Ridiculous hanged man, my sins confirm
your desecration; when I saw you seethe,
I felt my nausea mounting to my teeth,
the drying bile-stream of my wasted sperm.

Poor devil with sweet memories, your laws
are mine; before you, I too felt those jaws:
black panther, lancing crow, the Noah's Ark
that loved to chafe my flesh and leave their mark.

I'd lost my vision clinging to those shrouds,
I feared the matching blues of sky and sea;
all things were henceforth black with blood for me,
and plunged my heart in allegoric clouds . . .

Nothing stands upright in your land, oh Lust,
except my double, hanging at full length—
Oh God, give me the courage and the strength
to see my heart and body without disgust.

Baudelaire: Voyage à Cythère.

The Servant

My old nurse and servant, whose great heart
made you jealous, is dead and sleeps apart
from us. Shouldn't we bring her a few flowers?
The dead, the poor dead, they have their bad hours,
and when October, stripper of old trees,
poisons the turf and makes their marble freeze,
surely they find us worse than wolves or curs
for sleeping under mountainous warm furs . . .
These, eaten by the earth's black dream, lie dead,
without a wife or friend to warm their bed,
old skeletons sunk like shrubs in burlap bags—
and feel the ages trickle through their rags.
They have no heirs or relatives to chase
with children round their crosses and replace
the potted refuse, where they lie beneath
their final flower, the interment wreath.

The oak log sings and sputters in my chamber,
and in the cold blue half-light of December,
I see her tiptoe through my room, and halt
humbly, as if she'd hurried from her vault
with blankets for the child her sleepless eye
had coaxed and mothered to maturity.
What can I say to her to calm her fears?
My nurse's hollow sockets fill with tears.

Baudelaire: *La servante*.

The Game

Cheeks chalked, blacked lashes, eyes still terrible—
old bags glittering under chandeliers,
as they titter and make a waterfall
of stone and metal fall from their thin ears;

my hang-dog shadow joining in the queue,
as fixtures holding fifty candles light
the profiles of great men who used to write,
and here gasp out their ulcerous guts to screw;

crowding this gameboard, faces without lips,
lips white as teeth, false uppers without jaws,
bone fingers running through the youthful grips,
still fumbling empty pockets and false bras . . .

This is the sort of tableau of my doom
self-love imagines for my terminus;
stuck in a corner of the waiting-room,
I see myself withdrawn and lecherous—

envying the war-horses' running sores,
this one's torn nerves, that one's arthritic grace,
the graveyard gaiety of these old whores,
angling their flesh for traffic in my face—

envying those who scuttle character,
and crowd full sail into the blue abyss—
these drunk for blood, who in the end prefer
dishonor to death, and hell to nothingness.

Baudelaire: *Le jeu.*

The Voyage

(FOR T. S. ELIOT)

I.

For the boy playing with his globe and stamps,
the world is equal to his appetite—
how grand the world in the blaze of the lamps,
how petty in tomorrow's small dry light!

One morning we lift anchor, full of brave
prejudices, prospects, ingenuity—
we swing with the velvet swell of the wave,
our infinite is rocked by the fixed sea.

Some wish to fly a cheapness they detest,
others, their cradles' terror—others stand
with their binoculars on a woman's breast,
reptilian Circe with her junk and wand.

Not to be turned to reptiles, such men daze
themselves with spaces, light, the burning sky;
cold toughens them, they bronze in the sun's blaze
and dry the sores of their debauchery.

But the true voyagers are those who move
simply to move—like lost balloons! Their heart
is some old motor thudding in one groove.
It says its single phrase, "Let us depart!"

They are like conscripts lusting for the guns;
our sciences have never learned to tag
their projects and designs—enormous, vague
hopes grease the wheels of these automatons!

II.

We imitate, oh horror! tops and bowls
in their eternal waltzing marathon;
even in sleep, our fever whips and rolls—
like a black angel flogging the brute sun.

Strange sport! where destination has no place
or name, and may be anywhere we choose—
where man, committed to his endless race,
runs like a madman diving for repose!

Our soul is a three-master seeking port:
a voice from starboard shouts, "We're at the dock!"
Another, more elated, cries from port,
"Here's dancing, gin and girls!" Balls! it's a rock!

The islands sighted by the lookout seem
the El Dorados promised us last night;
imagination wakes from its drugged dream,
sees only ledges in the morning light.

What dragged these patients from their German spas?
Shall we throw them in chains, or in the sea?
Sailors discovering new Americas,
who drown in a mirage of agony!

The worn-out sponge, who scuffles through our slums
sees whiskey, paradise and liberty
wherever oil-lamps shine in furnished rooms—
we see Blue Grottoes, Caesar and Capri.

III.

Stunningly simple Tourists, your pursuit
is written in the tear-drops in your eyes!
Spread out the packing cases of your loot,
your azure sapphires made of seas and skies!

We want to break the boredom of our jails
and cross the oceans without oars or steam—
give us visions to stretch our minds like sails,
the blue, exotic shoreline of your dream!

Tell us, what have you seen?

IV.

　　　　　　　　　　"We've seen the stars,
a wave or two—we've also seen some sand;
although we peer through telescopes and spars,
we're often deadly bored as you on land.

The shine of sunlight on the violet sea,
the roar of cities when the sun goes down:
these stir our hearts with restless energy;
we worship the Indian Ocean where we drown!

No old chateau or shrine besieged by crowds
of crippled pilgrims sets our souls on fire,
as these chance countries gathered from the clouds.
Our hearts are always anxious with desire.

Desire, that great elm fertilized by lust,
gives its old body, when the heaven warms
its bark that winters and old age encrust;
green branches draw the sun into its arms.

Why are you always growing taller, Tree—
Oh longer-lived than cypress! Yet we took
one or two sketches for your picture-book,
Brothers who sell your souls for novelty!

We have salaamed to pagan gods with horns,
entered shrines peopled by a galaxy
of Buddhas, Slavic saints, and unicorns,
so rich Rothschild must dream of bankruptcy!

Priests' robes that scattered solid golden flakes,
dancers with tattooed bellies and behinds,
charmers supported by braziers of snakes . . ."

V.
Yes, and what else?

VI.
                    Oh trivial, childish minds!

You've missed the more important things that we
were forced to learn against our will. We've been
from top to bottom of the ladder, and see
only the pageant of immortal sin:

there women, servile, peacock-tailed, and coarse,
marry for money, and love without disgust
horny, pot-bellied tyrants stuffed on lust,
slaves' slaves—the sewer in which their gutter pours!

old maids who weep, playboys who live each hour,
state banquets loaded with hot sauces, blood and trash,
ministers sterilized by dreams of power,
workers who love their brutalizing lash;

and everywhere religions like our own
all storming heaven, propped by saints who reign
like sybarites on beds of nails and frown—
all searching for some orgiastic pain!

Many, self-drunk, are lying in the mud—
mad now, as they have always been, they roll
in torment screaming to the throne of God:
"My image and my lord, I hate your soul!"

And others, dedicated without hope,
flee the dull herd—each locked in his own world

hides in his ivory-tower of art and dope—
this is the daily news from the whole world!

VII.
How sour the knowledge travellers bring away!
The world's monotonous and small; we see
ourselves today, tomorrow, yesterday,
an oasis of horror in sands of ennui!

Shall we move or rest? Rest, if you can rest;
move if you must. One runs, but others drop
and trick their vigilant antagonist.
Time is a runner who can never stop,

the Wandering Jew or Christ's Apostles. Yet
nothing's enough; no knife goes through the ribs
of this retiarius throwing out his net;
others can kill and never leave their cribs.

And even when Time's heel is on our throat
we still can hope, still cry, "On, on, let's go!"
Just as we once took passage on the boat
for China, shivering as we felt the blow,

so we now set our sails for the Dead Sea,
light-hearted as the youngest voyager.
If you look seaward, Traveller, you will see
a spectre rise and hear it sing, "Stop, here,

and eat my lotus-flowers, here's where they're sold.
Here are the fabulous fruits; look, my boughs bend;
eat yourself sick on knowledge. Here we hold
time in our hands, it never has to end."

We know the accents of this ghost by heart;
our comrade spreads his arms across the seas;
"On, on, Orestes. Sail and feast your heart—
Here's Clytemnestra." Once we kissed her knees.

VIII.
It's time. Old Captain, Death, lift anchor, sink!
The land rots; we shall sail into the night;
if now the sky and sea are black as ink,
our hearts, as you must know, are filled with light.

Only when we drink poison are we well—
we want, this fire so burns our brain tissue,
to drown in the abyss—heaven or hell,
who cares? Through the unknown, we'll find the *new*.

Baudelaire: *Le voyage*.

Nostalgia

An autobiographical poem: Rimbaud remembers the small boy in a rowboat under the old walls of Charleville. His mother and sisters are on the bank. His father has just deserted them.

I.
The sucking river was the child's salt tears.
His eyes were blinded by white walls; the girls,
white lilies on white silk! The *Tricouleur*
hung from the walls restored by Joan of Arc—

wings of an angel! No, the gold stream slid,
breathing the underwater amber of its reeds . . .
His mother had the blue sky for parasol,
yet begged the arched bridge and the hills for shade.

II.
Then the walled surface swam with bubbles;
cloth of gold coverings piled the riverbed;
the sisters' faded grass-bruised pinafores
hung like willows; birds stepped from twig to twig.

Through noon, the river's spotted mirror steamed
off to the bare sky's perfect, burning sphere—
Oh Bride, your faith was purer than gold coins,
marsh marigolds, my hot and burning eyelid . . .

III.
The mother stood too stiffly in the field,
beclouded with the field-hands' shirts. She twirled
her parasol, and trampled on the weeds.
The sisters sat on the heraldic green,

and stared at red Morocco Missals, while
his father walked beyond the mountain, like
a thousand angels parting on the road.
She, cold and black, flew. Rushed after her lost man!

IV.
Nostalgia for his hairy arms—the grass
green in the holy April moonlight! Joy!
The riverbank's abandoned lumberyards
still fertilized the marsh with blocks and sawdust.

She wept below the parapet. The breath
of the dry poplars was the wind's alone;
the water had no bottom and no source;
a man in mud-caked hip-boots poled a barge.

V.
The dull eye drove the water out of reach—
still boat, oh too short arms! I could not touch
one or the other flower—the yellow burned me,
the cool blue was the ash-gray water's friend.

The reeds had eaten up the roses long ago;
each wing-beat shook the willows' silver dust.
My boat stuck fast; its anchor dug for bottom;
the lidless eye, still water, filled with mud.

Rimbaud: *Mémoire.*

The Poet at Seven

When the timeless, daily, tedious affair
was over, his Mother shut
her Bible; her nose was in the air;
from her summit
of righteousness, she could not see the boy:
his lumpy forehead knotted
with turmoil, his soul returned to its vomit.

All day he would sweat obedience.
He was very intelligent, but wrung,
and every now and then a sudden jerk
showed dark hypocrisies at work.
He would clap his hands on his rump,
and strut where the gloom of the hallway rotted
the hot curtains. He stuck out his tongue,
clenched his eyes shut, and saw dots.
A terrace gave on the twilight;
one used to see him up there in the lamplight,
sulking on the railing
under an abyss of air
which hung from the roof. His worst block
was the stultifying slump
of mid-summer—he would lock
himself up in the toilet and inhale
its freshness; there he could breathe.

When winter snowed under the breath of flowers,
and the moon blanched the little bower
behind the house, he would crawl
to the foot of the wall
and lie with his eyeballs squeezed to his arm,
dreaming of some dark revelation,
or listening to the legions of termites swarm
in the horny espaliers. As for compassion,

the only children he could speak to
were creepy, abstracted boys, who hid
match-stick thin fingers yellow and black with mud
under rags stuck with diarrhea.
Their dull eyes drooled on their dull cheeks,
they spoke with the selflessness of morons.
His Mother was terrified,
she thought they were losing caste. This was good—
she had the true blue look that lied.

At seven he was making novels
about life in the Sahara,
where ravished Liberty had fled—
sunrises, buffaloes, jungle, savannahs!
For his facts, he used illustrated weeklies,
and blushed at the rotogravures of naked, red
Hawaiian girls dancing.
A little eight year old tomboy,
the daughter of the next door workers,
came, brown-eyed, terrible,
in a print dress. Brutal and in the know,
she would jump on his back,
and ride him like a buffalo,
and shake out her hair.
Wallowing below
her once, he bit her crotch—
she never wore bloomers—
kicked and scratched, he carried back
the taste of her buttocks to his bedroom.

What he feared most
were the sticky, lost December Sundays,
when he used to stand with his hair gummed back
at a little mahogony stand, and hold
a Bible pocked with cabbage-green mould.
Each night in his alcove, he had dreams.
He despised God, the National Guard,
and the triple drum-beat
of the town-crier calling up the conscripts.

He loved the swearing
workers, when they crowded back, black
in the theatrical twilight to their wards.
He felt clean
when he filled his lungs with the smell—
half hay fever, half iodine—
of the wheat,
he watched its pubic golden tassels swell
and steam in the heat,
then sink back calm.

What he liked best were dark things:
the acrid, dank rings
on the ceiling, and the high,
bluish plaster, as bald as the sky
in his bare bedroom, where he could close
the shutters and lose
his world for hundreds of hours,
mooning doggedly
over his novel, endlessly
expanding with jaundiced skies,
drowned vegetation, and carnations
that flashed like raw flesh
in the underwater green
of the jungle starred with flowers—
dizziness, mania, revulsions, pity!
Often the town playground
below him grew loud with children;
the wind brought him their voices,
and he lay alone on pieces of unbleached canvas,
violently breaking into sail.

Rimbaud: *Les poètes de sept ans.*

The Drunken Boat

I felt my guides no longer carried me—
as we sailed down the virgin Amazon,
the redskins nailed them to their painted stakes
naked, as targets for their archery.

I carried Flemish wheat or Swedish wood,
but had forgotten my unruly crew;
their conversation ended with their lives,
the river let me wander where I would.

Surf punished me, and threw my cargo out;
last winter I was breaking up on land.
I fled. These floating river villages
had never heard a more triumphant shout.

The green ooze spurting through my centerboard
was sweeter than sour apples to a boy—
it washed away the stains of puke and rot-gut,
anchor and wheel were carried overboard.

The typhoon spun my silly needle round;
ten nights I scudded from the freighters' lights;
lighter than cork, I danced upon the surge
man calls the rolling coffin of his drowned.

Rudderless, I was driven like a plank
on night seas stuck with stars and dribbling milk;
I shot through greens and blues, where luminous,
swollen, drowned sailors rose for light and sank.

I saw the lightning turn the pole-star green,
currents, icebergs, and waterspouts. One night
the sunrise lifted like a flock of doves—
I saw whatever men suppose they've seen.

I saw the ocean bellowing on the land,
cattle stampeding with their tails on fire,
but never dreamed Three Marys walked the sea
to curb those frothing muzzles with a hand.

I saw the salt marsh boil, a whole whale rot
in some Louisiana bayou's muck,
cutting the blue horizon with its flukes—
bon-bons of sunlight and cold azure snot!

I was a lost boat nosing through the hulls
of Monitors and Hanseatic hulks;
none cared to gaff my wreckage from the bilge
and yellow beaks of the marauding gulls.

I would have liked to show a child those seas,
rocking to soothe the clatter of my sails
in irons on the equatorial line.
Like a woman, I fell upon my knees;

then heaven opened for the voyager.
I stared at archipelagoes of stars.
Was it on those dead watches that I died—
a million golden birds, Oh future Vigor!

I cannot watch these purple suns go down
like actors on the Aeschylean stage.
I'm drunk on water. I cry out too much—
Oh that my keel might break, and I might drown!

Shrunken and black against a twilight sky,
our Europe has no water. Only a pond
the cows have left, and a boy wades to launch
his paper boat frail as a butterfly.

Bathed in your languors, Waves, I have no wings
to cut across the wakes of cotton ships,
or fly against the flags of merchant kings,
or swim beneath the guns of prison ships.

Rimbaud: *Le bateau ivre.*

Eighteen-Seventy

I.
A POSTER OF OUR DAZZLING VICTORY AT SAARBRÜCKEN

In the center of the poster, Napoleon
rides in apotheosis, sallow, medalled, a ramrod
perched on a merrygoround horse. He sees life
through rosy glasses, terrible as God,

and sentimental as a bourgeois papa.
Four little conscripts take their nap below
on scarlet guns and drums. One, unbuckling, cheers
Napoleon—he's stunned by the big name!

Another lounges on the butt of his Chassepot,
another feels his hair rise on his neck.
A bearskin shako bounds like a black sun:

VIVE L'EMPEREUR! They're holding back their breath.
And last, some moron, struggling to his knees,
presents a blue and scarlet ass—to what?

II.
NAPOLEON AFTER SEDAN

The man waxy—he jogs along the fields
in flower, black, a cigar between his teeth.
The wax man thinks about the Tuileries
in flower. At times his mossy eye takes fire.

Twenty years of orgy have made him drunk:
he'd said: "My hand will snuff out Liberty,
politely, gently, as I snuff my stogie."
Liberty lives; the Emperor is out—

he's captured. Oh what name is shaking on
his lips? What plebescites? Napoleon
cannot tell you. His shark's eye is dead.

An opera glass on the horses at Compère . . .
he watches his cigar fume off in smoke . . .
soirées at Saint Cloud . . . a bluish vapor.

III.

TO THE FRENCH OF THE SECOND EMPIRE

You, dead in '92 and '93,
still pale from the great kiss of Liberty—
when tyrants trampled on humanity,
you broke them underneath your wooden shoes.

You were reborn and great by agony,
your hearts in rage still beat for our salvation—
Oh soldiers, sown by death, your noble lover,
in our old furrows you regenerate!

You, whose life-blood washed our soiled standards red,
the dead of Valmy, Italy, Fleurus,
thousands of Christs, red-bonneted . . . we

have let you die with our Republic, we
who lick the boots of our bored kings like dogs—
men of the Second Empire, I mean you!

IV.

ON THE ROAD

I walked on the great road, my two fists lost
in my slashed pockets, and my overcoat
the ghost of a coat. Under the sky, I walked,
I was your student, Muses. What affairs

we had together! My only pants were a big hole.
Tom Thumb, the dreamer, I was knocking off
my coupled rhymes. My inn was the Great Bear;
the stars rang like silver coins in my hand.

I heard them and I squatted on my hams,
September twilight on September twilight,
rhyming into the fairy-crowded dark.

The rain's cheap wine was splashing on my face.
I plucked at the elastics on my clobbered
shoes—one foot pressed tight against my heart.

V.

AT THE GREEN CABARET

For eight days I had been knocking my boots
on the road stones. I was entering Charleroi.
At the Green Cabaret, I called for ham,
half cold, and a large helping of tartines.

Happy, I kicked my shoes off, cooled my feet
under the table, green like the room, and laughed
at the naive Belgian pictures on the wall.
But it was terrific when the house-girl

with her earth-mother tits and come-on eyes—
no Snow Queen having cat-fits at a kiss—
brought me tarts and ham on a colored plate.

She stuck a clove of garlic in the ham,
red frothed by white, and slopped beer in my stein—
foam gilded by a ray of the late sun.

VI.

A MALICIOUS GIRL

In the cigar-brown dining room, perfumed
by a smell of shellac and cabbage soup,
I held my plate and raked together some
God-awful Belgian dish. I blew my soup,

and listened to the clock tick while I ate,
and then the kitchen opened with a blast;
a housemaid entered, God knows why—her blouse
half open, yellow hair in strings. She touched

a little finger trembling to her cheek,
where the peach-velvet changed from white to red,
and made a schoolgirl grimace with her lips . . .

She swept away the plates to clear my mind,
then—just like that—quite sure of being kissed,
she whispered, "Look, my cheek has caught a cold."

VII.

THE SLEEPER IN THE VALLEY

The swollen river sang through the green hole,
and madly hooked white tatters on the grass.
Light escaladed the hot hills. The whole
valley bubbled with sunbeams like a beer-glass.

The conscript was open-mouthed; his bare head
and neck swam in the bluish watercress.
He slept. The mid-day soothed his heaviness,
sunlight was raining into his green bed,

and baked the bruises from his body, rolled
as a sick child might hug itself asleep . . .
Oh Nature, rock him warmly, he is cold.

The flowers no longer make his hot eyes weep.
The river sucks his hair. His blue eye rolls.
He sleeps. In his right side are two red holes.

VIII.
EVIL

All day the red spit of the chain-shot tore
whistling across the infinite blue sky,
while the great captain saw his infantry
flounder in massed battalions into fire.

The criminal injustice that deceives
and rules us, lays our corpses end on end,
then burns us like the summer grass or leaves;
La Patrie is avaricious to this end!

She is a god that laughs at Papal bulls,
the great gold chalice and the thuribles.
She dozes while our grand hosannas drown

the guns and drums, and wakes to hear the grief
of widows or a mother who lays down
her great sou knotted in a handkerchief.

> Rimbaud: *L'éclatante victoire; Rages de Césars; Morts de quatre-vingt-douze;*
> *Ma Bohème; Au cabaret vert; La maline; Le dormeur du val; Le mal.*

The Lice-Hunters

The child, feverish, frowning, only saw red
finally, and begged the fairies for his life;
the royal sisters sat beside his bed;
each long and silver finger was a knife.

They laid the child beside the window's arch,
half-open. A glass of violets drank the blue;
he felt their wicked razor fingers march
through his thick hair to comb away the dew.

He heard their singing breath, and tried to breathe
the scent of rose and almond honey, hissed
and whistled through the fissures of their teeth,
sucking saliva from the lips he kissed.

He heard their eyebrows beating in the dark
whenever an electric finger struck to crush
a bloated louse, and blood would pop and mark
the indolence of their disdainful touch.

Wine of idleness had flushed his eyes;
somewhere a child's harmonica pushed its sigh
insanely through the wearied lungs—the rise
and dying of his ceaseless wish to cry.

Rimbaud: *Les chercheuses de poux.*

At Gautier's Grave

To you, gone emblem of man's happiness,
health! Do not think I raise this empty cup
and insane toast to nothingness, because
the non-existent corridor gives hope.
A golden monster suffers on the stem;
your apparition cannot comfort me,
I myself sealed you in your porphyry,
Gautier! The rite is for my hands to dash
their torch against your vault's thick iron gate.
We, who are here simply to celebrate
the absence of the poet, must confess
his sepulcher encloses him entire,
unless the burning glory of his craft,
a window where the light is proud to flash,
answer the mortal sun's pure fire with fire—
ashes to ashes in the common draft!

Marvelous, total, and alone, your boast
was such as false pride trembles to exhale—
that crowd already changing to the pale,
opaque unbeing of its future ghost.
But when fake mourning drapes the blazoned bier,
if one of these dead poets should appear,
serene, deaf even to my sacred verse,
and pass, the guest of his vague shroud, to be
the virgin hero of posterity—
I scorn the lucid horror of a tear.

A vast hole carried by a mass of fog,
the angry wind of words he did not say,
nothingness questions the abolished man:
the dream shrieks, "Say what the earth was, you,
its shadow! Space has no answer but this toy,
this voice whose clearness falters, 'I don't know.' "

The master, just by gazing, can reclaim
the restless miracle of paradise.
Once his voice alone was the final frisson
that gave the lily and the rose their name.
Does anything remain of this great claim?
No. Men, forget your narrow faiths, no shade
darkens our métier's artificial fire.

Thinking of you, I call on you: Remain—
Oh lost now in the gardens of this Star—
honor the calm disaster of our earth:
with drunken red words from the loving cup,
a solemn agitation on the air
the crystal gaze of diamonds and rain,
that falls, unfading, on the wilted flower,
the isolation of its sunlit hour.

His tombstone ornaments the garden path—
here is the only true and lasting light,
where the poet's casual, humble gesture ends
the dream that murders his humanity;
today on the great morning of his sleep,
when ancient death is now, as with Gautier,
only the closing of his sacred eyes,
a chance for patience, we too stand and see
this solid sepulcher holds all that hurt:
miserly silence and the massive night.

Mallarmé: *Toast funèbre*.

Helen

I am the blue! I come from the lower world
to hear the serene erosion of the surf;
once more I see the galleys bleed with dawn,
and shark with muffled rowlocks into Troy.
My solitary hands recall the kings;
I used to run my fingers through their beards;
I wept. They sang about their shady wars,
the great gulfs boiling sternward from their keels.
I hear the military trumpets, all that brass,
blasting commands to the frantic oars;
the rowers' metronome enchains the sea,
and high on beaked and dragon prows, the gods—
their fixed, archaic smiles stung by the salt—
reach out their carved, indulgent arms to me!

Valéry: *Hélène.*

A Roman Sarcophagus

The terrible Etruscan mater familias
with her lethal smile
and the reddish dust of her toga
still lounges at ease
like Madame Récamier on her tomb-lid.

In the beginning how familiar
the whirling water
of her pleats growing water-smooth
under the pressure of the breasts
spread like ox-horns!

What hinders our supposing
such arrest, posing and dominance
are momentary
once the corpse loses
its technicolor beauty?

Among the bangles, pious pictures, bits of glass,
this sarcophagus
once cradled something
gradually disintegrating
in a slowly dirtying slip.

Then the stone slopped it down.
Where's the intelligence
to galvanize this dead presence,
to put her to use
just once?

That would be water
glittering like geysers,

the tarpon's or marlin's mermaid flash,
water delivered
from the imperial aqueducts.

Rilke: *Römische Sarkophage.*

The Cadet Picture of My Father

(FOR VIOLA BERNARD)

There's absence in the eyes. The brow's in touch
with something far. Now distant boyishness
and seduction shadow his enormous lips,
the slender aristocratic uniform
with its Franz Josef braid; both the hands bulge
like gloves upon the saber's basket hilt.
The hands are quiet, they reach out toward nothing—
I hardly see them now, as if they were
the first to grasp distance and disappear,
and all the rest lies curtained in itself,
and so withdrawn, I cannot understand
my father as he bleaches on this page—

Oh quickly disappearing photograph
in my more slowly disappearing hand!

Rilke: *Jugend-Bildnis meines Vaters.*

Self-Portrait

The bone-build of the eyebrows has a mule's
or Pole's noble and narrow steadfastness.
A scared blue child is peering through the eyes,
and there's a kind of weakness, not a fool's,
yet womanish—the gaze of one who serves.
The mouth is just a mouth . . . untidy curves,
quite unpersuasive, yet it says its *yes*,
when forced to act. The forehead cannot frown
and likes the shade of dumbly looking down.

A still life, *nature morte*—hardly a whole!
It has done nothing worked through or alive,
in spite of pain, in spite of comforting . . .
Out of this distant and disordered thing
something in earnest labors to unroll.

Rilke: *Selbstbildnis aus dem Jahre 1906.*

Orpheus, Eurydice and Hermes

(FOR WILLIAM MEREDITH)

That's the strange regalia of souls.
Vibrant
as platinum filaments they went,
like arteries through their darkness. From the holes
of powder beetles, from the otter's bed,
from the oak king judging by the royal oak—
blood like our own life-blood, sprang.
Otherwise nothing was red.

The dark was heavier than Caesar's foot.

There were canyons there,
distracted forests, and bridges over air-pockets;
a great gray, blind lake
mooned over the background canals,
like a bag of winds over the Caucasus.
Through terraced highlands, stocked with cattle and patience,
streaked the single road.
It was unwinding like a bandage.

They went on this road.

First the willowy man in the blue cloak;
he didn't say a thing. He counted his toes.
His step ate up the road,
a yard at a time, without bruising a thistle. His hands fell,
clammy and clenched,
as if they feared the folds of his tunic,
as if they didn't know a thing about the frail lyre,
hooked on his left shoulder,
like roses wrestling an olive tree.

It was as though his intelligence were cut in two.
His outlook worried like a dog behind him,

now diving ahead, now romping back,
now yawning on its haunches at an elbow of the road.
What he heard breathed myrrh behind him,
and often it seemed to reach back to them,
those two others
on oath to follow behind to the finish.
Then again there was nothing behind him,
only the backring of his heel,
and the currents of air in his blue cloak.
He said to himself, "For all that, they are there."
He spoke aloud and heard his own voice die.
"They are coming, but if they are two,
how fearfully light their step is!"
Couldn't he turn round? (Yet a single back-look
would be the ruin of this work
so near perfection.) And as a matter of fact,
he knew he must now turn to them, those two light ones,
who followed and kept their counsel.

First the road-god, the messenger man . . .
His caduceus shadow-bowing behind him,
his eye arched, archaic,
his ankles feathered like arrows—
in his left hand he held *her*,
the one so loved that out of a single lyre
more sorrow came than from all women in labor,
so that out of this sorrow came
the fountain-head of the world: valleys, fields,
towns, roads . . . acropolis,
marble quarries, goats, vineyards.
And this sorrow-world circled about her,
just as the sun and stern stars
circle the earth—
a heaven of anxiety ringed by the determined stars . . .
that's how *she* was.

She leant, however, on the god's arm;
her step was delicate from her wound—
uncertain, drugged and patient.
She was drowned in herself, as in a higher hope,

and she didn't give the man in front of her a thought,
nor the road climbing to life.
She was in herself. Being dead
fulfilled her beyond fulfillment.
Like an apple full of sugar and darkness,
she was full of her decisive death,
so green she couldn't bite into it.
She was still in her marble maidenhood,
untouchable. Her sex had closed house,
like a young flower rebuking the night air.
Her hands were still ringing and tingling—
even the light touch of the god
was almost a violation.

A woman?
She was no longer that blond transcendence
so often ornamenting the singer's meters,
nor a hanging garden in his double bed.
She had wearied of being the hero's one possession.

She was as bountiful as uncoiled hair,
poured out like rain,
shared in a hundred pieces like her wedding cake.

She was a root, self-rooted.

And when the god suddenly gripped her,
and said with pain in his voice, "He is looking back at us,"
she didn't get through to the words,
and answered vaguely, "Who?"

Far there, dark against the clear entrance,
stood some one, or rather no one
you'd ever know. He stood and stared
at the one level, inevitable road,
as the reproachful god of messengers
looking round, pushed off again.
His caduceus was like a shotgun on his shoulder.

Rilke: *Orpheus. Eurydike. Hermes.*

Winter Noon

At the moment when I was still happy
(God forgive me my bombast!)
who punctured my brief joy?
You'll say a Milanese blonde
passing by, who laughed at me.
No, it was a balloon,
a sky-blue balloon drifting
through the blue of the winter noon.
The Italian heaven was never so blue:
there were puffy white clouds,
the sun burned the house-windows,
a string of smoke slipped
from one or two chimneys,
when the balloon took flight
over all things, all those divine things,
and escaped the inconsiderate hand
of the boy—(Surely he was weeping
in the middle of that crush
for his sorrow, his terrible sorrow)
between the Stock Exchange
and the Coffee House,
where I was killing time,
as I gaped at his balloon,
dipping and lifting . . .

Saba: *Mezzogiorno d'inverno.*

You Knocked Yourself Out

I.
Those unnumbered, ruthless, random stones,
tense, vibrating still, as if slung
by the smothered abysmal fire;
the terror of those Amazon cataracts cascading
down miles to the chaos of implacable embraces;
the rock's lockjaw above the sand's
detonating dazzle—do you remember?

The sky-line, a blinding china saucer?

Do you remember the mountain, that wounded giantess?
The stranded sand-pine
with its nets of roots as mineral as the shards they finger,
as it beetled above the down-slope, only
yawning to engulf the horizon shadows?
Cool that grotto's gullet filled
with salad leaves and butterflies—
do you remember it, dumb, delirious,
there just under the summit's rotunda stone,
three men's length tall?
A king-pin of flint, teetering,
immobile?

Quick wren. Greedy eyes drunk with wonder.
You zig-zagged from fiber to fiber
to conquer the height's speckled crown,
dare-devil, musical child,
and loitered there alone to spy into the lapis lazuli bayou,
where unearthly, moss-browed turtles
were rousing from the ooze.

There the tension of nature at its lowest,
submarine sublimities,
nihilist admonitions!

II.
You lifted arms like wings,
and gave the winds back their youth,
as you ran on the inertia of the stock-still air.

No one ever saw
your deft foot rest from the dance.

III.
Lucky grace,
how could you help knocking your brains out
on such horny blindness—
you, simple breath, crystal bubble,

a candle, too dazzling
for the shaggy, random, vandalistic
burning of the naked sun!

Ungaretti: *Tu ti spezzasti.*

Dora Markus

I.
It was where a plank pier
pushed from Porto Corsini into the open sea;
a handful of men, dull as blocks, drop,
draw in their nets. With a toss
of your thumb, you point out the other shore,
invisible, your true country.
Then we trailed a canal to the outlying shipyards,
silvered with sun and soot—
a patch of town-sick country, where depressed spring,
full of amnesia, was burning out.

Here where the old world's way of surviving
is subtilized by a nervous
Levantine anxiety,
your words flash a rainbow,
like the scales of a choking mullet.

Your restlessness makes me think
of migratory birds diving at a lighthouse
on an ugly night—
even your ennui is a whirlwind,
circling invisibly—
the let-ups non-existent.
I don't know how, so pressed, you've stood up
to that puddle of diffidence, your heart.
What saves you, perhaps,
is a charm, which you keep
near your lipstick, puff and nail-file—
a white mouse made of ivory . . .
Thus you exist.

[1926]

II.
In your own Carinthia now
your corsage is the crescent
hedges of flowering myrtle . . .
You sashay on the curb of a stagnant pond,
and watch the timid carp swallowing, swallowing,
or saunter under the lime trees,
and follow the kindling night
along the frowzy shorefront.
The purple and orange awnings of landings
and *pensioni* throw
a bonfire on the water.

Night blanketing
the fogging lake coves
brings only the catcalls of geese,
the put-put-put of the outboards.
The snow-white majolicas of your interior
have seen you alter,
and tell your fly-blown mirror
a story of cool miscalculations,
now engraved where no sponge can expunge.

That's your legend, Dora!
But it is written already
on the moist lips of sugar daddies
with weak, masculine side-burns,
in the ten inch gold frames
of the grand hotels—
it lives in the asthma
of the sprung harmonica
at the hour when daylight muddies, each day later.

It is written there!
The evergreen laurel lives on
for the kitchen, the voice doesn't change;
Ravenna is far away. A ferocious faith
distills its venom.

What does it want from you?
Not that you surrender
voice, legend or destiny . . .

[1939]

Montale: *Dora Markus.*

Day and Night

A feather floating from a feather-duster
can sketch your figure, or a sunbeam playing
hide and seek on my typescript, or the blinding semaphore
of a child's mirror, or a skylight on a roof.
Along the brick wall, knobby as a crocodile,
scrolls of vapor
prolong the steeple-tops of the poplars;
out on the sidewalk the hurdy-gurdy man's
ruffled parrot takes umbrage.
The night is like the sultry sulphur of Montecatini
on the little squares, on the footsteps; and always
this merciless parole for taking one's measure
in order to rise to the heroism of the quotidian,
the myopia of the incubus or succubus that cannot catch
the light of your eyes in the incandescent cave;
and always the same Saturday night ulcer of the multiplying family;
and the cancerous belly-aching on the veranda,
if a shotgun go off and redden your throat
and scatter your feathers,
Oh imperiled bird of the dawn . . .
And the hospitals and cloisters wake
to the reveille of military concerts.

Montale: *Giorno e notte.*

The Magnolia's Shadow

The shadow of the dwarf magnolia
is a scarecrow now that the turkey-wattle
blossoms are blown. Like something wired,
the cicada vibrates at timed intervals.
It is no longer the Easter of voices in unison,
Clizia, the season of the infinite deity,
who devours his faithful, then revives them in blood.
It was more facile to expend one's self,
and die at the first wing-flutter, at the first
hectic rumbling from the adversary—a nursery game.
The hard way begins now; but not for you,
eaten by sunlight, rooted—yet a fragile thrush,
flying high over those frogskin mudbanks,
not for you to whom zenith, nadir, capricorn
and cancer rush together, so that the war may be
inside you, and in your adorer, who sees on you
the stigmata of the Bridegroom—the shiver
of snowfall doesn't jar you. Others
shy backwards and hold back. The artisan's
subtle file shall be silent; the hollow husk
of the singer shall be powdered glass
under your feet; the shadow is neutral.
It's autumn, it's winter, it's the other
side of the sky, that leads you—there
I break water, a fish left high and dry
under the new moon.
> > > > > Goodbye.

> > > > Montale: *L'ombra della magnolia.*

Hitlerian Spring

A dense white cold of maddened moths
swaggers past parapet and lamp,
shaking a sheet upon the earth,
crackling like sugar underfoot.
Now the new season—
the nearing summer liberates
the thaw and chill
from stoneyard, lumberyard and orchard,
wood tossed by the river to its banks.

(An infernal possessor
motorcycles down the Corso;
hurrahing stooges and a jangle
of hooked crosses absorb and swallow
him—a thunderhead of light!)

                                The old shop
windows are shuttered, poor and harmless,
though even these are armed with cannon
and toys of war. This spring, the butcher
locks his creaking iron curtain—
once he would hook two goat's-heads crowned
with holly berries on his door . . .
they were a kind of ritual for
those mild young killers, unaware
the blood they spilled had been transformed
to a sick mangle of crushed wings.
Here barnacles and old mortgages
keep chiselling at the river-piles—
and no one, ahi, now is blameless!

The sirens and the tolling bells . . .
For nothing, then? On Saint John's Day,
the stinking roman candles scour

the air. Once more, spring! Now the slow
farewell, as sad as Baptism,
the mournful vigil of the horde,
the head brought in upon a board,
now diamond powder blurs the air,
and shakes down ice—the sky is like
Tobias looking at the sky,
seeing the seven seraphs flame.
Light rays and seeds are drifting down
through pollen hissing into fire,
through crushed and crooked fingers,
through the sharpness of driving snow,
the sirens and the tolling bells . . .

Clizia,
April's reopened wound is raw! . . .

Montale: *La primavera hitleriana.*

The Coastguard House

A death-cell? The shack of the coastguards
is a box over the drop to the breakers;
it waits for you without an owner,
ever since the mob of your thoughts
bullied a welcome,
and stayed on there, unrequited.
You didn't take it to heart.

For years the sirocco gunned the dead stucco with sand;
the sound of your laugh is a jagged coughing;
the compass, a pin-head, spins at random;
the dizzy dice screw up the odds.
You haven't taken my possession to heart;
another time has thinned your nostalgia;
a thread peels from the spool.

I hold an end of it,
but the house balks backward;
its sea-green weathercock
creaks and caws without pity.
I keep one end of the thread,
but you house alone
and hold your hollow breath there in the dark.

Oh the derelict horizon,
sunless except for the
orange hull of a lonely, drudging tanker!
The breakers bubble on the dead-drop.
You haven't taken my one night's possession to heart;
I have no way of knowing
who forces an entrance.

Montale: *La Casa dei doganieri.*

Arsenio

Roof-high, winds worrying winds
rake up the dust, clog the chimney ventilators,
drum through the bald, distracted little squares,
where a few senile, straw-hatted horses wheeze
by the El Dorado of the rooming houses' windows in the sun.
You are like an acid clash of castanets
disturbing by fits and starts our workaday hours,
today, as you go down
our main street, fronting the bay—
now you are sloshed with the dreary drizzle, now you dazzle us.

It's a sign of quite another orbit: you follow it.
A gusher of lead hangs over
the ungraspable gorges, and you go down,
more rootless than the winds.
A shower of salt spray, a whirlpool,
lifts, heavy with its element rebellious to the ether.
Your step through the pebbles is a creaking,
the mop-headed, beach-tossed seaweed snags you.
Iron link in a chain! Perhaps, powerless to walk,
this moment,
you finally evade finishing your journey's
all too well publicized delirium of inaction.

Here and there among the papery palm trees
you hear the wavering outcry
of the violins, dying as the thunder slams in
with the shudder of the shops closing metal shutters.
How imposing the storm now, when Sirius sparkles
garishly against the indigo heavens, far out
where the evening is already importunate.
Like some delicate tree entering the reddening light,
lightning etches a crash of pruned branches.
The strings of the two-bit orchestra grumble for silence.

You go down to a gloom that precipitates
and changes the siesta hour into night;
globelike lanterns rock on the gunnels of fishboats
in the offing, where a single darkening presence
clasps sea and heaven. Acetylene pulses
from a few perforated, rusty funnels.

                The sky trembles with raindrops.
The dry soil, turning to water, steams.
Everything near you is smoke,
a rustling hoes the earth,
capsizes the sopping pavilions,
douses the Chinese lanterns hissing on the esplanade.

You are flung aside
among wicker porch furniture and dank mats—
like a water-lily dragging its roots,
sticky, never sure-footed.
Hysterical with life, you stretch
towards an emptiness of suffocated sobbing.
You are knotted in the rings of the fish-net,
gulped by the gasping spent water . . .
Everything you grab hold of—
street, portico, walls and mirrors—
glues you to a paralyzed crowd of dead things.

If a word fells you,
if a gesture ruins you now, Arsenio,
it's a sign that this is the hour for letting go
of the life you were always disposed to throttle.
A wind carries its ashes to the stars.

                              Montale: *Arsenio.*

The Chess Player

At last with stubborn jabs of your fingers
you kill the red cigarette bulb in the china dish;
expiring spirals of smoke
crinkle like lamb's fleece toward the ceiling,
and encumber the knights and bishops
on the chessboard, who hold their positions—
stupefied. Smoke-ring after smoke-ring snakes upward,
more agile than the gold mines on your fingers.

A window opens. One puff is enough
to panic the smoke's heaven-flung mirage
of imperial arches and battlements;—
down below another world moves:
a man, bruised by the sores of the wolf,
ignores your incense:
all the torture and formulae
of your small, heraldic, chessboard world.

For a time, I doubted if you yourself even
made any sense of the game, its square,
hobbled moves through gunpowder
clouds of tobacco . . . Poise cannot
pay off the folly of death; the flash
of your eyes asks that an answering crash
pierce the smoke-screen
thrown up by the god of chance to befriend you.

Today, I know what you want. I hear
the hoarse bell of the feudal campanile.
The archaic ivory chessmen are terrified.
Like snowmen, they melt in your mind's white glare.

Montale: *Nuove stanze.*

News from Mount Amiata

I.
Come night,
the ugly weather's fire-cracker simmer
will deepen to the gruff buzz of beehives.
Termites tunnel the public room's rafters to sawdust,
an odor of bruised melons oozes from the floor.
A sick smoke lifts from the elf-huts and funghi of the valley—
like an eagle it climbs our mountain's bald cone,
and soils the windows.
I drag my table to the window,
and write to you—
here on this mountain, in this beehive cell
on the globe rocketed through space.
My letter is a paper hoop.
When I break through it, you will be imprisoned.

Here mildew sprouts like grass from the floor,
the canary cage is hooded with dirty green serge,
chestnuts explode on the grate.
Outside, it's raining.
There you are legendary.
Any legend falls short, if it confine you,
your gold-gated icon unfolding on gold.

II.
Magnesium flares light up the hidden summits;
but the narrow feudal streets below are too dark
for the caravan of black donkeys kicking up sparks.

You are devoted to precarious
sentiments and sediment—blackened architecture;
rectangular courtyards centered
on bottomless wells. You are led

by the sinister wings of nightbirds,
the infinite pit, the luminous gape of the galaxies—
all their sleight of hand and torture.
But the step that carries out into darkness
comes from a man going alone,
who sees nothing but the nearest light-chinked shutter.
The stars' pattern is too deep for him,
atmospheric ivy only chokes his darkness,
his campanile shuts its eye at two o'clock.

III.
Here on this mountain,
the world has no custom-barriers.
Let tomorrow be colder, let the north wind
shatter the stringy ribbons of old Missals,
the sandstone bastion of the barbarians.
When our sensations have no self-assurance,
everything must be a lens.
Then the polar winds will return clearer,
and convert us to our chains, the chains of the possible.

IV.
Today, the monotonous oratory of the dead,
ashes, lethargic winds—
a reluctant trickle drips
from the thatched huts.
Time is water.
The rain rains down black letters—
a *contemptu mundi*! What part of me does it bring you?

Now at this late hour
of my watch and your endless, prodigal sleep,
my tiny straw city is breaking up.
The porcupine sips a quill of mercy.

Montale: *Notizie dall' Amiata*.

The Eel

I.
The eel, the North Sea siren,
who leaves dead-pan Icelandic gods
and the Baltic for our Mediterranean,
our estuaries, our rivers—
who lances through their profound places,
and flinty portages, from branch to branch,
twig to twig, thinning down now,
ever snaking inward, worming
for the granite's heartland, threading
delicate capillaries of slime—
and in the Romagna one morning
the blaze of the chestnut blossoms
ignites its smudge in the dead water
pooled from chiselings
of the Apennines . . .
the eel, a whipstock, a Roman candle,
love's arrow on earth, which only
reaches the paradise of fecundity
through our gullies and fiery, charred streams;
a green spirit, potent only
where desolation and arson burn;
a spark that says everything
begins where everything is clinker;
this buried rainbow, this iris, twin sister
of the one you set in your eye's target center
to shine on the sons of men,
on us, up to our gills in your life-giving mud—
can you call her *Sister*?

II.
If they called you a fox,
it will be for your monstrous hurtle,
your sprint that parts and unites,
that kicks up and freshens the gravel,
(your black lace balcony, overlooking
the home for deformed children, a meadow,
and a tree, where my carved name quivers,
happy, humble, defeated)—
or perhaps only for the phosphorescent wake
of your almond eyes,
for the craft of your alert panic,
for the annihilation of dishevelled feathers
in your child's hand's python hug;
if they have likened you to the blond lioness,
to the avaricious demon of the undergrowth
(and why not to the filthy fish
that electrocutes, the torpedo fish?)
it is perhaps because the blind
have not seen the wings
on your delectable shoulder-blades,
because the blind haven't shot for
your forehead's luminous target,
the furrow I pricked there in blood,
cross, chrism, incantation,—and
prayer—damnation, salvation;
if they can only think of you
as a weasel or a woman,
with whom can I share my discovery,
where bury the gold I carry,
the red-hot, pot-bellied furnace raging
inside me, when, leaving me,
you turn up stairs?

Montale: *L'anguilla; Se t'hanno assomigliato.*

Little Testament

This thing the night flashes
like marshlight through the skull of my mind,
this pearl necklace snail's trail,
this ground glass, diamond-dust sparkle—
it is not the lamp in any church or office,
tended by some adolescent altar boy,
Communist or papist,
in black or red.
I have only this rainbow
to leave you, this testimonial
of a faith, often invaded,
of a hope that burned more slowly
than a green log on the fire.
Keep its spectrum in your pocket-mirror,
when every lamp goes out,
when hell's orchestra trembles,
and the torch-bearing Lucifer
lands on some bowsprit
in the Thames, Hudson or Seine—
rotating his hard coal wings,
half lopped by fatigue, to tell you, "Now."
It's hardly an heirloom or charm
that can tranquillize monsoons
with the transparent spider web of contemplation—
but an autobiography can only survive in ashes,
persistence is extinction.
It is certainly a sign: whoever has seen it,
will always return to you.
Each knows his own: his pride
was not an escape, his humility
was not a meanness, his obscure
earth-bound flash
was not the fizzle of a wet match.

Montale: *Piccolo testamento.*

Black Spring

A half-holiday for the burial. Of course, they punish
the provincial copper bells for hours;
terribly the nose tilts up like a tallow candle
from the coffin. Does it wish to draw breath
from its torso in a mourning suit? The last snow
fell somberly—white, then the roads were bread-crumbed with pebbles.
Poor winter, honeycombed with debts,
poured to corruption. Now the dumb, black springtime
must look into the chilly eye . . . from under the mould
on the roof-shingles, the liquid oatmeal
of the roads, the green stubble of life
on our faces! High in the splinter elm,
shrill the annual fledglings with their spikey necks.
They say to man that his road is mud,
his luck is rutted—there is nothing
sorrier than the marriage of two deaths.

Annensky.

September

The much-hugged rag-doll is oozing cotton from her ruined figure.
Unforgetting September cannot hide its peroxide curls of leaf.
Isn't it time to board up the summer house?
The carpenter's gavel pounds for new and naked roof-ribs.

The moment the sun rises, it disappears.
Last night the marsh by the swimming pool shivered with fever;
the last bell-flowers waste under the rheumatic dewdrop,
a dirty lilac stain souses the birches.

The woods are discomforted. The animals
head for the snow-stopped bear holes in the fairy tales;
behind the black park fences, tree trunks and pillars
form columns like a newspaper's death column.

The thinning birchwood has not ceased to water its color—
more and more watery, its once regal shade.
Summer keeps mumbling, "I am only a few months old.
A lifetime of looking back, what shall I do with it?

"I've so many mind-bruises, I should give up playing.
They are like birds in the bushes, mushrooms on the lawn.
Now we have begun to paper our horizon with them
to fog out each other's distance."

Stricken with polio, Summer, *le roi soleil*,
hears the gods' Homeric laughter from the dignitaries' box—
with the same agony, the country house
stares forward, hallucinated, at the road to the metropolis.

Pasternak.

For Anna Akhmatova

It seems I am choosing words that will stand,
and you are in them,
but if I blunder, it doesn't matter—
I must persist in my errors.

I hear the soiled, dripping small talk of the roofs;
the students' black boots drum eclogues on the boardwalks,
the undefined city takes on personality,
is alive in each sound.

Although it's spring, there's no leaving the city.
The sharp customers overlook nothing.
Day bends to its sewing until it weeps;
sunrise and sunset redden the same red eye.

You ache for the calm reaches of Ladoga,
then hurry off to the lake for a change
of fatigue. You gain nothing,
the shallows smell like closets full of last summer's clothes.

The dry wind dances like a dried-out walnut
across the waves, across your stung eyelids—
stars, branches, milestones, lamps. A white
seamstress on the bridge is always washing clothes.

I know that objects and eyesight vary greatly
in singleness and sharpness, but the iron
heart's vodka is the sky
under the northern lights.

That's how I see your face and expression.
This, not the pillar of salt, the "Lot's Wife" you pinned down
in rhyme five years ago to show up our fear,
limping forward in blinders, afraid of looking back.

How early your first dogged, unremitting idiom
took on life—no unassembled crumbs!
In all our affairs, your lines throb
with the high charge of the world. Each wire is a conductor.

                                                    Pasternak.

Mephistopheles

Every Sunday they left a circus of dust behind them,
as they poured out on the turnpike in stately, overcrowded carriages,
and the showers found nobody at home,
and trampled through the bedroom windows.

It was a custom at these staid Sunday dinners
to serve courses of rain instead of roastbeef;
on the baroque sideboard, by the Sunday silver,
the wind cut corners like a boy on a new bicycle.

Upstairs, the curtain rods whirled, untouched;
the curtains roared in salvos to the ceiling.
Outside the burghers kept losing themselves,
they showed up chewing straws by cowponds.

Earlier, when a long cortege of carriages
approached the city wall,
the horses would shy
from the shadows of the Weimar gallows.

The devil in blood-red stockings with rose rosettes
danced along the sunset-watered road—
he was as red
as a boiling lobster.

One snort of indignation
would have ripped the lid of heaven
from the skyline's low vegetation;
the devil's ribbons fluttered and danced.

The carriages swam through his eyes like road signs;
he scarcely lifted a finger in greeting.
He rolled on his heels, he trembled with laughter,
he sidled off hugging Faust, his pupil.

Pasternak.

The Seasons

I.

Now the small buds are pronged
to the boughs like candle-butts.
Steaming April! The adolescent park
simmers.

Like a lassoed buffalo, the forest
is noosed in the ropes of shrill feathered throats—
a wrestler, all gratuitous muscle,
caught in the pipes of the grand organ.

The shadows of the young leaves are gummy.
A wet bench streams in the garden.
Poetry is like a pump
with a suction-pad that drinks and drains up

the clouds. They ruffle in hoop-skirts,
talk to the valleys—
all night I squeeze out verses,
my page is hollow and white with thirst.

II.

The garden's frightful—all drip and listening.
The rain is loneliness.
A branch splashes white lace on the window.
Is there a witness?

The earth is swollen and smelly,
the pasture is a sponge;
as if it were August, the far off night ripens
and rots in the elm-dissected field.

No sound. No trespasser watches the night.
The rain is alone in the garden—
it starts up again, it drips
off roof and gutter.

I will drink the rain,
I, loneliness . . .
the rain weeps in the darkness.
Is there a witness?

But silence! Not even a wrinkling leaf.
No sign in the darkness,
only a swallowing of sobs and the swish of slippers . . .
in the interval, earth choking its tears . . .

III.
Summer says goodbye to the station.
Running in its photographer's black hood,
and blinding us with flash-bulbs, the thunder
takes a hundred souvenir snap-shots.

The lilac bush is a black scarecrow.
From hill and sky armfuls of lightning
crash on the station-agent's cottage
to smash it with light.

Waves of malevolence
lift the coal-dust from the roof;
the rain, coming down in buckets,
is like charcoal that smudges a drawing.

Something in my mind's
most inaccessible corners
registers the thunder's illumination,
stands up, and steadily blinks.

IV.
A driving rain whips the air.
The ice is scabby gray. You wait
for the sky to wake up.
Snow drones on the wind.

With unbuckled galoshes, with a muffler
flapping from his unbuttoned coat,
March bulls ahead, and makes rushes
at the frivolous, frenzied birds.

The season cannot miss you. It tries
to scrape up the candle-drippings in a snotty handkerchief—
it is safe now
to snatch off the night-caps of the tulips . . .

He is out of his senses, he musses his mop of hair.
He is buried in his mind's mush,
and stammers scurrilities
against me—my resurrection in the spring.

V.
Pinecones pop in the military gloom of our bedroom.
A gray smog boils in the overtime lightbulb.
The blue window simmers
over the snow-desert.
Our lips puff and stick.

Spring! I leave the street of astonished pines,
alarmed distances,
the awkward classical wooden house, apprehending its downfall—
the air blue as piles of faded sky-blue denim
lugged by the prisoners from their wards!

The age is breaking—pagan Rome,
thumbs down on clowns,
the wrestler's vain swansong to the grandstand—
on the true!
The overpaid gladiator must die in earnest.

Pasternak.

Sparrow Hills

Like water pouring from a pitcher, my mouth on your nipples!
Not always. The summer well runs dry.
Not for long the dust of our stamping feet, encore on encore
from the saxes on the casino's midnight bandstand.

I've heard of age—its obese warbling!
When no wave will clap hands to the stars.
If they speak, you doubt it. No face in the meadows,
no heart in the pools, no god among the pines.

Split your soul like wood. Let today froth to your mouth.
It's the world's noontide. Have you no eyes for it?
Look, conception bubbles from the bleached fallows;
fir cones, woodpeckers, clouds, pine needles, heat.

Here the city's trolley tracks give out.
Further, you must put up with peeled pine. The trolley poles are detached.
Further, it's Sunday. Boughs screwed loose for the picnic bonfire,
playing tag in your bra.

"The world is always like this," say the woods,
as they mix the midday glare. Whitsunday and walking.
All's planned with checkerberry couches, inspired with clearings—
the piebald clouds spill down on us, a country woman's house-dress.

Pasternak.

Wild Vines

Beneath a willow entwined with ivy,
we look for shelter from the bad weather;
one raincoat covers both our shoulders—
my fingers rustle like the wild vine around your breasts.

I am wrong. The rain's stopped.
Not ivy, but the hair of Dionysus
hangs from these willows. What am I to do?
Throw the raincoat under us!

                                        Pasternak.

In the Woods

A lilac heat sickened the meadow;
high in the wood, a cathedral's sharp, nicked groins.
No skeleton obstructed the bodies—
all was ours, obsequious wax in our fingers . . .

Such, the dream: you do not sleep,
you only dream you thirst for sleep,
that someone elsewhere thirsts for sleep—
two black suns singe his eyelashes.

Sunbeams shower and ebb to the flow of iridescent beetles.
The dragonfly's mica whirs on your cheek.
The wood fills with meticulous scintillations—
a dial under the clockmaker's tweezers.

It seemed we slept to the tick of figures;
in the acid, amber ether,
they set up nicely tested clocks,
shifted, regulated them to a soprano hair for the heat.

They shifted them here and there, and snipped at the wheels.
Day declined on the blue clock-face;
they scattered shadows, drilled a void—
the darkness was a mast derricked upright.

It seems a green and brown happiness flits beyond us;
sleep smothers the woods;
no elegiacs on the clock's ticking—
sleep, it seems, is all this couple is up to.

Pasternak.

The Landlord
(The Wedding)

Having crossed the curb in the courtyard,
the Landlord journeyed to the feast,
into the Bride's house—

with him departed the accordion player,
behind the bolted door of the Bride,
between one and seven.

The snatches of talk had quieted down,
but the sun rose blood red in the middle of the bed—
he wanted to sleep and sleep and sleep.

The accordion began to weep,
the accordion-player lay spread out on his instrument—
hearing the palms clapping, the shuffle of the shining serfs.

The feast's whole flourish jingled like silver in his hand,
again again again again,
the song of the broken accordion.

Rustling through the bed and the sleeper,
the noise, whistling and the cheering,
swam a white peahen.

She moved her hips,
and strutted out in the street,
this beautiful bird . . .

She shook her hair, she ruffled her breast feathers;
suddenly the noise of the game
is the stamping of a whole procession.

She dropped into the hole of the sun.

The sleepy courtyard grows businesslike,
horses stand up by the wooden well,
teamsters shout down the laughter of the feast.

A band of pigeons
blasts from the sky's blue bowl,
as if it were following the wedding party,

as if life were only an instant, of course,
the dissolution of ourselves into others,
like a wedding party approaching the window.

Pasternak.

Hamlet in Russia, A Soliloquy

"My heart throbbed like a boat on the water.
My oars rested. The willows swayed through the summer,
licking my shoulders, elbows and rowlocks—
wait! this might happen,

when the music brought me the beat,
and the ash-gray waterlilies dragged, and a couple of daisies blew,
and a hint of blue dotted a point offshore—
lips to lips, stars to stars!

My sister, life!
the world has too many people for us,
the sycophant, the spineless—
silently, like snakes in the grass, they sting.

My sister!
embrace the sky and Hercules
who holds the world up forever
at ease, perhaps, and sleeps at night

thrilled by the nightingales crying . . .

The boat stops throbbing on the water . . .

The clapping stops. I walk into the lights
as Hamlet, lounge like a student against the door frame,
and try to catch the far-off dissonance of life—
all that has happened, and must!

From the dark the audience leans its one hammering brow against me—
ten thousand opera glasses, each set on the tripod!
Abba, Father, all things are possible with thee—
take away this cup!

I love the mulishness of Providence,
I am content to play the one part I was born for . . .
quite another play is running now . . .
take me off the boards tonight!

The sequence of scenes was well thought out;
the last bow is in the cards, or the stars—
but I am alone, and there is none . . .
All's drowned in the sperm and spittle of the Pharisee—

To live a life is not to cross a field."

Pasternak.

Pigeons

(FOR HANNAH ARENDT)

The same old flights, the same old homecomings,
dozens of each per day,
but at last the pigeon gets clear of the pigeon-house . . .
What is home, but a feeling of homesickness
for the flight's lost moment of fluttering terror?

Back in the dovecote, there's another bird,
by all odds the most beautiful,
one that never flew out, and can know nothing of gentleness . . .
Still, only by suffering the rat-race in the arena
can the heart learn to beat.

Think of Leonidas perhaps and the hoplites,
glittering with liberation,
as they combed one another's golden Botticellian hair
at Thermopylae, friends and lovers, the bride and the bridegroom—
and moved into position to die.

Over non-existence arches the all-being—
thence the ball thrown almost out of bounds
stings the hand with the momentum of its drop—
body and gravity,
miraculously multiplied by its mania to return.

Rilke: *Die Tauben.*

For the Union Dead

(1964)

FOR MY FRIEND, WILLIAM ALFRED

NOTE

I want to make a few admissions and disclosures. My poems on Hawthorne and Edwards draw heavily on prose sentences by their subjects. "The Scream" owes everything to Elizabeth Bishop's beautiful, calm story, *In the Village*. "The Lesson" picks up a phrase or two from Rafael Alberti. "Returning" was suggested by Giuseppi Ungaretti's "Canzone." "The Public Garden" is a recasting and clarification of an old confusing poem of mine called "David and Bathsheba in the Public Garden." "Beyond the Alps" is the poem I published in *Life Studies*, but with a stanza restored at the suggestion of John Berryman. "Florence" steals a sentence from Mary McCarthy's book on Florence.

R.L.

Water

It was a Maine lobster town—
each morning boatloads of hands
pushed off for granite
quarries on the islands,

and left dozens of bleak
white frame houses stuck
like oyster shells
on a hill of rock,

and below us, the sea lapped
the raw little match-stick
mazes of a weir,
where the fish for bait were trapped.

Remember? We sat on a slab of rock.
From this distance in time,
it seems the color
of iris, rotting and turning purpler,

but it was only
the usual gray rock
turning the usual green
when drenched by the sea.

The sea drenched the rock
at our feet all day,
and kept tearing away
flake after flake.

One night you dreamed
you were a mermaid clinging to a wharf-pile,
and trying to pull
off the barnacles with your hands.

We wished our two souls
might return like gulls
to the rock. In the end,
the water was too cold for us.

The Old Flame

My old flame, my wife!
Remember our lists of birds?
One morning last summer, I drove
by our house in Maine. It was still
on top of its hill—

Now a red ear of Indian maize
was splashed on the door.
Old Glory with thirteen stars
hung on a pole. The clapboard
was old-red schoolhouse red.

Inside, a new landlord,
a new wife, a new broom!
Atlantic seaboard antique shop
pewter and plunder
shone in each room.

A new frontier!
No running next door
now to phone the sheriff
for his taxi to Bath
and the State Liquor Store!

No one saw your ghostly
imaginary lover
stare through the window,
and tighten
the scarf at his throat.

Health to the new people,
health to their flag, to their old
restored house on the hill!

Everything had been swept bare,
furnished, garnished and aired.

Everything's changed for the best—
how quivering and fierce we were,
there snowbound together,
simmering like wasps
in our tent of books!

Poor ghost, old love, speak
with your old voice
of flaming insight
that kept us awake all night.
In one bed and apart,

we heard the plow
groaning up hill—
a red light, then a blue,
as it tossed off the snow
to the side of the road.

Middle Age

Now the midwinter grind
is on me, New York
drills through my nerves,
as I walk
the chewed-up streets.

At forty-five,
what next, what next?
At every corner,
I meet my Father,
my age, still alive.

Father, forgive me
my injuries,
as I forgive
those I
have injured!

You never climbed
Mount Sion, yet left
dinosaur
death-steps on the crust,
where I must walk.

The Scream
(derived from Elizabeth Bishop's story *In the Village*)

A scream, the echo of a scream,
now only a thinning echo . . .
As a child in Nova Scotia,
I used to watch the sky,
Swiss sky, too blue, too dark.

A cow drooled green grass strings,
made cow flop, *smack, smack, smack*!
and tried to brush off its flies
on a lilac bush—all,
forever, at one fell swoop!

In the blacksmith's shop,
the horseshoes sailed through the dark,
like bloody little moons,
red-hot, hissing, protesting,
as they drowned in the pan.

Back and away and back!
Mother kept coming and going—
with me, without me!
Mother's dresses were black
or white, or black-and-white.

One day she changed to purple,
and left her mourning. At the fitting,
the dressmaker crawled on the floor,
eating pins, like Nebuchadnezzar
on his knees eating grass.

Drummers sometimes came
selling gilded red
and green books, unlovely books!

The people in the pictures
wore clothes like the purple dress.

Later, she gave the scream,
not even loud at first . . .
When she went away I thought
"But you can't love everyone,
your heart won't let you!"

A scream! But they are all gone,
those aunts and aunts, a grandfather,
a grandmother, my mother—
even her scream—too frail
for us to hear their voices long.

The Mouth of the Hudson

(FOR ESTHER BROOKS)

A single man stands like a bird-watcher,
and scuffles the pepper and salt snow
from a discarded, gray
Westinghouse Electric cable drum.
He cannot discover America by counting
the chains of condemned freight-trains
from thirty states. They jolt and jar
and junk in the siding below him.
He has trouble with his balance.
His eyes drop,
and he drifts with the wild ice
ticking seaward down the Hudson,
like the blank sides of a jig-saw puzzle.

The ice ticks seaward like a clock.
A Negro toasts
wheat-seeds over the coke-fumes
of a punctured barrel.
Chemical air
sweeps in from New Jersey,
and smells of coffee.

Across the river,
ledges of suburban factories tan
in the sulphur-yellow sun
of the unforgivable landscape.

Fall 1961

Back and forth, back and forth
goes the tock, tock, tock
of the orange, bland, ambassadorial
face of the moon
on the grandfather clock.

All autumn, the chafe and jar
of nuclear war;
we have talked our extinction to death.
I swim like a minnow
behind my studio window.

Our end drifts nearer,
the moon lifts,
radiant with terror.
The state
is a diver under a glass bell.

A father's no shield
for his child.
We are like a lot of wild
spiders crying together,
but without tears.

Nature holds up a mirror.
One swallow makes a summer.
It's easy to tick
off the minutes,
but the clockhands stick.

Back and forth!
Back and forth, back and forth—
my one point of rest
is the orange and black
oriole's swinging nest!

Florence

(FOR MARY MCCARTHY)

I long for the black ink,
cuttlefish, April, Communists
and brothels of Florence—
everything, even the British
fairies who haunted the hills,
even the chills and fever
that came once a month
and forced me to think.
The apple was more human there than here,
but it took a long time for the blinding
golden rind to mellow.

How vulnerable the horseshoe crabs
dredging the bottom like flat-irons
in their antique armor,
with their swordgrass blackbone tails,
made for a child to grab
and throw strangling ashore!

Oh Florence, Florence, patroness
of the lovely tyrannicides!
Where the tower of the Old Palace
pierces the sky
like a hypodermic needle,
Perseus, David and Judith,
lords and ladies of the Blood,
Greek demi-gods of the Cross,
rise sword in hand
above the unshaven,
formless decapitation
of the monsters, tubs of guts,
mortifying chunks for the pack.
Pity the monsters!
Pity the monsters!

Perhaps, one always took the wrong side—
Ah, to have known, to have loved
too many Davids and Judiths!
My heart bleeds black blood for the monster.
I have seen the Gorgon.
The erotic terror
of her helpless, big bosomed body
lay like slop.
Wall-eyed, staring the despot to stone,
her severed head swung
like a lantern in the victor's hand.

The Lesson

No longer to lie reading *Tess of the d'Urbervilles*,
while the high, mysterious squirrels
rain small green branches on our sleep!

All that landscape, one likes to think it died
or slept with us, that we ourselves died
or slept then in the age and second of our habitation.

The green leaf cushions the same dry footprint,
or the child's boat luffs in the same dry chop,
and we are where we were. We were!

Perhaps the trees stopped growing in summer amnesia;
their day that gave them veins is rooted down—
and the nights? They are for sleeping now as then.

Ah the light lights the window of my young night,
and you never turn off the light,
while the books lie in the library, and go on reading.

The barberry berry sticks on the small hedge,
cold slits the same crease in the finger,
the same thorn hurts. The leaf repeats the lesson.

Those Before Us

They are all outline, uniformly gray,
unregenerate arrowheads sloughed up by the path here,
or in the corners of the eye, they play
their thankless, fill-in roles. They never were.

Wormwood on the veranda! Plodding needles
still prod the coarse pink yarn into a dress.
The muskrat that took a slice of your thumb still huddles,
a mop of hair and a heart-beat on the porch—

there's the tin wastebasket where it learned to wait
for us playing dead, the slats it mashed in terror,
its spoor of cornflakes, and the packing crate
it furiously slashed to matchwood to escape.

Their chairs were *ex cathedra*, yet if you draw back the blinds,
(as full of windows as a fishnet now)
you will hear them conspiring, slapping hands
across the bent card-table, still leaf-green.

Vacations, stagnant growth. But in the silence,
some one lets out his belt to breathe, some one
roams in negligee. Bless the confidence
of their sitting unguarded there in stocking feet.

Sands drop from the hour-glass waist and swallow-tail.
We follow their gunshy shadows down the trail—
those before us! Pardon them for existing.
We have stopped watching them. They have stopped watching.

Eye and Tooth

My whole eye was sunset red,
the old cut cornea throbbed,
I saw things darkly,
as through an unwashed goldfish globe.

I lay all day on my bed.
I chain-smoked through the night,
learning to flinch
at the flash of the matchlight.

Outside, the summer rain,
a simmer of rot and renewal,
fell in pinpricks.
Even new life is fuel.

My eyes throb.
Nothing can dislodge
the house with my first tooth
noosed in a knot to the doorknob.

Nothing can dislodge
the triangular blotch
of rot on the red roof,
a cedar hedge, or the shade of a hedge.

No ease from the eye
of the sharp-shinned hawk in the birdbook there,
with reddish brown buffalo hair
on its shanks, one ascetic talon

clasping the abstract imperial sky.
It says:
an eye for an eye,
a tooth for a tooth.

No ease for the boy at the keyhole,
his telescope,
when the women's white bodies flashed
in the bathroom. Young, my eyes began to fail.

Nothing! No oil
for the eye, nothing to pour
on those waters or flames.
I am tired. Everyone's tired of my turmoil.

Alfred Corning Clark

(1916–1961)

You read the *New York Times*
every day at recess,
but in its dry
obituary, a list
of your wives, nothing is news,
except the ninety-five
thousand dollar engagement ring
you gave the sixth.
Poor rich boy,
you were unreasonably adult
at taking your time,
and died at forty-five.
Poor Al Clark,
behind your enlarged,
hardly recognizable photograph,
I feel the pain.
You were alive. You are dead.
You wore bow-ties and dark
blue coats, and sucked
wintergreen or cinnamon lifesavers
to sweeten your breath.
There must be something—
some one to praise
your triumphant diffidence,
your refusal of exertion,
the intelligence
that pulsed in the sensitive,
pale concavities of your forehead.
You never worked,
and were third in the form.
I owe you something—
I was befogged,
and you were too bored,
quick and cool to laugh.

You are dear to me, Alfred;
our reluctant souls united
in our unconventional
illegal games of chess
on the St. Mark's quadrangle.
You usually won—
motionless
as a lizard in the sun.

Child's Song

My cheap toy lamp
gives little light
all night, all night,
when my muscles cramp.

Sometimes I touch your hand
across my cot,
and our fingers knot,
but there's no hand

to take me home—
no Caribbean
island, where even
the shark is at home.

It must be heaven.
There on that island
the white sand shines
like a birchwood fire.

Help, saw me in two,
put me on the shelf!
Sometimes the little muddler
can't stand itself!

Epigram

(FOR HANNAH ARENDT)

Think of Leonidas perhaps and the hoplites
glittering with liberation,
as they combed one another's golden Botticellian
hair at Thermopylae—friends and lovers,
the bride and the bridegroom—
and moved into position to die.

Law

Under one law,
or two,
to lie unsleeping,
still sleeping on the battlefield . . .

On Sunday mornings,
I used to foray
bass-plugging out of season on
the posted reservoirs.

Outside the law.
At every bend I saw
only the looping shore
of nature's monotonous backlash.

The same. The same.
Then once, in a flash,
fresh ground, though trodden,
a man-made landscape.

A Norman canal
shot through razored green lawns;
black reflecting water arched
little sky-hung bridges of unhewn stone—

outside the law:
black, gray, green and blue,
water, stone, grass and sky,
and each unique set stone!

The Public Garden

Burnished, burned-out, still burning as the year
you lead me to our stamping ground.
The city and its cruising cars surround
the Public Garden. All's alive—
the children crowding home from school at five,
punting a football in the bricky air,
the sailors and their pick-ups under trees
with Latin labels. And the jaded flock
of swanboats paddles to its dock.
The park is drying.
Dead leaves thicken to a ball
inside the basin of a fountain, where
the heads of four stone lions stare
and suck on empty faucets. Night
deepens. From the arched bridge, we see
the shedding park-bound mallards, how they keep
circling and diving in the lanternlight,
searching for something hidden in the muck.
And now the moon, earth's friend, that cared so much
for us, and cared so little, comes again—
always a stranger! As we walk,
it lies like chalk
over the waters. Everything's aground.
Remember summer? Bubbles filled
the fountain, and we splashed. We drowned
in Eden, while Jehovah's grass-green lyre
was rustling all about us in the leaves
that gurgled by us, turning upside down . . .
The fountain's failing waters flash around
the garden. Nothing catches fire.

Lady Ralegh's Lament
(1618)

Sir Walter, oh, oh, my own Sir Walter—
the sour Tower and the Virgin Queen's garden close
are deflowered and gone now . . .
Horrible the connoisseur tyrant's querulous strut;
an acorn dances in a girdle of green oak leaves
up the steps to the scaffold to the block,
square bastard of an oak. Clearly, clearly,
the Atlantic whitens to merge Sir Walter's head,
still dangling in its scarlet, tangled twine,
as if beseeching voyage. Voyage?
Down and down; the compass needle dead on terror.

Going to and fro

It's authentic perhaps
to have been there, if now
you could loll on the ledge for a moment,
sunning like a couple,
and look down at the gaps—
if you could for a moment . . .

One step, two steps, three steps:
the hot-dog and coca-cola bar,
the Versailles steps,
the Puritan statue—
if you could get through the Central Park
by counting . . .

But the intestines shiver,
the ferry saloon thugs with your pain
across the river—pain,
suffering without purgation,
the back-track of the screw.
But you had instants,

to give the devil his due—
he and you
once dug it all out of the dark
unconscious bowels of the nerves:
pure gold, the root of evil,
sunshine that gave the day a scheme.

And now? Ah Lucifer!
how often you wanted your fling
with those French girls, Mediterranean
luminaries, Mary, Myrtho, Isis—
as far out as the sphinx!
The love that moves the stars

moved you!
It set you going to and fro
and up and down—
If you could get loose
from the earth by counting
your steps to the noose . . .

Myopia: a Night

Bed, glasses off, and all's
ramshackle, streaky, weird
for the near-sighted, just
a foot away.
                    The light's
still on an instant. Here
are the blurred titles, here
the books are blue hills, browns,
greens, fields, or color.
                              This
is the departure strip,
the dream-road. Whoever built it
left numbers, words and arrows.
He had to leave in a hurry.

I see
a dull and alien room,
my cell of learning,
white, brightened by white pipes,
ramrods of steam . . . I hear
the lonely metal breathe
and gurgle like the sick.
And yet my eyes avoid
that room. No need to see.
No need to know I hoped
its blank, foregoing whiteness
would burn away the blur,
as my five senses clenched
their teeth, thought stitched to thought,
as through a needle's eye . . .

I see the morning star . . .

Think of him in the Garden,
that seed of wisdom, Eve's
seducer, stuffed with man's
corruption, stuffed with triumph:
Satan triumphant in
the Garden! In a moment,
all that blinding brightness
changed into a serpent,
lay grovelling on its gut.

What has disturbed this household?
Only a foot away,
the familiar faces blur.
At fifty we're so fragile,
a feather . . .

The things of the eye are done.
On the illuminated black dial,
green ciphers of a new moon—
one, two, three, four, five, six!
I breathe and cannot sleep.
Then morning comes,
saying, "This was a night."

Returning

Homecoming to the sheltered little resort,
where the members of my gang
are bald-headed, in business,
and the dogs still know me by my smell . . .
It's rather a dead town
after my twenty years' mirage.

Long awash,
breaking myself against the surf,
touching bottom, rushed
by the green go-light
of those nervous waters, I found
my exhaustion, the light of the world.

Nothing is deader than this small town main street,
where the venerable elm sickens, and hardens
with tarred cement, where no leaf
is born, or falls, or resists till winter.

But I remember its former fertility,
how everything came out clearly
in the hour of credulity
and young summer, when this street
was already somewhat overshaded,
and here at the altar of surrender,
I met you,
the death of thirst in my brief flesh.

That was the first growth,
the heir of all my minutes,
the victim of every ramification—
more and more it grew green, and gave too much shelter.

And now at my homecoming,
the barked elms stand up like sticks along the street.
I am a foot taller than when I left,
and cannot see the dirt at my feet.

Yet sometimes I catch my vague mind
circling with a glazed eye
for a name without a face, or a face without a name,
and at every step,
I startle them. They start up,
dog-eared, bald as baby birds.

The Drinker

The man is killing time—there's nothing else.
No help now from the fifth of Bourbon
chucked helter-skelter into the river,
even its cork sucked under.

Stubbed before-breakfast cigarettes
burn bull's-eyes on the bedside table;
a plastic tumbler of alka seltzer
champagnes in the bathroom.

No help from his body, the whale's
warm-hearted blubber, foundering down
leagues of ocean, gasping whiteness.
The barbed hooks fester. The lines snap tight.

When he looks for neighbors, their names blur in the window,
his distracted eye sees only glass sky.
His despair has the galvanized color
of the mop and water in the galvanized bucket.

Once she was close to him
as water to the dead metal.

He looks at her engagements inked on her calendar.
A list of indictments.
At the numbers in her thumbed black telephone book.
A quiver full of arrows.

Her absence hisses like steam,
the pipes sing . . .
even corroded metal somehow functions.
He snores in his iron lung,

and hears the voice of Eve,
beseeching freedom from the Garden's
perfect and ponderous bubble. No voice
outsings the serpent's flawed, euphoric hiss.

The cheese wilts in the rat-trap,
the milk turns to junket in the cornflakes bowl,
car keys and razor blades
shine in an ashtray.

Is he killing time? Out on the street,
two cops on horseback clop through the April rain
to check the parking meter violations—
their oilskins yellow as forsythia.

Hawthorne

Follow its lazy main street lounging
from the alms house to Gallows Hill
along a flat, unvaried surface
covered with wooden houses
aged by yellow drain
like the unhealthy hair of an old dog.
You'll walk to no purpose
in Hawthorne's Salem.

I cannot resilver the smudged plate.

I drop to Hawthorne, the customs officer,
measuring coal and mostly trying to keep warm—
to the stunted black schooner,
the dismal South-end dock,
the wharf-piles with their fungus of ice.
On State Street
a steeple with a glowing dial-clock
measures the weary hours,
the merciless march of professional feet.

Even this shy distrustful ego
sometimes walked on top of the blazing roof,
and felt those flashes
that char the discharged cells of the brain.

Look at the faces—
Longfellow, Lowell, Holmes and Whittier!
Study the grizzled silver of their beards.
Hawthorne's picture,
however, has a blond mustache
and golden General Custer scalp.
He looks like a Civil War officer.

He shines in the firelight. His hard
survivor's smile is touched with fire.

Leave him alone for a moment or two,
and you'll see him with his head
bent down, brooding, brooding,
eyes fixed on some chip,
some stone, some common plant,
the commonest thing,
as if it were the clue.
The disturbed eyes rise,
furtive, foiled, dissatisfied
from meditation on the true
and insignificant.

Jonathan Edwards in Western Massachusetts

Edward's great millstone and rock
of hope has crumbled, but the square
white houses of his flock
stand in the open air,

out in the cold,
like sheep outside the fold.
Hope lives in doubt.
Faith is trying to do without

faith. In western Massachusetts,
I could almost feel the frontier
crack and disappear.
Edwards thought the world would end there.

We know how the world will end,
but where is paradise, each day farther
from the Pilgrim's blues for England
and the Promised Land.

Was it some country house
that seemed as if it were
Whitehall, if the Lord were there?
so nobly did he live.

Gardens designed
that the breath of flowers in the wind,
or crushed underfoot,
came and went like warbling music?

Bacon's great oak grove
he refused to sell,
when he fell,
saying, "Why should I sell my feathers?"

Ah paradise! Edwards,
I would be afraid
to meet you there as a shade.
We move in different circles.

As a boy, you built a booth
in a swamp for prayer;
lying on your back,
you saw the spiders fly,

basking at their ease,
swimming from tree to tree—
so high, they seemed tacked to the sky.
You knew they would die.

Poor country Berkeley at Yale,
you saw the world was soul,
the soul of God! The soul
of Sarah Pierrepont!

So filled with delight in the Great Being,
she hardly cared for anything—
walking the fields, sweetly singing,
conversing with some one invisible.

Then God's love shone in sun, moon and stars,
on earth, in the waters,
in the air, in the loose winds,
which used to greatly fix your mind.

Often she saw you come home from a ride
or a walk, your coat dotted with thoughts
you had pinned there
on slips of paper.

You gave
her Pompey, a Negro slave,
and eleven children.
Yet people were spiders

in your moment of glory,
at the Great Awakening—"Alas, how many
in this very meeting house are more than likely
to remember my discourse in hell!"

The meeting house remembered!
You stood on stilts in the air,
but you fell from your parish.
"All rising is by a winding stair."

On my pilgrimage to Northampton,
I found no relic,
except the round slice of an oak
you are said to have planted.

It was flesh-colored, new,
and a common piece of kindling,
only fit for burning.
You too must have been green once.

White wig and black coat,
all cut from one cloth,
and designed
like your mind!

I love you faded,
old, exiled and afraid
to leave your last flock, a dozen
Housatonic Indian children;

afraid to leave
all your writing, writing, writing,
denying the Freedom of the Will.
You were afraid to be president

of Princeton, and wrote:
"My deffects are well known;
I have a constitution
peculiarly unhappy:

flaccid solids,
vapid, sizzy, scarse fluids,
causing a childish weakness,
a low tide of spirits.

I am contemptible,
stiff and dull.

Why should I leave behind
my delight and entertainment,
those studies
that have swallowed up my mind?"

Tenth Muse

Tenth Muse, Oh my heart-felt Sloth,
how often now you come to my bed,
thin as a canvas in your white and red
check dresses like a table cloth,
my Dearest, settling like my shroud!

Yes, yes, I ought to remember Moses
jogging down on his mule from the Mount
with the old law, the old mistake,
safe in his saddlebags, and chiselled
on the stones we cannot bear or break.

Here waiting, here waiting for an answer
from this malignant surf of unopened letters,
always reaching land too late,
as fact and abstraction accumulate,
and the signature fades from the paper—

I like to imagine it must have been simpler
in the days of Lot,
or when Greek and Roman picturebook
gods sat combing their golden beards,
each on his private hill or mountain.

But I suppose even God was born
too late to trust the old religion—
all those settings out
that never left the ground,
beginning in wisdom, dying in doubt.

The Neo-Classical Urn

I rub my head and find a turtle shell
stuck on a pole,
each hair electrical
with charges, and the juice alive
with ferment. Bubbles drive
the motor, always purposeful . . .
Poor head!
How its skinny shell once hummed,
as I sprinted down the colonnade
of bleaching pines, cylindrical
clipped trunks without a twig between them. Rest!
I could not rest. At full run on the curve,
I left the cast stone statue of a nymph,
her soaring armpits and her one bare breast,
gray from the rain and graying in the shade,
as on, on, in sun, the pathway now a dyke,
I swerved between two water bogs,
two seines of moss, and stooped to snatch
the painted turtles on dead logs.
In that season of joy,
my turtle catch
was thirty-three,
dropped splashing in our garden urn,
like money in the bank,
the plop and splash
of turtle on turtle,
fed raw gobs of hash . . .

Oh neo-classical white urn, Oh nymph,
Oh lute! The boy was pitiless who strummed
their elegy,
for as the month wore on,
the turtles rose,
and popped up dead on the stale scummed

surface—limp wrinkled heads and legs withdrawn
in pain. What pain? A turtle's nothing. No
grace, no cerebration, less free will
than the mosquito I must kill—
nothings! Turtles! I rub my skull,
that turtle shell,
and breathe their dying smell,
still watch their crippled last survivors pass,
and hobble humpbacked through the grizzled grass.

Caligula

My namesake, Little Boots, Caligula,
you disappoint me. Tell me what I saw
to make me like you when we met at school?
I took your name—poor odd-ball, poor spoiled fool,
my prince, young innocent and bowdlerized!
Your true face sneers at me, mean, thin, agonized,
the rusty Roman medal where I see
my lowest depths of possibility.

What can be salvaged from your life? A pain
that gently darkens over heart and brain,
a fairy's touch, a cobweb's weight of pain,
now makes me tremble at your right to live.
I live your last night. Sleepless fugitive,
your purple bedclothes and imperial eagle
grow so familiar they are home. Your regal
hand accepts my hand. You bend my wrist,
and tear the tendons with your strangler's twist . . .
You stare down hallways, mile on stoney mile,
where statues of the gods return your smile.
Why did you smash their heads and give them yours?
You hear your household panting on all fours,
and itemize your features—sleep's old aide!
Item: your body hairy, badly made,
head hairless, smoother than your marble head;
Item: eyes hollow, hollow temples, red
cheeks rough with rouge, legs spindly, hands that leave
a clammy snail's trail on your soggy sleeve . . .
a hand no hand will hold . . . nose thin, thin neck—
you wish the Romans had a single neck!

Small thing, where are you? Child, you sucked your thumb,
and could not sleep unless you hugged the numb
and wooly-witted toys of your small zoo.

There was some reason then to fondle you
before you found the death-mask for your play.
Lie very still, sleep with clasped hands, and pray
for nothing, Child! Think, even at the end,
good dreams were faithful. You betray no friend
now that no animal will share your bed.
Don't think! . . . And yet the God Adonis bled
and lay beside you, forcing you to strip.
You felt his gored thigh spurting on your hip.
Your mind burned, you were God, a thousand plans
ran zig-zag, zig-zag. You began to dance
for joy, and called your menials to arrange
deaths for the gods. You worshipped your great change,
took a cold bath, and rolled your genitals
until they shrank to marbles . . .

                         Animals
fattened for your arena suffered less
than you in dying—yours the lawlessness
of something simple that has lost its law,
my namesake, and the last Caligula.

The Severed Head

Shoes off and necktie, hunting the desired
butterfly here and there without success,
I let nostalgia drown me. I was tired
of pencilling the darker passages,
and let my ponderous Bible strike the floor.
My house was changing to a lost address,
the nameplate fell like a horse-shoe from the door,
where someone, hitting nails into a board,
had set his scaffolding. I heard him pour
mortar to seal the outlets, as I snored,
watching the knobbed, brown, wooden chandelier
slicing the silence on a single cord.
In the low sun, about to disappear,
each branch was like a stocking-stretcher, cut
into a gryphon clawing upward. Here
and there, dull gilding pocked a talon. What
I imagined was a spider crab, my small
chance of surviving in this room. Its shut
windows had sunken into solid wall.
I nursed my last clear breath of oxygen,
there, waiting for the chandelier to fall,
tentacles clawing for my jugular. Then
a man came toward me with a manuscript,
scratching in last revisions with a pen
that left no markings on the page, yet dripped
a red ink dribble on us, as he pressed
the little strip of plastic tubing clipped
to feed it from his heart. His hand caressed
my hand a moment, settled like a toad,
lay clammy, comfortable, helpless, and at rest,
although his veins seemed pulsing to explode.
His suit was brushed and pressed too savagely;
one sleeve was shorter than his shirt, and showed
a glassy cuff-link with a butterfly

inside. Nothing about him seemed to match,
and yet I saw the bouillon of his eye
was the same color as his frayed mustache,
too brown, too bushy, lifted from an age
when people wore mustaches. On each lash,
a tear had snowballed. Then he shook his page,
tore it to pieces, and began to twist
and trample on the mangle in his rage.

"Sometimes I ask myself, if I exist,"
he grumbled, and I saw a sheet of glass
had fallen inches from us, and just missed
halving our bodies, and behind it grass-
green water flushed the glass, and fast fish stirred
and panted, ocean butterflies. A mass
of shadows followed them like moths, and blurred
tentacles, thirsting for a drop of life,
panted with calm inertia. Then I heard
my friend unclasp a rusty pocket-knife.
He cut out squares of paper, made a stack,
and formed the figure of his former wife:
Square head, square feet, square hands, square breasts, square back.

He left me. While the light began to fail,
I read my Bible till the page turned black.
The pitying, brute, doughlike face of Jael
watched me with sad inertia, as I read—
Jael hammering and hammering her nail
through Sisera's idolatrous, nailed head.

Her folded dress lay underneath my head.

Beyond the Alps

"Au-delà des Alpes est l'Italie," Napoleon 1797

(ON THE TRAIN FROM ROME TO PARIS, 1950, THE YEAR
PIUS XII DEFINED THE DOGMA OF MARY'S BODILY ASSUMPTION)

Reading how even the Swiss had thrown the sponge
in once again, and Everest was still
unscaled, I watched our Paris pullman lunge,
mooning across the fallow Alpine snow—
O bella Roma! I saw our stewards go
forward on tiptoe banging on their gongs.
Man changed to landscape. Much against my will,
I left the City of God where it belongs.
There the skirt-mad Mussolini unfurled
the eagle of Caesar. He was one of us
only, pure prose. I envy the conspicuous
waste of our grandparents on their grand tours—
long-haired Victorian sages accepted the universe,
while breezing on their trust funds through the world.

When the Vatican made Mary's Assumption dogma,
the crowds at San Pietro screamed *Papa!*
The Holy Father dropped his shaving glass,
and listened. His electric razor purred,
his pet canary chirped on his right hand.
The lights of science couldn't hold a candle
to Mary risen, gorgeous as a jungle bird!
But who believed this? Who could understand?
Pilgrims still kissed Saint Peter's brazen sandal.
The Duce's lynched, bare, booted skull still spoke.
God herded his people to the *coup de grâce*—
the costumed Switzers sloped their pikes to push.
Oh Pius, through the monstrous human crush . . .

I thought of Ovid. For in Caesar's eyes
that tomcat had the Number of the Beast,
and now where Turkey faces the red east,
and the twice-stormed Crimean spit, he cries:
"Rome asked for poets. At her beck and call,
came Lucan, Tacitus and Juvenal,
the *black republicans* who tore the tits
and bowels of the Mother Wolf to bits—
Then psychopath and soldier waved the rod
of empire over Caesar's salvaged bog . . .
Imperial Tiber, Oh my yellow dog,
black earth by the black Roman sea, I lie
with the boy-crazy daughter of the God,
il Duce Augusto. I shall never die."

Our mountain-climbing train had come to earth.
Tired of the querulous hush-hush of the wheels,
the blear-eyed ego kicking in my berth
lay still, and saw Apollo plant his heels
on terra firma through the morning's thigh—
each backward wasted Alp, a Parthenon,
fire-branded socket of the cyclops' eye . . .
There are no tickets to that altitude,
once held by Hellas when the Goddess stood,
prince, pope, philosopher and golden bough,
pure mind and murder at the scything prow—
Minerva the mis-carriage of the brain . . .

Now Paris, our black classic, breaking up
like killer kings on an Etruscan cup.

July in Washington

The stiff spokes of this wheel
touch the sore spots of the earth.

On the Potomac, swan-white
power launches keep breasting the sulphurous wave.

Otters slide and dive and slick back their hair,
raccoons clean their meat in the creek.

On the circles, green statues ride like South American
liberators above the breeding vegetation—

prongs and spearheads of some equatorial
backland that will inherit the globe.

The elect, the elected . . . they come here bright as dimes,
and die dishevelled and soft.

We cannot name their names, or number their dates—
circle on circle, like rings on a tree—

but we wish the river had another shore,
some further range of delectable mountains,

distant hills powdered blue as a girl's eyelid.
It seems the least little shove would land us there,

that only the slightest repugnance of our bodies
we no longer control could drag us back.

Buenos Aires

In my room at the Hotel Continentál
a thousand miles from nowhere,
I heard
the bulky, beefy breathing of the herds.

Cattle furnished my new clothes:
my coat of limp, chestnut-colored suede,
my sharp shoes
that hurt my toes.

A false fin de siècle decorum
snored over Buenos Aires
lost in the pampas
and run by the barracks.

All day I read about newspaper coups d'état
of the leaden, internecine generals—
lumps of dough on the chessboard—and never saw
their countermarching tanks.

Along the sunlit cypress walks
of the Republican martyrs' graveyard,
hundreds of one-room Roman temples
hugged their neo-classical catafalques.

Literal commemorative busts
preserved the frogged coats
and fussy, furrowed foreheads
of those soldier bureaucrats.

By their brazen doors
a hundred marble goddesses
wept like willows. I found rest
by cupping a soft palm to each hard breast.

I was the worse for wear,
and my breath whitened the winter air
next morning, when Buenos Aires filled
with frowning, starch-collared crowds.

Dropping South: Brazil

Walking and walking in a mothy robe,
one finger pushing through the pocket-hole,
I crossed the reading room and met my soul,
hunched, spinning downward on the colored globe.
The ocean was the old Atlantic still,
always the swell greened in, rushed white, and fell,
now warmer than the air. However, there
red flags forbade our swimming. No one swam.
A lawless gentleness. The Latin blonde,
two strips of ribbon, ripened in the sun,
sleeping alone and pillowed on one arm.
No competition. Only rings of boys
butted a ball to keep it in the air,
while inland, people starved, and struck, and died—
unhappy Americas, ah *tristes tropiques!*
and nightly in the gouges by the tide,
macumba candles courted *Yemanjá,*
tall, white, the fish-tailed Virgin of the sea,
corpselike with calla lilies, walking
the water in her white night gown. "I am falling.
Santa Maria, pray for me, I want to stop,
but I have lost my foothold on the map,
now falling, falling, bent, intense, my feet
breaking my clap of thunder on the street."

Soft Wood

(FOR HARRIET WINSLOW)

Sometimes I have supposed seals
must live as long as the Scholar Gypsy.
Even in their barred pond at the zoo they are happy,
and no sunflower turns
more delicately to the sun
without a wincing of the will.

Here too in Maine things bend to the wind forever.
After two years away, one must get used
to the painted soft wood staying bright and clean,
to the air blasting an all-white wall whiter,
as it blows through curtain and screen
touched with salt and evergreen.

The green juniper berry spills crystal-clear gin,
and even the hot water in the bathtub
is more than water,
and rich with the scouring effervescence
of something healing,
the illimitable salt.

Things last, but sometimes for days here
only children seem fit to handle children,
and there is no utility or inspiration
in the wind smashing without direction.
The fresh paint
on the captains' houses hides softer wood.

Their square-riggers used to whiten
the four corners of the globe,
but it's no consolation to know
the possessors seldom outlast the possessions,
once warped and mothered by their touch.
Shed skin will never fit another wearer.

Yet the seal pack will bark past my window
summer after summer.
This is the season
when our friends may and will die daily.
Surely the lives of the old
are briefer than the young.

Harriet Winslow, who owned this house,
was more to me than my mother.
I think of you far off in Washington,
breathing in the heat wave
and air-conditioning, knowing
each drug that numbs alerts another nerve to pain.

New York 1962: Fragment

(FOR E.H.L.)

This might be nature—twenty stories high,
two water tanks, tanned shingle, corseted
by stapled pasture wire, while bed to bed,
we two, one cell here, lie
gazing into the ether's crystal ball,
sky and a sky, and sky, and sky, till death—
my heart stops . . .
This might be heaven. Years ago,
we aimed for less and settled for
a picture, out of style then and now in,
of seven daffodils. We watched them blow:
buttercup yellow were the flowers, and green
the stems as fresh paint, over them the wind,
the blousy wooden branches of the elms,
high summer in the breath that overwhelms
the termites digging in the underpinning . . .
Still over us, still in parenthesis,
this sack of hornets sopping up the flame,
still over us our breath,
sawing and pumping to the terminal,
and down below, we two, two in one waterdrop
vitalized by a needle drop of blood,
up, up, up, up and up,
soon shot, soon slugged into the overflow
that sets the wooden workhorse working here below.

The Flaw

A seal swims like a poodle through the sheet
of blinding salt. A country graveyard, here
and there a rock, and here and there a pine,
throbs on the essence of the gasoline.
Some mote, some eye-flaw, wobbles in the heat,
hair-thin, hair-dark, the fragment of a hair—

a noose, a question? All is possible;
if there's free will, it's something like this hair,
inside my eye, outside my eye, yet free,
airless as grace, if the good God . . . I see.
Our bodies quiver. In this rustling air,
all's possible, all's unpredictable.

Old wives and husbands! Look, their gravestones wait
in couples with the names and half the date—
one future and one freedom. In a flash,
I see us whiten into skeletons,
our eager, sharpened cries, a pair of stones,
cutting like shark-fins through the boundless wash.

Two walking cobwebs, almost bodiless,
crossed paths here once, kept house, and lay in beds.
Your fingertips once touched my fingertips
and set us tingling through a thousand threads.
Poor pulsing *Fête Champêtre*! The summer slips
between our fingers into nothingness.

We too lean forward, as the heat waves roll
over our bodies, grown insensible,
ready to dwindle off into the soul,

two motes or eye-flaws, the invisible . . .
Hope of the hopeless launched and cast adrift
on the great flaw that gives the final gift.

Dear Figure curving like a questionmark,
how will you hear my answer in the dark?

Night Sweat

Work-table, litter, books and standing lamp,
plain things, my stalled equipment, the old broom—
but I am living in a tidied room,
for ten nights now I've felt the creeping damp
float over my pajamas' wilted white . . .
Sweet salt embalms me and my head is wet,
everything streams and tells me this is right;
my life's fever is soaking in night sweat—
one life, one writing! But the downward glide
and bias of existing wrings us dry—
always inside me is the child who died,
always inside me is his will to die—
one universe, one body . . . in this urn
the animal night sweats of the spirit burn.

Behind me! You! Again I feel the light
lighten my leaded eyelids, while the gray
skulled horses whinny for the soot of night.
I dabble in the dapple of the day,
a heap of wet clothes, seamy, shivering,
I see my flesh and bedding washed with light,
my child exploding into dynamite,
my wife . . . your lightness alters everything,
and tears the black web from the spider's sack,
as your heart hops and flutters like a hare.
Poor turtle, tortoise, if I cannot clear
the surface of these troubled waters here,
absolve me, help me, Dear Heart, as you bear
this world's dead weight and cycle on your back.

For the Union Dead

"Relinquunt Omnia Servare Rem Publicam."

The old South Boston Aquarium stands
in a Sahara of snow now. Its broken windows are boarded.
The bronze weathervane cod has lost half its scales.
The airy tanks are dry.

Once my nose crawled like a snail on the glass;
my hand tingled
to burst the bubbles
drifting from the noses of the cowed, compliant fish.

My hand draws back. I often sigh still
for the dark downward and vegetating kingdom
of the fish and reptile. One morning last March,
I pressed against the new barbed and galvanized

fence on the Boston Common. Behind their cage,
yellow dinosaur steamshovels were grunting
as they cropped up tons of mush and grass
to gouge their underworld garage.

Parking spaces luxuriate like civic
sandpiles in the heart of Boston.
A girdle of orange, Puritan-pumpkin colored girders
braces the tingling Statehouse,

shaking over the excavations, as it faces Colonel Shaw
and his bell-cheeked Negro infantry
on St. Gaudens' shaking Civil War relief,
propped by a plank splint against the garage's earthquake.

Two months after marching through Boston,
half the regiment was dead;
at the dedication,
William James could almost hear the bronze Negroes breathe.

Their monument sticks like a fishbone
in the city's throat.
Its Colonel is as lean
as a compass-needle.

He has an angry wrenlike vigilance,
a greyhound's gentle tautness;
he seems to wince at pleasure,
and suffocate for privacy.

He is out of bounds now. He rejoices in man's lovely,
peculiar power to choose life and die—
when he leads his black soldiers to death,
he cannot bend his back.

On a thousand small town New England greens,
the old white churches hold their air
of sparse, sincere rebellion; frayed flags
quilt the graveyards of the Grand Army of the Republic.

The stone statues of the abstract Union Soldier
grow slimmer and younger each year—
wasp-waisted, they doze over muskets
and muse through their sideburns . . .

Shaw's father wanted no monument
except the ditch,
where his son's body was thrown
and lost with his "niggers."

The ditch is nearer.
There are no statues for the last war here;
on Boylston Street, a commercial photograph
shows Hiroshima boiling

over a Mosler Safe, the "Rock of Ages"
that survived the blast. Space is nearer.
When I crouch to my television set,
the drained faces of Negro school-children rise like balloons.

Colonel Shaw
is riding on his bubble,
he waits
for the blessèd break.

The Aquarium is gone. Everywhere,
giant finned cars nose forward like fish;
a savage servility
slides by on grease.

Near the Ocean

(1967)

FOR BLAIR CLARK

NOTE

The theme that connects my translations is Rome, the greatness and horror of her Empire. My Juvenal and Dante versions are as faithful as I am able or dare or can bear to be. The Horace is freer, the Spanish sonnets freer still. How one jumps from Rome to the America of my own poems is something of a mystery to me.

I want to thank my wife, Stanley Kunitz, Philip Booth, Harris Thomas and William Arrowsmith for objections and suggestions.

R.L.

Near the Ocean

1. Waking Early Sunday Morning

O to break loose, like the chinook
salmon jumping and falling back,
nosing up to the impossible
stone and bone-crushing waterfall—
raw-jawed, weak-fleshed there, stopped by ten
steps of the roaring ladder, and then
to clear the top on the last try,
alive enough to spawn and die.

Stop, back off. The salmon breaks
water, and now my body wakes
to feel the unpolluted joy
and criminal leisure of a boy—
no rainbow smashing a dry fly
in the white run is free as I,
here squatting like a dragon on
time's hoard before the day's begun!

Vermin run for their unstopped holes;
in some dark nook a fieldmouse rolls
a marble, hours on end, then stops;
the termite in the woodwork sleeps—
listen, the creatures of the night
obsessive, casual, sure of foot,
go on grinding, while the sun's
daily remorseful blackout dawns.

Fierce, fireless mind, running downhill.
Look up and see the harbor fill:
business as usual in eclipse
goes down to the sea in ships—
wake of refuse, dacron rope,
bound for Bermuda or Good Hope,

all bright before the morning watch
the wine-dark hulls of yawl and ketch.

I watch a glass of water wet
with a fine fuzz of icy sweat,
silvery colors touched with sky,
serene in their neutrality—
yet if I shift, or change my mood,
I see some object made of wood,
background behind it of brown grain,
to darken it, but not to stain.

O that the spirit could remain
tinged but untarnished by its strain!
Better dressed and stacking birch,
or lost with the Faithful at Church—
anywhere, but somewhere else!
And now the new electric bells,
clearly chiming, "Faith of our fathers,"
and now the congregation gathers.

O Bible chopped and crucified
in hymns we hear but do not read,
none of the milder subtleties
of grace or art will sweeten these
stiff quatrains shovelled out four-square—
they sing of peace, and preach despair;
yet they gave darkness some control,
and left a loophole for the soul.

No, put old clothes on, and explore
the corners of the woodshed for
its dregs and dreck: tools with no handle,
ten candle-ends not worth a candle,
old lumber banished from the Temple,
damned by Paul's precept and example,
cast from the kingdom, banned in Israel,
the wordless sign, the tinkling cymbal.

When will we see Him face to face?
Each day, He shines through darker glass.
In this small town where everything
is known, I see His vanishing
emblems, His white spire and flag-
pole sticking out above the fog,
like old white china doorknobs, sad,
slight, useless things to calm the mad.

Hammering military splendor,
top-heavy Goliath in full armor—
little redemption in the mass
liquidations of their brass,
elephant and phalanx moving
with the times and still improving,
when that kingdom hit the crash:
a million foreskins stacked like trash . . .

Sing softer! But what if a new
diminuendo brings no true
tenderness, only restlessness,
excess, the hunger for success,
sanity of self-deception
fixed and kicked by reckless caution,
while we listen to the bells—
anywhere, but somewhere else!

O to break loose. All life's grandeur
is something with a girl in summer . . .
elated as the President
girdled by his establishment
this Sunday morning, free to chaff
his own thoughts with his bear-cuffed staff,
swimming nude, unbuttoned, sick
of his ghost-written rhetoric!

No weekends for the gods now. Wars
flicker, earth licks its open sores,
fresh breakage, fresh promotions, chance
assassinations, no advance.
Only man thinning out his kind
sounds through the Sabbath noon, the blind
swipe of the pruner and his knife
busy about the tree of life . . .

Pity the planet, all joy gone
from this sweet volcanic cone;
peace to our children when they fall
in small war on the heels of small
war—until the end of time
to police the earth, a ghost
orbiting forever lost
in our monotonous sublime.

2. Fourth of July in Maine

(FOR HARRIET WINSLOW)

Another summer! Our Independence
Day Parade, all innocence
of children's costumes, helps resist
the communist and socialist.
Five nations: Dutch, French, Englishmen,
Indians, and we, who held Castine,
rise from their graves in combat gear—
world-losers elsewhere, conquerors here!

Civil Rights clergy face again
the scions of the good old strain,
the poor who always must remain
poor and Republicans in Maine,
upholders of the American Dream,
who will not sink and cannot swim—
Emersonian self-reliance,
lethargy of Russian peasants!

High noon. Each child has won his blue,
red, yellow ribbon, and our statue,
a dandyish Union Soldier, sees
his fields reclaimed by views and spruce—
he seems a convert to old age,
small, callous, elbowed off the stage,
while the canned martial music fades
from scene and green—no more parades!

Blue twinges of mortality
remind us the theocracy
drove in its stakes here to command
the infinite, and gave this land
a ministry that would have made
short work of Christ, the Son of God,
and then exchanged His crucifix,
hardly our sign, for politics.

This white Colonial frame house,
willed downward, Dear, from you to us,
still matters—the Americas'
best artifact produced en masse.
The founders' faith was in decay,
and yet their building seems to say:
"Every time I take a breath,
my God you are the air I breathe."

New England, everywhere I look,
old letters crumble from the Book,
China trade rubble, one more line
unravelling from the dark design
spun by God and Cotton Mather—
our *bell età dell'oro*, another
bright thing thinner than a cobweb,
caught in Calvinism's ebb.

Dear Cousin, life is much the same,
though only fossils know your name
here since you left this solitude,
gone, as the Christians say, for good.
Your house, still outwardly in form
lasts, though no emissary come
to watch the garden running down,
or photograph the propped-up barn.

If memory is genius, you
had Homer's, enough gossip to
repeople Trollope's Barchester,
nurses, Negro, diplomat, down-easter,
cousins kept up with, nipped, corrected,
kindly, majorfully directed,
though family furniture, decor,
and rooms redone meant almost more.

How often when the telephone
brought you to us from Washington,
we had to look around the room

to find the objects you would name—
lying there, ten years paralyzed,
half blind, no voice unrecognized,
not trusting in the afterlife,
teasing us for a carving knife.

High New England summer, warm
and fortified against the storm
by nightly nips you once adored,
though never going overboard,
Harriet, when you used to play
your chosen Nadia Boulanger
Monteverdi, Purcell, and Bach's
precursors on the Magnavox.

Blue-ribboned, blue-jeaned, named for you,
our daughter cartwheels on the blue—
may your proportion strengthen her
to live through the millennial year
Two Thousand, and like you possess
friends, independence, and a house,
herself God's plenty, mistress of
your tireless sedentary love.

Her two angora guinea pigs
are nibbling seed, the news, and twigs—
untroubled, petrified, atremble,
a mother and her daughter, so humble,
giving, idle and sensitive,
few animals will let them live,
and only a vegetarian God
could look on them and call them good.

Man's poorest cousins, harmonies
of lust and appetite and ease,
little pacific things, who graze
the grass about their box, they praise
whatever stupor gave them breath
to multiply before their death—

Evolution's snails, by birth,
outrunning man who runs the earth.

And now the frosted summer night-dew
brightens, the north wind rushes through
your ailing cedars, finds the gaps;
thumbtacks rattle from the white maps,
food's lost sight of, dinner waits,
in the cold oven, icy plates—
repeating and repeating, one
Joan Baez on the gramophone.

And here in your converted barn,
we burn our hands a moment, borne
by energies that never tire
of piling fuel on the fire;
monologue that will not hear,
logic turning its deaf ear,
wild spirits and old sores in league
with inexhaustible fatigue.

Far off that time of gentleness,
when man, still licensed to increase,
unfallen and unmated, heard
only the uncreated Word—
when God the Logos still had wit
to hide his bloody hands, and sit
in silence, while his peace was sung.
Then the universe was young.

We watch the logs fall. Fire once gone,
we're done for: we escape the sun,
rising and setting, a red coal,
until it cinders like the soul.
Great ash and sun of freedom, give
us this day the warmth to live,
and face the household fire. We turn
our backs, and feel the whiskey burn.

3. The Opposite House

All day the opposite house,
an abandoned police stable,
just an opposite house,
is square enough—six floors,
six windows to a floor,
pigeons ganging through
broken windows and cooing
like gangs of children tooting
empty bottles.

Tonight, though, I see it shine
in the Azores of my open window.
Its manly, old-fashioned lines
are gorgeously rectilinear.
It's like some firework to be fired
at the end of the garden party,
some Spanish *casa*, luminous
with heraldry and murder,
marooned in New York.

A stringy policeman is crooked
in the doorway, one hand on his revolver.
He counts his bullets like beads.
Two on horseback sidle
the crowd to the curb. A red light
whirls on the roof of an armed car,
plodding slower than a turtle.
Deterrent terror!
Viva la muerte!

4. Central Park

Scaling small rocks, exhaling smog,
gasping at game-scents like a dog,
now light as pollen, now as white
and winded as a grounded kite—
I watched the lovers occupy
every inch of earth and sky:
one figure of geometry,
multiplied to infinity,
straps down, and sunning openly . . .
each precious, public, pubic tangle
an equilateral triangle,
lost in the park, half covered by
the shade of some low stone or tree.
The stain of fear and poverty
spread through each trapped anatomy,
and darkened every mote of dust.
All wished to leave this drying crust,
borne on the delicate wings of lust
like bees, and cast their fertile drop
into the overwhelming cup.

Drugged and humbled by the smell
of zoo-straw mixed with animal,
the lion prowled his slummy cell,
serving his life-term in jail—
glaring, grinding, on his heel,
with tingling step and testicle . . .

Behind a dripping rock, I found
a one-day kitten on the ground—
deprived, weak, ignorant and blind,
squeaking, tubular, left behind—
dying with its deserter's rich
Welfare lying out of reach:

milk cartons, kidney heaped to spoil,
two plates sheathed with silver foil.

Shadows had stained the afternoon;
high in an elm, a snagged balloon
wooed the attraction of the moon.
Scurrying from the mouth of night,
a single, fluttery, paper kite
grazed Cleopatra's Needle, and sailed
where the light of the sun had failed.
Then night, the night—the jungle hour,
the rich in his slit-windowed tower . . .
Old Pharaohs starving in your foxholes,
with painted banquets on the walls,
fists knotted in your captives' hair,
tyrants with little food to spare—
all your embalming left you mortal,
glazed, black, and hideously eternal,
all your plunder and gold leaf
only served to draw the thief . . .

We beg delinquents for our life.
Behind each bush, perhaps a knife;
each landscaped crag, each flowering shrub,
hides a policeman with a club.

5. Near the Ocean

(FOR E.H.L.)

The house is filled. The last heartthrob
thrills through her flesh. The hero stands,
stunned by the applauding hands,
and lifts her once head to please the mob . . .
No, young and starry-eyed, the brother
and sister wait before their mother,
old iron-bruises, powder, "Child,
these breasts . . ." He knows. And if she's killed

his treadmill heart will never rest—
his wet mouth pressed to some slack breast,
or shifting over on his back . . .
The severed radiance filters back,
athirst for nightlife—gorgon head,
fished up from the Aegean dead,
with all its stranded snakes uncoiled,
here beheaded and despoiled.

We hear the ocean. Older seas
and deserts give asylum, peace
to each abortion and mistake.
Lost in the Near Eastern dreck,
the tyrant and tyrannicide
lie like the bridegroom and the bride;
the battering ram, abandoned, prone,
beside the apeman's phallic stone.

Betrayals! Was it the first night?
They stood against a black and white
inland New England backdrop. No dogs
there, horse or hunter, only frogs
chirring from the dark trees and swamps.
Elms watching like extinguished lamps.
Knee-high hedges of black sheep
encircling them at every step.

Some subway-green coldwater flat,
its walls tattooed with neon light,
then high delirious squalor, food
burned down with vodka . . . menstrual blood
caking the covers, when they woke
to the dry, childless Sunday walk,
saw cars on Brooklyn Bridge descend
through steel and coal dust to land's end.

Was it years later when they met,
and summer's coarse last-quarter drought
had dried the hardveined elms to bark—
lying like people out of work,
dead sober, cured, recovered, on
the downslope of some gritty green,
all access barred with broken glass;
and dehydration browned the grass?

Is it this shore? Their eyes worn white
as moons from hitting bottom? Night,
the sandfleas scissoring their feet,
the sandbed cooling to concrete,
one borrowed blanket, lights of cars
shining down at them like stars? . . .
Sand built the lost Atlantis . . . sand,
Atlantic Ocean, condoms, sand.

Sleep, sleep. The ocean, grinding stones,
can only speak the present tense;
nothing will age, nothing will last,
or take corruption from the past.
A hand, your hand then! I'm afraid
to touch the crisp hair on your head—
Monster loved for what you are,
till time, that buries us, lay bare.

For Theodore Roethke
(1908–1963)

All night you wallowed through my sleep,
then in the morning you were lost
in the Maine sky—close, cold and gray,
smoke and smoke-colored cloud.

Sheeplike, unsociable reptilian, two
hell-divers splattered squawking on the water,
loons devolving to a monochrome.
You honored nature,

helpless, elemental creature.
The black stump of your hand
just touched the waters under the earth,
and left them quickened with your name . . .

Now, you honor the mother.
Omnipresent,
she made you nonexistent,
the ocean's anchor, our high tide.

Remember standing with me in the dark,
escaping? In the wild house? Everything—
I mad, you mad for me? And brought my ring
that twelvecarat lunk of gold there . . . Joan of Arc,
undeviating still to the true mark?
Robust, ah taciturn! Remember playing
Marian Anderson, Mozart's *Shepherd King*,
il re pastore? Hammerheaded shark,
the rainbow salmon of the world—your hand
a rose . . . And at the Mittersill, you topped
the ski-run, that white eggshell, your sphere, not land
or water—no circumference anywhere,
the center everywhere, I everywhere,
infinite, fearful . . . standing—you escaped.

Spring

(Horace, *Odes*, Book I, 4: *Solvitur acris hiems*)

Sharp winter melts and changes into spring—
now the west wind, now cables haul the boats
on their dry hulls, and now the cattle tire
of their close stalls, the farmer of his fire.
Venus leads dancers under the large moon,
the naked nymphs and graces walk the earth,
one foot and then another. Birds return,
they flash and mingle in mid-air. Now, now,
the time to tear the blossoms from the bough,
to gather wild flowers from the thawing field;
now, now, to sacrifice the kid or lamb
to Faunus in the green and bursting woods,
for bloodless death with careless foot strikes down
the peasant's hut and the stone towers of kings.
Move quickly, the brief sum of life forbids
our opening any long account with hope;
night hems us in, and ghosts, and death's close clay . . .
Sestius, soon, soon, you will not rush to beat
the dice and win the lordship of the feast,
or tremble for the night's fatiguing joys,
sleepless for this child, then for that one—boys
soon lost to man, soon lost to girls in heat.

Serving under Brutus

(Horace, *Odes*, Book II, 7: *O saepe mecum tempus in ultimum*)

O how often with me in the forlorn hope
under the proconsulship of Marcus Brutus,
Citizen! Who brought you back to Rome,
to our sultry gods and hot Italian sky?

My first friend, and my best, O Pompey,
how often have we drawn out the delaying day
with wine, and brightened our rough hair,
with Syrian nard!

With you too at Philippi, at that hysterical
mangling of our legions, when we broke
like women. Like an Egyptian,
I threw away my little shield.

I was afraid, but Mercury, the quick,
the subtle, found a way for me to escape.
And you? The wave of battle drew you under,
knocked you down into its troubled, bleeding surf.

Offer the Sky-god then this meal,
spread out your flesh worn out by war.
Enjoy this laurel tree, and don't forget me,
or spare the wine jars set aside for you.

Fill the frail goblets with red wine,
pour perfume from the fragile shells!
Who'll be the first to twist parsley
and myrtle with the coronets?

Throw down the dice. Throw down the dice—
Venus has chosen her master of the feast.
I'll drink like Alexander. It is sweet
to drink to fury when a friend's reprieved.

Cleopatra

(Horace, *Odes*, Book I, 37: *Nunc est bibendum*)

Now's the time to drink,
to beat the earth in rhythm,
toss flowers on the couches of the gods,
Friends!

Before this, it was infamous
to taste the fruit of the vine,
while Cleopatra with her depraved gangs,
germs of the Empire, plotted

to enthrone her ruin in the Capitol,
and put an end to Rome . . .
Impotent,
yet drunk on fortune's favors . . .

but Caesar tamed your soul:
you saw with a now sober eye
the scowling truth of his terror,
O Cleopatra, scarcely escaping,

and with a single ship, and scarcely
escaping from your limping fleet, on fire,
Cleopatra, with Caesar running on the wind,
three rising stands of oars, with Caesar

falling on you like a sparrow hawk
fallen on some soft dove or sprinting rabbit
in the winter field. And yet you sought
a more magnanimous way to die.

Not womanish, you scorned our swords,
you did not search for secret harbors.
Regal, resigned and anguished,
Queen, you even saw your house in ruin.

Poisonous snakes gave up their secrets,
you held them with practiced hands,
you showed your breasts. Then bolder, more ferocious,
death slipping through your fingers,

how could you go aboard Octavian's galleys,
how could you march on foot, unhumbled,
to crown triumphant Caesar's triumph—
no queen now, but a private woman?

The Vanity of Human Wishes
(A Version of Juvenal's Tenth Satire)

(FOR WILLIAM ARROWSMITH)

In every land as far as man can go,
from Spain to the Aurora or the poles,
few know, and even fewer choose what's true.
What do we fear with reason, or desire?
Is a step made without regret? The gods
ruin whole households for a foolish prayer.
Devoured by peace, we seek devouring war,
the orator is drowned by his torrential speech,
the gladiator's murdered by his skill
at murder. Wealth is worse; how many pile
fortune on fortune—like the Atlantic whale,
they bulk above the lesser fish and die.
For this in the dark years and at the word
of Nero, Seneca's high gardens fell;
Longinus died; a cohort of praetorians
besieged the Laterani. No soldiers purge
a garret. If you take a walk at night,
carrying a little silver, be prepared
to think each shadow hides a knife or spear.
You'll fear each wavering of the moonlit reed,
while beggars whistle in the robber's face.

Almost the first and last prayer made in all
the temples is for wealth: "Let my estate
stand first in Rome!" But who drinks arsenic
from earthenware? Fear death each time you lift
the jewelled goblet, or when vintage wine
purples the golden bowl.

                    Which wise man shall
I praise, Democritus or Heraclitus,
he who smiled or he who wept each time
he left his house? But the dry smile comes easy,

I marvel any finds sufficient tears.
Democritus could laugh till he was sick,
and yet in those days in his little town,
there were no fasces, litters, canopies,
no tribune bawling from the tribunal.
What if he'd seen the praetor riding high
in his triumphal car across the Circus,
dragging his palm-embroidered robes of Zeus,
a gold-stitched toga, and a cloud of dust?
What if he'd seen him in his cardboard crown,
a millstone that no mortal neck could bear—
there elbowed by a sweating German slave,
crowding the praetor to deflate his pride?
And now the eagle on its ivory staff,
the hornblowers, the herd of toadies mixed
with citizens of Rome, in snow-white robes,
his dearest friends, the lackeys in his pay.
Democritus could laugh at everything;
his neighbors' self-importance made him smile,
he even found amusement in their tears,
and by his courage and good humor proved
that honesty and wisdom can survive
the smothering air of a provincial town.
When Superstition shouted for his head,
he laughed, and left her hanging in her noose.

Why do we hunger so for vicious things?
Our wishes bend the statues of the gods.

How many men are killed by Power, by Power
and Power's companion, Envy! Your long list
of honors breaks your neck. Statues follow
the rope and crash, the axe cuts down the two-
wheeled chariot's wheels and snaps the horse's legs.
Fierce hiss the fires, the bellows roar, the head,
all-popular and adored by all once, burns—
Sejanus crackles, and his crude bronze face,
the second in the world, melts down to jars,
frying pans, basins, platters, chamber pots.

Hang out your streamers, lead the great chalked bull
to the high altar at the Capitol—
men lead Sejanus on a hook, and all
rejoice. "What flannel lips he has! No man,
I tell you, ever loved this man!" "But tell us,
what was his crime, friend? Who were the informers?
What witness swore away his life?" "No witness!
A wordy long epistle came from Capri."
"Tiberius spoke, enough, I'll hear no more."
But what about the Roman mob? Their rule
is always follow fortune and despise
the fallen. One thing's certain, if the gods
had spared Sejanus, if some accident
had choked Tiberius in his green old age,
the mob would hail Sejanus Caesar now.

Now that we have no suffrage left to sell,
we have no troubles; we who once conferred
legions, fasces, empires, everything,
are simply subjects; restlessly we ask
for two things: bread and circuses. But listen—
"I hear that many more are going to die."
"No doubt about it, they have built a fire."
"My closest friend, Brutidius, looked white
just now at Mars's altar, Caesar stirs,
I fear fresh heads will fall for negligence."
"Quick, Caesar's enemy is still exposed;
let's run; there's time to trample on the corpse."
"I'll bring my slaves for witnesses; no paid
accuser shall drag me haltered into court."
Thus, thus, the secret murmurs of the crowd—
would you be cheered and flattered like Sejanus?
Be rich as Croesus, give the ivory chair
to one, and armies to another? Would you be
Tiberius' right hand, while he sits and suns
himself at Capri, fed by eastern fags?
Surely you'd like to have his lances, cohorts,
blue-blooded knights and army corps of slaves.

Why not, friend? Even if you never wished
to murder, you would like to have the power.
But would you want to glitter and rise this high,
if ruin's counterweight must crush your life?

Who would prefer Sejanus' rod of office
to being mayor of Gabii, or Fidenae,
some rural aedile smashing crooked weights,
wearing a threadbare cloak at Ulubrae?
Let's say then that Sejanus was insane;
wanting authority and wealth, he added
story on story to his towering house—
so much the higher for the blinding crash!
What ruined Crassus, Pompey, he who scourged
Gaul and the torn Republic with his lash?
What brought them down? High places and the art
of climbing, wishes answered by the gods,
who send few kings to Pluto without wounds,
still fewer cherished by their people's love.

                              Each schoolboy
who cultivates Minerva with a penny fee,
and one poor slave to lug his satchel, prays through
the summer holidays for eloquence,
to be Demosthenes or Cicero.
Yet eloquence destroyed both orators,
this, this condemned and drowned them in its flood.
Eloquence lopped off Cicero's right hand,
and cut his throat, but no cheap shyster ever
dirtied the Roman rostrum with his blood.
"My consulate, how fortunate the state":
if this were all you wrote, you might have scorned
the swords and vengeance of Antonius.
Yes, all in all, I like such pompous verse
more than your force, immortal fifth Philippic!
Dark too the murder of the patriot Greek,
who stunned the men of Athens with his words,
and held the hushed assembly in his palm.

Under unfriendly gods and an ill star,
your blacksmith father raised and sent you forth,
red-eyed and sooty from the glowering forge,
from anvil, pincers, hammer and the coals
to study rhetoric, Demosthenes!

War souvenirs and trophies nailed to trees,
a cheek strap dangling from a clobbered helmet,
a breastplate, or a trireme's figurehead,
or captives weeping on the victor's arch:
these are considered more than human prizes.
For these Greek, Roman, and barbarian
commanders march; for these they pledge their lives
and freedom—such their thirst for fame, and such
their scorn of virtue, for who wants a life
of virtue without praise? Whole nations die
to serve the glory of the few; all lust
for honors and inscriptions on their tombs—
those tombs a twisting fig tree can uproot,
for tombs too have their downfall and their doom.

Throw Hannibal on the scales, how many pounds
does the great captain come to? This is he
who found the plains of Africa too small,
rich Carthage with her mercenary grip
stretched from Gibraltar to the steaming Nile
and back to Ethiopia, her stud
for slaves and elephants. He set his hand
firmly on Spain, then scaled the Pyrenees;
when snows, the Alps, and Nature blocked his road,
he derricked rocks, and split the mountainsides
with vinegar. Now Italy is his;
the march goes on. "Think nothing done," he says,
"until my Punic soldiers hack through Rome,
and plant my standard over the Subura's
whorehouses." What a face for painters! Look,
the one-eyed leader prods his elephant!
And what's the end? O glory! Like the others,

he is defeated, then the worried flight,
the great, world-famous client cools his heels
in royal anterooms, and waits on some
small despot, sleeping off a drunken meal.
What is the last day of this mighty spirit
whose valor turned the known world on its head?
Not swords, or pikes, or legions—no, not these,
his crown for Cannae and those seas of blood
is poison in a ring. March, madman, cross
the Alps, the Tiber—be a purple patch
for schoolboys, and a theme for declamation!

One world was much too small for Alexander,
racing to gain the limits of the globe,
as if he were a circling charioteer;
early however he reached his final city,
Babylon, fortified with frail dry brick.
A grave was all he wanted. Death alone
shows us what tedious things our bodies are.
Fleets climbed the slopes of Athos (such the lies
of Greek historians) yes, and paved the sea;
wheels rumbled down a boulevard of decks,
breakfasting Persians drank whole rivers dry—
that's how the perjured laureates puffed their songs.
But tell us how the King of Kings returned
from Salamis? Xerxes, whose amusement was
whipping the winds, and bragging how he'd drag
Neptune in chains, and branded to his throne—
a lovely master for the gods to serve!
Tell us of his return. A single ship,
scything for sea-room through the Persian dead.
That was his sentence for his dreams of glory.

"Give us long life, O God, and years to live,"
in sickness or in health, this is our prayer;
but age's ills are strong and never fail.
Look at the face, deformed and paralyzed,
unlike itself, its skin a hide, gone cheeks,

a thousand wrinkles like a mother ape.
But youth's unique: each boy is handsomer
than the next one, or cleverer, or stronger;
all old men look alike, their voices shake
worse than their fingers, every head is hairless,
each snivels like a child; they mess their bread,
their gums are toothless—how heavily they weigh
upon their wives, their children, and themselves!
Even the fortune-hunter turns them down,
now food and even wine are one more torture,
a long oblivion falls on intercourse,
the shy nerve, pumping, drops like a wet leaf,
though tickled through the night, it cannot rise.

What do you hope from your white pubic hairs?
Sex hounds you, when its power is gone. Or take
the loss of other senses—the best voice
strikes on the coughing ear like lead, the harp
of the best harpist screams like a ground knife.
What good are bosoms jingling with gold coins,
the best seat in the Colosseum, when you
can hardly tell a trumpet from a drum?
The boy announcing visitors or meals
half kills himself with baying in your ear.

Now only fevers warm the thinning blood,
diseases of all kinds lock hands and dance,
even their names escape you—let me list
the many lechers Oppia will love,
slow-coming Maura drain a day, how many
schoolboys Hamillus will crouch on, the partners
Hirrus will swindle, the sick men Themiston will kill
this autumn—I could more easily count
the villas bought up by the barber whose
razor once grated on my stiff young beard . . .
One man has a sagging shoulder, one a hernia,
another has a softening hipbone, and another
has cataracts; another's spoonfed: listen,
they yawn like baby swallows for their swill!

But the worst evil is the loss of mind;
we do not know our slaves, the friend we dined with,
then even our own children are forgotten.
"Who are they? Parasites!" The will's rewritten:
All goes to Phiale, so lulling are
the acrobatics of that quick, moist mouth
that used to sell her body in the streets.

Let's say you keep your mind, you'll live to see
your wife and sons laid out, the ashes of
brothers and sisters shut in marble urns.
These the rewards of living long: repeated
groaning that fills an empty house, yourself
in black, a ghost, disaster on disaster!
Nestor, if one believes the lines from Homer,
lived longer than a crow—how fortunate,
outwitting death and tasting the new wine
a hundred autumns! Was this all? Fate's grace,
and his long thread of years were all too much
for Nestor. He saw the beard of his son, Antilochus,
flame on the pyre, asked: "Why have I lived? What crime
have I committed?" Peleus felt the same
for his Achilles, and Laertes for
Odysseus. What of Priam? Would that he had died
the day when Paris launched his robber galley;
he would have met his city's shades, with Troy
still standing, Hector and all his sons on hand
to bear him on their shoulders, with Cassandra,
unravished, free to wail the song of mourning.
What good was his long life? He saw his house
fallen, all Asia burning—swords, then fire!
Then dropping his tiara, and putting on
armor, the poor old doddering soldier rushed
before the altar of his gods, and fell
like some old ox discarded by the plow,
craning his thin neck for the master's knife.
But Priam's death was human; Hecuba
survived him to die barking like a dog.

I pass by Mithridates; why repeat
Solon's old saws to Croesus—take our own men,
take Marius. Age brought him prison, exile,
weeks on his belly in Minturnae's marsh,
then back to Rome, his seventh consulship,
a few brief apoplectic days of blood.
Did Nature ever raise a Roman higher?
Did Rome? if he had died with all the pomp
of war, his army marshalled out to cheer him,
one foot descending on a Teuton's back?
How provident was the Campanian fever
for Pompey; but the tears of many cities,
all praying for his life, prevailed. He lived,
his stars preserved him, and a eunuch's slave
cut off his head. Was Lentulus so tortured?
Was Cethegus? Or even Catiline,
whose corpse lay undishonored on the field?

The nervous mother passing Venus' altar
prays for good-looking sons and lovelier daughters.
"Why not?" she says. "Latona bore Diana!"
Why not? And yet Lucretia's fate forbids
us to desire her face. Virginia
would swap her figure for Rutila's hump.
A handsome son has shy and trembling parents.

Luck seldom goes with beauty. But suppose
a simple household teaches him the fathers'
virtues and Sabine manners, say that nature
moreover makes him kind, intelligent,
with warm blood rising to his cheeks—
what better gifts can nature give the boy,
all-giving nature, gentler than his teachers?
And yet the boy will never be a man.
Some prodigal seducer will seduce
the parents—money never fails its giver.
No overweight tyrant castrates the deformed.
Trust Nero, Nero had an eye for beauty:
he never picked a spastic or a lout.

Let's say your son survives, and reaches twenty.
He'll look for softer and more practiced hands
than Nero's. He will fly to women. Would
you have him an adulterer like Mars,
almost as handsome, but no luckier,
his bronze foot kicking in the cripple's net?
Risk the worst punishments the laws allow
an injured husband? Often the revenge
outdoes the law: the cuckold chops the lover's
balls off, or jams a mullet up his arse.
Then let him choose a widow; soon he'll have
her money, all her unloved body has
to give. What can Catulla, what can Chloris
deny his swelling prick—sad sacks in heat,
their conscience washing out between their legs.
But beauty never hurts the good! Go ask
Bellerophon, go ask Hippolytus.
Chastity couldn't save their lives from Phaedra,
or Sthenoboea, faithful wives, then scorned
lovers screwed on to murder by their shame.

Now tell me what advice you have to give
the fellow Caesar's consort wants to marry—
the best man, the most beautiful, an old
patrician house could raise, soon caught, soon shoved
from life to death by Messalina's eyes.
She's long been seated, and her bridal veil
rustles, the lovers' bed of full-blown roses
rustles quite openly inside the garden;
by ancient rule, a dowry of a million
brass sesterces must now be counted—clerks,
lawyers, the thin-lipped priest, attend on tiptoe.
"What, did you want a hole-in-corner marriage?
The lady has a right to her religion.
What will you do? Speak up! Say no, you'll die
before the lamps are lit. Say yes, you'll live
until the city hears, and someone squeals
in Claudius's ear—he'll be the last in Rome
to know of his disgrace. Meanwhile obey

your love, if one or two days' life mean much—
whatever's best or costs the smallest effort,
to bring your fair white body to the sword."

There's nothing then to pray for? If you pray,
pray for the gods and Jupiter to help.
What's best, what serves us, only He can know.
We're dearer to the gods than to ourselves.
Hurried by impulse and diseased desire,
we ask for wives, and children by our wives—
what wives, what children, heaven only knows.
Still, if you ask for something, if you must
buy holy sausages and dedicate
the tripe of bulls at every altar, pray for
a healthy body and a healthy soul,
a soul that is not terrified by death,
that thinks long life the least of nature's gifts,
courage that takes whatever comes—this hero
like Hercules, all pain and labor, loathes
the lecherous gut of Sardanapalus.
Success is worshipped as a god; it's we
who set up shrines and temples in her name.
I give you simply what you have already.

Brunetto Latini

(Canto XV of Dante's "Inferno")

(FOR LILLIAN HELLMAN)

And now we walked along the solid mire
above a brook whose fuming mist protected
water and banks from the surrounding fire.
Just as the men of Flanders threw up huge
earthworks to stop the sea that always threatens
their fields and cattle between Ghent and Bruges,
or Paduans along the Brenta spread
out dykes to shield their towns and towers against
spring thawing the Carinzian watershed—
on such a plan the evil engineer,
whoever he was, had laid his maze of dykes,
though on a smaller scale, and with less care.
By now we'd gone much deeper underground,
and left the bleeding wood so far behind
I'd have seen nothing, if I'd looked around.

We met a company of spirits here,
trooping below us on the sand. Each one
stared closely at our faces. As men peer
at one another under the new moon,
or an old tailor squints into his needle,
these puckered up their brows and glowered. Soon,
I saw a man whose eyes devoured me, saying,
"This is a miracle." He seized my sleeve,
and as I felt his touch, I fixed my eyes
with such intensity on his crusted face
that its disfigurement could not prevent
my recognizing who he was. "Oh, Oh,"
I answered groaning, as I stretched my hand
to touch his arm, "are you here Ser Brunetto?"
He answered, "Do not be displeased, my Son,
if Brunetto Latini turn and walk a little
downward with you, and lets this herd pass on."

Then I, "I'll go with you, or we can sit
here talking as we used to in the past,
if you desire it, and my guide permit."

"O Son," he answered, "anyone who stands
still a moment will lie here a hundred years,
helpless to brush the sparks off with his hands.
Move on, I'll follow. Soon enough I must
rejoin my little group of friends who walk
with me lamenting their eternal lust."
Then since I dared not leave my bank and move
over the flames of his low path, I bent
my head to walk with reverence and love.
Then he, "What brings you here before your day?
Is it by accident, or Providence?
Who is this man who guides you on your way?"
I answered, "In the world that lies serene
and shining over us, I lost my path,
even before the first young leaves turned green.
Yesterday morning when my steps had come
full circle, this man appeared. He turned me round,
and now he guides me on my journey home."
"O Son," said he, "if you pursue your star,
you cannot fail to reach the glorious harbor.

And if the beautiful world, less sinister,
had let me live a little longer, I too
might have sustained your work and brought you comfort,
seeing how heaven has befriended you.
But that perverted and ungrateful flock
that held the hills with Catiline, and then
descended, hard and sterile as their rock,
to govern Florence, hate you for the good
you do; and rightly! Could they wish to see
the sweet fig ripen on their rotten wood?
Surely, they've earned their reputation: blind,
fratricidal, avaricious, proud.
O root their filthy habits from your mind!
Fortune will load such honors on your back

that Guelph and Ghibelline will hunger for you.
But beat them from the pasture. Let the pack
run loose, and sicken on the carcasses
that heap the streets, but spare the tender flower,
if one should rise above the swamp and mess—
some flower in which the fragile, sacred seed
of ancient Roman virtue still survives
in Florence, that vulture's nest of lies and greed."
"Master," I said, "you would not walk here now
cut off from human nature, if my prayers
had had an answer. I remember how
I loved you, sitting at your knees—all thought
fixed on your fatherly and gentle face,
when in the world, from hour to hour, you taught
me how a man becomes eternal. O
Master, as long as I draw breath and live,
men shall remember you and what I owe.
Your words about my future shall remain
with other prophecies I keep to give
a Lady, who if I reach her, will explain.
This much I know: If I can bear the stings
of my own heavy conscience, I will face
whatever good or evil Fortune brings.
This promise of good fortune has been made
before this; so, let Fortune whirl her wheel
at random, and the peasant work his spade."

Then Virgil, turning backward with one hand
lifted in wonder, mused at me, and said:
"He who knows how to listen shall understand."

Dwelling upon his words, I did not stop
eagerly briefing Ser Brunetto, and asked,
"Who are the most illustrious in your group?"
And he, "It's right to know a few of us,
but fitting I be silent on the rest;
our time's too short to squander on such dross.
In one word, we were scholars in our time,
great men of letters, famous in the world

we soiled and lost for our one common crime.
Priscian goes with us on this dismal turf,
and Francesco d'Accorso; you can see,
if you have any liking for such scurf,
the man the Servants' Servant chose to serve
him on the Arno, then on the Bacchilione,
where he laid down his ill-extended nerve.
I would say more to you, but must not stand
forever talking, speech must have an end.
I see fresh steam is stirring from the sand,
and men I would avoid are coming. Give
me no pity. Read my *Tesoro*. In
my book, my treasure, I am still alive."

Then he turned back, and he seemed one of those
who run for the green cloth through the green field
at Verona . . . and seemed more like the one
who wins the roll of cloth than those who lose.

The Ruins of Time

(Quevedo, *Miré los muros de la patria mía* and *Buscas en Roma a Roma, ¡O peregrino!*)
(Góngora, *Esta que admiras fábrica, esta prima* and *Menos solicitó veloz saeta*)

I.

I saw the musty shingles of my house,
raw wood and fixed once, now a wash of moss
eroded by the ruin of the age
turning all fair and green things into waste.
I climbed the pasture. I saw the dim sun drink
the ice just thawing from the bouldered fallow,
woods crowd the foothills, seize last summer's field,
and higher up, the sickly cattle bellow.
I went into my house. I saw how dust
and ravel had devoured its furnishing;
even my cane was withered and more bent,
even my sword was coffined up in rust—
there was no hilt left for the hand to try.
Everything ached, and told me I must die.

II.

You search in Rome for Rome? O Traveller!
in Rome itself, there is no room for Rome,
the Aventine is its own mound and tomb,
only a corpse receives the worshipper.
And where the Capitol once crowned the forum,
are medals ruined by the hands of time;
they show how more was lost to chance and time
than Hannibal or Caesar could consume.
The Tiber flows still, but its waste laments
a city that has fallen in its grave—
each wave's a woman beating at her breast.
O Rome! From all your palms, dominion, bronze
and beauty, what was firm has fled. What once
was fugitive maintains its permanence.

III.
This chapel that you gaze at, these stern tombs,
the pride of sculpture . . . Stop here, Passer-by,
diamonds were blunted on this porphyry,
the teeth of files wore smooth as ice. This vault
seals up the earth of those who never felt
the earth's oppression. Whose? If you would know,
stand back and study this inscription. Words
give marble meaning and a voice to bronze.
Piety made this chapel beautiful,
and generous devotion binds these urns
to the heroic dust of Sandoval,
who left his coat of arms, once five blue stars
on a gold field, to climb with surer step
through the blue sky, and scale the golden stars.

IV.
The whistling arrow flies less eagerly,
and bites the bull's-eye less ferociously;
the Roman chariot grinds less hurriedly
the arena's docile sand, and rounds the goal . . .
How silently, how privately, we run
through life to die! You doubt this? Animal
despoiled of reason, each ascending sun
dives like a cooling meteorite to its fall.
Do Rome and Carthage know what we deny?
Death only throws fixed dice, and yet we raise
the ante, and stake our lives on every toss.
The hours will hardly pardon us their loss,
those brilliant hours that wore away our days,
our days that ate into eternity.

History

(1973)

FOR FRANK BIDART AND STANLEY KUNITZ

History

History has to live with what was here,
clutching and close to fumbling all we had—
it is so dull and gruesome how we die,
unlike writing, life never finishes.
Abel was finished; death is not remote,
a flash-in-the-pan electrifies the skeptic,
his cows crowding like skulls against high-voltage wire,
his baby crying all night like a new machine.
As in our Bibles, white-faced, predatory,
the beautiful, mist-drunken hunter's moon ascends—
a child could give it a face: two holes, two holes,
my eyes, my mouth, between them a skull's no-nose—
O there's a terrifying innocence in my face
drenched with the silver salvage of the mornfrost.

Man and Woman

The sheep start galloping in moon-blind wheels
shedding a dozen ewes—is it faulty vision?
Will we get them back . . . and everything,
marriage and departure, departure and marriage,
village to family, family to village—
all the sheep's parents in geometric progression?
It's too much heart-ache to go back to that—
not life-enhancing like the hour a student
first discovers the authentic Mother
on the Tuscan hills of Berenson,
or of Galileo, his great glass eye
admiring the spots on the erroneous moon. . . .
I watch this night out grateful to be alone
with my wife—your slow pulse, my outrageous eye.

Bird?

Adrift in my sweet sleep . . . I hear a voice
singing to me in French, "*O mon avril.*"
Those nasals . . . they woo us. Spring. Not mine. Not mine. . . .
A large pileated bird flies up,
dropping excretions like a frightened snake
in Easter feathers; its earwax-yellow spoonbill
angrily hitting the air from side to side
blazing a passage through the smothering jungle—
the lizard tyrants were killed to a man by this bird,
man's forerunner. I picked up stones, and hoped
to snatch its crest, the crown, at last, and cross
the perilous passage, sound in mind and body . . .
often reaching the passage, seeing my thoughts
stream on the water, as if I were cleaning fish.

Dawn

The building's color is penny-postcard pale
as new wood—thirty stories, or a hundred?
The distant view-windows glisten like little cells;
on a wafer balcony, too thin to sit on,
a crimson blazer hangs, a replica
of my own from Harvard—hollow, blowing,
shining its Harvard shield to the fall air. . . .
Eve and Adam, adventuring from the ache
of the first sleep, met forms less primitive
and functional, when they gazed on the stone-ax
and Hawaiian fig-leaf hanging from their fig-tree. . . .
Nothing more established, pure and lonely,
than the early Sunday morning in New York—
the sun on high burning, and most cars dead.

In Genesis

Blank. A camel blotting up the water.
God with whom nothing is design or intention.
In the Beginning, the Sabbath could last a week,
God grumbling secrecies behind Blue Hill. . . .
The serpent walked on foot like us in Eden;
glorified by the perfect Northern exposure,
Eve and Adam knew their nakedness,
a discovery to be repeated many times . . .
in joyless stupor? . . . Orpheus in Genesis
hacked words from brute sound, and taught men English,
plucked all the flowers, deflowered all the girls
with the overemphasis of a father.
He used too many words, his sons killed him,
dancing with grateful gaiety round the cookout.

Our Fathers

That cloud of witnesses has flown like nightdew
leaving a bundle of debts to the widow and orphan—
the virus crawling on its belly like a blot,
an inch an aeon; the tyrannosaur,
first carnivore to stand on his two feet,
the neanderthal, first anthropoid to laugh—
we lack staying power, though we will to live.
Abel learned this falling among the jellied
creepers and morning-glories of the saurian sunset.
But was there some shining, grasping hand to guide
me when I breathed through gills, and walked on fins
through Eden, plucking the law of retribution from the tree?
Was the snake in the garden, an agent provocateur?
Is the Lord increased by desolation?

Walks

In those days no *casus belli* to fight the earth
for the familial, hidden fundamental—
on their walks they scoured the hills to find a girl,
tomorrow promised the courage to die content.
The willow stump put out thin wands in leaf,
green, fleeting flashes of unmerited joy;
the first garden, each morning . . . the first man—
birds laughing at us from the distant trees,
troubadours of laissez-faire and love.
Conservatives only want to have the earth,
the great beast clanking its chain of vertebrae. . . .
Am I a free man, if I have no servant?
If at the end of the long walk, my old dog dies of joy
when I sit down, a poor man at my fire?

King David Old

Two or three times a night, and for a month,
we wrang the night-sweat from his shirt and sheets;
on the fortieth day, we brought him Abishag,
and he recovered, and he knew her not—
cool through the hottest summer day, and moist;
a rankness more savage than all the flowers,
as if her urine caused the vegetation,
Jerusalem leaping from the golden dew;
but later, the Monarch's well-beloved shaft
lay quaking in place; men thought the world was flat,
yet half the world was hanging on each breast,
as two spent swimmers that did cling together—
Sion had come to Israel, if they had held. . . .
This clinch is quickly broken, they were glad to break.

Solomon's Wisdom

"Can I go on keeping a hundred wives at fifty,
still scorning my aging and dispirited life
what I loved with wild idealism young?
God only deals a king one hand to gamble,
his people chosen for him and means to lie.
I shiver up vertical like a baby pigeon,
palate-sprung for the worm, senility.
I strap the gross artillery to my back,
lash on destroying what I lurch against,
not with anger, but unwieldy feet—
ballooning like a spotted, warty, blow-rib toad,
King Solomon croaking, *This too is vanity;*
her lips are a scarlet thread, her breasts are towers—
hymns of the terrible organ in decay."

Solomon, the Rich Man in State

While still man, he drank the fruits of the world,
from the days of his youth to the night of death;
but here the matching of his fresh-cut flowers
is overdelicate and dead for death,
and his flowery coverlet lies like lead
asserting that no primitive ferment,
the slobbering poignance of the voyeur God,
will soil the wise man's earthly abandoned vestment
spread like King Solomon in the Episcopal morgue,
here at earth's end with nowhere else to go—
still sanguine, fit to serve a thousand wives,
a heaven that held the gaze of Babylon.
So calm perhaps will be our final change,
won from the least desire to have what is.

Old Wanderer

A nomad in many cities, yet closer than I
to the grace of 19th century Europe,
to the title of the intellectuals
boiling in Dostoyevsky's Petersburg—
more German than Germans, most Jewish of Jews, a critic
who talked—too much, and never stayed with a subject,
a small Jewish gentleman disliking Jews—
the ancient wailing wanderer in person.
Like Marx you like to splatter the Liberal Weeklies
with gibing multilingual communiqués
shooting like Italians all the birds that fly.
You voice your mother's anxious maternal warnings,
but it's no use humoring anyone who says
we'll sleep better under a red counterpane than a green.

Judith

"The Jews were much like Arabs, I learned at Radcliffe,
decay of infeud scattered our bright clans;
now ours is an airier aristocracy:
professors, solons, new art, old, New York
where only Jews can write an English sentence,
the Jewish mother, half Jew, half anti-Jew,
says, *literate, liberalize, liberate*!
If her husband dies and takes his lay in state,
she calms the grandeur of his marble hair.
Like Judith, she'd cut the Virgin Mary dead,
a jet-set parachute. Long before the Philistines,
Jewish girls could write: for Judith, knowing
Holofernes was like knocking out a lightweight—
smack! her sword divorces his codshead from the codspiece."

Israel 1

The vagabond Alexander passed here, *romero*—
did he make Israel Greek, or just Near East?
This province, still provincial, prays to the One God
who left his footmark on the field of blood;
his dry wind bleeds the overcharged barbed wires. . . .
Wherever the sun ferments our people from dust,
our blood leaps up in friendship a cold spring. . . .
Alexander learned to share the earth with God;
God learned to live in a heaven, wizened with distance,
a face thin as a sand-dollar in the pail of a child. . . .
Each year some prince of tyrants, King Ahab, says,
"If my enemies could only know me, I am safe."
But the good murderer is always blind;
the leopard enters the Ark and keeps his spots.

Israel 2

The sun still burns in Israel. I could have stayed there
a month longer and even stood conscription,
though almost a pacifist, and still unsure
if Arabs are black . . . no Jew, and thirty years
too old. I loved the country, her briskness, danger,
jolting between salvation and demolition. . . .
Since Moses, the long march over, saw the Mountain
lift its bullet-head past timberline to heaven:
the ways of Israel's God are military;
from X to X, the prophets, unto Marx;
reprisal and terror, voices benumbed in noise;
finally, no one tells us which is which . . .
till arms fuse and sand reverts to chemical,
semper idem and ubique, our God of Hosts.

Israel 3

Morale and teamsoul are hardly what we market
back home; it makes us tired to batter our old car
stalled on the crossroads, heads in, both headlights on
yacking directives like Julius Caesar's missiles.
We have no forum for Roman rhetoricians—
even doubt, the first American virtue,
has drawbacks, it can't cure anything.
Time's dissolutions leave no air to breathe. . . .
Israel is all it had to be, a garrison;
spend ten days there, or as I, three weeks,
you find the best and worst of countries . . . glass,
faith's icicle-point sharpened till invisible.
God finds his country as He always will . . .
nowhere easier than Israel to stand up.

Helen

"I am the azure! come from the underworld,
I hear the serene erosion of the surf;
once more I see our galleys bleed with dawn,
lancing on muffled oarlocks into Troy.
My loving hands recall the absent kings,
(I used to run my fingers through their beards)
Agamemnon drowned in Clytemnestra's bath, Ulysses,
the great gulf boiling sternward from his keel. . . .
I hear the military trumpets, all their brass,
blasting the rhythm to the frantic oars,
the rowers' metronome enchains the sea.
High on beaked vermillion prows, the gods,
their fixed archaic smiles smarting with salt,
reach out carved, indulgent arms to me."

Achilles to the dying Lykaon

"Float with the fish, they'll clean your wounds, and lick
away your blood, and have no care of you;
nor will your mother wail beside your pyre
as you swirl down the Skamander to the sea,
but the dark shadows of the fish will shiver,
lunge and snap Lykaon's silver fat.
Trojans, you will perish till I reach Troy—
you'll run in front, I'll scythe you down behind;
nor will your Skamander, though whirling and silver, save you,
though you kill sheep and bulls, and drown a thousand
one-hoofed horse, still living. You must die
and die and die and die and die—
till the blood of my Patroklos is avenged,
killed by the wooden ships while I was gone."

Cassandra 1

"Such clouds, rainbows, pink rainstorms, bright green hills,
churches coming and going through the rain,
or wrapped in pale greenish cocoons of mist—
so crazy I snapped my lighter to see the sun.
Famine's joy is the enjoyment. Who'll deny
the crash, delirious uterus living it up?
In the end we may see all things in a glance,
like speed-up reading; but tell me what is love?
I don't mind someone finding someone better—
I was doomed in Troy with my sister Polyxena
and Achilles who fought to their deaths through love—
Paris saw Achilles' vulnerable tendon . . .
a lover will always turn his back. Why did Paris
kill our sister with Achilles while he had her?"

Cassandra 2

"Nothing less needed than a girl shining a mirror
darkening with the foliage of May,
waiting the miracle of the polishing winds. . . .
I was not wise, or unique in any skill;
not unreasonably, Zeus became my enemy,
I knew God's shadow for the coming night;
I saw in the steam of the straw the barn would burn.
I did not wish to save myself by running.
Does Agamemnon lying in our blood remember
my pointed fingers painted with red ink,
the badge of my unfulfilled desire to be,
the happiness of the drop to die in the river—
how I, a slave, followed my king on the red carpet? . . .
The wave of the wineglass trembled to see me walk."

Orestes' Dream

"As I sleep, our saga comes out clarified:
why for three weeks mother toured the countryside,
buying up earthenware, big pots and urns,
barbarous potsherds, such as the thirsty first
archaeologists broke on their first digs . . . not *our* art—
kingly the clay, common the workmanship.
For three weeks mother's lover kept carving
chess-sets, green leaf, red leaf, as tall as urns,
modern Viking design for tribal Argos. . . .
When Agamemnon, my father, came home at last,
he was skewered and held bubbling like an ox,
his eyes crossed in the great strain of the heat—
my mother danced with a wicker bullshead by his urn.
Can I call the police against my own family?"

Clytemnestra 1

"After my marriage, I found myself in constant
companionship with this almost stranger I found
neither agreeable, interesting, nor admirable,
though he was always kind and irresponsible.
The first years after our first child was born,
his daddy was out at sea; that helped, I could bask
on the couch of inspiration and my dreams.
Our courtship was rough, his disembarkation
unwisely abrupt. I was animal,
healthy, easily tired; I adored luxury,
and should have been an extrovert; I usually
managed to make myself pretty comfortable. . . .
Well," she laughed, "we both were glad to dazzle.
A genius temperament should be handled with care."

Clytemnestra 2

"O Christmas tree, how green thy branches—our features
could only be the most conventional,
the hardwood smile, the Persian rug's abstraction,
the firelight dancing in the Christmas candles,
my unusual offspring with his usual scowl,
spelling the fifty feuding kings of Greece,
with a red, blue and yellow pencil. . . . I
am seasick with marital unhappiness—
I am become the eye of heaven, and hate
my husband swimming like vagueness, like a porpoise,
in the imperial purple of his heart. . . .
He now lies dead beneath the torches like a lion,
he is like the rich golden collection-plate,
O Christmas tree, how green thy branches were . . ."

Clytemnestra 3

No folly could secularize the sacred cow,
our Queen at sixty worked in bed like Balzac.
Sun, moon and stars lay hidden in the cornstalk,
where she moved she left her indelible sunset.
She had the lower jaw of a waterbuffalo,
the weak intelligence, the iron will.
In one night boys fell senile in her arms. . . .
Later, something unsavory took place:
Orestes, the lord of murder and proportion,
saw the tips of her nipples had touched her toes—
a population problem and bad art.
He knew the monster must be guillotined.
He saw her knees tremble and he enjoyed the sight,
knowing that Trojan chivalry was shit.

White Goddess

"I'm scratchy, I don't wear these torpedoes
spliced to my chest for you to lift and pose. . . .
As a girl, I had crushes on our Amazons;
after our ten hour hikes, I snorted ten hours
or more, I had to let my soul catch up—
men will never, I thought, catch up with such women. . . .
In the götterdämmerung of the Paris Opera,
I met my Goddess, a Gold Coast negro singing
Verdi's *Desdemona* in the ebbing gold.
When Othello strangled her, she died, then bowed,
saying with noble shyness, 'I appreciate
your co-operation with my shortcomings.
I wish you the love of God, and a friend . . .'
I never met a woman I couldn't make."

Ikhnaton and the One God

The mother-sobs of Hera who knows that any
woman must love her husband more than her,
constantly hated though inconstantly loved—
man thought twice about making marriage legal;
men triumphed, made a mangod; he was single,
a sapling who breathed refreshment from a flower,
its faded petals the color of fresh wood—
no tyrant, just a mediocre student,
his rule has the new broom and haste of the One God,
Ikhnaton with spikes of the gold sun in his hair.
The Jews found hope in his Egypt, the King's plan a small thing,
as if one were both drowning and swimming at the same time . . .
the *it-must-be* on the small child's grave:
"Say, Passerby, that man is born to die."

Aswan Dam

Had Pharaoh's servants slaved like Nasser's labor,
Egyptian manhood under Russian foremen,
the pyramid. . . . I saw the Russians and imagined
they did more tangible work in a day than all Egypt. . . .
Dr. Mohammed Abdullah Fattah al Kassas
fears the Dam will slow the downstream current,
dunes and sandbars no longer build up buffers
along the Delta and repulse the sea—
the Mediterranean will drown a million farms,
wild water hyacinths evaporate Lake Nasser,
snails with wormlike bloodflukes slide incurably
to poison five hundred miles of new canals. . . .
Rake-sailed boats have fished the fertile Nile;
Pharaoh's death-ship come back against the shore.

Down the Nile

Two in the afternoon. The restlessness.
Greek Islands. Maine. I have counted the catalogue
of ships down half its length, the beaks of the bowsprits. . . .
Yet sometimes the Nile is wet, and life's as painted:
those couples, one in love and marriage, swaying
their children and their slaves the height of children,
supple and gentle as giraffes or newts;
the waist still willowy, the paint still fresh;
decorum without conforming, no harness on
the woman, and no armor on her husband,
the red clay master with his feet of clay
catwalking lightly to his conquests, leaving
one model and dynasties of faithless copies—
we aging downstream faster than a scepter can check.

Sheep

But we must remember our tougher roots:
forerunners bent in hoops to the broiling soil,
until their backs were branded with the coin
of Alexander, God or Caesar—
as if they'd been stretched on burning chicken wire,
skin cooked red and hard as rusted tin
by the footlights of the sun—tillers of the desert!
Think of them, afraid of violence,
afraid of anything, timid as sheep
hidden in some casual, protective crevice,
held twelve dynasties to a burning-glass,
pressed to the levelled sandbreast of the Sphinx—
what were once identities simplified
to a single, indignant, collusive grin.

Sappho to a Girl

I set this man before the gods and heroes—
he sits all day before you face to face,
like a cardplayer. Your elbow brushes his elbow;
when you speak he hears you and your laughter
is water hurrying over the clear stones. . . .
If I see you a moment it's hollowness;
you are the fairest thing on this dark earth.
I cannot speak, I cannot see—
a dead whiteness trickling pinpricks of sweat.
I am greener than the greenest green grass—
I die. I can easily make you understand me—
a woman is seldom enslaved by what is best;
her servants, her children, the daily household ache—
the moon slides west, the Pleiades; I sleep alone.

The Spartan Dead at Thermopylae

A friend or wife is usually right I think
in her particular fear, though not in general—
who told the Spartans at Thermopylae
that their death was coming with the dawn?
That morning Xerxes poured wine to the rising sun . . .
in his army many men, but few soldiers,
it was not a god who threatened Greece but man. . . .
Leonidas and his three hundred hoplites
glittering with liberation, combed one another's
golden Botticellian hair at the Pass—
friends and lovers, the bride beside the bridegroom—
and moved into position to die.
Stranger, take this message to the Spartans:
"We lie here obedient to your laws."

Xerxes and Alexander

Xerxes sailed the slopes of Mount Athos (such
the lies of poets) and paved the sea with ships;
his chariots rolled down a boulevard of decks,
breakfasting Persians drank whole rivers dry—
but tell us how this King of Kings returned
from Salamis in a single ship
scything for searoom through his own drowned. . . .
One world was much too small for Alexander,
double-marching to gain the limits of the globe,
as if he were a runner at Marathon;
early however he reached the final goal,
his fatal Babylon walled with frail dry brick.
A grave was what he wanted. Death alone
shows us what tedious things our bodies are.

Alexander

His sweet moist eye missed nothing—the vague guerilla,
new ground, new tactics, the time for his hell-fire drive,
Demosthenes knotting his nets of dialectic—
phalanxes oiled ten weeks before their trial,
engines on oxen for the fall of Tyre—
Achilles . . . in Aristotle's annotated copy—
health burning like the dewdrop on his flesh
hit in a hundred calculated sallies
to give the Persians the cup of love, of brothers—
the wine-bowl of the Macedonian drinking bout . . .
drinking out of friendship, then meeting Medius,
then drinking, then bathing, then sleeping, then meeting Medius,
then drinking, then bathing . . . dead at thirty-two—
in this life only is our hope in Christ.

Death of Alexander

The young man's numinous eye is like the sun,
for three days the Macedonian soldiers pass;
speechless, he knows them as if they were his sheep.
Shall Alexander be carried in the temple
to pray there, and perhaps, recover? But
the god forbids it, "It's a better thing
if the king stay where he is." He soon dies,
this after all, perhaps, the "better thing.". . .
No one was like him. Terrible were his crimes—
but if you wish to blackguard the Great King,
think how mean, obscure and dull you are,
your labors lowly and your merits less—
we know this, of all the kings of old,
he alone had the greatness of heart to repent.

Poor Alexander, poor Diogenes

Alexander extended philosophy
farther than Aristotle or the honest man,
and kept his foot on everything he touched—
no dog stretching at the Indian sun.
Most dogs find liberty in servitude;
but this is a dog who justified his statue—
Diogenes had his niche in the Roman villas
honored as long as Rome could bear his weight—
cunis, cynic, dog, Diogenes.
Poor Diogenes growling at Alexander,
"You can do one thing for me, stand out of my sun."
When the schoolboys stole his drinking cup,
he learned to lap up water in his hands—
"No men in Athens . . . only Spartan boys."

The Republic

Didn't Plato ban philosopher-professors,
the idols of the young, from the Republic?
And diehard republicans? It wasn't just
the artist. The Republic! But it never was,
except in the sky-ether of Plato's thought,
steam from the horsedung of his city-state—
Utopia dimmed before the blueprint dried. . . .
America planned one . . . Herman Melville
fixed at that helm, facing a pot of coals,
the sleet and wind spinning him ninety degrees:
"I must not give me up then to the fire,
lest it invert my fire; it blinded me,
so did it me." There's a madness that is woe,
and there is a wisdom that is madness.

Rome

Rome asked for the sun, as much as arms can handle—
liquidation with principle, the proconsul's
rapidity, coherence, and royal *we*. . . .
Thus General Sulla once, again, forever;
and Marius, the people's soldier, was Sulla
doubled, and held the dirt of his low birth
as licence from the gods to thin the rich—
both pulled pistols when they heard foreign tongues,
praised defoliation of the East. . . .
Their faith was lowly, and their taxes high.
The emperor was killed, his métier lived—
Constantine died in office thanks to God.
Whether we buy less or more has long
since fallen to the archeologist's pick.

Hannibal 1. Roman Disaster at the Trebia

The dawn of an ill day whitens the heights.
The camp wakes. Below, the river grumbles and rolls,
and light Numidian horsemen water their horses;
everywhere, sharp clear blasts of the trumpeters.
Though warned by Scipio, and the lying augurs,
the Trebia in flood, the blowing rain,
the Consul Sempronius, proud of his new glory,
has raised the axe for battle, he marches his lictors.
A gloomy flamboyance reddens the dull sky,
Gallic villages smoulder on the horizon.
Far off, the hysterical squeal of an elephant. . . .
Down there, below a bridge, his back on the arch,
Hannibal listens, thoughtful, glorying,
to the dead tramp of the advancing Roman legions.

Hannibal 2. The Life

Throw Hannibal on the scales, how many pounds
does the First Captain come to? This is he
who found the plains of Africa too small,
and Ethiopia's elephants a unique species.
He scaled the Pyrenees, the snow, the Alps—
nature blocked his road, he derricked mountains. . . .
Now Italy is his. "Think nothing is done,
till Rome cracks and my standards fly in the Forum."
What a face for a painter; look, he's a one-eye.
The glory? He's defeated like the rest,
serves some small tyrant farting off drunken meals . . .
and dies by taking poison. . . . Go, Madman, cross
the Alps, the Tiber—be a purple patch
for schoolboys, and their theme for declamation.

Marcus Cato 234–149 B.C.

My live telephone swings crippled to solitude
two feet from my ear; as so often and so often,
I hold your dialogue away to breathe—
still this is love, Old Cato forgoing his wife,
then jumping her in thunderstorms like *Juppiter Tonans*;
his forthrightness gave him long days of solitude,
then deafness changed his gifts for rule to genius.
Cato knew from the Greeks that empire is hurry,
and dominion never goes to the phlegmatic—
it was hard to be Demosthenes in his stone-deaf Senate:
"Carthage must die," he roared . . . and Carthage died.
He knew a blindman looking for gold
in a heap of dust must take the dust with the gold,
Rome, if built at all, must be built in a day.

Marcus Cato 95–46 B.C.

As a boy he was brought to Sulla's villa, The Tombs,
saw people come in as men, and leave as heads.
"Why hasn't someone killed him?" he asked. They answered,
"Men fear Sulla even more than they hate him."
He asked for a sword, and wasn't invited back. . . .
He drowned Plato in wine all night with his friends,
gambled his life in the forum, was stoned like Paul,
and went on talking till soldiers saved the State,
saved Caesar. . . . At the last cast of his lost Republic,
he bloodied his hand on the slave who hid his sword;
he fell in a small sleep, heard the dawn birds chirping,
but couldn't use his hand well . . . when they tried to put
his bowels back, he tore them. . . . He's where he would be:
one Roman who died, perhaps, for Rome.

Horace: Pardon for a Friend

"Under the consulship of Marcus Brutus,
Citizen! We lived out Phillipi, the stampede
when two Republican legions broke like women,
and I threw away my little shield.
Minerva must have helped me to escape;
Pompey, the wave of battle sucked you under,
carried you bleeding in the frantic ebb—
to exile . . . and pardon. What brings you back to Rome,
our glum gods, our hot African sky?
Let us give this banquet to the gods—
do not spare the winejar at your feet.
We'll twist red roses in our myrtle garlands,
it's sweet to drink to fury when my friend is safe—
throw down the dice, and then throw down the dice."

Cicero, the Sacrificial Killing

It's somewhere, somewhere, thought beats stupidly—
a scarlet patch of Tacitus or the Bible,
Pound's Cantos lost in the rockslide of history?
The great man flees his greatness, fugitive husk
of Cicero or Marius without a toga,
old sheep sent out to bite the frosty stubble.
The Republic froze and fattened its high ranks,
the Empire was too much brass for what we are;
who asks for legions to bring the baby milk?
Cicero bold, garrulous in his den
chatting as host on his sofa of magazines;
a squad of state doctors stands by him winking . . .
he minds his hands shaking, and they keep shaking;
if infirmity has a color, it isn't yellow.

Ovid and Caesar's Daughter

"I was a modern, and in Caesar's eye,
a tomcat with the number of the Beast—
now buried where Turkey faces the red east,
or wherever Tomi my place of exile was.
Rome asked for art in earnest; at her call
came Lucan, Tacitus and Juvenal,
the black republicans who tore the tits
and bowels of the Mother Wolf to bits. . . .
Thieves pick gold
from the fine print and volume of the Colossus.
Because I loved and wrote too profligately,
Imperial Tiber, O my yellow Wolf,
black earth by the Black Roman Sea, I lie
libelled with the boy-crazy daughter of

Caesar Augustus who will never die."

Antony

"The headache, the night of no performance, duskbreak:
limping home by the fountain's Dionysiac gushes,
water smote from marble, the felon water,
the watery alcoholic going underground
to a stone wife. . . . We were an empire, soul-brothers
to Rome and Alexandria, their imperishable
hope to go beyond the growth of hope.
Am I your only lover who always died?
We were right to die instead of doing nothing,
fearfully backstepping in the dark night of lust.
My hand is shaking, and your breasts are breathing,
white bull's eyes, watchful knobs, in cups of tan
flat on the leather and horn of Jupiter—
daring to raise my privates to the Godhead."

Antony and Cleopatra

Our righteous rioters once were revelers,
and had the ear and patronage of kings:
if the king were Antony, he gave
army escorts, and never lost a servant.
At daybreak he fell from heaven to his bed:
next day he handled his winehead like old wine;
yet would notice the fleece of the cirrus, gold, distant,
maidenhair burning heaven's blue nausée,
and knew he lacked all substance: "If I could cure
by the Nile's green slot, a leaf of green papyrus—
I'll taste, God willing, the imperial wine no more,
nor thirst for Cleopatra in my sleep."
"You will drink the Nile to desert," she thinks.
"If God existed, this prayer would prove he didn't."

Cleopatra Topless

"If breast-feeding is servile and for the mammals,
the best breasts in the nightclub are fossils—
a single man couldn't go nearer than the bar;
by listing, I felt the rotations of her breeze;
dancing, she flickered like the family hearth.
She was the old foundation of western marriage. . . .
One was not looking for a work of art—
what do men want? Boobs, bottoms, legs . . . in that order—
the one thing necessary that most husbands
want and yet forgo. She's Cleopatra,
no victim of strict diet, but fulfilment—
chicken turtle climbing up the glass,
managing her invertebrae like hands—
the body of man's crash-love, and her affliction."

Nunc est bibendum, Cleopatra's Death

Nunc est bibendum, nunc pede liberum
the time to drink and dance the earth in rhythm.
Before this it was infamous to banquet,
while Cleopatra plotted to enthrone
her depravity naked in the Capitol—
impotent, yet drunk on fortune's favors!
Caesar has tamed your soul, you see with a
now sober eye the scowling truth of terror—
O Cleopatra scarcely escaping with a single ship
Caesar, three decks of oars—O scarcely escaping
when the sparrowhawk falls on the soft-textured dove. . . .
You found a more magnanimous way to die,
not walking on foot in triumphant Caesar's triumph,
no queen now, but a private woman much humbled.

Caligula 1

"I am like the king of a rain-country, rich
though sterile, young but no longer spry enough
to kill vacation in boredom with my dogs—
nothing cheers me, drugs, nieces, falconry,
my triple bed with coral Augustan eagles—
my patrician maids in waiting for whom
all princes are beautiful cannot put on
low enough dresses to heat my skeleton.
The doctor pounding pearls to medicine
finds no formula to cleanse a poisoned vein.
Not even our public happiness sealed with blood,
our tyrant's solace in senility,
great Caesar's painkiller, can strengthen my blood,
green absinthe of forgetfulness, not blood."

Caligula 2

My namesake, Little Boots, Caligula,
tell me why I got your name at school—
Item: your body hairy, badly made,
head hairless, smoother than your marble head;
Item: eyes hollow, hollow temples, red
cheeks roughed with blood, legs spindly, hands that leave
a clammy snail's trail on your scarlet sleeve,
your hand no hand could hold . . . bald head, thin neck—
you wished the Romans had a single neck.
That was no artist's sadism. Animals
ripened for your arenas suffered less
than you when slaughtered—yours the lawlessness
of something simple that has lost its law,
my namesake, not the last Caligula.

Empress Messalina's last Bridegroom

Tell me what advice you have to give
the fellow Caesar's consort wants to marry—
the last man, the most beautiful an old
patrician family has to offer . . . soon turned
from life to death by Messalina's eye.
She has long been seated, her bridal veil
is purple, her lover's bed of imperial roses
rustles invitingly, quite openly, in the garden—
now by ancient rule, her dowry of a million
sesterces is counted out—signatories,
lawyers, the green-lipped diviner, attend on tiptoe. . . .
"Say no, you'll die before the lamps are lit.
Say yes, you'll live till the city hears . . . her husband,
the Emperor Claudius last in Rome to know."

Weekly Juvenal, Late-Empire

In the days of Saturn, so he wrote,
Chastity still lingered on the earth—
a good son, soft-textured, eyes in the back of his head,
with a snobbish tassel on his plunger,
his apocalyptic disappointments
sobbing thunder for his melting caste—
poets' jamble-jangle to make confused thought deep . . .
Roma Meretrix, in your sick day
only women had the hearts of men.
Marx, a Juvenal in apotheosis, thought
the poor were Saturnians shaking us from below—
his romantic alchemy. He had no answer—
tomorrow-yesterday the world was young,
and parents had no children of their own.

Juvenal's Prayer

What's best, what serves us . . . leave it to the gods.
We're dearer to the gods than to ourselves.
Harassed by impulse and diseased desire,
we ask for wives, and children by those wives—
what wives and children heaven only knows.
Still if you will ask for something, pray for
a healthy body and a healthy soul,
a mind that is not terrified of death,
thinks length of days the least of nature's gifts—
courage that drives out anger and longing . . . our hero,
Hercules, and the pain of his great labor. . . .
Success is worshipped as a god; it's we
who set her up in palace and cathedral.
I give you simply what you have already.

Vita Brevis

The whistling arrow flies less eagerly,
and bites the bullseye less ferociously;
the Roman chariot grinds the docile sand
of the arena less violently to round the post. . . .
How silently, how hurriedly, we run
through life to die. You doubt this, animal
blinded by the light? Each ascending sun
dives like a cooling meteorite to its fall,
Licio. Did dead Carthage affirm what you deny?
Death only throws fixed dice, yet you will raise
the ante, and stake your life on every toss.
Those hours will hardly pardon us their loss,
those brilliant hours that wore away our days,
our days that ate into eternity.

The Good Life

To see their trees flower and leaves pearl with mist,
fan out above them on the wineglass elms,
life's frills and the meat of life: wife, children, houses;
decomposition burning out in service—
or ass-licking for medals on Caesar's peacock lawn,
tossing birdseed to enslaved aristocrats,
vomiting purple in the vapid baths.
Crack legions and new religions hold the Eagle—
Rome of the officers, dull, martyred, anxious to please.
Men might ask how her imperial machine,
never pleasant and a hail of gallstone,
keeps beating down its Caesars raised for murder,
though otherwise forgotten . . . pearls in the spiked necklace—
the price of slavery is ceaseless vigilance.

Rome in the Sixteenth Century

You come to Rome to look for Rome, O Pilgrim!
in Christian Rome there is no room for Rome,
the Aventine is its own mound and tomb;
her Capitol that crowned the forum rubble,
a laid out corpse her smart brick walls she boasted of;
her medals filed down by the hand of time
say more was lost to chance and time
than Hannibal or Caesar could consume.
Only the Tiber has remained, a small
shallow current which used to wash a city,
and now bewails her sepulcher. O Rome!
from all your senates, palms, dominions, bronze
and beauty, what was firm has fled. Whatever
was fugitive maintains its permanence.

Attila, Hitler

Hitler had fingertips of apprehension,
"Who knows how long I'll live? Let us have war.
We *are* the barbarians, the world is near the end."
Attila mounted on raw meat and greens
galloped to massacre in his single fieldmouse suit,
he never left a house that wasn't burning,
could only sleep on horseback, sinking deep
in his rural dream. Would he have found himself
in this coarsest, cruelest, least magnanimous,
most systematic, most philosophical . . .
a nomad stay-at-home: *He who has, has*;
a barbarian wondering why the old world collapsed,
who also left his festering fume of refuse,
old tins, dead vermin, ashes, eggshells, youth?

Mohammed

Like Henry VIII, Mohammed got religion
in the dangerous years, and smashed the celibates,
haters of life, though never takers of it—
changed their monasteries to foundries,
reset their non-activist Buddhistic rote
to the *schrecklichkeit* and warsongs of his tribe.
The Pope still twangs his harp for chastity—
the boys of the jihad on a string of unwitting camels
rush paradise, halls stocked with adolescent
beauties, both sexes for simple nomad tastes—
how warmly they sleep in tile-abstraction alcoves;
love is resurrection, and her war a rose:
woman wants man, man woman, as naturally
as the thirsty frog desires the rain.

Fame

We bleed for people, so independent and selfsuspecting,
if the door is locked, they come back tomorrow, instead of knocking—
hearts scarred by complaints they would not breathe;
it was not their good fortune to meet their love;
however long they lived, they would still be waiting.
They knew princes show kindness by humiliation. . . .
Timur said something like: "The drop of water
that fails to become a river is food for the dust.
The eye that cannot size up the Bosphorus
in a single drop is an acorn, not the eye of a man. . . ."
Timur's face was like the sun on a dewdrop;
the path to death was always under his foot—
this the sum of the world's scattered elements,
fame, a bouquet in the niche of forgetfulness.

Timur Old

To wake some midnight, on that instant senile,
clasping clay knees . . . in this unwarlike posture
meet your grandsons, a sheeted, shivering mound,
pressed racecar hideously scared, agog with headlight—
Timur . . . his pyramid half a million heads,
one skull and then one brick and then one skull,
live art that makes the Arc de Triomphe pale.
Even a modernist must be new at times,
not a parasite on his own tradition,
its too healthy sleep that foreshadows death.
A thing well done, even a pile of heads
modestly planned to wilt before the builder,
is art, if art is anything won from nature. . . .
We weep for the sword as much as for the victims—

fealty affirmed when friendship was a myth.

Northmen

These people were provincials with the wind
behind them, and a gently swelling birthrate,
scattering galleys and their thin crews
of pirates from Greenland to the lung of the Thames. . . .
The Skyfleets hover coolly in mirage;
our bombers are clean-edged as Viking craft,
to pin the Third World to its burning house. . . .
Charlemagne loved his three R's, and feared the future
when he saw the first Northmen row out on the Rhine:
we are begotten in sorrow to die in joy—
their humor wasn't brevity but too few words,
ravishment trailing off in the midnight sun,
illumination, then bewilderment,
the glitter of the Viking in the icecap.

End of the Saga

"Even if they murder the whole world,
we'll hit them so hard, they'll never tell the story."
Kriemhild was shouting, "If they get to the air,
and cool their coats of mail, we will be lost."
When the great hall was fired, we saw them kneel
beside their corpses, and drink the flowing blood—
unaccustomed to such drink, they thought it good,
in the great heat, it tasted cooler than wine.
They tried to lift their brothers from the fire,
they found them too hot to hold, and let them drop.
"O why are we so wet with our lifeblood?
Beines brichts, herzen nichts. . . ."
Kriemhild on horseback laughs at them, as well she may,
the house is burned, and all her enemies killed.

Death of Count Roland

King Marsilius of Saragossa
does not love God, he is carried to the shade of the orchard,
and sits reclining on his bench of blue tile,
with more than twenty thousand men about him;
his speech is only the one all kings must make,
it did to spark the Franco-Moorish War. . . .
At war's end Roland's brains seeped from his ears;
he called for the Angel Michael, his ivory horn,
prayed for his peers, and scythed his sword, Durendal—
farther away than a man might shoot a crossbow,
toward Saragossa, there is a grassy place,
Roland went to it, climbed the little mound:
a beautiful tree there, four great stones of marble—
on the green grass, he has fallen back, has fainted.

Eloise and Abelard

We know what orthodox analysis
could do with her, the talented, the taloned
cat hooked on the cold fish of Abelard.
They were one soul, but now her mind is dust,
and his assaulted ember is extinct.
After his imprisonment, energy came
to the woman such as she had never known,
sprinkling Paris like a fresh flow of blood,
old Sorbonne argot, shit on Saint Bernard
in love with his voice and sold to the police. . . .
Abelard's tortured debater's points
once flew to the mark, feathered with her ecstasy,
and stamping students, then he fell like lightning,
in love with *the dialectic*, his Minerva.

Joinville and Louis IX

"Given my pilgrim's scarf and staff, I left
the village of Joinville on foot, barefoot, in my shirt,
never turning my eyes for fear my heart would melt
at leaving my mortgaged castle, my two fair children—
a Crusader? Some of us were, and lived to be ransomed.
Bishops, nobles, and Brothers of the King
strolled free in Acre, and begged the King to sail home,
and leave the meaner folk. Sore of heart then,
I went to a barred window, and passed my arms through the bars
of the window, and someone came, and leant on my shoulders,
and placed his two hands on my forehead—Philip de Nemours?
I screamed, 'Leave me in peace!' His hand dropped by chance,
and I knew the King by the emerald on his finger:
'If I should leave Jerusalem, who will remain?' "

The Army of the Duc de Nemours

Yeats anxiously warned us not to lend a high
degree of reality to the Great War.
There are wars and wars, and some are high-notes
on the scale of sexual delirium
running the gamut of Moses' anathemas:
wantonness, sodomy, bestiality.
I am a Catholic because I am a wanton.
Italian mercenaries besieging Lyons
for the Duc de Nemours huzzaed great flocks
of goats before them—no billies, two thousand udders
decked out in green sportcoats fringed with gold.
They served a sound man for a mistress. Small war,
one far distant from our army mascots—
but who will tell us now what Lyons paid?

Dante 1

In his dark day, Dante made the mistake of treating
politicians as if they belonged to life,
not ideology. In his Vision
his poor souls eclipse the black and white of God.
A man running for his life will never tire:
his Ser Brunetto ran through hell like one
who ran for the green cloth through the green fields
at Verona, looking more like one
who won the roll of cloth, than those who lost. . . .
All comes from a girl met at the wrong time,
losing her color as she fared and brightened;
God and her love called Dante forth to exile
in midwintertime cold and lengthening days,
when the brief field frost mimics her sister, snow.

Dante 2

Torn darlings and professional sparring partners,
will we ever grow wiser or kinder in
the exercise of marriage—its death
like this summer landscape chilling under
the first influence of the evening star
winking from green to black—our bodies, black
before we even know that we are dead.
Dante loved Beatrice beyond her life,
with a loyalty outside anywhere;
all icy pandemonium . . . a girl
too early his enchanter and too late,
the hour half-over when every star was shining—
lightning piercing his marriage's slow fire,
some brightest prong, antennae of an ant.

Dante 3. Buonconte

"No one prays for me . . . Giovanna or the others."
What took you so far from Campaldino
we never found your body? "Where the Archiano
at the base of the Casentino loses its name
and becomes the Arno, I stopped running,
the war lost, and wounded in the throat—
flying on foot and splashing the field with blood.
There I lost sight and speech, and died saying *Maria*. . . .
I'll tell you the truth, tell it to the living,
an angel and devil fought with claws for my soul:
You angel, why do you rob me for his last word?
The rain fell, then the hail, my body froze,
until the raging Archiano snatched me,
and loosened my arms I'd folded like the cross."

Dante 4. Paolo and Francesca

And she to me, "What sorrow is greater to us
than returning from misery to the sweet time?
If you will know the first root of our love,
I'll speak as one who must both speak and weep.
On that day we were reading for dalliance
of Lancelot, and how love brought him down;
we were alone there and without suspicion,
often something we read made our eyes meet—
we lost color. A single moment destroyed us: reading
how her loved smile was kissed by such a lover.
He who never will be divided from me
came to me trembling, and kissed my shaking mouth.
That book and he who wrote it was a bawd,
a Galahalt. That day we read no further."

Dante 5. Wind

The night blowing through the world's hospital is human,
Francesca's strife and monotony blown
by the folly of Christendom that loathed her flesh—
seed winds, the youthful breath of the old world,
each a progression of our carnal pleasure
and a firm extension of the soul. . . .
The girl has been rowing her boat since early morning,
hard riding has never blistered her agile thighs.
The snail, a dewdrop, stumbles like the blind,
puts out his little horns to feel the sun.
In the garden of Allah, man still wears the beard,
the women are undressed, accepting love. . . .
They loved if one or two days of life meant much,
then an eternity of failed desire—

winds fed the fire, a wind can blow it out.

Canterbury

Regret those jousting aristocracies,
war-bright, though sportsmen, life a round of games;
sex horsed their chivalry, even when
the aggressor was only an artless dragon. . . .
The Black Prince clamps a missal in his hands,
rests, stone-chainmail, *imprimatur*, on his slab;
behind the spasms of his ruffian hand,
slept a public school and pious faith in murder—
gallantry sobered by suppression.
At Canterbury a guilty pilgrim may ask:
"Have I the right to my imagination?"
Here the great fighter Captain lies with those
who made it, those whom fate disdained to wound.
All's masonry . . . theirs the new day, as the old.

Coleridge and Richard II

Coleridge wasn't flatter-blinded by
his kinship with Richard II . . . a *feminine friendism*,
the constant overflow of imagination
proportioned to his dwindling will to act.
Richard unkinged saw shipwreck in the mirror,
not the King; womanlike, he feared
he must see himself more frequently to exist,
the white glittering inertia of the iceberg.
Coleridge had the cheering fancy only blacks
would cherish slavery for two thousand years;
though most negroes in 1800 London were
onwardlooking and further exiled
from the jungle of dead kings than Coleridge,
the one poet who blamed his failure on himself.

Dames du Temps Jadis

Say in what country, where
is Flora, the Roman,
Archipaida or Thais
far lovelier,
or Echo whose voice would answer
across the land or river—
her beauty more than human.
Where is our wise Eloise
and Peter Abelard
gelded at Saint Denis
for love of her—
Jehanne the good maid of Lorraine
the English burned at Rouen?
Where, mother of God, is last year's snow?

Bosworth Field

In a minute, two inches of rain stream through my dry
garden stones, clear as crystal, without trout—
we have gone down and down, gone the wrong brook.
Robespierre and Stalin mostly killed people they knew,
Richard the Third was Dickon, Duke of Gloucester,
long arm of the realm, goddam blood royal,
terrible underpinning of what he let breathe.
No wonder, we have dug him up past proof,
still fighting drunk on mortal wounds,
ready to gallop down his own apologist.
What does he care for Thomas More and Shakespeare
pointing fingers at his polio'd body;
for the moment, he is king; he is the king
saying: *it's better to have lived, than live.*

Cow

The moon is muffled behind a ledge of cloud,
briefly douses its bonfire on the harbor. . . .
Machiavelli despised those spuriously fought
Italian mounted-mercenary battles;
Corinthian tactics, Greek met Greek; one death,
he died of a stroke, but not the stroke of battle.
The Italians were not diehards even for peace—
our police hit more to terrorize than kill;
clubs break and minds, women hosed down stairs—
am I crippled for life? . . . A cow has guts,
screwed, she lives for it as much as we,
a three-day mother, then a working mother;
the calf goes to the calfpool. . . . When their barn has been burned,
cows will look into the sunset and tremble.

Sir Thomas More

Holbein's More, my patron saint as a convert,
the gold chain of *S*'s, the golden rose,
the plush cap, the brow's damp feathertips of hair,
the good eyes' stern, facetious twinkle, ready
to turn from executioner to martyr—
or saunter with the great King's bluff arm on your neck,
feeling that friend-slaying, terror-dazzled heart
ballooning off into its awful dream—
a noble saying, "How the King must love you!"
And you, "If it were a question of my head,
or losing his meanest village in France . . ."
then by the scaffold and the headsman's axe—
"Friend, give me your hand for the first step,
as for coming down, I'll shift for myself."

Anne Boleyn

The cows of Potter and Albert Cuyp are timeless;
in the depths of Europe, scrawly pastures
and scrawlier hamlets unwatered by paint or Hegel,
the cow is king. None of our rear-guard painters,
lovers of nature and haters of abstraction,
make an art of farming. With a bull's moist eye,
dewlap and misty phallus, Cuyp caught the farthest glisten,
tonnage and rumination of the sod. . . .
There was a whiteness to Anne Boleyn's throat,
shiver of heresy, *raison d'état*,
the windfall abandon of a Giorgione,
Renaissance high hand with nature—only the lovely,
the good, the wealthy serve the Venetian, whose art
knows nothing yet of husbandry and cattle.

Death of Anne Boleyn

Summer hail flings crystals on the window—
they wrapped the Lady Anne's head in a white handkerchief. . . .
To Wolsey, *the nightcrow*, but to Anthony Froude,
stoic virtue spoke from her stubborn lips and chin—
five adulteries in three years of marriage;
the game was hotly charged. "I hear say I'll
not die till noon; I am very sorry therefore,
I thought to be dead this hour and past my pain."
Her jailer told her that beheading was no pain—
"It is subtle." "I have a little neck,"
she said, and put her hands about it laughing.
They guessed she had much pleasure and joy in death—
no foreigners admitted. By the King's abundance
the scene was open to any Englishman.

Cranach's Man-Hunt

Composed, you will say, for our forever friendship,
almost one arm around our many shoulders,
a cloud darkens the stream of the photograph,
friends bound by birth and faith . . . one German outing.
We are game for the deer-hunt, aged five to ninety,
seniority no key to who will die
on this clearing of blown, coarse grass, a trap in the landscape,
a green bow in the bend of a choppy, lavender stream,
eighteen or nineteen of us, bounding, swimming—
stags and does . . . the Kaiser Maximilian
and the wise Saxon Elector, screened by one clump,
winch their crossbows . . . the horsemen, picadors,
whipped to action by their beautiful, verminous dogs . . .
this battle the Prince has never renounced or lost.

Charles V by Titian

But we cannot go back to Charles V
barreled in armor, more gold fleece than king;
he haws on the gristle of a Flemish word,
his upper and lower Hapsburg jaws won't meet.
The sunset he tilts at is big Venetian stuff,
the true Charles, done by Titian, never lived.
The battle he rides offstage to is offstage.
No St. Francis, he did what Francis shied at,
gave up office, one of twenty monarchs
since Saturn who willingly made the grand refusal.
In his burgherish monastery, he learned he couldn't
put together a clock with missing parts.
He had dreamed of a democracy of Europe,
and carried enemies with him in a cage.

Execution 1
(From Chidiock Tichborne 1568–86)

"I saw the world, and yet I was not seen;
fear comes more often now, and no less sharp
than in the year of my first razor and the death of God.
My tongue thickened as if anesthetized,
and I saw a painted fish blow live bubbles,
the wallpaper flowers drank plaster, turned to moss. . . .
The anachronistic axe sighs in its block;
a little further on, I will be nature,
my head a speck of white salt on a white plate,
lying on call forever, never called. . . .
At the Resurrection, will I start awake,
and find my head upon my shoulders again
singing the dawnless alba of the gerontoi?
Old age is all right, but it has no future."

Execution 2

"Asleep just now, just now I am awake—
my face the jack of hearts on a playing card;
my trousers are too bleached green; my coat wet leaf;
my fair young flesh sky-green of my sad vein.
I turn the card, and I am trees or grass—
last summer for the wondering mind, for seeing
the good servant's green grave outside the pale . . .
veined marble mantel, rolled rug, the sheeted den,
the old master covered with his pillowslip—
I searching as everyman for my one good deed,
crying love lost in my short apprenticeship,
regretting my long-vanished art of breathing,
knowing I must forget how to breathe through my mouth:
now I am dead, and just now I was made."

Marlowe

Vain surety of man's mind so near to death,
twenty-nine years with hopes to total fifty—
one blurred, hurried, still undecoded month
hurled Marlowe from England to his companion shades.
His mighty line denies his shady murder:
"How uncontrollably sweet and swift my life
with two London hits and riding my high tide,
drinking out May in Deptford with three friends,
one or all four perhaps in Secret Service.
Christ was a bastard, His Testament's filthily Greeked—
I died sweating, stabbed with friends who knew me—
was it the bar-check? . . . Tragedy is to die . . .
for that vacant parsonage, Posterity;
my plays are stamped in bronze, my life in tabloid."

Duc de Guise

The grip gets puffy, and water wears the stones—
O to be always young among our friends,
as one of the countless peers who graced the world
with their murders and *joie de vivre*, made good
in a hundred aimless amorous bondages. . . .
The irregular hero, Henri, Duc de Guise,
Pope and Achilles of the Catholic League,
whose canopy and cell I saw at Blois—
just before he died, at the moment of orgasm,
his round eyes, hysterical and wistful,
a drugged bull breathing, a cool, well-pastured brain,
the muscular slack of his stomach swelling
as if he were pregnant . . . his small sword unable
to encircle the circle of his killers.

Mary Stuart

They ran for their lives up nightslope, gained the car,
the girl's maxi-coat, Tsar officer's, dragged the snow,
she and he killed her husband, they stained the snow.
Romance of the snowflakes! Men swam up the night,
grass pike in overalls with scythe and pitchfork;
shouting, "Take the car, we'll smash the girl."
Once kings were on firstname terms with the poor,
a car was a castle, and money belonged to the rich. . . .
They roared off hell-wheel and scattered the weak mob;
happily only one man splashed the windshield,
they dared not pluck him, it was hard at night
to hold to the road with a carcass on the windshield—
at nightmare's end, the bedroom, dark night of marriage,
the bloodiest hands were joined and took no blood.

The Wife of Henri Quatre 1

"O cozy scuffles, soft obscenities,
wardrobes that dragged the exchequer to its knees,
cables of pearl and crazy lutes strung tight—
tension, groin and backbone! Every night
I kicked our pillows and embroidered lies
to famish the King's purse. I said his eyes
flew kiting to my dormer from the blue.
I was a sparrow. He was fifty-two. . . .
Alas, my brutal girlish moodswings drove
my Husband, wrenched and giddy, from the Louvre,
to sleep in single lodgings on the town. . . .
He feared the fate of kings who died in sport;
murder cut him short—
a kitchen-knife honed on a carriage-wheel."

The Wife of Henri Quatre 2

"I show no emotion, king must follow king;
the seasons circle, fall to laughing rings
of scything children. I rock my nightmare son,
I see his dimpled fingers clutch Versailles,
take ball and scepter; he asks the Queen to die.
And so I press a lover's palm to mine,
I am his vintage and his living vine,
oozing, entangling . . . a moment, a moment, a moment—
even a queen must divert her precious time.
Henri Quatre—how you used to look
for blood and pastime! If you ever loved
in this Kingdom where you let your scepter drop,
pardon the easy virtues of the earth. . . .
Your great nerve gone, Sire, sleep without a care."

Malherbe, L'Homme de Lettres

The duplicitous opportunism of
the unreconstructible master of plain French—
giving Horatian balance to your vengeance . . .
fierce and measuring with the best almost,
a winner by tying rivals in the ropes,
verse your chisel to make France a classic.
You took your disciples' measure, and kept them apart,
small enough to sing on the crown of your hat—
lay priest, a friend with bantam gaiety
neither wine or abstraction could corrupt—
your last profession of letters is writing letters,
writing a strayed friend's relenting wife:
"For an atheist Calvinist, you show
depths of compassion reserved the Virgin Mary."

Góngora, the Tomb of Cardinal Sandoval

This chapel that you gaze at, these stern tombs,
the pride of architecture . . . Ah traveller,
diamonds were blunted on this porphyry,
the teeth of files wore smooth as ice—this vault
seals up the dust of one who never let
the earth oppress him. Whose? If you would know,
stay and study this inscription. Words
give marble meaning and a voice to bronze.
Generous devotion binds this urn
with majesty and with propriety
to the heroic ashes of Sandoval,
who left his coat of arms, once five blue stars
on a gold field, to climb with surer step
through the blue sky, and scale the golden stars.

Spain Lost

Miré los muros de la patria mía

I saw the musty shingles of my house,
raw wood in place once, now a wash of moss
eroded by the ruin of the age
turning all fair and green things into waste.
I climbed the pasture. I saw the dim sun drink
the ice just thawing from the bouldered fallow,
scrub crowd the orchard, seize the summer's yield,
and higher up, the sickly cattle bellow.
I went into my house. I saw how dust
and ravel had devoured its furnishing;
even my stick was withered and more bent,
even my sword was coffined up in rust—
there was no hilt left for my hand to try.
Everything ached, and told me I must die.

Rembrandt

His faces crack . . . if mine could crack and breathe!
His Jewish Bridegroom, hand spread on the Jewish Bride's
bashful, tapestried, level bosom, is faithful;
the fair girl, poor background, gives soul to his flayed steer.
Her breasts, the snowdrops, have lasted out the storm.
Often the Dutch were sacks, their women sacks,
the obstinate, undefeated hull of an old scow;
but Bathsheba's ample stomach, her heavy, practical feet,
are reverently dried by the faithful servant,
his eyes dwell lovingly on each fulfilled sag;
her unfortunate body is the privilege of service,
is radiant with an homage void of possession. . . .
We see, if we see at all, through a copper mist
the strange new idol for the marketplace.

Milton in Separation

His wife was no loss to the cool and Christian Homer,
blind, paraphrasing Latin and pronouncing
divorce and *marriage* with hard, sardonic R's.
Through the blank strain of separation, he learned
he only cared for life in the straits. Her flight
put a live elbow in his marble Eve;
she filled a thirst for emptiness—
when she struck, he fell hookloose from her fireflesh,
free to serve what wooed him most, his writing,
the overobsession posterity must pay
on the great day when the eyelids of life lift,
and blind eyes shiver in the draft of heaven,
and goldfinch flame in the tinderbush—
to set the woods on fire and warm the glacier.

Marriage

Once the stoneaxe surrendered its Celt soul,
civilized marriage allowed a day for give-out,
four legs at Bible meeting on the loveseat. . . .
From the womb, I say, I scorned Leviathan,
found my intemperate, apocalyptic terms,
host to ten thousand ethnic sovereignties stuck
with strange tongues; the Garden open to all and free. . . .
Too long we've hungered for its ancient fruit,
marriage with its naked artifice;
two practised animals, and close to widow
and widower, greedily bending forward
for a last handgrasp of vermillion leaves,
clinging like bloodclots to the smitten branch—
fibrous growths . . . green, sweet, golden, black.

Samuel Pepys

A modern, except for double Sunday prayers,
Samuel Pepys knew what made the Navy float,
how to measure the baulks of timber, test hemp
for fray, what cloth could fly the English flag,
what made his wife fray, her butter-fingers with money,
on sufferance with her servants, her screwy periods
timed with her crushes on the Church of Rome.
Pepys was a religious stroller like Charles II,
old music, with no swerving for transcendence.
"Chance without merit brought me in, only work . . ."
He kept a sensual man's respect for sin.
By tears and prayers he cured himself of drink,
but not of glutting a woman with a look—
an inconsequential, not Hermetic, mind.

John Graham at Killiecrankie

"The Scotch Lords had the means to salmon fish,
the painter skill to paint them killing salmon,
sunrise or sunset, gray crag and brawling tarn,
poachers stripped, gashed, parceled to the birds. . . .
If we do not fight, we had better break up and die.
In the Highlands, wherever war is not a science,
we humbly ask for nerve in our commander.
Ours kicked off the one pair of shoes in the clan
to march us barefoot. The British drank the grass;
torrents of their redcoats and tartans raving down
the valley to the gorge of Killiecrankie. . . .
He waved his sword and opened a gap in his breastplate;
he won the battle, lost his life and Scotland.
If it's well with the King, it matters little to me."

Versailles

Smoke weakens the brilliant summer of Versailles;
marijuana fires fume in the King's back yard.
He breathes the green dust of the end of life,
as though he were in heaven—the peacock spins,
the revolution hasn't evolved to the King,
his cubist garden is square and cone and ball,
no imperfection to aid imagination.
Heaven might be this simple if we could go there,
and see the Sun-King spit into the wind of Versailles;
he cannot tell his left hand from his right,
he holds up two smooth stones, marked *left* and *right*. . . .
In the Hall of Mirrors, the heavy curtains lift,
a head higher, two heads, than the old shrunk dying King—
and dance spontaneously in the atheist air.

Peter the Great in France

"He saw us and Paris with open eyes—
no gloves, gold buttons, a brown coat mostly unbuttoned,
his frequent mouth-convulsions frightful to watch . . .
his hat on the table, never on his head,
even outdoors . . . an air of greatness
natural to him could not be mistaken.
What he drank was inconceivable: at meals,
a quart of brandy, two beers, two bottles of wine—
at Fontainebleau he nearly lost his horse.
For side he had a French interpreter,
though he spoke English and Latin like a consul. . . .
Peter, presented to the child Louis Quinze,
hoisted him up to his eye-level, and smiled—
the superiority of age was felt."

Bishop Berkeley

The Bishop's solipsism is clerical,
no one was much imperiled by his life,
except he sailed to New England and was Irish,
he wasn't an Attila or Rimbaud
driven to unhook his skull to crack the world.
He lived with quality, and thought the world
was only perceptions that he could perceive. . . .
In Mexico, I too caused my private earthquake,
and made the earth tremble in the soles of my feet;
a local insurrection of my blood,
its river system saying: I am I,
I am Whitman, I am Berkeley, all men—
calming my feet in a tub of lukewarm water;
the water that scalded one foot froze the other.

The Worst Sinner, Jonathan Edwards' God

The earliest sportsman in the earliest dawn,
waking to what redness, waking a killer,
saw the red cane was sweet in his red grip;
the blood of the shepherd matched the blood of the wolf.
But Jonathan Edwards prayed to think himself
worse than any man that ever breathed;
he was a good man, and he prayed with reason—
which of us hasn't thought his same thought worse?
Each night I lie me down to heal in sleep;
two or three mornings a week, I wake to my sin—
sins, not sin; not two or three mornings, seven.
God himself cannot wake five years younger,
and drink away the venom in the chalice—
the best man in the best world possible.

Watchmaker God

Say life is the one-way trip, the one-way flight,
say this without hysterical undertones—
then you could say you stood in the cold light of science,
seeing as you are seen, espoused to fact.
Strange, life is both the fire and fuel; and we,
the animals and objects, must be here
without striking a spark of evidence
that anything that ever stopped living
ever falls back to living when life stops.
There's a pale romance to the watchmaker God
of Descartes and Paley; He drafted and installed
us in the Apparatus. He loved to tinker;
but having perfected what He had to do,
stood off shrouded in his loneliness.

Christians

When I am oldfashioned, I hear words,
inner things in us the Lord God alone sees. . . .
David and Bathsheba will never tell me
I step on a thumbtack each time I go to a woman,
if Faith ceases to be a torture-machine, it stops—
I miss the white militia, the subtle schoolmen's
abstract-expressionist idea of salvation:
the haven of their heaven sure and uniform,
rest for the weary and sight for the blind.
Yet we were no kinder when we had the Faith,
and thought the massacred could be reformed,
and move like ironsides through the unwithering white,
squadron on squadron, stiff and sharp and pure—
they move in a body if they move at all.

Dies Irae

On this day of anger, when I am Satan's,
forfeited to that childless sybarite—
Our God, he walks with me, he talks with me,
in sleep, in thunder, and in wind and weather;
he strips the wind and gravel from my words,
and speeds me naked on the single way. . . .
You who save those you must save free; you, whose
least anger makes my faith derelict,
you came from nothing to the earth for me,
my enemies are many, my friends few—
how often do you find me, God, and die?
Once our Lord looked and saw the world was good—
in His hand, God has got us in His hand;
everything points to non-existence except existence.

Pompadour's Daughter

"Our family reunions in what new foreign bar?
Which lover will one's mother service this week?
Her shipowners, generals, peers were bell'Antonios,
almost by definition jerks, *les vieux*,
bantering insolence stuffed in wet footballs—
charging on her they did not cheer or shout; they growled. . . .
When I sought fame in Paris, I little knew
how near the fall was: speeches, lecture halls,
vast wombs of echoes bound by injured nerve.
I hoped I'd stay a woman if I only loved
one or two friends. I found a million friends. . . .
Now I want to marry the least man,
the top of whose husbandry is breeding flowers—
no sense in shouting truth from the wrong window."

Life and Civilization

Your skirt stopped half a foot above your knee,
diamonded your birthmarks by your black mesh tights;
and yet I see your legs as perfect legs—
who would want to finger or approach
the rumination in your figured sweater?
Civilization will always outdo life,
if toleration means to bear and hurt—
that's Locke, Voltaire; the Liberal dies for that,
bites his own lip to warm his icy tooth,
and faces all vicissitudes with calmness.
That's why there are none, that's why we're none,
why, unenlightened, we shiver once a moon
whenever Eros arcs into the Virgin—
as you, no virgin, made me bear myself.

Robespierre and Mozart as Stage

Robespierre could live with himself: "The republic
of Virtue without *la terreur* is a disaster.
Loot the châteaux, give bread to Saint Antoine."
He found the guillotine was not an idler
hearing *mort à Robespierre* from the Convention floor,
the high harsh laughter of the innocents,
the Revolution returning to grand tragedy—
is life the place where we find happiness,
or not at all? . . . Ask the voyeur
what blue movie is worth a seat at the keyhole. . . .
Even the prompted Louis Seize was living theater,
sternly and lovingly judged by his critics, who knew
a Mozart's insolent slash at folk could never
cut the gold thread of the suffocating curtain.

Saint-Just 1767–93

Saint-Just: his name seems stolen from the Missal. . . .
His chamois coat, the dandy's vast cravat
knotted with pretentious negligence;
he carried his head like the Holy Sacrament.
He thought only the laconic fit to rule
the austerity of his hideous cardboard Sparta.
"I shall move with the stone footsteps of the sun—
faction plagues the ebb of revolution,
as reptiles follow the dry bed of a torrent.
I am young and therefore close to nature.
Happiness is a new idea in Europe;
we bronzed liberty with the guillotine.
I'm still twenty, I've done badly, I'll do better."
He did, the scaffold, "Je sais où je vais."

Vision

Sloping, torn black tarpaper on a wet roof,
on several; here and there, an uprooted nail,
a downpour soaking the wooden gingerbread,
old ornamentation too labored for revival,
and too much for its time. My judge was there,
frizzled, powdered to perfection, sky-blue
Robespierre, or anyone's nameless, mercantile
American forefather of 1790—
his head bowed, a hand spiked on each sharp knee—
the cleansing guillotine peeps over his shoulder.
I climb the scaffold, knowing my last words
need not be audible or much to the point,
if my blood will blot my blackest mark—
what does having my life behind me mean?

Napoleon

Boston's used bookshops, anachronisms from London,
are gone; it's hard to guess now why I spent
my vacations lugging home his third-hand *Lives*—
shaking the dust from that stationary stock:
cheap deluxe lithographs and gilt-edged pulp
on a man . . . not bloodthirsty, not sparing of blood,
with an eye and *sang-froid* to manage everything;
his iron hand no mere appendage of his mind
for improbable contingencies . . .
for uprooting races, lineages, Jacobins—
the price was paltry . . . three million soldiers dead,
grand opera fixed like morphine in their veins.
Dare we say, he had no moral center?
All gone like the smoke of his own artillery?

Before Waterloo, the Last Night

And night and muffled creakings and the wheels
of the artillery-wagons circling with the clock,
Blücher's Prussian army passing the estate. . . .
The man plays the harpsichord, and lifts his eyes,
playing each air by ear to look at her—
he might be looking in a mirror for himself,
a mirror filled with his young face, the sorrow
his music made seductive and beautiful.
Suddenly everything is over. Instead,
wearily by an open window, she stands
and clasps the helpless thumping of her heart.
No sound. Outside, a fresh morning wind has risen,
and strangely foreign on the mirror-table,
leans his black shako with its white deathshead.

Waterloo

A thundercloud hung on the mantel of our summer
cottage by the owners, Miss Barnard and Mrs. Curtis:
a sad picture, half life-scale, removed and no doubt
scrapped as too English Empire for our taste:
Waterloo, Waterloo! You could choose sides then:
the engraving made the blue French uniforms black,
the British Redcoats gray; those running were French—
an aide-de-camp, Napoleon's perhaps,
wore a cascade of overstated braid,
there sabered, dying, his standard wrenched from weak hands;
his killer, a bonneted fog-gray dragoon—
six centuries, this field of their encounter,
death-round of French sex against the English *no* . . .
La Gloire fading to *sauve qui peut* and *merde*.

Leaving Home, Marshal Ney

Loved person, I'm never in the clear with conscience,
I hang by a kitetail. Old lovers used to stop
for the village's unreliable clock and bells;
their progress . . . more government, civil service,
the Prussian school, the Irish constable,
hardware exploding help on the city poor.
The *Ancien Régime* locked in place at the tap of a glove;
those long steel scoopnets lie rolled in the bureau. . . .
I hear the young voice of a fresher age and habit,
walking to fame or Paris: "You little knew
I could hardly put one foot before the other.
I passed through many varieties of untried being,
a Marshal of France, and shot for too much courage—
why should shark be eaten when bait swim free?"

Beethoven

Our cookbook is bound like Whitman's *Leaves of Grass*—
gold title on green. I have escaped its death,
take two eggs with butter, drink and smoke;
I live past prudence, not possibility—
who can banquet on the shifting cloud,
lie to friends and tell the truth in print,
be Othello offstage, or Lincoln retired from office?
The vogue of the vague, what can it teach an artist?
Beethoven was a Romantic, but too good;
did kings, republics or Napoleon teach him?
He was his own Napoleon. Did even deafness?
Does the painted soldier in the painting bleed?
Is the captive chorus of *Fidelio* bound?
For a good voice hearing is a torture.

While Hearing the Archduke Trio

None march in the Archduke's War, or worse lost cause,
without promise of plunder, murder, gallantry.
Marriage is less remunerative than war—
two waspheads lying on one pillowslip,
drowning, one toe just skating the sheet for bedrock.
The bright moonlight mackerels heaven in my garden,
fair flesh of the turtle given shape by shell,
Eve shining like an illuminated rib,
forsaking this garden for another bondage.
I so pray this pretty sky to stay:
my high blood, fireclouds, the first dew,
elms black on the moon, our birdhouse on a pipe. . . .
Was the Archduke, the music-patron, childless? Beethoven
married the single muse, her ear of flint.

Goethe

Goethe thought logical consistency
suited the genius of hypochondriacs,
who take life and art too seriously,
lacking the artist's germ of reckless charm.
"How can I perish, I do not exist. . . .
The more I understand particular things,"
he said, "the more I understand God."
He loathed neurotics for the harm they do,
and fettered *Te Deum laudamus* in his meter,
not *pauper amavi*. Take him, he's not copy—
past rationalism and irrationalism,
saved by humor and wearying good health,
hearing his daemon's cold corrosive whisper
chill his continuous ardor for young girls.

Coleridge

Coleridge stands, he flamed for the one friend. . . .
This shower is warm, I almost breathe-in the rain
horseclopping from fire escape to skylight
down to a dungeon courtyard. In April, New York
has a smell and taste of life. For whom . . . what?
A newer younger generation faces
the firing squad, then their blood is wiped from the pavement. . . .
Coleridge's laudanum and brandy,
his alderman's stroll to positive negation—
his passive courage is paralysis,
standing him upright like tenpins for the strike,
only kept standing by a hundred scared habits . . .
a large soft-textured plant with pith within,
power without strength, an involuntary imposter.

Leopardi, The Infinite

That hill pushed off by itself was always dear
to me and the hedges near
it that cut away so much of the final horizon.
When I would sit there lost in deliberation,
I reasoned most on the interminable spaces
beyond all hills,
the silence beyond my possibility.
Here for a little my heart is quiet inside me;
and when the wind lifts roughing through the trees,
I set about comparing my silence to those sounds,
I think about the infinite, the dead seasons,
this one that is present and alive,
the rumors we leave behind us, our small choice . . .
it is sweet to destroy my mind, and drown in this sea.

The Lost Tune

As I grow older, I must admit with terror:
I have been there, the works of the masters lose,
songs with a mind, philosophy that danced.
Their *vivace* clogs, I am too tired, or wise.
I have read in books that even woman dies;
a figure cracks up sooner than a landscape—
your subject was Maine, a black and white engraving,
able to enlarge the formal luxury of
foliage rendered by a microscope,
a thousand blueberry bushes marching up
the flank of a hill; the artist, a lady, shoots
her lover panting like a stag at bay;
not very true, yet art—had Schubert scored it,
and his singer left the greenroom with her voice.

Death and the Maiden

In Romantic painting, the girl is Body,
just as she must embody youth to die;
Death too must take a body to make a scene—
verismo has no tenor for death.
But in music . . . I've been thirty years
hearing the themes of Schubert's *Death and the Maiden*:
Schubert dying is death audible;
which theme is Maiden, which Death—*la femme fatale?*
Death will make melodrama of most of us,
change her chilled, unwilling audience to actors. . . .
These years of my dead friends, still mine—what other possession
allows no aging or devaluation?
Their names have kept their voice—*only in the movies,*
the maiden lives . . . in the madness of art.

Die Forelle

I lean on a bridgerail watching the clear calm,
a homeless sound of joy is in the sky:
a fisherman making falsecasts over a brook,
a two pound browntrout darting with scornful quickness,
drawing straight lines like arrows through the pool.
The man might as well snap his rod on his knee,
each shake of a boot or finger scares the fish;
trout will never hit flies in this brightness.
I go on watching, and the man keeps casting,
he wades, and stamps his feet, and muddies the water;
before I know it, his rod begins to dip.
He wades, he stamps, he shouts to turn the run
of the trout with his wetfly breathed into its belly—
broken whiplash in the gulp of joy.

Heine Dying in Paris 1

Every idle desire has died in my breast;
even hatred of evil things, even care
of my own distress and others.
What lives in me is death.
The curtain falls, the play is done;
my dear German public goes home yawning . . .
these good people—they're no fools—
eat their suppers and drink their glass of wine
quite happily—singing and laughing. . . .
That fellow in Homer's book was right,
he said the meanest little living Philistine
in Stuttgart-am-Neckar is luckier than I,
the golden haired Achilles, the dead lion,
prince of the shadows in the underworld.

Heine Dying in Paris 2

My day was luckily happier than my night;
whenever I struck the lyre of inspiration,
my people clapped; my lieder, all joy and fire,
pierced Germany's suffocating summer cloud.
Summer still glows, but my harvest is in the barn,
my sword's scabbarded in my spinal marrow,
and soon I must give up the half-gods
that made my world so agonizingly half-joyful.
My hand clangs to its close on the lyre's dominant;
my insolently raised champagne glass breaks at my lips. . . .
If I can forgive the great Aristophanes
and Author of Being his joke, he can forgive me—
God, how hatefully bitter it is to die,
how snugly one lives in this snug earthly nest!

Old Prints: Decatur, Old Hickory

Those awful figures of Yankee prehistory;
the prints were cheap once, our good faith came easy:
Stephen Decatur, spyglass screwed to raking
the cannonspout-smashed Bay of Tripoli—
because the Mohammedans believed in war.
Our country right or wrong—our commanders had no
commission to send their souls to paradise.
Others were more democratic: primitive, high-toned
President Jackson on his hobby horse,
watermelon-slice hat and ballroom sword;
he might have been the Tsar or Bolivar,
pillar of the right or pillar of the left—
Andrew Jackson, despite appearances,
stands for the gunnery that widened suffrage.

Northwest Savage

"With people like the great silent majority,
how can the great people get elected President?"
St. Paul and Lincoln Nebraska owe their rise
to W. H. Harrison, selfish little busybody
expelling Indians, legalizing slaves,
losing most of his battles with the Savage,
with numbers anything equal. No acid ate more
mechanically on vegetable fibre
than the whites in number. . . . Did the fish leaping
have leisure to see their waters had collapsed,
that even Jefferson's philanthropy
offered a great award for their extinction?
Landthirst, whiskeythirst. We flip extinct matches
at your rhinoceros hide . . . inflammable earth.

Henry and Waldo

Emerson is New England's Montaigne or Goethe,
cold ginger, poison to Don Giovanni—
see him on winter lecture-tours with Thoreau,
red flannels, one bowl of broken ice for shaving;
few lives contained such humdrum renunciations.
Thoreau, like Mallarmé and many others, found life
too brief for perfection, too long for comfort.
His friend would sooner take the arm of an elm,
yet he must have heard the voices on the river,
wood groans, water groans, gliding of bark canoes,
twilight flaking the wild manes of trees.
The color that killed him, us . . . perhaps a mouse,
zinc eating through the moonstalk, or a starling
lighting and pecking, a dash of poisonous metal.

Thoreau 1

God is the figure for environment,
all that I know, all that I fail to know;
who is mightier than the living God?
Other persons only met in books
have swallowed a bad name and made a comeback.
Students return to Othello and Macbeth,
Shakespeare's insomniac self and murderer,
his visionary captain trapped in scandal
by Shiva, the killer and a third of God.
No killer troubled Thoreau on his walk;
he thought never to see the piece of earth
that would bury him. God buried him.
He was forty-five, a good age for the lover;
the maker and destroyer had no quarrel.

Thoreau 2

He thought New England was corrupted by
too much communion with her saints,
our fears consoled and iced, no hope confirmed.
If the high sun wandered and warmed a winter day
and surprised the plodding circuit of our lives,
we winced and called it fickleness and fools-thaw—
"However bad your life, meet it, live it,
it's not as bad as you are." For Thoreau,
life in us was like water in a river:
"It may rise higher this year than all others."
Adrift there, dragging forty feet of line,
he felt a dull, uncertain, blundering purpose
jerking, slow to make up its mind, and knew
the light that blinds our eyes is not the sun.

Margaret Fuller Drowned

You had everything to rattle the men who wrote.
The first American woman? Margaret Fuller . . .
in a white nightgown, your hair fallen long
at the foot of the foremast, you just forty,
your husband Angelo thirty, your Angelino one—
all drowned with brief anguish together. . . . Your fire-call,
your voice, was like thorns crackling under a pot,
you knew the Church burdens and infects as all dead forms,
however gallant and lovely in their life;
progress is not by renunciation.
"Myself," you wrote, "is all I know of heaven.
With my intellect, I always can
and always shall make out, but that's not half—
the life, the life, O my God, will life never be sweet?"

Henry Adams 1850

Adams' connection with Boston was singularly cool;
winter and summer were two hostile lives,
summer was multiplicity, winter was school.
"We went into the pinewoods, netted crabs,
boated the saltmarsh in view of the autumn hills.
Boys are wild animals, I felt nature crudely,
I was a New England boy—summer was drunken,
poled through the saltmarsh at low tide,
the strong reds, greens, purples in children's Bibles—
no light line or color, our light was glare.
Already the Civil War darkened Faneuil Hall.
My refined, disquieting mind, I suppose
it had some function . . . sometimes by mishap
Napoleon's Old Guard were actually used in battle."

Colonel Charles Russell Lowell 1835–64

OCCASIONEM COGNOSCE

Hard to exhume him from our other Union martyrs;
though common now, his long-short, crisping hair,
the wire mustache, and manly, foppish coat—
more and more nearly looking like our sixties student. . . .
Twelve horses killed under him—his nabob cousin
bred and shipped replacements. He had, *gave* . . . everything
at Cedar Creek, his men dismounted, firing
repeating carbines; heading two vicious charges,
a slug collapsing his bad, tubercular lung:
fainting, loss of his voice above a whisper;
his general—any crusader since Moses—shouting:
"I'll sleep in the enemy camp tonight, or hell. . . ."
Charles had himself strapped to the saddle . . . bound to death,
his cavalry that scorned the earth it trod on.

Abraham Lincoln

All day I bang and bang at you in thought,
as if I had the license of your wife. . . .
If War is the continuation of politics—
is politics the discontinuation of murder?
You may have loved underdogs and even mankind,
this one thing made you different from your equals . . .
you, our one genius in politics . . . who followed
the bull to the altar . . . to death in unity.
J'accuse, j'accuse, j'accuse, j'accuse, j'accuse!
Say it in American. Who shot the deserters?
Winter blows sparks in the face of the new God,
who breathes-in fire and dies with cooling faith,
as the firebrand turns black in the black hand,
and the squealing pig darts sidewise from his foot.

George Eliot

A lady in bonnet, brow clearer than the Virgin,
the profile of a white rhinoceros—
like Emerson, she hated gardens, thinking
a garden is a grave, and drains the inkwell;
she never wished to have a second youth—
as for living, she didn't leave it to her servants,
her union, Victorian England's one true marriage,
one Victorian England pronounced *Mormonage*—
two virgins; they published and were childless. Our writers often
marry writers, are true, bright, clashing, though lacking
this woman's dull gray eyes, vast pendulous nose,
her huge mouth, and jawbone which forbore to finish:
George Eliot with Tolstoy's once inalienable eye,
George Eliot, a Countess Tolstoy . . . without Tolstoy.

Hugo at Théophile Gautier's Grave

I have begun to die by being alone,
I feel the summit's sinister cold breath;
we die. That is the law. None holds it back,
and the great age with all its light departs.
The oaks cut for the pyre of Hercules,
what a harsh roar they make
in the night vaguely breaking into stars—
Death's horses toss their heads, neigh, roll their eyes;
they are joyful because the shining day now dies.
Our age that mastered the high winds and waves
expires. . . . And you, their peer and brother, join
Lamartine, Dumas, Musset. Gautier,
the ancient spring that made us young is dry;
you knew the beautiful, go, find the true.

Baudelaire 1. The Abyss

Pascal's abyss moved with him as he moved—
all void, alas—activity, desires, words!
Above, below me, only space and shoal,
the spaces, the bat-wing of insanity.
I cuddle the insensible blank air,
I envy the void insensibility
and fear to sleep as one fears a great hole.
On my mind the raised hand of the Ultimate
traces his nightmare, truceless, uniform.
I have cultivated this hysteria
with terror and enjoyment till I see
only the infinite at every window,
vague, captivating, dropping who knows where. . . .
Ah never to escape from being and number!

Baudelaire 2. Recollection

Be calm, my Sorrow, you must move with care.
You asked for evening, it descends, it's here;
Paris is coffined in its atmosphere,
bringing some relief and others care.
Now while the common multitude strips bare,
feels pleasure's cat o'nine tails on its back,
accumulating remorse at the great bazaar—
give me your hand, my Sorrow. Let's stand back,
back from these people. Look, the defunct years dressed
in period costume crowd the balconies of the sky.
Regret emerges smiling from the river,
the sun, worked overtime, sleeps beneath an arch . . .
and like a long shroud stretched from east to west—
listen, my Dearest, hear the sweet night march!

Rimbaud 1. Bohemia

I walked on the great roads, my two fists lost
in my coat's slashed pockets; my overcoat too
was the ghost of a coat. Under the sky—
I was your student, Muses. What an affair
we had together! My only trousers were a big hole.
Tom Thumb, the stargazer. I brightened my steps with rhymes.
My inn was at the Sign of the Great Bear;
the stars sang like silver in my hands.
I listened to them and squatted on my heels,
September twilights and September twilights,
rhyming into the monster-crowded dark,
the rain splashing on my face like cheap wine.
I plucked the elastics on my clobbered boots
like lyrestrings, one foot squeezed tight against my heart.

Rimbaud 2. A Knowing Girl

In the cigar-brown dining room perfumed
with a smell of fruitbowls and shellac,
I was wolfing my plate of God knows what
Belgian dish. I sprawled in a huge chair,
I listened to the clock tock while I ate.
Then the kitchen door opened with a bang,
the housemaid came in . . . who knows why . . . her blouse
half-open and her hair wickedly set. She passed
her little finger trembling across her cheek,
pink and white peach bloom, and made a grimace
with her childish mouth, and coming near me
tidied my plates to make me free . . .
then—just like that, to get a kiss of course—
whispered, "Feel this, my cheek has caught a cold."

Rimbaud 3. Sleeper in the Valley

The river sings and cuts a hole in the meadow,
madly hooking white tatters on the rushes.
Light escalades the strong hills. The small
valley bubbles with sunbeams like a beerglass.
The young conscript bareheaded and open-mouthed,
his neck cooling in blue watercress;
he's sleeping. The grass soothes his heaviness,
the sunlight is raining in his green bed,
baking away the aches of his body. He smiles,
as a sick child might smile himself asleep.
O Nature, rock him warmly, he is cold.
The fields no longer make his hot eyes weep.
He sleeps in the sun, a hand on his breast lies open,
at peace. He has two red holes in his left side.

Rimbaud 4. The Evil

All day the red spit of the grapeshot smears
whistling across the infinite blue sky;
before the Emperor, in blue and scarlet,
the massed battalions flounder into fire.
The criminal folly that conspires and rules us
lays a hundred thousand corpses end on end—
O Nature, in your summer, your grass, your joy—
you made them, these poor dead men, in holiness! . . .
There's a God who laughs at damask altarcloths,
the great gold chalice, the fuming frankincense.
He dozes exhausted through our grand hosannah,
and wakes when mothers, brought together in pain,
and weeping underneath their old black hat,
give him the big penny they tied in their handkerchief.

Rimbaud 5. Napoleon after Sedan

(Rimbaud, the servant of the France he saved,
feared the predestined flow of his aesthetic
energies was to use the wrong direction;
he was looking for writing he needn't hate—)
Napoleon is waxy, and walks the barrack's unflowering
garden, a black cigar between his teeth . . .
a hand once able to stub out liberty.
His twenty years orgy has made him drunk.
Liberty jogs on, the great man stands,
he's captured. O what name is quaking on
his lip? What plebiscites? What Robespierre?
His shark's eye on the horses, the Grand Prix,
soirées at Saint Cloud, their manly vapor . . .
watching his cigar blue out in smoke.

La Lumière

In the blur of my glasses, you cannot fade—
your ruffle, electricity and your sure tongue . . .
richer now and much more radical.
The sun lights your windows it will never crash,
this blind snow, this blind light everywhere,
the sad, metallic sunlight of New York
throwing light on something about to die.
This light was familiar in the older cities;
it goes, disclosing less than leaves of artichokes—
a light that blinded kings who fled to London,
where Dickens might have played Napoleon's Nephew
cloaked in cigar smoke and the moans of girls,
a smell of chestnuts like a humidor . . .
watching exile chew his face from the mirror.

Mallarmé 1. Swan

Does the virgin, the alive, the beautiful day
dare tear for us with a mad stroke of its wing
the hard, neglectful lake hoarding under ice
a great glacier of flights that never fly?
The swan ruffles, remembers it is he,
fortitude that finds no raison d'être,
magnificence that gives itself no hope,
for never singing the country where one lives—
the great boredom blazing on sterile winter.
His whole neck shakes in his white agony
inflicted by the space the swan denies,
the horror of the ice that ties his wings,
the brilliance that led him to this grand asylum,
governed by staccato cries of grandeur.

Mallarmé 2. Gift of a Poem

I bring the child of an Idumean night,
a black thing bleeding, stumbling—its wings are plucked.
Through the window's gold and aromatic fire,
panes frosted by night, alas, and wearisome,
the dawn throws itself upon my sacred lamp—
palms! It reveals this relic to its father;
I try to cheer it with a hostile smile
that chills our blue and sterile solitude.
Nurse, Mother, with our child's innocence
and your cold feet, welcome this monster birth—
your voice is like viol and harpsichord.
Will your wilting fingers press a breast
flowing with solid whiteness, bringing woman
to lips the virgin azure has made hungry?

Main Street

They were talking much as usual only
laughing, talking rather too much and louder;
they had hoisted poplar trees to the people,
and the head of state with the head of a pig.
There was a lot of unclaimed space around.
The teenage police shook with chills-and-fever;
behind them, veterans of Sedan and Metz
fixed starry bayonets. It didn't look like a killing.
Like a dark worm, the eight-foot barricade;
a small mongrel with pipecleaner legs trots the top.
Joy! Indescribable apprehension. House-arrest
for women, children, foreigners and dogs.
Red-trousered, unpressed fatigues, the Communards
stand like empty wine-bottles on the table.

Lady Cynthia Asquith, 1916
(Written in Israel 1969)

"I am beginning to rub my eyes at the prospect of peace,
when we will have to know the dead are not
dead only for the duration of the war;
I am in glowing looks, I've never seen
myself in such keen color, even by daylight.
Strange to know suddenly in this slowly farewell war
that I know many more dead than I know living. . . ."
Turning the page in *Time* to see her picture,
I expect some London Judith: *no trespass.*
I touch your shutter-green sweater and breathing breasts:
Lady Cynthia Asquith, undying bulwark of British girl. . . .
Miracles were more common once than now,
but sleeping with this one cannot be maneuvered—
each stone a wall, an unexploded minefield.

Verdun

I bow down to the great goiter of Verdun,
I know what's buried there, ivory telephone,
ribs, hips bleached to parchment, a pale machinegun—
they lie fatigued from too much punishment,
cling by a string to friends they knew firsthand,
to the God of our fathers still twenty like themselves.
Their medals and rosettes have kept in bloom,
they stay young, only living makes us age.
I know the sort of town they came from, straight brownstone,
each house cooled by a rectilinear private garden,
a formal greeting and a slice of life.
The city says, "I am the finest city"—
landmass held by half a million bodies
for Berlin and Paris, twin cities saved at Verdun.

Hospital

We're lost if gossip is taken for gospel truth,
worse lost if we have found no truth in gossip—
we must take courses in what's alive and what isn't,
trips to the hospital. . . . I have seen stiffs
no one can distinguish from the living,
twitched by green fingers till they turn to flowers;
they are and are not—like the unknown soldier,
his archaic statue no barrage will wake. . . .
Others are strapped to cots, thrust out in hallways,
they are browner and flatter than we are,
they are whatever crinkles, plugged to tubes
plugged in jugs of dim blue doctored water,
a yard above them to lift their eyes to heaven—
they look dead, unlike the hero, and are alive.

Revenants

They come back sometimes, I know they do,
freed like felons on the first of May,
if there's a healthy bite in the south wind,
Spring the echo of God's single day.
They sun like earthworms on the puddly mall,
they are better equipped for everything than people,
except perhaps for living. When I meet them
covertly, I think I know their names:
Cousin So, Ancestral Mother-in-Law So . . .
I cannot laugh them into laughing back.
"Dead we have finally come to realize
what others must have known from infancy—
God is not about. We are less scared—
with misty bounds we scale the starry sheer."

Cadet-Picture of Rilke's Father

There's absence in the eyes. The brow's in touch
with something far, and his enormous mouth,
tempted, serious, is a boy's unsmiling . . .
modest, counting on future promotion, stiff
in his slender aristocratic uniform—
both hands bulge on the basket-hilt of his saber.
They are quiet and reach out to nothing.
I can hardly see them now, as if
they were the first to grasp distance and disappear.
All the rest is curtained in itself,
and so faded I cannot understand
my father as he bleaches on this page—
You quickly disappearing daguerreotype
in my more slowly disappearing hand.

Annensky: White Winter, Black Spring

Half-holiday for the burial. Of course we punished
our provincial copper bells for hours.
Terribly the nose tilted up like a tallow candle
from the coffin. Does he want
to draw breath from his torso in its morning suit?
We did not blow the candles until morning.
The snow fell somberly—now the roads are breadcrumbs.
Goodbye, poor winter honeycombed with debts—
now numb black spring looks at the chilly eye.
From under the mould on the roof shingles,
the liquid oatmeal of the roads,
the green stubble on our faces—life . . . in splinter elms
shrill the annual fledgelings with spikey necks.
They say to man his road is mud, or nothing.

Under the Tsar

No beer or washrag, half the lightbulbs bust,
still the baths are free, a treat for kings,
rows of tubs like churchpews infinite,
on each a reading-board, a pair of glasses,
a cake of scouring soap, and Marx in French.
When we have read our bible, we are washed—
the dirt of a lifetime cleaned from our fingernails;
our breasts, as the sons of Belial dreamed, are chests,
we are like our backs. We, who were wet and cold,
soak . . . dry for the first time in our lives.
But our hurt gums still leave a smear of blood on the apple;
we can't do all things, drink the spit of the snake
and meet the naked candor of the Tsar,
his slightly bald Medusa's pewter eye.

Romanoffs

Let's face it, English is a racist last ditch.
We plead guilty, the laws of history tell us
irrelevant things that happen never happened.
The Blacks and Reds survive, but who is White?
The word has fallen from the English tongue,
a class wiped out, their legacy, non-existence.
The new blade is too sharp, the old poisons.
Does arrogance give the ruler solitude
to study the desolation of his thought—
the starred cellar, where they shot and then dismembered
Tsar, Tsarina, the costly hemophilic children—
"Those *statesmen*," said Lenin, "sent 16 million to death."
Such fairy stories beguiled our brainwashed youth—
we, the Romanoffs with much to lose.

Dispossession

The paint is always peeling from the palace—
a man of eighty with the leg of iron,
striding fields shaved smooth as a putting green.
I see these far fields as easily as the present. . . .
How many of the enthusiasts are gone;
their strapped legs march, their impudent white standards
droop in the dust of the field, the gas of battle . . .
and the heart's moisture goes up like summer drought.
No passkey jingles on the sky's blue smoke-ring. . . .
The firemen smash holes in their own house;
yet dispossession isn't entirely our answer,
we yearn to swoop with the swallow's brute joy,
indestructible as mercy—round green weed
slipping free from the disappointment of the flower.

Rilke Self-Portrait

An old, long-noble people's unregressing
knack of holding is in the build of the eyebrow;
a scared blue child is peering through the eyes,
that now and then are humble like a woman's,
not servile . . . on occasion glad to serve.
A mouth made like a mouth, largish, in place,
less good at persuasion than for saying things.
Nothing wrong with the brow; it seldom frowns,
at home with quiet shadows, or looking down. . . .
As a thing that hangs together, the picture fails;
nothing is worked through yet or alive,
carried to enduring culmination—
as if hidden in accidents and stray things,
something unassailable were planned.

Muses of George Grosz

Berlin in the twenties left the world behind,
the iron glove of Prussia was unclenched,
elsewhere the music crept, and painting stank—
now our artists hurry to break windows,
as if we had beaten Germany at last.
Grosz' men are one man, old Marshal Hindenburg,
a close-cropped Midas feeling girls to gold.
His men never strip, his women always;
girls one meets at a Modern Language Annual,
pushing retirement, and outweighing men;
once the least of them were good for the game all night.
Grosz could swing the old sow by her tits:
the receding hairline of her nettled cunt
caught like a scalplock by a stroke of the brush.

The Poet

His teeth splayed in a way he'd notice and pity
in his closest enemies or friends.
Youth held his eye; he blinked at passing beauties,
birds of passage that could not close the gap.
His wife was high-blooded, he counted on her living—
she lived, past sixty, then lived on in him,
and often when he plotted lines, she breathed
her acrid sweetness past his imaginings.
She was still a magnificent handle of a woman—
did she have her lover as a novelist wished her?
No—hating someone nearer, she found her voice—
no wife so loved; though Hardy, home from cycling,
was glad to climb unnoticed to his study
by a circling outside staircase, his own design.

Scar-Face

By Lake Erie, Al Capone could set
his price on the moonshine that enflamed Chicago—
"Funny thing, in this our thing, a man
in this line of business has too much company."
He watched black and white men walk the tightrope,
and felt a high contempt for them all—poor fish,
sweating themselves to death for a starvation wage.
Little Caesar, like Julius Caesar, a rich man
knifed by richer. A true king serves the realm,
when he's equal to the man who serves his meal;
a gentleman is an aristocrat on bail. . . .
Splendor spread like gold leaf in your hand, Al,
made in the morning and by midday hard,
pushed by your fellow convicts to the wall.

Little Millionaire's Pad, Chicago

The little millionaire's is a sheen of copies;
at first glance most everything is French;
a sonata scored *sans rigueur*
is on a muddy-white baby grand piano,
the little plaster bust on it, small as a medallion,
is Franz Schubert below the colored blow-up
of the master's wife, executive-Bronzino—
his frantic touch to antique her! Out the window,
two cunning cylinder apartment towers—
below the apartments, six spirals of car garage,
below the cars, yachts at moorings—more Louis Quinze
and right than anything of the millionaire's,
except the small daughter's bedroom, perfect with posters:
"Do not enter. Sock it to me, Baby."

Wolverine, 1927

What did I know about the wolverine,
the Canada of Ernest Seton Thompson,
first great snow in the schoolbook, a Cartesian blank?
At the edge of the rumpled sky, a too-red glow,
a vertical iron rail, derrick or steeple,
trappers freighting on snowshoes through the snow,
track of the wolfpack wheelsaw to the church—
no need for preachers to tell me wolves eat meat,
improve the terror of the first trapped wolf. . . .
The wolverine, no critic of frontier justice,
learning the jaws meant him, was greatly tested,
hesitating to chew off his foot,
tasting the leisure of his double-choice . . .
our first undated leap in evolution.

Two Farmers

A nose flat-bent, no brave, cheeks razored wood—
Velázquez' self-portrait is James MacDonald,
Jim to grandfather, MacDonald to the children,
though always *Mr.* in our vocative.
Having a farmer then was like owning a car . . .
he sits on his lawn waiting a lift to the Old Men's Home—
saying? Here even the painter's speaking likeness fails;
nor could he paint my grandfather. I've overtaken
most of the elders of my youth, not this one,
yet I begin to feel why Grandpa knelt in the snow
so many weekends with his small grandson
sawing his cordwood for a penny a log—
Old Cato, ten years to live, preferring this squander
to his halcyon Roman credits from the Boom.

The Well

The stones of the well were sullenly unhewn,
none could deny their leechlike will to stay—
no dwelling near and four square miles of waste,
pale grass diversified by wounds of sand,
weeds as hard as rock and squeezed by winter,
each well-stone an illrounded ostrich egg,
amateurish for nature's artless hand . . .
a kind of dead chimney. Any furtive boy
was free to pitch the bucket, drinking glass
and funnel down the well . . . thin black hoops
of standing water. That well is bottomless;
plenty of elbowroom for the scuttled gear,
room at bottom for us to lie, undented. . . .
It's not the crowds, but crowding kills the soul.

First Things

Worse things could happen, life is insecure,
child's fears mostly a fallacious dream;
days one like the other let you live:
up at seven-five, to bed at nine,
the absolving repetitions, the three meals,
the nutritive, unimaginative dayschool meal,
laughing like breathing, one night's sleep a day—
solitude is the reward for sickness:
leafless, dusty February trees,
the field fretted in your window, all one cloth—
your mother harrowed by child gaiety. . . .
I remember that first desertion with fear;
something made so much of me lose ground,
the irregular and certain flight to art.

First Love

Two grades above me, though two inches shorter,
Leon Straus, sixthgrade fullback, his reindeer shirt—
passion put a motor in my heart.
I pretended he lived in the house across the street.
In first love a choice is seldom and blinding:
acres of whitecaps strew that muddy swell,
old crap and white plastic jugs lodge on shore.
Later, we learn better places to cast
our saffron sperm, and grasp what wisdom fears,
breasts stacked like hawknests in her boy friend's shirt,
things a deft hand tips on its back with a stick. . . .
Is it refusal of error breaks our life—
the supreme artist, Flaubert, was a boy before
the mania for phrases enlarged his heart.

The vaporish closeness of this two-month fog;
forty summers back, my brightest summer:
the rounds of Dealer's Choice, the housebound girls,
fog, the nightlife. Then, as now, the late curfew
boom of an unknown nightbird, local hemlock
gone black as Roman cypress, the barn-garage
below the tilted Dipper lighthouse-white,
a single misanthropic frog complaining
from the water hazard on the shortest hole;
till morning! Long dreams, short nights; their faces flash
like burning shavings, scattered bait and ptomaine
caught by the gulls with groans like straining rope;
windjammer pilgrims cowled in yellow hoods,
gone like the summer in their yellow bus.

Searching

I look back to you, and cherish what I wanted:
your flashing superiority to failure,
hair of yellow oak leaves, the arrogant
tanned brunt in the snow-starch of a loosened shirt—
your bullying half-erotic rollicking. . . .
The white bluffs rise above the old rock piers,
wrecked past insuring by two hurricanes.
As a boy I climbed those scattered blocks and left
the sultry Sunday seaside crowd behind,
seeking landsend, with my bending fishing rod
a small thread slighter than the dark arc of your eyebrow. . . .
Back at school, alone and wanting you,
I scratched my four initials, R.T.S.L.
like a dirty word across my bare, blond desk.

Shake of the electric fan above our village;
oil truck, refrigerator, or just men,
nightly reloading of the village flesh—
plotting worse things than marriage. They found dates
wherever summer is, the nights of the swallow
clashing in heat, storm-signal to stay home.
At night the lit blacktop fussing like a bosom;
Court Street, Dyer Lane, School, Green, Main Street
dropping through shade-trees to the shadeless haven—
young girls are white as ever. I only know
their mothers, sweatshirts gorged with tennis balls,
still air expiring from the tilting bubble—
I too wore armor, strode riveted in cloth,
stiff, a broken clamshell labeled man.

Joe Wardwell: Mink

In the unspoiled age, when they caught a cow-mink,
they made her urinate around the traps,
and every bull-mink hunting along the stream
went for the trap, and soon the mink were done—
the last we knew was in the freeze of '17,
a last bull making tracks in the snow for a last cow.
My friend, once professional, no longer traps:
"There're too many other ways to make a living"—
his, his army pension, and two working sons.
He builds houses for bluebirds, martins, swallows.
When a pair mates in one, it's like a match,
a catch, a return to his lost craft of trapping,
old China's hope to excel without progress. . . .
His money went to *Wildlife*; he killed too much.

1930's 3

The boys come, each year more gallant, playing chicken,
then braking to a standstill for a girl—
like bullets hitting bottles, spars and gulls,
echoing and ricochetting across the bay . . .
hardy perennials! Kneedeep in the cowpond,
far from this cockfight, cattle stop to watch us,
and having had their fill, go back to lapping
soiled water indistinguishable from heaven.
Cattle get onto living, but to *live*:
Kokoschka at eighty, saying, "If you last,
you'll see your reputation die three times,
or even three cultures; young girls are always here."
They *were* there . . . two fray-winged dragonflies,
clinging to a thistle, too clean to mate.

1930's 4

My legs hinge on my foreshortened bathtub
small enough for Napoleon's marching tub. . . .
The sun sallows a tired swath of balsam needles,
the color soothes, and yet the scene confines;
sun falls on so many, many other things:
Custer, leaping with his wind-gold scalplock,
half a furlong or less from the Sioux front line,
and Sitting Bull, who sent our rough riders under—
both now dead drops in the decamping mass. . . .
This wizened balsam, the sea-haze of blue gauze,
the distance plighting a tree-lip of land to the islands—
who can cash a check on solitude,
or is more loved for being distant . . . love-longing
mists my windshield, soothes the eye with milk.

Bobby Delano

The labor to breathe that younger, rawer air:
St. Mark's last football game with Groton lost on the ice-crust,
the sunlight gilding the golden polo coats
of boys with country seats on the Upper Hudson.
Why does that stale light stay? First Form hazing,
first day being sent on errands by an oldboy,
Bobby Delano, cousin of Franklin Delano Roosevelt—
deported soused off the Presidential yacht
baritoning *You're the cream in my coffee* . . .
his football, hockey, baseball letter at 15;
at 15, expelled. He dug my ass with a compass,
forced me to say "My mother is a whore."
My freshman year, he shot himself in Rio,
odious, unknowable, inspired as Ajax.

1930's 5

Timid in victory, chivalrous in defeat,
almost, almost. . . . I bow and watch the ashes
reflect the heraldry of an age less humbled,
though hardened with its nobles, serfs and faith—
(my once faith?) The fires men build live after them,
this night, this night, I elfking, I stonehands sit
feeding the wildfire wildrose of the fire
clouding the cottage window with my lust's
alluring emptiness. I hear the moon
simmer the mildew on a pile of shells,
the fruits of my banquet . . . a boiled lobster,
red shell and hollow foreclaw, cracked, sucked dry,
flung on the ash-heap of a soggy carton—
it eyes me, two pinhead, burnt-out popping eyes.

1930's 6

Months of it, and the inarticulate mist so thick
we turned invisible to one another
across our silence . . . rivals unreconciled,
each unbandaging a tender bloodsoaked foot
in the salmon-glow of the early lighted moon,
snuffed by the malodorous and frosty murk. . . .
Then the iron bellbuoy is rocking like a baby,
the high tide turning on its back exhausted—
colored, dreaming, silken spinnakers
flash in patches through the island pine,
like vegetating millennia of lizards
fed on fern or cropping at the treetops,
straw-chewers in the African siesta.
I never thought scorn of things; struck fear in no man.

1930's 7

The shore was pebbled with eroding brick,
seaweed in grizzling furrows—a surf-cast away,
a converted brickyard dormitory; higher,
the blacktop; higher yet, *The Osprey Nest*,
a bungalow, view-hung and staring, with washing
and picture-window. Whatever we cast out
takes root—weeds shoot up to litter overnight,
sticks of dead rotten wood in drifts, the fish
with a missing eye, or heel-print on the belly,
or a gash in the back from a stray hook—
roads, lawns and harbor stitched with motors,
yawl-engine, outboard, power mower, plowing
the mangle and mash of the monotonous frontier—
when the mower stopped clanking, sunset calmed the ocean.

For Archie Smith 1917–35
(Killed in a Car Wreck)

Our sick elms rise to breathe the peace of heaven,
at six the blighting leaves are green as mint,
the tree shadows blacker than trunk or branch—
Main Street's shingled mansards and square white frames
date from Warren G. Harding back to Adams—
old life! America's ghostly innocence.
I pipe-dream of a summer without a Sunday,
its steerage drive with children and Cousin Belle. . . .
I have driven when I ought not to have driven.
When cars were horse and buggy and roads dirt,
Smith made Sarasota from Princeton in three days.
A good fast driver is like the Lord unsleeping,
he never kills and he is never killed;
when he dies, a friend is always driving.

For Frank Parker 1. 1935

She never married, because she liked to talk,
"You watch the waves *woll* and *woll* and *woll* and *woll*,"
Miss Parker lisped. That's how we found Nantucket.
Wave-watching bored us, though we tried the surf,
hung dead on its moment of infinity,
corked between water, gravel and the gulls, smothered,
smitten from volition. When I breathe now,
I sometimes hear a far pant of gulls in my chest,
but death that summer was our classmate killed
in a wreck at Oak Bluffs near us . . . the first in our form. . . .
In your seascape Moses broke the Ten Commandments
on a shore of saltgrass, dune and surf,
repainted and repainted, till the colors aged,
a whirl of mud in the hand of Michelangelo.

For Frank Parker 2

The *Pisspot*, our sailing dory, could be moved
by sail and oar in tune . . . immovable
by either singly. The ocean died. We rocked
debating who was skipper, then shipped oars;
as we drifted I tried to put our rapture in verse:
When sunset rouged the sun-embittered surf.
This was the nearest we got to Melville's Nantucket,
though we'd been artist cottagers a month. . . .
The channel gripped our hull, we could not veer,
the boat swam shoreward flying our wet shirts,
like a birchlog shaking off loose bark and shooting:
And the surf thundered fireworks on the dunes.
This was the moment to choose, as school warned us,
whether to wreck or ride in tow to port.

1930's 8

"Nature never will betray us," the poet swore,
choosing peeled staff, senility and psalter
to scrounge Northumberland for the infinite. . . .
We burned the sun of the universal bottle,
and summered on a shorefront—the dusk seal
nightly dog-paddling on the hawk for fish,
whiskering the giddy harbor, a black blanket
splotched with spangles of the sky, the sky—
and somewhere the Brook Trout dolphin by the housepiles,
grow common by mid-vacation as hamburger,
fish-translucence cooked to white of an egg. . . .
Summer vacations surround the college winter,
the reach of nature is longer than a car—
I am no bigger than the shoe I fit.

The circular moon saw-wheels through the oak-grove;
below it, clouds . . . permanence of the clouds,
many as have drowned in the Atlantic.
It makes one larger to sleep with the sublime;
the Great Mother shivers under the dead oak—
such cures the bygone Reichian prophets swore to,
such did as gospel for their virgin time—
two elements were truants: man and nature.
By sunrise, the sky is nearer. Strings of fog,
such as we haven't seen in fifteen months,
catch shyly over stopping lobster boats—
smoke-dust the Chinese draftsman made eternal.
His brushwork wears; the hand decayed. A hand does—
we can have faith, at least, the hand decayed.

Anne Dick 1. 1936

Father's letter to your father said
stiffly and much too tersely he'd been told
you visited my college rooms alone—
I can still crackle that slight note in my hand.
I see your pink father—you, the outraged daughter.
That morning nursing my dark, quiet fire
on the empty steps of the Harvard Fieldhouse in
vacation . . . saying the start of *Lycidas* to myself
fevering my mind and cooling my hot nerves—
we were nomad quicksilver and drove to Boston;
I knocked my father down. He sat on the carpet—
my mother calling from the top of the carpeted stairs,
their glass door locking behind me, no cover; you
idling in the station wagon, no retreat.

Anne Dick 2. 1936

Longer ago than I had lived till then . . .
before the *Anschluss*, the ten or twenty million
war-dead . . . but who knows now off-hand how many?
I wanted to marry you, we gazed through your narrow
bay window at the hideous concrete dome
of M.I.T., its last blanched, hectic glow
sunsetted on the bay of the Esplanade:
like the classical seaport done by Claude,
an artist more out of fashion now than Nero,
his heaven-vaulting aqueducts, swords forged from plowshares,
the fresh green knife of his unloved mother's death. . . .
The blood of our spirit dries in veins of brickdust—
Christ lost, our only king without a sword,
turning the word *forgiveness* to a sword.

Father

There was rebellion, Father, and the door was slammed.
Front doors were safe with glass then . . . you fell backward
on your heirloom-clock, the phases of the moon,
the highboy quaking to its toes. My Father . . .
I haven't lost heart to say *I knocked you down*. . . .
I have breathed the seclusion of the life-tight den,
card laid on card until the pack is used,
old Helios turning the houseplants to blondes,
moondust blowing in the prowling eye—
a parental sentence on each step misplaced. . . .
You were further from Death than I am now—
that Student ageless in her green cloud of hash,
her bed a mattress half a foot off floor . . .
as far from us as her young breasts will stretch.

Mother and Father 1

If the clock had stopped in 1936
for them, or again in '50 and '54—
they are not dead, and not until death parts us,
will I stop sucking my blood from their hurt.
They say, "I had my life when I was young."
They must have . . . dying young in middleage;
often the old grow still more beautiful,
watering out the hours, biting back their tears,
as the white of the moon streams in on them unshaded;
and women too, the tanning rose, their ebb,
neither a medical, nor agricultural problem.
I struck my father; later my apology
hardly scratched the surface of his invisible
coronary . . . never to be effaced.

Mother and Father 2

This glorious oversleeping half through Sunday,
the sickroom's crimeless mortuary calm,
reprieved from leafing through the Sunday papers,
my need as a reader to think celebrities
are made for suffering, and suffer well. . . .
I remember flunking all courses but Roman history—
a kind of color-blindness made the world gray,
though a third of the globe was painted red for Britain. . . .
I think of all the ill I do and will;
love hits like the *infantile* of pre-Salk days.
I always went too far—few children can love,
or even bear their bearers, the never forgotten
my father, *my* mother . . . these names, this function, given
by them once, given existence now by me.

Returning

If, Mother and Daddy, you were to visit us
still seeing you as beings, you'd not be welcome,
as you sat here groping the scars of the house,
spangling reminiscence with reproach,
cutting us to shades you used to skim from Freud—
that first draft lost and never to be rewritten.
No one like one's mother and father ever lived;
when I see my children, I see them only
as children, only-children like myself.
Mother and Father, I try to receive you
as if you were I, as if I were you,
trying to laugh at my old nervewracking jokes . . .
a young, unlettered couple who want to leave—
childhood, closer to me than what I love.

Mother, 1972

More than once taking both roads one night
to shake the inescapable hold of New York—
now more than before fearing everything I do
is only (only) a mix of mother and father,
no matter how unlike they were, they are—
it's not what you were or thought, but you . . .
the choked oblique joke, the weighty luxurious stretch.
Mother, we are our true selves in the bath—
a cold splash each morning, the long hot evening loll.
O dying of your cerebral hemorrhage,
lost at Rapallo, dabbing your brow a week,
bruised from stumbling to your unceasing baths,
as if you hoped to drown your killer wound—
to keep me safe a generation after your death.

Father in a Dream

We were at the faculty dining table,
Freudianizing gossip . . . not of our world;
you wore your Sunday white ducks and blue coat
seeming more in character than life.
At our end of the table, I spattered gossip,
shook salt on my wine-spill; soon we were alone,
suddenly I was talking to you alone.
Your hair, grown heavier, was peacocked out in bangs;
"I do it," you said, "to be myself . . . or younger.
I'll have to make a penny for our classes:
calc and Kipling, and catching small-mouth bass."
Age had joined us at last in the same study.
"I have never loved you so much in all my life."
You answered, "Doesn't love begin at the beginning?"

To Daddy

I think, though I didn't believe it, you were my airhole,
and resigned perhaps from the Navy to be an airhole—
that Mother not warn me to put my socks on before my shoes.

Joan Dick at Eighty

"I opened, I shed bright musk . . . for eighty years?
I've lost the charms of a girl to charm the dragon,
the old flame-thrower dancing rounds to scatter fire. . . .
In my sleep last night, I was on a burning barge,
the angry water was calling me below;
it was jumping or dying at my post.
I had clasped you in my hands, I woke so—
who is washed white in the deep blue sea?
I have spent too much life travelling
from sister to sister each time they felt *down*;
they could never do with God, or without Him—
O His ears that hear not, His mouth that says not . . .
life never comes to us with both hands full;
the tree God touches hears the other trees."

Will Not Come Back
(Volverán)

Dark swallows will doubtless come back killing
the injudicious nightflies with a clack of the beak;
but these that stopped full flight to see your beauty
and my good fortune . . . as if they knew our names—
they'll not come back. The thick lemony honeysuckle,
climbing from the earthroot to your window,
will open more beautiful blossoms to the evening;
but these . . . like dewdrops, trembling, shining, falling,
the tears of day—they'll not come back. . . .
Some other love will sound his fireword for you
and wake your heart, perhaps, from its cool sleep;
but silent, absorbed, and on his knees,
as men adore God at the altar, as I love you—
don't blind yourself, you'll not be loved like that.

Second Shelley

The ceiling is twenty feet above our heads;
oak mantel, panels, oak linoleum tiles;
the book-ladders, brass rods on rollers, touch heaven—
in middle age, necessity costs more. . . .
Who can deduct these years? Become a student,
breathing rebellion, the caw and hair of Shelley,
his hectic hopes, his tremulous success—
dying, he left the wind behind him.
Here, the light of anarchy would harden in his eyes;
soon he starves his genius for denial,
thinks a clink in the heating, the chirp of birds,
and turns with the tread of an ox to serve the rich,
trusting his genius and a hand from his father
will lift his feet from the mud of the republic.

Ford Madox Ford

Taking Ford's dictation on Samuel Butler
in longhand: "A novelist has one novel, his own."
He swallowed his words, I garbled each seventh word—
"You have no ear," he said, "for civilized prose,
Shakespeare's best writing: *No king, be his cause never so spotless,
will try it out with all unspotted soldiers.*"
I brought him my loaded and overloaded lines.
He said: "You live a butterfly's existence,
flitting, flying, botching inspiration.
Conrad spent a day finding the *mot juste*; then killed it."
Ford doubted I could live and be an artist.
"Most of them are born to fill the graveyards."
Ford wrote my father, "If he fails as a writer, at least
he'll be head of Harvard or your English Ambassador."

Ford Madox Ford and Others

Ford could pick up talent from the flyspeck,
and had Goethe's gift for picking a bright girl;
most old masters only know themselves:
"The sun rises," they say, "and the sun sets;
what matters is our writing and reviews."
A joyful weariness cushions the worn-out chair,
one flight of stairs, one view of the one tree,
a heater more attentive than a dog—
praise, the last drink for the road, last welcome friend,
when we have buried all our enemies,
and lonely must descend to loneliness,
pronounce through our false teeth, affirm, eyes closed,
the sky above, the moral law within,
answering requests and plotting endless walks.

For Peter Taylor 1

On the great day, when the eyelid of life lifts—
why try to hide it? When we were at Kenyon,
Ezra Pound wrote me, "Amy Lowell
is no skeleton in anybody's closet."
Red leaves embered in the blue cool of fall,
the days we hoped to meet the Ohio girl,
beery, corny, the seductive verb,
mouth like a twat, vagina like a jaw,
small-mouth bass taking three hooks at a strike. . . .
We lost our fiancées on our first drive East—
stood-up by our girls in a wrong restaurant,
spare change ringing like sleighbells in our pockets—
fulfilling the prophecy of my first prize,
my nature cup for catching moths and snakes.

For Peter Taylor 2

Your doleful Kenyon snapshot—ham-squatting in bed,
jaw a bent lantern, your eyes too glossy;
chest syrups, wicked greens of diesel oil;
you the same green, except you are transparent.
At fifty, I can almost touch and smell
the pyjamas we were too sluttish to change,
and wore as winter underwear in our trousers,
thinking cleanliness was ungodliness.
You might have been sitting for your embalmer,
sitting upright, a First Dynasty mummy. . . .
You survive life's obliquities of health, though Adams
knew the Southerner, even as an animal, will lose.
Love teases. We're one still, shakier, wilder—
stuck in one room again, we want to fight.

To Allen Tate 1. 1937

My longest drive, two hundred miles, it seemed:
Nashville to Clarksville to the Cumberland,
March 1937, in *my* month Pisces,
Europe's last fling of impotence and anger—
above your fire the blood-crossed flag of the States,
a print of Stonewall Jackson, your shotgun half-cocked . . .
to shatter into the false windmills of the age.
The cornwhisky was whiter than the purest water;
you told dirty, stately setpieces in Cumberland patois;
you said your tenant with ten children had more art
than Merrill Moore. "Do they expect me to leave the South
to meet frivolous people like Tugwell and Mrs. Roosevelt?"
Ford, playing Russian Banker in the half-light, nagging,
"Don't show your cards, my dear Tate . . . it isn't done."

To Allen Tate 2. 1960's

On your enormous brow, a snowman's knob,
a ripped red tissuepaper child's birthday hat;
you squint, make out my daughter, then six or seven:
"*You* are a Southern *belle*; do you know why
you are a *Southern* belle?" (Stare, stupor, thumb in her mouth)
"Because your *mother* is a Southern belle."
Your eye wanders. "I love you now, but I'll love you
more probably when you are older." Harriet mutters,
"If you are still alive." We reach Gettysburg;
both too much the soldier from the Sourmash:
"I don't know whether to call you my son or my brother."
Ashtrays and icecubes deploy as Pickett's columns:
his flashing forest of slanting steel. You point:
"There, if Longstreet had *moved*, we would have *broke* you."

To Allen Tate 3. Michael Tate August 1967–July 1968

Each night, a star, gold-on-black, a muskellunge,
dies in the highest sphere that never dies. . . .
Things no longer usable for our faith
go on routinely possible in nature;
the worst is the child's death. Even his small gravestone,
the very, very old one, one century gone, two,
his *one-year* common as grass in auld lang syne
is beyond our scale of faith . . . and Michael Tate
gagging on your plastic telephone,
while the new sitter drew water for your bath,
unable to hear you gasp—they think: if there'd been
a week or two's illness, we might have been prepared.
Your twin crawls for you, ten-month twin . . . no longer
young enough to understand what happened.

To Allen Tate 4. A Letter from Allen Tate

This winter to watch the child of your old age;
and write, "He is my captor. As a young man,
I was too alert to let myself enjoy
Nancy's infancy as I do the little boy's."
Ah that was the mosses ago in your life, mine;
no New York flights this season. "As you must guess,
we're too jittery to travel after Michael's death."
You are still magisterial and cocky as when
you gave us young romantics our directive,
"Shoot when you get the chance, only shoot to kill."
Who else would sire twin sons at sixty-eight?
How sweet your life in retirement! What better than loving
a young wife and boy; without curses writing,
"I shall not live long enough to 'see him through.' "

Three Poems 1. Seal of the Fair Sex

"He was mother's beau before she spoke to boys—
our *Uncle* Harold. Now his eyes are going,
he pops in here twice a week with Maine delights,
his colorful, slightly aging garden truck,
his bounty to needy and unneedy since we knew him. . . .
Thirty raspberry bushes stacked on my sundeck,
then planted and meshed by himself in three small rows,
with three plastic lilies, his everlastings,
just like a grave—*for you to think of me,
when I lie uphill*. Do you find this amusing?
He is in love, I am the end-all crush.
When we are gone and dying, love is power,
love, in his hallucinated sunrise, keeps him . . .
it's all that kept off death at any time."

Three Poems 2. River Harbor

I sit desiring a more historic harbor,
wilds suiting our first Academy's pomp of youth,
or Aaron Burr's flirtation with frontiers—
we swing with our warpage to *fin de siècle*—
down river, down river, and none will go to town. . . .
Your wharfpiles leaking sawdust ran half a mile—
rot without burden. Your shack was a cookie-box,
your costly small motors moved electric-sculptures,
toys for the lover of Klee. Art for you was amusement,
child drowning the summer in puzzles and shady tennis. . . .
We lay under glass of a greenhouse at noon,
all visible for a fling of fifty miles,
North Haven, Stonington and Mount Desert—
your toy structures flecking in my eyes like flies.

Three Poems 3. Shipwreck Party

One misses Emerson drowned in Luminism,
his vast serenity of emptiness;
and FitzHugh Lane painting a schooner moored in Castine,
its bright flywings fixed in the topographical
severity of a world reworked as glass.
Tools are honest function, and even toys;
you puzzled out small devices, mini-motors,
set children and parents trotting in your trash,
you danced dressed as a beercan, crosscut, zany thing—
wit and too much contrivance for our yacht club brawl.
After the party, I heard your unmuffled car
loop the town, ten or twelve laps a minute—
a village is too small to lose a date
or need a hatchet to split hairs.

Hudson River Dream

I like trees, because I can never be at their eye-level;
not even when the stiff sash of the snowed-in farmhouse
slammed, as it always did, toward morning-rise;
I dreaming I was sailing a very small sailboat,
with my mother one-eighth Jewish, and *her* mother two-eighths,
down the Hudson, twice as wide as it is, wide as the Mississippi,
sliding under the pylons of the George Washington Bridge,
lacework groins as tall as twenty trees
(childhood's twice-as-wide and twice-as-high),
docking through the coalsmoke at a river café.
The Atlantic draws the river to no end. . . .
My knee-joints melted when I met you—
O why was I born of woman? Never to reach their eye-level,
seeing women's mouths while my date delays in the john.

Blood Test, 1931, After About Forty Years

Boarding, not bedding, at the Haven Inn,
I fourteen and just not missing breakfast
to catch you alone with coffee and stacked plates—
I dared not smile, so you didn't. You were eighteen,
you had been about, and were. . . .
Do the sheep your mother rented still mow the lawn
they dirty? Is her ruddy décolletage of just-forty . . .
She died that winter. . . . I watched you with my head half off—
all, all, the mind, the bones, the flesh, the soul . . .
gone in the peripheral flotsam of our live flow?
I see my blood pumped into crystal pipes,
little sticks like the firecrackers of live July—
ninetenths of me water, yet it's lousy stuff—
touch blood, it sticks, stains, drips, slides . . . and it's lukewarm.

Last Resort

The sunrise, the *cri de coeur*, my swat at age—
everyone now is crowding everyone
to stretch vacation until Indian Summer. . . .
Old People in thirty canebacks view Vermont,
a golf course, and the everlasting hills.
This club is open to all who worship health—
in quantity or inns, we terrify,
asking to linger on past fall in Eden.
Cold cracks the supple golf-shoe; we warm our cars,
burn the thruway to Boston and the world. . . . *Age*:
an old house sunk and glum, a smell of turtles,
my grandparents' bridal portrait fades to carbon—
youth that gave no youth, an old world marriage.
Didn't she love him when she loved his clothes?

Dream of Fair Ladies

Those maidens' high waists, languid steel and wedding cake,
fell, as waists must, and the white, white bust, to heel—
these once, the new wave; mostly they were many,
and would not let the children speak. They spoke
making a virtue of lost innocence.
They were never sober after ten
because life hit them, as it must by forty;
whenever they smoothed a dead cheek, it bled.
High-waisted maidens, languid steel and wedding cake . . .
they lost us on the road from chapel to graveyard.
Pace, pace, they asked for no man's seeding. . . .
Meeting them here is like ten years back home,
when hurting others was as necessary as breathing,
hurting myself more necessary than breathing.

Randall Jarrell 1. October 1965

Sixty, seventy, eighty: I would see you mellow,
unchanging grasshopper, whistling down the grass-fires;
the same hair, snow-touched, and wrist for tennis; soon doubles
not singles. . . . Who dares go with you to your deadfall,
see the years wrinkling up the reservoir,
watch the ivy turning a wash of blood
on your infirmary wall? Thirty years ago,
as students waiting for Europe and spring term to end—
we saw below us, golden, small, stockstill,
the college polo field, cornfields, the feudal airdrome,
the McKinley Trust; behind, above us, the tower,
the dorms, the fieldhouse, the Bishop's palace and chapel—
Randall, the scene still plunges at the windshield,
apples redden to ripeness on the whiplash bough.

Randall Jarrell 2

I grizzle the embers of our onetime life,
our first intoxicating disenchantments,
dipping our hands once, not twice in the newness . . .
coming back to Kenyon on the Ohio local—
the view, middle distance, back and foreground, shifts,
silos shifting squares like chessmen—a wheel
turned by the water buffalo through the blue
of true space before the dawn of days. . . .
Then the night of the caged squirrel on his wheel,
lights, eyes, peering at you from the overpass;
black-gloved, black-coated, you plod out stubbornly
as if in lockstep to grasp your blank not-I
at the foot of the tunnel . . . as if asleep, Child Randall,
greeting the cars, and approving—your harsh luminosity.

Munich 1938, John Crowe Ransom

Hitler, Mussolini, Daladier, Chamberlain,
that historic confrontation of the great—
voluble on one thing, they hated war—
each lost there pushing the war ahead twelve months.
Was it worse to choke on the puke of prudence,
or blow up Europe for a point of honor? . . .
John Crowe Ransom, Kenyon College, Gambier, Ohio,
looking at primitive African art on loan:
gleam-bottomed warriors of oiled brown wood,
waving broom-straws in their hands for spears;
far from the bearded, bronze ur-Nordic hoplites
of Athens and Sparta, not distant from their gods.
John said, "Well, they may not have been good neighbors,
but they haven't troubled the rest of the world."

Picture in *The Literary Life, a Scrapbook*

A mag photo, before I was I, or my books—
a listener. . . . A cheekbone gumballs out my cheek;
too much live hair. My wife caught in that eye blazes,
an egg would boil in the tension of that hand,
my untied shoestrings write my name in the dust. . . .
I lean against the tree, and sharpen bromides
to serve our great taskmaster, the New Critic,
who loved the writing better than we ourselves. . . .
In those days, if I pressed an ear to the earth,
I heard the bass growl of Hiroshima.
In the *Scrapbook*, it's only the old die classics:
one foot in the grave, two fingers in their Life.
Who would rather be his indexed correspondents
than the boy Keats spitting out blood for time to breathe?

Frederick Kuh, Manx Cat

(FOR JEAN STAFFORD)

Closer to us than most of our close friends,
the only friend we never quarrelled over,
the sole survivor of our first marriage, I see him
on catnip, bobtailed, bobbing like a rabbit,
streaking up the slender wand of a tree,
scratching the polished bark and glassy sprouts,
preferring to hang hooked than life a claw.
Windtoy, Lynxears, Furfall, you had eyes,
you lowered yourself to us, clockclaw, clickclaw—
to where no one backed down or lost a point.
Cats aren't quite lost despite too many lives.
Which of us will ever manage one,
or storm the heights and gracefully back down—
Jean, those years multiplied beyond subtraction?

Family Album

Those mute dinner parties, wife by husband,
no passenger having seniority over father,
rank won at the captain's table first day at sea—
INDISPENSABLE . . . like Franklin Roosevelt,
dying and solar on his fourth campaign—
coming to power by reaching public opinion—
the sad blandness of the silver voice;
he used time, time was his servant not his master. . . .
You learn to be yourself; at first it's freedom,
then paralysis, since you are yourself. . . .
Free in the teeth of the world's first army,
they snatched their third of a million men from Dunkirk;
for the first time England was spiritually in the war,
the defeat, like so many British retreats, a triumph.

Deutschland über Alles

Hitler, though we laughed, gave them the start,
the step forward, one had to give them that:
the Duce's, "Once they start marching, they'll never stop—"
the silver reichsmark sticking to the heel,
the knights corrupted by their purity,
made wilder by the wildness of the woodcut—
his eyes were glowing coals, a world gone dark,
the horde, on stopwatch, asked for earth and water,
settled for *lebensraum*, then *lebensraum*:
spaces, a space, the knight astride the eyetooth,
joy in the introversion of loneliness.
Who will contest the conqueror his dirt,
spaces enough to bury what he left,
the six million Jews gassed in the space to breathe?

In the Cage
(First Written 1944)

We short-termers file into the messhall
according to our houses—twos
of bleaching denim. A felon fairy
tinkles dinner-music blues,
blows kisses from his balustrade;
a canary chips its bars and screams.
We come from the prison cellar . . . spade,
pickax, hod for plaster, steam,
asbestos. To the anti-semite
black Bible-garbling Israelite
starving on wheatseeds for religion,
I am night, I am vanity. The cage
feeds our failed nerve for service.
Fear, the yellow chirper, beaks its cage.

Rats

That friend of the war years, the Israelite
on my masons' gang at our model jail,
held his hand over the postcard Connecticut
landscape, pocked by prisoners and a few safe human
houses, *Only man is miserable.*
He was wrong though, he forgot the rats. A pair
in an enclosure kills the rest, then breeds a clan.
Stranger rats with their wrong clan-smell stumble
on the clan, are run squeaking with tails and backs split open
up trees and fences—they die of nervous shock.
Someone rigged the enclosure with electric levers
that could give the rats orgasms. Soon they learned
to press the levers, did nothing else—still on the trip,
they died of starvation in a litter of food.

Hell

"Nth Circle of Dante—and in the dirt-roofed cave,
each family had marked off its yard of space;
no light except for coal fires laid in buckets,
no draft of air except the reek, no water,
no hole to hide the excrement. I walked,
afraid of stumbling on the helpless bodies,
afraid of going in circles. I lost the Fascist
or German deserters I was hunting . . . screaming
vecchi, women, children, coughing and cursing.
Then hit my foot on someone and reached out
to keep from falling or hurting anyone;
and what I touched was not the filthy floor:
a woman's hand returning my worried grasp,
her finger tracing my lifeline on my palm."

Streamers: 1970

The London windows bloomed with Christmas streamers
twenty-five days before their Christmas Day
I will not see if I can reach New York;
but I was divorced from my passport—
"The Home Office can't keep your passport, it isn't theirs,
it isn't yours even, it's God's, or Nixon's."
Everything gets lost in life's strip-tease—
who stripped for the guards at Auschwitz? They caught whores,
good Germans, and married them themselves for Hitler—
one assumes those marriages were consummated;
who'd marry a whore to read *Mein Kampf* in bed?
After the weddings they packed the wives in planes;
altitude gained, the girls were pushed outdoors—
their parachutes their streaming bridal veils.

Serpent

"When I was changed from a feeble cosmopolite
to a fanatical antisemite,
I didn't let you chew my time with chatter,
bury my one day's reasonable explanations
in your equal verisimilitude the next. . . .
But I got to the schools, their hysterical faith
in the spoken word, hypnotic hammer blows,
indelible, ineradicable,
the politician wedded to a mind—
I come once in a blue moon. . . . I my age,
its magical interpretation of the world,
enslaved to will and not intelligence. . . .
Soon it was obvious I didn't enjoy my war.
I'd no time for concerts, theater, to go to movies."

Words

Christ's first portrait was a donkey's head,
the simple truth is in his simple word,
lies buried in a random, haggard sentence,
cutting ten ways to nothing clearly carried. . . .
In our time, God is an entirely lost person—
there were two: Benito Mussolini and Hitler,
blind mouths shouting people into things.
After their Chicago deaths with girls and Lügers,
we know they gave a plot to what they planned.
No league against the ephemeral Enemy lasts;
not even the aristocracy of the Commune
curing the seven plagues of economics,
to wither daily in favor of the state,
a covenant of swords without the word.

Sunrise

There is always enough daylight in hell to blind;
the flower of what was left grew sweeter for them,
two done people conversing with bamboo fans
as if to brush the firefall from the air—
Admiral Onishi, still a cult to his juniors,
the father of the Kamikazes . . . he became a fish-hawk
flying our armadas down like game;
his young pilots loved him to annihilation.
He chats in his garden, the sky is zigzag fire.
One butchery is left, his wife keeps nagging him to do it.
Husband and wife taste cup after cup of Scotch;
how garrulously they patter about their grandchildren—
when his knife goes home, it goes home wrong. . . .
For eighteen hours you died with your hand in hers.

In the Forties 1

'46 and greenwood sizzling on the andirons,
two men of iron, two milk-faced British Redcoats.
June smoulders to greenness; in the sopping trees
the greenfrog whistles to the baser shush
of new leaves; thrush and robin go a-hunting,
heads cocked for earthworms sunning in the thaws. . . .
Friends came, new as the foliage of the season;
you came, unique in making me take walks.
One day we discovered—or did we—mounds
of the Abenaki, R.C. converts like me;
some humorist called them Praying Niggers, though
this helped them little with the English, who
scalped, killed and burned brave, squaw and child—then held
that field a moment . . . as we, newcomers, free.

In the Forties 2

The heron warps its neck, a broken pick,
to study its reflection in the glare
of the lily pads bright as mica, swarming
with plant-lice in the wood-red water.
I see you: your ballet glasses hold
the heron twisting by a fist of alder,
your figure's synonym—your chest so thin then,
the ribs stood out like bars. . . . The Puritan shone here,
lord of self-inflicted desiccation,
roaming for outlet through the virgin forest,
stalking the less mechanically angered savage—
the warpath to three wives and twenty children—
many of them, too many, Love, to count,
born like us to fill graveyards . . . thick as sticks.

In the Forties 3

By August, Brooklyn turned autumn, all
Prospect Pond could mirror. No sound; no talk;
dead matches nicked the water and expired
in target-circles of inverted sky,
nature's looking-glass . . . a little cold!
Our day was cold and short, love, and its sun
numb as the red carp, twenty inches long,
panting, a weak old dog, below a smashed
oar floating from the musty dock. . . . The fish
is fungus now; I wear a swollen face. . . .
I rowed for our reflection, but it slid
between my hands aground. There the squirrel,
a conservative and vegetarian,
keeps his roots and freehold, Love, unsliding.

F. O. Matthiessen 1902–50

Matthiessen jumping from the North Boston hotel,
breaking his mania barrier to despair;
a patriot like the Czech-student human torches?
Or manslaughter? Who knows whom he might have killed,
falling bald there like a shell. I'm scared
of hitting this street, his street so far to our left
in gala anti-Stalinist 1950—
I wouldn't murder and be murdered for my soul,
like Stonewall Jackson sucking the soul of a lemon. . . .
Mattie, his Yale *Skull and Bones* pin on the dresser,
torn between the homosexual's terrible love
for forms, and his anarchic love of man . . .
died, unique as the Union, lies frozen meat,
fast colors lost to lust and prosecution.

Sylvia Plath

A miniature mad talent? Sylvia Plath,
who'll wipe off the spit of your integrity,
rising in the saddle to slash at Auschwitz,
life tearing this or that, *I am a woman?*
Who'll lay the graduate girl in marriage,
queen bee, naked, unqueenly, shaming her shame?
Each English major saying, "*I* am Sylvia,
I hate marriage, I must hate babies."
Even men have a horror of giving birth,
mother-sized babies splitting us in half,
sixty thousand American infants a year,
U.I.D., Unexplained Infant Deaths,
born physically whole and hearty, refuse to live,
Sylvia . . . the expanding torrent of your attack.

Randall Jarrell

The dream went like a rake of sliced bamboo,
slats of dust distracted by a downdraw;
I woke and knew I held a cigarette;
I looked, there was none, could have been none;
I slept off years before I woke again,
palming the floor, shaking the sheets. I saw
nothing was burning. I awoke, I saw
I was holding two lighted cigarettes. . . .
They come this path, old friends, old buffs of death.
Tonight it's Randall, his spark still fire though humble,
his gnawed wrist cradled like *Kitten.* "What kept you so long,
racing the cooling grindstone of your ambition?
You didn't write, you *rewrote.* . . . But tell me,
Cal, why did we live? Why do we die?"

Theodore Roethke 1908–63

At Yaddo, you shared a bathroom with a bag
tree-painter whose boobs bounced in the basin,
your blues basin where you wished to plunge your head. . . .
All night, my friend, no friend, you swam in my sleep;
this morning you are lost in the Maine sky,
close, cold, gray, smoke and smoke-colored cloud.
Sheeplike, unsociable, reptilian, the shags
fly off in lines like duck in a shooting booth,
divers devolving to a monochrome.
You honored nature, helpless, elemental
creature, and touched the waters of the offing;
you left them quickened with your name: Ted Roethke. . . .
Omnipresent, the Mother made you nonexistent,
you, the ocean's anchor and high out-tide.

In Dreams Begin Responsibilities

My heater aches my head, it's cold outside,
it's bright outside, the sun tears stars in my shade . . .
the problem is to keep the dream a movie:
a hundred breasts are bursting the same black sweater,
like and unlike as the stars or the snowflakes.
Your dream had humor, then its genius thickened,
you grew thick and helpless, your lines were variants,
unlike and alike, Delmore—your name, Schwartz,
one vowel bedevilled by seven consonants . . .
one gabardine suit the color of sulphur,
scanning wide-eyed the windowless room of wisdom,
your notes on Joyce and porno magazines—
the stoplights blinking code for you alone
casing the bars with the eye of a Mongol horseman.

Tabletalk with Names 1970

"Why don't you write the things he should have written:
Nelson Rockefeller letching for his wife,
Delmore even hallucinating the room. . . ."
The boy wearing his black fleece mini-coat to lunch,
lace ragging his freshly laundered shirt,
his cufflinks sterling silver bottletops,
his longhand verses published in holograph.
"London is less terrible than New York,
but I will never storm the citadel."
He equally enjoyed the notables he taped:
Elsa Morante, Ezra, his Senator's wife.
"One of my lovely ladies." I must hold the table,
snapping at his questions like a queen,
another master's voice to fill the album.

Our Dead Poets

Their lines string out from nowhere, stretch to sorrow.
I think of the others who once had the top billing,
ironclads in our literary havoc,
now even forgotten by malice. "He exists,"
as an old Stalinist luminary said of a friend
sent to Siberia, "Cold helps him to compose."
As a child Jean Stafford stood on a chair to dress;
"It's so much easier." It's easier not to dress,
not brush our teeth, flick off unopened mail.
Sometimes for days I only hear your voices,
the sun of summer will not adorn you again
with her garment of new leaves and flowers . . .
her *nostalgie de la boue* that shelters ape
and protozoa from the rights of man.

For Ann Adden 1. 1958

Remember standing with me in the dark,
Ann Adden? In the mad house? Everything—
I mad, you mad for me? And brought my ring,
that twelve-carat lunk of gold there . . . Joan of Arc . . .
undeviating still from your true mark—
robust, ah taciturn! Remember our playing
Marian Anderson in Mozart's *Shepherd King*,
Il Re Pastore there? O Hammerheaded Shark,
the Rainbow Salmon of the World, your hand
a rose—not there, a week earlier! We stand,
sky-walking the eggshell by the Mittersill,
Pascal's infinite, perfect, fearful sphere—
the border nowhere, your center everywhere. . . .
And if I forget you, Ann, may my right hand . . .

For Ann Adden 2. Heidegger Student

"Have you ever lost a year off . . . somewhere?
The new owner can't give it back to us, can he?
Our terrible losses, but Harry Truman couldn't
lose a minute's sleep for Hiroshima—
a boy who slammed the paw of his mutt in the door of his car would. . . .
Twice I heard a rattling stress of cherry-stones,
saw from my bed, the man. My flight was Gothic
with steel-gloved hand, shoe filled with blood, and wings. . . .
And I killed my dragon—my doctor's thesis on Heidegger
in Germany, in German, for my German Prof.
I love Lenin, he was so feudal. *When I listen to Beethoven*,
he said, *I think of stroking people's hair;*
what we need are people to chop the head off.
The horizontal is the color of blood . . ."

For Ann Adden 3. 1968

"Dear Lowell, sitting sixty feet above the sea,
hearing my father build our house on this cliff,
sixty feet above the Penobscot Bay,
returning here from ten years exile in Europe,
waiting for our emigration papers, work cards . . .
I chanced to read your Adden poem in *Near the Ocean*.
You're older . . . an extending potency. . . .
What I'd like to say is humanity,
as if a cubist leapt to pharaohs in blackstone.
What I write to tell you is what a shining
remembrance for someone, you, to hold of me—
we aggrandize 1958,
the snow-capped, crazy, virginal year, I fled
America. We have a Viking son of three."

For Ann Adden 4. Coda

I want you to see me when I have one head
again, not many, like a bunch of grapes.
The universe moves beneath me when I move,
a stream of heady, terrified poured stone. . . .
On my great days of sickness, I was God—
cry of blood for high blood that gives both tyrant
and tyrannized their short half-holiday. . . .
Now the earth is solid, the sky is light,
yet even on the steadiest day, dead noon,
I have to brace my hand against a wall
to keep myself from swaying—swaying wall,
straitjacket, hypodermic, helmeted
doctors, one crowd, white-smocked, in panic, hit,
and bury me running on the cleated field.

T. S. Eliot

Caught between two streams of traffic, in the gloom
of Memorial Hall and Harvard's war-dead. . . . And he:
"Don't you loathe to be compared with your relatives?
I do. I've just found two of mine reviewed by Poe.
He wiped the floor with them . . . and I was *delighted*."
Then on with warden's pace across the Yard,
talking of Pound, "It's balls to say he only
pretends to be Ezra. . . . He's better though. This year,
he no longer wants to rebuild the Temple at Jerusalem.
Yes, he's better. '*You* speak,' he said, when he'd talked two hours.
By then I had absolutely nothing to *say*."
Ah Tom, one muse, one music, had one your luck—
lost in the dark night of the brilliant talkers,
humor and honor from the everlasting dross!

Ezra Pound

Horizontal on a deckchair in the ward
of the criminal mad. . . . A man without shoestrings clawing
the Social Credit broadside from your table, you saying,
". . . here with a black suit and black briefcase; in the brief,
an abomination, Possum's *hommage* to Milton."
Then sprung; Rapallo, and the decade gone;
and three years later, Eliot dead, you saying,
"Who's left alive to understand my jokes?
My old Brother in the arts . . . besides, he was a smash of a poet."
You showed me your blotched, bent hands, saying, "Worms.
When I talked that nonsense about Jews on the Rome
wireless, Olga knew it was shit, and still loved me."
And I, "Who else has been in Purgatory?"
You, "I began with a swelled head and end with swelled feet."

Fears of Going Blind

(FOR WYNDHAM LEWIS)

El Greco could paint a thunderstorm reflected
on a cufflink; Americans reflect
the space they peopled. . . . I see non sequitur:
Watch the stoplights, they are leopards' eyes;
what's the word for God, if he has four legs? . . .
Even the artist's vision picks up dirt,
the jelly behind the eyeball will leak out,
you will live with constellations of flusters,
comet-flashes from the outer corners;
see the failed surgeon exit with a smile,
they will not let you move your head for weeks,
your wife will hold up gin in a teacup to your mouth,
you will suck from a crooked straw—what depresses
me is they'll actually take my eyeball out.

Louis MacNeice 1907–63

A dozen children would visit half a dozen;
downstairs a lost child bullied the piano,
getting from note to note was jumping rail-ties;
the black keys showed bruises and turned white.
The outdoor games the child heard outside and missed
were as heavily hit and commonplace—
no need to be Bach to be what we are. . . .
Louis, watching his father, the Bishop, wade
a trout-stream barefoot, for the first time liked him:
"What poor feet!" Till thirty, he was afraid
a woman would roll on him, and smother him.
A month from his death, we talked by Epstein's bust
of Eliot; MacNeice said, "It is better
to die at fifty than lose our pleasure in fear."

William Carlos Williams

Who loved more? William Carlos Williams,
in collegiate black slacks, gabardine coat,
and loafers polished like rosewood on yachts,
straying stonefoot through his town-end garden,
man and flower seedy with three autumn strokes,
his brown, horned eyes enlarged, an ant's, through glasses;
his Mother, stonedeaf, her face a wizened talon,
her hair the burnt-out ash of lush Puerto Rican grass;
her black, blind, bituminous eye inquisitorial.
"Mama," he says, "which would you rather see here,
me or two blondes?" Then later, "The old bitch
is over a hundred, I'll kick off tomorrow."
He said, "I am sixty-seven, and more
attractive to girls than when I was seventeen."

Robert Frost

Robert Frost at midnight, the audience gone
to vapor, the great act laid on the shelf in mothballs,
his voice is musical and raw—he writes in the flyleaf:
For Robert from Robert, his friend in the art.
"Sometimes I feel too full of myself," I say.
And he, misunderstanding, "When I am low,
I stray away. My son wasn't your kind. The night
we told him Merrill Moore would come to treat him,
he said, 'I'll kill him first.' One of my daughters thought things,
thought every male she met was out to make her;
the way she dressed, she couldn't make a whorehouse."
And I, "Sometimes I'm so happy I can't stand myself."
And he, "When I am too full of joy, I think
how little good my health did anyone near me."

Stalin

Winds on the stems make them creak like things of man;
a hedge of vines and bushes—three or four
kinds, grape-leaf, elephant-ear and alder,
an arabesque, imperfect and alive,
a hundred hues of green, the darkest shades
fall short of black, the whitest leaf-back short of white.
The state, if we could see behind the wall,
is woven of perishable vegetation.
Stalin? What shot him clawing up the tree of power—
millions plowed under with the crops they grew,
his intimates dying like the spider-bridegroom?
The large stomach could only chew success. What raised him
was an unusual lust to break the icon,
joke cruelly, seriously, and be himself.

Harpo Marx

Harpo Marx, your hands white-feathered the harp—
the only words you ever spoke were sound.
The movie's not always the sick man of the arts,
yours touched the stars; Harpo, your motion picture
is still life unchanging, not nature dead.
You dumbly memorized an unwritten script. . . .
I saw you first two years before you died,
a black-and-white fall, near Fifth in Central Park:
old blond hair too blonder, old eyes too young.
Movie trucks and five police trucks wheel to wheel
like covered wagons. The crowd as much or little.
I wish I had knelt. . . . I age to your wincing smile,
like Dante's movie, the great glistening wheel of life—
the genius *happy* . . . a generic actor.

The Goldfish

The biggest cat sees all through eyefilm, yawns
dreamily, "Such a sweet little radical couple!"
And prays for the man to come without his wife.
Her decks of windows graze on Central Park,
her fortune flies from Zurich to meet the rent—
from her elevation the crowd is part of a movie.
"Is it as Marx dreamed, man is what he makes?"
She sighs, "The rich have muscle." Her windows watch
the unilluminating city lights,
as a goldfish might calculate the universe.
She sees the Old Left yielding place to New,
and eyes her guest, young, dissident, a trustee;
tonight he is single, he has everything,
swims in her like an eel in the Bay of Fundy.

Across Central Park

Home from you, and through the trodden tangle,
the corny birdwalk, the pubescent knoll,
rowboats three deep on the landing, tundra
from Eighty-First Street to my 15 Sixty-Seventh,
snow going from pepper and salt to brain-cell dull,
winter throwing off its Christmas decorations.
The afternoon has darkened in twenty minutes
from light to night—I think of seeing you
in General Eisenhower's Washington,
I in a Dickensian muffler, snow-sugared, unraveling. . . .
You've lived the season. In the waste loss
of revelations, your true voice has seared,
still yearningly young; and I, though never young
since our first meeting, am younger when we meet.

Che Guevara

(Central Park)

Week of Che Guevara, hunted, hurt,
held prisoner one lost day, then gangstered down
for gold, for justice—violence cracking on violence,
rock on rock, the corpse of our last armed prophet
laid out on a sink in a shed, revealed by flashlight. . . .
The leaves light up, still green, this afternoon,
and burn to frittered reds; our tree, branch-lopped
to go on living, swells with homely goiters—
under uniform sixteen story Park apartments . . .
the poor Latins much too new for our new world,
Manhattan where our clasped, illicit hands
pulse, stop my bloodstream as if I'd hit rock. . . .
Rest for the outlaw . . . kings once hid in trees
with prices on their heads, and watched for game.

Caracas 1

Through another of our cities without a center,
Los Angeles, and with as many cars
per foot, and past the 20-foot neon sign
for *Coppertone* on the cathedral, past the envied,
$700 per capita a year
in jerry skyscraper living slabs—to the White House
of El Presidente Leoni, his small men with 18-
inch repeating pistols, firing 45 bullets a minute,
two armed guards frozen beside us, and our champagne . . .
someone bugging the President: "Where are the girls?"
And the enclosed leader, quite a fellow, saying,
"I don't know where yours are, I know where to find mine". . . .
This house, this pioneer democracy, built
on foundations, not of rock, but blood as hard as rock.

Caracas 2

If words were handled like the new grass rippling,
far from planners, the vile writhings of our nerves . . .
One could get through life, though mute, with courage
and a merciful heart—two things, and the first thing:
humor . . . as the evicted squatter clings
with amused bravery that takes the form of mercy
to the Old Caracas Square—its shaky, one-man hovels,
its cathedral first spoiled in the age of Drake.
The church has hay in its courtyard; the hovel owns the Common—
no grass as green as the greens in the open sewer . . .
conservatives reduced to conservation:
communists committed to their commune—
artists and office-holders to a claque
of less than fifty . . . to each his venomous in-group.

Norman Mailer

The 9 a.m. man on the street is a new
phenomenon to me: he moves. He moves
in one direction for Fifth Avenue,
and up Fifth Avenue, simplex as pigeons,
as crocked with project, his heart, a watch,
imagining being paid for being on time. . . .
In Buenos Aires, the bourgeois is the clock,
his heart on Greenwich, the West's last Anglophile,
his constitutionals a reek of tweed—
being erratic isn't the only way
to be ourselves, or Norman Mailer—he wears
a wardrobe of two identical straight blue suits
and two blue vests . . . to prove monotony,
escape the many false faces I see as one.

Liberty and Revolution, Buenos Aires

At the *Hotel Continentál* I always
heard the bulky, beefy, breathing herd.
I had bought a cow suit and matching chestnut
flatter pointed shoes that hurt my toes.
That day cast the light of the next world: the bellow
of Juan Peron, the schoolgirls' Don Giovanni—
frowning starch-collared crowds, a *coup d'état*—
I missed it—of the leaden internecine soldier,
the lump of dough on the chessboard. . . . By darkening cypress,
the Republican martyrs lie in Roman temples;
marble goddesses calm each Liberal hero
still pale from the great kiss of Liberty. . . .
All night till my shoes were bloody—I found rest
cupping my soft palm to her stone breast.

Statue of Liberty

I like you like trees . . . you make me lift my eyes—
the treasonable bulge behind your iron toga,
the thrilling, chilling silver of your laugh,
the hysterical digging of your accursed spur,
Amazon, gazing on me, pop-eyed, cool,
ageless, not holding back your war-whoop—no chicken,
still game for swimming bare-ass with the boys.
You catch the frenetic spotlight we sling about
your lighthouse promontory, flights an inch
from combustion and the drab of ash. . . .
While youth lasts your flesh is never fallen—
high above our perishable flesh,
the icy foamrubber waterfall stands firm
metal, pear-pointing to eternity.

Can a Plucked Bird Live?

From the first cave, the first farm, the first sage,
inalienable the human right to kill—
"You must get used," they say, "to seeing guns,
to using guns." Guns too are mortal. Guns
failed Che Guevara, Marie Antoinette,
Leon Trotsky, the children of the Tsar—
chivalrous ornaments to power. Tom Paine said
Burke pitied the plumage and forgot the dying bird.
Arms given the people are always used against the people—
a dolphin of spirit poking up its snout
into the red steam of that limitless daybreak
would breathe the intoxication of Rimbaud. . . .
Are there guns that will not kill the possessor?
Our raised hands—fear made wise by anger.

The March 1

(FOR DWIGHT MACDONALD)

Under the too white marmoreal Lincoln Memorial,
the too tall marmoreal Washington Obelisk,
gazing into the too long reflecting pool,
the reddish trees, the withering autumn sky,
the remorseless, amplified harangues for peace—
lovely to lock arms, to march absurdly locked
(unlocking to keep my wet glasses from slipping)
to see the cigarette match quaking in my fingers,
then to step off like green Union Army recruits
for the first Bull Run, sped by photographers,
the notables, the girls . . . fear, glory, chaos, rout . . .
our green army staggered out on the miles-long green fields,
met by the other army, the Martian, the ape, the hero,
his new-fangled rifle, his green new steel helmet.

The March 2

Where two or three were flung together, or fifty,
mostly white-haired, or bald, or women . . . sadly
unfit to follow their dream, I sat in the sunset
shade of our Bastille, the Pentagon,
nursing leg- and arch-cramps, my cowardly,
foolhardy heart; and heard, alas, more speeches,
though the words took heart now to show how weak
we were, and right. An MP sergeant kept
repeating, "March slowly through them. Don't even brush
anyone sitting down." They tiptoed through us
in single file, and then their second wave
trampled us flat and back. Health to those who held,
health to the green steel head . . . to your kind hands
that helped me stagger to my feet, and flee.

Pacification of Columbia

Great dome, small domes or turbans, a child's blue sky,
exhalations of the desert sand—
my old jigsawpuzzle Mosque of Mecca
flung to vaultless consummation and consumed
by Allah—but the puzzle had no message. . . .
The destructive element emaciates
Columbia this Mayday afternoon;
the thickened buildings look like painted buildings,
Raphael's colossal classic sags on the canvas.
Horses, higher artistic types than their masters,
forage Broadway's median trees, as if
nature were liberation . . . the blue police
chew soundlessly by the burnished, nervous hides,
as if they'd learned to meet together in reason.

The Restoration

The old king enters his study with the police;
it's much like mine left in my hands a month:
unopened letters, the thousand dead cigarettes,
open books, yogurt cups in the unmade bed—
the old king enters his study with the police,
but all in all his study is much worse than mine;
an edge of malice shows the thumb of man:
frames smashed, their honorary honours lost,
all his unopened letters have been answered.
He halts at woman-things that can't be his,
and says, "To think that human beings did this!"
The sergeant picks up a defiled *White Goddess*,
or the old king's offprints on ideograms,
"Would a human beings do this things to these book?"

Leader of the Left

Though justice ascribe it to his blind ambition,
and blinder courage (both sowed their dirty germs)
not some ostracizing glandular imbalance—
the miracle of poverty opened his eyes;
his whole face took on a flesh of wood,
a slab of raw plastic grafted to his one
natural feature, scars from demonstrations
borne like a Heidelberg student for the New Left. . . .
His voice, electric, only burns low current;
by now he's bypassed sense and even eloquence—
without listening, his audience believe;
anticipating his sentence, they accept
the predestined poignance of his murder,
his Machiavellian Utopia of pure nerve.

The New York Intellectual

How often was his last paragraph recast?
Did Irving really want three hundred words,
such tact and tough, ascetic resonance,
the preposition *for*, five times in parallel,
to find himself "a beleaguered minority,
without fantasies of martyrdom,"
facing the graves of the New York Intellectuals,
"without joy, but neither with dismay"?
(Art was needed for this final sentence.)
Others read the obsequies with dismay.
What gifts or weakness changed the sick provincial
out-of-it West Side intellectual
to the great brazen rhetorician serpent,
swimming the current with his iron smile?

Historian's Daughter

"Yachts still out, though the saltmarsh is frost;
back for the funeral in my old town, New London,
I know the names of people not their faces.
What did I do to myself? I painted, often
using my hand for a brush. I could be someone,
though only a model, if I photographed.
My peer-group, students, graduates, hippies, mean less
to me than the wasp dropouts of sixty in bars.
But Father believed we needed a bracing man
like Harry Truman—Father was a bang
to do Japan with: he was never stoned,
never irrelevant; at each new airport,
he did five postcards, or recorded history—
our background had no grace for using sloth."

Worse Times

In college, we harangued our platitudes,
and hit democracy with Plato's corkscrew—
we demanded art as disciplined
and dark as Marx or Calvin's *Institutes*—
there was precedent for this argument:
flames from the open hearth of Thor and Saul,
beef frescoed on the vaults of cave and clan,
fleshpots, firewater, slung chunks of awk and man—
the missiles no dialectician's hand could turn.
Children have called the anthropoid, father;
he'd stay home Sunday, and they walked on coals. . . .
The passage from lower to upper middle age
is quicker than the sigh of a match in the water—
we too were students, and betrayed our hand.

Student

France died on the motionless lines of Marshal Joffre. . . .
We have found new saints and Roundhead cells
to guide us down the narrow path and hard,
standing on stilts to curse their black-ice heaven—
Marshal Stalin was something of an artist
at this vague, dreamlike trade of blood and guile—
his joke was death—meat stuck between his tooth
and gum began to stink in half a second.
If I could stop growing, I would stop at twenty,
free to be ill-at-ease again as everyone,
go a-whoring, a-kneeling before the masters,
wallpapering my unlocked cell with paper classics. . . .
Love at fifty is outdrinking the siren;
she sings the Kill-river of no cure.

Small College Riot

The bonfire is eating the green uprooted trees
and bakes cracks in the slabs of the Sixties piazza:
half-moon of students, coughing disk-hymns to pot;
the firemen leave a sizzle of black ink—
a second fire blazes in the facing corner.
On a glassed-in corridor, we professors—
fans of the Colosseum—wipe our glasses
primed for the gladiatorial matinee—
but won't someone move? The students move the firemen;
a boy in a wheelchair burns his lecture-notes,
and hangs his clothes to dry on the green fume—
naked . . . no shorts. Our guest speaker on Shelley
says, "If I met a student, I might have to kill him."
Four legendary oiltanks—are they under the fire?

Professor of Tenure

Wars have silenced half the classic tongues. . . .
The professor holds the chair of tenure,
ink licked from the warts and creases of his skin,
vapor of venom, commonplace and joy—
whenever he croaks, a rival has to plunge,
his girl with a taperecorder has total recall,
his students scribble—*Of course we have the bombs;*
what's wanting is the nerve to play the music,
smash East Germany and Poland in two days,
burn Russia with our nuclear typhoon,
blast Cairo, Damascus, China back to sand.
This Machiavel is one the world can buy;
he's held us to the rough these twenty years,
unchanging since he found no salad in change. . . .

The Spock Sentences in Boston

The black hardrubber bathtub stoppers at the Parker House
must have been ordered for their Majesties,
Edward VII and Queen Alexandra,
the weight and pull of William Howard Taft.
Things were made right in those days—18-carat
gold sky over Boston, brass beds in the jail.
That night I slept to the sawing of immense
machines constructing: saws in circles slicing
white crescents, shafts and blocks, as if Tyre and Sidon
were being reconstructed from salt *ab ovo*
in Boston to confound the intellect,
the treasonable defendant shouting: "Sell-out.
They have had all they can have, and have ruined
so much they will not safely ruin me."

Child-Pastel of Adrienne Rich

Trained at four to read a score by Mozart,
perched on *Plutarch's Lives* to reach the keyboard,
paid a raisin for each note struck true—
the painter of your pastel has graced and hurt you,
your true touch too attuned by your James Mill father. . . .
Then round, bowl-bobbed, married, a mother, came
the season of your rash fling at playing bourgeois. . . .
Self-starved now, one loose lock tossed: "The splendid must fall—
Montaigne, you bastard!" You'll rob the arsenal
to feed the needy, Toussaint, Fanon, Malcolm,
the Revolution's *mutilés de guerre*,
shirtless ones dying, or killing on the rooftops—
disabled veteran, how long will you bay with the hounds
and beat time with crutches? Your groundnote is joy.

Struggle of Non-Existence

Here on the bank where Darwin found his fair one,
and thirty kinds of weeds of the wood in flower,
and a blue shirt, a blue shirt, and our love-beads
rattling together to tell us we are young—
we found the fume-gray thistle far-gone in flower. . . .
God works inside us like the plowman worm
turning a soil that must have lost much sweetness
since Eden when the funk of Abel proved
the one thing worse than war is massacre. . . .
Man turns dimwit quicker than the mayfly,
fast goes the lucid moment of love-believed;
tissue sings to sinew, "Passerby . . .
dying beside you, I feel the live blood simmer
in our hands, and know we are alive."

The Revolution

The roaddust blinds us, tactics grow occult,
the terror of spending the summer with a child,
the revolution has happened in the mind,
a fear of stopping—when the soul, even the soul
of ruin, leaves a country, the country dies. . . .
"We're in a prerevolutionary situation
at Berkeley, an incredible, refreshing relief
from your rather hot-house, good prep-school Harvard riots.
The main thing is our exposure to politics;
whether this a priori will determine
the revolutionary's murder in the streets,
or the death of the haves by the have-nots, I don't know;
but anyway you should be in on it—
only in imagination can we lose the battle."

Youth

They go into the world, innocent, wordy, called
in all the directions I would want to go,
multiplying their twenties to the year 2000.
When I was young and closer to the Faith,
half my friends were leftists and professors
who could read the news when they were born,
they knew that kings must either reign or die.
Many a youth will turn from student to tiger,
seeking his final quarry in the grave—
our blasphemous, unavoidable last Mother
nourished on slow, cold debaucheries,
the bitter, dry pelt of feline undulation—
in her harlot's door of colored beads, she holds
youth old as Michelangelo to her bosom.

Trunks

The tree trunks in our headlights are bright white worms,
inside a truck-shed, white tires are hung like paintings;
the best photographer dare not retouch them—
not everyone accepts their claim to greatness.
*If blood doesn't spurt from my eyelashes, when
I meet a work of art, it isn't art—*
too much persuasion is famine, enough a miracle,
yet God is good, he sees us all as straw dogs.
Even the toothless, trodden worm can writhe—
in the night-moment, even a halt-pacifist,
nursed on leaflets and wheat-germ, hears the drum-step
of his kind whistle like geese in converging lines,
the police weeping in their fog of Mace,
while he plants the black flag of anarchy and peace.

For Mary McCarthy 1

Your eight-inch softwood, starblue floorboard, your house
sawn for some deadport Revolutionary squire. . . .
A friendly white horse doing small-point, smiling,
the weathered yeoman loveliness of a duchess,
enlightenment in our dark age though Irish,
our Diana, rash to awkwardness. . . .
Whose will-shot arrows sing cleaner through the pelt?
Have I said *will*, and not intelligence?
Leaving you I hear your mind, mind, mind,
stinging the foundation-termites, stinging
insistently with a battering ram's brass head of brass. . . .
I hide my shyness in bluster; you align
words more fairly, eighty percent on target—
we can only meet in the bare air.

For Mary McCarthy 2

"Dear Mary, with her usual motherly
solicitude for the lost overdog. . . ."
You sometimes seemed to stand by a white horse,
a Dürer Saint Joan armed by your college and by
that rougher university, the world. . . .
Since your travels, the horse is firmly yours;
you stare off airily through our mundane gossip
and still more mundane virtue, listen puzzled,
groan to yourself, and blurt an ice-clear sentence—
one hand, for solace, toying with the horse's mane. . . .
The immortals are all about us and above us;
for us *immortal* means another book;
there are too many . . . with us, the music stops;
the first violin stops to wipe the sweat from his brow.

For Mary McCarthy 3

"The land going down to the lake was choked with wild rose,
the sunset orchards were scarlet, the high swans, drunk
on making love, had bathed their aching heads;
the water was rebirth at first, then a winter:
no sun, or flower, or even hue for shadow. . . .
Exhaust and airconditioning klir in the city. . . .
The real motive for my trip is dentistry,
a descending scale: long ago, I used to drive
to New York to see a lover, next the analyst,
an editor, then a lawyer . . . time's dwindling choice.
But I can't quite make students all Seven Ages of Man.
Work means working; I fear I am one of the few
sane people living . . . not too stunning a sensation—
They want something different from understanding: belief."

The Going Generation

Our going generation; there are days
of pardon . . . perhaps to go on living in
the old United States of William James,
its once reposeful, now querulous, optimism.
I hear the catbird's coloratura cluck
singing fuck, fuck above the brushwood racket.
The feeder deals catfood like cards to the yearling
salmon in their stockpond by the falls.
Grace-days . . . it is less than heaven, our shelving
bulkhead of lawn black with binoculars,
eyelashes in the lenses that magnify
the rising bosom of the moon—drink, drink, and pitch
the old rings of Saturn like horseshoes round the light-globe . . .
in some tosses, it's heads you win and tails I lose.

Penelope

Manet's bourgeois husband takes the tiller at Cannes,
the sea is right, the virgin's cocky boater,
naive as the moon, streams with heartstring ribbons—
as if Ulysses were her husband for the Sunday. . . .
"Do clothes make the man, or a man the clothes?"
Ulysses whistles—enters his empty household,
the deserted hollowness of its polish,
cellar, womb, growths—heartless philanderer,
he wants his Penelope, and still pretends
he can change a silk purse to a sow's ear, thinks
something like this, or something not like this:
"How many a brave heart drowned on monologue
revives on ass, and lives for alcohol. . . .
Is it silk cuts scissors, or scissors silk?"

Ulysses

Shakespeare stand-ins, same string hair, gay, dirty . . .
there's a new poetry in the air, it's youth's
patent, lust coolly led on by innocence—
late-flowering Garden, far from Eden fallen,
and still fair! None chooses as his model
Ulysses landhugging from port to port for girls . . .
his marriage a cover for the underworld,
dark harbor of suctions and the second chance.
He won Nausicaa twenty years too late. . . .
Scarred husband and wife sit naked, one Greek smile,
thinking *we were bound to fall in love
if only we stayed married long enough—
because our ships are burned and all friends lost.*
How we wish we were friends with half our friends!

Before Repeal

O our repose, the goat's diminishing day—
the Romantic who sings, sings not in vain
Don Giovanni's farcical, brute leap. . . .
In New Orleans and just married, both our pajamas
hung out of reach and wrestling with the moisture
caught on the leather blade of the central fan—
our generation bred to drink the ocean
in the all-possible before Repeal;
all the girls were under twenty, and the boys
unearthly with the white blond hair of girls,
crawling the swimming pool's robin-egg sky.
Autumn deepens that color, warms vine and wire,
the ant's cool, amber, hyperthyroid eye,
grapes tanning on our tried entanglements.

Thanksgiving 1660 or 1960

When life grows shorter and daylightsaving dies—
God's couples marched in arms to harvest-home
and Plymouth's communal distilleries . . .
three days they lay at peace with God and beast. . . .
I reel from Thanksgiving midday into night:
the young are mobile, friends of the tossed waste leaf,
bellbottom, barefoot, Christendom's wild hair—
words are what get in the way of what they say.
None sleeps with the same girl twice, or marches homeward
keeping the beat of her arterial vein,
or hears the cello grumbling in her garden.
The sleeper has learned karate—Revolution,
drugging her terrible premenstrual cramps,
marches with unbra'd breasts to storm the city.

For Aunt Sarah

You never had the constitution to quarrel:
poised, warm and cool, distrusting hair and Hamlets,
yet infinitely kind—in short a lady,
still reaching for the turn of the century,
your youth in the solid golden age, when means
needed only to follow the golden mean
to love and care for the world; when businessmen
and their ancillary statesmen willingly gave up
health, wealth and pleasure for the gall of office—
converts to their only fiction, God.
But this new age? "They have no fun," you say. . . .
We've quarreled lightly almost fifty years,
Dear, long enough to know how high our pulse beats, while the young
wish to stand in our shoes before we've left them.

Flight in the Rain

Why did I say, I'm not afraid of flying,
death has no meaning in imagination?
Too much gets published without imagination. . . .
Tonight: the wing-tilt, air-bounce upright, lighted
Long Island mainstreets flashed like dice on the window;
raindrops, gut troutlines wriggling on the window—
the landing no landing—low circling at snailspace
exhausting a world of suburban similars. . . .
My delicate stomach says, *You were.* Says, *Pray*—
my mismanaged life incorrigible—
prayer can live without faith. God is *déjà vu,*
He hears the sparrow fall, heard years from here
in Rio, one propeller clunking off,
my *Deo gracias* on the puking runway.

Blizzard in Cambridge

Risen from the blindness of teaching to bright snow,
everything mechanical stopped dead,
taxis no-fares . . . *the wheels grow hot from driving*—
ice-eyelashes, in my spring coat; the subway
too jammed and late to stop for passengers;
snow-trekking the mile from subway end to airport . . .
to all-flights-canceled, fighting queues congealed
to telephones out of order, stamping buses,
rich, stranded New Yorkers staring with the wild, mild eyes
of steers at the foreign subway—then the train home,
jolting with stately grumbling: an hour in Providence,
in New Haven . . . the Bible. In darkness seeing
white arsenic numbers on the tail of a downed plane,
the smokestacks of abandoned fieldguns burning skyward.

The Heavenly Rain

Man at the root of everything he builds;
no nature, except the human, loves New York—
the clerk won't prove Aseity's existence
busing from helpless cause to helpless cause. . . .
The rain falls down from heaven, and heaven keeps
her noble distance, the dancer is seen not heard.
The rain falls, and the soil swims up to breathe;
a squatter sumac shafted in cement
flirts wet leaves skyward like the Firebird.
Two girls clasp hands in a clamshell courtyard, watch
the weed of the sumac failing visibly;
the girls age not, are always last year's girls
waiting for tomorrow's storm to wash
the fallen leaf, turned scarlet, back to green.

Misanthrope and Painter

"I'm *the misanthrope*, a woman who hates men—
men may be smarter but we are stronger.
We hate you mostly for the other woman,
yet even Desdemona dreams a faithless
Cassio will step into Othello's bed.
I am a painter, not a woman painter.
The only way Helen can fix her lyric palette
would be to throw herself under a truck.
Don't sell me your personality garbage, Baby;
when Rembrandt painted the last red spot on the nose
of a clown or Rembrandt, he disappeared in the paint.
That's my technique . . . I'm not nothing, Baby;
Rothko is invisible when I'm in the room.
You may have *joie de vivre*, but you're not twenty."

Redskin

Unsheathed, you unexpectedly go redskin,
except for two white torches, fruits of summer,
woman's headlights to guide us through the dark
to love the body, the only love man is.
Women look natural stripped to flesh, not man
equipped with his redemptive bat and balls—
Renoir, paralyzed, painted with his penis.
Endless, aimless consecutive sentences. . . .
Rain claws the skylight, a thousand fingernails,
icy, poorly circulating fingers
trickling all night from heaven to our skins . . .
our bodies sunburnt in the staining dawn. . . .
At wrath-break, when earth and ocean merge,
who wants to hold his weapon to the whale?

Thirst

The chilled glass of julep blows to pollen,
a cold wind, snow-touched, fans our steaming backs,
blows in and in, a thousand snow-years back,
above the Hudson's essence-steaming back,
the Great Arriviste in the metropolis. . . .
We have licked the acid of the saltmarsh,
salt craves its weight in water—thirst without bottom.
Your hand, a small monkey's, cannot lift your drink—
there'll be no more. We gasp, and fall asleep—
love's dissolution . . . we breathe no air from it,
only my heavy, secret and sad sighs.
Where is the tunnel that led to our only exit,
a hole soon filled with twenty slides of snow?
We were joined in love a thousand snow-years back.

New York

We must have got a lift once from New York
seven years back or so, it's hard to think,
gone like my Greek and box for butterflies. . . .
A pilgrim comes here from the outlands, Trinidad,
Port of Spain seeking a sister metropolis—
lands here, knowing nothing, strapped and twenty—
to parade the streets of wonder. . . . Plateglass
displays look like nightclubs blocks away;
each nightclub is heaven with a liveried tariff,
all the money, all the connection. . . . You have none,
you are triggered by the liberated girl,
whipped to that not unconquerable barricade
by our first categorical imperative, "Move,
you bastard, do you want to live forever?"

Sounds in the Night

Nothing new in them yet their old tune startles;
asked to adapt, they swear they cannot swerve:
machines are our only servants bound to serve,
metal, mortal and mechanical,
a dissonance more varied than New York birds
winging their clatter through the night air dirt.
Sleepless I drink their love, if it is love.
Miles below me, luminous on the night,
some simple court of wall-brick windowless,
and the grass-conservative cry of the cat in heat—
Who cares if the running stream is sometimes stopped—
inexhaustible the springs from which I flow.
Cats will be here when man is prehistory,
gone as Prohibition or mahjong.

Dream of Leak and Terra-Cotta

I would drown if I crossed these terra-cotta tiles—
drops strike with the tock of a townhall clock,
hitting more steadily than the minute hand—
like industry's doggéd, clogged pollution.
The toilet paper is squirled like a Moslem tile,
in the basin, a sad ringlet of my pubic hair—
an overweight, crested bathmat, squeezed
to a pierced pipe, and alchemized to water,
sprinkling bright drops of gin, dime-size and silver—
everything man-made is about to change to water. . . .
When I lifted the window, there was a view,
a green meadow pointing to a greener meadow,
to dogs, to deer, Diana out in war-skirt . . .
heaven paved with terra-cotta tile.

Fever

Desultory, sour commercial September
lies like a mustard plaster on the back—
Pavlov's dogs, when tortured, turned neurotics. . . .
If I see something unbelievable in the city,
it is the woman shopper out in war-paint—
the druggist smiles etherealized in glass. . . .
Sometimes, my mind is a rocked and dangerous bell;
I climb the spiral stairs to my own music,
each step more poignantly oracular,
something inhuman always rising in me—
a friend drops in the street and no one stirs.
Even if I should indiscreetly write
the perfect sentence, it isn't English—
I go to bed Lord Byron, and wake up bald.

Across the Yard: La Ignota

The soprano's bosom breathes the joy of God,
Brunnhilde who could not rule her voice for God—
her stately yellow ivory window frames
haven't seen paint or putty these twenty years;
grass, dead since Kennedy, chokes the window box.
She has to sing to keep her curtains flying;
one is pink dust flipped back to scarlet lining,
the other besmirched gauze; and behind them
a blown electric heater, her footlocker with Munich
stickers stood upright for a music stand.
Her doorbell is dead. No one has to hire her.
She flings her high aria to the trash like roses. . . .
When I was lost and green, I would have given
the janitor three months' rent for this address.

Elisabeth Schwarzkopf in New York

The great still fever for Paris, Vienna, Milan;
which had more genius, grace, preoccupations?
Loss of grace is bagatelle to pay
for a niche in the Pantheon or New York—
and as for Europe, they could bring it with them.
Elisabeth Schwarzkopf sings, herself her part,
Was ist Silvia, Die alte Marschallin,
until the historic rivers of both worlds,
the Hudson and the Danube burst their bar,
trembling like water-ivy down my spine,
from satyr's tussock to the hardened hoof. . . .
La Diva, crisped, remodelled for the boards,
roughs it with chaff and cardigan at recordings
like anyone's single and useful weekend guest.

Diamond Cutters

A terrible late October summer day;
we passed the diamond cutters and appraisers,
hole-in-the-corners on 47th Street—
trade ancient as the Ur-kings and their banks,
gambling empires for a grain of dust;
heaven in essence, crystal, hard and bright.
Herman Melville would have found a meaning,
while scuffing his final dogdays in New York,
fat from cousin dogfish and white whale,
unable to slumber from his metaphysics,
his mason's chisel on the throat of stone. . . .
We were boulevarding out the hour till lunch;
our conversation was inaudible to You,
eye brighter than the uncut sun at noon.

Candlelight Lunchdate

An oldtime sweatshop, remodelled purple brick—
candlelightbulbs twinkle in stormlamp chimneys;
the *Chez Dreyfus*, Harvard. The chimneys don't smoke,
their light is cruel; we are not highschool dates.
In college we hated the middle-aged, now we,
the late middles, are ten years their seniors,
caught by their swelling stream of traffic.
Say the worst, Harvard at least speaks English,
words are given a fighting chance to speak:
your hand now unattainable was not attained.
"You used to be less noisy." I kept your discards,
hairpins, buckles and beautiful dyed hairs—
we needn't be sick in mind, or believe in God,
to love the flesh of our youth, V-mouth of the pike.

Stoodup

Light takes on a meaning in the afternoon—
diamond windows of a Madison Avenue British pub,
one is streaming noonday, the other is dull;
reds gleam in the grand glass of the sporting prints:
blue beefy faces fired by the hunt and scotch,
Old England tarted up with boor and barmaid;
these reproductions urbanize the coarse. . . .
Sometimes color lines are blurred and dim
in the great city, and exotics mate.
It is not malevolence but inertia
that prevents our meeting obligations,
your active sloth that ties my willing hands—
two windows, two reflections, one bypasser
doubled and hurrying from his double life.

Two Walls

(1968, Martin Luther King's Murder)

Somewhere a white wall faces a white wall,
one wakes the other, the other wakes the first,
each burning with the other's borrowed splendor—
the walls, awake, are forced to go on talking,
their color looks much alike, two shadings of white,
each living in the shadow of the other.
How fine our distinctions when we cannot choose!
Don Giovanni can't stick his sword through stone,
two contracting, white stone walls—their pursuit
of happiness and his, coincident. . . .
At this point of civilization, this point of the world,
the only satisfactory companion we
can imagine is death—this morning, skin lumping in my throat,
I lie here, heavily breathing, the soul of New York.

Abstraction

Question: why do I write? Answer: if I stop,
I might as well stop breathing—superstition?
I want to write this without style or feeling—
4 a.m. to 7, I lay awake,
my mouth watering for some painless poison;
insomnia flings cowards small grains of courage,
they live to swell the overpopulation. . . .
Who has done this to me? Drink brought immortal
Faulkner, Crane and Hemingway themselves,
helped them plot on self-inspired to the end,
less awkward for their enemies than friends.
Their moment threw the dice out wrong,
or the chances befriended, not the choices—
the velocity of conversation.

Dissenting Academy

The Black Moslem's hack-moon hangs over WABC
TELEVISION, and its queue of stand-ins;
real trees, the sky-distempered, skim the heavens,
rooted in a nondescript, yellow brick tower—
my city! No zoned village curbs more coiffeured poodles,
our iron sings like a hundred kinds of birds.
The birds have left for the country. . . . In ivy-league colleges,
men breathe, and study darkens their small panes.
A professor has students to prime his pump
and wattles like a turkey to his grant—
each university is his universe. . . .
It's petty, and not worth writing home about,
why should anyone settle for New York?
Dying without death is living in a city.

Taxi Drivers

A green-leaf cushion is seat and back of my swivel-chair,
I swivel round past ceiling, walls, and locks—
an eerie study, bluegloss streaked with green.
They will never let me finish a sentence. . . .
The taxi drivers always hold the floor;
born with directions, crackling rolls of bills,
only wanting more juice to burn—unslowing
hacks condemned to keep in step with snails. . . .
How many voyagers have they talked to death—
safe from their fares in forts of gunproof plastic,
they daily run their course to the edge of culture,
the hem of Harlem. . . . I swing from wall to wall;
taxis dissect New York . . . some, unable
to see they're finished, go on into the wall.

Goiter Test, Utopia for Racoons

My goiter expert smiles like a racoon,
"O.K., you're rich and can afford to die."
He claws me a minute, claws his notes for five,
claws his notes three weeks, then claws me back;
he could crack my adam's apple like a walnut.
He washes his hands of me and licks his paws,
sipping his fountainpen for bubbly ink.
In a larger room in a greater hospital,
two racoons wear stethoscopes to count the pulse
of their geiger-counter and their thyroid scan;
they sit sipping my radioactive iodine
from a small zinc bottle with two metal straws.
What little health we have is stolen fruit.
What is the life-expectancy of a racoon?

Goiter Delirium, Werner von Urslingen

Half eggshell, half eggshell, white in a glass of water;
a whiteness swollen and doubled by the water,
soft goiters croaking in a plaster-cast,
heads flayed to the bone like Leonardo's felons,
heads thrust forward at me not to hear,
lipping with the astuteness of the deaf—
no skull so bald, this never had hair. I complain
like a bough asking severance from the dead tree—
it isn't me, I still to die and leave
my momentary thumbprint on the plaster-cast. . . .
This memento mori Dürer could have etched
or the landsknecht, Werner von Urslingen, who gave
his shield this motto, a German's faith in French:
L'ennemi de Dieu et de merci.

Under the Dentist

"When I say you *feel*, I mean you *don't*. This thing's
metaphysical not sensational:
you come here in your state of hypertension,
Bob . . . you lie quiet, be very, very good—
do you feel the jangling in your nerves?
You will feel the city jangling in your nerves,
a professor might even hear the cosmos jangle.
You watch news, the pictures will flick and jangle.
You don't have to be I.Q. or Maria Callas
to have feelings. Thinking burns out nerve;
that's why you cub professors calcify.
You got brains, why do you smoke? I stopped smoking, drinking,
not pussy . . . it's not vice. I drill here 8 to 5,
make New York at sunrise—I've got nerves."

Window-Ledge 1. The Bourgeois

Our house, forced, liberated, still on fire—
hand over hand on the noosed rope, the boy,
tanned, a cool crew haircut, nears my ledge,
smiling at me to mount his shoulders, swing
down fifty tiers of windows, two city blocks,
on that frail thread, his singed and tapering rope.
Looking down, our building is a tapered rope,
fat head, small base—Louis-Philippe, his pear-face
mirrored upside-down in a silver spoon.
I must go down the rope to save my life—
I am too big in the head. I solved this in my dream:
if forced to walk to safety on a tightrope,
if my life hung on my will and skill . . . better die.
The crowd in the street is cheering, when I refuse.

Window-Ledge 2. Gramsci in Prison

The only light I saw was sun reflected
off other windows from 3 p.m. to 4—
like Gramsci in a Roman prison reflecting
pessimism of intelligence, optimism of will. . . .
What I dreamed is not designed to happen—
to waken on the window's sloping ledge,
it soon apparent that I will not cling
hugging my shins and whistling daylight home
through the chalk and catlight of the ancient city,
Caesar's Rome of assassins and sunsick palms—
windows reflecting lightning without heat. . . .
I lived to the vibration of fulfilment,
falling past galleried windows to my bash—
I saw the world is the same as it has been.

Five Hour Political Rally

A design of insects on the rug's red acre,
one to each ten feet like the rich in graves;
the belly is like a big watermelon seed,
each head an empty pretzel, less head than mouth,
the wings are emblems, black as the ironwork
for a Goya balcony, lure and bar to love—
the darkeyed and protected Spanish girls
exhibited by the custom that imprisons.
Insects and statesmen grapple on the carpet;
all excel, as if each were the candidate;
all original or at least in person;
twenty first ballerinas are in the act.
Like insects they almost live on breath alone:
If you swallow me, I'll swallow you.

For Robert Kennedy 1925–68

Here in my workroom, in its listlessness
of Vacancy, like the old townhouse we shut for summer,
airtight and sheeted from the sun and smog,
far from the hornet yatter of his gang—
is loneliness, a thin smoke thread of vital
air. But what will anyone teach you now?
Doom was woven in your nerves, your shirt,
woven in the great clan; they too were loyal,
and you too were loyal to them, to death.
For them like a prince, you daily left your tower
to walk through dirt in your best cloth. Untouched,
alone in my Plutarchan bubble, I miss
you, you out of Plutarch, made by hand—
forever approaching your maturity.

For Robert Kennedy 2

How they hated to leave the unpremeditated
gesture of their life—the Irish in black, three rows
ranked for the future photograph, the Holy Name,
fiercely believed in then, then later held to
perhaps more fiercely in their unbelief. . . .
We were refreshed when you wisecracked through the guests,
usually somewhat woodenly, hoarsely dry. . . .
Who would believe the nesting, sexing tree swallow
would dive for eye and brain—this handbreadth insect,
navy butterfly, the harbinger of rain,
changed to a danger in the twilight? Will we
swat out the birds as ruthlessly as flies? . . .
God hunts us. Who has seen him, who will judge this killer,
his guiltless liver, kidneys, fingertips and phallus?

Assassin! (*Les Enfants du Paradis*)

The swinging of a bush, a bird, a fly,
even the shadow of these grows animate,
if anyone really wants to kill anyone. . . .
He waits. I wait. *I am a writer not a leader.*
But even a paranoid can have enemies. . . .
A hero might break his spine to better purpose,
like the two *apaches* in *Enfants du Paradis*
who ambush the Baron bathing in his bath-house.
No sport. The Baron (naked) sucks his hookah.
The first killer walks offscreen to his dark game;
the second waits. It's the fear which isn't screened.
The last shot is a dead arm dangling from the tub,
the assassin snaps and pockets the bowl of the hookah . . .
to prove in recollection that something gave.

For Eugene McCarthy

(July, 1968)

I love you so. . . . Gone? Who will swear you wouldn't
have done good to the country, that fulfillment wouldn't
have done good to you—the father, as Freud says:
you? We've so little faith that anyone
ever makes anything better . . . the same and less—
ambition only makes the ambitious great.
The state lifts us, we cannot raise the state. . . . All
was yours though, lining down the balls for hours,
freedom of the hollow bowling-alley,
the thundered strikes, the boys. . . . Picking a quarrel
with you is like picking the petals of the daisy—
the game, the passing crowds, the rapid young
still brand your hand with sunflecks . . . coldly willing
to smash the ball past those who bought the park.

Ocean

Mostly its color must adulterate,
sway, swelter; earth stands firm and not the sea,
one substance everywhere divisible,
great bosom of salt. It floats us—less and less
usable now we can fly like the angels.
We cannot stay alive without the ocean;
I think all marriages are like the ocean:
one part oxygen mates two parts hydrogen,
as if the formula existed everywhere
in us, as in the numinous Parnassus of chemistry.
The statesman mutters, "The problems of politics
are nothing. . . ." He was thinking of his marriage—
uncontrollable, law-ravaged like the ocean . . . God is
H_2O Who must forgive us for having lived.

Dream, the Republican Convention

That night the mustard bush and goldenrod
and more unlikely yellows trod a spiral,
clasped in eviscerating blue china vases
like friendly snakes embracing—cool not cold. . . .
Brotherly, stacked and mean, the great Convention
throws out Americana like dead flowers:
choices, at best, that hurt and cannot cure;
many are chosen, and too few were called. . . .
And yet again, I see the yellow bush rise,
the golds of the goldenrod eclipse their vase
(each summer the young breasts escape the ribcage)
a formation, I suppose, beyond the easel.
What can be is only what will be—
the sun warms the mortician, unpolluted.

Flaw

(Flying to Chicago)

My old eye-flaw sprouting bits and strings
gliding like dragon-kites in the Midwestern sky—
I am afraid to look closely, and count them;
today I am exhausted and afraid.
I look through the window at unbroken white cloud,
and see in it my many flaws are one,
a flaw with a tail the color of shed skin,
inaudible rattle of the rattler's disks.
God is design, even our ugliness
is the goodness of his will. It gives me warning,
the first scrape of the Thunderer's fingernail. . . .
Faust's soul-sale was perhaps to leave the earth,
yet death is sweeter, weariness almost lets
me taste its sweetness none will ever taste.

After the Democratic Convention

Life, hope, they conquer death, generally, always;
and if the steamroller goes over the flower, the flower dies.
Some are more solid earth; they stood in lines,
blouse and helmet, a creamy de luxe sky-blue—
their music savage and ephemeral.
After five nights of Chicago: police and mob,
I am so tired and had, clichés are wisdom,
the clichés of paranoia. . . . Home in Maine,
the fall of the high tide waves is a straggling, joshing
mell of police . . . they're on the march for me. . . .
How slender and graceful, the double line of trees,
slender, graceful, irregular and underweight,
the young in black folk-fire circles below the trees—
under their shadow, the green grass turns to hay.

From Prague 1968

Once between 6 and 7 a.m. at Harvard, we counted
ten jets, or maybe forty, one thunder-rivet
no one could sleep through, though many will.
In Prague on the eve of the *Liberation*, you woke
to the Russian troop-planes landing, chain on anvil,
and thought you were back at Harvard. I wish you were,
up and out on our tramp through the one museum.
You thought the best paintings between the Sienese
and Haitians were photographs. We've kept
up flirting since the fall of Harry Truman.
Even an old fool is flattered by an old girl,
tights, shoes, shirts, pinkthings, blackthings, my watch, your bra,
untidy exposures that cannot clash. . . . We lay,
talking without any need to say.

Election Night

Election Night, last night's Election Night,
without drinks, television or my friend—
today I wore my blue knitted tie to class.
No one understood that blue meant black. . . .
My daughter telephones me from New York,
she talks *New Statesman*, "Then you are a cop-out. Isn't
not voting Humphrey a vote for Nixon and Wallace?"
And I, "Not voting Nixon is my vote for Humphrey."
It's funny-awkward; I don't come off too well;
"You mustn't tease me, they clubbed McCarthy's pressroom."
We must rouse our broken forces and save the country:
I even said this in public. The beaten player
opens his wounds and hungers for the blood-feud
hidden like contraband and loved like whisky.

After the Election: From Frank Parker's Loft

We remember watching old Marshal Joffre or Foch
chauffeured in Roman triumph, though French, through Boston—
the same small, pawky streets, the Back Bay station,
though most of Boston's now a builders' dream,
white, unspoiled and blank. Here nothing has slid
since 1925. The Prudential Building
that saved so many incomes, here saves nothing.
From your window we see the *Thread and Needle Shoppe*,
where we stole a bad fifteen-dollar microscope,
and failed to make them pay back fifteen dollars. . . .
On the starry thruways headlights twinkle
from Portland, Maine to Portland, Oregon.
Nobody has won, nobody has lost;
will the election-winners ever pay us back?

Puzzle

A broad doorway, garage or warehouse door,
an asthmatic man panting into it to hide—
helpless place to hide, though two or three
off-duty policemen in earphones banquet on stools. . . .
The old team have the city. In an open car
elected and loser stand reflecting our smiles—
no insurance policy will accept them.
Disappointed we discover they're twins.
A voice moves like the ribs of a rake to reform the city.
Enamelled with joy and speechless with affliction—
Fra Angelico's *Last Judgment* . . . two
of the elect, two angels more restless than the rest,
swoop along a battlemented street
blank with the cobbled ennui of feudal Florence.

West Side Sabbath

(Breakfast)

WIFE, in her tower of *The New York Times*;
HUSBAND, rewriting his engagement-book. . . .
WIFE: Nixon's in trouble. HUSBAND: Another family
brawl? WIFE: Nixon has profounder troubles.
HUSBAND: You mean our National Peace Offensive?
WIFE: *Entre autres*. HUSBAND: When Nixon weighs in,
does he outweigh *The New York Sunday Times*?
WIFE: Say that twice, and I'll fly to San Juan with Bruce. . . .
Is our chance a monochrome Socialism,
Robespierre's gunpoint equality,
privilege slashed to a margin of survival?
Or the Student-Left's casually defined
anarchists' faith in playing the full deck—
who wants the monks without the fucking Maypole?

Eating Out Alone

The loneliness inside me is a place,
Harvard where no one might always be someone.
When we're alone people we run from change
to the mysterious and beautiful—
I am eating alone at a small white table,
visible, ignored . . . the moment that tries the soul,
an explorer going blind in polar whiteness.
Yet everyone who is seated is a lay,
or Paul Claudel, at the next table declaiming:
"L'Académie Groton, eh, c'est une école des cochons."
He soars from murdered English to killing French,
no word unheard, no sentence understood—
a vocabulary to mortify Racine . . .
the minotaur steaming in a maze of eloquence.

Painter

"I said you are only keeping me here
in the hospital, lying to my parents
and saying I am madder than I am,
because you only want to keep me here,
squeezing my last dollar to the pennies—
I'm saner than anyone in the hospital.
I had to say what every madman says—
a black phrase, *the sleep of reason mothers monsters*. . . .
When I am painting the canvas is a person;
all I do, each blot and line's alive,
when I am finished, it is shit on the canvas. . . .
But in his sketches more finished than his oils,
sketches made *after* he did those masterpieces,
Constable can make us *see* the breeze . . ."

In the American Grain

"Ninth grade, and bicycling the Jersey highways:
I am a writer. I was half-wasp already,
I changed my shirt and trousers twice a day.
My poems came back . . . often rejected, though never
forgotten in New York, this Jewish state
with insomniac minorities.
I am sick of the enlightenment:
what Wall Street prints, the mafia distributes;
when talent starves in a garret, they buy the garret.
Bill Williams made less than Band-Aids on his writing,
he could never write the King's English of *The New Yorker*.
I am not William Carlos Williams. He
knew the germ on every flower, and saw
the snake is a petty, rather pathetic creature."

Publication Day

"Dear Robert: I wish you were not a complete stranger,
I wish I knew something more about your mercy,
could total your minimum capacity
for empathy—this varies so much from genius.
Can you fellow-suffer for a turned-down book?
Can you see through your tragic vision, and
have patience with one isolated heart?
Do you only suffer for other famous people,
and socially comforting non-entities?
Has the thistle of failure a place in your affection?
It's important to know these things; in your equestrian
portrait by Mailer, I don't find these things. . . .
I write as a woman flung from a sinking ship—
one raft in the distance . . . you represent that raft."

Loser

"Now I'm almost impotent, I'm almost faithful;
that's why I stay here boozing off my marriage,
it has lasted more than thirty years'
nightly immersion in the acid bath.
The girl in bed was a mouth with two elastics,
a slit of blue daylight below the blowing shade—
my wife sat reading Simone de Beauvoir till day.
All marriages are alike . . . *sagesse de crise*!
Why was her toothpaste always in my tumbler?
For a true loser any good break is verbal,
we monopolize the low cards that lose tricks—
I have my place . . . if one is put in his place
enough times, he becomes his place . . .
the flatterer's all-forgiving, wounded smile."

The Winner

I had the talent before I played the game;
I made the black moves, then the white moves,
I just mulled through whole matches with myself—
it wasn't too social only mating myself. . . .
But this guy in West Berlin whispers a move in my ear,
or there's a guy with his head right over my board—
they weren't too communicative with high chess.
Are most of your friends from the chess world?
I have a few peripheral friends here and there
who are non-chess players, but it's strange,
if you start partying around, it doesn't go.
I try to broaden myself, I read the racetrack,
but it's a problem if you lose touch with life . . .
because they want two world leaders to fight it out hand to hand.

Keepsakes

"If once a winter with absent heart, you look,
then push my ingots underneath your checkstubs;
robbing children of trash was your great joke—
these are not rape, but things for Lost and Found:
bronze bosses, Arab dagger, thin true gold chain,
an ABC design almost too childish
for a child to spell. Can you still spell my name?
I was your gold mine rich with senseless power,
sluiced by your turbulent, pretentious meekness,
my passive willingness for the sullen delight.
Has too much skating cracked the ice? Do you still
swell your stomach with oracle, and say,
'Girls make things happen'—then rush to Boston with money
for first-hand exercise in this religion?"

The Just-Forties

Somewhere on the West Side with its too many
cleared lots ill-occupied with rusting cars,
I meet this innumerable acquaintance
masked in faces, though forward and familiar,
equipped for encounter like cops or Caesar's legions;
all seem to enjoy at least six men at once,
amateurs building up clienteles of love,
always one on the doorbell, another fleeing—
the Just-Forties, girls (Why is no man just forty?)
born too late for enriching memories:
President Harding, Prohibition, the boom market—
too experienced to be surprised,
and too young to know satiety,
the difficulty of giving up everything.

Under the Moon

In this wavy moonlight, we, like others,
too thoughtful clods, may learn from those we walk on:
star-nosed moles, their catatonic tunnels
and earthworks . . . only in touch with what they touch;
blind from their secret panic to dodge the limelight—
even a subway haunter could not envy
these vegetating and protective creatures,
forever falling short of man's short life. . . .
Through my fieldglasses, I aggrandize
a half-fledged robin with a speckled breast,
big as a pheasant . . . the invincible
syllogism advances from talon to talon.
No earthly ripple disturbs the moon, the ballbearing
utility of this bald and nearest planet. . . .

Moon-Landings

The moon on television never errs,
and shares the worker's fear of immigration,
a strange white goddess imprisoned in her ash,
entombed Etruscan, smiling though immortal.
We've clocked the moon; it goes from month to month
bleeding us dry, buying less and less—
chassis orbiting about the earth,
grin of heatwave, spasm of stainless steel,
gadabout with heart of chalk, unnamable
void and cold thing in the universe,
lunatic's pill with poisonous side-effects,
body whose essence is its excess baggage,
compressed like a Chinese dried caterpillar . . .
our hallucinator, the disenchantress.

Utopia

"Is Mao's China nearer the Utopia?"
"Only twelve or fifteen dynasties;
Mao still thinks it dishonorable to carry
firearms except for students, wars and birds."
"Are we altogether certain of that much here?"
"Mao is Establishment crowned to go down fanged,
old king-ape of the ape-horde preferring deference to justice."
"I prefer lying with a Canadian girl
on the American border, the belt of the earth,
each girl pretty as her Queen but not so rich."
"None must desert his cell for wife or friend."
"A wife is such a good thing I'd cry welcome,
welcome, even if she comes from hell. . . ."
"There's a strong shadow where there's too much light."

River God

The Aztecs gave their human sacrifice
credit-cards, dames, the usual pork of kings;
after a year, the king was cooled with palm-slash;
he never remembered he lost his heart—
man and the sun were succored by his blood. . . .
Mao had to find ways to economize on lepers;
each family had its leper, fed it like a pig—
if we purify, the waterlilies die?
Mao announced the people's plan for leprosy,
the lepers came bounding from the filth of hiding,
more than Ganges, or the popular cures of Christ. . . .
On dope like kings for the colorful boatride, the lepers
were launched out on the Yangtze with a thousand flowers—
the river god caught them in his arms when they drowned.

Killer Whale Tank

Even their immensity feels the hand of man. . . .
Forming himself in an S-curve before her,
swimming side by side and belly to belly
inches distant, each one stroking the other,
feather touch of a flipper across her belly;
he teases, nuzzles and lightly bites her nose,
and with a fluke titillates the vulva—
he awakes a woman. . . . With her closed mouth she rubs
his genital slit afire, and scoots away
a fraction of a second before explosion;
then, runs straight to him and will not turn aside,
seeking the common sleep that hands them back to life.
Whales meet in love and part in friendship—swoosh. . . .
The Killer's sorrow is he has no hands.

Sheik Without Six Wives in London

His whirlwind, a delirium of Eros—
English fairplay decrees *one legal wife*;
the Sheik hears the singular marriage laws
and screams . . . Henry the Eighth espoused monogamy
and shaved six wives to one. The Sheik writes postcards:
Westminster Abbey, Lambeth, House of Lords.
He writes, "Dear Lilith, English barbarity,
love Sheckle." He writes, "Dear Goneril, Dear Regan,
barbarity!" He writes, "My dear Hetaerae,
my six Rolls Royces snowed with parking tickets,
my harem zero." He sings to his last girl
knowing she wants a man, a lover and a poet,
not knowing they are mutually abhorrent—
"I am an iceberg melting in the ocean."

After the Play

"I've been married umpteen years," Ben said,
"I've walked where angels fear to tread,"
then lost his pace by popping up each second,
and held the restaurant spellbound stumbling
from the men's room seven times in twenty minutes,
to wreck his dinner, two computered dates,
and a fellow power man, fairweather friends,
gone waspish, buzzing, "This is impossible."
This, this. They left Ben confessing to the toilet. . . .
To hell with artists painting Cromwell's warts,
London bluedays, sidewalks smeared with dogmess,
pekinese and poodle, poodle and pekinese—
sometimes the palisades of garbage bags
are beautiful sunlit playgrounds of plastic balloons.

English-Speaking World

Loud conversation is sometimes overheard:
"Take Galbraith's *Affluent Society*,
we know it's cheap whiskey, he's the type
that overstructures the picnic to use his car.
It's bells for trotting teatrays on the lawn;
we've lost the freedom of the plutocrat,
once gone, he's really gone, he's bred not made."
In the pride of possession, the *New Statesman*
and the conservative are one at heart.
Dark time and darker hour for a weak faith
in the Socialist, egalitarian state.
In our time of overpopulation,
the homosexual is a savior—
Karl Marx orphaned his illegitimate child.

Loser

"Father directed choir. When it paused on a Sunday,
he liked to loiter out morning with the girls;
then back to our cottage, dinner cold on the table,
Mother locked in bed devouring tabloid.
You should see him, white fringe about his ears,
bald head more biased than a billiard ball—
he never left a party. Mother left by herself—
I threw myself from her car and broke my leg. . . .
Years later, he said, 'How jolly of you to have jumped.'
He forgot me, mother replaced his name, I miss him.
When I am unhappy, I try to squeeze the hour
an hour or half-hour smaller than it is;
orphaned, I wake at midnight and pray for day—
the lovely ladies get me through the day."

Monkeys

"You can buy cooler, more humdrum pets—
a monkey deprived of his mother in the cradle
feels the want of her affection so keenly
he either pines away or masters you
by literally hanging on your neck—
no ounce of your patience or courage is misplaced;
the worst is his air of boredom and neglect,
manifested in tail-chewing and fur-plucking.
The whole species is vulnerable to killing colds,
likes straw, hay or bits of a torn blanket,
a floortray thinly covered with sawdust,
they need trapezes, shelves, old rubber tires—
any string or beam will do to set them swinging—
these charming youngsters tend to sour with age."

Churchill 1970 Retrospective

For a time the splendid person's gone
from London—farewell Franklin, Josef, Winston,
boss's cigar and worker's overalls,
his stock still falling through the Christmas boom.
No Cromwell, though death to staff when high on brandy,
he jumped their flags like checkers on the war-map—
if he stumbled as a statesman, at least he could write.
Some British officer in Libya said,
"Out here we almost prefer Rommel to Churchill;
why is the PM such a shit to Wavell?"
They painted cardboard boxes to look like planes;
Churchill painted in mufti like Van Gogh—
icon still lighted by the fires of Dresden,
a worm like other writers, though a glow-worm.

De Gaulle's Chienlit

Seldom fine words without a virtue. He
who dumbly guns his government on virtue
is like the northern star, which keeps its place,
which keeps its place, and all the stars turn to it;
asks faithfulness and sincerity, though these
may undermine authority more than treason.
He, unseeing, says: a true man acts,
then speaks, speaks in obedience to his act:
what is good for the bee is good for the swarm.
Statecraft without labor is time lost—
and gambling with statecraft? It is perilous—
as if law could be the fulfilment of love,
as if freedom might be visible—free
to piss in any direction on your lawn.

De Gaulle est Mort

"When the French public heard de Gaulle was dead,
they popped champagne on all the squares—
even for Latins it was somehow obscene.
Was he their great man? Three days later
they read in the American press he was . . .
I kept asking those student questions you hate;
I remember a Paris taxi-driver told me:
'I would have popped champagne myself. . . . At last
France has someone better than Churchill to bury;
now he's dead, we know he defied America—
or would we have ditched them anyway?'
His choirgirls were pure white angels at Notre Dame;
I felt the Egyptians really wanted to eat
Nasser—de Gaulle, much bigger, was digested."

Lévi-Strauss in London

Lévi-Strauss, seeing two green plants in a cleft
of a cliff choosing diverse ammonites,
imagined a crevasse of millennia spanned—
when he told me this in English, our hostess spoke French;
I left the party with a severed head.
Since France gave the English their tongue, most civilized
Englishmen can muck along in French. . . .
I was so tired of camp and decoration,
so dog-tired of wanting social hope—
is *structuralism* the bridge from Marx to death?
Cézanne left his spine sticking in the landscape,
his slow brush sucked the resin from the pines;
Picasso's bullfighter's wrist for foil and flare—
they cannot fill the crack in everything God made.

Hedgehog

"All time and culture and my sorrows vocal—
I have ripened on remorse like Stilton cheese,
I regret the brush-off brilliance of my youth . . .
once conversant with French and Jean-Paul Sartre,
now too pompous to get through the doors I crashed,
lust the sublimation of my writing;
but I have never been a society-puppet,
Lady Chelsea her face lifted at eighty,
improved for profiles, paralyzed for friends,
or Giacometti's disciples, who let their teeth
fall out in homage to their toothless master.
I wasn't just a fashion-dog
defiling closed doors and asking, 'Am I in?'
No fool can pick me up and comb my quills."

Verlaine, Etc.

The tender Falstaffian ugh of Verlaine,
Those who have no minds have more than I,
only drunken words cold sober true.
Paul Valéry's assault on modesty,
To be understood is the worst disaster.
Aside from money, literary success
was small compensation for their vanity:
to be condemned by people who never read them,
to have been useful to poets devoid of talent.
What you should pray for is a thousand readers
none giving you a hint of his existence—
not the known shores tiding fan mail in and out. . . .
The muse is a loser, she is sort of sad dirty—
publication might just scour her clean.

Onionskin

It's fancy functional things love us best;
not butterfly useless or austere with use,
they touched my body to assume a body—
my half-pound silver ticker with two bopped lids,
whose splinter lever nicked my thumbnail, and set
time moving from six a.m. to six p.m.—
twice daily time stopped and its thin hands.
It goes a-begging, without me, it is lost.
Where is grandfather's gold snakehead watchchain?
The onionskin typing paper I bought by mistake
in Bucksport Maine last August? The last sheet
creasing cuts my finger and seems to scream
as if *Fortuna* bled in the white wood
and felt the bloody gash that brought me life.

The Nihilist as Hero

"All our French poets can turn an inspired line;
who has written six passable in sequence?"
said Valéry. That was a happy day for Satan. . . .
I want words meat-hooked from the living steer,
but a cold flame of tinfoil licks the metal log,
beautiful unchanging fire of childhood
betraying a monotony of vision. . . .
Life by definition breeds on change,
each season we scrap new cars and wars and women.
But sometimes when I am ill or delicate,
the pinched flame of my match turns unchanging green,
a cornstalk in green tails and seeded tassel. . . .
A nihilist wants to live in the world as is,
and yet gaze the everlasting hills to rubble.

In the Back Stacks
(Publication Day)

My lines swell up and spank like the bow of a yacht. . . .
Outside, no breakthrough for the Broadway bookstores,
outside, the higher voltage of studenten,
the Revolution seeking her professor. . . .
It's life in death to be typed, bound and delivered,
lie on reserve like the Harvard *British Poets*,
hanged for keeping meter. They died with Keats.
Is it enough to be a piece of thread
in the line from King David to Hart Crane?
We talked such junk all summer behind the stacks,
while the books lay incommunicado.
The anthology holds up without us,
outlasts the brass of Cleopatra's cheeks—
everything printed will come to these back stacks.

Reading Myself

Like thousands, I took just pride and more than just,
struck matches that brought my blood to a boil;
I memorized the tricks to set the river on fire—
somehow never wrote something to go back to.
Can I suppose I am finished with wax flowers
and have earned my grass on the minor slopes of Parnassus. . . .
No honeycomb is built without a bee
adding circle to circle, cell to cell,
the wax and honey of a mausoleum—
this round dome proves its maker is alive;
the corpse of the insect lives embalmed in honey,
prays that its perishable work live long
enough for the sweet-tooth bear to desecrate—
this open book . . . my open coffin.

Last Things, Black Pines at 4 a.m.

Imperfect enough once for all at thirty,
in his last days Van Gogh painted as if
he were hurling everything he had: clothes,
bed and furniture against the door
to keep out a robber—he would have roughened
my black pines imperceptibly withdrawing
from the blue black cold of morning sky,
black pines disengaging from blue ice—
for imperfection is the language of art.
Even the best writer in his best lines
is incurably imperfect, crying for truth, knowledge,
honesty, inspiration he cannot have—
after a show of effort, Valéry
and Trollope the huntsman are happy to drop out.

Playing Ball with the Critic

(FOR RICHARD BLACKMUR)

Writers can be taught to return the ball
to the police, smile and even like it;
the critics like it, smile, kick back the ball.
Our hurt blue muscles work like testicles;
how will we learn to duck and block the knock?
Is it a form of a force, or sentiment for form?
Your vision lacerates your syntax.
The logic is zealotry . . . In your first, best, book,
you don't distance yourself from the oddities of life. . . .
I wish I could saunter the grassy streets of old New York,
becoming every object I looked at,
stop for the unhurried, hear old Walt Whitman:
"If you will lend me a dollar, you will help
immortality to stumble on."

Outlaws, a Goodbye to Sidney Nolan

I see the pale, late glaze of an afternoon,
and chopped French conscripts of World War II
in stumps and berets playing *boules* at Pau—
what's more innocent than honorable foemen
giving their lives to kill the innocent?
Your Ned Kelly mugged and bloodied at Barracks Hall . . .
"My blood spoils the lustre of the paint on their gatepost;
when the outlaw reigns, your pockets swell;
it's double pay and double country girls. . . ."
Two rootstumps sit upright like skeletons of geese
sailing the outtide Penobscot on a saddle of drift;
five cormorants, their wing-noise like panting hounds—
Old Hand, we sometimes feel a frenzy to talk,
but truth, alas, is the father of knowing something.

Grasshoppers, for Stanley Kunitz 1970

Who else grew up in the shadow of your Worcester, Mass?
Why do I wake with a start of pathos to fear,
half-lifeless and groaning my andante—
see my no-Jew boarding school near Worcester,
class of '35 whittling . . . *our 35th*;
our pre-Prohibition summer cottage,
Buzzards Bay killing the grass for our croquet,
my homemade cases for fled skunk and turtle,
the old world black tie dinner without wine,
the lost generation sunset, its big red rose?
It is our healthy fifty years we've lost,
one's chance to break in print and love his daughter. . . .
We say the blades of grass are hay, and sing
the Joyful the creatures find no word to sing.

For Elizabeth Bishop (twenty-five years) 1. Water

At Stonington each morning boatloads of hands
cruise off for the granite quarry on the island,
leaving dozens of bleak white frame houses stuck
like oyster shells on the hill of rock. Remember?
We sit on the slab of rock. From this distance in time,
it seems the color of iris, rotting and turning purpler,
but it is only the usual gray rock
turning fresh green when drenched by the sea. . . .
The sea flaked the rock at our feet, kept lapping the matchstick
mazes of weirs where fish for bait were trapped.
You dreamed you were a mermaid clinging to a wharfpile,
trying to pull the barnacles with your hands.
We wish our two souls might return like gulls to the rock.
In the end, the water was too cold for us.

For Elizabeth Bishop 2. Castine Maine

Teenage patched jeans and softball—the Castine Common
looks like a cover for *The American Boy*.
My twelve-foot cedar hedge screens out the human.
North & South, Yarmouth to Rio, one Atlantic—
you've never found another place to live,
bound by your giant memory to one known longitude.
Britain's Georges rule your horoscope;
long live mad George Three in cap and bells,
king in your Nova Scotia, nowhere else—
a whitebeard, deaf and blind, singing Church of England
hymns he accompanied on his harpsichord.
"I wish I were a horse," you say, "or a Sicilian
sitting in my own Greenwich Village bar,
standing drinks . . . and never going outdoors."

For Elizabeth Bishop 3. Letter with Poems for Letter with Poems

"You are right to worry, only please DON'T,
though I'm pretty worried myself. I've somehow got
into the worst situation I've ever
had to cope with. I can't see the way out.
Cal, have you ever gone through caves?
I did in Mexico, and hated them.
I haven't done the famous one near here. . . .
Finally after hours of stumbling along,
you see daylight ahead, a faint blue glimmer;
air never looked so beautiful before.
That is what I feel I'm waiting for:
a faintest glimmer I am going to get out
somehow alive from this. Your last letter helped,
like being mailed a lantern or a spiked stick."

For Elizabeth Bishop 4

The new painting must live on iron rations,
rushed brushstrokes, indestructible paint-mix,
fluorescent lofts instead of French *plein air.*
Albert Ryder let his crackled amber moonscapes
ripen in sunlight. His painting was repainting,
his tiniest work weighs heavy in the hand.
Who is killed if the horseman never cry halt?
Have you seen an inchworm crawl on a leaf,
cling to the very end, revolve in air,
feeling for something to reach to something? Do
you still hang your words in air, ten years
unfinished, glued to your notice board, with gaps
or empties for the unimaginable phrase—
unerring Muse who makes the casual perfect?

Remembrance Day, London 1970's

Flipping the *Sundays* for notice of my new book,
I lost my place to a tall girl, a spine and ribs;
she bought every paper, even *News of the World*—
she had reason, her face on every front page:
Olympic runner, Lillian Board, and twenty,
told yesterday she is a cancer victim. . . .
In my coat I found a leaflet: "Our beloved
Ruth Fox . . . her first and last book, *Catch or Key,*
Journeys to far off lands or strolls at home,
was read by Frances Mintern Jones at the service
last Friday in the New England Poetry Club. . . ."
The remembered live, bagpipers in tan kilts,
their old officers in black suit, bowler and poppy,
their daughters on the sidewalk keeping their step.

Women, Children, Babies, Cows, Cats

"It was at My Lai or Sonmy or something,
it was this afternoon. . . . We had these orders,
we had all night to think about it—
we was to burn and kill, then there'd be nothing
standing, women, children, babies, cows, cats. . . .
As soon as we hopped the choppers, we started shooting.
I remember . . . as we was coming up upon one area
in Pinkville, a man with a gun . . . running—this lady . . .
Lieutenant LaGuerre said, 'Shoot her.' I said,
'You shoot her, I don't want to shoot no lady.'
She had one foot in the door. . . . When I turned her,
there was this little one-month-year-old baby
I thought was her gun. It kind of cracked me up."

Identification in Belfast
(I.R.A. Bombing)

The British Army now carries two rifles,
one with rubber rabbit-pellets for children,
the other's of course for the Provisionals. . . .
"When they first showed me the boy, I thought oh good,
it's not him because he is a blond—
I imagine his hair was singed dark by the bomb.
He had nothing on him to identify him,
except this box of joke trick matches;
he liked to have them on him, even at mass.
The police were unhurried and wonderful,
they let me go on trying to strike a match . . .
I just wouldn't stop—you cling to anything—
I couldn't believe I couldn't light one match—
only joke-matches. . . . Then I knew he was Richard."

Non-Violent

Honor . . . somehow our age has casually lost it;
but in the sick days of the code duello,
any quick killer could have called us out—
a million died in the Spanish war, ninetenths murdered—
viva la guerra, viva la muerte!
Could one be Christian and non-violent?
As boys, we never hoped to dig to China;
in the war, our unnegotiable few fell
the first to die for the unnegotiable flag,
pluming as crusaders from left to right. . . .
To die in my war of words, the lung of infinitude;
past history is immobile in our committed hands . . .
till Death drops his white marble scythe—Brother,
one skeleton among our skeletons.

Sound Mind, Sound Body

Mens sana? O at last; from twenty years
annual mania, their chronic adolescence—
mens sana in corpore insano.
Will I reach three score ten, or drop
the work half through? Each new birthday is the last?
Death is final and a fly-by-night,
the dirty crown on a sound fingernail.
On healthy days, I fall asleep mid-chapter—
death made Attila die of a nosebleed
on the first night of his child-bride. I linger,
I sun without sweating, hear out the old,
live on the dirt of family chronicle.
The married swallows on my work-barn scent
my kindred weakness, dare swoop me from their nest.

Those Older 1

They won't stay gone, and stare with triumphant torpor,
as if held in my fieldglasses' fog and enlargement,
in garments washed by the rainbow, and formal with time,
elders once loved by older elders in a Maytime
invisible to us as the Hittites. I'm too old
to date their coming or going—those *late* people:
Old Aunt Sarah and Cousin Belle. God stamped
them with one maiden name *for life*—blood-rich,
and constellations from the dancing heart.
Our first to die . . . so odd and light and dry . . .
children from a child's lost world . . . they left
hooded in snail-shells, the unassailable
deafness of their formidable asperity—
our girls . . . less than a toy, and more than a flower.

Those Older 2

No fence stands up between death and his object,
the guillotine sings the hollow green wilderness—
those older . . . I have had them fifty years;
they are gone astraying down a backward street,
not hearing the Dutchblight fritter the green elm—
old prunes and tarbone trees vulnerable to a breath,
forgetting why they put down roots near us to chill
a generation who feared exercise.
And I face faceless lines of white frame houses,
sanded, stranded, undarkened by shade or shutter . . .
mass military graveyard of those before us,
rich and poor, no trees in the sky—one white
stone multiplied a thousandfold and too close—
if I pass quickly, they melt to a field of snow.

I. A. Richards 1. Goodbye Earth

Sky-high on the cover of *Goodbye Earth*,
you flash and zigzag like a large hummingbird—
heavy socks and climber's knickerbockers,
sleeves rolled, shirt open at the throat;
an upended pick, your prisoner's ball and chain,
penetentially attached to your wrist.
Here while you take your breath, enthused, I see
the imperishable Byronics of the Swiss Alps
change to the landscape for your portrait, like you
casual, unconventional, innocent . . . earned
by gratuitous rashness and serpentine hesitation.
It is not a picture but a problem—
you know you will move on; the absolute,
bald peaks, glare-ice, malignly beckons . . . goodbye earth.

I. A. Richards 2. Death

This, our one intimate metaphysical—
today, tomorrow, death looks fairly on all.
Ivor, you knew the matter with this subject,
"My vanity won't let me believe in my death.
In our generous world-throw, ought but vanity,
death never catches those life speeds." You thought,
"A doubtful suicide should choose the ocean;
who knows, he might reach the other side?
If my coin falls heads, I'll see the other side. . . .
We still go foothill shuffling every weekened;
but climbing's dull past sixty unless you risk your life."
Hob-Alpine Spirit, you saved so much illusion
by changing its false coin to words—your shadow
on the blind bright heights . . . absconds to air.

For John Berryman 1

I feel I know what you have worked through, you
know what I have worked through—we are words;
John, we used the language as if we made it.
Luck threw up the coin, and the plot swallowed,
monster yawning for its mess of potage.
Ah privacy, as if we had preferred mounting
some rock by a mossy stream and counting the sheep . . .
to fame that renews the soul but not the heart.
The out-tide flings up wonders: rivers, linguini,
beercans, mussels, bloodstreams; how gaily they gallop
to catch the ebb—Herbert, Thoreau, Pascal,
born to die with the enlarged hearts of athletes at forty—
Abraham sired with less expectancy,
heaven his friend, the earth his follower.

For John Berryman 2
(January, After His Death)

Your Northwest and my New England are hay and ice;
winter in England's still green out of season,
here the night comes by four. *When will I see you,
John?* You flash back brightly to my mind,
a net too grandly woven to catch the fry.
Brushbeard, the Victorians waking looked like you . . .
last Christmas at the Chelsea where Dylan Thomas died—
uninterruptible, high without assurance,
of the gayest cloth and toughly twisted.
"I was thinking through dinner, I'll never see you again."
One year of wild not drinking, three or four books. . . .
Student in essence, once razor-cheeked like Joyce,
jamming your seat in the crew race, bleeding your ass—
suicide, the inalienable right of man.

Last Night

Is dying harder than being already dead?
I came to my first class without a textbook,
saw the watch I mailed my daughter didn't run;
I opened an old closet door, and found myself
covered with quicklime, my face deliquescent . . .
by oversight still recognizable.
Thank God, I was the first to find myself.
Ah the swift vanishing of my older
generation—the deaths, suicide, madness
of Roethke, Berryman, Jarrell and Lowell,
"the last the most discouraging of all
surviving to dissipate *Lord Weary's Castle*
and nine subsequent useful poems
in the seedy grandiloquence of *Notebook*."

Gods of the Family

My high blood less hotly burns its mortal coil,
I could live on, if free to leave the earth—
hoping to find the Greenbeard Giant, and win
springtide's circlet of the fickle laurel—
a wreath for my funeral from the Gallant Gangster.
I feel familiar cycles of pain in my back,
reticulations of the spawning cell,
intimations of our family cancer—
Grandmother's amnesia, Grandfather's cancered face
wincing at my adolescent spots—
with us no husband can survive his wife.
His widow tried to keep him alive by sending
blackbordered letters like stamps from Turkestan.
Where are they? They had three children, horses, Boston.

Red and Black Brick Boston

Life will not extend, though I'm in love;
light takes on meaning any afternoon
now, ten years from now, or yesterday.
The arctic brightness bakes the red bricks black,
a color too chequered to splash its happiness—
the winter sun is shining on something worthy,
begging the visible be eternal.
Eternity isn't love, or made for children;
a man and woman may meet in love though married,
and risk their souls to snatch a child's attention.
I glow with the warmth of these soiled red bricks,
their unalikeness in similarity,
a senseless originality for fact,
"Rome was," we told the Irish, "Boston is."

Death and the Bridge
(From a Landscape by Frank Parker)

Death gallops on a bridge of red rail-ties and girder,
a onetime view of Boston humps the saltmarsh;
it is handpainted: this the eternal, provincial
city Dante saw as Florence and hell. . . .
On weekends even, the local TV station's
garbage disposer starts to sing at daybreak:
keep Sunday clean. We owe the Lord that much;
from the first, God squared His socialistic conscience,
gave universal capital punishment.
The red scaffolding relaxes and almost breathes:
no man is ever too good to die. . . .
We will follow our skeletons on the girder,
out of life and Boston, singing with Freud:
"God's ways are dark and very seldom pleasant."

Outlook

On my rainy outlook, the great shade is up,
my window, five feet wide, is raised a foot,
most of the view is blanked by brick and windows.
Domestic gusts of noonday Sunday cooking;
black snow grills on the fire-escape's blacker iron,
like the coal that touched Isaiah's unclean tongue. . . .
I hear dead sounds ascending, the fertile stench
of horsedroppings from the war-year of my birth.
Since our '17, how many millions gone—
this same street, West Sixty-Seven, was here,
and this same building, the last gasp of true,
Nineteenth Century Capitalistic Gothic—
horsedroppings and drippings . . . hear it, hear the clopping
hundreds of horses unstopping . . . each hauls a coffin.

Memorial Day

Sometimes I sink a thousand centuries
bone tired then stone-asleep . . . to sleep ten seconds—
voices, the music students, the future voices,
go crowding through the chilling open windows,
fathomless profundities of inanition:
I will be dead then as the dead die here . . .
dáda, dáda dáda dá dá.
But nothing will be put back right in time,
done over, though through straight for once—not my father
revitalizing in a simple Rhineland spa,
to the beat of Hitler's misguiding roosterstep. . . .
Ah, ah, this house of twenty-foot apartments,
all all windows, yawning—the voice of the student singer's
Don Giovanni fortissimo sunk in the dead brick.

Ice

Iced over soon; it's nothing; we're used to sickness;
too little perspiration in the bucket—
in the beginning, polio once a summer. Not now;
each day the cork more sweetly leaves the bottle,
except a sudden falseness in the breath. . . .
Sooner or later the chalk wears out the smile,
and angrily we skate on blacker ice,
playthings of the current and cold fish—
the naught is no longer asset or disadvantage,
our life too long for comfort and too brief
for perfection—Cro-Magnon, dinosaur . . .
the neverness of meeting nightly like surgeons'
apprentices studying their own skeletons,
old friends and mammoth flesh preserved in ice.

End of a Year

These conquered kings pass furiously away;
gods die in flesh and spirit and live in print,
each library a misquoted tyrant's home.
A year runs out in the movies, must be written
in bad, straightforward, unscanning sentences—
stamped, trampled, branded on backs of carbons,
lines, words, letters nailed to letters, words, lines—
the typescript looks like a Rosetta Stone. . . .
One more annus mirabilis, its hero *hero demens*,
ill-starred of men and crossed by his fixed stars,
running his ship past sound-spar on the rocks. . . .
The slush-ice on the east bank of the Hudson
is rose-heather in the New Year sunset;
bright sky, bright sky, carbon scarred with ciphers.

For Lizzie and Harriet

(1973)

Summer

HARRIET, BORN JANUARY 4, 1957

Half a year, then a year and a half, then
ten and a half—the pathos of a child's fractions, turn-
ing up each summer. Her God a seaslug, God a queen
with forty servants, God—you gave up . . . things whirl
in the chainsaw bite of whatever squares
the universe by name and number. For
the hundredth time, we slice the fog, and round
the village with our headlights on the ground,
like the first philosopher Thales who thought all things water,
and fell in a well . . . trying to find a car
key. . . . It can't be here, and so it must be there
behind the next crook in the road or growth
of fog—there blinded by our feeble beams,
a face, clock-white, still friendly to the earth.

2.

HARRIET

A repeating fly, blueblack, thumbthick—so gross,
it seems apocalyptic in our house—
whams back and forth across the nursery bed
manned by a madhouse of stuffed animals,
not one a fighter. It is like a plane
dusting apple orchards or Arabs on the screen—
one of the mighty . . . one of the helpless. It
bumbles and bumps its brow on this and that,
making a short, unhealthy life the shorter.
I kill it, and another instant's added
to the horrifying mortmain of
ephemera: keys, drift, sea-urchin shells,
you packrat off with joy . . . a dead fly swept
under the carpet, wrinkling to fulfillment.

3.
ELIZABETH

An unaccustomed ripeness in the wood;
move but an inch and moldy splinters fall
in sawdust from the walls' aluminum-paint,
once loud and fresh, now aged to weathered wood.
Squalls of the seagull's exaggerated outcry
dim out in the fog. . . . *Pace, pace.* All day our words
were rusty fish-hooks—wormwood . . . Dear Heart's-Ease,
we rest from all discussion, drinking, smoking,
pills for high blood, three pairs of glasses—soaking
in the sweat of our hard-earned supremacy,
offering a child our leathery love. We're fifty,
and free! Young, tottering on the dizzying brink
of discretion once, you wanted nothing,
but to be old, do nothing, type and think.

4.
THESE WINDS   (HARRIET)

I see these winds, these are the tops of trees,
these are no heavier than green alder bushes;
touched by a light wind, they begin to mingle
and race for instability—too high placed
to stoop to the strife of the brush, these are the winds. . . .
Downstairs, you correct notes at the upright piano,
twice upright this midday Sunday torn from the whole
green cloth of summer; your room was once the laundry,
the loose tap beats time, you hammer the formidable
chords of *The Nocturne*, your second composition.
Since you first began to bawl and crawl
from the unbreakable lawn to this sheltered room, how often
winds have crossed the wind of inspiration—
in these too, the unreliable touch of the all.

5.

HARRIET

Spring moved to summer—the rude cold rain
hurries the ambitious, flowers and youth;
our flash-tones crackle for an hour, and then
we too follow nature, imperceptibly
change our mouse-brown to white lion's mane,
thin white fading to a freckled, knuckled skull,
bronzed by decay, by many, many suns. . . .
Child of ten, three-quarters animal,
three years from Juliet, half Juliet,
already ripened for the night on stage—
beautiful petals, what shall we hope for,
knowing one choice not two is all you're given,
health beyond the measure, dangerous
to yourself, more dangerous to others?

Through the Night

1.

Two buildings, scaffolds, go up across my street;
one owned by Harvard, the other owned by Harvard;
they keep on hammering from five till five.
Man shouting resounds on the steel ribs—
thus from a rib of the Ark and in his cups,
Noah harangued a world he said would drown. . . .
How could the reckless, authoritative young
bear me, if I had their life expectancy?
Their long hair, beads, jeans, are early uniforms—
like the generation of leaves, the race of man.
A girl straddles a car hood, and snuffs the dust of the headlights:
"I want to live," she screams, "where I can see."
The pale green leaf clings white to the lit night
and shakes a little on its stiff, tense twig.

2.

Nothing less nutritive than the thirst at Harvard—
it's as bad for me at fifty as nineteen—
the thirst for grown-ups, open cars and girls. . . .
While I was looking out a window
I saw you walking with the simple ones,
in the twilight, in the evening, in the black, in the night;
not painted or even loud—how earnestly,
I looked and found you lying on your bed;
you caught me and kissed me and stopped my rush,
your sinewy lips wide-eyed as the honeycomb,
we no longer needed to have lights.
On your record Alice Raveau's contralto
Orpheus sang, *Où vais-je sans Eurydice?*
dying in our undergrowth, dense beyond reward.

3.
The vague, dark new hallway, the darker stairway:
closed doors to bathroom, bedroom . . . to someone waiting?
Your snoring is like the rub of distant surf,
each footstep is a moral sentence. The round window
holds out its thin, black terminal disk of joy,
the blissfully brightening glimmer of immoral
redemption as I lie awake basking,
trying to extend the dark and unspent minute,
as the window frame gradually burns green;
four panes assuming the polar blue of day,
as my backbone swims in the sperm of gladness,
as your figure emerges from your body,
we are two species, even from outside—
a net trapped in the arms of another net.

4.
Gradually greener in the window frame:
the old oil, unfamiliar here, alive
in a hundred eighteenth-century lawns and landscapes—
Sir Joshua Reynolds might improve each fault:
the lonely hound, the stalwart, cow-faced girl,
the scarlet general, more oaken than his oaks—
leaf, trunk and park arranged as if pretence
alone were sacred—sudden success or money
both being somewhat in bad taste at Harvard—
one great window, one bright watching eye;
as achingly I awake to steal back home,
each house and scaffold, familiar, unfamiliar—
each shingle-touselled window is sheer face . . .
blindingly visible breasts freckle to brilliance.

The Charles River

1.

The sycamores throw shadows on the Charles,
as the fagged insect splinters, drops and joins
the infinite that scatters loosening leaves,
the long-haired escort and his short-skirted girl.
The black stream curves as if it led a lover—
my blood is pounding; in workaday times,
I take cold comfort from its heartelation,
its endless handstand round the single I,
the pumping and thumping of my overfevered wish. . . .
For a week my heart has pointed elsewhere:
it brings us here tonight, and ties our hands—
if we leaned forward, and should dip a finger
into this river's momentary black flow,
infinite small stars would break like fish.

2.

The circuit of snow-topped rural roads, eight miles
to ten, might easily have been the world's top,
the North Pole, when I trailed on spreading skis
my guide, his unerring legs ten inches thick in wool,
and pinched my earlobes lest they turn to snowdrops—
hard knocks that school a lifetime; yet I went on swiping
small things. That knife, yellow-snow with eleven blades,
where is it? Somewhere, where it will outlast me,
though flawed already when I picked it up. . . .
And now, the big town river, once straight and dead as its highway,
shrinks to country river, bankscrub, dry ice,
a live muskrat muddying the moonlight. You trail me,
Woman, so small, if one could trust appearance,
I might be in trouble with the law.

3.

No stars, only cars, the stars of man,
mount sky and highway; life is wild: ice straw
puts teeth in the shallows, the water smells and lives.
We walk a tightrope, this embankment, jewed—
no, yankeed—by highways down to a stubbly lip. . . .
Once—you weren't born then—an iron railing,
cheerless and dignified, policed this walk;
it matched the times, and had an esplanade,
stamping down grass and growth with square stone shoes;
a groan went up when the iron railing crashed. . . .
The Charles, half ink, half liquid coaldust,
bears witness to the health of industry—
wrong times, an evil dispensation; but who
can hope to enter heaven with clean hands?

4.

Seen by no visible eye, our night unbroken—
our motel bedroom is putty-gray and cold,
the shivering winds thrust through its concrete cube.
A car or two, then none; since midnight none.
Highways on three levels parallel the river,
roads patrol the river in her losing struggle,
a force of nature trying to breathe beneath
a jacket of lava. We lie parallel,
parallel to the river, parallel
to six roads—unhappy and awake,
awake and naked, like a line of Greeks,
facing a second line of Greeks—like them,
willing to enter the battle, and not come out . . .
morning's breathing traffic . . . its unbroken snore.

Harvard

1.

The parochial school's green copper dome like
a green summer grove above the defoliated playground;
clouds puff in cotton wads on a low Dutch sky—
the top of the school resembles a Place des Vosges. . . .
Lying in bed, I see a blind white morning
rise to mid-heaven in a gaggle of snow—
a silk stocking is coiling on a wire hanger
rapier-bright . . . they dangle from my tree,
a long throw for a hard cold day . . . wind lifting
the stocking like the lecherous, lost leg. . . .
The students, my swarm-mates, rise in their hundreds, and leave
the hive—they can keep time. I've slept so late,
I see my stubble whiten while I shave;
the stocking blows to smog, the steel coathanger stains.

2.

We inch by the Boston waterfront on icepools,
carparks make the harbor invisible,
our relationship advances, then
declines to private jokes, the chaff of lust. . . .
Dark days, fair nights . . . yet they fell short—
in a studio near the Back Bay Station, the skylight
angular, night-bluish, blear and spinsterish—
both fighting off muscular cramps, the same fatigue. . . .
Yet tonight means something, something we
must let go willingly, and smash:
all flesh is grass, and like the flower of the grass—
no! lips, breasts, eyes, hands, lips, hair-—
the overworked central heating bangs the frame,
as the milkhorse in childhood would clang the morning milkcan.

3.
MORNING

The great dawn of Boston lifts from its black rag;
from Thanksgiving to Christmas, thick arctic snow
thawing to days of moderate, night-black balm—
I cannot sleep, my veins are mineral,
dirt-full as the arteries of a cracked white cup;
one wearies of looking expectantly for the worse—
Chaucer's old January made hay with May.
In this ever more enlightened bedroom,
I wake under the early rising sun,
sex indelible flowers on the air—
shouldn't I ask to hold to you forever,
body of a dolphin, breast of cloud?
You rival the renewal of the day,
clearing the puddles with your green sack of books.

Sleep

1.

Four windows, five feet tall, soar up like windows,
rinsing their stained-glass angels in the void,
interminably alert for the four-hour stay till morning:
a watery dearth illuminated by
a light or two hung on a telephone pole;
an alley, ashcans, the usual Cambridge frame
clawed from packing crates, and painted dire,
frozen interminably to this four-hour verge. . . .
Heaven? The clock stops there as here—this flesh
elastic past the mind's agility,
hair coiled back on guard like the spring of a watch,
legs showing pale as wooden matches, lit
by four streak windows in the uncreating dawn
not night, not day, stealing brief life from both.

2.

Six straight hours to teach on less than three hours' sleep—
I shall be smitten by the hand of my cells,
and will not go down whiteheaded to my grave. . . .
I get to know myself, a spendthrift talker,
with no breath left to show in the last round. . . .
Back home, I sleep the hour hand round the clock
and enjoy the avarice of loneliness.
I lie like a hound, on bounds for chasing a hound,
short-tethered in a spare corner, nose on paws,
one eyelid raised to guard the bowl of water;
panting, "Better to die, than hate or fear,
better die twice than make ourselves feared or hated—
bad-livers live longer if the law's forgotten,
the happiest country has no history."

3.
An aquamarine bottle twinkles on a pane;
outside, a one-story factory with a troll chimney,
built in the age of novels and Fulton's steamboat,
condemned by law and Harvard, still on parole.
A tiger cat sentinelled on the record-player
spies on a second stretching from a carton-
dollhouse to bat a brass ball on a string.
The tree, untinselled, asymmetrical,
shoves up askewly blessing a small sprawl
of unsealed brownpaper Christmas packages.
Your child, she's nine, keeps shrewdly, inopportunely
reappearing—you standing up on your bed
in your Emily Dickinson nightgown, purely marveling
whether to be sensible or drown.

New York

1.
SNAKE

One of God's creatures, just as much as you,
or God; what other bends its back in crooks
and curves so gracefully, to yield a point;
brews a more scalding venom from cold blood;
or flings a spine-string noosed about their throats:
hysterical bird, wild pig, or screaming rabbit?
Often I see it sunning on bright, brisk days,
when the heat has ebbed from its beloved rocks;
it is seamless, scaled-down to its integrity,
coiled for indiscriminate malevolence.
Lately, its valor pushed it past man's patience;
stoned, raw-fleshed, it finds its hole—sentenced
to hibernate fifty years. . . . It will thaw, then kill—
my little whip of wisdom, lamb in wolf-skin.

2.
CHRISTMAS TREE

Twenty or more big cloth roses, pale rose or scarlet,
coil in the branches—a winning combination
for you, who have gathered them eight years or more:
bosom-blossoms from Caribbean steambath forests,
changeless, though changed from tree to tree, from Boston to here—
transplants like you. . . . Twenty small birds or more
nip the needles; a quail, a golden warbler—
the rest not great, except for those minnowy
green things, no known species, made of woven straw:
small dangling wicker hampers to tease a cat.
A fine thing, built with love; too unconventional
for our child to buy . . . the modesty
and righteousness of a woman's ego stripped naked:
"Because I lacked ambition, men thought me mad."

3.

NEW YEAR'S EVE

By miracle, I left the party half
an hour behind you, reached home five hours drunker,
imagining I would live a million years,
a million quarts drunker than the gods of Jutland—
live through another life and two more wives.
Life is too short to silver over this tarnish.
The gods, employed to haunt and punish husbands,
have no hand for trigger-fine distinctions,
their myopia makes all error mortal. . . .
My Darling, prickly hedgehog of the hearth,
chocolates, cherries, hairshirt, pinks and glass—
when we joined in the sublime blindness of courtship,
loving lost all its vice with half its virtue.
Cards will never be dealt to us fairly again.

4.

DEAR SORROW I

If I can't whistle in the dark, why whistle?
One doubts the wisdom of almighty God
casting weak husbands adrift in the hands of a wife.
We need the mighty diaphragm of Job
to jangle grandly. Pain lives in our free discussion,
like the Carlyles fighting meat from the mouth of their dog.
Luckily the Carlyles couldn't bear children—
ours sees me, "Genius, unwise, unbrilliant, weird,"
sees you, "Brilliant, unwise, unweird, nerves."
Barbaric cheek is needed to stay married. . . .
Lizzie, I wake to the hollow of loneliness,
I would cry out *Love, Love,* if I had words:
we are all here for such a short time,
we might as well be good to one another.

5.

DEAR SORROW 2

Each day more poignantly resolved on love,
though the stars in their courses war against us . . .
I have climbed to the last step of the stairs to look:
an open window roughs the central heat,
my lackluster pictures, Holbein's *Sir Thomas More*
and Audubon's *Bluejays*, shine in the January air—
more cries of the city than that woodsman could name. . . .
If we have loved, it's not returnable;
this room will dim and die as we dim and die,
its many secrets change to others' things.
Can I be forgiven the life-waste of my lifework?
Was the thing worth doing worth doing badly?
Man in the world, a whirlpool in a river—
soul cannot be saved outside the role of God.

6.

DEAR SORROW 3

We never see him now, except at dinner,
then you quarrel, and he goes upstairs. . . .
The old playground hasn't improved its asphalt base:
no growth, two broken swings, one OK—as was!
Our half century fought to stay in place.
But my eye lies, the precinct has turned hard,
hard more like a person than a thing.
Time that mends an object lets men go,
no doctor does the work of the carpenter.
It's our nerve and ideologies die first—
then we, so thumbed, worn out, used, got by heart.
Each new day I cherish a juster perspective,
doing all for the best, and therefore doing nothing,
fired by my second alcohol, remorse.

7.

DEAR SORROW 4

The hurt mother sleeps awake like a cat till daybreak
stretched on the mat by the bed of our breathy child . . .
her cat thrusts its small brown arm through a crack in the door,
then another arm, a brown nose, and the door sticks—
it is this waking daily to the fire of daybreak,
our twenty years of fractious will and feather. . . .
Do I romanticize if I think that I
can be as selfish a father as Karl Marx,
Milton, Dickens, Trotsky, Freud, James Mill,
or George II, a bad son and worse father—
the great lions needed a free cage to roar in. . . .
O when will I sleep out the storm, dear love,
and see at the end of the walk your dress glow
burnt-umber, as if you had absorbed the sun?

8.

HARRIET'S DREAM

"The broom trees twirped by our rosewood bungalow,
not wildlife, these were tropical and straw;
the Gulf fell like a shower on the fiber-sand;
it wasn't the country like our coast of Maine—
on ice for summer. We met a couple, not people,
squares asking Father if he was his name—
none ever said that I was Harriet. . . .
They were laying beach-fires with scarlet sticks and hatchets,
our little bungalow was burning—it
had burned, I was in it. I couldn't laugh,
I was afraid when the ceiling crashed in scarlet;
the shots were boom, the fire was fizz. . . . While sleeping
I scrubbed away my scars and blisters, unable
to answer if I had ever hurt."

9.

TERM-END   (HARRIET)

The term is finished and the air is lighter,
I recognize your faces in the room;
I touch your pictures, find you in the round.
We watch a dark strip of silence stalk in rippling,
the singed back of your clingy Burmese cat;
he sits pointing the window from the bedspread,
hooked on the nightlife flashing through the curtain—
we cannot hold the focus for a minute. . . .
The beautiful cat gives his hideous purr to show
he wants us in the house, not back with God.
I want to live on long enough to see you
live longer than even the obliquest cat—
but to know you are happy would mean to lead
your life for you, hold hard, and live you out . . .

10.

LEFT OUT OF VACATION

"Some fathers may have some consideration,
but he is so wonderfully eccentric,
drinking buttermilk and wearing red socks.
It was OK—not having him in Florida;
Florence is different, Mother—big deal, two girls
eating alone in the Italian restaurant!" . . .
Only God could destroy the wonders He makes,
and shelve you too among them, Charles Sumner Lowell,
shiny horsechestnut-colored Burmese Cat,
waggling your literary haunches like Turgenev,
our animal whose only friends are persons—
now boarded with cats in a cat-house, moved at random
by the universal Love that moves the stars
forever rehearsing for the perfect comeback.

11.
THE PICTURE   (ELIZABETH)

In New York, this is nature—twelve stories high,
two water tanks, tobacco-leaf shingle, girdled
by stapled pasture wire, while bed to bed,
we lie gazing into the ether's crystal ball,
sky and a sky and sky and sky, till death—
my heart stops . . . this might be heaven. At grandmother's
my terror of heaven was a scene from summer—
a picture, out of style now and then in,
of seven daffodils caught by the wind and still.
Buttercup yellow were the flowers, and green
the stems as fresh paint, over them the wind,
the blowzy wooden branches of the elms,
a sack of hornets sopping up the flame—
still over us, we still in parenthesis.

12.
SAME PICTURE

Still over us
high summer in the breath that overwhelms
the termites digging in the underpinning
down below
we two, two in one waterdrop
vitalized by one needledrop of blood,
up, up, up, up, and up
soon shot, soon slugged into the overflow—
and we two lying here,
one cell,
still over us our breath
sawing and pumping to the terminal,
no rest or stall
for the little wooden workhorse working here below.

Mexico

1.

The difficulties, the impossibilities . . .
I, fifty, humbled with the years' gold garbage,
dead laurel grizzling my back . . . like spines of hay;
you, some sweet, uncertain age, say twenty-seven,
untempted, unseared by honors or deception.
What help then? Not the sun, the scarlet blossom,
and the high fever of this seventh day,
the predestined diarrhea of the pilgrim,
the multiple mosquito spots, round as pesos.
Hope not for God here, or even for the gods;
the Aztecs knew the sun, the source of life,
will die, unless we feed it human blood—
we two are clocks, and only count in time . . .
the hand a knife-edge pressed against the future.

2.

Wishing to raise the cross of the Crucified King
in the monastery of Emmaus at Cuernavaca—
the monks, world-names for futurist crucifixes,
and avant-garde Virgins . . . like St. Paul, they earned
the cost of depth-transference by learning a craft.
A Papal Commission camped on them two years,
ruling analysis cannot be compulsory,
their cool Belgian prior was heretical, a fairy. . . .
We couldn't find his corpse removed by helicopter;
the cells were empty, but the art still sold;
lay-neurotics peeped out at us like deer,
orphans in spotless whitewashed cabins, named
Sigmund and *Karl*. . . . They live the life of monks,
one revelation healing the ravage of the other.

3.

The lizard rusty as a leaf rubbed rough
does nothing for days but puff his throat
for oxygen . . . and tongue up passing flies,
loves only identical rusty lizards panting:
harems worthy this lord of the universe—
each thing he does generic, and not the best.
We sit on a cliff like curs, chins pressed to thumbs—
how fragrantly our cold hands warm to the live coal!
The Toltec temples pass to dust in the dusk—
the clock dial of the rising moon, dust out of time—
two clocks set back to Montezuma's fate . . .
as if we still wished to pull teeth with firetongs—
when they took a city, they murdered everything,
till the Spaniards, by reflex, finished them.

4.

South of Boston, south of Washington,
south of any bearing . . . I walk the glazed moonlight:
dew on the grass and nobody about,
drawn on by my unlimited desire,
like a bull with a ring in his nose, a chain in the ring. . . .
We moved far, bull and cow, could one imagine
cattle obliviously pairing six long days:
up road and down, then up again passing the same
brick garden wall, stiff spines of hay stuck in my hide;
and always in full sight of everyone,
from the full sun to silhouetting sunset,
pinned by undimming lights of hurried cars. . . .
You're gone; I am learning to live in history.
What is history? What you cannot touch.

5.

Midwinter in Cuernavaca, tall red flowers
stand up on many trees; the rock is in leaf.
The sun bakes the wallbrick large as loaves of bread—
somewhere I must have met this feverish pink
and knew its message; or is it that I've walked
you past them twenty times, and now walk back?
This stream will not flow back, not once, not twice.
I've waited, I think, a lifetime for this walk.
The white powder slides out beneath our feet,
the sterile white salt of purity; even
your puffed lace blouse is salt. The red brick glides;
bread baked for a dinner never to be served. . . .
When you left, I thought of you each hour of the day,
each minute of the hour, each second of the minute.

6.

As if we chewed dry twigs and salt grasses,
filling our mouths with dust and bits of adobe,
lizards, rats and worms, we walk downhill,
love demanding we be calm, not lawful,
for laws imprison as much as they protect.
Six stone lions, allday drinkers, sit like frogs,
guarding the fountain; the three rusty arc-lights sweat;
four stone inkfish, too much sat on, bear the fountain—
no star for the guidebook . . . this city of the plain,
where the water rusts as if it bled,
and thirteen girls sit at the barroom tables,
then none, then only twenty coupled men,
homicidal with morality and lust—
devotion hikes uphill in iron shoes.

7.
We're knotted together in innocence and guile;
yet we are not equal, I have lived without
sense so long the loss no longer hurts,
reflex and the ways of the world will float me free—
you, God help you, must will each breath you take . . .
The lavatory breathes sweet shocking perfume.
In Cuernavaca the night's illusory houselights
watch everyone, not just the girls, in houses
like boxes on streets where buses eat the sidewalk.
It's New Year's midnight; we three drink beer in the market
from cans garnished with salt and lime—one woman, Aztec,
sings adultery ballads, and weeps because
her husband has left her for three women—
to face the poverty all men must face at the hour of death.

8.
Three pillows, end on end, rolled in a daybed
blanket—elastic, round, untroubled. For a second,
by some hallucination of my hand
I imagined I was unwrapping you. . . .
Two immovable nuns, out of habit, too fat to leave
the dormitory, have lived ten days on tea,
bouillon cubes and cookies brought from Boston.
You curl in your metal bunk-bed like my child,
I sprawl on an elbow troubled by the floor—
nuns packing, nuns ringing the circular iron stair,
nuns in pajamas scalloped through their wrappers,
nuns boiling bouillon, tea or cookies, nuns
brewing and blanketing reproval . . .
the soul groans and laughs at its lack of stature.

9.

No artist perhaps, you go beyond their phrases;
you were too simple to lose yourself in words . . .
Take our last day baking on the marble veranda,
the roasting brown rock, the smoking grass, the breath
of the world risen like the ripe smoke of chestnuts,
a cleavage dropping miles to the valley's body;
and the following sick and thoughtful day,
the red flower, the hills, the valley, the Volcano—
this not the greatest thing, though great; the hours
of shivering, ache and burning, when we charged
so far beyond our courage—altitude . . .
then falling back on honest speech;
infirmity's a food the flesh must swallow,
feeding our minds . . . the mind which is also flesh.

10.

Poor Child, you were kissed so much you thought you were walked on;
yet you wait in my doorway with bluebells in your hair.
Those other me's, you think, *are they meaningless in toto,*
hills coarsely eyed for a later breathless conquest,
leaving no juice in the flaw, mind lodged in mind?
A girl's not quite mortal, she asks everything. . . .
If you want to make the frozen serpent dance,
you must sing it the music of its mouth:
Sleep wastes the day lifelong behind our eyes,
night shivers at noonday in the boughs of the fir. . . .
Our conversation moved from lust to love,
asking only coolness, stillness, intercourse—
then days, days, days, days . . . how can I love you more,
short of turning into a criminal?

Eight Months Later

EIGHT MONTHS LATER

The flower I took away and wither and fear—
to clasp, not grasp the life, the light and fragile. . . .
It's certain we burned the grass, the grass still fumes,
the girl stands in the doorway, the red flower on the trees
where once the intermeshing limbs of Lucifer
sank to sleep on the tumuli of Lilith—
did anyone ever sleep with anyone
without thinking a split second he was God? . . .
Midsummer Manhattan—we are burnt black chips.
The worst of New York is everything is stacked,
ten buildings dance in the hat of one . . . half Europe
in half a mile. I wish we were elsewhere:
Mexico . . . Mexico? Where is Mexico?
Who will live the year back, cat on the ladder?

2.
DIE GOLD ORANGEN

I see the country where the lemon blossoms,
and the pig-gold orange glows on its dark branch,
and the south wind stutters from the blue hustings;
I see it; it's behind us, love, behind us—
the bluebell is brown, the cypress points too straight—
do you see the house, the porch on marble pillars?
The sideboard is silver, and the candles blaze;
the statue stands naked to stare at you.
What have I done with us, and what was done?
And the mountain, El Volcan, a climber of clouds?
The mule-man lost his footing in the cloud,
seed of the dragon coupled in that cave. . . .
The cliff drops; over it, the water drops,
and steams out the footprints that led us on.

Circles

WALK TO THE BARN   (HARRIET)

Nervous leaves twitter on the high wood elm,
this and that thing, grape-purple, skims the lawn—
our harmony is most alive and firm,
when three or four colors improve on black and white,
when six or seven words mean more than one . . .
Darling, this isn't us, I trapped in words,
you gagging on headoverheels inarticulation.
Or my barn . . . it's property uncouth as I.
Here nature seldom fears the hand of man,
the alders skirmish. You flame for a best friend—
is it always the same child or animal
impregnable in shell or coat of thorns,
punching you with embraces, holding out
a hestitant hand, unbending as a broom?

2.

DAS EWIG WEIBLICHE

Birds have a finer body and tinier brain—
who asks the swallows to do drudgery,
clean, cook, pick up a peck of dust per diem?
If we knock on their homes, they wince uptight with fear,
farting about all morning past their young,
small as wasps fuming in their ash-leaf ball.
Nature lives off the life that comes to hand—
if we could feel and softly touch their being,
wasp, bee and swallow might live with us like cats.
The boiling yellow-jacket in her sack
of felon-stripe cut short above the knee
sings home . . . nerve-wrung creatures, wasp, bee and bird,
guerillas by day then keepers of the cell,
my wife in her wooden crib of seed and feed. . . .

3.

OUR TWENTIETH WEDDING ANNIVERSARY I (ELIZABETH)

Leaves espaliered jade on our barn's loft window,
sky stretched on a two-pane sash . . . it doesn't open:
stab of roofdrip, this leaf, that leaf twings,
an assault the heartless leaf rejects.
The picture is too perfect for our lives:
in Chardin's stills, the paint bleeds, juice is moving.
We have weathered the wet of twenty years.
Many cripples have won their place in the race;
Immanuel Kant remained unmarried and sane,
no one could Byronize his walk to class.
Often the player outdistances the game. . . .
This week is our first this summer to go unfretted;
we smell as green as the weeds that bruise the flower—
a house eats up the wood that made it.

4.

OUR TWENTIETH WEDDING ANNIVERSARY 2

To our 20th. We live, two trees;
sometimes the green crack soonest in this soil
of granite and clamshells. Our first snapshot is still us,
ten or fifteen pounds inferior when
the Graces noosed you with my hard gold ring. . . .
The aging cling to life, even when dead:
Rameses keeps the hair of a young squaw—
but where is Pharaoh the day after tomorrow?
By setting limits, man has withdrawn from the monsters;
a metal rod and then another metal rod;
when the old are dying, they buy land,
savings no consideration. . . . You dive me,
graceful, higher, quicker . . . unsteady swallow
who will uproot the truth that cannot change.

5.

THE HUMAN CONDITION (HARRIET)

Should someone human, not just our machinery,
fire on sight, and end the world and us,
surely he'll say he chose the lesser evil—
our wars were simpler than our marriages,
sea monster on sea monster drowning Saturday night—
the acid shellfish that cannot breathe fresh air. . . .
Home things can't stand up to the strain of the earth.
I wake to your cookout and Charles Ives
lulling my terror, lifting my fell of hair,
as David calmed the dark nucleus of Saul.
I'll love you at eleven, twenty, fifty,
young when the century mislays my name—
no date I can name you can be long enough,
the impossible is allied to fact.

6.

THE HARD WAY (HARRIET)

Don't hate your parents, or your children will hire
unknown men to bury you at your own cost.
Child, forty years younger, will we live to see
your destiny written by our hands rewritten,
your adolescence snap the feathered barb,
the phosphorescence of your wake?
Under the stars, one sleeps, is free from household,
tufts of grass and dust and tufts of grass—
night oriented to the star of youth.
I only learn from error; till lately I trusted
in the practice of my hand. In backward Maine,
ice goes in season to the tropical,
then the mash freezes back to ice, and then
the ice is broken by another wave.

7.

WORDS FOR MUFFIN, A GUINEA-PIG

"Of late they leave the light on in my entry,
so I won't scare, though I never scare in the dark;
I bless this arrow that flies from wall to window . . .
five years and a nightlight given me to breathe—
Heidegger said spare time is ecstasy. . . .
I am not scared, although my life was short;
my sickly breathing sounded like dry leather.
Mrs. Muffin! It clicks. I had my day.
You'll paint me like Cromwell with all my warts:
small mop with a tumor and eyes too popped for thought.
I was a rhinoceros when jumped by my sons.
I ate and bred, and then I only ate,
my life zenithed in the Lyndon Johnson 'sixties . . .
this short pound God threw on the scales, found wanting."

8.

HEAT

For the first time in fifteen years, a furnace
Maine night that would have made summer anywhere,
in Brazil or Boston. The wooden rooms of our house
dry, redoubling their wooden farmhouse smell,
honest wooden ovens shaking with desire.
We feared the pressure was too curative. . . .
Outside, a young seal festers on the beach,
head snapped off, the color of a pig;
much lonelier, this formula for cures.
One nostril shut, my other attenuated—
it's strange tonight I want to pencil myself
do-its on bits of paper. I must remember
to breathe through my mouth. Breathe only from my mouth . . .
as my mouth keeps shutting out the breath of morning.

Late Summer

END OF CAMP ALAMOOSOOK   (HARRIET)

Less than a score, the dregs of the last day,
counselors and campers squat waiting for the ferry—
the unexpected, the exotic, the early
morning sunlight is more like premature twilight:
last day of the day, foreclosure of the camp.
Glare on the amber squatters, fire of fool's-gold—
like bits of colored glass, they cannot burn.
The Acadians must have gathered in such arcs;
a Winslow, our cousin, shipped them from Nova Scotia—
no malice, merely pushing his line of work,
herding guerillas in some Morality.
The campers suspect us, and harden in their shyness,
their gruff, faint voices hardly say hello,
singing, "Do we love it? *We love it.*"

2.

FAMILIAR QUOTATIONS   (HARRIET)

A poet, if all else fail . . . your words from nowhere:
on your first visit to a child—"I am too happy,
sometimes the little muddler can't stand itself."
Your transistor was singing Anton Webern—
what is it like? Rugged: if you can like this,
you can like anything. "It's like red ants,
a wild wolf . . . through the woods walking—
or spiders crying together without tears. . . .
Who made God? Did God the Father take Baby
Jesus to Central Park on Sunday?" What's true?
Christ imagined all men were his brothers;
He loved all men, he was you, and might have lived—
for love, he threw his lovely youth away.
"But you can't love everyone, your heart won't let you."

3.
BRINGING A TURTLE HOME

On the road to Bangor, we spotted a domed stone,
a painted turtle petrified by fear.
I picked it up. The turtle had come a long walk,
200 millennia understudy to dinosaurs,
then their survivor. A god for the out-of-power. . . .
Faster gods come to Castine, flush yachtsmen who see
hell as a city very much like New York,
these gods give a bad past and worse future to men
who never bother to set a spinnaker;
culture without cash isn't worth their spit.
The laughter on Mount Olympus was always breezy. . . .
Goodnight, little Boy, little Soldier, live,
a toy to your friend, a stone of stumbling to God—
sandpaper Turtle, scratching your pail for water.

4.
RETURNING TURTLE

Weeks hitting the road, one fasting in the bathtub,
raw hamburger mossing in the watery stoppage,
the room drenched with musk like kerosene—
no one shaved, and only the turtle washed.
He was so beautiful when we flipped him over:
greens, reds, yellows, fringe of the faded savage,
the last Sioux, old and worn, saying with weariness,
"Why doesn't the Great White Father put his red
children on wheels, and move us as he will?"
We drove to the Orland River, and watched the turtle
rush for water like rushing into marriage,
swimming in uncontaminated joy,
lovely the flies that fed that sleazy surface,
a turtle looking back at us, and blinking.

5.

WINSLOWS

"Cousin Cal—if your Liz is Kentucky Derby,
she is strictly the root of the Southern rose.
Our dear Winslows—Auntie (Liz Ross Winslow)
is giving out at ninety-three this August;
Uncle John swallowed only one bite of roast beef
at his ninetieth birthday dinner last month;
Mother's cataract glasses are good, but she can't
see to paint, though she is only eighty-six;
only Aunt Daisy Anne at ninety-five plus
is *indominateable*. Don't worry,
I'm not going to be a poet, I haven't suffered.
I've left the *Ashville Globe*, journalism's for the public;
I've got to write for me. George will support me;
haven't all great artists had a patron?"

6.

GROWTH   (HARRIET)

"I'm talking the whole idea of life, and boys,
with Mother; and then the heartache, when we're fifty. . . .
You've got to call your *Notebook*, *Book of the Century*,
but it will take you a century to write,
then I will have to revise it, when you die."
Latin, Spanish, swimming half a mile,
writing a saga with a churl named Eric,
Spanish, Spanish, math and rollerskates;
a love of party dresses, but not boys;
composing something with the bells of *Boris*:
"UNTITLED, would have to be the name of it. . . ."
You grow apace, you grow too fast apace,
too soon adult; no, not adult, like us. . . .
On the telephone, they say, "We're tired, aren't you?"

7.

THE GRADUATE   (ELIZABETH)

"Transylvania's Greek Revival Chapel
is one of the best Greek Revival things in the South;
the College's most distinguished graduate
was a naturalist, he had a French name like Audubon.
My sister Margaret, a two-bounce basketball
player and all-Southern Center, came home
crying each night because of 'Happy' Chandler,
the coach, and later Governor of Kentucky.
Our great big tall hillbilly idiots keep
Kentucky pre-eminent in basketball.
And how! Still, if you are somewhat ill-born,
you feel your soul is not quite first-class. . . ."
Never such shimmering of intelligence,
though your wind was short, and you stopped smoking.

8.

NO HEARING I. THE DIALOGUE

Old campaigner, we could surrender something,
not talking for a victory but survival;
quarrels seldom come from the first cause,
some small passage in our cups at dinner
rouses the Dr. Johnson in a wife—
a monologuist tries to think on his feet
while talking, maybe finds fine things, yet fails—
still, it's a privilege to earn the bullring.
We meet face to face in the 6 p.m. hour,
nursing two inches of family Bourbon
through two separate half-hours of television news,
heaven pumped in heartbeats to my head,
the red cherry rolling in the tumbler of sugared spirits . . .
in the days of the freeze, we see a minor sun.

9.
NO HEARING 2. ALCOHOL

I have been in the sun, and my lips keep twitching—
suddenly, no disinclination to murder—
these brown hours, they stream like water off my back.
I want to charge with bull-horns through the cedar hedge,
pretending left and right and wrong are wind. . . .
O to live in a small gone Horatian suburb
lost in its melancholy stream of traffic—
all for goodness, we both on in years. . . .
Mischievous fish-shapes without scale or eye
swim your leaf-green teagown, not maternal,
swirling six inches past your three-inch heel,
belling about you like a parachute—
Otello bellowing, the rug rolled up, a spate
of controversial spatter . . . then exhaustion.

10.
NO HEARING 3

Belief in God is an inclination to listen,
but as we grow older and our freedom hardens,
we hardly even want to hear ourselves . . .
the silent universe our auditor—
I am to myself, and my trouble sings.
The Penobscott silvers to Bangor, the annual V
of geese beats above the moonborne bay—
their flight is too certain. Dante found this path
even before his first young leaves turned green;
exile gave seniority to his youth. . . .
White clapboards, black window, white clapboards, black window, white
    clapboards—
my house is empty. In our yard, the grass straggles. . . .
I stand face to face with lost Love—my breath
is life, the rough, the smooth, the bright, the drear.

11.
NO HEARING 4

Discovering, discovering trees light up green at night,
braking headlights-down, ransacking the roadsides
for someone strolling, fleeing to her wide goal;
passing blanks, the white Unitarian Church,
my barn on its bulwark, two allday padlocked shacks,
the town pool drained, the old lighthouse unplugged—
I watch the muddy breakers bleach to beerfroth,
our steamer, THE STATE OF MAINE, an iceberg at drydock.
Your question, my questioner? It is for you—
crouched in the gelid drip of the pine in our garden,
invisible almost when found, till I toss a white raincoat
over your sky-black, blood-trim quilted stormcoat—
you saying *I would prefer not*, like Bartleby:
small deer trembly and steel in your wet nest!

12.
OUTLIVERS   (HARRIET AND ELIZABETH)

"If we could reverse the world to what it changed
a hundred years ago, or even fifty,
scrupulous drudgery, sailpower, hand-made wars;
God might give us His right to live forever
despite the eroding miracle of science. . . ."
"Was everything that much grander than it is?"
"Nothing seems admirable until it fails;
but it's only people we should miss.
The Goth, retarded epochs like crab and clam,
wept, as we do, for his dead child." We talk
like roommates bleeding night to dawn. You say,
"I hope, of course, you both will outlive me,
but you and Harriet are perhaps like countries
not yet ripe for self-determination."

13.

MY HEAVENLY SHINER   (ELIZABETH)

The world atop Maine and our heads is north,
zeroes through Newfoundland to Hudson Bay:
entremets chinois et canadiens.
A world like ours will tumble on our heads,
my heavenly Shiner, think of it curving on?
You quiver on my finger like a small
minnow swimming in a crystal ball,
flittering radiance on my flittering finger.
The fish, the shining fish, they go in circles,
not one of them will make it to the Pole—
this isn't the point though, this is not the point;
think of it going on without a life—
in you, God knows, I've had the earthly life—
we were kind of religious, we thought in images.

14.

IT DID   (ELIZABETH)

Luck, we've had it; our character the public's—
and yet we will ripen, ripen, know we once
did most things better, not just physical
but moral—turning in too high for love,
living twenty-four hours in one shirt or skirt,
breathless gossip, the breathless singles' service.
We could have done much worse. I hope we did
a hundred thousand things much worse! Poor *X's*,
chance went this way, that way with us here:
gain counted as loss, and loss as gain: our tideluck.
It did to live with, but finally all men worsen:
drones die of stud, the saint by staying virgin . . .
old jaw only smiles to bite the feeder;
corruption serenades the wilting tissue.

15.
SEALS

If we must live again, not us; we might
go into seals, we'd handle ourselves better:
able to dawdle, able to torpedo,
all too at home in our three elements,
ledge, water and heaven—if man could restrain his hand. . . .
We flipper the harbor, blots and patches and oilslick,
so much bluer than water, we think it sky.
Creature could face creator in this suit,
fishers of fish not men. Some other August,
the easy seal might say, "I could not sleep
last night; suddenly I could write my name. . . ."
Then all seals, preternatural like us,
would take direction, head north—their haven
green ice in a greenland never grass.

Our love will not come back on fortune's wheel—

in the end it gets us, though a man know what he'd have:
old cars, old money, old undebased pre-Lyndon
silver, no copper rubbing through . . . old wives;
I could live such a too long time with mine.
In the end, every hypochondriac is his own prophet.
Before the final coming to rest, comes the rest
of all transcendence in a mode of being, hushing
all becoming. I'm for and with myself in my otherness,
in the eternal return of earth's fairer children,
the lily, the rose, the sun on brick at dusk,
the loved, the lover, and their fear of life,
their unconquered flux, insensate oneness, painful "It was. . . ."
After loving you so much, can I forget
you for eternity, and have no other choice?

The Dolphin

(1973)

FOR CAROLINE

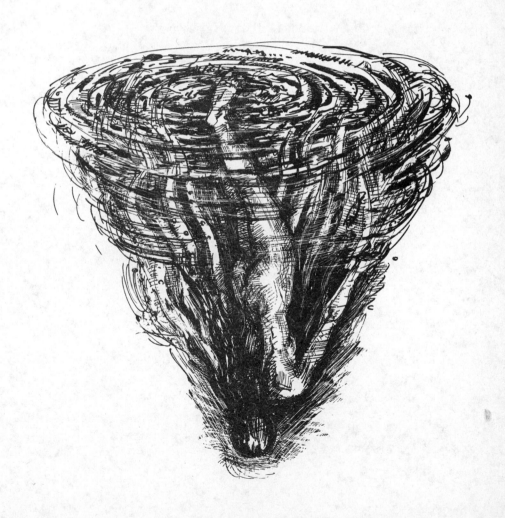

Fishnet

Any clear thing that blinds us with surprise,
your wandering silences and bright trouvailles,
dolphin let loose to catch the flashing fish . . .
saying too little, then too much.
Poets die adolescents, their beat embalms them,
the archetypal voices sing offkey;
the old actor cannot read his friends,
and nevertheless he reads himself aloud,
genius hums the auditorium dead.
The line must terminate.
Yet my heart rises, I know I've gladdened a lifetime
knotting, undoing a fishnet of tarred rope;
the net will hang on the wall when the fish are eaten,
nailed like illegible bronze on the futureless future.

Redcliffe Square

1.
LIVING IN LONDON

I learn to live without ice and like the Queen;
we didn't like her buildings when they stood,
but soon Victoria's manly oak was quartered,
knickknacks dropped like spiders from the whatnot,
grandparents and their unmarried staffs decamped
for our own bobbed couples of the swimming twenties,
too giddy to destroy the homes they fled.
These houses, no two the same, tremble up six stories
to dissimilar Flemish pie-slice peaks,
shaped by constructor's pipes and scaffolding—
aboriginal like a jungle gym.
Last century's quantity brick has a sour redness
that time, I fear, does nothing to appease,
condemned by age, rebuilt by desolation.

2.
WINDOW

Tops of the midnight trees move helter-skelter
to ruin, if passion can hurt the classical
in the limited window of the easel painter—
love escapes our hands. We open the curtains:
a square of white-faced houses swerving, foaming,
the swagger of the world and chalk of London.
At each turn the houses wall the path of meeting,
and yet we meet, stand taking in the storm.
Even in provincial capitals,
storms will rarely enter a human house,
the crude and homeless wet is windowed out.
We stand and hear the pummeling unpurged,
almost uneducated by the world—
the tops of the moving trees move helter-skelter.

3.

AMERICA FROM OXFORD, MAY 1970

The cattle have stopped on Godstow Meadow,
the peacock wheels his tail to move the heat,
then pivots changing to a wicker chair,
tiara of thistle on his shitty bobtail.
The feathertouch of May in England, but the heat
is American summer. Two weeks use up two months;
at home the colleges are closed for summer,
the students march, Brassman lances Cambodia—
he has lost his pen, his sword folds in his hand like felt.
Is truth here with us, if I sleep well?—
the ten or twelve years my coeval gives himself
for the new bubble of his divorce . . . ten or twelve years—
this air so estranged and hot I might be home. . . .
We have climbed above the wind to breathe.

4.

OXFORD

We frittered on the long meadow of the Thames,
our shoes laminated with yellow flower—
nothing but the soft of the marsh, the moan of cows,
the rooster-peacock. Before we had arrived,
rising stars illuminated Oxford—
the Aztecs knew these stars would fail to rise
if forbidden the putrifaction of our flesh,
the victims' viscera laid out like tiles
on fishponds changed to yellow flowers,
the goldfinchnest, the phosphorous of the ocean
blowing ambergris and ambergris,
dolphin kissing dolphin with a smirking smile,
not loving one object and thinking of another.
Our senses want to please us, if we please them.

5.
THE SERPENT

In my dream, my belly is yellow, panels
of mellowing ivory, splendid and still young,
though slightly ragged from defending me.
My tan and green backscales are cool to touch.
For one who has always loved snakes, it is no loss
to change nature. My fall was elsewhere—
how often I made the woman bathe in her waters.
With daylight, I turn small, a small snake
on the river path, arrowing up the jags.
Like this, like this, as the great clock clangs round,
and the green hunter leaps from turn to turn,
a new brass bugle slung on his invisible baldric;
he is groping for trout in the private river,
wherever it opens, wherever it happens to open.

6.
SYMPTOMS

I fear my conscience because it makes me lie.
A dog seems to lap water from the pipes,
life-enhancing water brims my bath—
(the bag of waters or the lake of the grave . . . ?)
from the palms of my feet to my wet neck—
I have no mother to lift me in her arms.
I feel my old infection, it comes once yearly:
lowered good humor, then an ominous
rise of irritable enthusiasm. . . .
Three dolphins bear our little toilet-stand,
the grin of the eyes rebukes the scowl of the lips,
they are crazy with the thirst. I soak,
examining and then examining
what I really have against myself.

7.

DIAGNOSIS: TO CAROLINE IN SCOTLAND

The frowning morning glares by afternoon;
the gay world in purple and orange drag,
Child-Bible pictures, perishables:
oranges and red cabbage sold in carts.
The sun that lights their hearts lights mine?
I see it burn on my right hand, and see
my skin, when bent, is finely wrinkled batwing.
Since you went, our stainless steelware ages,
like the young doctor writing my prescription:
The hospital. My twentieth in twenty years. . . .
Seatrout run past you in the Hebrides—
the gay are psychic, centuries from now,
not a day older, they'll flutter garish colors,
salmontrout amok in Redcliffe Square.

Hospital

SHOES

Too many go express to the house of rest,
buffooning, to-froing on the fringe of being,
one foot in life, and little right to that:
"I had to stop this business going on,
I couldn't attack my doctor anymore,
he lost his nerve for running out on life. . . ."
"Where I am not," we chime, "is where I am."
Dejection washes our pollution bare.
My shoes? Did they walk out on me last night,
and streak into the glitter of the blear?
I see two dirty white, punctured tennis-shoes,
empty and planted on the one-man path.
I have no doubt where they will go. They walk
the one life offered from the many chosen.

2.
JUVENILIA

Person, place and thing, once violated,
join the rubbish that predated nature;
boys race the hooded highway lights untimed,
and tiptoe through the treasuries of smashed glass,
scavenging for a lifelike hand or head.
I hoped to find girls in the wide, white squares;
I had no names or numbers—I could not meet them,
the women had suffered a fate worse than death—
weird in London of the bullhorn God.
No rocket goes as far astray as man. . . .
I'm on bounds, I mark my proofs, a sheaf of tapeworms,
sleek, untearable, interminable
paper that slices my finger like a knife—
one time in fifty, God will make a date.

3.
RIVAL

Is there an ur-dream better than words, an almost
work of art I commonplace in retelling
through the fearfullness of memory,
my perfunctory, all-service rhythms? . . .
For long, our taxi is changing into a van—
you-I . . . beefing we've not seen our driver.
He moves through the tan canvas-lapped bales of the van,
his step is careless, the bales begin to converge.
I am happy because I recognize
the man who assaulted you yesterday. . . .
Much later, the man's face, tan, a Chinese portrait,
floats symmetrical in a pool the same color.
It takes seconds to see the rival is dead,
the same water washes in and out of the mouth.

4.
STAIRWELL

Climbing from chair to chair to chair to chair,
I dare not look the stairwell in the eye;
its underpinning soils like carbon paper,
each step up would stop an athlete's heart—
the stairwell is hollow, bored, unbearable,
the same six words repeating on a disk:
marching for peace with paranoia marching,
marching for peace with paranoia marching . . .
ever at my heels and stormily.
Darling, we have halved the ailing summer.
Did the beheaded wish himself in half?
He was so airily cool and free and high—
or did he wish the opposite like us,
when we stitched two summer months in one?

5.

WALTER RALEIGH

Horseguard and Lifeguard, one loud red, one yellow,
colorful and wasteful and old hat. . . .
Americans can buy them on a postcard—
we do not see them with hallucinated eyes,
these horsemen, smartly antiqued and resurrected
from the blood of Crimea and Waterloo,
free to ramble London or trample France. . . .
Here sitting at your feet I feel no pressure
of analogies binding us to them.
Our omen is Raleigh kneeling for the axe—
he isn't going to die, it's not been painted.
Our Raleigh is a small boy in his velvet
and courting dress hearing an old buffer
lie about the toothless Spanish Main.

6.

DOUBLE-VISION

I tie a second necktie over the first;
no one is always waiting at the door,
and fills the window . . . sometimes a Burmese cat,
or maybe my Daughter on the shell of my glasses.
I turn and see persons, my pajama top
loose-knotted on the long thin neck of a chair—
make yourself at home. The cat walks out—
or does it? The room has filled with double-shadows,
sedation doubles everything I see. . . .
You can't be here, and yet we try to talk;
somebody else is farcing in your face,
we haggle at cross-purposes an hour.
While we are talking, I am asking you,
"Where is Caroline?" And you *are* Caroline.

Hospital II

"What a record year, even for us—
last March, I knew you'd manage by yourself,
you were the true you; now finally
your clowning makes visitors want to call a taxi,
you tease the patients as if they were your friends,
your real friends who want to save your image
from this genteel, disgraceful hospital.
Your trousers are worn to a mirror. . . . That new creature,
when I hear her name, I have to laugh.
You left two houses and two thousand books,
a workbarn by the ocean, and two slaves
to kneel and wait upon you hand and foot—
tell us why in the name of Jesus." Why
am I clinging here so foolishly alone?

2.
LETTER

"In London last month I encountered only
exhausted traffic and exhausting men—
the taxi driver might kill us, but at least he cared."
Cold summer London, your purer cold is Maine,
where each empty sweater and hollow bookcase hurts,
every pretext for their service gone.
We wanted to be buried together in Maine . . .
you didn't, "impractical, cold, out of touch."
The terrible postcards you bought and stamped for me
go off to Harriet, the Horseguards, the Lifeguards,
the Lord Mayor's Chariot, Queen Bess who could not bear—
true as anything else to fling a child. . . .
I shout into the air, my voice comes back—
nothing reaches your black silhouette.

3.

OLD SNAPSHOT FROM VENICE 1952

From the salt age, yes from the salt age,
courtesans, Christians fill the churchyard close;
that silly swelled tree is a spook with a twig for a head.
Carpaccio's Venice is as wide as the world,
Jerome and his lion lope to work unfeared. . . .
In Torcello, the stone lion I snapped behind you,
venti anni fa, still keeps his poodled hair—
wherever I move this snapshot, you have moved—
it's twenty years. The courtesans and lions
swim in Carpaccio's brewing tealeaf color.
Was he the first in the trade of painting to tell tales? . . .
You are making Boston in the sulfury a.m.,
dropping Harriet at camp, Old Love,
Eternity, You . . . a future told by tealeaves.

Caroline

FLASHBACK TO WASHINGTON SQUARE 1966

Two babies in your stroller, perhaps three,
all four of you in Bloomingdale polo coats;
they seemed to rush on one course, you another—
your brute joy in slanting them to the curb. . . .
We were Sunday people gone before we met.
We meet too many people, wives and husbands;
the family lasts, the child is never weaned,
parents never err in guessing wrong. . . .
How mean the drink-money for the hour of joy,
its breathy charity and brag of body. . . .
I hesitate to argue for our love unloosed—
we earn less credit than we burn,
though joy in the moment crowns credulity,
dying to be what we are.

2.

FRAGILITY

One foot in last year, one in last July,
the motionless month, the day that lasts a month.
We reach mid-journey, you lag by fifteen summers,
half a year more than Harriet's whole life.
The clock looks over my shoulder crazily.
This hospital is tinder . . . retards the sun,
melancholia sprinkles the blind root,
the cat nibbles little shoots foretelling rain,
sultry August is my wandering eye.
Hope grows less malign or thinks it might,
I wait for the hospital to catch on fire.
Keep me in your shadow . . . gold grizzling your undyed hair,
frail body of an athlete, her big hand—
your honor is humor and fragility.

3.
JULY-AUGUST

In hospital I read the news to sleep:
the Fourth of July, Bastille Day, the 16th
your Birthday . . . my two-month bankholiday.
August is summer lost in England.
Green nettles prick the oversoil with acid,
eat up the vestiges of last summer's clearing. . . .
One simultaneous sickness was enough
for us. From Brighton to Folkestone, the heads lie prone,
the patients mend, the doctors die in peace,
plucking the transient artificial flower—
the father fails to mail a single lobster
or salty nude to prove his pilgrimage.
I have no one to stamp my letters . . . I love you,
a shattered lens to burn the clinging smoke.

4.
MARRIAGE?

"I think of you every minute of the day,
I love you every minute of the day;
you gone is *hollow, bored, unbearable.*
I feel under some emotional anaesthetic,
unable to plan or think or write or feel;
mais ça ira, these things will go, I feel
in an odd way against appearances,
things will come out right with us, perhaps.
As you say, we got across the Godstow Marsh,
reached Cumberland and its hairbreadth Roman roads,
climbed Hadrian's Wall, and scared the stinking Pict.
Marriage? That's another story. We saw
the diamond glare of morning on the tar.
For a minute had the road as if we owned it."

5.

MORNING BLUE

The bathwater honks in and in, ten minutes, twenty,
twists of fire and cooling jobless bubbles;
I am exposed, keep guessing if I can take
the chill of the morning and its dressing.
The bathroom is a daub of daylight,
the beefy, flustered pigeons swish their quills—
in time the pigeons will forget the window;
I cannot—I, in flight without a ledge.
Up the carpetted stairway, your shoes clack,
clack nearer, and absentmindedly withdraw,
life withdrawn like a bad lead in poker.
Life *is* withdrawn, but after all it will be. . . .
It's safer outside; in the open air,
the car flying forward to hit us, has room to swerve.

Summer Between Terms

1.

The day's so calm and muggy I sweat tears,
the summer's cloudcap and the summer's heat. . . .
Surely good writers write all possible wrong—
are we so conscience-dark and cataract-blind,
we only blame in others what they blame in us?
(The sentence writes *we*, when charity wants *I*. . . .)
It takes such painful mellowing to use error. . . .
I have stood too long on a chair or ladder,
branch-lightning forking through my thought and veins—
I cannot hang my heavy picture straight.
I can't see myself . . . in the cattery,
the tomcats doze till the litters are eatable,
then find their kittens and chew off their breakable heads.
They told us by harshness to win the stars.

2.

Planes, trains, lorries simmer through the garden,
the reviewer sent by God to humble me
ransacking my bags of dust for silver spoons—
he and I go on typing to go on living.
There are ways to live on words in England—
reading for trainfare, my host ruined on wine,
my ear gone bad from clinging to the ropes.
I'd take a lower place, eat my toad hourly;
even big frauds wince at fraudulence,
and squirm from small incisions in the self—
they live on timetable with no time to tell.
I'm sorry, I run with the hares now, not the hounds.
I waste hours writing in and writing out a line,
as if listening to conscience were telling the truth.

Fall Weekend at *Milgate*

1.

The day says nothing, and lacks for nothing . . . God;
but it's moonshine trying to gold-cap my life,
asking fees from the things I lived and loved,
pilgrim on this hard-edge Roman road.
Your portrait is fair-faced with your honesty,
the painter, your first husband, made girls stare.
Your wall mirror, a mat of plateglass sapphire,
mirror scrolls and claspleaves, shows this face,
huge eyes and dawn-gaze, rumination unruffled,
unlearning apparently, since 1952. . . .
I watch a feverish huddle of shivering cows;
you sit making a fishspine from a chestnut leaf.
We are at our crossroads, we are astigmatic
and stop uncomfortable, we are humanly low.

2.

The soaking leaves, green yellow, hold like rubber,
longer than our eyes glued to the window can take;
none tumble in the inundating air. . . .
A weak eye sees a miracle of birth.
I'm counterclockwise . . . did we meet
last April in London, late fifties in New York?
Autumn sops on our windshield with huge green leaves;
the seasons race engines in America
burying old lumber without truce—
leaf-blight and street dye and the discard girl . . .
the lover sops gin all day to solve his puzzle.
Nature, like philosophers, has one plot,
only good for repeating what it does well:
life emerges from wood and life from life.

3.

Milgate kept standing for four centuries,
good landlord alternating with derelict.
Most fell between. We're landlords for the weekend,
and watch October go balmy. Midday heat
draws poison from the Jacobean brick,
and invites the wilderness to our doorstep:
moles, nettles, last Sunday news, last summer's toys,
bread, cheeses, jars of honey, a felled elm
stacked like construction in the kitchen garden.
The warm day brings out wasps to share our luck,
suckers for sweets, pilots of evolution;
dozens drop in the beercans, clamber, buzz,
debating like us whether to stay and drown,
or, by losing legs and wings, take flight.

Records

"... I was playing records on Sunday,
arranging all my records, and I came
on some of your voice, and started to suggest
that Harriet listen: then immediately
we both shook our heads. It was like hearing
the voice of the beloved who had died.
All this is a new feeling ... I got the letter
this morning, the letter you wrote me Saturday.
I thought my heart would break a thousand times,
but I would rather have read it a thousand times
than the detached unreal ones you wrote before—
you doomed to know what I have known with you,
lying with someone fighting unreality—
love vanquished by his mysterious carelessness."

In Harriet's Yearbook

You must be strong through solitude, said Fate,
for the present this thought alone must be your shelter—
this in your yearbook by your photograph.
Your bearing is a woman's not full woman,
bent to a straw of grass just plucked and held
like an eyetest card—you mature in blacking out.
A girl can't go on laughing all the time.
The other campgirls sway to your brooding posture,
they too must scowl to see a blade of grass;
yet you are out of focus and blurred like me,
separation stoops and fogs the lens—
one more humiliation to blow away,
only husked out in monosyllable—
profundities too shallow to expose.

Communication

"These communications across the sea,
but for once you were almost buoyant—
phone-conversations get so screwed . . . I wish
I had your lovely letter in my hand
delivered to me by the stately Alex
just the minute you hung up. I'm off
to Dalton to pick up Harriet's grades and record—
it is frightening to be a soul,
marked in the Book of Judgment once a month,
because you haven't lived much, and are alive.
Things go on, Pained Heart, another month is gone. . . .
She stayed up talking to us all last night,
giving three brainy women back their blast.
Age is nice . . . if that's your age . . . thirteen."

Dream

For months the heat of love has kept me marching,
now I am healthy, and I cannot stand;
women see through me like a head of cheese.
Boys on a gold enamelled goiterband:
boys in ultra-violet tights and doublets,
from the costume shop of Botticelli,
albino Absaloms; they probe my thicket
with pikes and wingnets, and I try to breathe,
I try to keep up breathing when I hide.
This is not Florence, or German mercenaries;
this is England, main artery of fighting—mercy was murder
at Towton when King Edward's heralds counted
twenty thousand Lancastrian dead in the field,
doubling the number killed to make the count.

Mermaid

1.

I have learned what I wanted from the mermaid
and her singeing conjunction of tail and grace.
Deficiency served her. What else could she do?
Failure keeps snapping up transcendence,
bubble and bullfrog boating on the surface,
belly lustily lagging three inches lowered—
the insatiable fiction of desire.
None swims with her and breathes the air.
A mermaid flattens soles and picks a trout,
knife and fork in chainsong at the spine,
weeps white rum undetectable from tears.
She kills more bottles than the ocean sinks,
and serves her winded lovers' bones in brine,
nibbled at recess in the marathon.

2.

Baudelaire feared women, and wrote, "Last night, I slept
with a hideous negress." Woe to Black Power,
woe to French women and the Academicians.
Why do I blush the moon with what I say?
Alice-in-Wonderland straight gold hair,
fair-featured, curve and bone from crown to socks,
bulge eyes bigger than your man's closed fist,
slick with humiliation when dismissed—
you are packaged to the grave with me,
where nothing's opened by the addressee . . .
almost a year and almost my third wife,
by accepting, by inviting, by surmounting,
rushing the music when the juice goes dead—
float like a butterfly and sting like a bee.

3.

Our meetings are no longer like a screening;
I see the nose on my face is just a nose,
your *bel occhi grandi* are just eyes
in the photo of you arranged as figurehead
or mermaid on the prow of a Roman dory,
bright as the morning star or a blond starlet.
Our twin black and tin Ronson butane lighters
knock on the sheet, are what they are,
too many, and burned too many cigarettes. . . .
Night darkens without your necessary call,
it's time to turn your pictures to the wall;
your moon-eyes water and your nervous throat
gruffs my directive, "*You must go now go.*"
Contralto mermaid, and stone-deaf at will.

4.

I see you as a baby killer whale,
free to walk the seven seas for game,
warm-hearted with an undercoat of ice,
a nerve-wrung back . . . all muscle, youth, intention,
and skill expended on a lunge or puncture—
hoisted now from conquests and salt sea
to flipper-flapper in a public tank,
big deal for Sunday children . . . My blind love—
on the Via Veneto, a girl
counting windows in a glass café,
now frowning at her menu, now counting out
neanderthals flashed like shorebait on the walk. . . .
Your stamina as *inside-right* at school
spilled the topheavy boys, and keeps you pure.

5.

One wondered who would see and date you next,
and grapple for the danger of your hand.
Will money drown you? Poverty, though now
in fashion, debases women as much as wealth.
You use no scent, dab brow and lash with shoeblack,
willing to face the world without more face.
I've searched the rough black ocean for you,
and saw the turbulence drop dead for you,
always lovely, even for those who had you,
Rough Slitherer in your grotto of haphazard.
I lack manhood to finish the fishing trip.
Glad to escape beguilement and the storm,
I thank the ocean that hides the fearful mermaid—
like God, I almost doubt if you exist.

The Mermaid Children

In my dream, we drove to Folkestone with the children,
miles of ashflakes safe for their small feet;
most coasts are sand, but this had larger prospects,
the sea drained by the out-tide to dust and dunes
blowing to Norway like brown paper bags.
Goodbye, my Ocean, you were never my white wine.
Only parents with children could go to the beach;
we had ours, and it was brutal lugging,
stopping, teasing them to walk for themselves.
When they rode our shoulders, we sank to our knees;
later we felt no weight and left no footprints. . . .
Where did we leave them behind us so small and black,
their transistors, mermaid fins and tails,
our distant children charcoaled on the sky?

They

Why are women a fraction more than us?
Lie with a woman and wake with Liberation,
her bondage is our lash, her labor our dismissal.
Her witness bugles to my dubious shade:
Woman victorious, animosity dead.
(Will the worm turn and sting her victor heel?)
Stendhal knew women deserved an education:
"No civilization rests on its best men,
its highest level, the mothers of its children—"
no vacation from shepherding the lost children . . .
if a mother no longer cares for her children,
civilization sinks to its institutions,
says, "Your fucking little psychopaths,
I didn't ask for them, they came for me."

The Friend

Your long arms antlered on the Goth-rude fireplace,
a frame ample and worthy of your wingspread . . .
whatever we say is for our hearts alone—
the first confidence of our two souls at school,
now seasoned with retrospective mercy.
Some meaning never has a use for words,
truth one couldn't tell oneself on the toilet,
self-knowledge swimming to the hook, then turning—
in Latin we learned no subject is an object.
"You say you'll remarry, you can't take none or two. . . .
All this makes me think of one thing, *you,*
at your age . . . think of it, it's the one big item
on your agenda—Do you really want
to live in the same room with anyone?"

In the Mail

"Your student wrote me, if he took a plane
past Harvard, at any angle, at any height,
he'd see a person missing, *Mr. Robert Lowell.*
You insist on treating Harriet as if she
were thirty or a wrestler—she is only thirteen.
She is normal and good because she had normal and good
parents. She is threatened of necessity. . . .
I love you, Darling, there's a black black void,
as black as night without you. I long to see
your face and hear your voice, and take your hand—
I'm watching a scruffy, seal-colored woodchuck graze
on weeds, then lift his greedy snout and listen;
then back to speedy feeding. He weighs a ton,
and has your familiar human aspect munching."

Doubt

I.

DRAW

The cardtable is black, the cards are played face down,
black-backs on a black cloth; and soon by luck
I draw a card I wished to leave unchosen,
and discard the one card I had sworn to hold.
Dreams lose their color faster than cut flowers,
but I remember the number on my card,
a figure no philosopher takes to bed. . . .
Should revelation be sealed like private letters,
till all the beneficiaries are dead,
and our proper names become improper Lives?
Focus about me and a blur inside;
on walks, things nearest to me go slow motion,
obscene streetlife rushes on the wheelrim,
steel shavings from the vacillating will.

2.

POINTING THE HORNS OF THE DILEMMA

From the dismay of my old world to the blank
new—water-torture of vacillation!
The true snakepit isn't monodrama Medea,
the gorgon arousing the serpents in her hair;
it's a room to walk with no one else, to walk,
take thought, unthink the thought and listen for nothing:
"She loves me too much to have my welfare at heart . . .
they just aren't up to your coming home
three weeks, then leaving for a year. They just aren't.
They can't stand much more of anything,
they are so tired and hurt and worn. They go on,
knowing your real sickness is a fretful
deafness to little children . . . and suspect
it's impossible for anyone to help you."

3.
CRITIC

Is my doubt, last flicker of the fading thing,
an honorable subject for conversation?
Do you know how you have changed from the true you?
I would change my trueself if I could:
I am doubtful . . . uncertain my big steps.
I fear I leave many holes for a quick knife
to take the blown rose from its wooden thorns.
A critic should save her sharpest tongue for praise.
Only blood-donors retain the gift for words;
blood gives being to everything that lives,
even to exile where tried spirits sigh,
doing nothing the day because they think
imagination matures from doing nothing,
hoping for choice, the child of vacillation.

Winter and London

CLOSED SKY

A hundred mornings greet the same closed sky,
one of nature's shows, one mantle wrapping
the dust of London with the dust of Europe—
in the interiors it is always night.
The clouds are welcome to us as insulation,
a silencer to the ultimate blue sky,
naked heaven's monologue with man.
In my country, the wettest Englishman
sparkles with approbation, magnifying
curious small things I could never see—
under closed sky, trifles are luminous,
gossip makes New York and London one,
one mouth . . . we use identical instruments
for putting up a house and pulling down.

2.
AT *OFFADO'S*

The Latin Quarter abuts on Belgravia,
three floors low as one, blocks built of blocks,
insular eighteenth century laying down
the functional with a razor in its hand,
construction too practical for conservation.
An alien should count his change here, bring a friend.
Usually on weekend nights I eat alone;
you've taken the train for *Milgate* with the children.
At *Offado's*, the staff is half the guests,
the guitar and singers wait on table,
the artist sings things unconsolable:
"Girls of Majorca. Where is my Sombrero?
Leave me alone and let me talk and love me—
a cod in garlic, a carafe of cruel rosé."

3.

FLOUNDER

In a day we pass from the Northern Lights
to doomsday dawns. Crowds crush to work at eight,
and walk with less cohesion than the mist;
the sky, without malice, is acid, Christmas lights
are needed to reveal the Thames. God sees—
wash me as white as the sole I ate last night,
acre of whiteness, back of Folkestone sand,
cooked and skinned and white—the heart appeased.
Soles live in depth, see not, spend not . . . eat;
their souls are camouflaged to die in dishes,
flat on their backs, the posture of forgiveness—
squinch-eyes, bubbles of bloodshot worldliness,
unable ever to turn the other cheek—
at sea, they bite like fleas whatever we toss.

4.

MASTODON

They splashed red on the Jews about to be killed,
then ploughed them back and forth in captured tanks;
the wood was stacked, the chainsaw went on buzzing.
In the best of worlds, the jailors follow the jailed.
In some final bog, the mastodon,
curled tusks raised like trumpets to the sky,
sunk to their hips and armpits in red mud,
splashed red for irreversible liquidation—
the heavens were very short of hearing then.
The price of freedom is displacing facts:
gnashed tusk, bulk-bruised bulk and a red splash.
Good narrative is cutting down description;
nature sacrifices heightening
for the inevitable closing line.

5.

FREUD

Is it honorable for a Jew to die as a Jew?
Even the German officials encouraged Freud
to go to Paris where at least he was known;
but what does it matter to have a following,
if no one, not even the concierge, says *good day*?
He took a house in London's amused humdrum
to prove that Moses must have been Egyptian—
"What is more monstrous than outliving your body?"
What do we care for the great man of culture—
Freud's relations were liquidated at Belsen,
Moses Cohn who had nothing to offer culture
was liquidated at Belsen. Must we die,
living in places we have learned to live in,
completing the only work we're trained to do?

6.

HARRIET'S DONKEY

On this blank page no worse, not yet defiled
by my inspiration running black in type,
I see your sepia donkey laugh at me,
Harriet's doodle, me in effigy,
my passport photo to America
that enflames the soul and irritates the eye—
M. de Maupassant va s'animaliser.
Gloomier exiles brought their causes here,
and children crying up and down the stairs;
Freud found his statue, older Jewish prophets
bit in until their teeth had turned to chalk,
found names in London and their last persona,
a body cast up lifeless on this shore. . . .
Family, my family, why are we so far?

During a Transatlantic Call

We can't swing New York on Harry Truman incomes—
the bright lights dragging like a ball and chain,
the Liberal ruined by the Liberal school.
This was the price of your manic flight to London—
the closed provincial metropolis, never
an asylum for the mercurial American mind. . . .
They say fear of death is a child's remembrance
of the first desertion. My daughter knows no love
that doesn't bind her with presents, letters, visits,
things outward and visible. . . . I've closed my mind
so long, I want to keep it closed, perhaps—
I have no faith in my right to will transcendence,
when a house goes, the species is extinct. . . .
They tell me to stop, they mustn't lose my money.

Exorcism

1.

What we love we are. As November
hardens the morning hoarfrost, I grow small;
slowly the bridal fury shows white teeth,
parading in invisible link mail—
greenness slurs into sterility,
the landscape is New England textile gray.
You point your finger: *What you love you are.*
I know what it is for a woman to be left,
to wait in the ante-room of apprehension:
Inasmuch as I am loved I am—
a woman romanticizing her exorcist,
two souls in a cocoon of mystery.
Your woman dances for you, child in arms,
she is dancing for you, Baby-Skull-Smile.

2.

This morning, as if I were home in Boston, snow,
the pure witchery-bitchery of kindergarten winters;
my window whitens like a movie screen,
glaring, specked, excluding rival outlook—
I can throw what I want on this blank screen,
but only the show already chosen shows:
Melodrama with her stiletto heel
dancing bullet wounds in the parquet.
My words are English, but the plot is hexed:
one man, two women, the common novel plot . . .
what you love you are. . . .
You can't carry your talent with you like a suitcase.
Don't you dare mail us the love your life denies;
do you really know *what you have done?*

Plotted

Planes arc like arrows through the highest sky,
ducks *V* the ducklings across a puckered pond;
Providence turns animals to things.
I roam from bookstore to bookstore browsing books,
I too maneuvered on a guiding string
as I execute my written plot.
I feel how Hamlet, stuck with the Revenge Play
his father wrote him, went scatological
under this clotted London sky.
Catlike on a paper parapet,
he declaimed the words his prompter fed him,
knowing convention called him forth to murder,
loss of free will and licence of the stage.
Death's not an event in life, it's not lived through.

The Couple

"Twice in the past two weeks I think I met
Lizzie in the recurrent dream.
We were out walking. *What sort of street*, you ask,
fair or London? It was our own street.
What did you hear and say? We heard ourselves.
The sidewalk was two feet wide. We, arm in arm,
walked, squelching the five-point oakleaves under heel—
happily, they melted under heel.
Our manner had some intimacy in my dream.
What were you doing on this honeymoon?
Our conversation had a simple plot,
a story of a woman and a man
versifying her tragedy—
we were talking like sisters . . . you did not exist."

Before Woman

BEFORE THE DAWN OF WOMAN

"Gazing close-up at your underjaw,
a blazon of barbaric decoration,
a sprinkle of black rubies, clots from shaving,
panting in measure to your wearied breath,
I see the world before the dawn of woman,
a jungle of long-horned males, their scab of rapine,
rhinoceros on Eden's rhinoceros rock. . . .
You hold me in the hollow of your hand—
a man is free to play or free to slack,
shifty past the reach of ridicule.
A woman loving is serious and disarmed,
she is less distracted than a pastured mare,
munching as if life depended on munching. . . .
Like the animals, I am humorless."

2.
DAY

Even a green parrot can talk one book,
sing up his second-rate, most writers do;
Christians and women have thought all men are evil,
though nothing living wholly disappoints God.
Living with you is living a long book
War and Peace, from day to day to day,
unable to look off or answer my name.
My springless step still stalks for youngman's wildweed,
the goldfinch-nest defying euphemism,
the God-borne instant never letting up.
Where will you take me in the fizz of winter?
Darling, the cork, though fat and black, still pulls,
new wine floods our prehistoric veins—
the day breaks, impossible, in our bed.

Artist's Model

1.

Hölderlin's thing with swan-scene and autumn
behind was something beautiful, wasn't it?
Manet's bottles mirrored behind his bar-girl
are brighter than the stuff she used to serve—
the canvas should support the artist's model.
Our children and theirs will have to pose for themselves;
we squeezed the juice, their job to eat the skin,
we put God on his knees, and now he's praying. . . .
When I sit in my bath, I wonder why
I haven't melted like a cube of sugar—
fiction should serve us with a slice of life;
but you and I actually lived what I have written,
the drunk-luck venture of our lives sufficed
to keep our profession solvent, was peanuts to live.

2.

"My cousin really learned to loathe babies,
she loved to lick the palate of her Peke,
as if her tongue were trying a liqueur—
what I say should go into your *Notebook.* . . .
I'd rather dose children on morphine than the churches.
When you are dying, and your faith is sick,
and you go on flapping in your sheets
like a cockroach fallen in a fishbowl;
you will look for the love you fumbled, and see
only religion caught naked in the searchlights—
Christians scream worse than atheists on the death-ward.
What is so infamous about it is
they shove your bed nearer the door to move the corpse;
you know damn well it isn't for fresh air."

3.

"*If it were done, 'twere well it were done quickly—*
to quote a bromide, your vacillation
is acne." And we totter off the strewn stage,
knowing tomorrow's migraine will remind us
how drink heightened the brutal flow of elocution. . . .
We follow our script as timorously as actors,
divorced from making a choice by our need to act.
"If you woke and found an egg in your shoe,
would you feel you'd lost this argument?"
It's over, my clothes fly into your borrowed suitcase,
the good day is gone, the broken champagne glass
crashes in the ashcan . . . private whims, and illusions,
too messy for our character to survive.
I come on walking off-stage backwards.

4.

Our dream has been more than life is solid—
I touch your house, the price of the furniture,
the two round marble tables big as millwheels
in your parlor unvulgarized by clutter-comforts.
But I can say more than this about you,
equal your big eyes to a silver tablespoon,
hindsight cannot romance their anger away—
bite of dog or dolphin, laughing and meant.
In my dream of misinterpretation,
your midnight taxi meets the midnight train—
one person removed, the household falls askew
from the children's tea to toilet paper.
I read in the floorboards' unintelligible worm-script
the blanks for all our birthdays . . . yours by summer.

Mermaid Emerging

The institutions of society
seldom look at a particular—
Degas's snubnosed dancer swings on high,
legging the toplights, never leaving stage,
enchanting lovers of art, discerning none.
Law fit for all fits no one like a glove. . . .
Mermaid, why are you another species?
"Because, you, I, everyone is unique."
Does anyone ever make you do anything?
"Do this, do that, do nothing; you're not chained.
I am a woman or I am a dolphin,
the only animal man really loves,
I spout the smarting waters of joy in your face—
rough-weather fish, who cuts your nets and chains."

Marriage

1.

ANGLING

Withdrawn to a third your size, and frowning doubts,
you stare in silence through the afterdinner,
when wine takes our liberty and loosens tongues—
fair-face, ball-eyes, profile of a child,
except your eyelashes are always blacked,
each hair colored and quickened like tying a fly.
If a word amuses you, the room includes your voice,
you are audible; none can catch you out,
your flights are covered by a laughing croak—
a flowered dress lost in the flowered wall.
I am waiting like an angler with practice and courage;
the time to cast is now, and the mouth open,
the huge smile, head and shoulders of the dolphin—
I am swallowed up alive . . . I am.

2.

TIRED IRON

Mulch of tired iron, bullet-stitch of straffing planes—
surely the great war of our youth was hollow;
still it had cleanness, now the smelly iron,
the war on reeds, the grand *noyades* of the rice-fields.
We promised to put back Liberty on her feet . . .
I can't go on with this, the measure is gone:
a waterfall, the water white on green,
like the white letters on my olive keyboard—
to stray with you and have you with me straying,
flesh of my body, saved by our severalness—
you will not marry, though disloyal to woman
in your airy seizures of submission,
preferring to have your body broken to being
unbreakable in this breaking life.

3.
GRUFF

The sky should be clearing, but it cannot lighten,
the unstable muck flies through the garden trees,
there's morning in my heart but not in things.
We've almost made a marriage like our parents—
the poise of disaster! Our love means giving the wheel
a shake that scatters spurs of displaced bone
in the heel of the driver's hand; it means to turn
right angle on ourselves, on our external star.
We might have married as Christ says man must not
in heaven where marriage is not, and giving
in marriage has the curse of God and Blake.
I am in bondage here, and cannot fly;
when marriage is surmounted, what is left?
"Heaven, if such things are," you gruff into the phone.

4.
LEAF-LACE DRESS

Leaf-lace, a simple intricate design—
if you were not inside it, nothing much,
bits of glinting silver on crinkled lace—
you fall perhaps metallic and as good.
Hard to work out the fact that makes you good,
whole spirit wrought from toys and nondescript,
though nothing less than the best woman in the world.
Cold the green shadows, iron the seldom sun,
harvest has worn her swelling shirt to dirt.
Agony says we cannot live in one house,
or under a common name. This was the sentence—
I have lost everything. I feel a strength,
I have walked five miles, and still desire to throw
my feet off, be asleep with you . . . asleep and young.

5.

KNOWING

This night and the last, I cannot play or sleep,
thinking of Grandfather in his last poor days.
Caroline, he had such naked nights,
and brought his *tortures of the damned* to breakfast—
when his son died, he made his grandchildren plant trees;
his blood lives, not his name. . . . We have our child,
our bastard, easily fathered, hard to name . . .
illegibly bracketed with us. My hand
sleeps in the bosom of your sleeping hands,
firm in the power of your impartial heat.
I'm not mad and hold to you with reason,
you carry our burden to the narrow strait,
this sleepless night that will not move, yet moves
unless by sleeping we think back yesterday.

6.

GOLD LULL

This isn't the final calm . . . as easily,
as naturally, the belly of the breeding
mother lifts to every breath in sleep—
I feel tomorrow like I feel today
in this gold lull of sleep . . . the muzzled lover
lies open, takes on the world for what it is,
a minute more than a minute . . . as many a writer
suffers illusions that his phrase might live:
power makes nothing final, words are deeds.
President Lincoln almost found this faith;
once a good ear perhaps could hear the heart
murmur in the square thick hide of Lenin
embalmed, wide-eyed in the lull that gives a mother
courage to be merciful to her child.

7.
GREEN SORE

We wake too early, the sun's already up,
the too early chain-twitter of the swallows fatigues,
words of a moment's menace stay for life:
not that I wish you entirely well, far from it.
That was my green life, even heard through tears. . . .
We pack, leave *Milgate*, in a rush as usual
for the London train, leaving five lights burning—
to fool the burglar? Never the same five lights.
Sun never sets without our losing something,
keys, money—not everything. "Dear Caroline,
I have told Harriet that you are having a baby
by her father. She knows she will seldom see him;
the physical presence or absence is the thing."—
a letter left in a page of a book and lost.

8.
LETTER

"I despair of letters. You say I wrote H. isn't
interested in the thing happening to you now.
So what? A fantastic untruth, misprint, something;
I meant the London scene's no big concern, just you. . . .
She's absolutely beautiful, gay, etc.
I've a horror of turmoiling her before she flies
to Mexico, alone, brave, half Spanish-speaking.
Children her age don't sit about talking *the thing*
about their parents. I do talk about you,
and I have never denied I miss you . . .
I guess we'll make Washington this weekend;
it's a demonstration, like all demonstrations,
repetitious, gratuitous, unfresh . . . just needed.
I hope nothing is mis-said in this letter."

9.

HEAVY BREATHING

Your heavier breathing moves a lighter heart,
the sun glows on past midnight on the meadow,
willing, even in England, to stretch the day.
I stand on my head, the landscape keeps its place,
though heaven has changed. Conscience incurable
convinces me I am not writing my life;
life never assures which part of ourself is life.
Ours was never a book, though sparks of it
spotted the page with superficial burns:
the fiction I colored with first-hand evidence,
letters and talk I marketed as fiction—
but what is true or false tomorrow when surgeons
let out the pus, and crowd the circus to see us
disembowelled for our afterlife?

10.

LATE SUMMER AT *MILGATE*

An air of lateness blows through the redone bedroom,
a sweetish smell of shavings, wax and oil;
the sun in heaven enflames a sanded floor.
Age is our reconciliation with dullness,
my varnish complaining, *I will never die*.
I still remember more things than I forgo:
once it was the equivalent of everlasting
to stay loyal to my other person loved—
in the fallen apple lurked a breath of spirits,
the uninhabitable granite shone
in Maine, each rock our common gravestone. . . .
I sit with my staring wife, children . . . the dour Kent sky
a smudge of mushroom. In temperate years the grass
stays green through New Year—I, my wife, our children.

11.

NINTH MONTH

For weeks, now months, the year in burden goes,
a happiness so slow burning, it is lasting;
our animated nettles are black slash
by August. Today I leaned through lunch on my elbows,
watching my nose bleed red lacquer on the grass;
I see, smell and taste blood in everything—
I almost imagine your experience mine.
This year by miracle, you've jumped from 38
to 40, joined your elders who can judge:
woman has never forgiven man her blood.
Sometimes the indictment dies in your forgetting.
You move on crutches into your ninth month,
you break things now almost globular—
love in your fullness of flesh and heart and humor.

12.

BEFORE HOSPITAL

I ask doggishly into your face—
dogs live on guesswork, heavens of submission,
but only the future answers all our lies—
has perfect vision. A generation back,
Harriet was this burdensome questionmark—
we had nowhere then to step back and judge the picture. . . .
I fish up my old words, *Dear* and *Dear Ones*;
the dealer repeats his waterfall of cards—
will the lucky number I threw down
come twice? Living is not a numbers game,
a poor game for a father when I am one. . . .
I eat, drink, sleep and put on clothes up here,
I'll get my books back when we've lived together—
in this room on which all other rocks bear down.

13.

ROBERT SHERIDAN LOWELL

Your midnight ambulances, the first knife-saw
of the child, feet-first, a string of tobacco tied
to your throat that won't go down, your window heaped
with brown paper bags leaking peaches and avocados,
your meals tasting like Kleenex . . . too much blood is seeping . . .
after twelve hours of labor to come out right,
in less than thirty seconds swimming the blood-flood:
Little Gingersnap Man, homoform,
flat and sore and alcoholic red,
only like us in owning to middle-age.
"If you touch him, he'll burn your fingers."
"It's his health, not fever. Why are the other babies so pallid?
His navy-blue eyes tip with his head. . . . Darling,
we have escaped our death-struggle with our lives."

14.

OVERHANGING CLOUD

This morning the overhanging clouds are piecrust,
milelong Luxor Temples based on rich runny ooze;
my old life settles down into the archives.
It's strange having a child today, though common,
adding our further complication to
intense fragility.
Clouds go from dull to dazzle all the morning;
we have not grown as our child did in the womb,
met Satan like Milton going blind in London;
it's enough to wake without old fears,
and watch the needle-fire of the first light
bombarding off your eyelids harmlessly.
By ten the bedroom is sultry. You have double-breathed;
we are many, our bed smells of hay.

15.

CARELESS NIGHT

So country-alone, and O so very friendly,
our heaviness lifted from us by the night . . .
we dance out into its diamond suburbia,
and see the hill-crown's unrestricted lights—
all day these encroaching neighbors are out of sight.
Huge smudge sheep in burden becloud the grass,
they swell on moonlight and weigh two hundred pounds—
hulky as you in your white sheep-coat, as nervous to gallop. . . .
The Christ-Child's drifter shepherds have left this field,
gone the shepherd's breezy too predictable pipe.
Nothing's out of earshot in this daylong night;
nothing can be human without man.
What is worse than hearing the late-born child crying—
and each morning waking up glad we wake?

16.

MORNING AWAY FROM YOU

This morning in oystery Colchester, a single
skeleton black rose sways on my flour-sack window—
Hokusai's hairfine assertion of dearth.
It wrings a cry of absence. . . . My host's new date,
apparently naked, carrying all her clothes
sways through the dawn in my bedroom to the shower.
Goodmorning. My nose runs, I feel for my blood,
happy you save mine and hand it on,
now death becomes an ingredient of my being—
my Mother and Father dying young and sixty
with the nervous systems of a child of six. . . .
I lie thinking myself to night internalized;
when I open the window, the black rose-leaves
return to inconstant greenness. A good morning, as often.

Another Summer

WILDROSE

A mongrel image for all summer, our scene at breakfast:
a bent iron fence of straggly wildrose glowing
below the sausage-rolls of new-mown hay—
Sheridan splashing in his blue balloon tire:
whatever he touches he's told not to touch
and whatever he reaches tips over on him.
Things have gone on and changed, the next oldest
daughter bleaching her hair three shades lighter with beer—
but if you're not a blonde, it doesn't work. . . .
Sleeping, the always finding you there with day,
the endless days revising our revisions—
everyone's wildrose? . . . And our golden summer
as much as such people can. When most happiest
how do I know I can keep any of us alive?

2.
DOLPHINS

Those warmblooded watchers of children—*do not say*
I have never known how to talk to dolphins,
when I try to they just swim away.
We often share the new life, *the new life*—
I haven't stilled my New England shades by combing
the Chinese cowlicks from our twisted garden,
or sorted out the fluff in the boiler room,
or stumbled on the lost mouth of the cesspool.
Our time is shorter and brighter like the summer,
each day the chill thrill of the first day at school.
Coughs echo like swimmers shouting in a pool—
a mother, unlike most fathers, must be manly.
Will a second dachshund die of a misborn lung?
Will the burned child drop her second boiling kettle?

3.
IVANA

Small-soul-pleasing, loved with condescension,
even through the cro-magnon tirades of six,
the last madness of child-gaiety
before the trouble of the world shall hit.
Being chased upstairs is still instant-heaven,
not yet your sisters' weekends of voluntary scales,
accompanying on a recorder carols
rescored by the Sisters of the Sacred Heart in Kent.
Though burned, you are hopeful, accident cannot tell you
experience is what you do not want to experience.
Is the teenager the dominant of ache?
Or flirting seniles, their conversation three noises,
their life-expectancy shorter than the martyrs?
How all ages hate another age,

and lifelong wonder what was the perfect age!

4.
ALIMONY
(A Dream in the Future)

3, 4, and then 5 children, fortunately
fortune's hostages and not all ours—
the sea comes in to us, we move it outward. . . .
I'm somewhere, nowhere; four Boston houses I grew from,
slash-brick expressionist New England fall;
I walk, run, gay with frost . . . with Harriet . . .
a barracuda settlement. (Santo Domingo,
quick divorces, solid alimony,
its dictator's marina unsafe because of sharks
checking in twice daily like grinning, fawning puppies
for our sewage, even for their own excrement. . . .)
"I am not sure I want to see her again."
Harriet laughing without malice . . . with delight:
"That's how mother talks about you."

5.

THE NEW   (CAROLINE)

The one moment that says, *I am, I am, I am. . . .*
My girlfriends tell me I must stay in New York,
one never has such new friends anywhere;
but they don't understand,
wherever he is is my friend.

Leaving America for England

1.

AMERICA

My lifelong taste for reworking the same water—
a day is day there, America all landscape,
ocean monolithic past weathering;
the lakes are oceans, nature tends to gulp. . . .
Change I earth or sky I am the same;
aging retreats to habit, puzzles repeated
and remembered, games repeated and remembered,
the runner trimming on his mud-smooth path,
the gamefish fattening in its narrow channel,
deaf to the lure of personality.
May the entertainment of uncertainty
help me from seeing through anyone I love. . . .
Overtrained for England, I find America . . .
under unmoved heaven changing sky.

2.

LOST FISH

My heavy step is treacherous in the shallows—
once squinting in the sugared eelgrass for game,
I saw the glass torpedo of a big fish,
power strayed from unilluminating depth,
roaming through the shallows worn to bone.
I was seven, and fished without a hook.
Luckily, Mother was still omnipotent—
a battered sky, a more denuded lake,
my heavy rapier trolling rod bent *L*,
drowned stumps, muskrat huts, my record fish,
its endless waddling outpull like a turtle. . . .
The line snapped, or my knots pulled—I am free
to reach the end of the marriage on my knees.
The mud we stirred sinks in the lap of plenty.

3.

TRUTH

Downstairs the two children's repeating piano duet,
when truth says goodmorning, it means goodbye.
The scouring voice of 1930 Oxford,
"Nothing pushing the personal should be published,
not even Proust's *Research* or Shakespeare's *Sonnets*,
a banquet of raw ingredients in bad taste. . . .
No Irishman can understate or drink. . . .
W. B. Yeats was not a gent,
he didn't tell the truth: *and for an hour,*
I've walked and prayed—who prays exactly an hour?
Yeats had bad eyes, saw nothing . . . not even peahens:
What has a bard to do with the poultry yard?
Dying, he dished his stilts, wrote one good poem,
small penance for all that grandeur of imperfection."

4.

NO TELLING

(FOR CAROLINE)

How much less pretentiously, more maliciously
we talk of a close friend to other friends
than shine stars for his festschrift! Which is truer—
the uncomfortable full dress of words for print,
or wordless conscious not even no one ever sees?
The best things I can tell you face to face
coarsen my love of you in solitary.
See that long lonesome road? It must end
at the will and second of the end-all—
I am still a young man not done running around. . . .
The great circuit of the stars lies on jewellers' velvet;
be close enough to tell me when I will die—
what will love do not knowing it will die?
No telling, no telling . . . not even a last choice.

5.

SICK

I wake now to find myself this long alone,
the sun struggling to renounce ascendency—
two elephants are hauling at my head.
It might have been redemptive not to have lived—
in sickness, mind and body might make a marriage
if by depression I might find perspective—
a patient almost earns the beautiful,
a castle, two cars, old polished heirloom servants,
Alka-Seltzer on his breakfast tray—
the fish for the table bunching in the fishpond.
None of us can or wants to tell the truth,
pay fees for the over-limit we caught, while floating
the lonely river to senility
to the open ending. Sometimes in sickness,

we are weak enough to enter heaven.

6.

FACING ONESELF

After a day indoors I sometimes see
my face in the shaving mirror looks as old,
frail and distinguished as my photographs—
as established. But it doesn't make one feel
the temptation to try to be a Christian.

Foxfur

"I met Ivan in a marvelous foxfur coat,
his luxurious squalor, and wished you one . . . your grizzled
knob rising from the grizzled foxfur collar.
I long to laugh with you, gossip, catch up . . . or down;
and you will be pleased with Harriet,
in the last six months she's stopped being a child,
she says God is just another great man,
an ape with grizzled sideburns in a cage.
Will you go with us to *The Messiah*,
on December 17th, a Thursday,
and eat at the *Russian Tearoom* afterward?
You're not under inspection, just missed. . . .
I wait for your letters, tremble when I get none,
more when I do. Nothing new to say."

On the End of the Phone

My sidestepping and obliquities, unable
to take the obvious truth on any subject—
why do I do what I do not want to say,
able to understand and not to hear?
Your rapier voice—I have had so much—
hundred words a minute, piercing and thrilling . . .
the invincible lifedrive of everything alive,
ringing down silver dollars with each word. . . .
Love wasn't what went wrong, we kept our daughter;
what a good father is is no man's boast—
to be still friends when we're no longer children. . . .
Why am I talking from the top of my mouth?
I am talking to you transatlantic,
we're almost talking in one another's arms.

Cars, Walking, etc., an Unmailed Letter

"In the last three days Sheridan learned to walk,
and left the quadruped behind—for some reason
small pets avoid him. . . ." Who shakes hands with a dead friend?
I see a huge, old rattling brown paper bag,
a picture, no fact; when I try to unwrap it,
it slips in my hands. It is our old car
resurrected from the must of negligence,
warning like Hector's Ghost from the underground—
the car graveyard . . .
I do not drive in England, yet in my thought,
our past years, especially the summers, are places
I could drive back to if I drove a car,
our old Burgundy Ford station-wagon summer-car,
our fourth, and first not prone to accident.

Flight to New York

I.
PLANE-TICKET

A virus and its hash of knobby aches—
more than ever flying seems too lofty,
the season unlucky for visiting New York,
for telephoning kisses transatlantic. . . .
The London damp comes in, its smell so fertile
trees grow in my room. I read Ford's *Saddest Story*,
his *triangle* I read as his student in Nashville.
Things that change us only change a fraction,
twenty-five years of marriage, a book of life—
a choice of endings? I have my round-trip ticket. . . .
After fifty so much joy has come,
I hardly want to hide my nakedness—
the shine and stiffness of a new suit, a feeling,
not wholly happy, of having been reborn.

2.
WITH CAROLINE AT THE AIR-TERMINAL

"London Chinese gray or oyster gray,
every appalling shade of pitch-pitch gray—
no need to cook up far-fetched imagery
to establish a climate for my mood. . . .
If I have had hysterical drunken seizures,
it's from loving you too much. It makes me wild,
I fear. . . . We've made the dining-room his bedroom—
I feel unsafe, uncertain you'll get back.
I know I am happier with you than before.
Safer . . ." The go-sign blazes and my plane's
great white umbilical ingress bangs in place.
The flight is certain. . . . Surely it's a strange joy
blaming ourselves and willing what we will.
Everything is real until it's published.

3.
PURGATORY

In his portrait, mostly known from frontispiece,
Dante's too identifiable—
behind him, more or less his height, though less,
a tower tapering to a fingerend,
a snakewalk of receding galleries:
Purgatory and a slice of Europe,
less like the fact, more like the builder's hope.
It leans and begs the architect for support,
insurance never offered this side of heaven.
The last fifty years stand up like that;
people crowd the galleries to flee
the second death, they cry out manfully,
for many are women and children, but the maker
can't lift his painted hand to stop the crash.

4.
FLIGHT

If I cannot love myself, can you?
I am better company depressed . . .
I bring myself here, almost my best friend,
a writer still free to work at home all week,
reading revisions to his gulping wife.
Born twenty years later, I might have been prepared
to alternate with cooking, and wash the baby—
I am a vacation-father . . . no plum—
flown in to New York. . . . I see the rising prospect,
the scaffold glitters, the concrete walls are white,
flying like Feininger's skyscraper yachts,
geometrical romance in the river mouth,
conical foolscap dancing in the sky . . .
the runway growing wintry and distinct.

5.

NEW YORK AGAIN

After London, the wind, the eye, my thoughts
race through New York with gaping coarse-comb teeth,
the simple-minded streets are one-way straight,
no queues for buses and every angle right,
a bunchy London with twenty times the soaring;
it is fish-shaped, it is modern, it is metal,
austerity assuaged with melodrama,
an irritable reaching after fact and reason,
a love of features fame puts up for sale—
love is all here, and the house desolate.
What shall I do with my stormy life blown towards evening?
No fervor helps without the favor of heaven,
no permissive law of nature picks up the bill—
survival is talking on the phone.

6.

NO MESSIAH

Sometime I must try to write the truth,
but almost everything has fallen awry
lost in passage when we said goodbye in Rome.
Even the licence of my mind rebels,
and can find no lodging for my two lives.
Some things like death are meant to have no outcome.
I come like someone naked in my raincoat,
but only a girl is naked in a raincoat.
Planesick on New York food, I feel the old
subway reverberate through our apartment floor,
I stop in our Christmas-papered bedroom, hearing
my *Nolo*, the non-Messianic man—
drop, drop in silence, then a louder drop
echoed elsewhere by a louder drop.

7.

DEATH AND THE MAIDEN

Did the girl in *Death and the Maiden* fear marriage?
No end to the adolescence we attained
by overworking, then struggled to release—
my bleak habit of counting off minutes on my fingers,
like pages of an unrequested manuscript—
that brilliant onetime moment we alone shared,
the leftovers from God's picnic and old times.
Why do I weep for joy when others weep?
One morning we saw something, half weed, half wildflower,
rise from the only thruhole in the barn floor—
it had this chance in a hundred to survive.
We knew that it was someone in disguise,
a silly good person . . . thin, peelnosed, intruding,
the green girl who doesn't know how to leave a room.

8.

NEW YORK

A sharper air and sharper architecture—
the old fashioned fishingtackle-box skyscrapers,
flesh of glass and ribs of tin . . . derisively
called *modern* in 1950, and now called modern.
As if one had tried to make polar bears
live in Africa—some actually survived,
curious, strong meat permutations of polar bear. . . .
It wasn't so once, O it wasn't so,
when I came here ten or twenty years ago. . . .
Now I look on it all with a yellow eye;
but the language of New Yorkers, unlike English,
doesn't make me fear I am going deaf. . . .
Last night at four or five, whenever I woke up,
I found myself crying—not too heavily.

9.

SLEEPLESS

Home for the night on my ten years' workbed,
where I asked the facing brick for words, and woke
to my conscious smile of self-incrimination,
hearing then as now the distant, panting siren,
small as a harbor boat patrolling the Hudson,
persistent cry without diminishment
or crescendo through the sleepless hours.
I hear its bland monotony, the voice
that holds, and never shortcircuits the transcendence
I fiddled for imperiously and too long.
All my friends are writers. Do I deserve
to sleep, because I gave myself the breaks,
self-seeking with persistent tenderness
rivals seldom lavish on a brother?

10.

NEW YORK

I can move around more . . . through the thirty years
to the New York of Jean Stafford, Pearl Harbor, the Church?
Most of my old friends are mostly dead,
entitled to grow infirm and lap the cream—
if time that hurt so much improved a little?
Our onslaught, not wholly Pyrrhic, to launch Harriet
on the heart-turning, now savage, megapolis. . . .
A friendly soft depression browns the air,
it's not my glasses needing a handkerchief . . .
it's as if I stood tiptoe on a chair
so that I couldn't help but touch the ceiling—
almost obscenely, complaisantly on the phone with
my three wives, as if three-dimensional space were my breath—
three writers, none New Yorkers, had their great years there.

11.

CHRISTMAS

All too often now your voice is too bright;
I always hear you . . . commonsense and tension . . .
waking me to myself: truth, the truth, until
things are just as if they had never been.
I can't tell the things we planned for you this Christmas.
I've written my family not to phone today,
we had to put away your photographs.
We had to. We have no choice—we, I, they? . . .
Our Christmas tree seems fallen out with nature,
shedding to a naked cone of triggered wiring.
This worst time is not unhappy, green sap
still floods the arid rind, the thorny needles
catch the drafts, as if alive—I too,
because I waver, am counted with the living.

12.

CHRISTMAS

The tedium and déjà-vu of home
make me love it; bluer days will come
and acclimatize the Christmas gifts:
redwood bear, lemon-egg shampoo, home-movie-
projector, a fat book, sunrise-red, inscribed
to me by Lizzie, "Why don't you lose yourself
and write a play about the fall of Japan?"
Slight spirits of birds, light burdens, no grave duty
to seem universally sociable
and polite. . . . We are at home and warm,
as if we had escaped the gaping jaws—
underneath us like a submarine,
nuclear and protective like a mother,
swims the true shark, the shadow of departure.

Dolphin

My Dolphin, you only guide me by surprise,
captive as Racine, the man of craft,
drawn through his maze of iron composition
by the incomparable wandering voice of Phèdre.
When I was troubled in mind, you made for my body
caught in its hangman's-knot of sinking lines,
the glassy bowing and scraping of my will. . . .
I have sat and listened to too many
words of the collaborating muse,
and plotted perhaps too freely with my life,
not avoiding injury to others,
not avoiding injury to myself—
to ask compassion . . . this book, half fiction,
an eelnet made by man for the eel fighting—

my eyes have seen what my hand did.

Day by Day

(1977)

Part One

Ulysses and Circe

I.

Ten years before Troy, ten years before Circe—
things changed to the names he gave them,
then lost their names:
Myrmidons, Spartans, soldier of dire Ulysses . . .
Why should I renew his infamous sorrow?
He had his part, he thought of building
the wooden horse as big as a house
and ended the ten years' war.
"By force of fraud," he says, "I did
what neither Diomedes, nor Achilles son of Thetis,
nor the Greeks with their thousand ships . . .
I destroyed Troy."

II.

What is more uxorious than waking at five
with the sun and three hours free?
He sees the familiar bluish-brown river
dangle down her flat young forearm,
then crisscross. The sun rises,
a red bonfire,
weakly rattling in the lower branches—
that eats like a locust and leaves the tree entire.
In ten minutes perhaps,
or whenever he next wakes up,
the sun is white as it mostly is,
dull changer of night to day,
itself unchanged, in war or peace.
The blinds give
bars of sunlight, bars of shade,
but the latter predominate
over the sincerity of her sybaritic bed.
She lies beside him,

a delicious, somnolent log. She says,
"Such wonderful things are being said to me—
I'm such an old sleeper, I can't respond."

III.
O that morning might come without the day—
he lies awake and fears the servants,
the civilities
of their savage, assiduous voices.
It's out of hand . . . her exotic palace
spun in circles no sober Greek can navigate.
He is afraid the whining, greasy animals
who bury chewed meat beneath his window
are only human, and will claim
his place of honor on the couch.
His heart is swallowed in his throat;
it is only an ache of the mind,
the twilight of early morning . . .
"Why am I my own fugitive,
because her beauty
made me feel as other men?"

IV.
She stands, her hair
intricate and winding as her heart.
They talk like two guests
waiting for the other
to leave the house—
her mongrel harmony
of the irreconcilable.
Here his derelict choice
changes to necessity;
compassion is terror,
no schism can split
the ruthless openness
of her yielding character.
Her eyes well,

and hypnotize
his followers,
the retarded animals.
They cannot stay awake,
and keep their own hours,
like degenerates
drinking the day in,
sweating it out in hysterical submission.

Young,
he made strategic choices;
in middle age he accepts
his unlikely life to come;
he will die like others as the gods will,
drowning his last crew
in uncharted ocean,
seeking the unpeopled world beyond the sun,
lost in the uproarious rudeness of a great wind.

On Circe's small island,
he grew from narrowness—
by pettiness,
he ennobled himself to fit the house.
He dislikes everything
in his impoverished life of myth.

The lotus brings a nostalgia
for the no-quarter duels he hated;
but she is only where she is.
Her speech is spiced with the faded slang
of a generation younger than his—
now the patois of the island.
Her great season goes with her;
the gorgeous girls she knew
are still her best friends,
their reputations lost like Helen's,
saved by her grace.

She is a snipper-off'er—
her discards lie about the floors,
the unused, the misused,
seacoats and insignia,
the beheaded beast.

She wants her house askew—
kept keys to lost locks,
unidentifiable portraits, dead things
wrapped in paper the color of dust . . .

the surge of the wine before the quarrel.

Slight pleasantries leave lasting burns—
the air in the high hall simmers
in the cracked beams with a thousand bugs;
though this is mid-autumn,
the moment when insects die
instantly as one would ask of a friend.

On his walk to the ship,
a solitary tree suddenly
drops half its leaves;
they stay green on the ground.
Other trees hold. In a day or two,
their leaves also will fall,
like his followers,
stained by their hesitation
prematurely brown.

V.
"Long awash and often touching bottom
by the sea's great green go-light
I found my exhaustion
the light of the world.

Earth isn't earth
if my eyes are on the moon,
her likeness caught
in the split-second of vacancy—

duplicitous,
open to all men, unfaithful.

After so many millennia,
Circe,
are you tired
of turning swine to swine?

How can I please you,
if I am not a man?

I have grown bleak-boned with survival—
I who hoped to leave the earth
younger than I came.

Age is the bilge
we cannot shake from the mop.

Age walks on our faces—
at the tunnel's end,
if faith can be believed,
our flesh will grow lighter."

VI.
Penelope

Ulysses circles—
neither his son's weakness,
nor passion for his wife,
which might have helped her, held him.
She sees no feat
in his flight or his flight back—
ten years to and ten years fro.

On foot and visible,
he walks from Long Wharf home.
Nobody in Ithaca knows him,
and yet he is too much remarked.
His knees run quicker than his feet,
his held-in mouth is puffy,
his eye is a traveled welcomer.
He looks for his lighthouse,
once so aggressively white—
a landmark, now a marina.
How white faced and unlucky-looking
he was twenty years ago,
even on the eve of his embarkation
and carnival of glory,
when he enticed Penelope
to dance herself to coma in his arms.
Risk was his métier.
His dusty, noontime road is home now;
he imagines her dashing to him
in the eager sacklike shift
she wore her last month pregnant.
Her then unspectacled eyes were stars—
a cornered rabbit . . . Today his house
is more convivial and condescending;
she is at home,
well furnished with her entourage,
her son, her son's friends, her lovers—
the usual chaos of living well,
health and wealth in clashing outfits—
only infirmity could justify
the deformity . . .
He has seen the known world,
the meanness and beacons of men;
the full heat of his pilgrimage
assumes the weight
and gravity of being alive.
He enters the house,
eyes shut, mouth loose.
The conjugal bed is just a step;

he mistakes
a daughter for her mother.
It is not surprising.
The men move him away—
a foolish but evil animal.
He is outdoors;
his uninvited hands are raw, they say
I love you through the locked window.
At forty, she is still
the best bosom in the room.
He looks at her,
she looks at him admiring her,
then turns to the suitors—knowing
the lying art of the divine Minerva
will not make him
invincible as he was,
her life ago, or young . . .
Volte-face—
he circles as a shark circles
visibly behind the window—
flesh-proud, sore-eyed, scar-proud,
a vocational killer
in the machismo of senility,
foretasting the apogee of mayhem—
breaking water to destroy his wake.
He is oversize. To her suitors,
he is Tom, Dick, or Harry—
his gills are pleated and aligned—
unnatural ventilation-vents
closed by a single lever
like cells in a jail—
ten years fro and ten years to.

Homecoming

What was is . . . since 1930;
the boys in my old gang
are senior partners. They start up
bald like baby birds
to embrace retirement.

At the altar of surrender,
I met you
in the hour of credulity.
How your misfortune came out clearly
to us at twenty.

At the gingerbread casino,
how innocent the nights we made it
on our *Vesuvio* martinis
with no vermouth but vodka
to sweeten the dry gin—

the lash across my face
that night we adored . . .
soon every night and all,
when your sweet, amorous
repetition changed.

Fertility is not to the forward,
or beauty to the precipitous—
things gone wrong
clothe summer
with gold leaf.

Sometimes
I catch my mind
circling for you with glazed eye—

my lost love hunting
your lost face.

Summer to summer,
the poplars sere
in the glare—
it's a town for the young,
they break themselves against the surf.

No dog knows my smell.

Last Walk?

That unhoped-for Irish sunspoiled April day
heralded the day before
by corkscrews of the eternal
whirling snow that melts and dies
and leaves the painted green pasture marsh—
and the same green . . . We could even imagine
we enjoyed our life's great change then—
hand in hand with balmy smiles
graciously belittling our headlong reverse.

We walked to an artificial pond
dammed at both ends to reflect the Castle—
a natural composition for the faded colorist
on calm bright days or brighter nights.
At first we mistook the pond for a lull in the river—
the Liffey, torrential, wild,
accelerated to murder,
wider here than twenty miles downhill to Dublin—
black, rock-kneed, crashing on crags—
by excessive courage married to the ocean.

"Those swans," you said, "if one loses its mate,
the other dies. This spring a Persian exile
killed one cruelly, and its mate
refused to be fed—
It roused an explosion of xenophobia
when it died."
Explosion is growing common here;
yet everything about the royal swan
is silly, overstated, a luxury toy
beyond the fortunate child's allowance.

We sat and watched a mother swan
enthroned like a colossal head of Pharaoh
on her messy double goose-egg nest of sticks.
The male swan had escaped
their safe, stagnant, matriarchal pond
and gallanted down the stout-enriched rapids to Dublin,
smirking drunkenly, racing bumping,
as if to show a king had a right to be too happy.

I meant to write about our last walk.
We had nothing to do but gaze—
seven years, now nothing but a diverting smile,
dalliance by a river, a speeding swan . . .
the misleading promise
to last with joy as long as our bodies,
nostalgia pulverized by thought,
nomadic as yesterday's whirling snow,
all whiteness splotched.

Suicide

You only come in the tormenting
hallucinations of the night,
when my sleeping, prophetic mind
experiences things
that have not happened yet.

Sometimes in dreams
my hair came out in tufts
from my scalp,
I saw it lying there
loose on my pillow like flax.

Sometimes in dreams
my teeth got loose in my mouth . . .
Tinker, Tailor, Sailor, Sailor—
they were cherrystones,
as I spat them out.

I will not come again to you,
and risk the help I fled—
the doctors and darkness and dogs,
the hide and seek for me—
"Cuckoo, cuckoo. Here I am . . ."

If I had lived
and could have forgotten
that eventually it had to happen,
even to children—
it would have been otherwise.

One light, two lights, three—
it's day, no light is needed.
Your car I watch for never comes,

you will not see me peeping for you
behind my furtively ajar front door.

The trees close branches and redden,
their winter skeletons are hard to find;
a friend seldom seen
is not the same—
how quickly even bad cooking eats up a day.

I go to the window,
and even open it wide—
five floors down, the trees are bushes and weeds,
too contemptible and small
to delay a sparrow's fall.

Why haven't you followed me here,
as you followed me everywhere else?
You cannot do it
with vague fatality
or muffled but lethal sighs.

Do I deserve credit
for not having tried suicide—
or am I afraid
the exotic act
will make me blunder,

not knowing error
is remedied by practice,
as our first home-photographs,
headless, half-headed, tilting
extinguished by a flashbulb?

Departure

Intermissa, Venus, diu

"Waiting out the rain,
but what are you waiting for?
The storm can only stop
to get breath to begin again . . .
always in suspense to hit
the fugitive in flight.
Your clothes, moth-holed
with round cigarette burns,
sag the closet-pole.
Your books are rows of hollow suits;
'Who lives in them?'
we ask acidly,
and bring them down
flapping their paper wrappers.
So many secondary troubles,
the body's curative diversions;
but what does it matter,
if one is oneself, has something
past criticism to change to?
Not now as you were young . . .
Horace in his fifties held
a Ligurian girl
captive in the sleep of night,
followed her flying across the grass
of the Campus Martius, saw her lost
in the Tiber he could not hold.
Can you hear my first voice,
amused in sorrow,
dramatic in amusement . . .
catastrophies of description
knowing when to stop,
when not to stop?
It cannot be replayed;
only by exaggeration

could I tell the truth.
For me, neither boy
nor woman was a help.
Caught in the augmenting storm,
choice itself is wrong,
nothing said or not said tells—
a shapeless splatter of grounded rain . . .
Why, Love, why, are a few tears
scattered on my cheeks?"

Part Two

Our Afterlife I

(FOR PETER TAYLOR)

Southbound—
a couple in passage,
two Tennessee cardinals
in green December outside the window
dart and tag and mate—
young as they want to be.
We're not.
Since my second fatherhood
and stay in England,
I am a generation older.
We are dangerously happy—
our book-bled faces
streak like red birds,
dart unstably,
ears cocked to catch
the first shy whisper of deafness.
This year killed
Pound, Wilson, Auden . . .
promise has lost its bloom,
the inheritor reddens
like a false rose—
nodding, nodding, nodding.
Peter, in our boyish years,
30 to 40,
when Cupid was still the Christ of love's religion,
time stood on its hands.

Sleight of hand.

We drink in the central heat
to keep the cold wave out.
The stifled telephone that rings in my ear
doesn't exist.
After fifty,

the clock can't stop,
each saving breath
takes something. This is riches:
the eminence not to be envied,
the account
accumulating layer and angle,
face and profile,
50 years of snapshots,
the ladder of ripening likeness.

We are things thrown in the air
alive in flight . . .
our rust the color of the chameleon.

Our Afterlife II

Leaving a taxi at Victoria,
I saw my own face
in sharper focus and smaller
watching me from a puddle
or something I held—*your* face
on the cover of your *Collected Stories*
seamed with dread and smiling—
old short-haired poet
of the first Depression,
now back in currency.

My thinking is talking to you—
last night I fainted at dinner
and came nearer to your sickness,
nearer to the angels in nausea.
The room turned upside-down,
I was my interrupted sentence,
a misdirection tumbled back alive
on a low, cooling black table.

The doctors come more thickly,
they use exact language
even when they disagree on the mal-diagnosis
in the surgeon's feather-touch.

Were we ever weaned
from our reactionary young masters
by the *schadenfreude* of new homes?

America once lay uncropped and golden,
it left no tarnish on our windshield . . .
In a generation born under Prohibition,
the Red Revolution, the Crash,
cholesterol and bootleg—

we were artisans
retained as if we were workers
by the charities of free enterprise.

Our loyalty to one another sticks like love . . .

This year for the first time,
even cows seem transitory—
1974
of the Common Market,
the dwarf Norman appletree
espaliered to a wall.
The old boys drop like wasps
from windowsill and pane.
In a church,
the Psalmist's glass mosaic Shepherd
and bright green pastures
seem to wait
with the modish faithlessness
and erotic daydream
of art nouveau for our funeral.

Louisiana State University in 1940

(FOR ROBERT PENN WARREN)

The torch-pipes wasting waste gas all night,
O Baton Rouge, your measureless student prospects,
rats as long as my forearm regrouping toward
the sewage cleansing on the open canals—
the moisture mossing in the green seminar room
where we catnapped,
while Robert Penn Warren talked three hours
on Machiavelli . . . the tyrannicide
of princes, Cesare Borgia, Huey Long,
citing fifty English and Italian sources—
our dog-eat-dog days in isolationist America,
devouring Stalin's unmeasured retreats,
as if we had a conscience to be impartial.

"How can you beat a country
where every boy of twelve can fix a motorcycle?"
Red, you could make friends with anyone,
criminals, or even showy writer giants
you slaughtered in a review . . .

my dangerous ad hominem simplifications.

Your reminiscences have more color than life—
but because, unlike you, I'm neither novelist
nor critic, I choose your poetry:
Terror, Pursuit, Brother to Dragons, Or Else.
Can poetry get away with murder,
its terror a seizure of the imagination
foreign to our stubborn common health?
It's the authentic will to spoil,
the voice,
haunted not lost,
that lives by breaking in
berserk with inspiration,

not to be shaken without great injury,
not to be quieted by ingenious plotting—
the muse,
"rattling her crutch that puts forth a small bloom, perhaps white . . ."
an old master still engaging the dazzled disciple.

For John Berryman

(After reading his last *Dream Song*)

The last years we only met
when you were on the road,
and lit up for reading
your battering *Dream*—
audible, deaf . . .
in another world then as now.
I used to want to live
to avoid your elegy.
Yet really we had the same life,
the generic one
our generation offered
(*Les Maudits*—the compliment
each American generation
pays itself in passing):
first students, then with our own,
our galaxy of grands maîtres,
our fifties' fellowships
to Paris, Rome and Florence,
veterans of the Cold War not the War—
all the best of life . . .
then daydreaming to drink at six,
waiting for the iced fire,
even the feel of the frosted glass,
like waiting for a girl . . .
if you had waited.
We asked to be obsessed with writing,
and we were.

Do you wake dazed like me,
and find your lost glasses in a shoe?

Something so heavy lies on my heart—
there, still here, the good days
when we sat by a cold lake in Maine,

talking about the *Winter's Tale*,
Leontes' jealousy
in Shakespeare's broken syntax.
You got there first.
Just the other day,
I discovered how we differ—humor . . .
even in this last *Dream Song*,
to mock your catlike flight
from home and classes—
to leap from the bridge.

Girls will not frighten the frost from the grave.

To my surprise, John,
I pray *to* not for you,
think of you not myself,
smile and fall asleep.

Jean Stafford, a Letter

Towmahss Mahnn: that's how you said it . . .
"That's how Mann must say it," I thought.

I can go on imagining you
in your Heidelberry braids and Bavarian
peasant aprons you wore three or four years
after your master's at twenty-one.

How quickly I run through my little set
of favored pictures . . . pictures starved to words.
My memory economizes so prodigally
I know I have suffered theft.

You did miracles I blushed to acknowledge,
outlines for novels more salable than my poems,
my ambiguities lost seven cities down.
Roget's synonyms studded your spoken and written word.

Our days of the great books, scraping and Roman mass—
your confessions had such a vocabulary
you were congratulated by the priests—
I pretended my impatience was concision.

Tortoise and hare
cross the same finishing line—
we learn the spirit is very willing to give up,
but the body is not weak and will not die.

You have spoken so many words and well,
being a woman and you . . . someone must still hear
whatever I have forgotten
or never heard, being a man.

Since 1939

We missed the declaration of war,
we were on our honeymoon train west;
we leafed through the revolutionary thirties'
Poems of Auden, till our heads fell down
swaying with the comfortable
ungainly gait of obsolescence . . .
I miss more things now,
am more consciously mistaken.
I see another girl reading Auden's last book.
She must be very modern,
she dissects him in the past tense.

He is historical now as Munich,
and grew perhaps
to love the rot of capitalism.

We still live
with the devil of his derelictions
he wished to disdain
in the mischievous eccentricity of age.

In our unfinished revolutionary now,
everything seems to end and nothing to begin . . .
The Devil has survived his hollow obits,
and hobbles cursing to his demolition,
a moral heaviness no scales can weigh—
a regurgitation like spots
of yellow buttercups . . .

England like America has lasted
long enough to fear its past,
the habits squashed like wax,
the gay, the prosperous,
their acid of outrage . . .

A decade or so ago,
cavalier African blacks piled
their small English cemetery and dump
to suffocation with statues,
Victorias, Kitcheners, Belfast mercenaries
drained white by rule and carved in soap . . .
caught by the marked cards that earned their keep—
the sovereign misfortune to surpass.

Did they put on too much color like a great actress
for the fulfillment of the dress rehearsal . . .
Did they think they still lived,
if their spirit carried on?

We feel the machine slipping from our hands,
as if someone else were steering;
if we see a light at the end of the tunnel,
it's the light of an oncoming train.

Square of Black

On this book, large enough to write on,
is a sad, black, actual photograph
of Abraham Lincoln and Tad in 1861,
father and son,
their almost matching silver watchchains,
as they stare into the blank ledger,
its murders and failures . . . they.
Old Abe, and old at 52—
in life, in office, no lurking illusion,
clad for the moment in robes of splendor,
passed him unchallenged . . .
Only in a dream was he able to hear
his voice in the East Room of the White House
saying over his own dead body:
"Lincoln is dead."

Dreams, they've had their vogue,
so alike in their modernist invention,
so dangerously distracted by commonplace,
their literal insistence on the letter,
trivia indistinguishable from tragedy—
his monstrous melodrama terminating
at a playhouse . . . dreaming, overhearing
his own voice,
the colloquial sibilance of the circuit-court,
once freedom, the law and home to Lincoln—
shot while sleeping through the final act.

Fortunately
I only dream inconsequence.
Last night I saw a little
flapping square of pure black cloth.
It flew to the corners of my bedroom,
hugging, fluttering there coquettishly—

a bat, if wing and pelt could be one-color black.
It was a mouse. (So my dream explained.)
It taught me to feed and tame it
with nagging love . . . only existing
in my short dream's immeasurable leisure.

Fetus

(Front-page picture, *Boston Globe*, February 1975)

The convicted abortion-surgeon
and his Harvard lawyers are Big League,
altruistic, unpopular men lost in the clouds
above the *friendly* municipal court.
The long severe tiers of windows
are one smear of sunlight multiplied;
the new yellow brick has a cutting edge.

"The law is a sledgehammer,
not a scalpel."

The court cannot reform the misstep
of the motionless moment . . .
So many killers are cleared of killing,
yet we are shocked a fetus can be murdered—
its translucence looms to attention
in bilious X-ray
too young to be strengthened
by our old New England hope of heaven
made unsentimental by our certainty in hell.

Our germ—
no number in the debtbook
to say it lived
once unembarrassed by the flesh.

When the black arrow arrives on the silver tray,
the fetus has no past,
not even an immovable wall of paintings—
no room to stir its thoughts,
no breathless servility
overacting the last day,
writhing like a worm

under the contradicting rays of science—
no scared eye on the audience.

Wrap me close, but not too close—
when we wake to our unacceptable age,
will we find our hearts enlarged
and wish all men our brothers—
hypocrites pretending to answer
what we cannot hear?

How much we carry away with us
before dying,
learning we have nothing to take,
like the fetus, the homunculus,
already at four months one pound,
with shifty thumb in mouth—

Our little model . . .

As I drive on, I lift my eyes;
the focus is spidered
with black winter branches
and blackened concrete stores
bonneted for Easter with billboards . . .
Boston snow contracting
like a yellow surgical bandage—
the slut of struggle.
The girl high on the billboard
was ten years my senior in life;
she would have teased my father—
unkillable, unlaid,
disused as the adolescent tan on my hand.
She is a model, and cannot lose her looks,
born a decade too soon for any buyer.

Art of the Possible

"Your profession of making what can't be done
the one thing you can do . . ."

In my parents' townhouse,
a small skylight-covered courtyard,
six feet by nine,
lit two floors of bathrooms—
their wanton windows clear glass above,
and modestly glazed below.
There for a winter or so,
when eleven or twelve,
one year short
of the catastrophic brink of adolescence,
I nightly enjoyed my mother bathing—
not lust, but the lust of the eye.

We sit drinking and forking clams,
a man and a woman three years younger,
table companions for twenty years,
raking over the roster of our acquaintance—
grateful our student euphemisms hide
our trembling hands afraid to lift a fork in public.
"Father Freud brainwashed you to hate your mother."
We stand to leave,
your breasts touch my chest;
under our clothes, our bodies
are but as bodies are.
On the thin ice of our hard age
malignant with surprises,
everything inside us stings, yet chills
knowing the affliction of seduction . . .
Tomorrow
the unbecoming oneness of our ravished body
melts in the light of day.

No engagement, I go . . .
darkness straightens the limping hand,
insomnia finds a hundred justifications
for the inexcusable phrase.
After many lives in marriage,
bedrooms blood-temperature,
my joy in making this room arctic—
a solitary barrenness
finds the cold spots in the bed,
and cherishes their expiring chill.

In the Ward

(FOR ISRAEL CITKOVITZ)

Ten years older in an hour—

I see your face smile,
your mouth is stepped on without bruising.
You are very frightened by the ward,
your companions are chosen for age;
you are the youngest
and sham-flirt with your nurse—
your chief thought is scheming
the elaborate surprise of your escape.

Being old in good times is worse
than being young in the worst.

Five days
on this grill, this mattress
over nothing—
the wisdom of this sickness
is piously physical,
ripping up memory
to find your future—
old beauties, old masters
hoping to lose their minds before they lose their friends.

Your days are dark,
your nights imaginary—
the child says,
heaven is a big house
with lots of water and flowers—
you go in in a trunk.

Your feet are wired above your head.

If you could hear the glaring lightbulb
sing
your old modernist classics—
they are for a lost audience.

Last year
in buoyant unrest,
you gathered two or three young friends
in the *champagne room*
of your coldwater flat,
to explore the precision
and daimonic lawlessness
of Arnold Schönberg born
when music was still imperfect science—
Music,
its ever retreating borderlines of being,
as treacherous, perhaps, to systems,
to fecundity,
as to silence.

Die Sprache ist unverstanden
doch nicht unverständlich?

If you keep cutting your losses,
you have no loss to cut.

Nothing you see now
can mean anything;
your will is fixed on the lightbulb,
its blinding impassivity
withholding disquiet,
the art of the possible
that art abhors.

It's an illusion death or technique
can wring the truth from us like water.

What helpless paperishness,
if vocation
is only shouting what we will.

Somewhere your spirit
led the highest life;
all places matched
with that place
come to nothing.

Burial

(FOR ———)

Six or seven swallows drag the air,
their fast play of flight unbroken
as if called by a voice—
the flies become fewer about my head.

A longwinded wasp stumbles on me,
marauding, providing, as if about to sting—
patting, smelling me, caught
in the carnivorous harmony of nature.

The small girl has set a jagged chip
of sandstone on the grave of a crow,
chalked with white Gothic like a valentine:
"For Charlie who died last night."

Your father died last month,
he is buried . . . not too deep to lie
alive like a feather
on the top of the mind.

Ear of Corn

At the head of his table
the wine baron
looks like the old Stravinsky.

There's green on the bread;
all the beautiful girls he knew
are old maids or dead.

One must admire him,
so assured of his triumphant return,
of making it abundantly,
yet spoiling his hopeless odds by talking.

He is drunk on his own wine,
his hundreds of servants filling 14 glasses
in chronological vintage at each place
with incantations of the price.
"It's a sacrilege for *me* to say it . . .
they mustn't hear me . . .
the best drink is a rum-banana daiquiri!"

He is not lacking in love,
someone's young wife is on his right—
"Have you ever returned to a childhood house,
and found it unchanged?
It makes one so angry . . . it's so shrunk,
one wishes it wiped out—if it *is* wiped out,
that, of course, is another kind of catastrophe."

The girl hears and feels maternal.
His eyes never leave her lips.
She cannot cure his hallucination
he can bribe or stare
any woman he wants into orgasm . . .

He fills her ear
with his old sexual gramophone.

Like belief,
he makes nothing happen.

He, she, or she or she—
she is a stream,
one of the bubbles . . . one of the sparks
that flashed from the miscellaneous dish he gobbled.

Her face is delicate and disgusted,
as if she had been robbed, raped,
or repudiated by her mother—
a discarded ear of corn
lying in a sink,
leaf and cornsilk flipped to show
the golden kernels are browned . . .
his first image of a girl who refused.

His great lethargy calms him:
hypnos kai hydor,
Scotch and water—
he no longer asks for love.

Is this the substance hoped for,
after a grasshopper life of profit—
to stand shaking on fine green legs,
to meet the second overflowing of Eros,
himself younger in each young face;
and see in that mirror
a water without the life of water,
a face aging
to less generosity than it had?

Off Central Park

(FOR E.H.)

Here indeed, here for a moment,
here ended—that's new.

Another new thing, your single wooden dice,
three feet high,
and marked with squares like a chessboard,
stands laughing at us on the threshold.

Our light intimacy of reference is unbroken.

The old movables keep their places;
they are more confidently out of style
in their unhurried, almost routine decline.

I can give the dates when they entered our lives:

Cousin Belle's half-sofa,
her carrot dangled before famished heirs,
is twenty years lighter.

The small portrait of Cousin Cassie,
corsetted like the Empress Eugénie
and willed to father when I was seven,
is now too young for me to talk to.

In the bookcase, my Catholic theology,
still too high for temptation—
the same radical reviews
where we first broke into print
are still new to us.

Your gilt urchin-faced angels hang like stars
in the cramped bathroom under the stairs—
they see everything that happens there.

Fast and fallen New York—as if I were home,
I go to the bureau for fresh shirts;
the drawers have the solidity of Spanish kings,
observers of successive peaks of decadence,
set on racks in identical bass-viol coffins—
but only a breath, yours, holds anything together,
a once superfluous, now supernatural, spirit,
the thread and sentence of life we mended 50 times.

Our old world . . . nine-tenths invisible—
here we made over what we were before we met . . .

Outside,
I pass Harriet's subteenager playground,
half-modernized,
then interrupted, as if by a stroke of senility.

The sun of comfort shines on the artist,
the same Academician from our building . . .
he is repeating his *Mont Sainte-Victoire*—
why should a landscape painter
ever leave Central Park?
his subject lies under his nose . . .
his prison?

"After so much suffering," you said,
"I realize we couldn't have lasted
more than another year or two anyway."

Death of a Critic

I.
Dull, disagreeable and dying,
the old men—
they were setups for my ridicule,
till time, the healer, made me theirs.

In the old New York, we said,
"If life could write,
it would have written like us."
Now the lifefluid goes
from the throwaway lighter,
its crimson, cylindrical, translucent
glow grows pale—
O queen of cities, star of morning.

The age burns in me.

The path is cleared and cleared each year,
each year the brush closes;
nature cooperates with us,
then we cooperate no more.

II.
The television's ocean-green square
loved and searched as no human face . . .

In my disconnected room,
I improve talking to myself.
I convalesce. I do not enjoy
polemic with my old students,
and place a board across the arms of my chair
to type out letters
they burn for fear of my germs.

Disciples came like swallows from Brazil,
or airborne book reviews from London.
On sleepless nights, when my tragedy
delights the dawdling dawnbirds, I ask
where are their unannounced, familiar faces
I could not recognize.

The students whose enthusiasm
burned holes in the transitory
have graduated to not having been.
It would never do
to have them come back to life again,
they would have the fool's heartiness of ghosts . . .
without references or royalties,
out of work.

Now that I am three parts iced-over,
I see the rose glow in my heater.
In moments of warmth, I see
the beauty who made summer
Long Island tropical.
From the nineties to Nixon,
the same girl, the same bust,
still consciously unwrinkled.
On my screen,
her unspeakable employer
offers her to me nightly,
as if she were his daughter.

Did their panic make me infallible?
Was my integrity my unique
understanding of everything I damned?

Did the musician, Gesualdo,
murder his wife to inherit
her voice of the nightingale?

My criticism survives its victims
buried in the Little Magazines

that featured us concurrently,
the barracuda and his prey.
My maiden reviews,
once the verbal equivalent of murder,
are now a brief, compact pile,
almost as old as I.
They fall apart sallowing,
their stiff pages
chip like dry leaves
flying the tree that fed them.

Under New York's cellular façades
clothed with vitreous indifference,
I dwindle . . . dynamite no more.

I ask for a natural death,
no teeth on the ground,
no blood about the place . . .
It's not death I fear,
but unspecified, unlimited pain.

Endings

(FOR HARRIET WINSLOW)

The leap from three adjectives to an object
is impossible—

legs purple and white
like purple grapes on marble.

The change was surprising though laughable
in the 24 years since my first childish
visit to you in Washington—
my foot now touched the first rung of the ladder,
the sharpest pencil line,
far from my Potomac School, my ABC's
with Miss Locke and Miss Gay.

Our arms reached out to each other
too full of drinks . . .
You joked of your blackouts,
your abstractions,
comic and monumental
even for Washington.
You woke wondering why
you woke in another room,
you woke close to drowning.
Effects are without cause;
your doctors found nothing.
A month later you were paralyzed
and never unknotted . . .

A small spark tears at my head,
a flirting of light brown specks in the sky,
explosive pinpricks,
an unaccountable lapse of time.

When I close my eyes, the image is too real,
the solid colors and perspective of life . . .
the tree night-silvered above a bay becomes
the great globe itself, an eye deadened to royal blue
and buried in a jacket of oak leaves.

Why plan; when we stop?

The wandering virus never surmounts the cluster
it never joined.

My eyes flicker, the immortal
is scraped unconsenting from the mortal.

Part Three

DAY BY DAY

FOR CAROLINE

I

The Day

It's amazing
the day is still here
like lightning on an open field,
terra firma and transient
swimming in variation,
fresh as when man first broke
like the crocus all over the earth.

From a train, we saw cows
strung out on a hill
at differing heights,
one sex, one herd,
replicas in hierarchy—
the sun had turned
them noonday bright.

They were child's daubs in a book
I read before I could read.

They fly by like a train window:
flash-in-the-pan moments
of the Great Day,
the *dies illa*,
when we lived momently
together forever
in love with our nature—

as if in the end,
in the marriage with nothingness,
we could ever escape
being absolutely safe.

Domesday Book

Let nothing be done twice—

When Harold fell
with an arrow in his eye at Hastings,
the bastard Conqueror taxed
everything in his Domesday Book:
ox, cow, swine,
the villages and hundreds
his French clerks tore to shreds
and fed
to berserk hawk and baron.
His calculated devastation,
never improvidently
merciful to the helpless,
made anarchy anachronism
and English a speech for serfs.

England/Scotland/Ireland
had better days—
now the elephantiasis of the great house
is smothered in the beauty of its English garden
changed already to a feathery, fertile waste,
lawns drenched with the gold-red sorrel.
The hectic, seeded rose
climbs a neglected gravel drive
cratered to save the children from delivery vans.
The beef-red bricks and sky-gray stones
are buried in the jungle leaf of June—
wildflowers take root in the kitchen garden.

The dower house goes with the house,
the dowager with her pale, white cup of tea
she inspired with brandy.

Lathom House, Middleton Manor,
New Hall, Silverton,
Brickling with its crinkled windows
and rose-pink gables
are converted to surgeries, polytechnics,
cells of the understaffed asylum
crumbling on the heads of the mad.

The country houses that rolled
like railways are now
more stationary than anthills—
their service gone. Will they fall
under the ax of penal taxes
they first existed to enact . . .
too grand for any gallery?
Will the house for pleasure
predecease its predecessor,
the cathedral,
once outshone in art and cost?

Cold chimneystacks and greening statuary
outlive the living garden
parceled to irreversible wilderness
by one untended year—
from something to nothing . . .
like King Charles who lost his head
and shared the luck and strange
fibered Puritan violence
of his antagonist, the Protector,
whose carcass
they drew on a hurdle to Tyburn,
hanged and buried under the gallows.

If they have you by the neck, a rope will be found.

Nulle terre sans seigneur.

The old follies, as usual, never return—
the houses still burn

in the golden lowtide steam of Turner.
Only when we start to go,
do we notice the outrageous phallic flare
of the splash flowers that fascinated children.

The reign of the kingfisher was short.

We Took Our Paradise

We took our paradise here—
how else love?

These three weeks the weather
has accreted reek
like a bathroom mirror:
hills, cows, molehills,
the oceanless inland . . .

the harvest
we whistle from grass.

The struck oak that lost
a limb that weighed a ton
still shakes green leaves
and takes the daylight,
as if alive.

Can one bear it; in nature
from seed to chaff no tragedy?

Folly comes from something—
the present, yes,
we are in it;
it's the infection
of things gone . . .

the Atlantic rattling paper
I haven't heard three years.

Why does a man love a woman
more than women?

Lives

Summer is like Hope
to engrave free verse on bronze—
in this room,
the air is blocked by its walls;
I cannot walk to old friends,
as if there were doors.

In the end,
in tagging distance,
I am afraid of falling back,
becoming a child according to the Gospel,
acting with more demand
than I was able to full flower—
in sum
the Great Cycle is the ponderous strum
of this final year.

How could you love, and you so young?

My unhealthy generation—
their lives never stopped stopping,
with ursine step,
one foot bleeding,
without a crutch—
snapdragons,
half-amiable and gallant . . .

their week was so short
they could see it move.

Yet I take joy in remembering the pains
we took to give the ringing statement—
the calendared slip of the scissors
was only poisonous in thought.

It would take a tree-surgeon
to know the blond-faced wheat
and comfortable fleshed-out trees
are crumbling to sawdust.

This August is like a woman
who gets men without moving.

The Spell

Sometimes I begin to fear a dead
lost spirit who claimed he could haunt—
perhaps he could hex me . . . only by haunting himself.
What help were his sermons,
his genius for unrhetorical wit,
his metaphysical grandiosity,
or the hard antisocial ritual he laid on himself,
like a snail's shell to be at home anywhere
and always comfortably himself?
Age came, and then infirmity,
a boyish precocity eagerly willing
to take a joke or two and quote a hundred.
He was not ruled by measure,
or comfortably himself,
when he made
his verse the echo of his conscious mind.
Or when at appointed hours,
he brightly hectored the visitors
in his lodgings, that clean cliff of books
above a wash of trash.
We almost expected a miracle,
when on good days at the dot of six
he changed
his room-chilled black coffee
to spirits in our bitter mugs.
He once changed English to his own demotic.
He was more madly, innocently, at home
on bachelor afternoons,
when he cut short the cocktail hour,
expelled his guests,
and sat down in the ebbing twilight
to the early supper of a child . . .
an old choirboy chirping in his stall,
too tipsy to manage his knife,

free to drink or not to drink . . .
Comme le bon dieu le veut, le temps s'envole.
He was not my double, and haunts me.
He died
generously drinking, too disciplined for a friend.

This Golden Summer

This golden summer,
this bountiful drought,
this crusting bread—
nothing in it is gold.

Its fields have the yellow-white hair
of Patriarchs who lived
on two goats and no tomorrow—
a fertility too rich to breathe.

Our cat, a new mother, put a paw
under my foot, as I held a tray;
her face went white, she streaked screaming
through an open window, an affronted woman.

Is our little season of being together
so unprecarious, I must imagine
the shadow around the corner . . .
downstairs . . . behind the door?

I see even in golden summer
the wilted blowbell spiders
ruffling up impossible angers,
as they shake threads to the light.

We have plucked the illicit corn,
seen the Scriptural
fragility of flowers—
where is our pastoral adolescence?

I will leave earth
with my shoes tied,
as if the walk
could cut bare feet.

Milgate

Yearly, connubial swallows nest
in the sky-flung gutter and stop its mouth.
It is a natural life. Nettles
subdue the fugitive violet's bed,
a border of thistles hedges the drive;
children dart like minnows. They dangle
over the warm, reedy troutbrook.

It's a crime
to get too little from too much.

In mirage, meadow turns to lawn,
in the dredged cowpond, weed is water,
half-naked children beautify,
feud and frighten the squabbling ducks—
from vacation to vacation,
they broaden out to girls, young ladies,
a nightlife on two telephones.

The elderflower is champagne.

Age goes less noticed in humbler life—
the cedar of Lebanon dumbly waves
one defoliated millennial stump;
the yew row, planted under Cromwell
with faith and burnish, keeps its ranks,
unpierceably stolid, young, at ease.

August flames in the rusty sorrel,
a bantam hen hatches wild pheasant chicks,
the dog licks ice cream from a cone;
but mostly the cropped, green, sold-off pastures
give grace to the house, to *Milgate Park*,
its name and service once one in Bearsted,

till uselessness brought privacy,
splendor, extravagance, makeshift
offered at auction for its bricks—
yet for a moment saved by you,
and kept alive another decade,
by your absentminded love,
your lapwing's instinctive elegance,
the glue of your obdurate Ulster will—
Milgate,
enclosures to sun and space to cool,
one mural varied in fifty windows,
sublime and cozy, stripped of creeper,
its severity a blaze of salmon-pink,
its long year altered by our small . . .
easy to run as things made to run.

Realities

Who knows if the live season
will add tomorrow to today?

Young we identified
the sounds of the summer night,
the mating birds,
roadsters and sex
of the incumbent generation.

How little we cost then—
and so many submitted to pain,
and even joy, to bring us here—
they now solid
because we are solid,
we their only outcome.

Their faces, no longer faces, adorn
the golden age of photographs—
thinking, like us, their autumn
the autumn of the world.

Houses grew with them,
increasing like the great conch's
roselipped, steepled shell—
left calcifying in gardens,
where their children multiplied . . .
I cannot believe myself them,
my children more skeptical than I,
misunderstanding those who misunderstood—
hanging on to power by a fingernail.

If I could go through it all again,
the slender iron rungs of growing up,
I would be as young as any,
a child lost
in unreality and loud music.

Ants

Ants
are not under anathema to make it new—
they are too small and penny-proud
to harm us much or hold the human eye
looking downward on them,
like a Goth watching a game of chess.

On this tenth hot day,
the best of a drought summer,
the unthinking insects
leave their heated hills:
warrior, honey-cow and slave.
The earth is rock;
the ants waver
with thread antennae
emptily . . . as if one tactic
did for feeding or seeking
barren fields for drill.

Ants are amazing but not exemplary;
their beehive hurry excludes romance.

Once in time out of mind,
on such a warm day as this,
the ant-heads must have swarmed beyond
the illusive shimmer of the ant-hill,
and crowned slavery with socialism.
They invented the state before and after
Plato's grim arithmetic—a state
unchanging, limited, beyond our reach,
decadence, or denial . . .
their *semper eadem* of good fortune.
Yet not always the same;
the ants repair it yearly,

like the Chinese traditional painter
renewing his repertory flowers—
each touch a stroke for tradition.

They are the lost case of the mind.

I lie staring under an old oak,
stubby, homely, catacombed by ants,
more of a mop than a tree.
I fear the clumsy boughs will fall.
Is its weak, wooden heart strong enough
to bear my weight if I should climb
from knob to knob to the top?
How uneasily I am myself,
as a child I found the sky too close.
Why am I childish now and ask
for daffy days when I tried to read
Walden's ant-war aloud to you for love?

Sheridan

Another day of standstill heat,
old American summer, Old Glory,
only the squeaking, floppy lapwings
and garrulous foreign colony of jackdaws
are English, all else is American.
Placed chestnut trees flower mid-cowfield,
even in harvest time, they swear,
"We always had leaves and ever shall."

Sheridan, you gleam and stall in the heat,
mislaying as many things as people;
your whole plastic armory, claymore,
Nazi helmet, batwings, is lost.
But who would hide weapons that do
everything true weapons should, but hurt?
"You're Mr. Loser," you say, "you lost our guns."
You say it in Kentish cockney: *weir* guns.

How unretentive we become,
yet weirdly naked like you. Today
only the eternal midday separates
you from our unchangeably sunset
and liver-invigorated faces. High-hung,
the period scythe silvers in the sun,
a cutting edge, a bounding line,
between the child's world and the earth—

Our early discovery that only children grow.

Marriage

I.
We were middle-class and verismo
enough to suit Van Eyck,
when we crowded together in Maidstone,
patriarch and young wife
with our three small girls
to pose in Sunday-best.
The shapeless comfort of your flowered frock
was transparent against the light,
but the formal family photograph in color
shows only a rousing brawn of shoulder
to tell us you were pregnant.

Even there, Sheridan, though unborn,
was a center of symmetry;
even then he was growing in hiding
toward gaucheness and muscle—
to be a war-
chronicler of vast inaccurate memory.
Later, his weird humor
made him elf and dustman,
like him, early risers.
This summer, he is a soldier—
unlike father or mother,
or anyone he knows,
he can choose both sides:
Redcoat, Minuteman, or George the Third . . .
the ambivalence of the Revolution that made him
half-British, half-American.

II.
I turn to the *Arnolfini Marriage*,
and see
Van Eyck's young Italian merchant
was neither soldier nor priest.
In an age of Faith,
he is not abashed to stand weaponless,
long-faced and dwindling
in his bridal bedroom.
Half-Jewish, perhaps,
he is freshly married,
and exiled for his profit to Bruges.
His wife's with child;
he lifts a hand,
thin and white as his face
held up like a candle to bless her . . .
smiling, swelling, blossoming . . .

Giovanni and Giovanna—
even in an age of costumes,
they seem to flash their fineness . . .
better dressed than kings.

The picture is too much like their life—
a crisscross, too many petty facts,
this bedroom
with one candle still burning in the candelabrum,
and peaches blushing on the windowsill,
Giovanni's high-heeled raw wooden slippers
thrown on the floor by her smaller ones . . .
dyed *sang de boeuf*
to match the restless marital canopy.

They are rivals in homeliness and love;
her hand lies like china in his,
her other hand
is in touch with the head of her unborn child.
They wait and pray,
as if the airs of heaven

that blew on them when they married
were now a common visitation,
not a miracle of lighting
for the photographer's sacramental instant.

Giovanni and Giovanna,
who will outlive him by 20 years . . .

The Withdrawal

I.
Only today and just for this minute,
when the sunslant finds its true angle,
you can see yellow and pinkish leaves spangle
our gentle, fluffy tree—
suddenly the green summer is momentary . . .
Autumn is my favorite season—
why does it change clothes and withdraw?

This week the house went on the market—
suddenly I wake among strangers;
when I go into a room, it moves
with embarrassment, and joins another room.

I don't need conversation, but you to laugh with—
you and a room and a fire,
cold starlight blowing through an open window—
whither?

II.
After sunfall, heaven is melodramatic,
a temporary, puckering, burning green.
The patched-up oak
and blacker, indelible pines
have the indigestible meagerness of spines.

One wishes heaven had less solemnity:
a sensual table
with five half-filled bottles of red wine
set round the hectic carved roast—
Bohemia for ourselves
and the familiars of a lifetime
charmed to communion by resurrection—

running together in the rain to mail a single letter,
not the chafe and cling
of this despondent chaff.

III.
Yet for a moment, the children
could play truant from their tuition.

IV.
When I look back, I see a collapsing
accordion of my receding houses,
and myself receding
to a boy of twenty-five or thirty,
too shopworn for less, too impressionable for more—
blackmaned, illmade
in a washed blue workshirt and coalblack trousers,
moving from house to house,
still seeking a boy's license
to see the countryside without arrival.

Hell?

Darling,
terror in happiness may not cure the hungry future,
the time when any illness is chronic,
and the years of discretion are spent on complaint—

until the wristwatch is taken from the wrist.

II

Logan Airport, Boston

Your blouse,
Concord grapes on white,
a souvenir you snatched at the airport,
shone blindingly up the gangway
to a sky overcrowded at rush-hour.
Below the flying traffic,
thin, dwindling yellow trees were feverish,
as if frightened
by your limitless prospect on the blue.

I see you, you are hardly there—
it's as though I watched a painter
do sketches of your head
that by some consuming fire
erased themselves,
until I stared at a blank sheet.

Now in the brown air of our rental,
I need electricity even on fair days,
as I decamp from window to window
to catch the sun.
I am blind with seeing;
the toys you brought home like groceries
firetrap on the stairs.

Is it cynical to deliquesce,
as Adam did in age,
though outwardly goldleaf,
true metal, and make-up?

Our mannerisms harden—
a bruise is immortal,
the instant egg on my shin
I got from braking a car
too sharply a year ago
stays firm brown and yellow,
the all-weather color for death.

I cannot bring back youth with a snap of my belt,
I cannot touch you—
your absence is presence,
the undrinkable blaze
of the sun on both shores of the airport.

Bright sun of my bright day,
I thank God for being alive—
a way of writing I once thought heartless.

Wellesley Free

(A reading)

I.

The new blower machine
puffs lost leaves from the yard
with a muffled clang—
whirs my head like the barber,
when my hair was short enough to cut.
The best machine can be wrecked

at 56.
I balance on my imbalance,
and count the black and white steps
to my single room.
Space is mere clearance
since you flew to Europe.

Our boys' school train would pass Wellesley
without slowing. We weren't free.

The girls go airily into the night;
boys are temporary
and rev their cars
and cough out the midnight bells
and leave the College for Women
lighter without men.

II.

I have fallen from heaven.
In my overnight room,
3 French windows to the right,
and 3 to the left
cast bright oblique reflections
unnerving with their sparkle.

Coleridge,
the author of *Dejection*,
thought
genius is the discovery
of subjects remote
from my life.

I cannot read.
Everything I've written
is greenish brown,
as if the words
refused to sound.
A lemon-squeezer night—

I cannot sleep solo,
I loathe age with terror,
and will be that . . .
eat the courage of my selfishness
unredeemed by the student's
questionmark potential . . .

70° outside,
and almost December.

To Mother

I've come a third time
to live in your dour, luxurious Boston;
I almost lifted the telephone to dial you,
forgetting you have no dial.
Your exaggerating humor,
the opposite of deadpan,
the opposite of funny to a son,
is mine now—
your bolting blood, your lifewanting face,
the unwilled ruffle of drama in your voice.

You were
Josephine Beauharnais, la femme militaire.

The humpback brick sidewalks of Harvard
kick me briskly,
as if allowed the license of age;
persons who could hardly walk or swallow,
when I was a student,
angrily grate like old squirrels
with bandages of white hair about their ears.
I see myself change in my changed friends—
may I live longer, yet break no record.

Becoming ourselves,
we lose our nerve for children.

One crummy plant can inspire a whole room—
yours were not crummy—bulb, sheath, seductive stem,
the lily that lifts its flag a moment
puckering on the white pebbles of a whiter pot.
Your parlor was a reproach. I wish I were there with you,
the minutes not counted, but not forever—

you used to brush mantelpiece and banister
with the forefinger of a fresh white glove for dust.

"Why do we keep expecting life to be easy,
when we know it never can be?"

I enjoyed hearing scandal on you. Much came
from others, your high-school friends, themselves now dust.
It has taken me the time since you died
to discover you are as human as I am . . .
if I am.

Robert T. S. Lowell

Son

I futilely wished
to meet you at my age;
the date never came off.
It would take two lifetimes
to pick the crust
and uncover the face
under our two menacing,
iconoclastic masks.

Father

You had your chance to meet me.
My father died before I was born.
I was half orphaned . . . such a son
as the stork seldom flings to ambition.

I lay
in the lee of my terrible elders;
the age had a largeness I lacked,
an appetite that forgave everything . . .
our Spanish War's oversubscribed,
battle-bright decks.

At fourteen
I enlisted at Annapolis.

At twenty-seven
I proposed in uniform
and married your mother—
a service I served with even wistfulness,
enslaved by the fire I courted.

I only wished idly
with dilated eyes
to relive my life.

Your game-leg beagle would tiptoe to my room,
if she heard you were asleep—
loneliness to loneliness!

You think that having
your two children on the same floor this fall,
one questioning, one climbing and breaking,
is like living on a drum
or a warship—it can't be that,
it's your life, and dated like mine.

For Sheridan

We only live between
before we are and what we were.

In the lost negative
you exist,
a smile, a cypher,
an old-fashioned face
in an old-fashioned hat.

Three ages in a flash:
the same child in the same picture,
he, I, you,
chockablock, one stamp
like mother's wedding silver—

gnome, fish, brute cherubic force.

We could see clearly
and all the same things
before the glass was hurt.

Past fifty, we learn with surprise and a sense
of suicidal absolution
that what we intended and failed
could never have happened—
and must be done better.

Bright Day in Boston

Joy of standing up my dentist,
my X-ray plates like a broken Acropolis . . .

Joy to idle through Boston,
my head full of young Henry Adams
and his unnoticed white silk armband,
worn for a day to free the slaves.

An epoch ago the instant
when one could live anywhere
unendangered, unendangering
anything but respect . . .

Impregnable and out of place
on the sunny side of the old Mall,
now housing for students—
their blouses coquetting in the purple glass
of the great bastion-bayed mansion
of Augustus Lowell,
martinet of his mills and lover of roses . . .

No one has troubled to file away
the twisted black iron window-bars,
their taunt of dead craft.

For no reason, the slender streetlamps,
of identical delicate iron
and weak as candles,
flicker all day.

In a city of murder, an American city.

This house, that house—
I have lived in them all,
straight brick without figure.

My fluids command my heart
to go out to the loser—always;
but it is murder to pity the rich,
even when they are as gone
as Hector, tamer of horses—
always doomed to return,
to be with us always like the poor.

Grass Fires

In the realistic memory
the memorable must be forgone;
it never matters,
except in front of our eyes.

I made it a warning,
a cure, that stabilized nothing.
We cannot recast the faulty drama,
play the child,
unable to align
his toppling, elephantine script,
the hieroglyphic letters
he sent home.

I hold big kitchen matches to flaps of frozen grass
to smoke a rabbit from its hole—
then the wind bites them, then they catch,
the grass catches, fire everywhere,
everywhere
inextinguishable roots,
the tree grandfather planted for his shade,
combusting, towering
over the house he anachronized with stone.

I can't tell you how much larger
and more important it was than I,
how many summers before conscience
I enjoyed it.

My grandfather towered above me,
"You damned little fool,"
nothing to quote, but for him original.
The fire-engines deployed with stage bravado,
yet it was I put out the fire,

who slapped it to death with my scarred leather jacket.
I snuffed out the inextinguishable root,
I—
really I can do little,
as little now as then,
about the infernal fires—
I cannot blow out a match.

Phillips House Revisited

A weak clamor like ice giving . . .

Something sinister and comforting
in this return after forty years' arrears
to death and Phillips House . . .
this irreverent absence of pain,
less than the ordinary that daily irks—
except I cannot entirely get my breath,
as if I were muffled in snow,
our winter's inverted gray sky
of frozen slush,
its usual luminous lack of warmth.

This room was brighter then
when grandfather filled it,
brilliant for his occasion
with his tallness, reddish tan and pain.

Twice he was slipped
champagne and oysters
by a wild henna-dyed niece by marriage
he had promised to cut.

This seemed good to him and us.

He could still magnetize the adolescent.

I too am passed my half-bottle . . .
no oyster.

But these forty years grandfather would insist
have turned the world on its head—
their point was
to extinguish him like a stranded crab.

He needed more to live than I,
his foot could catch hold anywhere
and dynamite his way to the gold again—
for the world is generous to the opportune,
its constantly self-renewing teams of favorites.

St. Mark's, 1933

The fourth form dining-table
was twenty feet by four,
six boys to a side;
at one end, Mr. Prendie the Woodchuck,
dead to the world, off picking daisies;
at the other end, another boy.
Mid-meal, they began
to pull me apart.
"Why is he always grubbing in his nose?"
"Because his nose is always snotty."
"He likes to wipe his thumb in it."
"Cal's a creep of the first water."
"He had a hard-on for his first shower."
"He only presses his trousers once a term."
"Every other term." "No term."
Over the years I've lost
the surprise and sparkle of that slang
our abuse made perfect.
"Dimbulb." "Fogbound." "Droopydrawers."
"The man from the Middle West."
"Cal is a slurp."
"A slurp farts in the bathtub."
"So he can bite the bubbles."
How did they say my face
was pearl-gray like toe-jam—
that I was foul
as the gymsocks I wore a week?
A boy next to me breathed my shoes,
and lay choking on the bench.

"Cal doesn't like everyone."
"Everyone doesn't like Cal."
"Cal,
who is your best friend at this table?"

"Low-ell, Low-ell"
(to the tune of *Noël, Noël*).

This was it, though I bowdlerize . . .
All term I had singled out classmates,
and made them listen to and remember
the imperfections of their friends.
I broke one on the other—
but who could break them,
they were so many,
rich, smooth and loved?

I was fifteen;
they made me cry in public.
Chicken?

Perhaps they had reason . . .
even now
my callous unconscious drives me
to torture my closest friend.

Huic ergo parce, Deus.

To Frank Parker

Forty years ago we were here
where we are now,
the same erotic May-wind blew
the trees from there to here—

the same tang of metal in the mouth,
the dirt-pierced wood of Cambridge.

Sometimes
you are so much younger than your face,
I know I am seeing your old face—
the hampered Henry James
mockery of your stutter,
your daily fear of choking, dying—
in school, loudness not words
gave character to the popular boy's voice.

We looked in the face of the other
for what we were.
Once in the common record heat
of June in Massachusetts,
we sat by the school pool
talking out the soul-lit night
and listened to the annual
unsuffering voice of the tree frogs,
green, aimless and wakened:
"I want to write." "I want to paint."

Was it I wanted you to paint? . . .

Age is another species,
the nothing-voiced. The very old
made grandfather look vulgarly young,
when he drove me to feed them at their home.

We will have their thoughtful look,
as if uncertain
who had led our lives.

The past changes more than the present.

Wherever there's grass, there is pollen,
the asthma of high summer—
the inclination to drink, not eat . . .

"Let us go into the garden,
or shall I say the yard?"
Why have you said this twice, Frank?
The garden has no flowers,
or choice of color,
the thick wet clump of grass
thins to red clay,
like an Indian's shaved and tufted head,
or yours—
we once claimed alliance with the Redskin.
What is won by surviving,
if two glasses of red wine are poison?

Morning after Dining with a Friend

(Some weeks after Logan Airport)

Waking wifeless is now a habit—
hearing the human-abstract rush of traffic,
another night, another day
entertaining nothing but my thoughts—

Why have I twisted your kind words
and tortured myself till morning?

My brain keeps flashing back last night—
a booth in the Greek restaurant,
now fronting the Boston Combat Zone—
"We'd be mad not to take a taxi back."

"I think Frost liked me better
but found you more amusing."

I met you first at the old Met Opera Club,
shy, correct, in uniform,
your regulation on active duty
substitute for black-tie—

Poet and aviator
at 36,
the eternal autumn of youth.

That image has gained body;
yet shrinks back this morning
to its greener Platonic shade,
the man of iron—

not drinking, terrified
of losing your mind . . .

turning to me, calm
by a triumph of impersonation:

"If you could come a little nearer
the language of the tribe."

Return in March

Tannish buds and green buds,
hidden yesterday, pioneers today.
The Georgian thirties' Harvard houses
have shed their brashness in forty years;
architecture suffers decline with dignity
and requisitions its atmosphere—
our hope is in things that spring.

Tonight in the middle of melting Boston,
a brick chimney tapers, and points a ladder
of white smoke into the blue-black sky.

Suburban Surf

(After Caroline's return)

You lie in my insomniac arms,
as if you drank sleep like coffee.

Then,
like a bear tipping a hive for honey,
you shake the pillow for French cigarettes.

No conversation—
then suddenly as always cars
helter-skelter for feed like cows—

suburban surf come alive,

diamond-faceted like your eyes,
glassy, staring lights
lighting the way they cannot see—

friction, constriction etc.
the racket killing
gas like alcohol.

Long, unequal whooshing waves
break in volume,
always very loud enough to hear—

méchants, mechanical—

soothe, delay, divert
the crescendo always surprisingly attained
in a panic of breathlessness—

too much assertion and skipping
of the heart to greet the day . . .
the truce with uncertain heaven.

A false calm is the best calm.

In noonday light,
the cars are tin, stereotype and bright,
a farce
of their former selves at night—
invisible as exhaust,
personal as animals.

Gone
the sweet agitation of the breath of Pan.

III

Turtle

I pray for memory—
an old turtle,
absentminded, inelastic,
kept afloat by losing touch . . .
no longer able to hiss or lift
a useless shield against the killer.

Turtles age, but wade out amorously,
half-frozen fossils, yet knight-errant
in a foolsdream of armor.
The smaller ones climb rocks to broil in comfort.

Snapping turtles only submerge.
They have survived . . . not by man's philanthropy.

I hunted them in school vacations.
I trampled an acre of driftstraw
floating off the muskrats' loose nests.
Here and there, a solitary turtle
craned its brown Franciscan cowl
from one of twenty waterholes.
In that brew, I stepped
on a turtle's smooth, invisible back.
It was like escaping quicksand.
I drew it in my arms by what I thought was tail—
a tail? I held a foreleg.
I could have lost a finger.

This morning when
the double-brightness of the winter sun
wakes me from the film of dreaming,

my bedroom is unfamiliar. I see
three snapping turtles squatted on my drifting clothes—
two rough black logs . . . the third is a nuzzler
dressed in see-through yellow tortoiseshell,
a puppy squeaking and tweaking
my empty shirt for milk.

They are stale and panting;
what is dead in me wakes their appetite.
When they breathe, they seem to crack apart,
crouched motionless on tiptoe
with crooked smiles
and high-school nicknames on their tongues,
as if they wished to relive
the rawness that let us meet as animals.
Nothing has passed between us but time.

"You've wondered where we were these years?
Here are we."

They lie like luggage—
my old friend the turtle . . . Too many pictures
have screamed from the reel . . . in the rerun,
the snapper holds on till sunset—
in the awful instantness of retrospect,
its beak
works me underwater drowning by my neck,
as it claws away pieces of my flesh
to make me small enough to swallow.

Seventh Year

Seven years ago, my instantly dispelled
dream of putting the place on its feet—

never again—I see it clearly,
but with the blind glass eyes of a doll.

This early January
the shallow brown lakes on the drive
already catch
the first spring negative of the birds.

The burnished oxweight cows
now come closer to us and crash
foot over foot through vine and glass—

lowing to one another with the anxious
human voice of a boy calling cows.

We are at least less run-down
than Longfellow's house on Brattle Street,
where only his bearded bust of Zeus,
his schoolday self, is young,

where the long face of his wife
who burned to death
ages as if alive

as Longfellow, whose hand held
the dismissive laurel bough
that hides his grave.

The New England Augustans
lived so long one thought
the snow of their hair would never melt.

Where is Hart Crane,
the disinherited, the fly by night,
who gave
the drunken Dionysus firmer feet?

To each the rotting natural to his age.

Dividing the minute we cannot prolong,
I stand swaying at the end of the party,
a half-filled glass in each hand—
I too swayed
by the hard infatuate wind of love
they cannot hear.

Shaving

Shaving's the one time I see my face,
I see it aslant as a carpenter's problem—
though I have gaunted a little,
always the same face
follows my hand with thirsty eyes.

Never enough hours in a day—
I lie confined and groping,
monomaniacal,
jealous of even a shadow's intrusion—
a nettle
impossible to deflect . . .
unable to follow the drift
of children, their blurting third-degree.

For me,
a stone is as inflammable as a paper match.

The household comes to a stop—
you too, head bent,
inking, crossing out . . . frowning
at times with a face open as a sunflower.

We are lucky to have done things as one.

Runaway

You would sit like a folded beach-chair
in the tallest, hardest armchair . . .
out of character churchly—
or prop your left elbow on a rug
before the soiling fire
that turned your fingernails to coal.
Winterlong
and through the fleeting cool Kentish summer—
obstinately scowling
to focus your hypnotic, farsighted eyes
on a child's pale blue paper exam book—
two dozens . . . carpeting an acre of floor,
while a single paragraph in your large,
looping, legible hand exhausted a whole book.
A born athlete; now a half hour typing
with your uncorrected back
made a week's infection certain.
Out of your wreckage, beauty, wealth,
gallantries, wildness, came your book,
Great Granny Webster's
paralyzing legacy of privation,
her fey Celtic daughter's
death in an asylum,
your Aunt Veronica's manicly gay
youthful, then ultimate, suicide,
your father's betrayal of you,
rushing to his military death in Burma,
annexed for England
by his father's father, the Viceroy . . .
There's so much else—our life.
At the sick times, our slashing,
drastic decisions made us runaways.

Caroline in Sickness

Tonight the full moon is stopped by trees
or the wallpaper between our windows—
on the threshold of pain,
light doesn't exist,
and yet the glow is smarting
enough to read a Bible
to keep awake and awake.
You are very sick,
you remember how the children,
you and your cousin,
Miss Fireworks and Miss Icicle,
first drove alone with learners' cards
in Connemara, and popped a paper bag—
the rock that broke your spine.
Thirty years later, you still suffer
your spine's spasmodic, undercover life . . .
Putting off a luncheon,
you say into the telephone,
"Next month, if I'm still walking."
I move to keep moving;
the cold white wine is dis-spirited—
Moon, stop from dark apprehension . . .
shine as is your custom,
scattering this roughage to find sky.

Stars

I.
Caged in fiction's iron bars,
I give this voice to you
with tragic diction to rebuke the stars—
it isn't you, and yet it's you.

"Will you, like Goethe, fall
to oblivion in my arms;
then talk about the stars?
Say they light militant campfires,
storm heaven while I sleep?
Not now—
my spine is hurting me,
I can only lie face down,
a gross weight innocent—
if you will let me sleep—
of seduction, speech, or pain.
I'm too drugged to do anything,
or help you watch the sky.
I am indifferent to the stars—
their ranks are too docile and mathematical
to regroup if once scattered
like comatose sheep . . .
I am indifferent—
what woman has the measure of a man,
who only has to care about himself
and follow the stars'
extravagant, useless journey across the sky,
to divert me from the absence of the sun?
Because they cannot love, they need no love."

II.
If you heard God is dead,
the old monopolist,
who made us to take us apart—
would you stand upright in spite of your spine?

"I sleep,
an old walnut soaked in rum,
too slippery for the stars to crack
in their rigid, identical glass wheels . . .
If God is dead,
how can I be certain another old man
will drop again from the stars,
from sixty thousand fathoms away,
and halt by the post of my bed—
motionless with ill-omened power?
A new old lover
might hurt a thousand times worse . . .
But my beloved
is godlike, tantalizing,
made in the image of a man
too young to be frightened of women.
He can only appear in all my dreams."

Seesaw

The night dark before its hour—
heavily, steadily,
the rain lashes and sprinkles
to complete its task—
as if assisting
the encroachments of our bodies
we occupy but cannot cure.

Sufferer, how can you help me,
if I use your sickness
to increase my own?

Will we always be
one up, the other down,
one hitting bottom, the other
flying through the trees—
seesaw inseparables?

Ten Minutes

The single sheet keeps shifting on the double bed,
the more I kick it smooth, the less it covers;
it is the bed I made.
Others have destinations, my train is aimless.
I know I will fall off into the siding and thistle—
imagining the truth will hide my lies.

Mother under one of her five-minute spells
had a flair for total recall,
and told me, item by item, person by person,
how my relentless, unpredictable selfishness
had disappointed and removed
anyone who tried to help—
but I cannot correct the delicate compass-needle
so easily set ajar.

I am companionless;
occasionally, I see a late, suicidal headlight
burn on the highway and vanish.
Now the haunted vacancy fills with friends—
they are waspishly familiar and aggrieved,
a rattling makeshift of mislaid faces,
a whiplash of voices. They cry,
"Can you love me, can you love me?
Oh hidden in your bubble and protected by your wife,
and luxuriously nourished without hands,
you wished us dead,
but vampires are too irreplaceable to die."

They stop, as cars that have the greenlight
stop, and let a pedestrian go . . .
Though I work nightshift,
there's no truth in this processing of words—
the dull, instinctive glow inside me

refuels itself, and only blackens
such bits of paper brought to feed it . . .

My frightened arms
anxiously hang out before me like bent L's,
as if I feared I was a laughingstock,
and wished to catch and ward you off . . .
This is becoming a formula:
after the long, dark passage,
I offer you my huddle of flesh and dismay.
"This time it was all night," I say.
You answer, "Poseur,
why, you haven't been awake ten minutes."

       •   •   •

I grow too merry,
when I stand in my nakedness to dress.

Visitors

To no good
they enter at angles and on the run—
two black verticals are suddenly four
ambulance drivers in blue serge,
or the police doing double-duty.
They comb our intimate, messy bedroom,
scrutinize worksheets
illegible with second-thoughts,
then shed them in their stride,
as if they owned the room. They do.
They crowd me and scatter—inspecting
my cast-off clothes for clues?
They are fat beyond the call of duty—
with jocose civility,
they laugh at everything I say:
"Yesterday I was thirty-two, a threat
to the establishment because I was young."
The bored woman sergeant
is amused by the tiger-toothed samurai
grinning on a Japanese hanging—
"What would it cost? Where could I buy one?"

I can see through the moonlit dark;
on the grassy London square,
black cows ruminate in uniform,
lowing routinely like a chainsaw.
My visitors are good beef, they too make
one falsely feel the earth is solid,
as they hurry to secretly telephone
from their ambulance. Click, click, click,
goes the red, blue, and white light
burning with aristocratic negligence—
so much busywork.
When they regroup in my room, I know

their eyes have never left their watches.
"Come on, sir." "Easy, sir."
"Dr. Brown will be here in ten minutes, sir."
Instead, a metal chair unfolds into a stretcher.
I lie secured there, but for my skipping mind.
They keep bustling.
"Where you are going, Professor,
you won't need your Dante."
What will I need there?
Is that a handcuff rattling in a pocket?

I follow my own removal,
stiffly, gratefully even, but without feeling.
Why has my talkative
teasing tongue stopped talking?
My detachment must be paid for,
tomorrow will be worse than today,
heaven and hell will be the same—
to wait in foreboding
without the nourishment of drama . . .
assuming, then as now,
this didn't happen to me—
my little strip of eternity.

Three Freuds

By the faint Burne-Jones
entrance window to *The Priory*,
is a bearded marble bust
of dear, dead old Dr. Wood blanche-white,
no name for comedy,
but our founder anticipating me
like an intuitive friend
or doorman in the cold outside his home.
He looks like Sigmund Freud,
too high on bonhomie,
cured by his purgatory of mankind.
Inside the window, is a live patient,
a second bearded Freud,
no Freud, though polished
as the vacant monolith of Dr. Wood . . .
The old boy is not artificial
or disinterested,
yet rudderless and titled,
when he queues at the cold buffet
to pluck up coleslaw in his hands.
When you emerge
it may seem too late.
You chose to go
where you knew I could not follow.

Home

Our ears put us in touch with things unheard of—
the trouble is the patients are tediously themselves,
fussing, confiding . . . committed voluntaries,
immune to the outsider's horror.
The painter who burned both hands
after trying to kill her baby, says,
"Is there no one in Northampton
who goes to the Continent in the winter?"
The alcoholic convert keeps smiling,
"Thank you, Professor, for saving my life;
you taught me homosexuality is a heinous crime."
I hadn't. I am a thorazined fixture
in the immovable square-cushioned chairs
we preoccupy for seconds like migrant birds.

"Remarkable breakdown, remarkable recovery"—
but the breakage can go on repeating
once too often.

Why is it so hard for them to accept
the very state of happiness is wrong?

Cups and saucers stamped with the hospital's name
go daily to the tap and are broken.
In the morgue and hospice of the National Museum,
our poor bones and houseware
are lucky to end up in bits and pieces
embalmed between the eternal and tyrants,
their high noses rubbed rough.
How quickly barred-windowed hospitals and museums go—
the final mover has all the leisure in the world.

We have none. Since nature,
our unshakable mother, will grow impatient with us,
we might envy museum pieces

that can be pasted together or disfigured
and feel no panic of indignity.

At visiting hours, you could experience
my sickness only as desertion . . .
Dr. Berners compliments you again,
"A model guest . . . we would welcome
Robert back to Northampton any time,
the place suits him . . . he is so strong."
When you shuttle back chilled to London,
I am on the wrong end of a dividing train—
it is my failure with our fragility.

If he has gone mad with her,
the poor man can't have been very happy,
seeing too much and feeling it
with one skin-layer missing.

    •   •   •

The immovable chairs have swallowed up the patients,
and speak with the eloquence of emptiness.
By each the same morning paper lies unread:
January 10, 1976.
I cannot sit or stand two minutes,
yet walk imagining a dialogue
between the devil and myself,
not knowing which is which or worse,
saying,
as one would instinctively say Hail Mary,
I wish I could die.
Less than ever I expect to be alive
six months from now—
1976,
a date I dare not affix to my grave.

The Queen of Heaven, I miss her,
we were divorced. She never doubted
the divided, stricken soul
could call her Maria,
and rob the devil with a word.

Shadow

I must borrow from Walt Whitman to praise this night,
twice waking me smiling, mysteriously in full health,
twice delicately calling me to the world.
Praise be to sleep and sleep's one god,
the Voyeur, the Mother,
Job's tempestuous, inconstant I AM . . .
who soothes the doubtful murmurs of the heart.

Yet to do nothing up there but adore,
to comprehend nothing but the invisible night—
fortunately the narcoticized
Christian heaven cannot be dreamed or staffed.

If I had a dream of hell
it would be packing up a house
with demons eternally asking
thought-provoking questions.

I have watched the shadow of the crow,
a Roman omen,
cross my shaking hand,
an enigma even for us to read,
a crowsfoot scribble—
when I was with my friend,
I never knew that I had hands.

A man without a wife
is like a turtle without a shell—

this pending hour, this tapeworm minute,
this pending minute, I wait for you to ring—
two in unhealth.

Yet the day is too golden for sleep,
the traffic too sustained . . .
twang-twang of the asylum's leaden bass—
those bleached hierarchies,
moving and shifting like white hospital attendants,
their single errand to reassure the sick.

Notice

The resident doctor said,
"We are not deep in ideas, imagination or enthusiasm—
how can we help you?"
I asked,
"These days of only poems and depression—
what can I do with them?
Will they help me to notice
what I cannot bear to look at?"

The doctor is forgotten now
like a friend's wife's maiden-name.
I am free
to ride elbow to elbow on the rush-hour train
and copy on the back of a letter,
as if alone:
"When the trees close branches and redden,
their winter skeletons are hard to find—"
to know after long rest
and twenty miles of outlying city
that the much-heralded spring is here,
and say,
"Is this what you would call a blossom?"
Then home—I can walk it blindfold.
But we must notice—
we are designed for the moment.

Shifting Colors

I fish until the clouds turn blue,
weary of self-torture, ready to paint
lilacs or confuse a thousand leaves,
as landscapists must.

My eye returns to my double,
an ageless big white horse,
slightly discolored by dirt
cropping the green shelf diagonal
to the artificial troutpond—
unmoving, it shifts as I move,
and works the whole field in the course of the day.

Poor measured, neurotic man—
animals are more instinctive virtuosi.

Ducks splash deceptively like fish;
fish break water with the wings of a bird to escape.

A hissing goose sways in stationary anger;
purple bluebells rise in ledges on the lake.

A single cuckoo gifted with a pregnant word
shifts like the sun from wood to wood.

All day my miscast troutfly buzzes about my ears
and empty mind.

But nature is sundrunk with sex—
how could a man fail to notice, man
the one pornographer among the animals?
I seek leave unimpassioned by my body,
I am too weak to strain to remember, or give
recollection the eye of a microscope. I see

horse and meadow, duck and pond,
universal consolatory
description without significance,
transcribed verbatim by my eye.

This is not the directness that catches
everything on the run and then expires—
I would write only in response to the gods,
like Mallarmé who had the good fortune
to find a style that made writing impossible.

Unwanted

Too late, all shops closed—
I alone here tonight on *Antabuse*,
surrounded only by iced white wine and beer,
like a sailor dying of thirst on the Atlantic—
one sip of alcohol might be death,
death for joy.
Yet in this tempting leisure,
good thoughts drive out bad;
causes for my misadventure, considered
for forty years too obvious to name,
come jumbling out
to give my simple autobiography a plot.

I read an article on a friend,
as if recognizing my obituary:
"Though his mother loved her son consumingly,
she lacked a really affectionate nature;
so he always loved what he missed."
This was John Berryman's mother, not mine.

Alas, I can only tell my own story—
talking to myself, or reading, or writing,
or fearlessly holding back nothing from a friend,
who believes me for a moment
to keep up conversation.

I was surer, wasn't I, once . . .
and had flashes when I first found
a humor for myself in images,
farfetched misalliance
that made evasion a revelation?

Dr. Merrill Moore, the family psychiatrist,
had unpresentable red smudge eyebrows,

and no infirmity for tact—
in his conversation or letters,
each phrase a new
paragraph,
implausible as the million
sonnets he rhymed into his dictaphone,
or dashed on windshield writing-pads,
while waiting out a stoplight—
scattered pearls, some true.
Dead he is still a mystery,
once a crutch to writers in crisis.
I am two-tongued, I will not admit
his Tennessee rattling saved my life.
Did he become mother's lover
and prey
by rescuing her from me?
He was thirteen years her junior . . .
When I was in college, he said, "You know
you were an unwanted child?"
Was he striking my parents to help me?
I shook him off the scent by pretending
anyone is unwanted in a medical sense—
lust our only father . . . and yet
in that world where an only child
was a scandal—
unwanted before I am?

That year Carl Jung said to mother in Zurich,
"If your son is as you have described him,
he is an incurable schizophrenic."

In 1916
father on sea-duty, mother with child
in one house with her affectionate mother-in-law,
unconsuming, already consumptive . . .
bromidic to mother . . . Mother,
I must not blame you for carrying me in you
on your brisk winter lunges across
the desperate, refusey Staten Island beaches,

their good view skyscrapers on Wall Street . . .
for yearning seaward, far from any home, and saying,
"I wish I were dead, I wish I were dead."
Unforgivable for a mother to tell her child—
but you wanted me to share your good fortune,
perhaps, by recapturing the disgust of those walks;
your credulity assumed we survived,
while weaklings fell with the dead and dying.

That consuming love,
woman's everlasting *cri de coeur*,
"When you have a child of your own, you'll know."
Her dowry for her children . . .

One thing is certain—compared with my wives,
mother was stupid. Was she?
Some would not have judged so—
among them, her alcoholic patients,
those raconteurish, old Boston young men,
whose fees, late in her life
and to everyone's concern,
she openly halved with Merrill Moore.
Since time out of mind, mother's gay hurting
assessments of enemies and intimates
had made her a formidable character
to her "reading club," seven ladies,
who since her early twenties
met once a week through winters
in their sitting rooms for confidence and tea—
she couldn't read a book . . .
How many of her statements began with,
But Papá always said or *Oh Bobby* . . .
if she Byronized her father and son,
she saw her husband as a valet sees through a master.

She was stupider than my wife . . .
When I was three months,
I rocked back and forth howling
for weeks, for weeks each hour . . .

Then I found the thing I loved most
was the anorexia Christ
swinging on Nellie's gaudy rosary.
It disappeared, I said nothing,
but mother saw me poking strips of paper
down a floor-grate to the central heating.
"Oh Bobby, do you want to set us on fire?"
"Yes . . . that's where Jesus is." I smiled.

Is the one unpardonable sin
our fear of not being wanted?
For this, will mother go on cleaning house
for eternity, and making it unlivable?
Is getting well ever an art,
or art a way to get well?

The Downlook

For the last two minutes, the retiring monarchy
of the full moon looks down on the first chirping sparrows—
nothing lovelier than waking to find
another breathing body in my bed . . .
glowshadow halfcovered with dayclothes like my own,
caught in my arms.

Last summer nothing dared impede
the flow of the body's thousand rivulets of welcome,
winding effortlessly, yet with ambiguous invention—
safety in nearness.

Now the downlook, the downlook—small fuss,
nothing that could earn a line or picture
in the responsible daily paper we'll be reading,
an anthology of the unredeemable world,
beyond the accumulative genius of prose or this—
a day that sharpens apprehension by dulling;
each miss must be a mile,
if one risk the narrow two-lane highway.

It's impotence and impertinence to ask directions,
while staring right and left in two-way traffic.

There's no greater happiness in days of the downlook
than to turn back to recapture former joy.

Ah loved perhaps before I knew you,
others have been lost like this,
yet found foothold
by winning the dolphin from the humming water.

How often have my antics
and insupportable, trespassing tongue
gone astray and led me to prison . . .
to lying . . . kneeling . . . standing.

Thanks-Offering for Recovery

The airy, going house grows small
tonight, and soft enough to be crumpled up
like a handkerchief in my hand.
Here with you by this hotbed of coals,
I am the *homme sensuel*, free
to turn my back on the lamp, and work.
Something has been taken off,
a wooden winter shadow—
goodbye nothing. I give thanks, thanks—
thanks too for this small
Brazilian *ex voto*, this primitive head
sent me across the Atlantic by my friend . . .
a corkweight thing,
to be offered *Deo gratias* in church
on recovering from head-injury or migraine—
now mercifully delivered in my hands,
though shelved awhile unnoticing and unnoticed.
Free of the unshakable terror that made me write . . .
I pick it up, a head holy and unholy,
tonsured or damaged,
with gross black charcoaled brows and stern eyes
frowning as if they had seen the splendor
times past counting . . . unspoiled,
solemn as a child is serious—
light balsa wood the color of my skin.
It is all childcraft, especially
its shallow, chiseled ears,
crudely healed scars lumped out
to listen to itself, perhaps, not knowing
it was made to be given up.
Goodbye nothing. Blockhead,
I would take you to church,
if any church would take you . . .
This winter, I thought
I was created to be given away.

Epilogue

Those blessèd structures, plot and rhyme—
why are they no help to me now
I want to make
something imagined, not recalled?
I hear the noise of my own voice:
The painter's vision is not a lens,
it trembles to caress the light.
But sometimes everything I write
with the threadbare art of my eye
seems a snapshot,
lurid, rapid, garish, grouped,
heightened from life,
yet paralyzed by fact.
All's misalliance.
Yet why not say what happened?
Pray for the grace of accuracy
Vermeer gave to the sun's illumination
stealing like the tide across a map
to his girl solid with yearning.
We are poor passing facts,
warned by that to give
each figure in the photograph
his living name.

APPENDIX

Translations

Rabbit, Weasel, and Cat

(Adapted from La Fontaine)

Dame Weasel one fine morning stole
into young Rabbit's furnished hole;
it was an easy trick to play,
the master had stepped out to pay
his courtship to Aurora and the day,
and taste the clover and the dew.
Gobbling all that he could chew,
the rabbit trots home to his burrow—
the weasel's nose is pointing through the window.
The dislodged rabbit gives a shout,
"My God, what's this? This needle-snout?
Dame Weasel, leave, you have no choice,
don't make me raise my voice—
shall I call out the rats?"
The weasel answers, "Property
belongs to the present occupant.
An ignoble *casus belli*,
this hole I can only enter on my belly—
suppose it were Versailles!
Tell me, Friend, on what condition
is a holding handed down
to John or Henry's son,
or you, and not to me?"
The rabbit cited religion and tradition.
"There's law," he said, "that renders me
binding dominion of this habitation.
It came from James and Peter down to me.
The first possessor, is there better law?"
"Let's go then to an honest judge,"
Dame Weasel answered, "to Rabinagruge."
This old cat lived in sanctity,
a holy man of a cat,
pudgy and sleek-furred
from sipping at his pot of fat—

an expert in legality.
"Come nearer, Children," the old cat purred;
"I'm deaf, alas, for who can fight the years?"
The litigants came close, they had no fears.
Seeing them stand within arm's reach,
the cat plopped a soft paw on each,
and by breaking their necks, made peace.
This is the fate
of little nations that appeal to great.

George III

(This too is perhaps a translation, because I owe so much to Sherwin's brilliant Uncorking Old Sherry, *a life of Richard Brinsley Sheridan.—R.L.)*

Poor George,
afflicted by two Congresses,

ours and his own that regularly
and legally had him flogged—

once young George, who saw
his lost majority of our ancestors

dwindle to a few inglorious Tory refugee
diehards who fled for him to Canada—

to lie relegated to the ash-heap,
unvisited in this bicentennial year—

not a lost cause, but no cause.

In '76, George was still King George,
the one authorized tyrant,

not yet the mad, bad old king,

who whimsically picked the pockets of his page
he'd paid to sleep all day outside his door;

who dressed like a Quaker, who danced a minuet
with his appalled apothecary in Kew Gardens;

who did embroidery with the young court ladies,
and criticized them with suspicious bluntness;

who showed aversion for Queen Charlotte, almost
burned her by holding a candle to her face.

It was his sickness, not lust for dominion
made him piss purple, and aghast

his retinue by formally bowing to an elm,
as if it were the Chinese emissary.

George—

once a reigning monarch like Nixon,
and more exhausting to dethrone . . .

Could Nixon's court,
could Haldeman, Ehrlichman, or Kissinger

blame their king's behavior
on an insane wetnurse?

Tragic buffoonery
was more colorful once;

yet how modern George is,
wandering vacated chambers of his White House,

addressing imaginary congresses,
reviewing imaginary combat troops,

thinking himself dead and ordering black clothes:
in memory of George, for he was a good man.

Old, mad, deaf, half-blind,

he talked for thirty-two hours
on everything, everybody,

read Cervantes and the Bible aloud
simultaneously with shattering rapidity . . .

Quand on s'amuse, que le temps fuit—

in his last lucid moment,
singing a hymn to his harpsichord,

praying God for resignation
in his calamity he could not avert . . .

mercifully unable to hear
his drab tapes play back his own voice to him,

morning, noon, and night.

Arethusa to Lycotas

(Propertius, Book IV, 3)

Arethusa sends her Lycotas this command:
if I can call you, always absent, mine.
If some letters have an uncertain outline,
they're proofs I write you with a dying hand.

Bactra twice-visited, you rushed to see
the taunting Neurican on his armored horse,
the wintry Getae, Britain's painted cars,
the sunburnt Hindo by his sultry sea.

Is this our marriage? Hymen was gone when I
a stranger to love, and afraid of freedom, chose
the ominous torch that lit me to your house—
the coronet on my hair was set awry.

May whoever cut tentstakes from the harmless ash,
or carved the hoarse-complaining trumpet from bone—
die worse than Ocnus, who sits aslant to twine
his rope in hell forever to feed the ass.

Does the breastplate bruise your soft white flesh,
are your civil hands blistered by the war spear?
Better these hurt you than some girl should scar
your neck with toothmarks for my tears to heal.

Now sharper nights attend the evening star,
the blanket will not stay put on my bed—
I could kiss your dull weapons you left here dead . . .
the birds, that herald morning, sing no more.

I know the painted world of maps, I know
which way the Araxes you will ford must flow,
how far without water a Parthian horse will fly—
I've placed your almost polar city, Dai.

I know which lands the sun hurts, which the frost—
which wind will blow you home to Italy.
My older sister and old nurse swear to me
it's only the heavy winter holds you fast.

Hippolyta was lucky, she could enter the ring
barebreasted; a captain's helmet hid her curls.
I wish our Roman camps admitted girls,
I'd be faithful baggage for your soldiering.

Mountains would not frighten me with height,
or Jupiter chaining the high streams with ice.
All love is great—a wife has greater love,
Venus blows on this flame that it may live.

All's dead here—at rare Kalends, a lonely housemaid
opens the Lares on her perfunctory round;
I wait for the whine of Craugus, the small hound;
he is only claiming your place in my bed.

If the barn-owl scream from the neighboring oak,
or wine is sprinkled on the spluttering lamps,
that day requires we kill the first-year lambs;
blackmail hurries the stately priest to work.

I've no cause to shine in bridal attire,
make crystals glitter like waterdrops on my ears;
I hang shrines with flowers, the crossroad with green firs;
marjoram crackles in the ancestral fire.

Is glory taking Bactra's walls by force,
or tearing the turban from a perfumed king,
while the bow twangs from their hypocrite flying horse,
and lead scatters like hailstones from the twisted sling?

When their young men are gone, and slavery heals
their widows, and the spear without a head
drags at your triumphant horse's heels—
remember the vow that binds you to our bed.

If you come back to me by day or night,
and make us for the moment man and wife,
I'll bring your arms to the Capua Gate, and write:
From a girl grateful for her husband's life.

Last Poems

(1977)

Executions

My executions begin at 10 P.M.
and end with dawn.

I sit under the royal oak
raising most, condemning few
with an inaudible whisper to my guard—
these six years, these sixteen years . . .
it doesn't matter, the count was lost.

Besides the necessity to keep awake,
what is life without the relief of love?
Love to the mind is wind to the sea—
a saintly, two-tongued wife. . . .
I too have loved—an incumbent husband
all wives can imagine dead.

These days when I give judgment,
I look spruce and unchanging,
I wear a fine suit of gold—
two slaves to fan me
and carry me in a huge armchair
shaking in their hands,
as I count the steps downward
from my throne: 25, 24, 23.

I escape . . . everything,
intermittently, I forget
my intolerable, metallic heat,
my distrusted gaiety the day
I decided to decline . . . and live.
I can point out myself, the culprit,
with my palsied, pedagogic scepter.

Night executions spare me
the agony of early rising.

Loneliness

A stonesthrow off,
seven eider ducks
float and dive in their watery commune . . .
a family, though not a marriage—
we have learned not to share.
We were
so by ourselves and calm this summer,
I would wish to live forever,
like the small boy on the wharf
marching alone, far ahead of the others,
still anxiously flapping
their particolored sails in the calm.

Summer Tides

Tonight
I watch the incoming moon swim
under three agate veins of cloud,
casting crisps of false silver-plate
to the thirsty granite fringe of the shore.
Yesterday, the sun's gregarious sparklings;
tonight, the moon has no satellite.
All this spendthrift, in-the-house summer,
our yacht-jammed harbor
lay unattempted—
pictorial to me like your portrait.
I wonder who posed you so artfully
for it in the prow of his Italian skiff,
like a maiden figurehead without legs to fly.
Time lent its wings. Last year
our drunken quarrels had no explanation,
except everything, except everything.
Did the oak provoke the lightning,
when we heard its boughs and foliage fall? . . .
My wooden beach-ladder swings by one bolt,
and repeats its single creaking rhythm—
I cannot go down to the sea.
After so much logical interrogation,
I can do nothing that matters.
The east wind carries disturbance for leagues—
I think of my son and daughter,
and three stepdaughters
on far-out ledges
washed by the dreaded clock-clock of the waves . . .
gradually rotting the bulwark where I stand.
Their father's unmotherly touch
trembles on a loosened rail.

Appendices

APPENDIX I:

Land of Unlikeness

(1944)

INDE ANIMA DISSIMILIS DEO
INDE DISSIMILIS EST ET SIBI.
S. BERNARD

INTRODUCTION

There is no other poetry today quite like this. T. S. Eliot's recent prediction that we should soon see a return to formal and even intricate metres and stanzas was coming true, before he made it, in the verse of Robert Lowell. Every poem in this book has a formal pattern, either the poet's own or one borrowed, as the stanza of "Satan's Confession" is borrowed from Drayton's "The Virginian Voyage," and adapted to a personal rhythm of the poet's own.

But this is not, I think, a mere love of external form. Lowell is consciously a Catholic poet, and it is possible to see a close connection between his style and the formal pattern. The style is bold and powerful, and the symbolic language often has the effect of being *willed*; for it is an intellectual style compounded of brilliant puns and shifts of tone; and the willed effect is strengthened by the formal stanzas, to which the language is forced to conform.

A close reader of these poems will be able to see two general types, or extremes which it is the problem of the poet to unite, but which I believe are not yet united: this is not a fault, it merely defines the kind of poet that Lowell, at this early stage, seems to be. On the one hand, the Christian symbolism is intellectualized and frequently given a savage satirical direction; it points to the disappearance of the Christian experience from the modern world, and stands, perhaps, for the poet's own effort to recover it. On the other hand, certain shorter poems, like "A Suicidal Nightmare" and "Death from Cancer," are richer in immediate experience than the explicitly religious poems; they are more dramatic, the references being personal and historical and the symbolism less willed and explicit.

The history of poetry shows that good verse does not inevitably make its way; but unless, after the war, the small public for poetry shall exclude all except the democratic poets who enthusiastically greet the advent of the slave-society, Robert Lowell will have to be reckoned with. Christopher Dawson has shown in long historical perspective that material progress may mask social and spiritual decay. But the spiritual decay is not universal, and in a young man like Lowell, whether we like his Catholicism or not, there is at least a memory of the spiritual dignity of man, now sacrificed to mere secularization and a craving for mechanical order.

—ALLEN TATE

The Park Street Cemetery

In back of the Athenaeum, only
The dead are poorer. Here frayed
Cables wreathe the spreading obelisk,
And a clutter of Bible and weeping willows
Preserves the stern surnames: Adams,
Otis, Hancock, Mather, Revere;
Franklin's mother rests in hope.

Dusty leaves and the frizzled lilac
Liven this elder's garden with baroque
And prodigal embellishments; but the ground
Has settled *in saecula saeculorum*;
The dead cannot see Easter crowds
On Boston Common, or Beacon Hill
Where the Irish hold the Golden Dome.

What are Sam Adams or Cotton Mather?
The stocks and Paradises of the Puritan Dracos,
New World eschatologies
That fascinated like a Walpurgis Nacht,
And the Promised Land foreseen in Plymouth?
The graveyard's face is painted with facts
And filagreed swaths of forget-me-nots.

In Memory of Arthur Winslow

I.

DEATH FROM CANCER

This Easter, Arthur Winslow, less than dead
Your people set you up in Phillips House
To settle off your wrestling with the crab
Whose claws drop flesh on your serge yatching-blouse
Until longshoreman Charon come and stab
Through your adjusted bed
And crush the crab. On Boston Basin shells
Hit water by the Union Boat Club's wharf;
You ponder why the coxes' squeakings dwarf
The *resurrexit Dominus* of all the bells;

Grandfather Winslow, look, the swanboats coast
That island in the Public Gardens, where
The bread-stuffed ducks are brooding, where with tub
And strainer the mid-Sunday Irish scare
The sun-struck shallows for the dusky chub,
This Easter, and the Ghost
Of risen Jesus walks the waves to run
Arthur upon a trumpeting black swan
Beyond Charles River to the Acheron
Where the wide waters and their voyager are one.

II.

DUNBARTON

The stones are yellow and the grass is grey
When we ride you to the Dunbarton Hill
In a mortician's Packard limousine;
The dozen Winslows and the Starks half fill
The granite plot and the dwarfed pines go green
From watching for the day
When the great year of the little yoeman come
Bringing the Mayflower Compact and the faith
That made the Pilgrim Makers take a lathe
To point their wooden steeples lest the Word be dumb.

O fearful Witnesses, your day is done:
The minister, Kingsolving, waves your ghosts
To the shades, evergreen, the pilgrims' home;
The first selectman of Dunbarton posts
Wreathes of New Hampshire pine-cones on your chrome
Box where the mirrored sun
Is booming: "Arthur, no one living has reached
Dunbarton. Are only poor relations left
To hold an empty bag of pine-cones?" Cleft,
Broken down boulders sprawl out where our fathers preached.

III.

FIVE YEARS LATER

This Easter, Arthur Winslow, five years gone,
I come to bury you and not to praise
The craft that netted a million dollars, late
Mining in California's golden bays
Then lost it all in Boston real estate;
Then from the train, at dawn,
Leaving Columbus in Ohio, shell
On shell of our stark culture struck the sun
To fill my head with all our fathers won
When Cotton Mather wrestled with the fiends from Hell.

You must have hankered for our family's craft:
The block-house Edward made, the Governor,
At Marshfield, and the slight coin-silver spoons
Some Winslow hammered thinner than Revere,
And General Stark's coarse bas-relief of bronze
Set on your granite shaft
In rough Dunbarton; for what else could bring
You, Arthur, to the veined and alien West,
But devil's notions that your gold, at least,
Would give back life to men who whipped the British King?

IV.

A PRAYER FOR MY GRANDFATHER TO OUR LADY

"Mother, for these three hundred years or more
Neither our clippers nor our slavers reached
The haven of your peace in this Bay State:
Neither my father nor his father. Beached
On these dry flats of fishy real estate,
O Mother, I implore
Your scorched, blue thunderbreasts of love to pour
Buckets of blessings on my burning head
Until I rise like Lazarus from the dead:
Lavabis nos et super nivem dealbabor.

"On Copley Square I saw you hold the door
To Trinity, Kingsolving's Church, and saw
The painted Paradise of harps and lutes
Sink like Atlantis in the Devil's jaw
And knock the Devil's teeth out by the roots;
But when I strike for shore
I find no painted idols to adore:
Hell is burned out, heaven's harp-strings are slack.
Mother, run to the chalice, and bring back
Blood on your finger-tips, for Lazarus who was poor."

A Suicidal Nightmare

Tonight and crouching in your jungle-bed,
O tiger of the gutless heart, you spied
The maimed man stooping with his bag;
And there was none to help. Cat, you saw red,
And like a grinning sphinx, you prophesied
Cain's nine and outcast lives are in the bag.

Watching the man, I spun my borrowed car
Into the bog. I'd left the traveled road
And crashed into a lower bog;
And that was why the catapulting fur,
A wooly lava of abstractions, flowed
Over my memory's inflated bag.

The maimed man stooped and slung me on his back:
My borrowed car flopped quacking in the flood,
It foundered in the lowest bog.
Man, why was it your rotten fabric broke?
"Brother, I fattened a caged beast on blood
And knowledge had let the cat out of the bag."

On the Eve of the Feast of the Immaculate Conception

(1942)

Mother of God, whose burly love
Turns swords to plowshares, come, improve
      On the big wars
And make this holiday with Mars
Your Feast Day, while Bellona's bluff
Courage or call it what you please
      Plays blindman's buff
      Through virtue's knees.

Freedom and Eisenhower have won
Significant laurels where the Hun
      And Roman kneel
To lick the dust from Mars' bootheel
Like foppish bloodhounds; yet you sleep
Out our distemper's evil day
      And hear no sheep
      Or hangdog bay!

Bring me tonight no axe to grind
On wheels of the Utopian mind:
      Six thousand years
Cain's blood has drummed into my ears,
Shall I wring plums from Plato's bush
When Burma's and Bizerte's dead
      Must puff and push
      Blood into bread?

Oh, if soldiers mind you well
They shall find you are their belle
      And belly too;
Christ's bread and beauty came by you,
Celestial Hoyden, when our Lord
Gave up the weary Ghost and died,
      You shook a sword
      From his torn side.

Over the seas and far away
They feast the fair and bloody day
        When mankind's Mother,
Jesus' Mother, like another
Nimrod danced on Satan's head.
The old Snake lopes to his shelled hole;
        Man eats the Dead
        From pole to pole.

The Boston Nativity

Now at the spun world's Hub
I listen to unchristian carollings
While Boston Common, Hill and Country Club,
    Charlestown and King's
   Chapel sing Christmas Day
   To my dead baby's clay.

Doctors pronounce him dead.
Dead as the gods and oaths of yesterday;
See how the carrion puffs out his death's head!
    Progress can't pay
   For burial. The Town Hall
   Shall be his box and pall.

Child, the Mayflower rots
In your poor bred-out stock. Brave mould, here all
The Mathers, Eliots and Endicots
    Brew their own gall,
   Here Concord's shot that rang
   Becomes a boomerang.

"Peace and goodwill on earth"
Liberty Bell rings out with its cracked clang.
If Baby asks for gifts at birth,
    Santa will hang
   Bones of democracy
   Upon the Christmas Tree.

So, child, unclasp your fists,
And clap for Freedom and Democracy;
No matter, child, if the Ark Royal lists
    Into the sea;
   Soon the Leviathan
   Will spout American.

Cradle of Freedom, rock your little man:
"Peace, peace," the sheepish angels sing,
While Santa, the benighted Magian,
Throws sheepskins on my carrion king,
Jesus, the Maker of this holiday,
Ungirds his loins' eternal clay.

The Bomber

Bomber climb out on the roof
Where your goggled pilots mock,
With positive disproof,
David's and Sibyl's bluff.
"Will God put back the clock
Or conjure an Angel Host
When the Freedoms police the world?"
O Bomber your wings are furled
And your choked engines coast.
The Master has had enough
Of your trial flights and your cops
And robbers and blindman's buff,
And Heaven's purring stops
When Christ gives up the ghost.

The air is gassy and dry,
Bomber climbing the crest
Of the daredevil sky;
For this is the clinker day
When the burnt out bearings rest,
And we give up the Ghost.
At dawn like Phaeton
To the demolishing sun
You hurtled the hollow boast
Until you lost your way.
Now you dive for the global crust.
How can frail wings and clay
Beat down the biting dust
When Christ gives up the ghost?

Bomber like a god
You nosed about the clouds
And warred on the wormy sod;
And your thunderbolts fast as light
Blitzed a wake of shrouds.
O godly Bomber, and most
A god when cascading tons
Baptized the infidel Huns
For the Holy Ghost,
Did you know the name of flight
When you blasted the bloody sweat
And made the noonday night:
When God and Satan met
And Christ gave up the ghost?

Concord Cemetery After the Tornado

Buzzard's Bay had spun
Back the tidal wave
In its almighty tide;
But Concord, by the grave
Of Waldo Emerson,
Rumbles from side to side
Taunting the typhoon's groan
And then turns down her thumb;
There, like Drake's drum,
Winds' wings beat on stone.

What does this rubble say,
O Woman out in the rain?
"Concord, you loved the heart
Without a body." Brain
And brass are come to clay
While the professors cart
Our guts to Babylon,
There godless Greece and Rome
Bay to the plastered Dome:
"Winds' wings beat on stone."

In the dry winds of noon,
Ralph Waldo Emerson,
Judging the peaceful dead
Of Concord, takes the sun
From every gravestone. Soon
Angels will fear to tread
On that dead Lion's bones,
In their huge, unhewn hide,
Rattling to wind and tide:
"Winds' wings beat on stone!"

Salem

In Salem seasick spindrift drifts or skips
To the canvas flapping on the seaward panes
Until the knitting seaman stabs at ships
Nosing like sheep of Morpheus through his brain's
Asylum. Seaman, seaman, how the draft
Lashes the oily slick about your head,
Beating up whitecaps! Seaman, Charon's raft
Dumps its damned goods into the harbor-bed,
Where sewage sickens the rebellious seas.
Remember, seaman, Salem fishermen
Once hung their nimble fleets on the Grand Banks.
Where was it that New England bred the men
Who quartered the Leviathan's fat flanks
And fought the British lion to his knees?

Concord

Gold idles here in its inventor's search
For history, for over city ricks,
The Minute Man, the Irish Catholics,
The ruined Bridge and Walden's fished-out perch,
The belfry of the Unitarian Church
Rings out the Hanging Jesus. Crucifix,
How can your whited spindling arms transfix
Mammon's unbridled industry, the lurch
For forms to harness Heraclitus' stream!
This Church is Concord, where the Emersons
Washed out the blood-clots on my Master's robe
And then forgot the fathers' flintlock guns
And the renown of that embattled scream
Whose echo girdled the imperfect globe.

Napoleon Crosses the Beresina

"And wheresoever you see Eagles, look for the bodies."

Here Charlemagne's stunted shadow plays charades
With pawns and princes whose play-cannister
Shivers the Snowman's bones, and the Great Bear
Shuffles away to its ancestral shades;
And here Napoleon Bonaparte parades,
Hussar and cuirassier and grenadier
Over the tombstone steppes to Russia. Here,
The Eagles fly, the Occident invades
The Holy Land of Russia. Lord and Glory
Of dragonish, unfathomed waters, rise!
Although your Beresina cannot gnaw
These soldier-plumed pontoons to matchwood, ice
Is tuning them to tumbrels, until snow
Blazes its carrion-miles to Purgatory.

Scenes from the Historic Comedy

I.

THE SLOUGH OF DESPOND

At sunset only swamp
Afforded pursey tufts of grass . . . these gave,
I sank. Each humus-sallowed pool
Rattled its cynic's lamp
And croaked: "We lay Apollo in his grave;
Narcissus is our fool."

My God, it was a slow
And brutal push! At last I struck the tree
Whose dead and purple arms, entwined
With sterile thorns, said: "Go!
Pluck me up by the roots and shoulder me;
The watchman's eyes are blind."

My arms swung like an axe.
And with my morning sword I lopped the knot;
The labyrinthine East was mine
But for the asking. Lax
And limp, the creepers caught me by the foot,
And then I toed their line;

I walk upon the Flood:
My way is midden; there is no way out;
Now how the Dead Sea waters swell,—
The tree is down in blood!
All of the bats of Babel flap about
The rising sun of Hell.

II.

Harlot, your day is done,
Leper, who turned your back on Jordan, bawl:
"I am the Mistress of the Sea."
The sea of Babylon
Is broken, waters clamber up her wall.
O Jesus, set my people free!

This is the gala day
When girdled Satan runs the Golden Gate;
His charioteers are stupefied,
His footmen stumble. *Yea*
Is *nay*. O Harlot, the clay feet of state
Are gone with time and tide.

Star-gazers flee. The Sign
Of the hanged Savior turns our weather-vanes;
The life-boats run white flags. You say:
"No sorrow is like mine;
The Lord rides home in scarlet and his reins
Are flaming on this joyful day."

The little lions run
Whimpering to the Wounded Shepherd's crook;
Their golden manes are pliant wool.
Woe unto Babylon,
No one will hold her rampant Lion. Look,
Her waters are like a dead pool!

III.

FROM PALESTINE

O apes of Lucifer
Who thawed his hands with borrowed Charity,
You split our Cross for stovewood. Fire
Is all that you can stir

For love or money out of Galilee;
The *Lignum Vitae* is your pyre.

Britain is wooden; gas
Blows on the wind until her ghost is laid
In Jacob's Well; her bastions break
As the charred Angels blaze
All manmarks from this world man never made.
Armadas whelm the Roman Lake.

Wet from your mummy-box,
Moses, go down, go down where British bones
Relinquish their Egyptian tomb
And hunt the desert fox;
Where painted Highlanders with stocks and stones
Stamp Allah from his hearth and home.

Love is the final fire,
And makes the King of Kings his servant's slave;
Deep deep in Mithra's sweating pit
Europa strips for hire;
"I am," I said, "my foot is in the grave:
The sunset of the West is lit."

Dea Roma

Augustus mended you. He hung the tongue
Of Tullius upon your rostrum, lashed
The money-lenders from your Senate House;
Then Brutus bled his forty-six percent
For *Pax Romana*. Quiet as a mouse
Blood licks your Greek cosmetics with its tongue.

Some years, your legions soldiered through this world
Under the eagles of Lord Lucifer;
But human torches lit the soldier home,
And victims dyed your purple crucifix:
All of the roads and sewers wound to Rome;
Satan is pacing up and down the world.

How many butchers and philosophers
Dirtied the Babylonian purple! Blood
Ran in through pipes of public aqueducts;
Vandal patricians squatted on Rome's lid,
Until Maxentius, floundering in the mud,
Wiped out the scandal of philosophers.

Now sixteen centuries, Eternal City,
Are squandered since the inflated pagan flowed
Under the Milvian Bridge; from the dry Dome
Of Michaelangelo, your Fisherman
Walks on the waters of a draining Rome
To bank his catch in the Celestial City.

Christ for Sale

In Greenwich Village, Christ the Drunkard brews
Gall, or spiked bone-vat, siphons His bilged blood
Into weak brain-pans and unseasons wood:
His auctioneers are four hog-fatted Jews.
In furs and bundlings of vitality,
Cur ladies, ho, swill down the ichor in this Dye.

Drying upon the crooked nails of time,
Dirty Saint Francis, where is Jesus' blood,
Salvation's only Fountainhead and Flood?
These drippings of the Lamb are Heaven's crime.
Queens, Brooklyn and Manhattan, come and buy:
Gomorrah, had you known the wormwood in this Dye!

Us still our Savior's mangled mouth may kiss
Although beauticians plaster us with mud:
Dog of the veins, your nose is stopped with blood;
Women are thirsty, let them lap up this:
The lunchers stop to spit into Christ's eye.
O Lamb of God, your loitering carrion will die.

The Crucifix

How dry Time screaks in its fat axle-grease,
As sure November strikes us through the ice
And the Leviathan breaks water in the rice
Fields, at the poles, at the Hot Gates to Greece;
It's time: the worldly angels strip to tease
And wring out bread and butter from their eyes,
To wipe away the past's idolatries;
Tomorrow's seaways lurch through Sodom's knees.
"The Ark of State is sinking. Run, rat, run,"
Our Captain warns us till we run upon
Our father Adam. Adam, if the land
Becomes the incarnation of the hand
That builds Jerusalem out of clay, how can
War ever change our new into old man?
Get out from under my feet, old man. Let me pass;
On Ninth Street through the Hallowe'en's soaped glass
I picked at an old Bone on two crossed sticks
And found, to *Via et Vita et Veritas*,
A stray dog's signpost is a crucifix.

The Wood of Life
(Good Friday, 1942)

Who raises up this royal banner
Whose wooden mystery so shines?
O Anvil of our Death's designs,
Who hammers here Life's Spanner?
Hebrews bind a Lamb for slaughter
And on this chopping block
Pour out the blood of royal stock:
They christen Life in blood and water;
This is that secret immolation
Foretold by David's trumpet strains,
On this wood the Monarch reigns
Whose freedmen fly to every nation.
Dangerous and refulgent Tree,
King's purple covers up your taint,
What the worm and human want
Wrung from the first man's extacy.
Here are scales whose Reckoning-weight
Outweighs the apple's fell dejection;
Our cornerstone, the Jew's Rejection.
O royalest bier of state,
Wealth from the waters you deliver,
All Argo overshot or Ark secured,
Most blessed Arc, your beams have cured
The Golden Fleece. Cold Comfort, shiver!
Christ Crucified is all our reason
And most in this dark hour
We will invoke, O Cross, your power,
Our prime, at best, is Passion's season.

Satan's Confession

I.
THE GARDEN

The laurels are cut down,
The Son of Darkness mourns;
   Old Adam's funeral wreath,
   Once crossed with death,
Is Jesus' crown,
King Jesus' Crown of thorns.

Adam, you idle-rich
Image of the Divine;
   Tell me, what holds your hand?
   Fat of the land.
My wife's a bitch;
My Garden is Love's Shrine.

His Garden Wall is high,
Stout is his Garden Wall;
   Not high enough nor stout
   To keep snakes out;
Nick bends the Tree,
The Woman takes the Fall.

When providential wit,
At loggerheads with Sin,
   Expels the swilling fool
   To hard-knock's School,
O Hypocrite,
What is your medicine?

The Hypocrite will plaster
Brimstone of the Abyss
   On Adam's every whim;
   And life and limb
Abjure their Master:
Man is a syphilis!

Come, Good Physician, let
Your Body out to Hell,
   The sky is out of reach.
   O dying Leech;
Your own Blood-let
Has made Corruption well!

II.

THE FRUIT

The laurels are cut down,
The Son of Darkness cries;
   Old Adam's mortal wreath,
   The prize of Death,
Is Jesus' Crown,
Jack's beanstalk to the skies.

Now Heaven's Three-fold Power
Sends down its Public Curse
   To act His bloody Mime;
   Vainglorious Time
Has told His hour;
Christ kicks in the womb's hearse.

Then born, the little Boy
Bawls in the bestial straw;
   O Holy Mother, strap
   God to thy pap,
For this gaunt Toy
Will suckle Israel's Law.

Into the wilderness
His Spirit drives poor Christ,
    Still dripping Jordan's balm.
    In Jesus' palm,
Satan confess,
Lies your back-stabbing wrist!

Christ's thirtieth year has passed,
His body knows its strength;
    Our Lord has had His fill
    Of Passion's swill;
The Cross is last,
Spread-eagling his Man's length.

He drains His poisoned cup;
Thorns, nails and spearhead comb
    The Scapegoat till His blood
    Becomes a flood . . .
The Game is up,
Old Batwings circles home.

III.
THE TREE

The laurels are cut down,
The Son of Darkness mourns;
    Old Adam's funeral wreath,
    Once crossed with Death,
Is Being's crown,
The Scapegoat's Crown of Thorns.

The worms in Eden's Tree
Gorged on rotten spice,
    And played the devil's parts,
    Until this Heart's
Indignity
Brought serpents to their knees.

Bow down your boughs, tall Tree:
Give your tough in'ards ease.
    Will natural rigor shun
    Creation's Son,
Activity
Hold up its wooden knees?

O faithful Cross, among
All trees the only Wood;
    What other Tree could breed
    Leaf, flower or seed
Worthy to dung
Christ's body in its blood?

No other timbers would
Give passage to the Goat,
    When, Sole Ark, you swirled,
    O shipwrecked World,
Through fire and flood,
And made the deadman float.

The laurels are cut down,
The roots of sin are bowed,
    Christ nails them to the Wood,
    Where Adam's blood
Is a king's crown,
King Jesus' purple shroud.

IV.
ENVOY

I praise the Trinity;
From Death three Eagles fly;
    Sire, Son and Paraclete,
    A blind world greet;
One Charity
Reverbs the three-fold I.

Christmas Eve in the Time of War

(A Capitalist Meditates by a Civil War Monument)

"He neither shall be rocked
    In silver nor in gold
But in a wooden cradle
    That rocks upon the mould."

Tonight a blackout. Twenty years ago
I strung my stocking on the tree—if Hell's
Inactive sting stuck in the stocking's toe,
Money would draw it out. Stone generals
Perching upon a pillar of dead snow,
Two cannon and a cairn of cannon balls,
Livid in the unfinished marble, know
How Christmas drunkards left them in the cold,
While Christ the King is rocking on the mould.

A blizzard soaps our dirty linen, all
The crowsfoot feathers mossing Mars' brass hat
Whiten to angels' wings, but the War's snowfall
Has coffered the good-humored plutocrat
Who rattled down his brass like cannon balls
To keep the puppets dancing for the state.
Tonight the venery of capital
Hangs the bare Christ-child on a tree of gold,
Tomorrow Mars will break his bones. I am cold,

War's coddling will not warm me up again.
Brazenly gracious, Mars is open arms,
The sabers of his statues slash the moon:
Their pageantary understanding forms
Anonymous machinery from raw men,
It rides the whirlwind, it directs the drums.
I bawl for Santa Claus and Hamilton,
To break the price-controller's strangle-hold.
I ask for bread, my father gives me mould.

Tonight in Europe and America
All lights are out. Tonight the statesmen lurch
Into some shuttered houseboat, mosque or bar;
Blue lines of boys and girls are on the march:
The Child has come with water and with fire.
Stone Generals, do you tremble for your perch?
Tonight our ruler follows his own Star;
Pretorians shake the Magi's Star for gold.
How can I spare the Child a crust of mould,

His stocking is full of stones! Stone men at war,
Give me the garish summer of your bed—
Flaring poinsettia, sweet william, larkspur
And black-eyed susan with her frizzled head:
My child is dead upon the field of honor:
His blood has made the golden idol glimmer.
"I bring no peace, I bring the sword," Christ said,
"My nakedness was fingered and defiled."
But woe unto the rich that are with child.

Cistercians in Germany

Here corpse and soul go bare. The Leader's headpiece
Capers to his imagination's tumblings;
The Party barks at its unsteady fledglings
To goose-step in red-tape, and microphones
Sow the four winds with babble. Here the Dragon's
Sucklings tumble on steel-scales and puff
Billows of cannon-fodder from the beaks
Of bee-hive camps, munition-pools and scrap-heaps,
And here the serpent licks up Jesus' blood,
Vahalla vapors from the punctured tank.
Rank upon rank the cast-out Christians file
Unter den Linden to the Wilhelmsplatz,
Where Caesar paws the gladiator's breast;
His martial bumblings and hypnotic yawp
Drum out the pastors of these aimless pastures;
And what a muster of scarred hirelings and scared sheep
To cheapen and popularize the price of blood!

But who will pipe of pastors, herds and hirelings
Where a strait-laced mechanic calls the tune?
Here the stamped tabloid, ballot, draft or actress
Consumes all access and all faculties
For spreading blandishments or terror. Here
Puppets have heard the civil words of Darwin
Clang clang, while the divines of screen and air
Twitter like Virgil's harpies eating plates,
And lions scamper up the rumps of sheep.
The Shepherd knows his sheep have gone to market;
Sheep need no pastoral piping for the kill,
Only cold mutton and a fleecing.

The milch-goat gave two tuns of mead a day:
Germans, you swallow this. Flint-headed hearts,
You have forgotten Adam's fault and howl:

"Who was this man who sowed the dragon's teeth,
This fabulous or fancied patriarch
Who sowed so ill for his descent? This ulcer
Our ghettoes isolate but cannot purge?
God's blood be on the bankers and the Jews."
Yesterday pagan Junkers smashed our cells,
We lift our bloody hands to wizened Bernard,
To Bernard gathering his canticle of flowers,
His soul a bridal chamber fresh with flowers,
And all his body one extatic womb,
And through the trellis peers the sudden Bridegroom.

The Drunken Fisherman

Wallowing in this bloody sty,
I cast for fish that pleased my eye
(Truly, Jehovah's bow suspends
No pots of gold to weight its ends);
Only the blood-mouthed rainbow trout
Rose to my bait. They flopped about
My canvas creel until the moth
Corrupted its unstable cloth.

A calendar to tell the day;
A handkerchief to wave away
The gnats; a couch unstuffed with storm
Pouching a bottle in one arm;
A whiskey bottle full of worms;
And bedroom slacks; are these fit terms
To mete the worm whose gilded rage
Havocs the in'ards of old age?

Once fishing was a rabbit's foot:
O wind blow cold, O wind blow hot,
Let suns stay in or suns step out:
Life danced a jig on the sperm-whale's spout:
The fisher's fluent and obscene
Catches kept his conscience clean.
Children, the raging memory drools
Over the glory of past pools.

Now the hot river, ebbing, hauls
Its bloody waters into holes;
A grain of sand inside my shoe
Mimics the moon that might undo
Man and Creation too; remorse,
Stinking, has puddled up its source;
Here tantrums thrash to a whale's rage.
This is the pot-hole of old age.

Is there no way to cast my hook
Out of this dynamited brook?
The Fisher's sons must cast about
When shallow waters peter out.
I will catch Christ with a greased worm,
And when the Prince of Darkness stalks
My bloodstream to its Stygian term . . .
On water the Man-fisher walks.

Children of Light

Our Fathers wrung their bread from stocks and stones
And fenced their gardens with the Redman's bones;
Embarking from the Nether Land of Holland,
Pilgrims unhouseled by Geneva's night,
You planted here the Serpent's seeds of light;
And here the pivoting searchlights probe to shock
The riotous glass houses built on rock,
And candles gutter in a hall of mirrors,
And light is where the ancient blood of Cain
Is burning, burning the unburied grain.

Leviathan

When the ruined farmer knocked out Abel's brains,
Our Father laid great cities on his soul,
      A monolithic mole
To bury man and yet to praise him. Cain's
Life-blood shall drown the Serpent in his Hole.

When Israel turned from God's wise fellowship,
He sent us Canaan or Exile, Ark or Flood,
      At last, for brotherhood,
Our Savior and His saving Heart. The Ship
Of State is asking Christ to walk on blood:

Great Commonwealth, roll onward, roll
On blood, and when the ocean monsters fling
      Out the satanic sting,
Or like an octopus constrict my soul,
Go down with colors flying for the King.

APPENDIX II:

Akhmatova and Mandelstam

(from *Poets on Street Corners*, 1968)

ANNA AKHMATOVA

Requiem

I wasn't under a new sky,
its birds were the old familiar birds.
They still spoke Russian. Misery
spoke familiar Russian words.

1961

BY WAY OF INTRODUCTION

In the terrible years of the Yezhovshchina, I spent seventeen months in the
prison lines at Leningrad. Once, someone somehow recognized me. Then
a woman standing behind me, her lips blue with cold, who had of course
never heard of me, woke up from the stupor that enveloped us, and asked
me, whispering in my ear (for we only spoke in whispers): "Could you
describe this?"
I said, "I can."
Then something like a smile glided over what was once her face.

APRIL I, 1957

DEDICATION

Grief turns the Neva to green glass,
soon the abiding hills are dust,
and yet the prison locks stand fast,
the convict, kicking in his lair,
breathes the consuming air.

For someone somewhere, a fresh wind;
for someone the low sun is a live coal,
but we know nothing. Blind and small,

we hear the keys clang through wards,
the sleepwalk of the guards.

Up, out, as if for early Mass—
when we prowled through wild Leningrad,
we were more breathless than the dead,
and lower than the sun. Low fog,
soon leveled out to fog.

We hoped! The verdict? . . . only tears,
each one cut off from everyone,
rudely cut off, tripped up, thrown down,
blood siphoned from the heart. Dead stone,
she walks still, sways . . . alone.

Oh two years' hell-black, line-up nights,
cry, cry, for your imprisoned friend,
clothe him from the Siberian wind,
shine in the haloed moon's snow eye . . .
I say good-bye, good-bye.

MARCH 1940

INTRODUCTION

Then only the hollow, smiling dead
dared to draw breath and sing;
by blocks and prisons, Leningrad
throbbed like a useless wing.

There convict regiments, miles long,
and mad with suffering,
heard engines hiss their marching song,
the cattle cars' wheel-ring.

The star of death stood over us;
Russia convulsed, as ominous
removal trucks and black
police boots broke her back.

1.

They led you off at dawn. I followed,
as if I walked behind your bier.
In the dark rooms, the children bellowed,
wax melted in the icon's glare.

Cold the small icon's final kiss,
cold the lined forehead's greenish sweat—
like the wives of the Streltsis,
I'll howl beneath the Kremlin's gate.

1935

2.

The dragging Don flows slow, so slow,
the orange moon climbs through a window.

Its hat is slanted on its brow,
the yellow moon has met a shadow.

This woman is alone,
no one will give the dog a bone.

Her husband's killed, her son's in prison;
Kyrie eleison!

3.

Myself! No, she is someone else,
I couldn't take it. Light
no lanterns in these death cells—
black cloths for windows . . . night!

4.

Think back on Tsarskoe's play world, soon
outgrown, soon dated, show-off child—
the tree house built to reach the moon . . .
Oh what has happened to that child?

Number 300 in the queues
of women lugging food and news
for felons. . . . Will your scalding tear
burn an ice hole in the new year?

No sound. A prison poplar waves
over the deadly closeness, waves
of white leaves whiten in the wind—
what innocent lives have reached the end!

5.
For one month, five months, seventeen,
I called you back. I screamed
at the foot of the executioner.
You are my son, my fear.

Thoughts rush in circles through my head;
I can't distinguish white from red,
who is a man, and who a beast,
or when your firing squad will rest.

Here there are only musty flowers,
old clock hands tramping out the hours,
old incense drifting from a censer,
and somewhere, boot steps leading nowhere.

See, see, it pins us down from far;
now looking straight into my eye,
"Move quickly, be prepared to die,"
says the huge star.

6.
These weeks are lightweight runners. Light
of foot, they skin the oblivious snow.
Son, tell me how the white-capped night
looks through your prison window.

"It watches with the owl's hard eye,
or chokes the air with its white snow.
It speaks to us of Calvary,
it speaks of death."

1939

7.
THE VERDICT

At last the silent judge spoke out,
and struck us with his stony word—
but never mind, I will make out,
I was prepared.

Stones, chores . . . I'll manage. Splitting rock
stops the split mind from looking back.
I can forget you now and then,
turn stone, and learn to live again—

or else? The woods' hot rustle, boughs
bursting, a window flying open . . .
I had long had a premonition
of this clear day and empty house.

SUMMER 1939

8.
TO DEATH

You will come anyway, so why not now?
I wait for you. Now truly miserable,
I've turned my lights off and unlocked the door.
You are so simple and so wonderful.

Come to me in whatever shape you will:
a poison-bomb shell, or the typhus mist—
housebreaker, coming from behind to kill,
lifting a clubbed revolver in your fist.

Come to me as your own invention, Fate,
familiar to the point of nausea here—
I want to see the top of the blue hat,
the cringing stupor of the janitor.

All's one now. In Siberia,
rivers are ice, the pole star shines from far,
and the blue rays of my beloved's eye
burn through the daily torture. Let me die.

AUGUST 19, 1939
THE HOUSE ON THE FONTANKA

9.
MADNESS

Already madness—on my breast
are three black moles. I see a fox:
two ears, black muzzle. Let me rest,
this bed I lie on is a pine box.

So simple and so wonderful!
Careful to stress each syllable
the allegoric voices hiss,
I lie decoding images.

I've breathed in red wine from the air!
Now sickness gathers up its gains,
and kicks me as I kneel in prayer,
and nothing of my own remains—

no, not my son's shy smile of wonder
that turned the bars to lines of shadow,
the woods' hot rustle, summer thunder,
our whispers at the prison window—

no, not the roughhouse of the boys,
birch boughs filled with the new birds,
light noises changing to a voice,
the ache of the last words.

MAY 4, 1940
THE HOUSE ON THE FONTANKA

10.

THE CRUCIFIXION

"Mother, do not cry for me as I lie in my grave . . ."

I.

When angel choirs proclaimed his agony,
and fire destroyed the April sky,
Christ questioned, "Why have you forsaken me?"
and told his Mother not to cry.

II.

Magdalen fought and hit the officer,
the loved disciple stood like stone—
all this, God, but your Mother weeps alone;
none dares or cares to look at her.

1940–1943

EPILOGUE

I.

An Assyrian sculptor carved your spear
and skewered flanks. Oh, lioness—
I've seen their faces die like grass,
the lowered eyelid's tick of fear.

I've seen the sick-blond curls grow rough,
snow rot the brown, smiles disappear
from soft, obedient mouths, as fear
suppressed its dry, embarrassed cough.

I pray for you, companions, all
who stood in lines with heavy feet,
come winter's cold or summer heat,
under the red and blinding wall.

II.
And now the requiem hour has come,
I see you, hear you, feel you. Some
marched to their deaths in cheering ranks,
others have faded into blanks.

Some, coming to Siberia, said,
"Why worry, this is home at last."
Some lived. I'd write their names in red
forever, but the list is lost.

I've made a sort of elegy
drawn from the scattered words they spoke.
Braced for the terror's second stroke,
now and always, I hear their cry.

Tomorrow's the memorial day,
a hundred million people pray
through my tired mouth and lethargy:
"Remember me, remember me."

Friends, if you want some monument
gravestone or cross to stand for me,
you have my blessing and consent,
but do not place it by the sea.

I was a sea-child, hardened by
the polar Baltic's grinding dark;
that tie is gone: I will not lie
a Tsar's child in the Tsarist park.

Far from your ocean, Leningrad,
I leave my body where I stood
three hundred hours in lines with those
who watched unlifted prison windows.

Safe in death's arms, I lie awake,
and hear the mother's animal roar,
the black truck slamming on its brake,
the senseless hammering of the door.

Ah, the Bronze Horseman* wipes his eye
and melts, a prison pigeon coos,
the ice goes out, the Neva goes
with its slow barges to the sea.

MARCH 1940

*The statue of Peter the Great astride a horse, which stands in the heart of Leningrad on the quays above the Neva River.

OSIP MANDELSTAM

Somehow we got through the miles of Moscow,
left the Sparrow Hills, and found the small, familiar church.
Our open sled was filled with straw, and roughly hooded
with coarse, frozen cloth that hurt us.

Then in Uglitch the children played knucklebones.
When we drove through it, I reached for my lost hat,
the air smelled like bread left in the oven,
three candles were melting in the chapel.

They were not three candles but three meetings—
one of them had been blessed by the Lord Himself.
There couldn't be a fourth—Rome was so far away,
and the Lord had never really been Himself there.

Our sled stuck in a black rut,
and people shuffled by us to stare.
The men were all bones, the women were crows.
They gossiped and wasted time by the door.

Birds blackened the bare distance with spots—
his tied hands were icy. The Tsarevitch's
body was like a frozen sack when they drove him in,
and set fire to the reddish straw.

                                        1916

I spoke with a child's gibberish to authority,
I was afraid to eat oysters,
I looked at the guardsmen out of the corner of my eye.

Everyone tortured me about this,
but how could I sulk in the foolish beaver miter of a bishop
by the Egyptian porticoes of the banks?

No gypsy girl ever danced for me
under the crackle of hundred-ruble bills
in a café high over the lemon-yellow Neva.

Far from the sirens and the ominous crush of events,
I shivered at the oncoming wave of murders,
and fled to the nymphs of the Black Sea.

I had to put up with much pain and anguish
from the famous beauties of the day,
those delicate, continental ladies.

Why then does this city move me like an old Mass,
when its fires and ice storms only make it
more arrogant, self-loving, empty and youthful?

Is it because I saw the naked, red-haired
Lady Godiva in some old picture book?
Lady Godiva, I do not remember. Lady Godiva.

1931

In the name of the higher tribes of the future,
in the name of their foreboding nobility,
I have had to give up my drinking cup at the family feast,
my joy too, then my honor.

This cutthroat wolf century has jumped on my shoulders,
but I don't wear the hide of a wolf—
no, tuck me like a cap in the sleeve
of a sheepskin shipped to the steppes.

I do not want to eat the small dirt of the coward,
or wait for the bones to crack on the wheel.
I want to run with the shiny blue foxes
moving like dancers in the night.

There the Siberian river is glass,
there the fir tree touches a star,
because I don't have the hide of a wolf
or slaver in the wolf trap's steel jaw.

                                        1931

Preserve my words forever for their aftertaste of misfortune and smoke,
for their tar of collective patience and conscientious work—
water in the wells of Novgorod must be black and sweetened
to reflect a star with seven fins at Christmas.

Oh my Fatherland, my friend, my rough helper,
remember your unrecognized brother, the apostate from the people's
    family—
I have promised to build you forests of log wells,
such as the Tartars built to lower the princes in wooden buckets.

If only your executioners, those frozen blocks, could love me,
as the Tsar Peter, a deadly marksman, loved the balls he bowled on the
    lawn—
for your love, I'll walk through life in an iron shirt,
for my execution, I'll walk the woods like Peter, and find a handle for the
    axe.

MAY 3, 1931

No, I will not hide from the great mess
behind the coachman's back of Moscow;
I am hanging on the outside of a terrifying time, a moving bus.
I do not know why I live.

You and I, we will go to Avenues "A" and "B,"
and see who is going to die first—
Oh Moscow, she huddles like a scared sparrow,
then she swells like a sponge cake.

She has just time to threaten from behind a corner.
You do as you wish, I am not afraid—
who has enough heat in his gloves to hold the reins and ride
around Moscow, the whore, her ribbon of boulevards?

                                        1931

My eyelash prickles—a tear boils up from my chest.
I'm not afraid. I know what's on the calendar—a storm.
Someone marvelous is hurrying me on to forget everything.
It's stuffy here. It's boring how much I want to live.

At the first noise I lift my head from the bunks.
I look around me wildly, half asleep.
I am like a convict singing his rough song,
when morning blues a gray strip above his prison.

1931
MOSCOW

Fragments

Now that I have learned to be discreet,
now that I am brown and brittle for my harvest,
shall I go on pretending
death was much closer in my childhood?

The children still grow drowsy with apprehension,
and hurt all over when they are forced to eat;
but I have lost my taste for sulking,
I am alone no matter where I look.

I look at sky and fields, sky and fields.
What more do I want? Suddenly I am squinting
like a nearsighted sultan at his turquoise ring.
The earth is just another book—so bookish.

I too am earth, this dear, dear earth
that tortures me like talk or music.
My God, help me to live through this night.
I fear for my life, my life, your slave. . . .

Living in Petersburg is to sleep in a coffin.
But I am no longer a child!
The grave can teach
the cripple to run in circles.

Look, my lips cake
and crack like red clay.
I am everyone speaking
for the sky to remain sky.

You and I will sit for a while in the kitchen.
The white kerosene smells sweetly.

A sharp knife, a loaf of bread.
Why don't you pump the petroleum stove tight?

You can collect some strings,
and tie up our basket before sunrise,

then we will escape to the railway station.
No one will find us.

The Turkish Woman

Everything rests on your small shoulders:
the sidelong glances of conscience,
our dangerous, wolfish simplicity—
my words, like a drowned woman, are dumb.

Red fins shining, red gills fanning,
their wondering mouths rounded in wordless
and famished O's, the fish fin here and there.
Take this, feed them the half-risen bread of your flesh!

But we are not goldfish swimming round the globe,
and bubbling when we meet by a water fern;
ours the heat of the warm-blooded body, little ribs
vain as wishbones, the wet, white glitter of the eyeball.

I am gathering poppies from the dangerous fields
of your eyebrows. I love
your tiny, fluttering fish-gill red lips,
as a janissary loves his pitiful, small crescent moon.

Dear Turkish woman, do not be angry,
we will be tied together in a strong sack
and thrown into the Black Sea. I'll do it myself,
while drinking your words, their black water.

Maria, comfort those who must die;
death must be frightened off, and put to sleep.
I stand on a steep cliff by the sea.
Go away from me, stand off—another minute!

FEBRUARY 1934
MOSCOW

Stalin*

We live. We are not sure our land is under us.
Ten feet away, no one hears us.

But wherever there's even a half-conversation,
we remember the Kremlin's mountaineer.

His thick fingers are fat as worms,
his words reliable as ten-pound weights.

His boot tops shine,
his cockroach mustache is laughing.

About him, the great, his thin-necked, drained advisors.
He plays with them. He is happy with half-men around him.

They make touching and funny animal sounds.
He alone talks Russian.

One after another, his sentences hit like horseshoes! He
pounds them out. He always hits the nail, the balls.

After each death, he is like a Georgian tribesman,
putting a raspberry in his mouth.

1934
MOSCOW

*This poem is said to have caused Mandelstam's arrest in 1934.

Chapayev

1.

Unreeling, speaking from the wet film—
they must have had a shepherd of sounds for the fish—
the loud images were moving in
upon me—and upon all, upon you too . . .

They had given up their privileged smallness,
their teeth gripped the deadly last cigarettes.
The brand new White Russian officers
stood against the open loins of the steppes.

A low roaring was heard—airplanes
streaking in burning to the very end—
an English razor blade, large enough to shave a horse,
scraped Admiral Kolchak's cheek.

After me, Oh land, refit me—
the heat of the fixed earth is beautiful—
Chapayev's smoking rifle has jammed.
Help me, untie me, separate me . . .

2.

Passing the dragon with five heads. For five whole days,
I shrank back, I was proud of our huge open spaces rising like dough.
Sleep had swallowed the sounds, but sound wore through my sleep.
Behind us, the harnessed highways rushed and ran us down.

A five-headed dragon. Our cavalry, drunk with dancing, riding on;
our infantry, a fur-capped, blacktopped mass, widening,
rushing like an aorta, power in the white night—no, knives!
They slashed our eyeballs to strips of flesh like pine needles.

If only I had an inch of blue sea, as little as a needle's eye,
enough for the lowest cardholders, convicts chained two and two, to hoist
    sail,
but this is a plain Russian tale without a drink to go with it, or a wooden
    spoon.
Hey, who are those three boys coming out of the iron gates of the GPU!

To keep Pushkin's wonderful goods from falling to parasites,
our youthful lovers of his white-toothed verse
were becoming learned, a tribe of Pushkin-specialists with pistols . . .
If only I had an inch of blue sea, as little as a needle's eye!

The train was going toward the Urals. Commander Chapayev spoke
from the sonorous screen into our open mouths—
Oh to clear the tall wooden fence, go through the screen, and drown . . .
Like Chapayev, to drown, to die on one's own horse!

JUNE 1935
VORONEJ

To the Memory of Olga Vaxel

Is it possible to praise a dead woman?
She was an alien to her people and full of strength.
The power of her love for a stranger
brought her to a hot and violent grave.

The firm black swallows of her eyebrows
swoop down at me from the grave.
They tell me they've lain too long
In their cold bed at Stockholm.

Your people were proud of an ancestor's violin—
Your neck bending over its neck improved its looks.
When you opened your mouth to laugh,
you too looked more Italian, and better-looking.

I keep your heavy memory,
wild one, little bear, Mignon . . .
But the wheels of the mills are fast in winter,
the horn of the postman is thinly blowing.

JULY 1935
VORONEJ

The Future

My body, all I borrowed from the earth,
I do not want it to return here—
some flour-white butterfly.
My body, scratched and chewed with thought,
I want it to become a street, a land—
it was too full of vertebrae.

The dark green pine needles howling in the wind
look like funeral wreaths thrown into the water . . .
how our pastimes and life were drained away!
when we sat like galley slaves at our gruelling benches—
bodies spread against a backdrop of green pine,
red flags colored like the A B C's of a child!

The comrades of the last contingent are on the move;
no conversation; on their shoulders,
the exclamation points of rifles.
From the heights of the sky, a thousand guns,
brown eyes, blue eyes; no one sets the step—men, men, men!
Who will follow after them?

JULY 21, 1935
VORONEJ

The Unknown Soldier

1.
Let this air here be a witness
to his distant, pounding heart
out in the trenches—all-seeing, hungry air:
ocean without a window, matter.

Those stars—how inquisitive
their looks at all times—but why inquire
into the downfall of the judge and witness,
into an ocean without a window, matter?

The heavy-booted sower aches in his joints
from the rain, the nameless manna,
the forest of crosses dotting
the ocean like a suicide battalion.

The thin, cold people will kill,
or they will starve, or they will freeze to the wires.
The unknown soldier expatiates on his rest
in the unknown graves.

Oh thin little swallow who has all
but forgotten how to fly, teach me
how to handle this airy grave,
without wings, without a rudder.

Ah, Michael Lermontov killed for sport!
I'll give you a strict accounting,
tell how huddled flesh is broken by the grave,
by an ocean without a window, matter.

2.
These worlds go on proscribing us,
as they rustle through their frost-killed vineyards,

as they hover like a mirage of golden, stolen Meccas,
taletelling children,
wet, poisonous berries,
crashing pavilions or stars—
like the golden fat of the stars.

3.
Through the ether measured in decimals,
light-time congeals to one beam,
the numbers grow transparent with pain,
a mothlike summation of zeros.

Beyond this battlefield, a field, then fields—
like a triangular flight of cranes,
the news flies ahead on its lighted beam of dust.
Everything is lit up by yesterday's casualties.

Napoleon, the small star of Austerlitz,
has wizened in his black oystershell;
the Mediterranean swallow squints,
the infected sand of Egypt sinks back to Nile.

The news flies ahead on its lighted beam of dust,
says, "I am not Waterloo, Leipzig,
the Battle of the Nations.
I am something novel that will light the world."

4.
The Arabian fireworks flutter like mixed horse food,
light-time congeals to one beam,
a single bayonet pushed by oblique footsteps,
stuck like a hair on my retina.

A million men killed at knockdown prices
have serviced the trail to nothingness—
good night to them, my best wishes
from these mass graves of mammoth molehills.

The sky over these trenches is the incorruptible
Robespierre fed on important deaths;
my lips kiss nothingness . . .
Out of you, after you, O high-priced sky!

Over the shell holes, the earth masses, and the trenches
where the unknown soldier lagged a little in the dark,
hunches the genius of nothingness,
frowning, infected, humiliated.

5.
How beautifully the butchered infantry sings,
how beautifully the night sings,
over the thick smile of Good Soldier Schweik,
over Don Quixote's frail bird leg of a lance,
over the birdlike rushes of the robber barons.
The cripple makes friends with the runner,
both will have work enough on their hands,
and the crutches beat with the dry clatter
of rain against the century's caterpillar wheels—
this is friendship . . . all over the world.

6.
Is this why the skull develops
such an imposing dome—a handbreadth and a handbreadth?
Are the beloved eyes opened
as a breakthrough for the battalions?
The skull grows pompous with life—
a handbreadth and another handbreadth.

Its suture is as neat as a zipper.
It rises like Santa Sophia, the Dome,
rounded with thought, the self of its dream,
mosaic of the stars,
the cup of cups, the homeland of homelands,
the cap of joy, bald Shakespeare's father.

7.

Clarity and its possibility of outline
are pricked with red. Things run home,
and the sky swarms with their disappearance
whitening with lazy afterlight.

The only shell hole ahead of us is miscalculation,
only the superfluous is close to us.
We fight for the everyday air,
this glory should not serve as an example.

We hold our consciousness in reserve,
day-by-day life is half dead—
is it really me finishing this drink,
eating my own head toasting on the grill?

The dress shirt of joy is starched with our blood,
the stars are pricked in red.
Night, stepmother of those herds of stars,
hear what is, what will be!

8.

The aortas fill with blood,
and a dull grumble rises from the ranks:
"I was born in ninety-four."
"I was born in ninety-two."
Along with the others I too crumple
the used-up year of my birth in my fist.
My blood leaves my throat dry.
I murmur, "I was born on a January night
in the year ninety-one,
unenviable year, unenviable century,
my barbed wire of fire."

1937

APPENDIX III:

Magazine Versions

Beyond the Alps

(On the train from Rome to Paris)

Reading of how the Swiss have thrown the sponge
In once again and Everest is still
Unscaled, I watch our Paris pullman lunge
Mooning across the fallow Alpine snow;
O bella Roma! It's against my will,
Like the tri-lingual Roman cooks who go
Forward on tiptoe, banging on their gongs;
I leave the City of God where it belongs.
O gods, when the breast-thumping blimp unfurled
The eagle of Cæsar, he was one of us
Only, pure prose, and less miraculous
Than those grand tours that our grand parents made
Immortal, when the artist followed trade,
While breezing on his trust fund through the world.

O just to dog the crowd! *Papa, Papa,*
Papa, Papa, l'Assunta, Libertà:
New England Puritan, you could only see
A sort of bread and circus piety—
St. Peter's idols, white as death and hope,
Turned ultra-violet, when you cheered the Pope,
Who wiped his glasses, backed against a wall,
And watched the Reds and Blackshirts merge to scrawl
Morte Americani in full view—
The lights had washed them a cerulean blue,
Like Virgins signing on the dotted line:
"No peace on earth." Here saints believe and act;
Bricks turn to gold by fiat. They resign
God's Mother risen to the realm of fact?

The Holy Father drops his looking glass
And listens. His electric razor purrs,
His pet canary chirps on his left hand.
God's in his heaven; Mary's back in furs;
Blackmarket princes liquidate their stock.
O Father, you believe? You understand
Why God, who broke this Roman boot on rock,
Still herds his people to the coup de grace?
Lion of Judah, when the evil eye
Of Satan, cloak and dagger gone, shall die,
There where your Switzers slope their pikes and push,
O Pius, through the monstrous human crush—
Will Cæsar, lynched and booted to blind shape,
Clear the Piazza with a whiff of grape?

I thought of Ovid, for in Cæsar's eyes,
That Tomcat had the number of the Beast.
Where the young Turks are facing the red east,
And the twice-stormed Crimean spit, he cries:
"Rome asked for poets. At her beck and call,
Came Lucan, Tacitus and Juvenal,
The black republicans who tore the teats
And bowels of the mother wolf to bits.
Beneath a psychopath's divining rod,
Deserts interred the Cæsar-salvaged bog.
Imperial Tiber, O my yellow dog,
Black earth by the black Roman sea, I lie
With the boy-crazy daughter of the God,
Il duce Augusto. I shall never die."

Life is for children. At the hospital,
Sister Angelica received my call
Bluely, and put me in your shoes a mile
From nowhere, Santayana. When you died,
True to your boyish shyness of the Bride,
No shock of recognition made her smile.
While the rash Texan Thomist, sent to task
Your old Franciscan wrapper's mongol mask,
Loiters, I see your child's red pencil pass

Bleeding deletions on the proofs you hold
Under your throbbing magnifying glass,
That worn arena, where the whirling sand
And broken-hearted lions lick your hand,
Refined as yellow as a lump of gold.

"Spirit gives life," you say, "will letters kill
The calm eccentric, if by heaven's will
He found the Church too good to be believed?
I died, the nuns will tell you, *as I lived.*
That's how they rime and riddle what I wrote
Of Christ, whose faith is too pragmatical
To nurse illusion. Jesus wept, when Paul,
Who sowed the winds with dogma, missed the boat.
I preached the truth was what my hand could reach,
And gave the bottomless Evangel soul.
Essence took heart and landscape from my speech.
Dying, I fancied the Blue Sisters pressed
Like geese-girls, hissing, *Rome must give her best.*
Let Curtius in full armor fill the hole!"

My mountain-climbing train has come to earth.
Tired by the querulous hush-hush of the wheels,
The blear-eyed ego, kicking in my berth,
Lies still, and sees Apollo plant his heels
On terra firma through Aurora's thigh—
Fire-branded socket of the cyclop's eye.
O Machiavellian vision charged with good,
Dog-star of Athens, when the Goddess stood—
Prince, Pope, philosopher and golden bough,
Pure mind and murder at the scything prow—
Minerva, the miscarriage of the brain:
Decipher Europe! Vibrate through my pane . . .
Now Paris, our black classic, breaking up
Like killer kings on an Etruscan cup.

Buenos Aires

In my room at the Hotel Continental
a thousand miles from nowhere,
I heard
the bulky, beefy breathing of the herds.

Cattle furnished my new clothes;
my coat of limp, chestnut-colored suede,
my sharp shoes
that hurt my toes.

A false fin de siecle decorum
snored over Buenos Aires,
lost in the pampas
and run by the barracks.

Old strong men denied apotheosis,
bankrupt, on horseback, welded to their horses, moved
white marble rearing moon-shaped hooves,
to strike the country down.

Romantic military sculpture
waved sabers over Dickensian architecture,
laconic squads patrolled the blanks
left by the invisible poor.

All day I read about newspaper *coup d'états*
of the leaden, internecine generals—
lumps of dough on the chessboard—and never saw
their countermarching tanks.

Along the sunlit cypress walks
of the Republican Martyrs' graveyard,
hundreds of one-room Roman temples
hugged their neo-classical catafalques.

Literal commemorative busts
preserved the frogged coats
and fussy, furrowed foreheads
of those soldier bureaucrats.

By their brazen doors
a hundred marble goddesses
wept like willows. I found rest
by cupping a soft palm to each hard breast.

That night I walked the streets.
My pinched feet bled in my shoes. In a park
I fought off seduction from the dark
python bodies of new world demigods.

Everywhere, the bellowing of the old bull—
the muzzled underdogs still roared
for the brute beef of Peron,
the nymphets' Don Giovanni.

On the main square
a white stone obelisk
rose like a phallus
without flesh or hair—

always my lighthouse
homeward to the hotel!
My breath whitened the winter air,
I was the worse for wear.

When the night's blackness spilled,
I saw the light of morning
on Buenos Aires filled
with frowning, starch-collared crowds.

Washington

The heavy spokes of this wheel
touch the sore spots of the earth.

On the Potomac, swan-white
power launches keep breasting the sulphurous wave.

Otters slide and dive and slick back their hair.
Raccoons clean their meat in the creek.

In some hole of a museum, Commander Carpenter
still bombs the first German U-boat.

The circles are held by green statues, tough as weeds.
I cannot name the names, or number the dates,

or count the circles—
circle on circle, like rings on a tree.

They come here bright as dimes,
and die disheveled and soft.

MAY 1964

Waking Early Sunday Morning

Oh to break loose, like the chinook
salmon jumping and falling back,
nosing up to the impossible
stone and bone-crushing waterfall—
raw-jawed, weak fleshed there, stopped by ten
steps of the roaring ladder, and then
to clear the top on the last try,
alive enough to spawn and die.

Stop, back off. The salmon breaks
water, and now my body wakes
to feel the unpolluted joy
and criminal leisure of a boy—
no rainbow smashing a dry fly
in the white run is free as I,
here squatting like a dragon on
time's hoard before the day's begun!

Time to grub up and junk the year's
output, a dead wood of dry verse:
dim confession, coy revelation,
liftings, listless self-imitation,
whole days when I could hardly speak,
came pluming home unshaven, weak
and willing to read anyone
things done before and better done.

Fierce, fireless mind, running down hill.
Look up and see the harbor fill:
business as usual in eclipse
goes down to the sea in ships—
wake of refuse, dacron rope,
bound for Bermuda or Good Hope,
all bright before the morning watch,
the wine dark hulls of yawl and ketch.

I watch a glass of water wet
with a fine fuzz of icy sweat,
silvery colors touched with sky,
serene in their neutrality—
yet if I shift, or change my mood,
I see some object made of wood,
background behind it of brown grain,
to darken it, but not to stain.

Oh that the spirit could remain
tinged but untarnished by its strain!
Better dressed and stacking birch,
or lost with the Faithful at Church—
Oh anywhere, but somewhere else!
And now the new electric bells,
clearly chiming, "Faith of our fathers,"
and now the congregation gathers.

Oh Bible chopped and crucified
in hymns we hear but do not read,
none of the milder subtleties
of grace or art will sweeten these
stiff quatrains shovelled out four-square—
they sing of peace, and preach despair;
yet they gave darkness their control,
and left a loophole for the soul.

No, put old clothes on, and explore
the corners of the woodshed for
its dregs and dreck: tools with no handle,
ten candle-ends not worth a candle,
old lumber banished from the Temple,
damned by Paul's precept and example,
cast from the kingdom, banned in Israel,
the wordless sign, the tinkling cymbal.

Empty, irresolute, ashamed,
when the sacred texts are named,
I lie here on my bed apart,
and when I look into my heart,
I discover none of the great
subjects: death, friendship, love and hate—
only old china doorknobs, sad,
slight, useless things to calm the mad.

Oh to break loose now. All life's grandeur
is something with a girl in summer . . .
elated as the President
girdled by his establishment
this Sunday morning, free to chaff
his own thoughts with his bear-cuffed staff,
swimming nude, unbuttoned, sick
of his ghost-written rhetoric!

No weekends for the gods now. Wars
flicker, earth licks its open sores,
fresh breakage, fresh promotions, chance
assassinations, no advance.
Only man thinning out his kind
sounds through the Sabbath noon, the blind
swipe of the pruner and his knife
busy about the tree of life.

Oh hammering military splendor,
top-heavy Goliath in full armor—
little redemption in the mass
liquidations of their brass,
elephant and phalanx moving
with the times and still improving,
when that kingdom hit the crash:
a million foreskins stacked like trash . . .

Sing softer! But what if the new
diminuendo brings no true
tenderness, only restlessness,
excess, the hunger for success,
sanity of self-deception
fixed and kicked by reckless caution,
while I listen to the bells—
Oh anywhere, but somewhere else!

Pity the planet, all joy gone
from this sweet volcanic cone;
peace to our children when they fall
in small war on the heels of small
war—until the end of time
to police the earth, a ghost
orbiting forever lost
in our monotonous sublime.

In the Ward

Ten years older in an hour—

I see your face smile,
your mouth is stepped on without bruising.
You are very frightened by the ward,
your companions were chosen for age;
you are the youngest
and sham-flirt with the nurse—
your chief thought is scheming
the elaborate surprise of your escape.

Being old in good times is worse
than being young in the worst.

Five days
on this grill, this mattress
over nothing—
the wisdom of this sickness
is piously physical,
ripping up memory
to find your future—
old beauties, old masters
who lost their friends before they lost their minds.

Your days are dark,
and night is light—
here the child says:
heaven is a big house
with lots of water and flowers—
you go in in a trunk.

Your feet are wired above your head—

If you could hear the glaring lightbulb
sing

your old modernist classics . . .
They are for a lost audience.

Last year
in buoyant unrest,
you gathered two or three young friends
in the *champagne room*
of your coldwater flat
to explore the pedantry
and daimonic lawlessness
of Arnold Schoenberg
born when music was still imperfect science—
his ever-retreating borderlands of being
that could not console.

If you keep cutting your losses,
you have no loss to cut.

Nothing you see now
can mean anything;
your will is fixed on the lightbulb,
it's blinding impassivity
with-holding disquiet—
the art of the possible
that art abhors.

It's an illusion death or technique
can wring the truth from us like water.

What helpless paperishness,
if vocation
is only shouting what we will.

Somewhere your spirit
led the highest life;
all places matched
with that place
come to nothing.

APPENDIX IV:

Two Sequences from *Notebook*

Those Older

1.
They won't stay gone, rising with royal torpor,
as if held in my binoculars' fog and enlargement,
casting the raindrops of the rainbow: children;
loved by their still older elders in a springtide
invisible to us as the Hittites. We're too near now
to date their comings and goings—those *late* people:
Cousin Susie and Cousin Belle. Fate stamped
them with their maiden name *for life*—blood-rich,
and constellations from the dancing heart.
Our first to die . . . so odd and light and dry,
they seemed foreshadows of some earlier, strange creation,
hooded in snail-shells, the unassailable
deafness of their formidable asperity—
our girls . . . less than a toy, and more than a flower.

2.
Another was a man in his middle life
from the days of his youth till the day of his death;
and yet the matching of his fresh-cut flowers
was over-delicate and dead for death,
as if the flowery coverlet lay like lead,
asserting that no primitive ferment
or slobbering poignance of the voyeur God
would ever corrupt or soil his earthly vestment
spread like King Solomon in the Episcopal morgue,
sanguine, still ready for his thousand lovers. . . .
Here at world's end, here with nowhere else to go,
lie those before us, and those just before us:
less than a toy, and more than a flower . . .
rich and poor, the poor . . . no trees in the sky.

3.
No fence stands up between us and our object:
approaching nearer, nailing down the old,
and free to pick those neither ripe nor young,
as the hollow green wilderness sings the guillotine,
sings those before us. . . . I have had them fifty years:
all those grander, or finer, or simply older,
gone astraying down a backward street, the trees,
late-lopped, tar-boned, old prunes like stumps of martyrs;
and even this dead timber is bulldozed rootless,
and we face faceless lines of white frame houses,
sanded, stranded, undarkened by shade or shutter—
rich and poor . . . no trees in the sky—their stones,
so close they melt to a field of snow, as we pass,
won from the least desire to have what is.

Long Summer

1.

At dawn, the crisp goodbye of friends; at night,
enemies reunited, who tread, unmoving,
like circus poodles dancing on a ball—
something inhuman always rising on us,
punching you with embraces, holding out
a hesitant hand, unbending as a broom;
heaping the bright logs brighter, till we sweat
and shine as if anointed with hot oil:
straight alcohol, bright drops, dime-size and silver. . . .
Each day more poignantly resolved to stay,
each day more brutal, oracular and rooted,
dehydrated, and smiling in the fire,
unbandaging his tender, blood-baked foot,
hurt when he kicked aside the last dead bottle.

2.

Humble in victory, chivalrous in defeat,
almost, almost. . . . I bow and watch the ashes
blush, crash, reflect: an age less privileged,
burdened with its nobles, serfs and Faith.
Possessors. The fires men build live after them,
this night, this night, I elfin, I stonefoot,
walking the wildfire wildrose of those lawns,
filling this cottage window with the same
alluring emptiness, hearing the simmer
of the moon's mildew on the same pile of shells,
fruits of the banquet . . . boiled a brittle lobster-
shell-red, the hollow foreclaw, cracked, sucked dry,
flung on the ash-heap of a soggy carton—
two burnt-out, pinhead, black and popping eyes.

3.

Months of it, and the inarticulate mist so thick
we turned invisible to one another
across the room; the floor, aslant, shot hulling
through thunderheads, gun-cotton dipped in pitch,
Salmon-glow as the early lighted moon,
snuffed by the malodorous and frosted murk—
not now! Earth's solid and the sky is light,
yet even on the steadiest day, dead noon,
the sun stockstill like Joshua's in midfield,
I have to brace my hand against a wall
to keep myself from swaying—swaying wall,
straitjacket, hypodermic, helmeted
doctors, one crowd, white-smocked, in panic, hit,
stop, bury the runner on the cleated field.

4.

Here nature seldom feels the hand of man,
our alders skirmish. I flame for the one friend—
is it always the same child or animal
impregnable in shell or coat of thorns,
only kept standing by a hundred scared habits—
turtle the deft hand tips on its back with a stick?
I think of all the ill I do and will;
love hits like the polio of better days;
I always went too far. A day, that's summer;
whitecaps for acres strew the muddy swell.
I stand between tides; quickly bit by bit
the old crap and white plastic jugs lodge on the shore,
the ocean draws out the river to no end:
most things worth doing are worth doing badly.

5.

The vaporish closeness of this two-month fog;
thirty-five summers back, the brightest summer:
the Dealer's Choice, the housebound girls, the fog;
fog lifting. Then, as now, the after curfew
boom of an unknown nightbird, local hemlock
gone black as Roman cypress, the barn-garage
below the tilted Dipper lighthouse-white,
a single misanthropic frog complaining
from the water hazard on the shortest hole;
till morning! Short dreams, short shrift—one second, bright
as burning shavings, scattered bait and ptomaine
caught by the gulls with groans like straining rope;
windjammer pilgrims cowled in yellow hoods,
making for harbor in their yellow bus.

6.

The Romantic that springs, springs not in vain
in Don Giovanni's farcical, brute leaps . . .
O my repose, the goat's diminishing day.
Once in New Orleans when the ceiling fan
wrestled the moisture, and one pajama leg
hung out of reach, caught on a leather blade—
our generation bred to drink the ocean
in the all-possible before Repeal;
all girls then under twenty, and the boys
unearthly with the white blond hair of girls,
crawling the swimming pool's robin's-egg sky;
safe, and in reach. The fall warms vine and wire,
the ant's cool, amber, hyperthyroid eye,
grapes tanning on these tried entanglements.

7.

Shake of the electric fan about our village;
oil truck, refrigerator, or just man,
nightly reloading of the village flesh—
there are worse things than marriage. Men find dates
whenever summer is on, these nights of the swallow
clashing in heat, storm-signal to stay home.
On Court Street, Dyer Lane, School, Green and Main,
the moon-blanched blacktop fusses like a bosom,
dropping through shade-trees to the shadeless haven—
woman's as white as ever. One only knows
mothers, the sweatshirt gorged with tennis balls,
still air expiring from the lavish arc—
we too wore armor, strode riveted in cloth,
stiff as the broken clamshell labeled man.

8.

They come, each year more gallant, playing chicken,
then braking to a standstill for a girl;
soft bullets hitting bottles, spars and gulls,
echo and ricochet across the bay—
hardy perennials. Kneedeep in the cowpond,
far from this cockfight, cattle stop and watch us,
then, having had their fill, go back to lapping
soiled water indistinguishable from heaven.
The cattle get through living, but to *live*:
Kokoschka at eighty, saying, "If you last,
you'll see your reputation die three times,
and even three cultures; young girls are always here."
They *were* there . . . two fray-winged dragonflies,
clinging to a thistle, too clean to mate.

9.

The shore is pebbled with eroding brick,
seaweed in grizzled furrows—a surf-cast away,
a converted brickyard dormitory; higher,
the blacktop; higher yet, a fish-hawk's nest,
a bungalow, view-hung and staring, with wash
and picture-window—here, like offshoots that
have taken root. Grass shooting overnight,
sticks of dead rotten wood in drifts, the fish
with missing eyes, or heel-print on the belly,
or a gash in the back from a stray hook;
the lawns, the paths, the harbor—stitched with motors,
yawl-engine, outboard, power mower, plowing
the mangle and mash of the monotonous frontier,
bottles of dirt and lighted gasoline.

10.

Two in the afternoon. The restlessness.
Greek Islands. Maine. I have counted the catalogue
of ships down half its length: the blistered canvas,
the metal bowsprits, once pricking up above
the Asian outworks like a wedge of geese,
the migrant yachtsmen, and the fleet in irons. . . .
The iron bell is rocking like a baby,
the high tide's turning on its back exhausted,
the colored, dreaming, silken spinnakers
reach through the patches in the island pine,
as if vegetating millennia of lizards fed
on fern and cropped the treetops . . . or nation of gazelles,
straw-chewers in the African siesta. . . .
I never thought scorn of things; struck fear in no man.

11.

Up north here, in my own country, and free—
look on it with a jaundiced eye, you'll see
the manhood of the sallowing south, *noblesse*
oblige turned redneck, and the fellaheen;
yet sometimes the Nile is wet; life's lived as painted:
those couples, one in love and profit, swaying
their children and their slaves the height of children,
supple and gentle as giraffes or newts;
the waist still willowy, and the paint still fresh;
decorum without hardness; no harness on
the woman, and no armor on the husband,
the red clay Master with his feet of clay,
catwalking lightly through his conquests, leaving
one model, dynasties of faithless copies.

12.

Both my legs hinged on the foreshortened bathtub,
small enough to have been a traveler's . . .
sun baking a bright swath of balsam needles,
soft yellow hurts; and yet the scene confines;
sun falls on so many, many other things:
someone, Custer, leaping with his wind-gold scalplock,
a furlong or less from the old-style battle,
Sitting Bull's, who sent our hundreds under
in the Indian Summer—Oh that wizened balsam,
this sunlit window, the sea-haze of gauze blue
distance plighting the tree-lip of land to islands—
wives split between a playboy and a drudge.
Who can help us from our nothing to the all,
we aging downstream faster than a scepter can check?

13.

Everyone now is crowding everyone
to put off leaving till the Indian Summer;
and why? Because everyone will be gone—
we too, dull drops in the decamping mass,
one in a million buying solitude. . . .
We asked to linger on past fall in Eden;
there must be good in man. Death bears us. Life
keeps our respect by keeping at a distance—
death we've never outdistanced as the Apostle boasted . . .
stream of heady, terrified poured stone,
suburban highway, rural superhighway,
sprig of skunkweed, mast of scrub . . . the rich poor—
we are loved by being distant; love-longing
mists the windshield, soothes the eye with milk.

14.

Mischievous fish-shapes without scale or eye
swimming your leaf-green teagown, maternal, autumnal,
swirling six inches past the three-inch heel,
collapsing on us like a parachute,
in a spate of controversial spatter . . . then
exhaustion. We hunger for the ancient fruit,
marriage with its naked artifice;
two practiced animals, close to widower
and widow, greedily bending forward
for the first handgrasp of vermilion leaves,
clinging like bloodclots to the smitten branch—
summer afield and whirling to the tropics,
to the dogdays and dustbowl—men, like ears of corn,
fibrous growths . . . green, sweet, golden, black.

15.

Iced over soon; it's nothing; we're used to sickness;
too little perspiration in the bucket—
in the beginning, polio once a summer. Not that;
each day now the cork more sweetly leaves the bottle,
except a sudden falseness in the breath,
passive participation, dogged sloth,
angrily skirting greener ice, the naught
no longer asset or advantage. Sooner
or later, and the chalk wears out the smile,
this life too long for comfort and too brief
for perfection—Cro-Magnon, dinosaur—
the neverness of meeting nightly like surgeons'
apprentices studying their own skeletons,
old friends and mammoth flesh preserved in ice.

APPENDIX V:

Uncollected Poems

The Cities' Summer Death

The summer hospital enframes
In its fashionable windows
Boats brow-beaten by varnished storms
And curbed-off grass where no cows browse.

Grandfather feathery as thought
Furls his flurried wrapper and floats
Off his adjustable bed
Wafted on somnolent swan-boats.

Cancer ossifies his features,
The starved skeleton shows its teeth,
Flamingo crackling embroiders
Italian bones with shameless froth.

But the honking untainted swans
Float over the deathly stream
And the aghast oarsmen of Charon's
Ferry raise their skeleton rhythm.

The Dandelion Girls

As home-made candles with fuzzy wicks
Bent birches sprout out of a knob
Where brilliant clouds have surged away—
Clouds are luxuriantly grey.

Slackly curling below this knob
A stagnant brook is stiff with swirls;
By its charred stump three sirens twist
Buttery blooms in their rancid curls.

If wishes were white horses I
Under the sirenic eyes should lie;
Or fluctuate on that charming stream
As a windy wave-walking Christ;

Or as an urchin with bare feet,
Birch stick, bent pin and tattered shirt
Flaunting his lanky fishing line
And chub from an opposing bank.

But I dreamt sirens drank me in
As bawdy watchers of the stage;
On me harsh birches, nursing dew,
Showered their warm humidity.

Sublime Feriam Sidera Vertice

In compensation for blind circumstance,
Nature charged brute devotions to the soul,
      A patriot patrol,
To underwrite human designs, that man's
Least action seem to take a righteous role.

Finding instead satanic partnership,
Nature put out a fall, an Ark, a Flood,
      Like as a common good
Christ Jesus and his golden rule . . . the ship
Of state has learned Christ how to sail on blood.

Great Commonwealth, sail on and on and roll
On blood, on my free blood; my heart misgave,
      Confessed itself a slave,
And Hegel proved State an invested soul,
Oh mortmain, patron and gaoler of the grave.

Pentecost, 1942

Day breaks, the Dove is flying and His words
Tongue the dead air with burning. Over sea,
Our flying fortresses unload their birds
Beyond Charybdis on soft Sicily
And atrophy the Pentecostal sky
Above the fuselage of Messerschmitt
And Fokker. The pilot, falling from on high,
Suddenly full of burning, screams: "A hit."
Palermo, city where the Arab blazed
Jihad, these ashes are our curses hurled
Head-foremost at the mobile underworld
Whose shadows stretch their fingers out to kill
Crusaders and their idols. God be praised,
All passes through the darkness of His will.

Monte Cassino

Angels of peace and joy go round the clock
Proclaiming that Emmanuel is come;
But the cold shepherd hides behind his flock,
And the steel feathers whistle down and bomb
Monte Cassino Abbey, where we pray:
"Where shall we run to? O where shall we hide?
The Angels' wings are flaming on this day,
The riders of the sky are stupefied
With justice. Father Shepherd, let us run
And find a place of hiding from the face
Of our Redeemer." "But, my dearest son,
My son," you whisper, "there's no hiding-place,
Though in the armor of obedience,
Michael, the Fowler, fly to your defense."

Caron, Non Ti Crucciare

"And with Him they crucify two thieves, the one on His right hand, the other on His left."

I.

My beauty is departed: they will square
My hands and feet, and Omar's coarse-hair tent
Towers above the Kedron's Torrent, Sent,
Ben Himnon and the hide-bound outlands where
The little fox runs shivering to its lair,
Fearful lest the short-sighted Orient
Mistake it for this shambles of dissent
Where the red victims of the gallows stare
And dazzle the trenched highways with their blood.
My brothers, if I call you brothers, see:
The blood of Abel, crying from the dead
Sticks to my shaven skull and eyes. What good
Are *lebensraum* and bread to Israel dead
And rotten on the cross-beams of the Tree?

II.

This is the hour of darkness and the clocks
Of Heaven bawl and falter and the Ram
Kicks over his loose traces, earthquake rocks
The stolid temple of Jerusalem,
Whose cornerstone is rocking with a will
To scatter Jew and Roman to the wind;
The wolves steal up on tiptoe for the kill.
Our beauty is departed. All have sinned.
We are a chosen people. Satan, be still;
We huddled against the gallows lest we die.
O why did God climb out on this bald hill,
That Young Man, worse than prodigal, and lie
Upon the gallows of our brotherhood?
The wolves go round in circles in the wood.

III.

I wandered footloose in the wastes of Nod
And damned the day and age when I was born.
I weary of this curse, Almighty God,
Which solely falls on my cleft heel and horn;
My shepherd brother led the lepers back
To Jordan. Then I strayed to Babylon
Where gold-dust sands the sidewalks, lost the track
Of Abel through the fallow to thy Son.
Here merchants trim the sheep and goats in mills
Where woolen turns to gold and dollar bills:
The merchants spare us in the golden net
Of Mammon. O Jerusalem, I said,
If I forget thee, may my hand forget
Her cunning. Let the stranger eat my bread.

IV.

"There is a woman, if you find her, Son,"
My worldly father whispered, "Where each street
Bubbles and bursts with houses of concrete,
There you shall know the whore of Babylon."
In this way Cain's instruction was begun,
Mother of God, before I could repeat
An *Ave* or know the fabulous clay feet
Of Babylon are dynamite and gun;
Mother of God, I lie here without bail.
Instruct a lasher of the sheep and goat
In Jonah, who three nights of midnights lay
Buried inside the belly of the whale,
Then, grappling Nineveh by its mule's throat,
Hauled a great city to the Scapegoat's hay.

V.

Behind his sliding window, Dives sits
To turn out Lazarus, if he should knock;
Wealth is a weighty sorrow. But my wits
Are addled by the sepulchre, the rock,
By splinters of the Godhead in a head
That knows the devils Saul and Joshua smote
From Salem repossess their old homestead
And keep up open-house to feast the Goat;
O tame and uniform conceits of man
And human reason, you should light the night
By burning! Goat-foot Satan, I have lain,
Clutching my nothing close as death, tonight
And heard you hooting, when our women ran;
Your goat horns rattle on the whited pane.

VI.

We saw Mount Sinai and the Holy Land
In Egypt, compound of black earth and green
Between a powdered mountain and red sand
Scoured by the silver air-lines: we have seen
The sworded Seraphim, the serpent-tree,
The apple, once more distant than light-years,
Falling like burning brands about our ears.
The hydra-headed delta choked with sea;
On that sarcophagus of the Nile's mud
And mummies, the Destroyer clamped a lid,
Weightier than King Cheops' pyramid,—
Coffin within a coffin. In whose blood,
Or Jordan, will our spiked and burdened hands
Cup water for a mummy and his lands?

VII.

But peace, in Israel bearded elders keep
The peace as they have always kept it. No
Wolves break into these pastures where the sheep
Wait for the hireling hind to shear them. O
People, let us sleep out this night in peace.
Jehovah nods, the doors of Janus slam,
Cocks on the weathervanes will never cease
Crowing for our defilement of the Lamb.
Lamb in the manger, come into our house:
Here you may find and buy all you can eat,
Dirt cheap. On high, till cockcrow, Lord of Hosts,
The gallows' bird is singing to his spouse,
And mad-cap Lamb is gambolling in the street
And splatters blood on the polluted posts.

VIII.

Virgil, who heralded this golden age,
Unctuous with olives of perpetual peace,
Had heard the cackle of the Capitol Geese,
And Caesar toss the sponge and patronage
Of Empire to his prostituted page.
The gold is tarnished and the geese are grease,
Jason has stripped the sheep for golden fleece,
The last brass hat has banged about the stage.
But who will pipe a new song? In our land
Caesar has given his scarlet coat away.
But who will pipe a new song? In our land
Caesar has given his crown of thorns away.
But who will pipe the young sheep back to fold?
Caesar has cut his throat to kill the cold.

IX.

God is my shepherd and looks after me.
See how I hang. My bones eat through the skin
And flesh they carried here upon the chin
And lipping clutch of their cupidity;
Now here, now there, the sparrow and the sea
Gull splinter the groined eyeballs of my sin,
Caesar, more beaks of birds than needles in
The fathoms of the Bayeux Tapestry;
Our beauty is departed. Who'll discuss
Our scandal, for we are terror and speak:
"Remember how the Dove came down to us,
Broke through your armor of imperial bronze
And beat with olive-branch and bleeding beak
And picked the Lord's Anointed to the bones."

X.

I made this Babel. Pushed against the wall,
With splintered hands and knees and sky-sick blood,
I pieced together scaffolding, O God,
To swing my cloven heels into the tall
Third heaven of heavens, where the Prophet Paul
Fathoms that Jacob's Ladder is the wood
Of Christ the Goat, whose hanging is too good
For my unnourished horns, gone wooden, all
Splintered. God even of the goats, that was:
The fearful night is over and the mist
Is clearing from the undemolished shore
Of Paradise, where homing angels pass
With the dunged sheep into the manger. Christ
Swings from this Tower of Babel to the floor.

The Panther
(After Rilke)

This deck-walk-counting-up of bars
Has tired his vision. Paws uncurled,
He sees a hundred thousand bars;
Behind the filing bars no world.

The supple, prowling, cushioned stride
Cuts close and closer to the center.
His atoms dance about a center.
A great will stands there stupefied.

Sometimes the pupil blinks its shutter.
No sound. A negative must flutter
That sinewed stillness, float and drop—
Must find the heart and stop.

APPENDIX VI:

Poems in Manuscript

The Tartars
(After Li Po)

Last year they scorched the valley of Son-Kan,
This year the Leek Hills; and their horses go
Nosing out ashes in the bone-white snow:
Nowhere and nowhere and nowhere. To the Han,
The latest dynasty, we've marched to man
The walls. The Great Wall stands, the beacons burn;
The beacons burn: the Tartars will not turn
Their horses' heads of bone. It all began
Before our fathers, and their fathers said:
"It all began before our fathers." "Peace,"
A whitened war-horse whinnies on his knees
From nowhere, as the turkey-buzzards seize
The looping blue intestines of the dead
And fasten them as garlands on the trees.

The Broom

(After Leopardi)

Here on the dry back
of the sleepless mountain,
Vesuvius, the killer,
uncheered by flower or shrub—
you spread your lonely brush,
and spice the waste. A while ago, I saw
you stretch your stems and beautify
the villas buckled round
this city, in its hour the queen of mortals.
The speechless, grave façades
seem to keep faith with the spoiled Empire
and leave a record. Once again, I meet
you on this soil, companion
of dull places and the world's abandoned,
affliction's clinging friend.
These slopes are scoured
with sterile grit and paved with solid lava
that echoes to the pilgrim's foot.
Here the snakes
nest and unwind to find the sun;
rabbits duck
into their cavernous, familiar burrows—
these were cheerful little towns and tended fields.
Once they grew blond with corn
and trembled with the mooing cattle.
Here were gardens and great villas,
welcome asylums for the idleness
of statesmen, famous cities, crushed
and crushing out their people
when floods of lava thundered
from the mountain's burning mouth.
While ruin deadens everything

around you, gentle flower,
you send up fragrance to the sky,
as if you pitied man's misfortunes,
and wished to heal the waste.

El Desdichado
(After Gérard de Nerval)

I am the widower, the destitute,
the Prince of Aquitaine whose tower is gone,
the shadow. My star is death. My starry lute
carries my melancholia's black sun.

You who have cheered me in the tomb's dark night
give me the flower that used to cool my brows,
Pausilippo, and the Aegean's light,
the arbor where the vine supports the rose.

Am I Apollo or love? Lusignan, or Biron?
My queen's kisses still burn and blind my eye,
I've swum in grottoes where the siren sings.

Twice victor, I have crossed the Acheron,
held Orpheus' lyre, supported on its strings
now the saint's anguish, now the fairy's cry.

Christ in the Olive Grove

(After Gérard de Nerval)

> God is dead, heaven is empty . . .
> Weep, children, you have no father!
> JOHN PAUL RICHTER

I.

When the Lord lifted up his wasted hands,
as poets do, beneath the sacred trees,
he was long lost in wordless agonies,
he thought he was betrayed by his weak friends.

He turned and looked at those who lay at rest,
dreaming of being prophets, sages, kings,
dog-tired, and only thinking foolish things.
He cried aloud, "No, God does not exist!"

They slept. "Friends, do you know my Father's word?
I've scaled his heaven, I have walked his ways,
broken, bleeding, and sick for many days.

I have deceived you, Brothers: void, void, void!
The God behind my altar is destroyed;
there is no God!" They slept and never heard.

II.

He went on, "All is dead. I've scoured the sky,
and lost my foothold in the Milky Way—
longer than life, its fertile veins display
gold sand and silver waves that blind the eye.

Air-wave on air-wave breaks on those waste shores,
the troubled eddies of a roughened sea;
a vague breath moves those vagabonds, the stars;
no spirit lives in that immensity.

Seeking the eye of God, I only found
an empty socket, black and bottomless;
the night that rules this world grows thicker there.

A frail rainbow bends over that close air,
sill of the void, shadow of nothingness,
where worlds and systems sink without a sound.

III.
Motionless destiny, speechless reverse,
frigid necessity! . . . Chance that must flow
through dead lands under an immortal snow,
chilling by steps the whitening universe,

first force, first force, you know not what you do—
these burnt-out suns, dashed each on each like earth!
How can a breathless, dying world renew
another fresh world's life-line cut at birth?

Father inside me, do I feel your drive?
Have you the strength to breathe your death and live?
What if your own anathema that slew

the angel of the night abolished you.
I feel that I alone suffer and cry,
alas, if I die, everything will die."

IV.
None heard the eternal victim groan and shake,
giving the world his flooded heart in vain.
Fainting, defeated, bleeding from each vein,
he called the only person left awake.

"Judas," he cried, "you know the price I'll bring;
I suffer, friend, this hard earth, this long hour . . .
Hurry, and sell me, end this bargaining;
come, for your crime at least gives you this power."

But Judas, ill and thoughtful, walked away;
shaken and discontented with his pay,
he read his darkness written on the wall.

Pilate alone appeared to hear the call,
watching for Caesar through the merciless night.
"Go, catch the fool," he told some satellite.

V.
Christ was this fool, this God who'd lost his use,
drowned Icarus remounting to the sky,
Phaeton broken by the bolt of Zeus,
lovely, dead Atys saved by Cybele.

The augur pricked the victim's flank and groaned,
the earth grew drunken with the precious blood,
the universe leaned on its axes, stunned,
snow-white Olympus seemed to fall, then stood.

"Zeus, Zeus," cried Caesar, "what is this strange birth?
Who is the new God forced upon the earth?
If he's not God, at least he is a devil."

The old gods kept their peace and turned away;
only one person could explain the evil—
he who gave souls to the children of clay.

Bellosguardo

(After Montale)

Oh how faint the twilight hubbub rising from
that stretch of landscape arching towards the hills—
the even trees along its sandbanks glow
for a moment, and talk together tritely;
how clearly this life finds a channel there
in a fine front of columns flanked by willows,
the wolf's great leaps through the gardens past the fountains
spouting so high the basins spill—this life
for everyone no longer possessed with our breath—
and how the sapphire last light is born again
for men who live down here; it is too sad
such peace can only enlighten us by glints,
as everything falls back with a rare flash
on steaming sidestreets, crossed by chimneys, shouts
from terraced gardens, shakings of the heart,
the long, high laughter of people on the roofs,
too sharply traced against the skyline, caught
between the wings and tail, massed branchings, cloud-
ends, passing, luminous, into the sky
before desire can stumble on the words.

Flux

(After Montale)

The children with their little bows
terrify the wrens into holes.
Sloth grazes the lazy, thin blue
sky-painted trickle of the stream—
rest from the stars for the barely
living walkers on the white roads.
Tall steeples of poplars tremble
and overtop the hardened hill
surveyed by a statue, Summer—
stonings have made her negro-nosed,
and on her there grows a redness
of creeper, a humming of drones.
The wounded goddess does not look,
and everything is bending to
follow the flotilla of paper boats
descending slowly down the trough.
An arrow glistens in the air,
fixes in a stake, and quivers.
Life's this squandering of banal
occurrence; vain, rather than cruel.
They come back, if a season's gone,
a minute, these tribes of children
with bow or sling, and find the dead
features unaltered, even if
the fruit they grasped no longer hangs
dead on the young bough. The children
come back again . . . like this. One day,
the circle that controls our life
will return with the past for us,
distant, fragmented and vivid,
thrown up on an unmoving screen
by an unrevealed projector.
And still the hazy, pale blue vault
vacantly bridges the teeming

watercourse. Only the statue
knows what plunging, lost, entangled
things die in the burning ivy.
All is arched for the great descent:
the channel surges on wildly,
its mirrors crinkle; small schooners
are speeded, caught and wrecked in the
eddies of soap-foamed waste. Goodbye—
stones whistle through the thinning branch,
and gasping luck makes off again,
an hour slips, its faces dissolve . . .
life is cruel, rather than vain.

Boats on the Marne
(After Montale)

Joy of the bobber heading for the drift
drawn by the small, white arch-stones of the bridge,
the full moon drained of color by the sun—
the boats are nimble on the Marne, retarded
by autumn and the city's sluggish drone;
and if you touch the meadows with your oar,
the butterfly catcher will reach you with his net;
each ivied swelling and espaliered wall,
a wash of red, retells the dragon's blood.

It's easy to hear their voices on the river,
bursts from the banks, the twilight of canoes
and couples gliding under breezy manes
of chestnut trees, but who can hear the filing-in
of seasons, each measured out its brandy for
the vast, untrampled dawn? Where's the great wait?
How measure their invading emptiness?

This is the dream: a huge and endless day
returns to pour its glare, almost unmoving,
below the bridges, then, at every turn,
man and his good works struggle to the surface,
and float, and vague tomorrow veils its horror . . .
But the dream was more than this, and its reflection,
still fleeing on the water, swims below
some swinging nest, unreachable, pure air
and silence; and high above the gathered cry
of noonday hangs another morning, morning
over evening and evening over morning—
and the great turmoil is a great rest.
                          Here then?
Here the enduring color is a mouse
dancing among the rushes, or the starling,

a dash of poisonous metal, sinking in
the smoke-mist of the bank.
                              "Another day,"
we'll say. Or what will *you* say? Ask this day
where it will carry us, this mouth, this river,
writhing into a single gush?
                              It's night:
we can go lower, explore the depths, and rest,
until the rising constellations burn.

Beowulf

[The following stanzas are fragments from an unfinished poem. Lowell be-
gan writing a sonnet; but after the third stanza, the sestet, he abandoned it.
The lines that follow the asterisk are blank verse, and begin by adapting lines
from the sonnet.]

Grendel's right arm and shoulder hung in chains
gave me some solace in the feud with fate;
I was the hero, savior of the Danes,
though lonelier without the fiend to hate;

once more I track the blood-trail through the wood,
I feel the red mist rusting on my hand,
and see the tide has risen stained with blood;
Grendel's mother still holds the harassed land.

All sorts of serpents swam about the pool,
making a trial of the bobbing ice,
and others straddled shelves of the ravine,
maturing plans for murder as they roll;
an endless forenoon furthered their design.
And bored, I stab at bellies with my spear.

*

I saw the tide was rising stained with blood,
and felt the red steam rusting on my hand;
time after time the horn resounded, failed,
my foot-troop moved into position, stared.
All sorts of serpents swam about the pool,
making a trial of the current's force;
others straddled shelves in the ravines,
maturing thoughts of murder as they basked;
an endless forenoon ripened their design.
They sank, sullenly, for their blood was up.

I hit one in the belly with my spear,
weaker and weaker grew its surging fight,
washed up on shore, we killed it with our steel.
A piece of flotsam lying beneath a cliff.
My men looked hard upon this visitor.

I was not anxious for my life, put on
my battered chain-mail, twisted link by link
to stand all tests or pressures of the pool.
The helmet clamped upon my head was set
with boar-heads, riveted with brazen tusks,
certain to pierce and flash into the depths
as I descended. In my hand a sword, steel etched
with acid, hardened by the blood of battle.

A ground swell rose and held me in its glass;
the noon was afternoon before I touched
bottom and grasped the features of that land.
There starving for a fight, and starved for meat,
and wild with weeping for her murdered son—
came Grendel's mother, fifty years the queen,
summer and winter of that under land.
She knew at once some mortal from the world
above had reconnoitered her domain.
She made a lunge at me and held me close
against her scummy scales. Her ugly hands
fumbled the ring-tight meshes of my mail
and found no entrance, but I could not move
or draw my sword, as down we went,
sea-monster[s] gnashed my warshirt with their teeth,
first one and then another charged and crashed,
grappling and hounding me, and I survived.

Three Poems for *Kaddish*

[Sometime in the early 1960's, Lowell began to collaborate with Leonard Bernstein on Bernstein's third symphony, *Kaddish*. Three poems were written before the collaboration was broken off. Bernstein in the end wrote his own text.]

I.

Brothers, we glory in this blinding hour,
our loins are quickened by the heat of power,
we think the sun draws nearer day by day.
All creatures now obey
the motions of our uncreating hands.
Our whole world is a Caribbean sea,
we bake our hearts out on the sands.
We worship thee, Oh bathers' sun,
and in our terror ask if Solomon
in all his beauty was arrayed like thee.

God hung the rainbow in the sky,
the sign of his contrition and our peace.
He knew man's self-dominion would increase.
We need no help from Providence to die.

Because we were forgetful of God's ways,
will he rejoice and watch our planet run
like a black coffin round the sun
with frigid repetitions of his praise?

I think our little span has reached its end,
that henceforth only ruin will regard
the breathless planets and the sun descend
aeons around an earth whose crust is hard.

They ask me to sing a song;
I, the lily of Sharon, the rose of the valleys,

I, the wasted!
How can I sing a new song,
rolled stem and blossom
in this strange land?

Can God destroy us in the act of praise?

II.
Who understands the fierce intelligence
that gazed upon the ancient world and found
nothing but disease and violence
ruled the imagination of its mind?

The heavens opened and the waters roared,
cities and peoples crashed before the flood.
How shall we sing the praises of the Lord,
who looked upon this work and found it good?

Was God sure
that our extinction was our only cure?

Men saw the heavens' open windows pour
destruction on the land for forty days;
from sun to sun, they filled the earth with praise,
but now we know the Lord of Hosts is poor.

Father, we watch creation's downward curve,
and think the fevers of our sickness shake
your old head, and destroy its inner nerve;
the knotted muscles of your forehead break.

Poor little Father, we have stained your grace,
and heaped our coals of conscience on your head,
and now you hardly dare to show your face,
for in our dying, you are surely sad.

Look in our fallible and foolish glass,
your own face stares at you like withered grass!

III.
Winter and darkness settle on the land;
above the river, green, avenging ice
advances and resumes its old command,
our north and south poles hold us in a vise.
The sun has dropped, and there is nothing here
but frozen fishermen whose lanterns burn
above the ice-holes. Listen, you will hear
the saber-tooth and mastodon return,
dazed monarchs of this arctic wilderness
they rule with shaggy, crushing stubbornness.

The sun has dropped. We listen for a sign:
the manna scattered from God's hand like bread,
a pillar of fire to show our path and shine,
a hero with a rainbow on his head.
No, none of these. The sun has dropped. We must
suffer the silence of the dead machine,
whose self-repairing wheels need no unseen
mechanic, when they grind us into dust.
The system runs on its own steam. The clock-
maker has no surprises for the clock.

Yet still we stand and sing into the cold,
and trust we never can annihilate
the old, established order of the world;
we know that by creating we create.
Poor little Father, are you looking down
on us without volition to resist?
Our hands have turned creation on its head.
Oh Father, do not bite your lip and frown;
it hardly matters now if we made God,
or God made us. Both suffer and exist.

The Seasons

I stood, Augustus's statue—both my hands
upraised, palms up, as if to catch the rain,
gave weight and measure to my happy lands—
a king's touch, for each motion of my brain
gave some sick subject his supreme desire.
Out on the lake, an island lay afire
with swarming roses, burnished orchard trees,
boughs weighed by yellow apples to the ground.
I, Dionysus in an arbor, charmed
the nymphs and graces dancing without sound.
Out on the lake the coupled swans were drunk;
my handclap made them plunge; out there a head,
drinking the sacred, sobering water, sank.
A sunk
body kept tossing on its bed
of mud. This world, my world—
Oh sick of heart! I felt the winter freeze
the sunshine into ice. The seasoned shades
of fruit-trees in the autumn sunset fled.
The roses had departed on the wind,
the roses had departed to despair—
swans plunging through my mind,
the clatter of their feathers in the wind.

Diffugere Nives

(Horace, Book IV, 7)

The snow flies, green comes back to the fields,
trees cluster into leaf,
and earth accepts vicissitude;
the loud river shrinks to its banks.

The Grace and her twin sisters
dance naked again—
hope for nothing, the year warns us,
and the hour that seizes our day.

The hard soil softens in spring rain, spring
trampled down by summer, itself about to die;
then appley autumn throws away its fruit,
soon winter comes inert.

Moons change, the world repairs its loss;
but we? When we go down
to Father Aeneas and Rome's peasant kings,
we are dust and shadow.

Who knows if the live season will add
a tomorrow to today?
All you spend on your sympathetic soul
will tantalize your inheritor's warm hands.

When you have died and splendid Minos
summons you to justice;
then, Torquatus, neither your birth,
eloquence or piety will give you back your life.

Diana couldn't rescue her chaste
Hippolytus from the infernal shades;
nor was Theseus able to loose Pirithoos
from his oblivious chains.

Vivamus

(Catullus, 5)

These severe rumors—
but let us live and love.
Our brief light
is not like the sun
able to die one day
and rise the next.
For us, the night
is compulsory and forever.

Then give me a thousand kisses,
then a hundred, then a hundred,
then a thousand, then . . .
We'll grow confused,
we have so many on our hands.
The malicious,
having no sum,
will imagine a Guinness record.

Balloon

It takes just a moment
for the string of the gas balloon
to tug itself loose from the hand.

If its string could only be caught in time
it could still be brought down
become once more a gay toy
safely tethered in the warm nursery world
of games, and tears, and routine.

But once let loose out of doors
being gas-filled the balloon can do nothing but rise
although the children who are left on the ground may cry
seeing it bobbing out of human reach.

On its long cold journey up to the sky
the lost balloon might seem to have the freedom of a bird.
But it can fly only as a slave
obeying the pull to rise which it cannot feel.

Having flown too high to have any more use as a plaything
who will care if it pays back its debt and explodes
returning its useless little pocket of air
to an uncaring air it has never been able to breathe.

Fragment

[The final stanza of an unfinished poem that Lowell was working on the week before he died]

Christ,
may I die at night
with a semblance of my faculties,
like the full moon that fails.

APPENDIX VII:

"After Enjoying Six or Seven Essays on Me"

(Robert Lowell's Final Essay on His Work)

☙

I am not an authoritative critic of my own poems, except in the most pressing and urgent way. I have spent hundreds and hundreds of hours shaping, extending and changing hopeless or defective work. I lie on a bed staring, crossing out, writing in, crossing out what was written in, again and again, through days and weeks. Heavenly hours of absorption and idleness . . . intuition, intelligence, pursuing my ear that knows not what it says. In time, the fragmentary and scattered limbs become by a wild extended figure of speech, something living . . . a person.

I know roughly what I think are my better poems, and more roughly and imperfectly why I think they are; and roughly too, which are my worst and where they fail. I have an idea how my best fall short. To have to state all this systematically, and perhaps with controversial argument, would be a prison sentence to me. It would be an exposure. But which is one's good poem? Is it a translation? Can one write something that will sing on for years like the sirens, and not know it?

Reading other critics on me, as I have the pleasure of doing here,* gives me the surprise of seeing my poems through eyes that are not mine. Younger, older . . . refreshingly different and perhaps keener eyes . . . mercifully through the eyes of another, for a poem changes with each inspection. Variability is its public existence. Yet variety has limits; no one could call *Macbeth* or my *Quaker Graveyard* hilarious minuets. That would take an insensately amusing theorist.

Politics? We live in the sunset of Capitalism. We have thundered nobly against its bad record all our years, yet we cling to its vestiges, not just out of greed and nostalgia, but for our intelligible survival. Is this what makes our art so contradictory, muddled and troubled? We are being proven in a sort of secular purgatory; there is no earthly paradise on the horizon. War, nuclear bombs, civil gangsterism, race, woman—the last has always been the writer's most unavoidable, though not only, subject, one we are too seriously engaged in to be fair, or . . . salvationists.

It seems our insoluble lives sometimes come clearer in writing. This happens rarely because most often skill and passion are lacking, and when these

Salmagundi, Spring 1977.

are not lacking it happens rarely because the goddess Fortuna grudgingly consents. It is easier to write good poems than inspired lines.

Influences: I assume this is a live subject. When I began to publish, I wrote literally under the rooftree of Allen Tate. When I imitated him, I believed I was imitating the muse of poetry. When I erred, I failed, or accidentally forced myself to be original. Later, I was drawn to William Carlos Williams and Elizabeth Bishop. I can't say how much I hope I learned. Yet I differed so in temperament and technical training (particularly with Williams) that nothing I wrote could easily be confused with their poems. How many poets I wish I could have copied, the Shakespeare of *The Winter's Tale*, the Wordsworth of the *Ruined Cottage*, the Blake of "Truly my Satan . . . ," the Pound of the best Pisan Cantos. Baudelaire? Hardy? Maybe I have. The large poet of the nineteenth century who attracts and repels us is Robert Browning. Who couldn't he use, Napoleon III, St. John, Cardinal Manning, Caliban? He set them in a thousand meters. Nor was his ear deficient—take the opening of *Andrea del Sarto*, hundreds of lines of *Christmas Eve*, all of the *Householder*, most of *Mr. Sludge the Medium*. And yet Browning's idiosyncratic robustness scratches us, and often his metrical acrobatics are too good. One wishes one could more often see him plain, or as he might have been rewritten by some master novelist, Samuel Butler or George Eliot, though not in her Italian phase. Yet perhaps Browning's poems will outlast much major fiction. Meanwhile he shames poets with the varied human beings he could scan, the generosity of his ventriloquism.

Looking over my *Selected Poems*, about thirty years of writing, my impression is that the thread that strings it together is my autobiography, it is a small-scale *Prelude*, written in many different styles and with digressions, yet a continuing story—still wayfaring. A story of what? Not the "growth of a poet's mind." Not a lesson and example to be handed to the student. Yet the mind must eventually age and grow, or the story would be a still-life, the pilgrimage of a zombie. My journey is always stumbling on the unforeseen and even unforeseeable. From year to year, things remembered from the past change almost more than the present.

Those mutilating years are often lenient to art. . . . If only one's selected poems could keep their figure like Madame Bovary!

I haven't said what I wished to write in poems, the discordant things I've tried. It isn't possible, is it? When I was working on *Life Studies*, I found I had no language or meter that would allow me to approximate what I saw or remembered. Yet in prose I had already found what I wanted, the conventional style of autobiography and reminiscence. So I wrote my autobiographical poetry in a style I thought I had discovered in Flaubert, one that used images and ironic or amusing particulars. I did all kinds of tricks with meter and the avoidance of meter. When I didn't have to bang words into rhyme and count, I was more nakedly dependent on rhythm. After this in the *Union Dead*, I used the same style but with less amusement, and with more composition and stanza-structure. Each poem was meant to stand by itself. This stronger structure would probably have ruined *Life Studies*, which would have lost its novelistic flow. Later on in *For the Union Dead*, free verse subjects seemed to melt away, and I found myself back in strict meter, yet tried to avoid the symbols and heroics of my first books. After that I wrote a long sequence in Marvell's eight line four foot couplet stanza. God knows why, except that it seemed fit to handle national events. Indeed the stanza was a Godsent task that held me almost breathing couplets all one summer and deep into the next autumn. Shine compensated for the overcompression. For six years I wrote unrhymed blank verse sonnets. They had the eloquence at best of iambic pentameter, and often the structure and climaxes of sonnets, with one fraction of the fourteen lines balanced against the remaining fraction. Obscurity and confusion came when I tried to cram too much in the short space. Quite often I wasn't obscure or discontinuous. I had a chance such as I had never had before, or probably will again, to snatch up and verse the marvelous varieties of the moment. I think perfection (I mean outward coherence not inspiration) was never so difficult. Since then, I have been writing for the last three years in unrhymed free verse. At first I was so unused to this meter, it seemed like tree-climbing. It came back—gone now the sonnet's cramping and military beat. What I write almost always comes out of the pressure of some inner concern, temptation or obsessive puzzle. Surprisingly, quite important things may get said. But sometimes what is closest to the heart has no words but stereotypes. Stereotypes are usually true, but never art. Inspired lines from nowhere roam through my ears . . . to make or injure a poem. All my poems are written for catharsis; none can heal melancholia or arthritis.

I pray that my progress has been more than recoiling with satiation and disgust from one style to another, a series of rebuffs. I hope there has been increase of beauty, wisdom, tragedy, and all the blessings of this consuming chance.

AFTERWORD:

On "Confessional" Poetry

Because Robert Lowell is widely, perhaps indelibly associated with the term "confessional," it seems appropriate and even necessary to discuss how "confessional" poetry is not confession. How Lowell's candor is an illusion created by art. He always insisted that his so-called confessional poems were in significant ways invented. The power aimed at in *Life Studies* is the result not of accuracy but the illusion of accuracy, the result of arrangement and invention.

Life Studies, *Heart's Needle* (both 1959), *Kaddish* (1960) and then *Ariel* (1965) generated a flood of unvarnished poems about family that M. L. Rosenthal christened "confessional." Lowell winced at the term. It implies helpless outpouring, secrets whispered with an artlessness that is their badge of authenticity, the uncontrolled admission of guilt that attempts to wash away guilt. Or worse: confession of *others'* guilt; litanies of victimization. But there is an honorific meaning to the word *confession*, at least as old as Augustine's *Confessions*: the most earnest, serious recital of the events of one's life crucial in the making of the soul. Candor in the *Confessions* is not simply self-laceration, not covert self-promotion or complaint. Bad "confessional" poems breathe the air of the Saturday confession box or the rituals of talk therapy, rather than Augustine.

The problem that Lowell faced at the end of "Life Studies" is how to end a work that has no obvious narrative conclusion. How to make, in Dr. Johnson's words at the end of *Rasselas*, a "Conclusion in Which Nothing Is Concluded." Films usually end biography with a triumphant public event, a reversal of the hero's losses: Marjorie Lawrence sings Isolde again; Jolson performs again to cheers, after years of silence. The little room of four poems that Lowell made at the end of "Life Studies" substitutes crystallization, concentration, emblem for the assertion of triumph.

The final section of the book *Life Studies* is a sequence of poems also titled "Life Studies." The shape of this sequence is my subject.

The sequence is divided into two numbered parts. This is a striking, decisive act: the two parts are of very unequal length. There are eleven poems in part one (the first is six pages), and only four in part two (none more than two pages). Part one is organized chronologically: there are large gaps in elapsed time between poems, but the forward movement of time underlies the whole. Part one begins in childhood and ends with the adult Lowell's emergence from a mental hospital. This generates no note of triumph. The final line of the entire section of eleven poems is: "Cured, I am frizzled, stale and small."

The first poem of part two immediately announces that it is not placed here simply because it is the next stage of autobiography: for the only time in the sequence, Lowell explicitly breaks chronology. (He is forty-one at the end of part one, but forty now.)

Part two as a whole exists in a kind of suspended time. The forward movement of time doesn't determine the relation of the four poems to one another. The first and last ("Memories of West Street and Lepke" and "Skunk Hour"), though located in specific settings, are synoptic, are overviews. They frame two short poems ("Man and Wife" and "To Speak of Woe That Is in Marriage") that thematically make a kind of unit, locked together as two sides of the same thing.

"Memories of West Street and Lepke" contrasts the poet's present, the bewilderingly "tranquilized *Fifties*," with his youth, his "seedtime." The world then was charged with intensities (he was jailed as a conscientious objector, after "I made my manic statement"), but no less opaque. The poem ends with an image of the imprisoned Lepke:

> Flabby, bald, lobotomized,
> he drifted in a sheepish calm,
> where no agonizing reappraisal
> jarred his concentration on the electric chair—
> hanging like an oasis in his air
> of lost connections. . . .

In this passage the voice of the poem suddenly imagines the inner life of Lepke: in a world of "lost connections," the electric chair appears "like an oasis." But the syntax drifts and floats as the poet imagines Lepke drifting and floating. Is it the electric chair that is "hanging like an oasis," or Lepke himself and his world "full / of things forbidden the common man"? Lowell's temporary identification with Lepke unnerves. The final words, "lost connections," resonate through the entire sequence like summary, like prophecy: the sequence too is both *drifting* and *concentrated*.

"Skunk Hour" dramatizes, perhaps for the first time in the history of lyric, the moment when the mind sees, acknowledges its insanity: "My mind's not right." The focus of "Memories of West Street and Lepke" is time, retrospect; here the territory is place, community, the world of a small Maine town. In this town the poet can make breezy insider jokes ("we've lost our summer millionaire") but more deeply is a voyeur, an outsider. "My mind's not right" triggers an abyss of self-loathing that possesses the grandeur of self-knowledge, the afflatus/stoicism of Satan: "I myself am hell." Then immediately this is undercut: "nobody's here— //only skunks . . ." In the final image, the skunks who rule the night ("They march on their soles up Main Street") refuse to scare when discovered in their world of garbage:

> I stand on top
> of our back steps and breathe the rich air—
> a mother skunk with her column of kittens swills the garbage pail.
> She jabs her wedge-head in a cup
> of sour cream, drops her ostrich tail,
> and will not scare.

When I first read these lines, the final lines of the book, the mother skunk's *not* scaring seemed itself scary: an emblem of how the world resists the poet, refusing to be shaped or bent by his needs and will. Now I think that the opposite is more true. The consciousness of these poems has not "scared" before experience, before events in the poet's life that poetry traditionally has found impossible to handle as fact, as autobiography. The skunks are "moonstruck," *lunatic* like the poet. Like the skunks, the poet surveys, is kept alive by, feeds on the fallen world that he is and has found.

"Man and Wife" and "To Speak of Woe That Is in Marriage," placed between "Lepke" and "Skunk Hour," are mirror-images of one another. First the husband, then the wife speak not of marriage in general, but of their specific marriage. The two titles, however, insist on generality: the two poems together allow the reader to peer beneath the surface of a daguerreotype labelled "Man and Wife." At the end of each poem, the *other* partner in the marriage looms over the person who speaks—enormous, engulfing, impossible to move or deflect. She is the Atlantic Ocean breaking over the head of her husband. He is an elephant stalled over his wife. Within the body of each poem, their plights are different; the range of tones is very different; but the final parallel images suggest a terrible equilibrium.

Lowell has shaped the structure of part two, then, in this way: poems one and four (both overviews) stand like pylons or plateaus framing two short poems that mirror each other as two unreconciled but joined sides of the same thing. The structure feels "free-standing"; unlike part one, part two does not thrust the reader *forward* in chronological time. Everything is more densely emblem. The reader has the sensation of conclusion, within a structure where identification with skunks is the closest thing to new wisdom, or triumph.

Lowell in his *Paris Review* interview with Frederick Seidel says that the illusion of "reality" in a "confessional" poem *is an aesthetic effect*. Seidel: "These poems, I gather from what you said earlier, did take as much working over as the earlier ones." Lowell's response:

> They were just as hard to write. They're not always factually true. There's a good deal of tinkering with fact. You leave out a lot, and emphasize this and not that. Your actual experience is a complete flux. I've invented facts and changed things, and the whole balance of the poem was something invented. So there's a lot of artistry, I hope, in the poems. Yet there's this thing: if a poem is autobiographical—and this is true of any kind of autobiographical writing and of historical writing—you want the reader to say, This is true. In something like Macaulay's *History of England*, you think you're really getting William III. That's as good as a good plot in a novel. And so there was always that standard of truth which you wouldn't ordinarily have in poetry—the reader was to believe he was getting the *real* Robert Lowell.

What fascinates in these sentences is the forthrightness with which Lowell treats the sensation that the autobiographical or historical writer aims at, *This is true*, as an aesthetic effect—as possessing power *because* the writing gives the reader the illusion that it is true. *Life Studies* aims at this effect. The illusion that the poem is not art but a report on life, that the reader is getting "the *real* Robert Lowell," is not a central concern in all of Lowell's books (not central, for example, to *Near the Ocean* or *Lord Weary's Castle*), but lies at the heart of the power of autobiography and history. Art that constantly reminds one that it is art, that it is constructed and could have been constructed in another way, forgoes this power (ideally, for power of another kind).

The "realist" author serves an accuracy that is not the accuracy of fact: Lowell says in the final paragraph of the same interview, "Almost the whole problem of writing poetry is to get it back to what you really feel." That takes, he says, "maneuvering." Here is an example of maneuvering, from

"To Speak of Woe That Is in Marriage":

> It's the injustice . . . he is so unjust—
> whiskey-blind, swaggering home at five.
> My only thought is how to keep alive.
> What makes him tick? Each night now I tie
> ten dollars and his car key to my thigh. . . .

I've taught this poem many times in class, and I always ask the class—why does she tie ten dollars and his car key to her thigh? (I teach at Wellesley College, so this is asked of a group of women.) The answers usually are about evenly divided between the idea that she does this to protect her escape if he again becomes violent, and the idea that she thereby requires sexual intimacy from him before he can escape and (in the words of the poem) "free-lanc[e] out along the razor's edge." Each motive is possible (she fears him; she is fascinated by him), and they are opposites. I don't think that, from the poem, one can know which is true. Does *she* know? Are both true?

I once brought this passage up with Lowell. He smiled rather sheepishly and said that his wife had never done that, that it was told him by the wife of Delmore Schwartz.

Crucial to the texture of a Lowell poem, throughout his career, are these images or actions or *things* that resist a single meaning, that haunt because, dense with meaning, they also elude meaning. Autobiography promises that the walls of a house will dissolve, the veil that separates us from what is real will be at last lifted. In a Lowell poem what the reader is offered with at times startling candor is an invented world dense with the luminous opacity of life.

—F.B.

Notes

Glossary

Chronology

Selected Bibliography

Acknowledgments

Index of Titles

NOTES

The *Notes* provide literary and historical references, cross-references, translations of foreign-language words, and (in our judgment) significant variants. Proper names and places that appear again and again in Lowell are listed in the *Glossary*, or cross-referenced. Alternate published versions of complete poems can be found either here or in the *Appendices*. The *Notes* do not offer interpretations of the poems, though problematic passages trigger exceptions; choice of what to annotate is, of course, itself interpretation. The *Notes* do not attempt to account for all the textual changes that Lowell publicly made. Indeed, as John Unterecker pointed out, "by so publicly reorganizing and revising published work, Lowell made a true *Complete Poems* virtually impossible" (Rudman, xiv). Many fine scholars and critics have written on Lowell's poems. The first book, Hugh B. Staples' *Robert Lowell: The First Twenty Years*, remains one of the most useful. We have stolen from it generously. The pages that follow often rely on the two full-length biographies, by Ian Hamilton and Paul Mariani. For a list of books and collections of essays consulted, see *Selected Bibliography*.

We use Arabic numerals for stanza and line of poem, and Roman numerals for the section (if there is one): 2.1 is stanza two, line one, and III.2.1 is section three, stanza two, line one. For sonnet sequences, we provide sequence title, the number of the particular sonnet (including title if it has one), and line number: "Charles River" 4.5 is sonnet number four, line five of that sequence.

Here are the abbreviations used in the *Notes* when referring to Lowell's books:

LOU	*Land of Unlikeness*
LWC	*Lord Weary's Castle*
MK	*The Mills of the Kavanaughs*
LS	*Life Studies*
IM	*Imitations*
FTUD	*For the Union Dead*
NTO	*Near the Ocean*
HIS	*History*
DOL	*The Dolphin*
FLH	*For Lizzie and Harriet*
SP	*Selected Poems* (revised)
DBD	*Day by Day*
CPR	*Collected Prose*

LORD WEARY'S CASTLE (1946)

The copy-text is the second printing (Harcourt, Brace). Four poems were changed for the second printing, as detailed below.

Lambkin: In the anonymous Scottish ballad "Lamkin," Lord Weary refuses to pay the stonemason Lamkin for building his castle; in revenge for this betrayal, Lamkin kills Weary's wife and child. "Lord Weary's castle is a house of ingratitude, failure of obligation, crime and punishment" (Berryman, 288). (For a Homeric parallel, see opening note to "The Death of the Sheriff" p. 1024.) Lamkin asks the child's nurse to fetch a basin to catch the wife's blood; the nurse replies:

> 'There need nae bason, Lamkin,
>   lat it run through the floor;
> What better is the heart's blood
>   o the rich than o the poor?'

> (*The English and Scottish Popular Ballads*, ed. Child [93A])

EPIGRAPH

"Suscipe, Domine . . . innocuos": "Receive, O Lord, these gifts for the commemoration of Thy Saints, that just as their passion made them glorious, so may our devotion free us of sin," from the Secret of the Mass for the finding of the body of St. Stephen Protomartyr, celebrated August 3. St. Stephen (d. c. A.D. 36) was the first Christian martyr, condemned by the Sanhedrin for proselytizing for the new religion; Saul of Tarsus (later, St. Paul) approved of the execution (see Acts 6–7). See "Colloquy in Black Rock" p. 11, and headnote p. 1007.

THE EXILE'S RETURN

The poem uses images and phrases from Thomas Mann's short story "Tonio Kröger" (*Stories of Three Decades*, trans. H. T. Lowe-Porter [1936]). The story begins, "The winter sun, poor ghost of itself, hung milky and wan behind layers of cloud above the huddled roofs of the town. In the gabled streets it was wet and windy and there came in gusts a sort of soft hail, not ice, not snow" (85).

2–3 Hôtel/ De Ville: town hall.
8 Holstenwall: " 'All right; let's go over the wall,' [Tonio] said with a quaver in his voice. 'Over the Millwall and the Holstenwall, and I'll go as far as your house' " (86).
15 The Yankee commandant: The first printing reads, "The bristling podestà" (podestà: Italian for a mayor or local administrative head).
21 Rathaus: Town hall.
24 Lasciate ogni speranza, voi ch'entrate (Abandon all hope, you who enter here); inscription over the Gate of Hell, Dante, *Inferno*, III.9.

THE HOLY INNOCENTS

The Holy Innocents: Herod slaughtered the children of Bethlehem, trying to destroy the infant Jesus; see Matthew 2:16–18. The Feast is celebrated on December 28.

1.1ff The setting of the poem is Damariscotta Mills, Maine, where Lowell lived in the winter of 1945 (Staples, 96); St. Patrick's Church, not St. Peter's (1.6), is nearby.
1.7 "These are they which were not defiled with women; for they are virgin" (Revelation 14:4). (All biblical references are to the King James version, unless otherwise specified.)

2.2 "[I]t out-Herods Herod, pray you avoid it" (Hamlet's instructions to the Players, *Hamlet*, III.ii. 13–14).

COLLOQUY IN BLACK ROCK

Black Rock and its mudflats, Black Mud, are situated near Bridgeport, Connecticut, on Long Island Sound; Lowell lived there after his imprisonment for draft resistance (1944), working "in a Catholic cadet nurses' dormitory, mopping corridors and toilets" (Lowell, *CPR* 279). Bridgeport's large Hungarian population, many of whom worked at the Sikorski helicopter factory, attended St. Stephen's Catholic Church. St. Stephen is Hungary's first king and patron saint; the first Christian martyr, who died by stoning, is also named Stephen (Acts 7:59; see note to Epigraph, 1006). The poem was originally titled "Pentecost." About the composition of this poem, Lowell writes, "I hadn't written a line for a year, and had just come home one evening from mopping floors as a conscientious objector. I was strolling about and staring at the low-tide litter and wishing. That the War were over, and that the [transformative] event in the last stanza would lift me out of my pails of dirty water. Then the lyrical outline came" (Mariani, 116). A Black Rock neighbor writes that Lowell stayed at a "big yellow stucco [rooming] house sitting on the edge of the dump. . . . More often than not the residue of the dump actually came up to the doorstep. What is interesting is that standing on the steps of that house, one was in a position to see the spire of St. Stephen's to the right and the spire of St. Peter's to the left" (letter from Maureen Maguire, *Black Rock News*, 1 Jan. 1978).

2.1 T. S. Eliot (Lowell's editor at Faber) was bothered by "detritus," which makes this a four-beat line; in *Poems 1938–49* (Faber and Faber) Lowell made changes in response to Eliot, as well as other revisions in this and other poems. None of the changes were ever incorporated in later collections.

3.5 A year and a day: Lowell's sentence for refusing the draft, "the extra day making him in the eyes of the law a felon" (Mariani, 108).

5.1 Jesus—who fished for men's souls—walked on the sea (John 6:19).

5.2 kingfisher: A bird with a crested head, identified with "halcyon" (fabled bird "that was supposed to have had the power to calm the wind and the waves during the winter solstice while it nested on the sea," *American Heritage Dictionary*). See the final line of "Domesday Book" in *DBD*, 766.

5.2–3 Corpus Christi: Body of Christ. "Services at St. Stephen's are held in Hungarian, and on the Sunday following Corpus Christi Day the feast is celebrated by a special procession and mass. . . . [T]he 'drum-beat of St. Stephen's choir' is an echo of [a] religious parade" (Staples, 42).

5.4 *Stupor Mundi*: Wonder of the World (epithet of Frederick II [1194–1250], Holy Roman Emperor).

CHRISTMAS IN BLACK ROCK

2.7 Glory to God in the highest (Luke 2:14).

3.9 Furies: spirits of punishment, avenging wrongs, especially those done to kindred.

NEW YEAR'S DAY

The setting of the poem is Damariscotta Mills, Maine.

2.6 church: See note to "The Holy Innocents" 1.1ff, 1006.

2.7 St. Peter, the distorted key: In Matthew 16:19 Jesus says to Peter, "And I will give unto thee the keys of the kingdom of heaven: and whatsoever thou shalt bind on earth shall be bound in heaven: and whatsoever thou shalt loose on earth shall be loosed in heaven."

3.3 *Puer natus est*: [Unto us] a child is born (Isaiah 9:6). Part of the Introit of the Mass for the Feast of the Circumcision (January 1).

THE QUAKER GRAVEYARD IN NANTUCKET

The body of Warren Winslow, Lowell's cousin, was never recovered after his Navy destroyer, *Turner*, sank from an accidental explosion in New York harbor during World War II (Williamson, *Pity the Monsters*, 35, n. 14).

Epigraph: Genesis 1:26 (Douay version).

In 1963, Lowell spoke about *Moby Dick*: "If I have an image for [America], it would be one taken from Melville's *Moby Dick*: the fanatical idealist who brings the world down in ruin through some sort of simplicity of mind. I believe that's in our character and in my own personal character; I reflect that it's a danger for us. It's not all on the negative side, but there's power there and energy and freshness and the possibility of ruin" (Meyers, *Interviews*, 77). He later states, "I always think there are two great symbolic figures that stand behind American ambition and culture. One is Milton's Lucifer and the other is Captain Ahab: these two sublime ambitions that are doomed and ready, for their idealism, to face any amount of violence" (Meyers 105). See Herman Melville's *Moby Dick* (ch. 16): "Some of these same Quakers are the most sanguinary of all sailors and whale-hunters. They are fighting Quakers; they are Quakers with a vengeance." For an early poem titled "To Herman Melville," see 1011. Lowell's comments on this poem quoted below are from a letter to Shozo Tokunaga, his Japanese translator, Jan. 10, 1969, unless another source is specified.

I.1–12 See "The Shipwreck," chapter one of Thoreau's *Cape Cod* (1864): "I saw many marble feet and matted heads as the clothes were raised, and one livid, swollen, and mangled body of a drowned girl . . . the coiled-up wreck of a human hulk, gashed by the rocks or fishes, so that the bone and muscle were exposed, but quite bloodless,—merely red and white,—with wide-open and staring eyes, yet lustreless, dead-lights; or like the cabin windows of a stranded vessel, filled with sand. . . ."

I.1 Madaket: A harbor on the western shore of Nantucket Island; during college, Lowell spent two summers there.

I.10 dead-lights: Heavy glass portholes.

I.14 barks: " 'bark' means take the bark or skin off" (Lowell).

I.15 Ahab's void: In *Moby Dick*, Ahab is captain of the whaling ship the *Pequod*. " 'Void' is Ahab's death or absence" (Lowell).

I.18 dreadnaughts: "pun on a heavy warship and the literal meaning of the words, implying hubris" (Lowell).

I.19 deity: " 'Deity,' the devil, the god of war" (Lowell).

I.22 earth-shaker: Poseidon, god of earthquakes and of water.

I.22–23 " 'Chaste,' in the sense of inhuman, sterile, 'steel' like a warship" (Lowell).

II.7 Large racing sailboats, called S-boats, sailed from Siasconset, Nantucket Island.

II.11 lead squids: Artificial bait.

III This section did not appear in the first magazine version (*Partisan Review* 12, no. 2 [1945], 170–73), but was included in "Passages from the Quaker Graveyard" (*Partisan Review* 13, no. 1 [1946], 76–78).

III.5 westward: Many editors consider this a misprint for "eastward." "Someone in Nantucket once told me if I kept going east I'd come to Spain (enemy of England) maybe 'westward' should be 'eastward,' but I meant looking west toward New England! You know 'Castles in Spain' are illusory hopes or possessions" (Lowell).

III.7 " 'Eel grass' is grasslike seaweed growing mostly in the shoals, not weeds on ship; 'water-clock' is really the globe, a kind [of] round clock, touched by the hours, changes of season" (Lowell).

III.15 " 'Wooden' etc. a cliché maybe: a simpler less complicated older time. . . . [I]t's also pre-stee[l] ships. Also, stiff" (Lowell).

III.18 Of IS, the whited monster: The magazine version and *LWC* first printing read: "Of Is, the swashing castle." In Exodus 3:14 God, from a burning bush, tells Moses: "I AM THAT I AM"; Gerard Manley Hopkins writes "what Christ is, / . . . IS immortal diamond" ("That Nature is a Heraclitean Fire"); Etienne Gilson writes, "It is because God is beautiful that things are beautiful . . . because He IS that they are" (*The Spirit of Medieval Philosophy* [1936], 133). "I think Lowell also means to retain by the word IS a reference to Christ (*I*esus *S*alvator)" (Staples, 102).

III.19 In the sperm-whale's slick: The first printing reads: "In the monster's slick".

III.24 The *Partisan Review* version ends with three additional lines:

> And the waters overwhelmed us, slick
> And salt went over our souls,
> The waters of the proud went over our souls.

IV.1.1 whaleroad: From the Old English kenning *hrónrad* ("riding place of the whale"); the ocean.

IV.1.10 *Clamavimus*: We have cried. "Out of the depths have I cried unto thee, O Lord" (Psalms 130:1).

IV.2.4 " 'Crabs' maybe Eliot, but I got it from Corbière in a poem about Paris. 'Quaker Grave-yard' began as a translation of that poem, then black turned into blue and nothing but this is left of the original" (Lowell). Cf. Corbière, "Paris Nocturne," stanza 1. This is a translation by Kenneth Koch and Georges Guy:

> —It is the sea: dead calm—and the spring tide
> With a far-off roaring has departed.
> The surge will come back rolling in its noise—
> Do you hear the scratching of the crabs of night?

IV.2.8 "I am poured out like water" (Psalms 22:14).

IV.2.9 The mast-lashed master of Leviathans: "Ahab, who, however, becomes finally lashed to the white whale itself" (Staples, 102). Cf. Odysseus, lashed to a mast as he listens to the Sirens (*Odyssey*, XII).

V Two stanzas first printed as Part V of "Passages from the Quaker Graveyard" (*Partisan Review*) were later revised and retitled "Buttercups" (p. 22). For these lines, see notes to "Buttercups" (1013).

V See *Moby Dick* chapters 61 ("Stubb Kills a Whale") and 67 ("Cutting In").

V.3–4 Woods Hole, Martha's Vineyard: Other launching points for ships.

V.6 Jehoshaphat: In Hebrew, the valley of decision or judgment. "Let the heathen be wakened, and come up to the valley of Jehoshaphat: for there will I sit to judge all the heathen round about. . . . Multitudes, multitudes in the valley of decision: for the day of the Lord is near in the valley of decision" (Joel 3:12, 14). "The valley of judgment. The world, according to some prophets and scientists, will end in fire" (Lowell, "Author's Note," in *Modern Poetry*, ed. K. Friar and J. M. Brinnin [1951], 520).

V.9 "Stubb slowly churned his long sharp lance into the fish, and kept it there, carefully churning and churning" (*Moby Dick*, ch. 61).

V.10 swingle: A wooden, swordlike instrument.

V.15 "When the morning stars sang together, and all the sons of God shouted for joy" (Job 38:7).

V.17 "A red arm and hammer hovered backwardly uplifted in the open air, in the act of nailing the flag faster and yet faster to the subsiding spar" of the *Pequod* as it sank (*Moby Dick*, chapter 135, "The Chase—Third Day").

V.17 In LWC, "Hide,"; according to Lowell, the comma after "Hide" is a consistent misprint (Williamson, *Pity the Monsters*, 42, n.20). "No comma after 'hide'; Jonah a type of Christ, but Christ by my bitter jugglery becomes the whale not the Whaleman" (Lowell).

V.18 Jonas Messias: Jonas Messiah; "for as Jonas was three days and three nights in the whale's belly; so shall the Son of man be three days and three nights in the heart of the earth" (Matthew 12:40).

VI The Carmelite Monastery of Walsingham, in Norfolk, England, was a popular shrine to Mary in pre-Reformation days; it was destroyed in 1538. "The road to the shrine is a quiet country lane shaded with trees, and lined on one side by a hedgerow. On the other, a stream flows down beneath the trees, the water symbol of the Holy Spirit, 'the waters of Shiloah that go softly,' the 'flow of the river making glad the city of God' " (E. I. Watkin, *Catholic Art and Culture* [1947], 177).

VI.1.4 munching: "[T]his word is never used the way I use it. The grass or leaves by the lane could be munched, I guess by some twist I made the lane become its cows" (Lowell).

VI.1.8–10 Shiloah . . . Sion: "or if Sion hill / Delight thee more, and Siloa's brook that flowed / Fast by the Oracle of God" (Milton, *Paradise Lost*, I.10–12). Sion: "The name came to signify God's holy hill at Jerusalem (Psalms 2:6), Jerusalem itself (Isaiah 1:27), and allegorically the heavenly city (Hebrews 12:22, Revelation 14:1)" (*The Oxford Dictionary of the Christian Church*, 1977).

VI.2.6 *Non est species, neque decor*: [There is] neither form nor comeliness. "[H]e hath no form nor comeliness; and when we shall see him, there is no beauty that we should desire him" (Isaiah 53:2). "[T]here is no comeliness or charm in that expressionless face with heavy eyelids" (Watkin, *Catholic Art and Culture*, 177).

VI.2.8 "Nostalgia locates desire in the past where it suffers no active conflict and can be yearned toward pleasantly. History is the antidote to this. . . . Warren Wilson drowns, the Quakers drown, the wounded whale churns in an imagination of suffering and violence which it is the imperative of the poem to find release from, and each successive section of the poem is an attempt to discover a way out. . . . What the Lady of Walsingham represents is past contention. She's just there. The method of the poem simply includes her among its elements, past argument, as a possibility through which all the painful seeing in the poem can be transformed and granted peace. She floats; everything else in the poem rises and breaks, relentlessly, like waves" (Robert Hass, 5; 6; 22–23).

VII The following lines were printed as section VII of "Passages from the Quaker Graveyard" in *Partisan Review*:

> And now that the long smother snaps your spine
> Across Poseidon's shins
> To banquet the disgusting gulls and terns
> Of the debauched Atlantic, Sailor, and spins
> Your green-eyed liquefaction to the sterns
> Of the ships of the line
> At drydock; will the sun,
> Descending, harnessed, harrassed, huge,
> Horse up the ocean, spun,
> In the fiery deluge,
> World-wide? The tide, my cousin, turns again

And the corrosive smoulder of its mould
Burns out the babble of the world's untold
Kyrie in the cordage of your brain,
The knock and knowledge of the rainbow's fouled
And halcyon summer. You are dead and gone
Where loud-mouthed terror howled:
"How slowly time's lubricious feathers move;
O when will the long, dallying day have done
And lend me leave to come unto my love?"

[14 *Kyrie: Kyrie Eleison* (Lord have mercy [upon us], a Greek litany in the Roman Catholic Mass).]

VII.5 shoal-bell: A warning of shallow waters.

VII.8 "Dagon his name, sea monster, upward man / And downward fish" (Milton, *Paradise Lost*, I.462–63).

VII.10 clippers: Clipper ships (the fast sailing ships of the mid-nineteenth century).

VII.11 bell-trap: Bell-shaped fish trap (John Frederick Nims, *The Harper Anthology of Poetry*, 1981, 679) or, according to Anzilotti's conversation with Lowell, the bell or ball discharging the water siphon in a toilet tank (Anzilotti, 64).

VII.17 "I will set my bow in the clouds, and it shall be the sign of a covenant between me and between the earth" (God's promise to Noah not to flood the earth again, Genesis 9:13, Douay version).

Many elements from "The Quaker Graveyard in Nantucket" appeared earlier in this unpublished poem:

TO HERMAN MELVILLE
(From Salem, Mass.)

Here is the whaleroad, Herman, and the King
Who scoured the whalers' bones on sand and shell
And stirred the troubled waters in whirlpools
To send the Pequod packing off to hell
Where Charon stowed it on his ship of fools:
The ocean towering
Hellward upon the white, unshriven whale,
Spouting out blood and water, as it rolls,
Sick as a dog, on these Atlantic shoals;
Clamare de profundis and the sirens wail.

You are the sea, the depths where the high tide
Mutters to its hurt self, mutters and ebbs,
Waves wallow in their wash, go out and out;
Do you hear the kicking of the horseshoe crabs?
The sperm-whale breaching? Its enormous snout,
Wobbling from side to side,
Turns to this setting sun where whirlpools swirl,
Grinding with black waters and white teeth,
To snap up gobbets from this blubber-sheath.
Shall I sheet it with a leper's skin of pearl?

Herman, you sleep and knit your hands. Off-shore,
The whale-boat, tacking for its staved-in ton,
Tilts on a global tornado, all this orb
Of ocean bowls the sick Leviathan,
A snarling ball, harpoon and line and barb,
To our Atlantic shore.
Herman, while Moby Dick, our shield from hell,
Is flapping his fat flukes about his ears,
He thrashes in our tackle and he hears
His gun-blue ticker beating like a silver bell.

He is white oil; unwashed Diogenes,
Lantern in hand, comes here to fill his tubs;
The lubber comes to fish in this white slick;
His skull of guts is but a can of grubs!
The milk-white whale is belly-up. Quick, quick,
Salem is on her knees,
The whale is tossed upon the Devil's horns;
O mast-lashed Master of Jerusalem,
I am poured out like water. Ark of Shem,
Save me from the whale's mouth and the horns of unicorns.

[Houghton Library ms, bMS Am 1905 2048. 1.10 Clamare de profundis: Psalms 130:1. 4.1
Diogenes: See headnote to "Poor Alexander, Poor Diogenes" 1079. 4.9 Shem: Noah's son,
forefather of the Hebrews.]

THE FIRST SUNDAY IN LENT

Lent, the period of penitence between Ash Wednesday and the day before Easter.

I.2.3–5 Bunker Hill, Gettysburg: Revolutionary War and Civil War battlegrounds.
I.2.6 Lüger: German pistol.
I.2.8 The first printing reads: "In a stained print of Waterloo to trap"; the preceding line ends
with no punctuation.
I.3.9 "He will overshadow thee with his shoulders and under his wings shalt thou trust" (from
the Mass for the First Sunday in Lent; see Psalms 91:4).
II.1.9 Ares: Greek god of war, of warlike frenzy.
II.1.9 LWC, "lanes,"; the comma after "lanes" did not appear in the magazine version (Kenyon
Review 13 [1946]).

CHRISTMAS EVE UNDER HOOKER'S STATUE

Joseph Hooker (1814–1879), Union Army general during the Civil War, nicknamed "Fight-
ing Joe"; soon after the disastrous Union defeat at Chancellorsville, he resigned command of
the Army of the Potomac, serving in lesser posts until retirement. His statue is on the south lawn
of the Massachusetts State House. An early version of the poem was published as "The Capital-
ist's Meditation by the Civil War Monument, 1942" (Partisan Review 10 [1943]; for this ver-
sion, see p. 1153), then in Land of Unlikeness revised as "Christmas Eve in the Time of War"
(p. 887).

1.1 blackout: In World War II, during an air raid drill, after warning sirens an entire city was required to extinguish all lights visible to enemy aircraft; in addition, the gilded dome of the Massachusetts State House (1.7), across from the Common (2.6), was overpainted in black.

2.2 his fruitless star: The star of Bethlehem.

2.9 "Or what man of you, if his son asks him for bread, will give him a stone?" (Matthew 7:9).

3.7 Melville (writing about Manassas) in his poem "The March into Virginia" from *Battle-Pieces*: "All wars are boyish, and are fought by boys, / The champions and enthusiasts of the state."

BUTTERCUPS

An earlier version was published as Part V of "Passages from the Quaker Graveyard" (*Partisan Review* 13 [1946], 77).

2.2 Ancrem Winslow: John Ancrum Winslow (1811–1873), American naval officer, commander of the Pacific squadron (1870–1872), and Lowell's maternal ancestor.

2.10 red dragoon: British soldier. See "Waterloo" in *HIS*, 475.

Ancrum Winslow is called Anselm Winslow in the magazine version:

> When you were children, the northeasters ripped
> The rotten canvas from your model-boats
> And Bremen dinghys in Nantucket. What
> You were was camouflaged in spangled coats,
> But the blank salvos of Versailles had stripped
> You in their bluster and your teeth were cut
> On a barbaric broom-pole's butt,
> Churning into your thin
> Blue-blooded chin;
> There was cold steel behind the horseplay. But
> Even your stolid prescience sensed the time
> Was ripe to take a broom
> And clear this room
> Our vestibule to crime:
>
> Recall the shadows its doll-curtains rained
> On Anselm Winslow's ponderous plate from blue
> Canton, the breaking of the haggard tide
> On the gigantic print of Waterloo,—
> The blacks and whites obscurely waterstained
> With a curled scar across the glass. You cried
> To see the Emperor's eagle-standard slide
> From the gloved cuirassier
> Staff-officer
> With golden leaf cascading down his side;
> And a dragoon, his plough-horse rearing, swayed
> Back on his reins to crop
> The buttercup
> Bursting upon the braid.

[1.5 Versailles: Possibly the Treaty of Versailles (1919), ending World War I: the treaty did not, as many thought, bring lasting peace or make standing armies irrelevant. 2.3 Canton: The city in China now called Guangzhou; known for blue-and-white porcelain.]

IN MEMORY OF ARTHUR WINSLOW

An elegy for Lowell's maternal grandfather. See "In Memory of Arthur Winslow" in *LOU*, 862; the first three poems in the sequence "Life Studies" from *LS*, 163–71; and "Phillips House Revisited" in *DBD*, 798. A version of Part I was published as "Death from Cancer on Easter" in *Sewanee Review* 51 (1943), 392.

I.1.2 Phillips House: The private, posh wing of Massachusetts General Hospital in Boston.
I.1.3 crab: The Latin word for crab is "cancer."
I.1.9 coxes: The coxswains of the racing shells.
I.1.10 *resurrexit dominus*: The Lord has risen.
I.2.1 swanboats: Flat pleasure-boats with a front shaped like a swan, their back like a swan's wing and tail; they circle the pond in Boston's Public Garden.
I.2.7 "With seven wounds walks on the waves to bear" (magazine version).
I.2.10 "Where timbers draw no water for the voyager" (magazine version).
II Dunbarton, New Hampshire, where Lowell's maternal ancestors, the Winslows and Starks, are buried. After the first publication of this poem, the cemetery was moved to a different location in Dunbarton; Lowell is buried there. For information on and photo of the Stark cemetery, see Corbett, 156–58, 86. Lowell describes the original cemetery in *CPR*, 348.
II.1.10 Word: In John 1:1, "the Word was with God and the Word was God"; in John 1:14, "the Word became flesh and dwelt among us."
III.1.2 I came to mourn you, not to praise: Cf. Shakespeare, *Julius Caesar* III.ii.71.
III.2.2 Edward Winslow (1595–1655), one of the founders of the Plymouth Colony, three times governor. Winslow "built at Marshfield the first block-house, a structure of heavy timbers used for military defense, with sides loopholed and pierced for gunfire" (Heymann, 290).
III.2.4 the Sheriff: Edward Winslow III (1669–1753), who was "once sheriff for George the Second" (see "Dunbarton" 4.12–14 in *LS*, p. 168); "a high sheriff and a noted silversmith, whose fine silverwork is among the silver most valued by American collectors" (Heymann, 290).
III.2.4 Revere: Paul Revere (1735–1818), silversmith and Revolutionary patriot.
III.2.5 John Stark (1728–1822), Revolutionary War general. Stark "in 1759 founded the New Hampshire township of Starkstown, later renamed Dunbarton" (Heymann, 290).
IV The model for this section is Villon's "Ballade pour Prier Nostre Dame," in which the poet in his mother's voice speaks a prayer to Our Lady. In Lowell's lines, "presumably, in the first stanza, the poet is speaking, but the alteration of the pronoun to the plural in the last line ('lavabis *nos*') indicates a modulation to the voice of Arthur Winslow" (Staples, 97). Later, Lowell did a version of the Villon poem; see "Villon's Prayer for His Mother to Say to the Virgin" in *IM*, 212.
IV.1.3 Bay State: Massachusetts.
IV.1.9 Lazarus: The Lazarus whom Jesus raised from the dead; see John 11.
IV.1.10 "Wash us, and I shall be whiter than snow"; an adaptation of Psalms 51:7, changing the second word of the Vulgate from "me" to "nos" (us).
IV.2.3–5 Trinity Episcopal Church does not show this scene; the lines adapt a passage from the Villon noted above (Fein, 185). See Villon's "Prayer for His Mother to Say to the Virgin" 4.3–6, p. 213.
IV.2.10 Lazarus: The beggar who "died, and was carried by the angels into Abraham's bosom: the rich man also died, and was buried; And in hell he [the rich man] lifted up his eyes, being

in torments, and seeth Abraham afar off, and Lazarus in his bosom. And he cried and said, Father Abraham, have mercy on me, and send Lazarus, that he may dip the tip of his finger in water, and cool my tongue; for I am tormented in this flame" (Luke 16:22–24).

WINTER IN DUNBARTON

"My father" in this poem is Lowell's grandfather, Arthur Winslow. "He was my Father. I was his son" ("Dunbarton" 3.1 in *LS*, 168). For the graveyard, see note to "In Memory of Arthur Winslow" II, p. 1014.

3.5 coke-barrel: A barrel that holds coal.

MARY WINSLOW

Lowell's maternal grandmother (d. 1944), married to Arthur Winslow.

1.7 rigid Charles: The frozen Charles River.
2.9 Glass what they're not: our Copley ancestress: I.e., mirror or reflect "the portrait by John Singleton Copley (who had married a Winslow) of our ancestor, Sarah Waldo" (Stuart, 204; the portrait [titled "Mrs. Samuel Waldo" (Sarah Erving), 1764–65] is reproduced on 226).

SALEM

See "Salem" in *LOU*, 873.

4 Morpheus: The god of dreams.
11 Great Banks: Lowell presumably intends "Grand Banks," the enormous shallow fishing area off Newfoundland.

CONCORD

Site of an opening engagement in the American Revolution (April 19, 1775). For magazine version, see note to "Concord" in *LOU*, 1152. See Emerson's "Concord Hymn."

3 Minute Man: Statue (by Daniel Chester French) of one of the militiamen, ordinary citizens ready to take up arms in a minute, who fought the British in 1775; the statue is at Old North Bridge.
4 ruined bridge: Old North Bridge; see "Concord Hymn" 1.1, 2.3. Walden: Thoreau's pond, near Concord.
9 Heraclitus: Pre-Socratic philosopher who said, "You cannot step into the same river twice" (DK 12).
13–14 For King Philip, see note to "At the Indian Killer's Grave" 1.4 (p. 1021).
14 Cf. "Here once the embattled farmers stood, / And fired the shot heard round the world" ("Concord Hymn" 3–4).

CHILDREN OF LIGHT

"The children of this world are in their generation wiser than the children of light" (Luke 16:8). See "Children of Light," *LOU*, 893.

1 "When all our fathers worshiped stocks and stones" (Milton, "On the Late Massacre in Pied-
mont," 4). "*Stocks and stones* is a little joke on Milton's Piedmontese sonnet—it was the
Catholics according to Milton who were idolators and worshipped stones" (Lowell, letter,
June 26, 1967). See also Jeremiah 2:26–27.

3–5 After a decade in Holland, many English Separatists (their beliefs derived from John
Calvin of Geneva) sailed to Massachusetts on the Mayflower (1620); later they were called
Pilgrims.

5 Serpent's seeds: see note to "At the Indian Killer's Grave" 5.2 (p. 1022).

7 "*Glass houses,* people who live in glass houses shouldn't throw stones etc. of the proverb—
expensive houses later built by [a] plutocratic civilization with sea-views" (Lowell, letter,
June 26, 1967).

9 Cain: Cain was forced by God to wander after killing his brother Abel (Genesis 4:12–14).

REBELLION

The narrative underlying this poem is told in "Anne Dick 1. 1936" (*HIS*, 509); see also, from the
same volume, "Father" (p. 510) and "Mother and Father 1" (p. 511).

18 Dives: Rich man (Latin); commonly used name for the unnamed rich man in the parable of
Lazarus, Luke 16:19–31.

AT A BIBLE HOUSE

9–10 Mennonites are the German-language Protestant evangelical sect working as farmers
in Pennsylvania. Doukabors, a Russian separatist sect living in Canada. Both groups are
fiercely independent and pacifist.

THE DRUNKEN FISHERMAN

For first version, written when Lowell was in college, see note to "The Drunken Fisherman" in
LOU, 1154.

1.3 Jehovah's bow: See note to "The Quaker Graveyard in Nantucket" VII. 17, p. 1011.

5.3 Fisher's: Christ's. "Follow me and I will make you become fishers of men" (Mark 1.17).

5.4 peter: A pun on Peter, the chief Apostle, a fisherman before following Jesus.

5.5 I will catch Christ with a greased worm: "[T]he fish is a symbol of Christ. . . . It came into use
in the second century, but neither its origin nor its meaning have so far been completely elu-
cidated" (*The Oxford Dictionary of the Christian Church*, 514).

5.7 Stygian: See *Glossary* for Styx.

5.8 Man-Fisher: Christ, fisher of men, walked on the sea (John 6:19).

THE NORTH SEA UNDERTAKER'S COMPLAINT

See Pieter Bruegel the Elder's painting, *Gloomy Day* (1565).

3 Weser: A river in northwestern Germany.

10 Angelus: A Roman Catholic prayer recited three times daily, preceded by the ringing of a bell.

11 St. Gertrude's: See note to "The Blind Leading the Blind" 1.10 p. 1023.

12–14 Here is the ending of the magazine version (*The Nation* 162 [1946]):

To wail with the dead bell the martyrdom
Of two more parish priests, the phosphorous
Shriveled to glory when they babbled *fire*.

NAPOLEON CROSSES THE BEREZINA

"The poem pictures Napoleon's forces as they prepare to cross the Beresina River on their way to Moscow, unaware that the same river is to be the scene of their crushing defeat in the retreat from Russia in November, 1812" (Staples, 99). See "Napoleon Crosses the Beresina" in *LOU*, 875, and "Russia 1812" in *IM*, 229.

Epigraph: Matthew 24:28: "For wheresoever the carcase is, there will the eagles be gathered together."

1–4 "Charlemagne's stunted shadow" performs a charade, as Napoleon does crossing the river toward Russia; the "play-canister" holding the chess pieces, though making the "Snowman" shiver, leaves the "Great Bear" of Russia retreating unharmed to its homeland, whose "shades" are left to annihilate invading troops.

13 tumbrils: Crude carts that carried prisoners to the guillotine during the French Revolution.

THE SOLDIER

The source is Dante, *Purgatorio*, V.85–129. In 1289, Dante (a Florentine Guelph) fought the Ghibelline faction, which included Buonconte da Montefeltro, at Campaldino near the Archiano River; Buonconte died there. See "Dante 3. Buonconte" in *HIS*, 454, and "Home" 9 in *DBD*, 825.

1 Magazine version (*Common Sense* 14 [1945]): "In time of war I could not save my skin."
8 Fleeing on foot and bloodying the plain (*Purgatorio*, V.99).
10 "Till Spring he rotted there, and then the flood" (magazine version).

WAR

Based on Rimbaud's "Le mal." See Rimbaud's "Eighteen-Seventy" VIII in *IM*, 268, and "Rimbaud 4. The Evil" in *HIS*, 489.

3 Sire: Napoleon III.

CHARLES THE FIFTH AND THE PEASANT

"This poem is a synthesis of Valéry's 'César' (*Album de vers anciens*) and Titian's portrait of Charles V, Holy Roman Emperor" (Staples, 90). For Charles V and Titian's equestrian portrait, see headnote to "Charles V by Titian" p. 1089.

1.8 Word: See note to "In Memory of Arthur Winslow" II.1.10 p. 1014.
2.6 Ark: Parodic of the peasant's boat. Deluge of the King: "Après moi le déluge" (after me the deluge; Louis XV).

The time of Lowell's poem is the last evening before the battle of Waterloo (1815), as the protagonist waits to join the troops massing against Napoleon. Its source, Rilke's "Letzter Abend" ("The Last Evening"), is set before another battle; it is dedicated to Julie Frelfrau von Nordeck zur Rabenau, whose first husband died in the battle of Königgrätz in 1866. See "Before Waterloo, the Last Night" in *HIS*, 475.

2 Blücher: Gebhard Leberecht von Blücher, Prussian field marshal (1742–1819).
5 Scylla: A sea-monster, living in a cave opposite Charybdis (a whirlpool); she devours sailors, seizing them from passing ships.
10 Abel: See note to "Children of Light" 9 p. 1016.
14 shako: A stiff cylindrical military dress hat with short visor and plume.

FRANCE

From the Gibbet: Cf. Villon's "L'épitaphe Villon" ("Ballade des pendus"). See "Villon's Epitaph" in *IM*, 214.

8 The Bayeux Tapestry, France, depicts William the Conqueror's invasion of England (1066); an embroidery, not tapestry (therefore made with "needles," 7).
12 After Cain killed Abel, "the Lord set a mark upon Cain" (Genesis 4:15).
13 *lebensraum*: Living space. In 1938 Adolf Hitler demanded *lebensraum*, a unified "living space" for all German peoples; this expansionism led to World War II.

1790

In his memoirs, General Thiebault describes Louis XVI, as he walked out early one morning with two companions, killing a spaniel that ran too close to him. "[A]s the animal turned to run to its mistress, the King, who had a large cane in his hand, broke its back with a blow of his cudgel. Then, amid the screams and tears of the lady, and as the poor little beast was breathing its last, the King, delighted with his exploit, continued his walk, slouching rather more than usual, and laughing like any lout of a peasant" (*The Memoirs of Baron Thiebault*, trans. Butler [1896], I, 89–90).

1.1 Maundy Thursday: The Thursday before Easter, celebrating Jesus' institution of the Eucharist; according to tradition, on this day rulers wash the feet of the poor.
2.10 Champ de Mars: Field of Mars (god of war), a military parade ground in Paris.

BETWEEN THE PORCH AND THE ALTAR

Joel 2:17 "Between the porch and the altar, the priests, the Lord's ministers, shall weep, and shall say: Spare, O Lord, spare Thy people" (from the Epistle for the Mass of Ash Wednesday). The Revised Standard Version translates "porch" as "vestibule." See also Jean Stafford's story "Between the Porch and the Altar" (first published in *Harper's*, June 1945).

I.12 Aeneas searching through the burning ruins of Troy (*Aeneid*, II.752ff).
II.1 The farmer: "The statue of the Minute-Man" (Lowell quoted in Staples, 88). Emerson in "Concord Hymn" calls the militiamen "embattled farmers" (1.3). See note to "Concord" 3 p. 1015.
II.8 Never to have lived is best: Sophocles, *Oedipus at Colonus*, 1224. Compare "Heine Dying in Paris" I.13–14 in *IM*, 227.

II.9 Man tasted Eve with Death: "According to ancient tradition, immediately after the fall, Adam and Eve knew that they must die, and they performed the sexual act, these two becoming inextricably intertwined" (George P. Elliott, in Staples, 88).

II.15–16 St. Patrick banished the snakes from Ireland.

III " 'Katherine's Dream' was a real dream. I found that I shaped it a bit, and cut it, and allegorized it, but still it was a dream someone had had" (Lowell, *CPR*, 241–42). "Details" of "Stafford's story . . . recall 'Katherine's Dream' " (Yenser, 334 n.29).

IV According to Lowell, the opening scene takes place in an imaginary Boston nightclub, "in which there is an ice-skating floorshow" (Staples, 88).

IV.25 *Dies amara valde*: Day bitter above all [others]; "the Day" (23) when God "shall come to judge the world with fire." Latin from the Responsory of the Mass on Ash Wednesday. (In the Requiem Mass, this text is not part of the opening "Dies irae" sequence, but appears in "Libera me.") See note to "The Day" 4.4 on p. 1143, and "St. Mark's, 1933" 6.1 on p. 1146.

IV.25–26 Here the Lord / Is Lucifer in harness: "The region where Lucifer is Lord is Hell; in the Bible, harness usually means armor" (George P. Elliott, in Staples, 88).

TO PETER TAYLOR ON THE FEAST OF THE EPIPHANY

Epiphany, celebrated on January 6, commemorates the revelation of the divine nature of Christ to the Gentiles; associated with the Magi, the Wise Men who sought the King of the Jews and found the infant Jesus, bringing him gold, frankincense, myrrh (Matthew 2:1–12).

5 The Whore of Babylon, "with whom the kings of the earth have committed fornication, and the inhabitants of the earth have been made drunk with the wine of her fornication" (Revelation 17:2; see 17:1–5). "The beast that carrieth her, which hath the seven heads and ten horns" (Revelation 17:7); "behold a great red dragon, having seven heads and ten horns" (Revelation 12:3).

7 Magazine version (*The Nation* 162 [1946]): "We glitter: where the little minds recall".

12 this town: Probably Black Rock, Connecticut; there is an airplane factory in nearby Bridgeport (Staples, 106). See "Colloquy in Black Rock" p. 11.

AS A PLANE TREE BY THE WATER

From the Apocrypha, Ecclesiasticus 24:14: "I was exalted like a palm-tree in Engaddi, and as a rose-plant in Jericho, as a fair olive-tree in a pleasant field, and grew up as a plane-tree by the water." In the magazine version (*Partisan Review* 13 [1946], 78), the refrain at the end of each stanza reads: "The flies are on the plane tree in the streets." For reproduction of a manuscript version, see Miehe, 84ff.

1.3 Babel: Babylonian city, where Noah's descendants tried to build a tower (2.5) to reach heaven; as punishment, the words of the builders became incomprehensible (Genesis 11:1–9).

3.4 Massabieille: A grotto near Lourdes, site of St. Bernadette's vision of the Virgin Mary.

3.5–6 The grave / Is . . . swallowed up in Christ: "Death is swallowed up in victory" (I Corinthians 15:54).

3.7 When Joshua's people shouted, the walls of the city of Jericho fell (Joshua 6:20).

3.8–10 The *Partisan Review* version reads:

> To our Atlantic are singing: "Sing, Wall.
> Sing for the exaltation of the King."
> The flies are on the plane tree in the streets.

See "The Crucifix" in *LOU*, 881.

4 hot gates: Thermopylae; see headnote to "The Spartan Dead at Thermopylae" p. 1078.
11 Adam: In Hebrew, Adam means "clay."
13 Temple: The first Temple of Jerusalem was destroyed by the Babylonians in 586 B.C., the stone Second Temple by Roman troops in A.D. 70; thereafter Temple worship ceased.
18 *Via et Vita et Veritas:* "Jesus saith unto him, I am the way, the truth, and the life: no man cometh unto the Father, but by me" (John 14:6).

DEA ROMA

Dea Roma: The Goddess Rome. See "Dea Roma" in *LOU*, 879.

1.2 Tullius: Marcus Tullius Cicero (see note to "Cicero, the Sacrificial Killing" 5, p. 1081). In the Second Triumvirate (43 B.C.), Augustus agreed to Mark Antony's demand that Cicero be killed; after Cicero's execution, his head and right hand were impaled on the rostra (the speaker's platform) in the Roman Forum.
1.4 Brutus bled his forty-six per cent: The pro-Republican assassin of Julius Caesar had, years before Caesar's death, "lent money to the town [of Salamis in Cyprus] at 48 percent interest, and was prepared to go to any length to recover the debt" (*The Oxford Companion to Classical Literature* [1937], 82). The collapse of the Republican cause after Brutus' death at Philippi meant a (temporary) end to civil war.
1.5 *Pax Romana*: The Roman peace.
3.2–3 Maxentius, pagan Emperor of Rome (306–312). Constantine, after seeing in the sky (according to Eusebius of Caesarea) a burning cross inscribed with the words "In this sign thou shalt conquer," in A.D. 312 defeated Maxentius at the Milvian Bridge. In 313 he made Christianity a lawful religion.
3.4 Michelangelo: He designed and supervised the construction of the Dome of St. Peter's Basilica in Vatican City (1546–1564).

THE GHOST

Based on Sextus Propertius' *Elegies* 4.7. Propertius' lover is called "Cynthia" in his four books of poems (her real name was probably Hostia).

2.7 Lethe: The river of forgetfulness in the Underworld; souls that return to earth must first drink from it.
3.4 Rome has seven hills.
3.9 Notus: The southwest wind.
5.1 Pompilia's Chloris: Accused by Cynthia of being a poisoner, as is Nomas (5.4).
5.3 Pluto: See note to "The Mills of the Kavanaughs" 11.13 p. 1027.
5.8 Thracians: People from Thrace, in Asia Minor; considered barbaric outsiders in both Greece and Rome. "[T]heir savage methods of fighting, their human sacrifices, their habits of tattooing and of eating butter, made them appear barbarous to the Greeks" (*The Oxford Classical Dictionary* [1949], 901).
5.8 My golden bust: Cynthia's image in gold.
8.3 Anio: A river rising in the Sabine country and joining the Tiber just north of Rome.

8.5 Herakles: Known for his prodigious strength, simple living, and valor; he also, in a fit of madness, killed his wife and children (in Latin, Hercules).
9.5 dog: Cerberus, the three-headed dog guarding the entrance to Hades.

IN THE CAGE

Lowell was imprisoned for draft resistance, 1943–1944. For background, see note to "Memories of West Street and Lepke" 2.3 on p. 1041. Later version: "In the Cage," *HIS*, 526.

6 "In the poem, prison is seen as a coal-mine. . . . The canaries beating their bars are the canaries that miners used to take down the pit to detect dangerous escapes of gas" (Raban, *Selection*, 164).
10 Black conscientious objector, member of a religious group named "The Israelites." "They had found a text in the Bible which said, 'But I am black though my brother is white.' This convinced them that the people of the Old Testament were Negroes. The Israelites believed that modern Jews were imposters" (Lowell, *CPR*, 362). See note to "The Mouth of the Hudson" 2.2–4 p. 1058.

AT THE INDIAN KILLER'S GRAVE

The "Indian killer" is in part Lowell's ancestor John Winslow, for whom (along with his wife, Mary Winslow) there is a cenotaph (2.18) in King's Chapel Burying Ground, Boston. But the Indian killer of the title is essentially generic, a collective figure—the "Pilgrim fathers" (3.3) whose heritage Lowell ponders in Boston's oldest cemetery, "[t]his garden of the elders" (2.2). For earlier versions of parts of this poem, see "The Park Street Cemetery" (p. 861) and "Cistercians in Germany" (p. 889) in *LOU*.

Epigraph: From Nathaniel Hawthorne's "The Gray Champion" (par. 3) in *Twice Told Tales* (tenses slightly changed).
1.3 Jehoshaphat: See note to "The Quaker Graveyard in Nantucket" V.6 on p. 1009.
1.4 King Philip: Metacomet, chief sachem of the Wampanoags; the colonists called him King Philip. On King Philip's War (1675–1676): "This war, caused by the colonists' territorial expansionism, was the bloodiest of all the wars between the newcomers and native Americans. . . . [T]he leader of the colonists' military forces was Josiah Winslow, commander-in-chief and governor of Plymouth Colony, and Lowell's direct ancestor on his mother's side. . . . Winslow and his men burned villages of men, women, and children, and caused the virtual annihilation of the Narragansetts" (Axelrod, *Life*, 69–70). In 1676 King Philip was killed. "After Philip's body was quartered and decapitated, his head was exhibited on a pole in Plymouth for twenty years. His wife and children were sold into slavery in the West Indies" (Fein, 195).
1.7 An old well in the graveyard is covered by a metal cage. "The diabolical-looking octagonal metal cage has nothing to do with burials; it's a vent shaft for the subway" (Harris and Lyon, *Boston* [1999], 92).
1.11 Grace-with-wings and Time-on-wings: Insignia on the top borders of tombstones.
2.7–8 "The chapel, founded in 1686, was the first Anglican church in Puritan Boston to serve the British officers dispatched to the city by the king. No Puritan would sell land to the crown, so the governor appropriated a corner of the cemetery" (Harris and Lyon, *Boston*, 92).
2.15 The Massachusetts State House has a golden dome.
2.19 John and Mary Winslow: John died in 1674, a year before King Philip's War, so cannot be

among the "veterans" mentioned in Hawthorne's epigraph. The brother of Governor Edward Winslow, he became a wealthy merchant and shipowner; in 1637, helped raise money to support troops fighting the Pequin Indians; in 1638, served on a jury that condemned three white men to death for murdering an Indian; in 1653, served on Plymouth's "Council of War." (Josiah Winslow, his brother Edward's son, was the first commander-in-chief in King Philip's War.) In sum, Lowell chooses as his emblematic "Indian killer" not a famous soldier in the Indian Wars, but a successful Puritan businessman, a "good citizen" whose religious convictions and mercantile habits inevitably led to the near-extinction of New England's Native American tribes. Mary Chilton (later, John's wife) at age 12 was the first female Mayflower passenger to go ashore at Plymouth Rock.

3.5 dragon: At the Apocalypse (see note to "To Peter Taylor on the Feast of the Epiphany" 5 on p. 1019).

3.8ff "The address of King Philip to the Indian killers in the poem is also the address of Lowell to his ancestors" (Fein, 196).

3.16 *raca*: Fool (Aramaic; see Matthew 5:22).

3.20 Your election: Predestination; here, Puritan belief in selection (by the Divine Will) for salvation.

4.1 man-hole: A grave.

5.2 the man who sowed: Like Cadmus who killed a dragon, then sowed its teeth from which an army sprang up. The army fought until only five warriors survived; with these five Cadmus founded Thebes.

5.6 The four writers of the Gospels.

5.8 "The image here of the magical mother twining flowers into the warlock of Philip's severed head—consoling and restoring—is both gothic and poignant" (Bell, 26).

5.8–11 "The 'Cistercians' ['Cistercians in Germany'] wasn't very close to me, but the last lines seemed felt; I dropped the Cistercians and put a Boston graveyard in" (Lowell, *CPR*, 247).

MR. EDWARDS AND THE SPIDER

This poem employs passages from Jonathan Edwards' *Of Insects*, his sermons "Sinners in the Hands of an Angry God" (based on Ezekiel 22:14) and "The Future Punishment of the Wicked." The source of the stanzaic structure is Donne's "A Nocturnal on St. Lucy's Day."

1.1 "[S]o flying for Nothing but their Ease and Comfort they Suffer themselves to Go" ("The Habits of Spiders" in *Of Insects*, written when Edwards was eleven).

2.1 "Art thou in the hands of the great God, who . . . when fixed time shall come, will shake all to pieces?" ("The Future Punishment of the Wicked").

2.9 "Can thine heart endure, or can thine hands be strong, in the days that I shall deal with thee?" (Ezekiel 22:14).

3.2 The underside of the Black Widow, a poisonous female spider, has an hourglass design.

4.1–2 Windsor Marsh is near East Windsor, Connecticut, where Edwards grew up. "You have often seen a spider . . . when thrown into the midst of a fierce flame" ("The Future Punishment of the Wicked").

5.2 Josiah Hawley: Edwards' uncle (see note to line 4, next poem).

AFTER THE SURPRISING CONVERSIONS

"I hope that the source of 'After the Surprising Conversions' will be recognized" (Lowell's Note to *LWC*). The poem is mainly derived from the conclusion to Jonathan Edwards' letter known as "Narrative of Surprising Conversions" (November 6, 1736), describing the religious revival he had led in Northhampton, Mass. The passage begins, "In the latter part of May, it began to be very sensible that the Spirit of God was gradually withdrawing from us, and after this time Satan seemed to be more let loose, and raged in a dreadful manner. The first instance wherein it appeared, was a person putting an end to his own life by cutting his throat." The passage ends, "And many who seemed under no melancholy, some pious persons, who had no special darkness or doubts about the goodness of their state—nor were under any special trouble or concern or mind about anything spiritual or temporal—had it urged upon them as if somebody had spoke to them, Cut your own throat, now is a good opportunity. Now! Now!"

3 Ascension Day is celebrated in May or early June, on the Thursday forty days after Easter.
4 sensible: Evident. A gentleman: probably Edwards' uncle Josiah Hawley, who committed suicide. "The Devil took the advantage, and drove him into despairing Thoughts" (from Edwards' letter).

THE SLOUGH OF DESPOND

The Slough of Despond is near the City of Destruction in John Bunyan's Puritan allegory, *The Pilgrim's Progress* (1678). This poem is a revision of Part I of "Scenes from the Historic Comedy" in *LOU*, 876.

1.4 cynic's lamp: Like that carried by Diogenes. See headnote to "Poor Alexander, Poor Diogenes" on p. 1079.
1.5–6 "Diogenes, in a world denied the objective light of Phoebus Apollo, discovers narcissists where he would find honest men" (Yenser, 15).
3.2–4 the knot: Gordian knot. The legend was that whoever could untie it would gain the empire of Asia; Alexander the Great with his sword cut it, and did.
4.1 I.e., like Jesus (John 6:19).
4.5 bats of Babel: See note to "As a Plane Tree by the Water" 1.3 on p. 1019.

THE BLIND LEADING THE BLIND

"If the blind lead the blind, both shall fall into the ditch" (Matthew 15:14). The poem is inspired by Pieter Bruegel the Elder's painting on this subject, *The Parable of the Blind* (1568).

1.6 Hildesheim: A city in northwestern Germany, with splendid Romanesque buildings, many of which were heavily damaged in World War II.
1.10 St. Gertrude's: "Another of Lowell's imaginary churches—presumably here the edifice which appears in the painting's background" (Staples, 89). St. Gertrude's also appears in "The North Sea Undertaker's Complaint" 11, p. 36.

THE FENS

The Fens are a drained swampland in northeast England confiscated from Catholic monasteries by Henry VIII. See William Cobbett's *Rural Rides*, passage dated April 9, 1830: "To Crowland I went. . . . Here I was in the heart of the fens. The whole country as *level* as the table on which I am now writing. . . . The land is covered with beautiful grass, with sheep lying about upon it as fat as hogs stretched out sleeping in a stye. . . . What a contrast between these and the heath-covered sand-hills of Surrey. . . . *Here* [in the Fens] the grasping system takes *all* away, because it has the means of coming at the value of all: *there* [in Surrey], the poor man enjoys *something*: because he is thought too poor to have anything: he is there allowed to have what is deemed *worth nothing*; but here, where every inch is valuable, not one inch is he permitted to enjoy" (II [1930], 239).

2.5 rack-renting system: The widespread practice of charging exorbitant rent for farming land.
2.7 mast: Nuts accumulated on the ground that serve as food for pigs.
2.9 See the anonymous ballad "The Baily Beareth the Bell Away."

THE DEATH OF THE SHERIFF

Epigraph: "Perhaps you ask what was the fate of Priam?" (*Aeneid*, II.506). King Priam, killed during the fall of Troy, was the son of Laomedon. Laomedon had hired Poseidon, god of the sea, to build the walls of Troy, but then ("like Lord Weary in the ballad" [Staples, 93]) refused to pay him. As Troy fell, Poseidon with his trident broke up the city's walls and foundations. See *Aeneid*, II.506–634.
I *Noli Me Tangere*: Touch me not; Christ's warning to Mary Magdalene (John 20:17). See also Thomas Wyatt's "Whoso List to Hunt" 13, and note to "Flight to New York" 6.12 p. 1139.
I.2.5 tabula rasa: clean slate.
I.3.6 Our aunt, his mother: "This seems to imply that the love affair is incestuous" (Staples, 93); the lovers are cousins of the dead sheriff.
II.1.3 Poseidon is shown destroying the walls of Troy (*Aeneid*, II.608–12).
II.1.9 *Parmachenie Belle*: a variety of fishing-fly for catching trout, named after Lake Parmachenee in Maine.
II.2.5 In *Aeneid*, II.567–69, Aeneas discovers Helen, whose flight to Troy with Paris caused the war, hiding in Troy's ruins near the shrine of Vesta, goddess of the hearth.
II.2.8 Seeing the corpse of Priam, Aeneas fears for his father, wife and son (*Aeneid*, II.560–63).
II.2.9 Banquet Apollo: The gods, not simply the Greeks, have destroyed Troy (*Aeneid*, II.608–18); if Aeneas kills Helen, he can "let" the gods (in revenge for the actions of Laomedon) feed on his family. Her death will "satiate the fire" (II.2.10).
II.3.2 *Pura per noctem in luce*: "in pure radiance, [gleaming] through the night" (*Aeneid*, II.590). In the *Aeneid*, this describes Venus, not Helen; Venus prevents her son Aeneas from killing Helen.
II.3.4 shield: The shield of Aeneas, covered mostly with scenes from future Roman wars (*Aeneid*, VIII.626–728).

THE DEAD IN EUROPE

1.3 Lombard crown: The dominance of the Northern Italian towns once constituting the Kingdom of Lombardy was for centuries in dispute.
1.6 jellied fire: Incendiary bombs, such as the Allies dropped on the city of Dresden during World War II.

WHERE THE RAINBOW ENDS

"Much of the imagery of the poem is taken from the book of Revelation. See especially Revelation 4:7–8; 6 (*passim*); 8:7–9; 9:3; 12:14; 15:6; 19:8–9" (Staples, 107). For the rainbow, see note to "The Quaker Graveyard in Nantucket" VII. 17, p. 1011. For a draft of the poem set not in Boston but Brooklyn, see below.

1.3 slates: Slate gravestones.
1.8 Ararat: Mountain where Noah's ark landed (Genesis 8:4).

1.10 The wild ingrafted olive and the root: See Romans 11:17.

2.2 Pepperpot: Longfellow Bridge, the "salt and pepper" bridge spanning the Charles River between Cambridge and Boston, whose towers resemble canisters used to hold salt and pepper.

2.3 In *LWC*, there is no punctuation at the end of this line; the period appears in *SP*.

2.3–5 In the first printing, line 2.3 ends in a comma, and lines 4–5 read:

> The tree-dabbed suburb where construction mans
> The wrath of God. About the chapel, piles

3.4 the furnace-face of IS: The first printing reads "the furnace face of Is". See "The Quaker Graveyard in Nantucket" III.18, p. 16, and corresponding note, p. 1009.

3.9–10 Stand and live / The dove has brought an olive branch to eat: The dove bringing an olive branch signalled to Noah the end of the Flood (Genesis 8:11). These lines are engraved on Lowell's father's tombstone in Dunbarton, New Hampshire; see note to "In Memory of Arthur Winslow" II, p. 1014.

An early draft of this poem has a different title, and locale:

PENTECOST

We saw the sky as yellow, red and brown,
Not blue, in Brooklyn where the ghetto wore
Its oriental sordor on its sleeve
And the torn hang-dog of the rabbi tore
The crucified and spouting meat. O leave
Our sorrows and bow down,
Gnarled graftings on our patriarchal root;
O seed of Abraham, your daily bread
Is a religion and life from the dead:
The wild, ingrafted olive strangles the true shoot.

The bus has brought us at a turtle's pace,
Where Brooklyn Bridge, ironic rainbow, spans
East River and its seven scorched earth miles,
The City where disintegration bans
The fear of God. And now the bishop smiles,
Light thunders to his face,
We stand with children for the photograph.
The children with their Sabbath-smiles are bold
About this temple where the Dove is sold,
In Brooklyn where St. Patrick is the rainbow's laugh.

In Brooklyn serpents whistle at the cold.
The choir goes up the altar-steps and sings,
"Hosannah to the Lion, Lamb and Beast
Who fans the furnace-face of Is with wings."
We breathe the ether of the marriage-feast;
At the high altar, gold
And bric-a-brac. We kneel and the wings beat
Our cheeks. What can the Dove of Jesus give

You now but Wisdom, Exiles. Stand and live,
The fire-tongued Dove has brought an olive-branch to eat.

[Houghton Library, bMS Am 1905 2058. 1.3 sordor: Physical or moral sordidness. 1.8 seed of Abraham: The Hebrews.]

THE MILLS OF THE KAVANAUGHS (1951)

The copy-text is the second printing (Harcourt, Brace).

THE MILLS OF THE KAVANAUGHS

A synopsis of this long and difficult poem: "[It] is told from the point of view of Anne, a poor girl from a family of thirteen children, who is first adopted by the Kavanaughs and then married to the youngest son, Harry. . . . Joining the Navy prior to Pearl Harbor, her husband returns from the war on the verge of a nervous breakdown; he attempts and fails to suffocate his wife in bed one night because she speaks aloud, while asleep, to a man in a dream; Harry fears that she has committed adultery. Shortly thereafter, greatly distraught, he [dies]. Anne, left alone in the Kavanaugh garden near her husband's grave amid Grecian statuary, reflects on the Kavanaugh myth, their heritage of success and failure, sometimes addressing her dead husband, sometimes not. . . . Ovid's mythological account of Persephone in *Metamorphoses* V [337–571] is brought into play by the poet's use of a four-part organization in imitation of Persephone's circle of seasons. Spring (stanzas 1–7) dates Anne's meeting with Harry; summer (8–15) recalls their courtship; autumn (16–22) reflects the course of their marriage; and winter (23–38) is the season of his manic depression and collapse" (Heymann, 381–82). "The [final] five stanzas record Anne's thoughts as she gets into her boat and rows down the millstream. Her quest for the meaning of her life is a coda that summarizes the meaning of the poem. It is a review of the history of the Kavanaughs, her marriage ('Even in August it was autumn') and her future ('Love, I gave / Whatever brought me gladness to the grave')" (Staples, 58).

The magazine version (*Kenyon Review* 12 [1951], 1–39) "contains numerous allusions to the Virgin Mary and to St. Patrick, who are somewhat unsuccessfully superimposed upon the myth of Pluto and Persephone upon which the whole poem is based. These are all omitted in the later [book] version. . . . Lowell selects those parts of the myth most useful to his purpose, rejects others and subordinates the whole to his own imagination" (Staples, 55, 61).

Lowell radically shortened the poem in *Selected Poems* (1976), reducing it to its final five stanzas. The present text is the original book version. An early manuscript draft was titled "The Kavanaughs of the Mills."

Epigraphs: From Matthew Arnold's poem "Dover Beach" (1867) and William Carlos Williams' book of essays *In the American Grain* (1925).

1.1 Douay Bible: An English translation of the Latin Vulgate, published in Douai, France (1609); also known as the Douay-Rheims Bible; for many years it was the standard Catholic version.

1.4 *Sol*, her dummy: "She pretends that the Bible she has placed in the chair opposite her is her opponent" (Lowell's introductory note).

1.9 Bacchanals: revelers; participants in a Bacchanalia.

2.10 Harding: Warren Harding, U.S. president (1921–23).

2.12 Saco: A river in southern Maine.

2.13 Charles the First: King of England (reigned 1625–1649).

2.14 Hearst: William Randolph Hearst (1863–1951), newspaper magnate and politician, known for his scurrilous "yellow journalism."

3.11 *verboten*: Forbidden.

4.11 Daphne: Huntress pursued by Apollo; she was changed into a laurel tree, which he then worshipped.

6.5 Ceres: Goddess of earth and agriculture; Persephone's mother [Greek name, Demeter].

6.14 her renewal: Persephone's return each year from the underworld signals the spring (see 11.5–6).

6.15 setter: Irish setter.

7.2 the children: Anne and Harry as youngsters (Staples, 57).

8–10 "[A]lthough we may say that Anne is *principally* related to Persephone in the clutches of Pluto as she reconstructs the swimming scene [with Harry] (stanzas 8–10), she is also Cyane whose body melts down to water (*Metamorphoses* V 425–37) and Arethusa yielding to Alpheus after she is turned into a river (*Metamorphoses* V 557–641)" (Staples, 62).

9.6 *Nella miseria*: In misery. From the Paolo and Francesca episode in Dante's *Inferno*, (V. 121–23): "No sadness / Is greater than in misery to rehearse // Memories of joy" (*The Inferno of Dante*, trans. Pinsky [1994], 53). See "Dante 4. Paola and Francesca" in *HIS*, 455.

9.7–12 Adapted from lines excised from the Faber and Faber version of "David and Bathsheba in the Public Garden"; see note I.2.12ff., p. 1030.

11.3 Avernal: In or of Avernus. Avernus is the lake where Hades, driving the chariot that carried the "ambushed" Persephone, opened a passage to the underworld; here, synonymous with the underworld. See *Metamorphoses*, V.420–24.

11.13 Hades: Latin name, Pluto; king of the underworld. He seized Persephone as she was gathering flowers and dragged her down to the underworld, making her queen there. When she ("violated bride" 11.8) ran from him, Hades pursued ("thundered at her heel" 11.14).

13.2 Bowdoin: Bowdoin College, in nearby Brunswick, Maine.

13.13 daub: crude, amateurish painting.

14.16 *Cut down we flourish*: The motto of Lowell's maternal ancestors, the Winslows. Cf. John 12.24: "if [a grain of wheat] dies, it bears much fruit."

15 See "In the Forties 1" in *HIS*, 530.

15.1 fire-dogs: Andirons.

15.2 Hessians: German mercenaries hired by the British to fight the colonials during the War of Independence.

15.8 *praying niggers*: Demotic for the Abenaki Indians (see Lowell's introductory note, p. 73).

15.10 *Miserere*: Musical setting of Psalms 51, which begins, *Miserere mei Deus* (Have mercy on me, O God).

17.4 December: The attack on Pearl Harbor was December 7, 1941.

18.11 Their martyr's rubric: Here, blood-red leaves.

19.2 Thomas Macaulay (1800–1859) wrote *Essay on Clive* (prose), *Lays of Ancient Rome* (verse).

19.5 Lucretia: The noblewoman Lucretia committed suicide after being raped, forcing the expulsion of Tarquinus from Rome (510 B.C.).

19.8 and yet she'd: "she" is Anne.

20.7 The Magi: The three wise men who visited the infant Jesus.

20.14 glüg: A kind of wassail, spiced wine and whiskey ("grain").

27.4 dry-flies: Lures that sit on the water's surface.

29.3 The depressed and paranoid Saul befriended and attacked David (Samuel I and II).

31.7–16 All the references to Harry's suicide that are explicit in the magazine version (*Kenyon Review*) have been excised in the book version. In the end, Harry dies "outside the Church" (37.9), but whether this is because he has literally killed himself is unclear. Harry's desire to die is clear: "You must bury me / As if you gloried in my liberty" (31.9–10).

32.3 Hallows': Halloween. Patience: A game of solitaire.

34 See "In the Forties 2" in *HIS*, 530.

34.12 Adams: John Adams, U.S. president (1797–1801).

34.12 Romish: Roman Catholic.

34.16 The quotation mark ending this stanza was inadvertently left out of all previous printings of the complete text; this was finally corrected in *Selected Poems*.

35.5 Fragonard: Jean-Honoré Fragonard (1732–1806), French rococo painter primarily of romance and garden scenes.

36 See "In the Forties 3" in *HIS*, 531.

36.2–4 Matches are being thrown in the millpond, making "target-circles" near the "bobber" (the float on a fishing line).

37.10 Harry Tudor: King Henry VIII of England broke with Rome and established the Anglican Church; in Catholic eyes, he died "outside the church" (37.9).

38.3 After Napoleon's defeat (Waterloo, 1815), the Bourbon Louis XVIII ruled until his death (1824).

38.3–12 Death: Hades, "God's brother" (38.7) because he is the brother of Zeus (chief of the gods, father of Persephone).

38.8 Death whipped his horses through the startled sod: the moment when Hades in his chariot opens the route to the underworld (see note to 11.3, p. 1027).

38.12 Thracian field: See note to "The Ghost" 5.8 p. 1020.

FALLING ASLEEP OVER THE AENEID

In this poem the dreamlike phantasmagoria of "an old man's" sleep merges with a version of the funeral of Pallas in the *Aeneid*, XI.22–99. The Trojans have arrived in Italy, after the fall of Troy and much deprivation; Pallas is the son of an Italian ally. Pallas has been killed in battle by Turnus, king of the Rutulians, who opposes the Trojan presence in Italy.

5 lictor: An attendant to a magistrate.

7 Ares: The Greek and Trojan god of war, identified by the Romans with Mars.

15 Dido: Queen of Carthage who, in love with Aeneas, killed herself when he sailed for Italy (*Aeneid* IV.663).

17 Punic: Carthaginian.

22 Child of Aphrodite: Aeneas' mother is Aphrodite (Venus).

45 bitter river: Styx.

65 elephants of Carthage: Prefiguring the Carthaginian Hannibal's march on Rome, using elephants (218–211 B.C.).

66 Turms: Troops of thirty or thirty-two horsemen.

76 My Uncle Charles: Lowell's distant cousin, Charles Russell Lowell, killed in the Civil War. In the version from *Kenyon Review* 10 (1948), this line ends with a comma.

77 Phillips Brooks: Brooks (1835–1893) was an Episcopal bishop, minister of Boston's Trinity Church, and an author. Grant: Ulysses S. Grant, Civil War general, later U.S. president.

85 young Augustus: Many Romans, including Virgil, were grateful for the peace the grand-nephew of Julius Caesar brought to the Empire after many years of civil war. When Octavian, after the defeat of Antony and Cleopatra, became Augustus (27 B.C.), he was thirty-six years old.

HER DEAD BROTHER

I.1.1 Lion of St. Mark's: A great winged lion on a clock tower guards St. Mark's Square, Venice; emblem of the power of the Venetian Republic.

I.1.10 Achilles dead: "I would rather follow the plow as thrall to another / man, one with no land allotted him and not much to live on, / than be a king over all the perished dead" (*The Odyssey of Homer*, trans. Lattimore [1967], XI. 489–91).

I.2.4 crocking: Soiling with color.

I.2.5 Sheepscot: A river in southern Maine.

I.2.8 scotching: Crushing.

I.3.3 Stowe: A town in Vermont.

I.3.6 As false as Cressid: Shakespeare, *Troilus and Cressida*, III.ii.183. Cressid (Cressida) was a Trojan woman who pledged fidelity to Troilus, then betrayed him.

I.3.10 Packard: A car.

II.1.5 *Water Witch*: Model ship in a bottle, replica (Yenser, 85) of a boat left in Boston Harbor. It is also the title of James Fenimore Cooper's romantic novel (1830), featuring a small boat called *Water Witch*.

II.2.9 Stygian: Of the Styx.

II.3.5–6 running dead / Before the wind: The wind had been blowing from the stern.

MOTHER MARIE THERESE

The young nun who speaks the poem remembers Mother Marie Therese, drowned Mother Superior of her convent. (The Austrian Empress Maria Theresa [1717–1780] was Marie Antoinette's mother; Mother Marie Therese, also aristocratic, is fictional.) "I don't believe anybody would think my nun was quite a real person. She has a heart and she's alive, I hope, and she has a lot of color to her and drama, and has some things that Frost's characters don't, but she doesn't have their wonderful quality of life" (Lowell, *CPR*, 265).

1 Maris Stella House: Presumably their convent. Maris Stella: Star of the sea.

2 Mother's: The Mother Superior's.

4 Pio Nono: Pope Pius IX (1792–1878).

8 Carthage: A (fictional) nearby coastal town.

18 friends of Cato: I.e., friends of the rulers of this world.

24 Probationers: Those preparing to become nuns.

28 Bourbon: The ruling family of France and Spain.

38 In *The Mills of the Kavanaughs*, this line ends with a comma.

46 Proserpina: Daughter of Zeus and Demeter who, picking flowers, was carried off by Hades and made Queen of the Underworld; Greek name, Persephone. After the intervention of Demeter, she returned to the earth six months each year.

48 Candle, Book and Bell: A phrase signifying the ceremony of excommunication from the Roman Catholic Church; here, the nun expels (half-expels) "flowers and fowling pieces" from her life.

52 Canuck: French Canadian patois.

54 *Action Française*: A right-wing nationalist French daily newspaper.

55 soi-disant: Self-styled; here, the King is pretender to the throne.

57 Bridegroom: When a nun makes final vows, she becomes a Bride of Christ; a gold ring is placed on her finger.

59 Hohenzollern: The ruling family of Prussia and imperial Germany until 1918.

66 An émigrée in this world and the next: Kafka, "The Hunter Gracchus" (Staples, 55).

71 The Feast of (Saint) Louis IX (1214–1270), king of France, celebrated on August 25.

76 Saint Denis' Head and Queen Mary's Neck (81) seem to be Canadian promontories. Although there is a Queen Mary's Church in Herring Neck, Newfoundland, "certainly the geography is fictional; indeed, there is a kind of grisly humor attached to such formations as *St. Denis' Head* and *Queen Mary's Neck*, when the manner of death of St. Denis and Marie Antoinette

is taken into consideration" (Staples, 99). St. Denis (died c. A.D 250) reportedly walked with his head in his hands after his beheading.

83 Montcalm: Louis-Joseph de Montcalm-Gozon, French general who successfully led French forces in the French and Indian War, until 1759, when the British under General James Wolfe (86) defeated him; both Montcalm and Wolfe were killed.

83–84 on Abraham's / Bosom: I.e, in heaven. The site of the battle in which Montcalm and Wolfe were killed is called the Plains of Abraham.

86 The Huron tribe, converted by French Jesuit missionaries in the early seventeenth century, were decimated by the Iroquois in 1649, then dispersed (Jesuit priests [87] were also killed).

95 Boom: Floating barrier of logs.

96 Frontenac: Louis de Buade, Comte de Frontenac (1622–1698), French soldier and twice colonial ruler of New France (Great Lakes region and Eastern Canada); in the first French and Indian War, he attacked Boston.

108 *Contra naturam*: Against nature.

111 Advent: From Latin "Adventus," coming (i.e., of Christ).

128 *venite*: Come! "O come, let us sing unto the Lord" (Psalms 95:1).

129 Cf. the final line of "The Servant" in *IM*, 248: "My nurse's hollow sockets fill with tears."

DAVID AND BATHSHEBA IN THE PUBLIC GARDEN

David, king of Judah and Israel, saw Bathsheba washing herself, then seduced and impregnated her while her husband Uriah the Hittite was away. He tried to establish Uriah as the father of their child, then had him killed in battle, and married her (II Samuel 11:2–27). Lowell raided this poem for "The Public Garden" in *FTUD*, 341.

I.1.9 lion-fountain: The fountain with four stone lions in Boston's Public Garden. The emblem of David's kingdom Judah was the lion.

I.2.2 Levant: Land bordering the eastern Mediterranean.

I.2.12ff In the Faber and Faber *Poems 1938–49*, the following stanza appears between stanzas two and three (stanza two ends with a colon); Bathsheba is speaking:

> I knew these circles after Joab killed
> Uriah in the shock of battle. Sharp
> Arrows transfix me! You will harp
> Of women? We are called
> To succour Israel if his foot shall slide."
> "I knew you from my roof-top: bubbles filled
> Uriah's fountain, and we splashed. We died
> In Adam, while the grass-snake slid appalled
> To summer, while Jehovah's grass-green lyre
> Was rustling all about us in the leaves
> That gurgled by us, upside-down." "Earth grieves:
> Unspeakable the groanings when it catches fire!

II.1.5 Abishag: The servant woman brought in to warm old King David's bed.

II.2.8 Joab: David's general; he later slew Absalom, David's rebellious son.

II.3.9 the harper's fingers: David was a harper.

Based on Werfel's poem "Der Dicke Mann im Spiegel."

2.4 The version in *Poetry* 70 (1947) reads: "The Yellow-fingered King".
3.4 pursey: Short-winded, swollen, heavy, puckered (*OED*).
5.2 meerschaum: A kind of clay, used in making the bowl of a pipe.
6.2 beaver: A visor on a helmet.

THANKSGIVING'S OVER

Lowell radically shortened this poem in *Selected Poems*, reducing it to the opening fourteen lines, followed by the final stanza.

1.3 the El: An elevated train line.
2.4 Christophers: St. Christopher medals, worn as talismans.
3.4 In *The Mills of the Kavanaughs*, there is a comma after "needle-point"; it did not appear in *Partisan Review* 17 (1950).
3.25–26: The stanza break came after "flocks" (rather than "hemlocks") in both the Faber and Faber *Poems 1938–49* and *Partisan Review* versions.
4.8 *Primavera*: Spring; Botticelli's painting *Primavera* (1477–1478) includes Venus and the Three Graces.
4.11 lying-in house: A hospital for giving birth.
4.13 kneeler: A board or cushion for kneeling in prayer.
5.17 *Nein*: no.
6.4 St. Francis of Assisi (1182–1226) once preached to the birds.
6.10 *Come unto us, our burden's light*: Matthew 11:30, "My yoke is easy, and my burden light."
6.15 beads: Rosary beads.
6.16 *Miserere*: Have mercy. From Psalms 51:1: *Miserere mei Deus* (Have mercy on me, O God).

LIFE STUDIES (1959)

The copy-text is the second American printing (Farrar, Straus and Cudahy), which differs in significant ways from the first Faber and Faber edition, published a few months earlier. The English edition did not include "91 Revere Street"; also see "Dunbarton" below. About *Life Studies*, Lowell said in 1964: "I wanted to see how much of my personal story and memories I could get into poetry. To a large extent, it was a technical problem, as most problems in poetry are. But it was also something of a cause: to extend the poem to include, without compromise, what I felt and knew" (Meyers, *Interviews*, 85).
    For Elizabeth: Elizabeth Hardwick.

PART ONE
BEYOND THE ALPS

This poem symbolically encapsulates Lowell's journey from *Lord Weary's Castle* to *Life Studies*. "Crossing the Alps," as early as 1953, is an emblem: reviewing Robert Penn Warren's long poem *Brother to Dragons*, Lowell says that modern poetry "could absorb everything—everything, that is, except plot and characters, just those things long poems usually relied upon." Now Warren "has crossed the Alps and, like Napoleon's shoeless army, entered the fat, populated river bottom of the novel" (*CPR*, 68).

In *For the Union Dead*, Lowell cites Napoleon as the source of the title "Beyond the Alps." (Lowell first uses the phrase in "Falling Asleep over the Aeneid," line 68 [1947].) For other versions of the poem, see Appendix III, p. 927, and *FTUD*, 364. An early draft carries the subtitle "for George Santayana" (Houghton Library, bMS Am 1905 2182).

Prefatory note: *Mary's bodily assumption*: On November 1, 1950, Pope Pius XII "declared it as a matter of divinely revealed dogma that the Blessed Virgin Mary 'having completed her earthly course was in body and soul assumed into heavenly glory,' to deny which would incur the wrath of Almighty God and the Holy Apostles" (*The Oxford Dictionary of the Christian Church*, 949).

1.2 The Swiss made this attempt in 1952.

1.5 O beautiful Rome!

1.7 Life: "Man" in the Faber and Faber version. Lowell returned to "Man" in *FTUD* but retained "Life" in *SP*.

1.8 City of God: Rome. The phrase echoes Augustine's book *The City of God* (A.D. 413–426).

1.13 "I accept the universe": Attributed to Margaret Fuller (1810–1850). Carlyle's reported response: "By God! she'd better." (For Margaret Fuller, see "Margaret Fuller Drowned" in *HIS*, 484.) In *SP*, Lowell replaced "accepted" with "bought".

2.2 San Pietro: The square before St. Peter's Basilica in Vatican City. *Papa*: "Pope" (Italian); "papá" means "father," and was printed in *SP* in error.

2.10 Saint Peter's brazen sandal: Part of the bronze statue of St. Peter in the Basilica, kissed in reverence by the faithful.

2.11 The Duce: Mussolini; caught escaping after his government fell, he and his mistress were gunned down and hanged head downward from a streetlamp in Milan (1945).

2.12 *coup de grâce*: A mortal, killing stroke.

2.13 Switzers: The Pope's official guards, from Switzerland.

3.4 Apollo plant his heels: Phoebus Apollo, the sun god, at dawn.

3.6 Parthenon: A temple honoring Minerva (in Greek, Athena), the "Goddess" of 3.9; she helped Odysseus blind the Cyclops (*Odyssey* IX). "Minerva was the goddess of both arts and war" (Raban, *Selection*, 165).

3.9 Hellas: Greece; here, ancient Greece.

3.10 golden bough: The branch carried by Aeneas that allowed him to pass safely through the underworld (*Aeneid*, VI.136ff).

3.12 Minerva, the miscarriage of the brain: Minerva was born, clothed in full armor, directly from the head of Zeus.

4.1 Now Paris, our black classic, breaking up: The train's destination. Rome was the symbolic home of Lowell's early Roman Catholicism, as well as of the universalist politics underlying the city's ecclesiastical and imperialist past; now Lowell arrives at a new city, "our black classic"—no less violent, but secular, the home of radical, fragmenting political and artistic revolution. (Cf. "exiled here / in Paris, its Black Sea" in "The Swan" 1.7.1–2 in *IM*, 243.)

4.2 "The 'killer kings on an Etruscan cup' are the black-figure paintings on the vases which the Etruscans buried with their dead in ceremonial tombs. Great battles and scenes from mythology were recorded in a frieze around the body of the vase; and the black paint was subsequently scored with an awl to reveal details" (Raban, *Selection*, 166). "Etruscan art, formally dependent upon Greek art, is equally complex for, while the forms are recognizably Hellenized, the underlying spirit still retains a barbaric energy quite opposed to the Greek search for perfection in harmony" (*The New Columbia Encyclopedia*, 1975). Etruscan civilization predated the Roman.

Marie de Médicis (1573–1642), daughter of Florentine banker Francesco de' Medici, in 1600 married Henri IV (1553–1610), king of France and Navarre; her son ruled as King Louis XIII (1610–1643). She was twice excluded from court (1617–1622 and 1631–1642) for attempting to control government policy.

See "The Wife of Henri Quatre 1" and "2" in *HIS*, 463 and 464.

5.2 Finisterre: Literally, "land's end," the promontory of northwest Spain extending into the Atlantic ocean.

5.6 Saint Denis: The royal abbey in the town of Saint-Denis, north of Paris, where most of the kings and queens of France are buried, including Henri IV and Marie de Médicis.

5.7 Carrara: Sculpted from Carrara marble.

INAUGURATION DAY: JANUARY 1953

1.1 Stuyvesant: A square in New York City named after Peter Stuyvesant, Dutch colonial governor who surrendered New Amsterdam to the British (1664).

1.3 El: An elevated train line.

1.8 Cold Harbor: Site in Virginia of Ulysses S. Grant's victory over Robert E. Lee (June 1864); Grant, however, lost five times as many soldiers.

2.4 Ike: Like Grant, Dwight Eisenhower ("Ike") became president of the U.S. after serving as commander of the Army.

2.5 mausoleum: The most popular memorial to Grant is his tomb, in New York City.

A MAD NEGRO SOLDIER CONFINED AT MUNICH

1.2 Kraut DP: German displaced person.

2.2 Koenigsplatz: King's square.

3.2 *Fräulein*: A young woman. Outing shirts: made from outing flannel.

Here is the magazine version of stanzas four and five (*Partisan Review* 20 [1953], 632):

> You are my true-love, though your talk went wrong.
> Thus we are married, child; and when I drew
> You underneath my overturned canoe,
> I hugged you to my heart where toys belong.
>
> Six times I knew you—like a trolley-pole
> Sparking at contact, your electric shock—
> The power-house! . . . The sergeant calls our roll.
> He counts the spoons. We file before the clock,

Part Two
91 REVERE STREET

Lowell lived here with his parents, on Boston's Beacon Hill, from age eight to ten (1925–1927). In 1927 the family moved to 170 Marlborough Street; in 1930 he became a boarding student at St. Mark's School in Southborough, Massachusetts.

121 *ci-devant*: Former; an aristocrat who lost his title in the French Revolution. *Parvenu*: Upstart.

122 motto: Cf. "For the Union Dead" 10.4, p. 377.

122 wandering Jew: Condemned to wander the earth until Judgment Day, for mocking Christ on the day of Crucifixion (medieval legend).

122 *homo lupus homini*: Man [is] wolf to man.

123 *parti pris*: Prejudice or bias.

123 Jordan Marsh: Boston department store.

123 *chasseurs d'Alpine*: Mountain soldiers of the French army.

124 *pro tem*: Short for *pro tempore*: temporary.

124 Brahmin: Member of an old, patrician Boston family.

124 Hub of the Universe: Local nickname for Boston.

125 Tommies: British soldiers.

125 *vino rosso*: Red wine.

126 plebe: Naval Academy freshman.

126 *hors de combat*: Outside the fight or contest; disabled.

127 Siegfried . . . Valhalla: In Richard Wagner's opera tetralogy *Der Ring des Nibelungen* (1853–1874), the body of the German warrior Siegfried is not carried to the stronghold of the gods, Valhalla, by Brunnhilde. In the final opera, Brunnhilde joins Siegfried's body on his funeral pyre; the fire god then travels to Valhalla, which he destroys by flame.

127 Abbé Liszt: Franz Liszt (1811–1886), the most famous piano virtuoso of his time, as well as composer; Wagner's father-in-law. He took minor orders (therefore "Abbé") in 1861.

127 Mother's hero: Siegfried, who kills the dragon guarding the hoard of the Rheingold.

127 Sarah Bernhardt: In 1901 the French stage actress starred in Edmond Rostand's *L'Aiglon*, about Napoleon's son.

129 Ludendorff: Erich Ludendorff (1865–1937), German general and military strategist of World War I.

129 *sturm und drang*: "Storm and stress," German romantic literary movement (c. 1765–1785).

129 Japanese hotel: Frank Lloyd Wright designed the Imperial Hotel (constructed 1916–1922) in Tokyo; it was famous not only for its architectural design but for withstanding the 1923 earthquake.

130 swan boats: See note to "In Memory of Arthur Winslow" I.2.1 on p. 1014.

130 *Ein, zwei, drei*: one, two, three. "*BEER*" rhymes with *vier*, four.

132 pirates' chorus: From Gilbert and Sullivan's *The Pirates of Penzance* (1879).

132 Scollay Square: A shabby area of "tattooing parlors, shooting galleries, and burlesque" (Walter Muir Whitehill, *Boston: A Topographic History*, 1968, 201).

133 my first school: Potomac School, near Washington, D.C.

133 Riverside Press: Publisher and printing house in Cambridge, Massachusetts. Rudy Vallee: American crooner. Hampton Institute: A historically black college in Virginia.

133 Admiral William Sims (1858–1936), American commander of operations in European waters, World War I.

134 *dummkopf*: Blockhead; stupid, foolish.

135 *Beau Geste*: A silent film with Ronald Colman (1926).

136 *in ovo*: Unformed ("in the egg").

137 Sacco and Vanzetti: Italian immigrants to Massachusetts convicted and executed (1927) for robbery and murder; many felt that the evidence was insufficient, and that they were persecuted for being anarchists. Lowell's cousin Abbott Lawrence Lowell, president of Harvard, was asked by the governor of Massachusetts to head a committee to review the case. The committee concluded that Sacco and Vanzetti's trial had been fair; their executions followed.

137 King Log: A fable in which frogs, asking Jupiter for a king, are sent a log. When they complain of its inertness, they are sent a stork, which devours them.

138 Filene's Basement: The discount portion of a department store in Boston.

138 Bill Tilden: tennis champion. Capablanca: José Raúl Capablanca, Cuban chess grand master.

138 Sir Thomas Lipton: British tea merchant and yachtsman (1850–1931). His ships, all named *Shamrock*, raced five times unsuccessfully in the America's Cup sailing race ("Cup Defender races").

138 Harkness: Cf. Lowell, *CPR*, 357.

139 I usually manage: See "Clytemnestra 1" 11–12, p. 431, and corresponding note, p. 1077.

140 Mahan: Alfred Thayer Mahan (1840–1914), American naval officer, influential naval historian.

140 skipper a flivver: Be the commander of (drive) an old or cheap car.

142 *climacteric*: See note to " 'To Speak of Woe That Is in Marriage' " 13 p. 1045.

143 remember the *Maine*: Rallying cry of the Spanish-American War, prompted in part by the blowing up of the U.S. destroyer *Maine* (1898).

143 cigar-chawing: Amy Lowell smoked cigars.

143 *Patterns*: Amy Lowell's most famous poem.

143 *outrée*: Eccentric.

143 the Duse: Eleonora Duse (1858–1924), celebrated Italian actress.

144 *cits*: Citizens, i.e., civilians.

144 broking gangs: Stockbrokers.

144 Harkness: "With [Harvard President Abbott Lawrence] Lowell's encouragement a New York oil magnate, Edward S. Harkness, donated $12 million to Harvard . . . for the establishment of seven Georgian residence centers" (Heymann, 44).

144 Bull Moose Party: Theodore Roosevelt's Bull Moose Party, formally called the Progressive Party (1912), advocated many social reforms.

144 Curley: Four-time Mayor James Michael ("Boss") Curley ran the Irish political machine in Boston.

144 Bolshies: Bolsheviks, the Communist forces who won the Russian Revolution (1917).

144 Béla Kun-Whon: Hungarian Communist leader (1886–1937); he ruled Hungary for four months in 1919.

144 Etretat: A town on the Normandy coast of France.

144 "The Croix de Guerre": The War Cross, French medal given for outstanding military service.

144 *vers de société*: Urbane, ironic verse.

144 "Tommy" Atkins!: Harkness has turned "Admiral Ledyard Atkinson" into the generic name given to the regular British soldier (originally the fictitious name used in sample forms for privates in the British army; therefore British soldiers are "Tommies").

145 Somerset Club: An exclusive men's club on Beacon Hill.

147 Oyez: Hear ye!

147 *bête noire*: Someone or something especially disliked or avoided.

148 *coup de théâtre*: An unexpected, dramatic event that overturns the given.

148 patroon: A landholder (under the original Dutch system) in New York.

148 Robert Livingston: A patrician New York lawyer and diplomat (1746–1813), minister to France who helped negotiate the Louisiana Purchase (1803).

PART THREE
FORD MADOX FORD

Lowell served informally as Ford's personal secretary (August–September 1937). In 1962, Lowell wrote: "Something planned and grand, and something helter skelter and unexpected seemed to come together in this poem. I thought for a long time I would never catch the tone and the man; now I think I have perhaps" (*Poet's Choice*, ed. Engle and Langland [1962], 164). See "Ford Madox Ford" and "Ford Madox Ford and Others" in *HIS*, p. 515 and 516.

1.2 birdie: In golf, for any hole, one stroke under par.

1.3 Lloyd George: David Lloyd George (1863–1945), prime minister of Great Britain (1916–1922).

1.5 Hueffer: Ford Madox Ford's original surname; his father was a German music critic, Francis Hueffer. After serving with the British Army in World War I (during which he was gassed and shell-shocked), in 1919 he changed "Hueffer" to "Ford." Niblick: Nickname for a nine iron, inappropriate for putting.

1.14 Georgian Whig magnificoes: Aristocrat reformers.

1.15 Somme: French battleground in World War I, as were Nancy and Belleau Wood (1.18).

1.34–35 Washington Square and Stuyvesant Square, New York City.

1.41 Brevoort: A hotel in New York, frequented by artists. In Dutch, "voort" means "ford" (shallow place where a body of water can be crossed).

FOR GEORGE SANTAYANA

George Santayana (1863–1952), philosopher, novelist, poet. Born in Spain, educated largely in the United States, Santayana taught philosophy at Harvard from 1889 until 1912, when he returned to Europe. "I used to visit George Santayana in 1950 and 1951 in Rome. He was just under ninety, I was just over thirty. He took a fancy to my craggy, dark, apocalyptic poetry because I was both an old Bostonian and an apostate Catholic" (Lowell, *CPR*, 205). Before they met, Santayana praised Lowell's poems; there was an extensive correspondence between them. For Lowell's brief essay on Santayana, see *CPR* 205–6. The magazine version of "Beyond the Alps" contains passages that became part of this poem (see Appendix III p. 927, and note p. 1157).

1.11–14 Santo Stefano Rotondo is the church on the grounds of the convent of the Blue Sisters of the Little Company of Mary, in Rome. Santayana lived in a nursing home attached to this convent.

2.3 Ser Brunetto: See headnote to "Brunetto Latini" p. 1072.

2.3–5 These lines are based on Dante's *Inferno*, XV.121–24; see "Brunetto Latini" 120–23 in *NTO*, 416, and "Dante 1" in *HIS*, 453.

2.7 Alcibiades: Handsome, traitorous Athenian soldier and politician, who professes his love for the philosopher Socrates in Plato's dialogue *The Symposium* (215b ff). As implied by the references both to Brunetto Latini and to Santayana's "long pursuit" of Alcibiades, Santayana was homosexual.

2.9 fleeting virgins: Like Daphne, who when pursued by Apollo was changed into a laurel tree (as a wreath, once conferred on poets, heroes, victors).

2.15 galleys: Printer's proofs.

TO DELMORE SCHWARTZ

The time of this poem is the year that Lowell and his wife Jean Stafford lived with Delmore Schwartz in Cambridge, Massachusetts. In later years Schwartz's mental problems increasingly alienated him from friends and jobs. A few days after Schwartz's death in 1966, Lowell wrote to Elizabeth Bishop that 1946 had been

> an intimate gruelling year . . . Jean and he and I, sedentary, indoors souls, talking about books and literary gossip over glasses of milk, strengthened with Maine vodka. . . . Delmore in an unpressed mustard gaberdine, a little winded, husky-voiced, unhealthy, but with a carton of varied vitamin bottles, the color of oil, quickening with Jewish humor,

and in-the-knowness, and his own genius, every person, every book—motives for everything, Freud in his blood, great webs of causation, then suspicion, then rushes of rage. He was more reasonable then, but obsessed, a much better mind, but one already chasing the dust—it was like living with a sluggish, sometimes angry spider—no hurry, no motion, Delmore's voice, almost inaudible, dead, intuitive, pointing somewhere, then the strings tightening, the roar of rage—too much, too much for us! Nothing haunts me more than breaking with friends. I used to think he was the only one I broke with. (Mariani, 134)

For a later poem on Schwartz, see "In Dreams Begin Responsibilities" in *HIS*, p. 533.

2.16–17 "Freude" in German means "joy."

2.25–26 Schwartz is quoting and changing lines from Wordsworth's "Resolution and Independence": "We Poets in our youth begin in gladness; / But thereof come in the end despondency and madness" (48–49). After reading Lowell's poem, Schwartz wrote to Lowell that he had looked up what he had written in 1946: "We poets in our youth begin in sadness / But thereof come, for some, exaltation, / ascendancy and gladness" (Mariani, 475, n.93).

2.27 In 1946, Stalin had not yet suffered cerebral hemorrhages.

WORDS FOR HART CRANE

Hart Crane: American poet (1899–1932).

1.8 *Catullus redivivus*: Catullus restored to life.

An earlier version of this poem was titled "Epitaph of a Fallen Poet" (*Partisan Review* 20 [1953], 39):

> When England gives the laurel to some dope
> Or screw who scrubs Catullus' tongue with soap,
> Perhaps he will consider why I took
> This crooked turn, instead of Uncle Sam's
> Good offices that only health can buy.
> Because I knew my classics like a book,
> Stranger from England, tell the British: I,
> *Catullus Redivivus,* once the rage
> Of Rome and Paris, used to play your role
> Of homosexual wolfing the stray lambs
> Who hunger by the Place de la Concorde.
> My profit was a pocket with a hole.
> Who asks for X, the Shelley of the age,
> Must pay pound sterling for his bed and board.

PART FOUR: LIFE STUDIES
MY LAST AFTERNOON WITH UNCLE DEVEREUX WINSLOW

" 'Rock' was my name for Grandfather Winslow's country place at Rock, Massachusetts. An avenue of poplars led from the stable to the pine grove. . . . The letter paper at Rock bore the name 'Chardesa,' taken from the names of my grandfather's three children—Charlotte [Lowell's mother], Devereux, and Sarah" (*CPR*, 359–60). Devereux was "named for the North Carolina

Devereuxs on their mother's side" (Mariani, 28). For the prose genesis of this poem, see *CPR*, 359–61.

I.1.5 Fontainebleau: town on the Seine, with former royal residence. Mattapoisett: "Fashionable summer watering spot" (Mariani, 34), on Buzzards Bay, southern coast of Massachusetts. Puget Sound: inlet of the Pacific, Washington State ("Father['s] ten years' dream of moving from Boston to Puget Sound," *CPR*, 354).

I.1.8 Norman: "Just like those poplars one sees in Normandy, was [Lowell's] explanation" (Anzilotti, 64).

I.2.7 root-house: A half-sunken storage shed for root vegetables and bulbs.

I.2.12 silver mine: See headnote to "Grandparents," p. 1039.

I.2.13 *Stukkert am Neckar*: Stuttgart, Germany, on the Neckar River.

III. For drafts of this section, see Axelrod, *Life*, 247. Here is the magazine version of part III from *Botteghe Oscure* 23 (1959), 207–8:

> Up in the air,
> by the sunset window in the billiards-room,
> my Great Aunt Sarah
> was learning the *Overture to the Flying Dutchman,*
> and thundered on the keyboard of her dummy piano.
> With gauze skirts like a boudoir table,
> accordion-like, yet soundless,
> it had been bought to spare the nerves
> of my Grandmother Winslow,
> tone-deaf, quick as a cricket—
> now grousing through a paper-bound *Zola*, and saying:
> "Why does Sally thump forever
> on a toy no one can hear?"
>
> Forty years earlier,
> twenty, auburn-headed, a virtuoso
> wept over by Liszt,
> Aunt Sarah, the Winslows' only "genius,"
> had lifted her archaic Athenian nose,
> and jilted an Astor.
> Each morning she had practiced
> on the grand piano at Symphony Hall,
> deathlike in the off-season summer—
> its naked Greek statues draped with purple
> like the saints during Holy Week . . .
> On the concert day, Miss Winslow could not appear.
>
> Now her investments were made by her Brother.
> Her career
> was a danger-signal for the nieces.
> High above us,
> Aunt Sarah lifted a hand
> from the dead keys of the dummy piano,
> and declaimed grandly:
> "Barbarism lies behind me;
> mannerism is ahead."

III.1.4 Great Aunt Sarah (Winslow), the sister of Lowell's grandfather, Arthur Winslow.

III.1.6 dummy piano: A soundless piano for practicing.

III.1.12 "Auction": Auction bridge.

III.1.15 Tauchnitz: Inexpensive editions of American and British authors.

IV.1.7 troubling the waters: "For an angel went down at a certain season into the pool, and troubled the water" (John 5:4).

IV.2.9 Mr. Punch: Cartoon figure from the cover of the London satiric magazine *Punch, or, The London Charivari*.

IV.2.11 *La Belle France*: France personified as the toga-clad figure of a woman.

IV.2.18 veldt: Open country. The poster depicts a scene from the South African Boer War (1899–1902), between the British and the Dutch-descended Afrikaners.

IV.3.8 Agrippina: mother of Nero, murdered by Nero. "I would beg my Uncle Devereux to read me more stories about that Emperor, who built a death barge for his mother, one that collapsed like a bombarded duck blind!" (*CPR*, 361).

IV.3.9 Golden House: Nero's Domus Aurea, palace built after the great fire of Rome (A.D. 64).

DUNBARTON

In the Faber and Faber edition (published before the American), the present first stanza is printed as the final stanza. For information on the graveyard, see note to "In Memory of Arthur Winslow" II on p. 1014. For a related poem, see "Two Farmers" in *HIS*, 500.

7.5 fauve: Violent, intense colors (as used by the Fauvist painters, 1898–1908).

GRANDPARENTS

Lowell's maternal grandparents: "Arthur Winslow [was] a six-foot self-made millionaire who had gone as a youth to Stuttgart, Germany, instead of to Boston Latin, for his schooling. . . . Back home, he went west to Colorado as a mining engineer to rip his fortune from the mountains, marry Mary Devereux of Raleigh, North Carolina, and return east" (Mariani, 28).

1.9 Pierce Arrow: An elegant large automobile.

1.13 "They Are All Gone into the World of Light!," title and first line of a poem (1655) by Henry Vaughan.

2.6 the song "Summertime," from the opera *Porgy and Bess* by George and Ira Gershwin and DuBose Heyward (1935).

2.8 *Ancien Régime*: The old order (term for the aristocracy overturned by the French Revolution).

COMMANDER LOWELL

Lowell's father, the third Robert Traill Spence Lowell. "At twenty, Bob had graduated Annapolis with the class of '07. He was an engineer, a sliderule man, a wizard in math and the nascent science of radio" (Mariani, 30).

Lowell said of the genesis of this poem: "[W]hen I was writing *Life Studies*, a good number of the poems were started in very strict meter, and I found that, more than the rhymes, the regular beat was what I didn't want. . . . ['Commander Lowell'] is largely in couplets, but I originally wrote perfectly strict four-foot couplets. With that form it's hard not to have echoes of Marvell. That regularity just seemed to ruin the honesty of sentiment, and became rhetorical; it said, 'I'm a poem'—though it was a great help when I was revising, having this original skeleton. I could keep the couplets where I wanted them and drop them where I didn't; there'd be a form to come back to" (*CPR*, 243).

1.7–8 The archduchess Marie-Louise Hapsburg married Napoleon in 1810.

4.9 Menninger: Karl Menninger (1893–1990), psychiatrist and author.

4.13 *à la clarté déserte de sa lampe*: "In the deserted light of his lamp"; adapted from Stéphane Mallarmé's poem "Brise Marine." The passage, in Roger Fry's translation, reads:

> Nothing, not old gardens reflected in eyes
> Will keep back this heart that is plunged in the sea
> O nights! Nor the deserted light of the lamp
> On the empty paper which its whiteness protects
> Nor even the young woman suckling her child.

(Staples, 91)

5.12 Yangtze: River in China; Lowell's father served there during the Chinese Civil War (Mariani, 30).

TERMINAL DAYS AT BEVERLY FARMS

Beverly Farms, a seaside town on Boston's North Shore.

FATHER'S BEDROOM

See *CPR*, 355, for another version of this scene.

FOR SALE

4–10 See *CPR*, 354, for another description of this cottage.

SAILING HOME FROM RAPALLO

Rapallo: Resort on the Italian Riviera, where Charlotte Winslow Lowell died. For Lowell on his mother's last days, see *CPR*, 349–50, and Hamilton, 202–3.

2.2 Gulf of Genoa.

2.6 *spumante*: Sparkling wine.

2.9 *Risorgimento*: A style characteristic of the period of Italy's national revival, national consolidation (mid-nineteenth century); heavy, showy, with much sculpted detail.

2.10 the *Invalides*: The army mausoleum housing Napoleon's tomb in Paris.

3.16 *Occasionem cognosce*: Recognize the opportunity, or, more colloquially, "Seize your chance."

4.4 *panettone*: A tall, sweet Italian holiday bread. Lowell writes that his mother's body "shone in her bridal tinfoil" (*CPR*, 350); Mariani claims that "her body [was] wrapped in cellophane" (22). Anzilotti gives a paraphrased exchange between himself and Lowell: "The *panettone* that we know in Italy is not wrapped in tinfoil. Perhaps [Lowell] meant *panforte?* Yes, this is what he had in mind, the dark and hard Sienese panforte I had sent him as a Christmas present" (64).

DURING FEVER

2.8 Triskets: Triscuits, thrice-baked crackers.
3.1ff For a prose version, see *CPR*, 355–56.
3.9 *putti*: Cupid-like children in Italian art.
4.3–8 Lowell describes this scene in *CPR*, 297–98.

WAKING IN THE BLUE

For an early draft of this poem, see Hamilton, 244–46. For Lowell's prose about another psychiatric hospital (Payne Whitney Clinic), see *CPR*, 346–63 *passim*.

1.1 B. U.: Boston University. A draft of the poem was seen by Donald Junkins while Lowell was a patient at McLean's, mid-December 1957; during this period Lowell taught in the B.U. English Department, and Junkins was his student (Mariani, 262).
1.3 *The Meaning of Meaning*: A book co-authored by critic I. A. Richards and linguist C. K. Ogden. A draft of this poem used instead *Semantics and Social Relations* (Houghton bMS Am 1905 2539).
1.8 Cf. John Crowe Ransom, "Winter Remembered": "A cry of Absence, Absence, in the heart" (3).
3.1 McLean's: A private psychiatric hospital in Belmont, Massachusetts.
3.3 Porcellian: An exclusive student club at Harvard College.

HOME AFTER THREE MONTHS AWAY

2.2 In 1954, when Lowell was confined in a Cincinnati hospital, Elizabeth Hardwick wrote to him from New York: "I hope you are feeling well. We all think of you constantly, darling, and long to have 'Richard himself again so that we may resume the even tenor of our ways.' (I've never learned where that comes from or even if it is correctly quoted.)" (April 19, 1954). Lowell may also possibly have known this passage from Colley Cibber's adaptation of Shakespeare's *Richard III* (V.3.118–121).

> Hence babbling Dreams, you threaten here in vain;
> Conscience avant, *Richard's* himself again:
> Hark! the Shrill Trumpet sounds, to Horse, away,
> My Soul's in Arms, and eager for the Fray.

2.4 levee: A reception held by an eminent person upon rising from bed.
3.1 "Consider the lilies of the field, how they grow; they toil not, neither do they spin" (Matthew 6:28).

MEMORIES OF WEST STREET AND LEPKE

For an unpublished draft of the poem, see below.

1.4 "hardly passionate Marlborough Street": "William James once gave his classes this example of understatement: 'Marlborough Street is hardly a passionate street'" (letter from Lowell to W. C. Williams, April 19, 1957).
2.2 seedtime: "fair seed-time had my soul" (Wordsworth, *The Prelude*, I.301).
2.3 C.O.: Conscientious objector. Lowell refused to register for the armed services in 1943 and

was jailed for five months in Danbury, Connecticut, after spending ten days in New York City's West Street Jail. In an interview twenty-five years later, Lowell said to V. S. Naipaul: "I was a Roman Catholic at the time, and we had a very complicated idea of what was called 'the unjust war.' This policy of bombing German cities seemed to be clearly unjust. So I refused to go to the army and was sent to jail" (Mariani, 106). For Lowell's public letter announcing his refusal to register, see *CPR*, 367–70.

3.2 At West Street, Louis "Lepke" Buchalter (the head of Murder Incorporated) and two extortion racketeers from a theatrical union, William Bioff and George Browne, were imprisoned. Browne had earlier been convicted of pandering. Buchalter (1897–1944) was convicted of murder in 1941, and electrocuted three years later. "Lepke" is from the Yiddish word "Lepkeleh" ("Little Louis").

4.7 *Murder Incorporated*: The public nickname for Lepke's "murder for hire" syndicate. As inmate Jim Peck recalls, "Lowell was in a cell next to Lepke, you know, Murder Incorporated, and Lepke says to him: 'I'm in for killing. What are you in for?' 'Oh, I'm in for refusing to kill.' And Lepke burst out laughing" (Hamilton, 91). Peck's story may be apocryphal, mistaking Robert Lowell for fellow war-resister Lowell Naeve; see Philip Metres, "Confusing a Naive Robert Lowell and Lowell Naeve: 'Lost Connections' in 1940s War Resistance at West Street Jail and Danbury Prison," *Contemporary Literature*, vol. 41 #4, pp. 661–692.

4.13 lobotomized: Metaphorical; Buchalter was not physically lobotomized.

4.15 agonizing reappraisal: A phrase made famous by John Foster Dulles, President Eisenhower's secretary of state (1953–1959). "[H]is insistence upon the establishment of the European Defense Community (EDC) threatened to polarize the free world, when in 1953 he announced that failure to ratify EDC by France would result in an 'agonizing reappraisal' of the United States' relations with France" (*Encyclopaedia Brittanica*).

Here is a draft of this poem:

MY SEASON IN HELL
(West Street Jail, 1943)

Though I cannot reread my manic statement,
Telling off the state and president,
And sent to all my relatives and friends,
Once for months my head rang with the glory
Of my refusal to serve in the army.
I was as if levitated to transcendence, when
I sat waiting sentence in the bull pen
Beside a negro boy with curlicues
Of marijuana in his hair.
My short sentence was a year.
An extra day, though, was given me
To make my trespass a felony.

On the roof of the West Street Jail is a short
Enclosure like a children's soccer court—
Here once a day I watched the Hudson River
Through sooty, home-made, barbed entanglements
And faded khaki-colored tenements.
There, the New York Bundists, four and four,
Marched with unjaded esprit de corps.

Their rounds were like Gran[d]pa's constitutionals on the Charles.
Their leader looked quite like King Charles—
He had a black van dyke,
And a stiff upper lip that seemed to quiver
Silhouetted against the ruined Reich.
His second in command,
More of a Sancho Panza,
Used to play American jazz on the jail piano—
Like a catbird, though,
That warbles perfect thrush, then spoils the show
With a great crested fly-catcher's *ach, ach,*
He would eventually fart and bang out Bach.

Lepke was softer,
A slumping, inconspicuous man.
In his little hour
Ruling with a Himmler's dispassionate, vicarious power,
His genius had made *Murder Incorporated* work
Its ass off liquidating in New York.
Now he was on the shelf and spared
Our cruel traumas of self-analysis.
No wife's visit, or discussions with Jehovah's Witnesses
Jarred his concentration on the electric chair
That hung like an oasis in his air
Of lost connections. Perhaps he had pull—
His barren, little cell was full
Of things forbidden the common man:
A portable radio, a dresser, two toy American flags
Tied together with a ribbon of palm.
He drifted in a sheepish calm,
And looked like myself,
Grown flabby, bald and lobotomized.
His job was piling towels on a rack.
He was easily recognized.
Prisoners kept pointing out his back.
His cell door hung open like a loose grin.
Usually, nobody bothered to lock him in.

Houghton Library ms, bMS Am 1905 2203

[*My Season in Hell*: echoing the title of Arthur Rimbaud's poem in prose and verse *Une saison en enfer* (1873). 2.6 Bundists: American pro-Nazi paramilitary group, most of whose members were of German descent; it disintegrated after America entered World War II. 2.9 King Charles: Probably Charles I of England—cf. the portrait by Anthony Van Dyck (1635). 2.14 Sancho Panza: pragmatic, buffoonish servant in *Don Quixote* (1605). 2.16 Catbird: A songbird that imitates the calls of other birds. 3.4 Himmler: Heinrich Himmler (1900–1945), Hitler's second in command, head of the SS. 3.5 *Murder Incorporated*: next to this line Lowell wrote "like General Motors".]

1.1 *Miltown*: a popular tranquilizer in the 1950s.
1.17 the Rahvs: Philip Rahv, editor of the *Partisan Review,* and his wife, Nathalie.

Here is an early draft of this poem, entitled "Holy Matrimony":

> At last the trees are green on Marlborough Street,
> Blossoms on our Saucer Magnolia ignite
> Now for their feverish five days' white. . . .
> Last night I held your hands, *Petite,*
> Subtlest of all God's creatures, still pure nerve,
> Still purer nerve than I,
> Who, hand on glass
> And heart in mouth,
> Outdrank the Rahvs once in the heat
> Of Greenwich Village, and sat at your feet—
> Too boiled and shy
> And poker-faced to make a pass,
> While the shrill verve
> Of your invective scorched the solid South.
>
> That time is gone; we've lost
> The *thirties'* single talent for seeing red
> On every issue everywhere;
> The Trotskyite, the Stalinist,
> MacLeish's *irresponsibles* . . . even F.D.R.
> Is gone;
> Nothing has come instead;
> Though now the South is casus belli for
> A civil war,
> My Nashville Tennessee Agrarian
> Masters are teaching metrics in the Middle West.
>
> On [a] warm spring night though, we can hear the outcry,
> If our windows are open wide,
> I can hear the South End,
> The razor's edge
> Of Boston's negro culture. They as we
> Refine past culture's possibility,
> Fear homicide,
> Grow horny with alcohol, take the pledge . . .
> At forty why pretend
> It's just the others, not ourselves, who die?
>
> You turn your back,
> Sleepless, you hold
> Your pillow to your hollows like a child,
> Your merciless Racinian *tirade*
> Breaks like the Atlantic on my head:

"It's the injustice . . . you are so unjust.
There's nothing accommodating, nice or kind—
But *What can I do for you?* What can I do for you,
Shambling into our bed at two
With all the monotonous sourness of your lust,
A tusked heart, an alcoholic's mind,
And blind, blind, blind
Drunk! Have pity! My worst evil
Is living at your level.
My mind
Moves like a water-spider . . .
The legs stick and break in your slough.
Why prolong our excruciation now?
What is your purpose. Each night now I tie
Ten dollar

Houghton Library, bMS Am 1905 2204

[The manuscript ends here. Hamilton reproduces this draft (265–66), but omits the second stanza. 2.5 MacLeish: Archibald MacLeish (1892–1982), poet, playwright, lawyer, Librarian of Congress, and assistant secretary of state. 2.5 *irresponsibles*: In *The Nation* (May 18, 1940; published as a small book the same year) Archibald MacLeish characterized the intellectuals of the 1920s and 1930s as "The Irresponsibles," because they failed to anticipate or meet assaults on Western culture from the right and the left. 2.8 casus belli: An occasion that justifies war. 2.10 Agrarian: A group of Southern writers who decried the industrialization of the American South and advocated a return to older values; it included poets John Crowe Ransom, Allen Tate, and Robert Penn Warren, Lowell's teachers and friends. 4.4 Racinian: see note on "Dolphin" 1.2, p. 1139.]

"TO SPEAK OF WOE THAT IS IN MARRIAGE"

The title is from the Wife of Bath: "Experience, though noon auctoritee / Were in this world, is right y-nogh for me / To speke of wo that is in mariage" (opening of "The Wife of Bath's Prologue," Chaucer, *The Canterbury Tales*). The epigraph is a spliced quotation from Schopenhauer's *The World as Will and Idea*, trans. Haldane and Kemp [1909]:

[I]s not the definite determination of the individualities of the next generation a much higher and more worthy end than those exuberant feelings and supersensible soap bubbles of theirs? . . . For it is the future generation, in its whole individual determinateness, that presses into existence by means of those efforts and toils ("The Metaphysics of the Love of the Sexes," vol. 3, ch. 44, p. 342).

" 'To Speak of Woe That Is in Marriage' . . . started as a translation of Catullus's *siqua recordanti benefacta* [LXXVI]. I don't know what traces are left, but it couldn't have been written without Catullus" (Lowell, *CPR*, 254). For an early draft, in which "Man and Wife" and " 'To Speak of Woe That Is in Marriage' " were part of the same poem, see "Holy Matrimony," p. 1044–45. When first published (*Partisan Review* XXV [1958]), the poem was not enclosed in quote marks.

13 climacteric: A period or critical moment when physiological changes take place in the body; here, the male equivalent of menopause.

Lowell writes: "The dedication is to Elizabeth Bishop, because rereading her suggested a way of breaking through the shell of my old manner. Her rhythms, idiom, images, and stanza structure seemed to belong to a later century. 'Skunk Hour' is modelled on Miss Bishop's 'The Armadillo.' . . . Both 'Skunk Hour' and 'The Armadillo' use short line stanzas, start with drifting description, and end with a single animal." The setting is Castine, "a declining Maine sea town [near Nautilus Island]. I move from the ocean inland" ("On 'Skunk Hour,' " *CPR*, 226). Lowell's essay discusses other sources, poems by Hölderlin and Annette Droste-Hülshoff; the essay as a whole is of extraordinary interest, but too long to be reproduced here.

Axelrod (*Life*, 247) prints a draft.

3.6 Lowell writes that the "red fox stain" is "meant to describe the rusty reddish color of autumn on Blue Hill, a Maine mountain near where we were living. I had seen foxes playing on the road one night, and I think the words have sinister and askew suggestions" (*CPR*, 229).

5.1–6 Lowell: "This is the dark night. I hoped my readers would remember John of the Cross' poem ['The Dark Night of the Soul']. My night is not gracious, but secular, puritan, and agnostical. An Existential night" (*CPR*, 226).

5.2 Tudor Ford: A two-door sedan (Ford named the four-door model the Fordor).

5.2 the hill's skull: Golgotha, the hill where Jesus was crucified, is Hebrew for "skull" (from the shape of the hill).

5.3 I watched for love-cars: Lowell writes that the anecdote of "watching the lovers was not mine," but "about Walt Whitman in his old age" (*CPR*, 228). In the early 1970s, Elizabeth Bishop told Frank Bidart that the source of the anecdote was Logan Pearsall Smith's *Unforgotten Years* (1939):

> Almost every afternoon my father would take Walt Whitman driving in the Park; it was an unfailing interest to them to drive as close as they could behind buggies in which pairs of lovers were seated, and observe the degree of slope towards each other, or "buggy-angle," as they called it, of these couples; and if ever they saw this angle of approximation narrowed to an embrace, my father and Walt Whitman, who had ever honored that joy-giving power of nature symbolized under the name of Venus, would return home with happy hearts. (99)

6.2 careless Love: The blues song "Careless Love" has many verses; we have no information regarding which version or performance Lowell might have had in mind. Here is a verse recorded by Big Joe Turner in February 1941:

> Love, O Love, O careless Love . . .
> You worried my mother until she died
> You caused my father to lose his mind
> You worried my mother until she died
> You made my father lose his mind.

6.3 "The 'sob in each blood-cell' is meant to have a haggard, romantic profilish exaggerated quality—true, but in the rhetoric of destitution, here the more matter of fact descriptive style gives out, won't do, and there's only the stagey for the despair. Then one leaves it for the skunk vision. Most people take the skunks as cheerful [but] they are horrible blind energy, at the same time . . . a wish and a fear of annihilation, i.e., dropping to a simpler form of life, and a hopeful wish for that simpler energy" (Lowell, letter to John Berryman, March 18, 1962; Mariani 491, n.66).

6.5 "Which way I fly is hell; my self am hell" (Satan, in Milton's *Paradise Lost*, IV.75).

Regarding the ending Lowell writes, "Somewhere in my mind was a passage from Sartre or Camus about reaching some point of final darkness where the one free act is suicide. Out of this comes the march and affirmation, an ambiguous one, of my skunks in the last two stanzas" (*CPR*, 226).

IMITATIONS (1961)

The copy-text is the second Farrar, Straus and Cudahy printing, with corrections from *The Voyage & other versions of poems by Baudelaire* (1968); from the second Faber and Faber edition of *Imitations* (new edition, 1971); and from *Poets on Street Corners* (ed. Olga Carlisle, 1968).

INTRODUCTION

12 I have tried to write alive English: Cf. Dryden's "Dedication" of his verse translation of Virgil's *Aeneid* (1697): "I have endeavour'd to make *Virgil* speak such *English*, as he wou'd himself have spoken, if he had been born in *England*, and in this present Age." In his 1680 essay on "Ovid and the Art of Translation," Dryden (echoing Cowley) uses the term "imitation": "I take imitation of an author . . . to be an endeavour of a later poet to write like one who has written before him, on the same subject; that is, not to translate his words, or be confined to his sense, but only to set him as a pattern, and to write as he supposes that author would have done, had he lived in our age, and in our country." (Dryden then goes on to advocate a kind of translation less free than "imitation," though not wholly literal.)

After Lowell's Introduction, the following Acknowledgments appear:

> I have been so free with my texts that it is perhaps an impertinence for me to thank those people, more expert in languages than I, for their scattered help. Corrections in my Italian were made by Alfredo Rizzardi and Renato Poggioli; in my French by Jackson Mathews, T. S. Eliot and Elizabeth Bishop; in my German by Hannah Arendt. Russian trots were given me by Mrs. Roman Jakobson, Mrs. Olga Carlisle and Nicolas Nabokov. Swarms of published translations were useful and irritating to me. General stylistic suggestions were made by my wife, Stanley Kunitz, Mary McCarthy, William Alfred, I. A. Richards, Adrienne Rich and William Meredith.

THE KILLING OF LYKAON

1 Opening lines of the *Iliad*.
2 See *Iliad*, XXI.99–135. The Greek half-god Achilles, after mourning the death of his friend Patroklos, now in rage kills many Trojans, including Lykaon.
4.2 Skamander: The chief river of the Trojan plain.

THREE LETTERS TO ANAKTORIA

The speaker throughout is Sappho.

II.1.3 The Persian fleet was defeated by the Greeks at Salamis (480 B.C.).
II.2.5 Persepolis: The capital of Persia.
II.3.1–4 Helen was carried away by Paris to Troy, prompting the Trojan War.

CHILDREN

In the magazine version (*Hudson Review* 12 [1959], 57–58), the final two stanzas are both spoken by the warning voice, as they are in *The Penguin Book of German Verse* (1957).

THE GREAT TESTAMENT

Villon seems to have intended the title "Le testament," but this poem is generally known as "Le grand testament."

3.6 Monastic orders of great severity.

7.3–8 Ecclesiastes 11:9–10.

14.5 Jacques Coeur: "One of the wealthiest individuals France has ever seen" (Anthony Bonner, *The Complete Works of François Villon*, trans. Bonner [1964], 193).

15.4 Psalms 103:16.

17.7 cone or horse-hair hats: "Conical hats worn by the noblewomen of the day"; "the fashion for the bourgeoisie . . . consisted of a horse-hair lined headdress onto which a hood was affixed" (Bonner, 194).

18.1 I.e., even Helen of Troy.

BALLAD FOR THE DEAD LADIES

Titled simply "Ballade" in the sources, this poem is generally known as "Ballade des dames du temps jadis" ("Ballad of the Ladies of Times Gone By"). See "Dames du Temps Jadis" in *HIS*, 457.

2.5 Buridan: Jean Buridan (1300–1358) "was not only a famous fourteenth-century professor at the University of Paris but also the hero of an equally famous legend. When he was a student, it began to be noised about that the Queen of France (and Navarre) [Jeanne de Navarre] was inviting students to her palace bordering on the Seine, giving them fine meals, sleeping with them and then having them tossed to a watery death in the river. Buridan managed to get himself an invitation, and everything the rumors said turned out to be true. For three days they ate, drank, listened to sweet music and made love. Then came his time to be tossed out the window; but Buridan had arranged for a barge full of hay to pass beneath the palace. As he landed in it, his fellow-students guiding the barge dropped a large rock into the river to reassure the Queen. Being a kill-joy lot, modern scholars have proved that this story is a fabrication" (Anthony Bonner, *The Complete Works of François Villon*, trans. Bonner [1964], 194).

3.1 Queen Blanche: Blanche de Castille, mother of Louis IX.

3.3 Bertha Big Foot and Beatrice are "heroines of a medieval *Chanson de geste, Hervi de Metz*. The first was the legendary wife of Pépin le Bref and mother of Charlemagne" (Bonner, 194).

THE OLD LADY'S LAMENT FOR HER YOUTH

Villon's title is "La vieille en regrettant le temps de sa jeunesse"; also known as "Les regrets de la belle Hëaulmière." "The Belle Hëaulmière (Beautiful Armoress) in her youth was one of the better known beauties and demi-mondaines of Paris. She was born around 1375. . . . When Villon knew her (before his departure from Paris in 1456) she must have been around eighty, certainly old and decrepit enough to merit the complaints Villon puts in her mouth" (Anthony Bonner, *The Complete Works of François Villon*, trans. Bonner, 196).

VILLON'S PRAYER FOR HIS MOTHER TO SAY TO THE VIRGIN

As with "Ballad for the Dead Ladies" (see note, above), simply titled "Ballade" in the sources; generally known as "Ballade pour Prier Nostre Dame." Lowell used Villon's poem as a model for section IV of "In Memory of Arthur Winslow" (see note p. 1014).

2.4 "her" in our text replaces "him" (*IM*) based on Lowell's handwritten correction in a copy of the Faber and Faber edition (1971).

3.2 St. Mary of Egypt (fifth century), actress, courtesan, desert eremite.

3.3–5 Theophilus: "Hero of a legend very popular in the Middle Ages. To regain his job he made a pact with the devil, but then was redeemed by Our Lady" (Anthony Bonner, *The Complete Works of François Villon*, trans. Bonner, 198).

4.3–5 Cf. "In Memory of Arthur Winslow" IV.2.2–5, p. 25.

VILLON'S EPITAPH

Titled in the sources "L'épitaphe Villon"; generally known as "Ballade des pendus" ("Ballade of the Hanged"). See "France" in *LWC*, 42.

THE INFINITE

See "Leopardi, The Infinite," in *HIS*, 478.

SYLVIA

5.3–4 Marie-Antoinette / stage-set: The Queen of France had a pastoral setting (comprised of several buildings) constructed at Versailles; there she could dress as a shepherdess.

SIC TRANSIT

Sic transit gloria mundi: "Thus passes the glory of the world."

11.14–15 Belchen and Blauen are two mountains.

HEINE DYING IN PARIS

I.12 Doric: The oldest and simplest of the three orders of Greek architecture.

I.13–14 "Never to have lived is best" (Sophocles, *Oedipus at Colonus*, 1224).

II. See "Heine Dying in Paris 1" in *HIS*, 480.

II.2.1 That fellow: The shade of Achilles. See note to "Her Dead Brother" I.1.10 on p. 1028.

II.2.3 Stukkert-am-Neckar: Stuttgart, Germany, on the Neckar River.

III. See "Heine Dying in Paris 2" in *HIS*, 481.

III.1.3 Chosen People: Heine was of Jewish descent, but espoused a Romantic and sensual philosophy at odds with his background.

III.2.4–5 God the Creator as comic playwright; the poet as creator, but on a smaller scale.

III.2.4–6 The version of these lines from *The Nation* 190 (April 23, 1960), 349, reads:

> Mortal, I witness earth's abstruse acumen,
> Her sugared leasehold on life:
> Mid-summer's frail and green-juice bird's-nest.

Napoleon's Grand Army began its march on Russia with 422,000 men; 110,000 reached Moscow; only 10,000 returned from Russia. See "Napoleon Crosses the Berezina" in *LWC*, 37.

1.36 Attila the Hun (A.D. 406–453) at the irresistible "dawn" of his strength; in 216 B.C. at Cannae, Hannibal cut to pieces a Roman army of more than 50,000 men. (Their successes, in turn, were illusory: each failed to take the city of Rome, goal of both campaigns.)

1.41 Ney: Marshal Michel Ney commanded the rear guard of Napoleon's army in its retreat; see "Leaving Home, Marshal Ney" in *HIS*, 476.

1.43 *qui vive*: A sentinel's challenge (literally, "[long] live who?"), intended to discover to which party the person challenged belongs, and properly requiring an answer in the form "(vive) le roi," "(vive) la France," etc. (*OED*).

2.10 *lèse-majesté*: treason, or an affront to another's dignity (literally, "violated majesty").

AT GAUTIER'S GRAVE

See "Hugo at Théophile Gautier's Grave" in *HIS*, 486.

3.4 the pyre of Hercules: Wearing the poisoned Nessus shirt that cannot be removed, in agony Hercules had himself carried to the summit of Mt. Oeta and placed on a pyre, then persuaded Polas, father of Philoctetes, to light it.

3.10 Authors, Hugo's contemporaries.

CHARLES BAUDELAIRE

Lowell wrote Elizabeth Bishop: "I've just been doing some Baudelaire in meter as strict as his, and have never had such a work-out. Three poems have about killed me. I think he is unlike any of the later Baudelairean French poets—in him the fire comes from the descent of his Racinian rhetoric into the material of Flaubert and Balzac, or something of the sort, so that if you remove the finish he's gone, though still rich in a flat prosy way. . . . I never realized that such wonder could be done with a sentence, moving through its terrible balances and metric and so seldom turning into a mere fireworks of syntax" (August 9, 1960).

MY BEATRICE

In Dante's *Vita Nuova* and *Divine Comedy*, Beatrice remains inaccessible but loved, guiding the soul who loves her from profane desires to religious vision.

SPLEEN

See "Caligula 1" in *HIS*, 444.

3 Fénelon: French theologian and writer (1651–1715), who wrote *Maxims of the Saints* (1697) and other works advocating Quietism. Apologues: Moral fables.

THE FLAWED BELL

2.3 piously to repeat: This is "to piously repeat" in *IM*; our reading is from *The Voyage*.

MEDITATION

See "Baudelaire 2. Recollection" in *HIS*, 487.

THE INJURED MOON

1.4 Cynthia: The moon goddess.
3.3 Endymion: A young shepherd of great beauty, Endymion was pursued by the moon goddess (called, in this myth, Selene), who visited him nightly when he was asleep.

THE ABYSS

See "Baudelaire 1. The Abyss" in *HIS*, 487.

1 Blaise Pascal (1623–1662), French mathematician, scientist, philosopher. "We sail within a vast sphere, ever drifting in uncertainty, driven from end to end. When we think to attach ourselves to any point and to fasten to it, it wavers and leaves us; and if we follow it, it eludes our grasp, slips past us, and vanishes for ever. Nothing stays for us. This is our natural condition, and yet most contrary to our inclination; we burn with the desire to find solid ground and an ultimate sure foundation whereon to build a tower reaching to the Infinite. But our whole groundwork cracks, and the earth opens to abysses" (Pascal, *Pensées*, trans. Trotter [1941], no. 72 ["Man's disproportion"], 25).

THE SWAN

I.1.1ff For Andromache, Baudelaire follows Virgil (*Aeneid*, III.294–329). The widow of Hector, after the fall of Troy she was the slave of Pyrrhus (son of Achilles); later Pyrrhus gave her to his slave the seer Helenus, son of Priam.
I.1.3 when Racine's tirades scourged: His *Andromaque* was first performed in 1667.
1.2.2 the new Carrousel: "The area between the two wings of the Louvre and the Carrousel Arch. . . . [I]t had been a warren of small streets, but in Baudelaire's time the area was cleared for a monumental square" (James McGowan, *Charles Baudelaire: The Flowers of Evil*, trans. McGowan [1993], 371).
II.1.2 *arrondissements* razed *en bloc*: Parisian neighborhoods torn down all at once.
II.4.2 Jeanne Duval: A mixed-race Parisian actress who was Baudelaire's lover.

VOYAGE TO CYTHERA

Cythera: Greek island, chief center of the cult of Aphrodite, goddess of love.

5.3 The quotation marks ending this line did not appear in *IM*; correction from *The Voyage*.
15.3–4 The version from *Partisan Review* 28 (1961), no. 2, 193–95, reads:

> Oh God, give me the courage and the strength
> To contemplate my body without disgust.

THE SERVANT

1.5 October: We have added the comma after this word.
2.8 Cf. the final line of "Mother Marie Therese" in *MK*, 99.

II.6.4 The Emperor Tiberius became a recluse on the island of Capri, where he supervised legendary debaucheries; the Blue Grotto is located there.

VII.3.1 Wandering Jew: See note to "91 Revere Street," 122 p. 1034.

VII.3.4 retiarius: A gladiator armed with a net. All earlier editions have printed "retarius."

VII.6.1 lotus-flowers: In the *Odyssey* IX, Odysseus and his men land upon the coastline of the lotus-eaters, who live in a drugged, indolent state; once his sailors taste the lotus-flower, they long never to leave.

ARTHUR RIMBAUD

For Lowell on Rimbaud, see *CPR*, 134–37.

NOSTALGIA

I.1.3 *Tricouleur*: The French flag (literally, "tricolor").

II.2.3 Bride: The mother as bride (the French is, *"ta foi conjugale, ô l'Epouse!"* [your conjugal faith, O Spouse]).

III.2.1 Prayer books bound in red morocco.

THE DRUNKEN BOAT

8.3 Three Marys: "In the Camargue, on an island at the mouth of the Rhône, is the little town of Les Saintes-Maries-de-la-Mer, where according to tradition, the three Maries—Marie Jacobé, Marie-Salomé and Marie-Madeleine—with their black servant Sara, Lazarus and Saint Maximin landed after being buffeted by the waves and suffering a fate similar to that of Rimbaud's *bateau ivre.* . . . The feast of 'Trois Maries' [is] 25 May" (Enid Starkie, *Arthur Rimbaud* [1961], 136).

10.2 Monitors: Iron-clad warships (nineteenth century). Hanseatic: The Hanseatic League was an association of free towns, organized for trade.

13.2 I.e., heroic figures, against a backdrop of spare grandeur, as in the theater of Aeschylus (Greek playwright, 525–426 B.C.).

EIGHTEEN-SEVENTY

I. *A Poster*

The poster celebrates the early, small French victory at Saarbrücken during the Franco-Prussian War (1870–1871); but in the next few weeks, the French were driven back.

3.1 Chassepot: French breech-loading gun; French generals believed that with such advanced weaponry they would easily defeat the Prussians.

3.3 shako: See note to "The Shako" 14 on p. 1018.

4.1 VIVE L'EMPEREUR: Long live the Emperor!

II. *Napoleon after Sedan*

France suffered a major defeat at Sedan, a few months after the beginning of the Franco-Prussian War. Napoleon III was captured there; four days later he was declared deposed by a bloodless revolution in Paris. Finally released by the Prussians, he lived in exile in England until his death. See "Rimbaud 5. Napoleon After Sedan" in *HIS*, 490.

1.1 Tuileries: Napoleon III's chief residence in Paris, burned during the Paris Commune (1871); the formal gardens, near the Louvre, survive.
4.4 Saint-Cloud was a royal chateau outside Paris, destroyed during the Franco-Prussian War.

III. *To the French of the Second Empire*
 The revolution of 1848 brought France the Second Republic; in 1852, Louis Napoleon Bonaparte, president of the Republic, declared himself Emperor Napoleon III, and created the Second Empire.

1.1 I.e., those who died in the early years of the French Revolution.
2.3 sown: "sewn" in *IM*.
3.2 Sites of battles during the Revolutionary and Napoleonic wars.

IV. *On the Road*
 See "Rimbaud 1. Bohemia" in *HIS*, 488.

V. *At the Green Cabaret*

1.1 Charleroi: In Belgium.

VI. *A Malicious Girl*
 See "Rimbaud 2. A Knowing Girl" in *HIS*, 488.

VII. *The Sleeper in the Valley*
 See "Rimbaud 3. Sleeper in the Valley" in *HIS*, 489.

VIII. *Evil*
 See "War" in *LWC*, 39, and "Rimbaud 4. The Evil" in *HIS*, 489.

1.3 great captain: Napoleon III.
2.4 *La Patrie*: The nation.
3.1 Papal bulls: Official documents issued by the Pope, bearing Papal seals.
4.3 sou: A French coin, worth about a penny.

HELEN

See "Helen" in *HIS*, 428.

A ROMAN SARCOPHAGUS

1.1 Etruscan mother of a family.
1.5 For this image (not in Rilke) Lowell is almost certainly thinking of the portrait of Madame de Récamier by Jacques-Louis David. Julie Récamier (1777–1849) was a celebrated beauty and the hostess of a salon frequented by powerful literary and political figures.

THE CADET PICTURE OF MY FATHER

Viola Bernard: Lowell's psychiatrist. See "Cadet-Picture of Rilke's Father" in *HIS*, 494.

5 Franz Josef: Emperor of Austria and King of Hungary (b. 1830–d.1916).

See "Rilke Self-Portrait" in *HIS*, 497.

2.1 *nature morte*: French term for a still life (literally, "dead nature").

ORPHEUS, EURYDICE AND HERMES

Hermes, messenger god who carries the caduceus, conducts souls of the dead to the Underworld; here, he is conducting Eurydice out.

YOU KNOCKED YOURSELF OUT

A manuscript version is titled "You Dashed your Brains Out / Giuseppe Ungaretti's elegy for his son, dead in Brazil" (Houghton Library, bMS 1905 2782).

DORA MARKUS

I.1.2 Porto Corsini: The port of Ravenna, Italy.
II.1.1 Carinthia: A province of Austria.
II.1.10 *pensioni*: Small hotels.

DAY AND NIGHT

1.10 Montecatini: A resort spa in Tuscany.

THE MAGNOLIA'S SHADOW

6 Clizia: A pseudonym (drawn from Ovid) of Montale's beloved.

HITLERIAN SPRING

Hitler and Mussolini met in Florence on May 9, 1938, the feast day of St. John the Evangelist, patron saint of Florence.

2.1 infernal possessor: Hitler.
2.2 Corso: Avenue.
3.4–5 the butcher / locks his creaking iron curtain: "The holiday, declared in Hitler's honor, of the butchers" (Jonathan Galassi, *Eugenio Montale: Collected Poems 1920–1954*, trans. Galassi [1998], 583).
3.6–7 two goat's-heads crowned / with holly berries: St. John's Day is normally celebrated not only with fireworks ("roman candles" 4.3), but by wreathing slaughtered goats with flowers and berries.
4.10 Tobias: Son of Tobit, in the Apocryphal Book of Tobit, he is protected by seven angels during "his perilous journey to a faraway land, the consummation of a happy marriage, and a safe return trip home" (William Arrowsmith, *Eugenio Montale: The Storm and Other Things*, trans. Arrowsmith [1985], 196).
5.1 Clizia: See note to "The Magnolia's Shadow," above.

THE COASTGUARD HOUSE

Montale's title translates to "The House of the Customs Men."

THE CHESS PLAYER

Montale wrote that "Nuove stanze" (New Stanzas), could be titled "Love, chess, and wartime vigil" (Jonathan Galassi, *Eugenio Montale: Collected Poems 1920–1954*, trans. Galassi [1998], 525).

NEWS FROM MOUNT AMIATA

Mount Amiata: An extinct volcano in southern Tuscany.

I.1.6 funghi: Mushrooms.
IV.1.7 a *contemptu mundi*: Writing that expresses contempt for the material world, modeled on Bernard of Cluny's poem *De contemptu mundi* (c. 1140).

THE EEL

Under one title, Lowell's poem joins two separate poems by Montale: Part I is "L'anguilla" (The Eel); Part II, "Se t'hanno assomigliato" (If they've compared you).

I.11 Romagna: North-central region of Italy just above the Apennines (I.15), the mountain range running the length of the Italian peninsula.

LITTLE TESTAMENT

"The title imitates the 'testaments' of Francois Villon, the diminutive adjective characteristically undercutting the summary implications of the noun" (Jonathan Galassi, *Eugenio Montale: Collected Poems 1920–1954*, trans. Galassi [1998], 608).

BLACK SPRING

For another version, see "Annensky: White Winter, Black Spring" in *HIS*, 495.

BORIS PASTERNAK

With the help of Olga Carlisle, Lowell revised many of the versions of Pasternak included in *Imitations*; in 1968, he published them in her volume *Poets on Street Corners*. We have used the *Poets on Street Corners* versions here. Two other poems—"September" and "The Seasons"—were not revised later; we print the *Imitations* texts. For Lowell's versions of Akhmatova and Mandelstam, also published in *Poets on Street Corners*, see Appendix II, p. 897.

SEPTEMBER

6.1 *le roi soleil*: The Sun King, Louis XIV of France (1638–1715).

FOR ANNA AKHMATOVA

3.3–4 The *IM* version reads:

> You bend to your sewing until you weep;
> sunrise and sunset redden your swollen eyes.

4.1 Ladoga: A large lake in Russia.

7.2 Told by two angels not to look back, Lot and his wife fled the destruction of Sodom and Gomorrah; looking back, she was turned to salt (Genesis 19:17–26).

8.2 took on life: "hardened" (*IM*).

MEPHISTOPHELES

4.1ff Version from *IM*:

> Later, when the long cortege of carriages
> approached the city wall,
> the horses shied
> from the shadow of the Gothic gallows.

4.4 Weimar gallows: Buchenwald is near Weimar, and just outside the crematorium was a gallows.

SPARROW HILLS

1.4 on the casino's midnight bandstand: "in the casino's midnight gazebo" (*IM*).

3.1 froth to your mouth: "froth from your mouth" (*IM*).

THE LANDLORD

The Wedding: This subtitle did not appear in *IM*.

6.3 peahen: "peacock" in *IM*; in stanzas 7–9, all pronouns "she" and "her" appear in *IM* as "he" and "his."

HAMLET IN RUSSIA, A SOLILOQUY

For this poem we have used the title from *IM*, but the text from *Poets on Street Corners*. Here is Olga Carlisle's Note, which accompanied the poem (titled simply "Hamlet") in *Poets on Street Corners* (91):

> This English version of "Hamlet" is as much a poem *about* Boris Pasternak as an adaptation *from* Boris Pasternak. An extremely free adaptation—or rather "imitation," as Robert Lowell calls it—it is based on three poems by Pasternak. Two of the poems, written in 1917, are from *My Sister Life*. The third is titled "Hamlet" and is from *Poems from Doctor Zhivago*. It was written in 1946, according to a close and knowledgeable friend of Pasternak's. Robert Lowell points out that the new English "Hamlet" tells us of the Russian poet's life in a way that he himself might not have perceived it. It opens with a pastoral version of youth, a boating scene which could have been depicted by an

Impressionist. The poem ends tragically with the poet's crucifixion by the mob. In the adapter's interpretation, the clapping of the river ripples and that of the audience which greets the poet about to enact his own tragic ending merge with each other, providing a transition for poems belonging to very different periods and moods.

3.4 silently: "politely" (*IM*).
8.3 Abba: Father.
9.4 boards: "hooks" (*IM*).

PIGEONS

Lowell's placement of Rilke's poem at the end of *IM* breaks the chronological arrangement of the book. The original was written as a letter-poem to Erika Mitterer; the German begins: "Taube, die draussen, blieb" ("Dove that ventured outside"). Hannah Arendt (1906–1975): German-American philosopher.

3 This stanza is not in Rilke's original; later Lowell reprinted it as "Epigram" in *FTUD*, 339. For annotation, see notes to "The Spartan Dead at Thermopylae" p. 1078.

FOR THE UNION DEAD (1964)

The copy-text is the second Farrar, Straus and Giroux printing.

In an interview, Lowell said: "In *For the Union Dead*, I modified the style of *Life Studies*—free-verse stanzas, each poem on its own and more ornately organized. Then came metrical poems, more plated, far from conversation, metaphysical. My subjects were still mostly realism about my life. I also wrote one long public piece, the title poem" (*CPR*, 269). Elsewhere he said: "*For the Union Dead* is more mixed, and the poems in it are separate entities. I'm after invention rather than memory, and I'd like to achieve some music and elegance and splendor, but not in any programmatic sense. Some of the poems may be close to symbolism" (Meyers, *Interviews*, 85).

WATER

Addressed to Elizabeth Bishop. See "For Elizabeth Bishop (twenty-five years) 1. Water" in *HIS*, p. 593.

THE OLD FLAME

Addressed to Lowell's first wife, Jean Stafford. The setting is Damariscotta Mills, Maine.

2.3 In *FTUD* "stars" was "stripes"; earlier and later versions—*Partisan Review* 29 (1962), no. 3; the Farrar, Straus and Giroux *Selected Poems*—print "stars".
2.5 In *Partisan Review* and the Faber and Faber *Selected Poems* (1965), the color is "old-red-schoolhouse-red." (Clarity would perhaps be increased if the phrase read "old-red-schoolhouse red.")

MIDDLE AGE

3 Cf. "The Lord's Prayer": "[F]orgive us our trespasses, As we forgive those who trespass against us" (from *The Book of Common Prayer*, 1929).

4.2 Mount Sion: Or Zion, hill in Jerusalem conquered by King David, the City of David; symbolic of Jerusalem, the Promised Land, God's holy hill.

THE SCREAM

"A scream, the echo of a scream, hangs over that Nova Scotian village. No one hears it; it hangs there for ever, a slight stain in those pure blue skies" (opening of Elizabeth Bishop's story "In the Village"). First published in *The New Yorker* (December 19, 1953), the story appears in *Questions of Travel* (1965).

5.4 The Babylonian king Nebuchadnezzar went temporarily mad: "he was driven from men, and did eat grass as oxen" (Daniel 4:33).
7.4–5 See "Familiar Quotations" in *FLH*, 634.

THE MOUTH OF THE HUDSON

2.2–4 Lowell drew this image from his memory of imprisonment during World War II. He writes: "we would sit around barrels filled with burning coke and roast wheat seeds" (*CPR*, 361–62). The Israelites mentioned in "In the Cage" were part of this group; see Mariani, 113 and 472, (n. 9), as well as "In the Cage" in *LWC*, 55, and *HIS*, 526. Also see "Rats" in *HIS*, 527.

FALL 1961

For an early draft of this poem, see Miehe, 122.

2.3 "Across the nation last week, there was endless conversation about the threat of nuclear war" between the United States and the Soviet Union (*Time*, September 29, 1961; 13); opposing troops engaged in a stand-off as the Berlin Wall was built, and both countries resumed nuclear testing. (For more on the "historical moment," see Steven Axelrod, "Robert Lowell and the Cold War," *The New England Quarterly*, September 1999, 349–52.)
4.1 shield: The North American Air Defense Command engaged in an exercise called "Sky Shield II" against a simulated Russian nuclear attack on October 14, 1961.
4.3–5 See "Familiar Quotations" in *FLH*, 634.
5.1 "The purpose of playing . . . is, to hold as 'twere the mirror up to nature" (Hamlet's instructions to the Players, III.ii.20–22).

FLORENCE

Among her many books, novelist and critic Mary McCarthy wrote *The Stones of Florence* (1959).

1.1 black ink: "When disturbed, cuttlefish eject a cloud of dark brown ink from an ink sac for protection. . . . The ink . . . has been used as the artist's pigment, sepia" (*The New Columbia Encyclopedia* 1975).
3.6 Perseus, David and Judith: Great decapitators. Perseus beheaded Medusa ("the Gorgon," 3.20); David beheaded Goliath; Judith beheaded Holofernes. Statues of Perseus, David and Judith are in the Piazza della Signoria in Florence ("Where the tower of the Old Palace / pierces the sky" [3.3–4]).

THE LESSON

1.1 Novel by Thomas Hardy (1891).

THOSE BEFORE US

4.1 *ex cathedra*: From the seat of authority (literally, "from the chair").

EYE AND TOOTH

1.2 the old cut cornea: Lowell had suffered a corneal abrasion from a contact lens. He described this poem as "my farewell to contact lenses" (Hamilton, 293).

1.3 "now we see through a glass, darkly; but then face to face" (I Corinthians 13.12).

3.1ff "When I woke up this morning, something unusual for this summer was going on!— pinpricks of rain were falling in a reliable, comforting simmer. Our town was blanketed in the rain of rot and the rain of renewal. New life was muscling in, everything growing moved on its one-way trip to the ground. I could feel this, yet believe our universal misfortune was bearable and even welcome. An image held my mind during these moments and kept returning—an old-fashioned New England cottage freshly painted white. I saw a shaggy, triangular shade on the house, trees, a hedge, or their shadows, the blotch of decay. The house might have been the house I was now living in, but it wasn't; it came from the time when I was a child, still unable to read, and living in the small town of Barnstable on Cape Cod. Inside the house was a bird book with an old stiff and steely engraving of a sharp-shinned hawk. The hawk's legs had a reddish-brown buffalo fuzz on them; behind was the blue sky, bare and abstracted from the world. In the present, pinpricks of rain were falling on everything I could see, and even on the white house in my mind, but the hawk's picture, being indoors I suppose, was more or less spared. Since I saw the picture of the hawk, the pinpricks of rain have gone on, half the people I once knew are dead, half the people I now know were then unborn, and I have learned to read. An image of a white house with a blotch on it—this is perhaps the start of a Williams poem" (Lowell, *CPR*, 37–38).

7.3–4 "Eye for eye, tooth for tooth, hand for hand, foot for foot" (Exodus 21:24).

8.1ff See Deuteronomy 28:65.

ALFRED CORNING CLARK

A classmate at St. Mark's School.

1.10 unreasonably: "unseasonably" in *FTUD*; "unreasonably" in *Partisan Review* 29 (1962), no. 1, and *SP* (1977).

CHILD'S SONG

5.3–4 see "Familiar Quotations" in *FLH*, 634.

EPIGRAM

These lines appear as stanza three of "Pigeons" (*IM*), 316; for annotation, see notes to "The Spartan Dead at Thermopylae" (*HIS*), 1078.

"One law for civic man, another for the imagination" (Raban, *Selection*, 172).

2.3 " 'Bass-plugging' is fishing for the freshwater bass with an imitation dead-fish made out of colored wood and metal" (Raban, *Selection*, 172).

THE PUBLIC GARDEN

See "David and Bathsheba in the Public Garden" in *MK*, 100.

1.9 swanboats: See note to "In Memory of Arthur Winslow" I.2.1, p. 1014.

LADY RALEGH'S LAMENT

Sir Walter Ralegh (1554?–1618) died on the block; his fortunes declined with the accession to the throne (1603) of King James I (probably the "connoisseur tyrant," 4), who succeeded Queen Elizabeth, the "Virgin Queen" (2).

10 beseeching voyage: Ralegh had headed many expeditions; for his final one, in 1616 he was released from imprisonment in the Tower to search for gold on the Orinoco River, in South America.

GOING TO AND FRO

"And the Lord said unto Satan, Whence comest thou? Then Satan answered the Lord, and said, From going to and fro in the earth, and from walking up and down in it" (Job 1:7). A draft of this poem (Houghton Library bMS Am 1905 2745) is titled "For Nerval or Someone."

5.4 Mary, Myrtho, Isis: Myrtho is a name, derived from "myrtle," invented by Gérard de Nerval (1808–1855) in his sonnet "Myrtho" (*Gérard de Nerval: Selected Writings*, trans. Sieburth [1999], 403); wreaths of myrtle crowned the victors in the ancient Olympic games. Isis is the wife of Osiris, the slain god of Egyptian mythology; to return him to life, she reassembled the scattered bits of his dead body. From Nerval's "Aurélia":

> I turned my thoughts to the eternal Isis, sacred mother and bride; all my aspirations, all my prayers gathered into her magic name; I felt myself come back to life in her, and at times she appeared to me in the guise of the ancient Venus, at times she took on the features of the Christian Virgin. (Sieburth, 308)

Mary the mother of Jesus is "the Christian Virgin."

5.6–6.1 The love that moves the stars / moved you!: "[T]he magnetic rays that emanate from me or from others flow directly through the infinite chain of creation whose transparent network is in continuous communication with the planets and the stars" (Sieburth, 307). Also cf. the final line of Dante's *Commedia* (Paradiso, XXXIII.143).

6.4 The Houghton draft reads:

> Nerval got loose from the dark
> by counting his steps to the noose.

Nerval was hospitalized several times for severe mental breakdowns. During the final weeks of his life he lived on the streets of Paris without fixed address; at the age of forty-six, he hanged himself in the rue de la Vieille-Lanterne.

MYOPIA: A NIGHT

The magazine version of this poem is significantly different; see *Encounter*, August 1964.

3.1 the morning star: Lucifer, another name for Satan (4.1ff).

RETURNING

" 'Returning' was suggested by Giuseppe Ungaretti's 'Canzone' " (Lowell's introductory Note, 319). See "Walks" in *HIS*, 424, and "Ulysses and Circe" V and "Homecoming" in *DBD*, 713 and 720.

1.4 the dogs still know me by my smell: Cf. *Odyssey* XVII.300ff.

HAWTHORNE

For Lowell on Hawthorne, see *CPR*, 188–91.
   Many details of the first two stanzas are drawn from "The Customs House," Hawthorne's introduction to his novel *The Scarlet Letter*.

5.2 Lowell: James Russell Lowell. Henry Wadsworth Longfellow (1807–1882), Oliver Wendell Holmes (1809–1894) and John Greenleaf Whittier (1807–1892) were prominent New England "men of letters." For Lowell on J. R. Lowell and Longfellow, see *CPR*, 194–96.
6.2–5 From Hawthorne's romance *Septimus Felton* (1871).

JONATHAN EDWARDS IN WESTERN MASSACHUSETTS

Several passages use phrases from works by Edwards: "Of Insects," "Personal Narrative," "Sarah Pierrepont," and "Sinners in the Hands of an Angry God"; and from Sir Francis Bacon's essays (as cited below).

5.3 *Whitehall*: "Whitehall, the Royal Palace, becomes the metaphor for any country house imbued with the presence of God" (Mazzaro, *Themes*, 132).
6 "And because, the *Breath* of Flowers, is farre Sweeter in the Aire, (where it comes and Goes, like the Warbling of Musick) then in the hand" (Bacon, "Of Gardens").
7.3 when he fell: In 1621, Bacon pleaded guilty to accepting bribes as Lord Chancellor; he spent the next five years, until his death, writing in retirement.
7.4 "In Fame of Learning, the Flight will be slow, without some Feathers of *Ostentation*" (Bacon, "Of Vaine-Glory").
11.1 Bishop Berkeley; see headnote to "Bishop Berkeley" in *HIS*, 1092.
11.4 Sarah Pierrepont: Edwards' wife.
12.1ff "They say there is a young lady who is beloved of that Great Being, who ... comes to her and fills her mind with exceeding sweet delight, and that she hardly cares for anything. . . . She will sometimes go about from place to place, singing sweetly, and ... loves to be alone, walking in the fields and groves, and seems to have some one invisible always conversing with her" (Edwards, "Sarah Pierrepont," quoted in Mazzaro, *Themes*, 132).

16.2 Great Awakening: A widespread series of religious revivals in the American Colonies, mid-eighteenth century; begun in New England (1734–1735) by Edwards' preaching in Northampton, Massachusetts.

16.2–4 "Alas, how many . . .": From Edwards' "Sinners in the Hands of an Angry God."

17.3 you fell from your parish: In 1750 Edwards' congregation dismissed him from Northampton.

17.4 "All rising to *Great Place*, is by a winding Staire" (Bacon, "Of Great Place").

23.2ff From Edwards' letter to the Board of Trustees of the College of New Jersey (now Princeton University).

TENTH MUSE

There are nine Muses in Greek mythology.

1.1 Sloth: one of the seven Deadly Sins. In 1964, Stanley Kunitz said: "Only once did he ever complete a poem in a day. That was 'The Tenth Muse,' a poem about sloth!" (Meyers, *Interviews*, 89). Lowell writes: "sloth is the safest cure of all vices" (*CPR*, 132).

2.1ff Moses brought the Ten Commandments, the "old law" inscribed on stone, down from Mt. Sinai (Exodus 20).

4.2 Lot: See note to "For Anna Akhmatova" 7.2 p. 1056.

CALIGULA

"Cal" was Lowell's nickname, the name used by his closest friends. Lowell to Bishop: "Dear Elizabeth; (You must be called that; I'm called Cal, but I won't explain why. None of the prototypes are flattering: Calvin, Caligula, Caliban, Calvin Coolidge, Calligraphy—with merciless irony)" (August 1, 1947). Many details in this poem are drawn from the portrait of Caligula by Suetonius, *Lives of the Caesars*. Caligula: "little boots" in Latin.

See the "Caligula" poems in *HIS*, 444 and 445.

1.3 "The whole poem unfolds that altogether convincing hesitation in 'like you'—a verb or not?" (Christopher Ricks, *Critics on Robert Lowell*, ed. Price, 99).

3.10 Adonis was gored by a boar.

3.13 Caligula declared himself a god.

THE SEVERED HEAD

Lowell wrote that this poem was "a pure Tate pastiche"; its model is Allen Tate's "The Buried Lake" (Axelrod, *Life*, 153).

1.11 In *FTUD*, there is a comma after "chandelier," deleted here.

3.3 Jael: See Judges 4 and 5. The Hebrew woman Jael "put her hand to the nail, and her right hand to the workmen's hammer; and with the hammer she smote [the sleeping] Sisera, she smote off his head, when she had pierced and stricken through his temples" (5:26). Sisera was a defeated Canaanite captain, seeking refuge with Jael. [In class, Lowell used the second telling of the encounter of Jael and Sisera (Judges 5:20–31), King James Version, as an example of great writing. F.B.]

Lowell's introductory Note: " 'Beyond the Alps' is the poem I published in *Life Studies*, but with a stanza restored at the suggestion of John Berryman." See *LS* 113, and Appendix III, 927, for other versions; "Ovid and Caesar's Daughter" in *HIS*, 442, is a revision of stanza three.

Au-delà des Alpes est l'Italie: "Beyond the Alps is Italy"; Napoleon is echoing Livy, *History* XXI, 30. (Lowell's train travels in the *opposite* direction from Napoleon's "shoeless army" eager to plunder Italy; see headnote p. 1031.)

For additional annotation, see notes to the *LS* "Beyond the Alps," pp. 1031–32.

3: Lowell never ceased tinkering with this stanza. It appears in the magazine version of the poem (Appendix III, p. 927), then was cut from *LS* (1959). In *FTUD* (1964) he rewrote it. In the 1972 Faber and Faber *LS* it was again rewritten, and for the only time included in the text of "Beyond the Alps" opening the book. In *HIS* (1973), Lowell again recast it, this time under a separate title ("Ovid and Caesar's Daughter," p. 442). In the *SP* "Beyond the Alps" (1976), the stanza is gone.

After *FTUD*, in each version the number of lines assigned to the voice of Ovid is different. Here is the 1972 revision:

> I thought of Ovid. For in Caesar's eyes
> that tomcat had the Number of the Beast,
> and now where Turkey faces the red east,
> and the twice-stormed Crimean spit, he lies.
> Rome asked for poets. At her beck and call,
> came Lucan, Tacitus and Juvenal,
> the *black republicans* who tore the tits
> and bowels of the Mother Wolf to bits.
> Killer and army-commander waved the rod
> of empire over the Caesars' salvaged bog . . .
> "Imperial Tiber, Oh my yellow dog,
> black earth by the black Roman sea, I lie
> with the boy-crazy daughter of the God,
> *il duce Augusto*. I shall never die."

3.6 Roman writers; critics of Roman history, of the excesses following the fall of the Republic.
3.8 The mythic founders of Rome, Romulus and Remus, were nursed by a wolf.
3.14 *il duce*: The leader (Italian); *il Duce*: Mussolini. *Augusto*: Augustus Caesar.

JULY IN WASHINGTON

For an early version, "Washington," see Appendix III, p. 932.

1.1 this wheel: Pierre-Charles L'Enfant planned Washington, D.C. (1791) so that federal buildings are in a central location and broad, diagonal avenues radiate out from this center.
4.1 circles: Traffic circles, with statues and greenery in the center.
5.2 Cf. "the meek shall inherit the earth" (Psalms 37:11).
6.1 " 'The Elect,' the old American Calvinist doctrine of a community of saints existing by divine grace, have turned into 'the elected' " (Raban, *Selection*, 174).
8.2 delectable mountains: Cf. "il dilettoso monte" (Dante, *Inferno*, I. 77).

BUENOS AIRES

Lowell visited Brazil in summer 1962, then in September briefly went to Argentina. On December 24, 1962, Lowell wrote Bishop from the United States: "I guess I was beginning to go off during the last two weeks in Brazil, and this must have been painful for you to watch or at least sense. When I got to Buenos Aires, my state zoomed sky-high and I am glad you didn't see it. It's hard for the controlled man to look back on the moment of chaos and claim. I shan't try, but it was all me, and I am sorry you were touched by it."

Some months before Lowell's visit to Argentina, Dr. Arturo Frondizi, the Argentine president, had been arrested by the military, who then assumed power.

For the magazine version, see Appendix III, p. 930. See also "Liberty and Revolution, Buenos Aires" in *HIS*, 544.

DROPPING SOUTH: BRAZIL

Lowell wrote Bishop (December 24, 1962) that he had finished a poem about "dropping in a dream on the Copacabana beach."

1.10 two strips of ribbon: A bikini.
1.15 *tristes tropiques*: Melancholy tropics; title of 1955 book by Claude Lévi-Strauss.
1.17 *macumba*: An Afro-Brazilian religion.
1.21 *Santa Maria*: "Yemanjá" in *Kenyon Review* 26 (Winter 1964), 25.

SOFT WOOD

1.2 Scholar Gypsy: In Matthew Arnold's poem, the title figure leaves Oxford to join a band of gypsies; centuries later, he is seen, or perhaps seen.
6.1 my window: Lowell in this poem conjoins two Castine residences. His studio was a converted seaside barn; he described it as being "right on the bay, which on one side looks like a print of Japan and other side like a lake in Michigan as the rocky islands with pine trees ease off into birches and meadows" (Corbett, 41). Harriet Winslow's "house" (7.1) was in the center of town; for photos, see Mariani 320 and 224.
7.1 Harriet Winslow: Lowell's cousin Harriet was "completely incapacitated now by strokes and slowly dying" (Mariani, 315).

NEW YORK 1962: FRAGMENT

E.H.L.: Elizabeth Hardwick Lowell. See "The Picture" and "Same Picture" in *FLH*, 623.

17–19 "Still, still, still. Whenever Lowell uses the word 'still' we know that something is about to change, if not for the character in the poem, then for the poet. 'Still' connotes a cross between persistence and despair. The dual meanings of the word seem to be at loggerheads" (Mark Rudman, 22).

THE FLAW

"Like 'Eye and Tooth' [p. 334] and 'Flaw (Flying to Chicago)' [in *HIS*, 574] this poem elaborates, in the style of a metaphysical conceit, the image of the hairline cut on the cornea of Lowell's eye. . . . The flaw [is] shaped like a question mark" (Raban, *Selection*, 174–75). "I kept seeing a little black nit or gnat worrying oddly over any white surface I looked at. At times it became a hair with little legs" (Lowell, letter, November 1, 1970).

1.2 A country graveyard: "the harbour's graveyard" in *Encounter* 21 (1963), no. 5, 51.

1.4 essence: French for "gasoline."

4.5 *Fête Champêtre*: A village festival.

6.2 "how will I hear your answer in the dark?" (*Encounter*).

NIGHT SWEAT

1.3 living: "lying" (*Kenyon Review* 26 [1964], 25).

1.3 tidied room: "furnished room" (*Encounter* 21 [1963], no. 5, 51).

1.12 will to die: "wish to die" (*Kenyon Review*).

1.13–14 Cf. "May our heirs seal us in a single urn, / A single spirit never to return" (Yvor Winters' "The Marriage").

2 In *SP* Lowell eliminated the break between stanzas, which is restored here. See Introduction (p. xiv) for discussion of this change.

2.1 Behind me! You!: "Get thee behind me, Satan" (Matthew 16:23).

FOR THE UNION DEAD

A brief recital of the poem's historical background: President Lincoln began admitting African-American soldiers into the Union forces in 1863. The 54th Regiment of Massachusetts Volunteer Infantry became the first black regiment recruited in the North. Robert Gould Shaw, a twenty-six-year-old white officer from a prominent abolitionist Boston family, volunteered for its command. The 54th Regiment became famous for leading an unsuccessful assault on Fort Wagner, South Carolina (July 18, 1863). In the hard-fought battle, the Regiment lost more than 250 soldiers, including Shaw. The heroic charge, coupled with so many casualties, made the regiment a household name throughout the North, and helped spur black recruiting. Augustus Saint-Gaudens' bronze bas-relief monument commemorating Shaw and his men, which faces the Massachusetts State House, was dedicated in 1897.

Lowell's poem was originally titled "Colonel Shaw and the Massachusetts' 54th," and appeared as the final poem in the first paperback edition of *Life Studies* (Vintage, 1960). It was published under its present title in *The Atlantic Monthly* 206 (1960), no. 5. Lowell read the poem at the Boston Arts Festival, June 1960, held near the Augustus Saint-Gaudens monument. Lowell's great-grand-uncle, the poet James Russell Lowell, had written a poem about Robert Gould Shaw, "Memoriae Positum R.G.S.," published in 1864; a passage from it is inscribed on the Shaw monument:

> Right in the van of the red rampart's slippery swell
> With heart that beat a charge he fell forward as fits a man
> But the high soul burns on to light men's feet
> Where death for noble ends makes dying sweet.

In 1928, Robert Lowell's mentor Allen Tate wrote "Ode to the Confederate Dead." For a list of prior poems, speeches, and other sources, see Axelrod, *Life*, 268–69, n.33; Doreski adds several more (*Shifting Colors*, 242, n.5). Doreski prints manuscript passages, a complete draft (97–109) and two statements about the poem made by Lowell (94–95, 109).

In 1960, reading the poem for the first time in public, Lowell began with a prepared statement: "My poem, *The Union Dead*, is about childhood memories, the evisceration of our modern cities, civil rights, nuclear warfare and more particularly, Colonel Robert Shaw and his Negro regiment, the Massachusetts 54th. I brought in early personal memories because I wanted to avoid the fixed, brazen tone of the set-piece and official ode" (Doreski, 109). In 1964, Lowell wrote in the *Village Voice*: "I lament the loss of the old Abolitionist spirit: the terrible injustice, in the past and in the present, of the American treatment of the Negro is of the greatest urgency to me as a man and as a writer" (letter to the editor, November 19, 1964, 4). In 1969, Lowell wrote: "In 1959 I had a message. Since then the blacks have perhaps found their 'break,' but the landscape remains" (Doreski, 95).

    Relinquunt . . . Publicam: The inscription on Saint-Gaudens' sculpture reads: "Omnia relinquit servare rempublicam" ("he leaves all behind to protect [preserve, save] the state"). Lowell in his epigraph changes the Latin so that "he" becomes "they." "Omnia relinquit servare rempublicam" is the motto of the Society of the Cincinnati (Washington, D.C.); the phrase is attributed to Henry Knox. The Society's members are descended from Revolutionary War officers; Shaw, had he survived his father, would have been eligible for membership.

1.3 cod: Until 1974, the unofficial symbol of Massachusetts; in that year it became official.

7.4 "so true to nature that one can almost hear them breathing" (from William James' speech at the dedication of the monument).

10.1 He is out of bounds now: "Our wall of circumstance / Cleared at a bound, he flashes o'er the fight" (J. R. Lowell, "Memoriae Positum R.G.S." III.2.7–8).

10.2 "choose life and die": cf. Deuteronomy 30:19 ("therefore choose life, that both thou and thy seed may live," KJV).

10.4 Cf. "91 Revere Street," p. 122, paragraph 2 (final sentence).

12.1 "the abstract soldiers'-monuments have been reared on every village green" (William James' speech).

13.4 After the charge, there were "many anonymous and widely circulated pieces of doggerel, one of which purported to describe Fort Wagner's commanding officer ordering his troops to bury Shaw 'with his niggers' " (Axelrod, *Life*, 164). "I am thankful they buried him 'with his niggers.' They were brave men and they were his men" (Colonel Charles Russell Lowell). Charles Russell Lowell Jr. married Josephine Shaw, Colonel Shaw's sister, after Shaw's death; he also died in the Civil War. See "Colonel Charles Russell Lowell 1835–64" in *HIS*, 485.

15.1 Mosler Safe: An advertisement for this safe read: "The Hiroshima Story Comes to Life, with a Bang"; the first atomic bomb was dropped on Hiroshima, 1945.

15.4 The poem was written during the period of forced school desegregation in the South; nine African-American school-children attempting to attend an all-white high school in Little Rock, Arkansas, had to be escorted by Federal troops (September 1957).

17 "The poem . . . finally circles back to its memory of childhood, at which there dawns, un-voiced, the fear that the Aquarium's tanks are now dry because the sea-world has broken loose. . . . How right to eschew a hyphen in 'giant finned' " (Christopher Ricks, in *Critics on Robert Lowell*, ed. Price, 98).

NEAR THE OCEAN (1967)

The copy-text is the first Farrar, Straus and Giroux printing.

    In the main text, we print the version of Lowell's Note that appears in the FSG paperback and Faber and Faber editions. In the FSG hardback edition, which contained illustrations by Sidney Nolan, Lowell alludes to Nolan: "How one jumps from Rome to the America of my own poems is something of a mystery to me. Perhaps the bridge is made by the brilliant drawings of Sidney Nolan. May my lines throw some light on his!"

    Lowell writes: "My next book, *Near the Ocean*, starts as public. I had turned down an invitation to an Arts Festival at the White House because of Vietnam. This brought more publicity than poems, and I felt miscast, felt burdened to write on the great theme, private though almost 'global.' . . . [T]he meter I chose, Marvell's eight-line stanza . . . hummed in my mind summer till fall. It's possible to have good meter yet bad intention or vice versa—*vers de société*, or gauche sprawl. All summer, as I say, the steady, hypnotic couplet beat followed me like a dog. I liked that. After two months, I had two poems, one a hopeless snakeskin of chimes. My last piece ['Near the Ocean,' section V of the sequence of the same title], my most ambitious and least public, was a 'Dover Beach,' an obscure marriage-poem set in our small Eastern seaboard America" (*CPR*, 269–70).

NEAR THE OCEAN

1. WAKING EARLY SUNDAY MORNING

See Appendix III, p. 933, for the magazine version of this poem.

2.5 I.e., a rainbow trout biting a fishing lure that sits on the water's surface. "A dry fly floats on the surface, that's the generic name for this kind of fly, unlike a *wet* fly" (Lowell, quoted in Anzilotti, 62–63).

4.3–4 "They that go down to the sea in ships, that do business in great waters; These see the works of the Lord, and his wonders in the deep" (Psalms 107:23–24).

6.5 anywhere, but somewhere else!: Cf. Baudelaire's prose-poem "Any Where Out of the World" (he gave it this English title) in *Le Spleen de Paris* (1864; Axelrod, *Life*, p. 270, n.54.).

8.3–8 This passage offers a sequence of things or representations that, though once useful, once powerful, now are remnants. Unexplicit, "wordless," their power is the power of things once believed, of again wearing "old clothes." The last line quotes St. Paul: "Though I speak with the tongues of men and of angels, and have not charity, I am become as sounding brass, or a tinkling cymbal" (I Corinthians 13:1). For those animated by conviction, such things or arts offer merely tantalizing, seductive surfaces, signs without substance like the graven images condemned in the Hebrew Bible. Paul, who damned the "unrighteous" (see I Corinthians 6:9–10), was himself banished, an "example" (Acts 19–20; Yenser, p. 347, n.10). According to Lowell, the pun on "cymbal-symbol" is found in Paul's Greek text (Williamson, *Pity the Monsters*, 122). [F.B.]

9.1–2 "[N]ow we see through a glass, darkly; but then face to face" (I Corinthians 13:12).

9.7 Lowell tried to use the china doorknobs as early as "Skunk Hour": "I began to feel that real poetry came, not from fierce confessions, but from something almost meaningless but imagined. I was haunted by an image of a blue china doorknob. I never used the doorknob, or knew what it meant, yet somehow it started the current of images in my opening stanzas" (written in 1964; *CPR*, 228).

10.2–8 Goliath: The Philistine giant slain by David. King Saul asked David to bring him one hundred foreskins of Philistines, instead of a dowry, to marry the King's daughter Michal (I Samuel 18:25–27).

12.3 President Lyndon B. Johnson.

12.6 bear-cuffed: I.e., playfully slapped with an open hand. "[T]he bear was Johnson, the President, who cuffed his aides" (Lowell in conversation, paraphrased by Anzilotti, 65).

14.6 "Our official doctrine is that we must be prepared to police the world" (Walter Lippmann, *Newsweek*, May 24, 1965, 23).

14.8 Cf. "The Voyage" VII.1.2–4 in *IM*, 254. Perhaps "monotonous sublime" is an inversion of each term of Shelley's phrase "intense inane" (*Prometheus Unbound*, III.iv.204), spoken by the "Spirit of the Hour":

The loftiest star of unascended Heaven
Pinnacled dim in the intense inane.

2. FOURTH OF JULY IN MAINE

2.2 Clergy active in the Civil Rights movement (late 1950s and 1960s).

2.7 See Emerson's essay "Self-Reliance."

6.3 China trade: New England merchant ships carried American goods such as leather to China, Chinese tea, ceramic wares and silk back; the China trade flourished between the late eighteenth century and mid-nineteenth century.

6.5 Cotton Mather: American Puritan clergyman and writer (1663–1728). "Mather, the Salem witch hanger, was a professional man of letters employed to moralize and subdue. His truer self was a power-crazed mind bent on destroying darkness with darkness, on applying his cruel, high-minded, obsessed intellect to the extermination of witch and neurotic. His soft, bookish hands are indelibly stained with blood. . . . His face is not on a postage stamp" (Lowell, *CPR*, 183).

6.8 *bell'età dell'oro*: Golden age.

8.3 Trollope's Barchester: Many of Anthony Trollope's novels were set in the fictional town of Barchester; see, e.g., *Barchester Towers* (1857).

10.6 Nadia Boulanger (1887–1979) French conductor and teacher; here, her recordings are played on a Magnavox record-player (10.8).

15.1 converted barn: See note to "Soft Wood" 6.1 on p. 1064.

16.1 This line rewrites the final line of John Crowe Ransom's "Of Margaret": "Of that far away time of gentleness." Lowell wrote Ransom that he had reworked his line (July 26, 1968).

16.5 Logos: Word. See John 1:1.

3. THE OPPOSITE HOUSE

1.2 police stable: "police station" in *The New York Review of Books* (April 18, 1965).

2.5 José Antonio Primo de Rivera, the Falangist leader, appealed for clemency for his brother and brother's wife: "Life is not a firework one lets off at the end of a garden party" (Hugh Thomas, *The Spanish Civil War*, 352).

2.7 *casa*: Literally, "house"; but with some of the larger implications of the French *maison*.

3.9 *Viva la muerte!*: Long live death! (Falangist general Millán Astray's motto in the Spanish Civil War [Thomas, 354]).

4. CENTRAL PARK

This poem carries echoes of William Carlos Williams' "Sunday in the Park" section of *Paterson* II (Axelrod, *Life*, 190; Mariani, 338–39).

4.6 Cleopatra's Needle: A stone obelisk in Central Park.

4.8–10 From *The New York Review of Books* (March 31, 1966):

> Then night, the night—Oh jungle hour,
> the rich in his slit-windowed tower . . .
> Oh Pharaohs starving in your foxholes,

Lowell described this poem as "a nightmarish, obscure reverie on marriage, both vengeful and apologetic" (Mariani, 336). E.H.L.: Elizabeth Hardwick Lowell.

1.4 her once head: Decapitated head; like Perseus lifting Medusa's head in Bernini's statue (Florence). In *NTO*, "her head"; "her once head" in *SP*.

1.7 old iron-bruises: A pun on "Old Ironsides," nickname of the U.S.S. *Constitution*, moored in Boston Harbor. "[A] sort of pun; the old lady is hard as iron, her complexion is like bruises from something hard, rather the color of old iron" (Lowell, quoted in Anzilotti, 62).

2.5 gorgon head: Medusa's head (see Glossary).

6 *The New York Review of Books* version (March 31, 1966):

> Or was it later? Long recovered,
> dead sober, cured! As usual smothered
> by the closed, diminished scene,
> they met once, crossed the gritty green,
> then passed elms dried to bark, washed out
> in summer's coarse last quarter drought.
> (They're young still!) She put on a face.
> Dehydration browned the grass.

6.3 hardveined elms: "like us with hardening of the arteries" (Lowell, quoted in Anzilotti, 62).

FOR THEODORE ROETHKE

Roethke died of a heart attack while diving into a swimming pool.

See "Theodore Roethke 1908–63" in *HIS*, 533.

1958

See "For Ann Adden 1. 1958" in *HIS*, 535.

7–8 Marian Anderson: American contralto (1897–1993). Anderson never recorded or broadcast anything from *Il re pastore* (8), Mozart's dramatic "serenata" (1775). In 1955, she was in the news as the first African-American to sing at the Metropolitan Opera; she debuted as, then recorded, Ulrica in Verdi's *Un ballo in maschera*. Perhaps *Il re pastore* (with its connotations of pastoral harmony) has been confused with, or by intention substituted for Ulrica's invocation to Satan, "Re dell'abisso" (King of the Abyss). The poem is made up of vertiginous shifts, extravagant judgments suddenly reversed as in delirium, abysses that open as opposites abruptly pass: "Hammerheaded shark" (8) immediately followed by "the rainbow salmon of the world" (9). The *History* revision makes clear that in the original "1958" Lowell probably did not intend merely a serial listing of recordings: the new line reads, "Marian Anderson in Mozart's *Shepherd King*" (7). [F.B.]

10 Mittersill: Mittersill Resort, in Franconia, New Hampshire.

10 In the magazine version (*Harper's*, September 1966) line 10 was the final line, and reads: "a rose. Remember? And we stood, still stand?" In *NTO*, Lowell changed line 10, and added four more lines, making the poem a sonnet.

11–13 "The whole visible world is only an imperceptible atom in the ample bosom of nature. No idea approaches it [i.e., nature]. We may enlarge our conceptions beyond all imaginable space; we only produce atoms in comparison with the reality of things. It is an infinite sphere, the center of which is everywhere, the circumference nowhere" (Pascal, *Pensées*, trans. Trotter [1941], no. 72 ["Man's disproportion"], 22). "St. Augustine described the nature of God as a circle whose center was everywhere and its circumference nowhere" (Emerson, "Circles").

SPRING

12 Faunus: God of fields and shepherds, protector of poets.

SERVING UNDER BRUTUS

A note on the circumstances of Horace's poem: "Horace, and this Pompey, had been in the army of Brutus and Cassius, fighting against Octavian (Augustus) [for the restoration of the Republic]. Philippi is the disastrous battle that ended the cause of Brutus and Cassius, who committed suicide. Horace's property was confiscated but he was allowed to go to Rome, where he later came into favor with Augustus. This real or fictitious Pompey was evidently forgiven later and had been allowed to return to Italy only a short time before the occasion, real or fictitious, of the poem" (Ferry, *Odes of Horace* [1997], 328). See "Horace, Pardon For a Friend," *HIS*, 441.

2.4 nard: A balm made from spikenard.

CLEOPATRA

"The occasion of this poem is the news of the final defeat and the deaths of Antony and Cleopatra (30 B.C.E.)" (Ferry, *Horace*, 327). See "Nunc est bibendum, Cleopatra's Death" in *HIS*, 444.

3.1 Capitol: One of the hills of Rome, with several temples, crowned by the temple of Jupiter. "At all periods it constituted less a part of the inhabited area of the city than a citadel and sanctuary: it is mentioned chiefly in connection with religious observances, especially triumphs, and with military operations" (*The Oxford Classical Dictionary*, 164).
5.3 running on the wind: Sailing with the wind coming over the stern of the boat.
9.1 Octavian: Caesar.

THE VANITY OF HUMAN WISHES

Juvenal's poem is known simply as the Tenth Satire; Lowell uses the title of Samuel Johnson's great "imitation" of the poem (1749), set in London, not Rome. Juvenal: born A.D.c. 55 or 60, died in or after 127. See "Hannibal 2. The Life" (439), "Weekly Juvenal, Late-Empire" (446), and "Juvenal's Prayer" (446), all in *HIS*. William Arrowsmith: American scholar and translator (1924–1992).

1.14–15 Nero exiled jurist Cassius Longinus on trumped-up charges; he forced the philosopher Seneca to commit suicide after the "Conspiracy of Piso" was discovered (A.D. 65).
1.16 Laterani: Presumably, followers of senator Plautius Lateranus, also implicated in the "Conspiracy of Piso" against Nero.
3.2–6 Greek philosopher Democritus (c. 460–c. 370 B.C.), famous for his theory that everything is atoms and void, was known in Rome as the "laughing philosopher." Heraclitus (fl. c. 500 B.C.)—because of a misinterpretation of his view that "all things flow" like rivers, as well as Theophrastus' assertion that he was melancholic—was known as the "weeping philosopher."

5.8 Sejanus: Roman soldier who gained power when Tiberius Caesar withdrew from Rome to the island of Capri, until Tiberius, warned of his plans to seize the throne, sent a letter to the senate, leading to Sejanus' arrest and execution (A.D. 31).

7.9–10 The first Triumvirate (begun in 60 B.C.) was composed of Crassus, Pompey the Great, and Julius Caesar ("he who scourged / Gaul . . .").

8.5 Demosthenes: See note on 8.16 below, and reference to the "Philippics" in note to "Alexander" 3 p. 1078. Cicero: see note to "Cicero, the Sacrificial Killing" 5 p. 1081, and to "Dea Roma" 1.2 p. 1020.

8.11 "My consulate": Cicero's "Poem on His Consulate" has often been derided. It is the "pompous verse" referred to below (14).

8.12 you: Cicero.

8.13 Antonius: Mark Antony, who had Cicero executed because of Cicero's speeches (the "Philippics") attacking him.

8.16 patriot Greek: Demosthenes; he committed suicide rather than be arrested by the Greek ruler Antipater (322 B.C.).

11 See "Hannibal 2. The Life" in HIS, 439.

11.14 Subura: A noisy, crowded slum area in Rome. ("Suburva" in NTO; correction from magazine version, Encounter, December 1966, p. 92.)

11.25 Cannae: See note to "Russia 1812" 1.36 on p. 1050.

12.8–16 The Persian king Xerxes dug a canal through the peninsula of Mt. Athos; he later lashed the waters of the Hellespont (to punish Neptune) after his defeat by Greece at Salamis (480 B.C.).

16.7–30 Nestor, the aged leader in the Iliad (I.250ff); his son Antilochus was killed by Paris. Peleus and Achilles, Laertes and Odysseus: fathers and sons. King Priam was killed during the destruction of Troy (Aeneid, II.506–58). Paris's abduction of Helen across the sea prompted the war, and therefore the death of Priam's children: Hector (killed by Achilles), Cassandra (made concubine by Agamemnon, later killed by Clytemnestra). After Priam's death, some accounts hold that his wife, Hecuba, was turned into a dog.

17.1 Mithridates: Mithradates VI Eupator (120–63 B.C.), king of Pontus (in Turkey). After several defeats, the last by Roman general Pompey, his subjects (led by his son) revolted; he died by the sword of a guard.

17.2 According to a chronologically impossible story told by Herodotus (1.29ff), when Greek statesman and poet Solon was asked by King Croesus if he, the king, was not the happiest man he had ever seen, Solon replied: "Call no man happy before his death" (c. 555 B.C.).

17.2 our own men: I.e., Romans.

17.3 Marius: Gaius Marius (c. 157–86 B.C.); see "Rome" 5 in HIS, 438, and corresponding note, p. 1080.

17.11–15 Pompey, murdered as he stepped off a boat.

17.15 Lentulus: A member of Catiline's conspiracy to overthrow the Senate, strangled on Cicero's orders (December 5, 63 B.C.).

17.16 Cethegus: Another member of the Catiline conspiracy, condemned to death in 63 B.C.

18.3 Latona: Titaness who with Jupiter conceived Diana, goddess of the hunt.

18.4–6 Lucretia committed suicide after being raped; Virginia, relentlessly pursued by the seducer Appius, was killed by her father.

20.4 Mars The god of war seduced Venus, and was caught by her crippled husband, Vulcan.

20.17–20 Sthenoboea, wife of Proetus, king of Argos, was in love with Bellerophon, who refused her; she accused him of rape, then killed herself. Phaedra slandered her son-in-law Hippolytus after he rejected her advances, whereupon her husband and Hippolytus's father, Theseus, had Hippolytus killed. When his innocence was revealed, she committed suicide.

21.2 Caesar's consort: Messalina. Although married to the Emperor, Messalina forced Gaius Silius, the consul designate, to divorce his wife and then married him (47–48 A.D.); both were executed. Tacitus (*Annals*, 11.12 and 26ff) says Silius instigated the marriage ceremony. See "Empress Messalina's Last Bridegroom" in *HIS*, 445.

22 See "Juvenal's Prayer" in *HIS*, 446.

22.10–11 See "Sound Mind, Sound Body," p. 597.

22.15 Hercules: The half-human son of Jupiter; he had to complete twelve labors to expiate the crime of killing his wife and children.

22.16 Sardanapalus: Legendary, sybaritic king of Assyria (found in the *Persica* of the Greek historian Ctesias); some scholars identify him with Ashurbanipal, who reigned 668–627 B.C..

BRUNETTO LATINI

Brunetto Latini (c. 1212–1294) was a diplomat and scholar, whose didactic poem *Il Tesoretto* (*The Little Treasury*) may have served as a model for Dante's *Commedia*. Dante says that he "taught me how a man becomes eternal," but many contemporary scholars argue that he was not literally Dante's teacher. Ser Brunetto ("Ser," a customary term of respect) shares a "low path" with other sodomites, such as Andrea de' Mozzi; see note below [6.13–15]. See "Dante 1" in *HIS*, 453, and "For George Santayana" 2.3–5 in *LS*, 155.

Lillian Hellman (1905–1984), American dramatist; in her play *The Children's Hour* (1934), a malicious child accuses two of her teachers of being lesbian.

3.12 this man: Virgil, the Roman poet (70–19 B.C.).

4.5 perverted and ungrateful flock: descendants of the people of the hill town of Fiesole, the headquarters of Catiline's army (see note to "The Vanity of Human Wishes" 17.15 p. 1071). The Romans destroyed Fiesole and then founded Florence in the plains below, inviting the surviving Fiesolans to live there.

4.15 Guelph and Ghibelline: Parties favoring the Italian Pope and the German Holy Roman Emperor, respectively, who contended for control of Florentine politics. Dante was a Guelph; but after the defeat of the Ghibellines, the Guelphs in turn divided into Black Guelph and White Guelph. The Black Guelphs, with the help of Pope Boniface VIII, eventually exiled hundreds of White Guelphs, including Dante. "Dante was virtually a Ghibelline, a fanatical one. His *Commedia* is a Ghibelline epic. . . . I am suggesting that the *Commedia*, like *Paradise Lost*, is in part hermetic, and means at times the opposite of what it asserts" (Lowell, *CPR*, 216–17).

4.33 with other prophecies I keep: Prophecies that Dante has heard earlier in the *Inferno*, from Ciacco about Florentine factions exiling their opponents (VI.64ff), from Farinata about Dante's own exile (X. 79–81).

4.34 a Lady: Beatrice—Dante cannot refer to her directly here (see *Beatrice* Portinari in the Glossary).

6.10–11 Priscian and d'Accorso, distinguished scholars of the day.

6.13–15 Servants' Servant: A term for the Pope (servus servorum Dei: "the servant of the servants of God"); here, an ironic reference to Pope Boniface VIII. Boniface transferred Bishop Andrea de' Mozzi ("the man") from Florence to Vicenza, where he died. Arno: river in Florence. Bacchilione: river in Vicenza.

6.20 *Tesoro*: Italian title (meaning "treasure") of Latini's French work *Li livres dou tresor*, an encyclopedia of history, natural science, ethics, rhetoric, and political science.

7.1–4 A reference to Verona's annual foot race, with naked runners; the winner was given a bolt of green cloth.

Line one of each sonnet translates the Spanish title listed by Lowell.

This sequence was published as "Four Spanish Sonnets" in *Poetry* 103 (1963), nos. 1–2. The first two poems were titled "Ruins" and the second two, "Time." Each of the four poems had a subtitle: "His House"; "Rome"; "For the Chapel of Our Lady of the Sacristy, in the holy Church of Toledo, the burial place of Cardinal Sandoval"; "A Roman Street."

I See "Spain Lost" in *HIS*, 465.

II See "Rome in the Sixteenth Century" in *HIS*, 448.

II.3 Aventine: One of the seven hills of Rome.

II.5 Capitol: See note to "Cleopatra" 3.1 p. 1070.

III See "Góngora, the Tomb of Cardinal Sandoval" in *HIS*, 465.

III.11 Sandoval: Francisco Gómez de Sandoval y Rojas (1553–1623), prime minister to Philip III of Spain (1578–1621); he was made a cardinal in 1618 before being ousted from power. Góngora was Philip's chaplain.

IV See "Vita Brevis" in *HIS*, 447.

HISTORY (1973)

After *Near the Ocean*, Lowell began writing unrhymed blank verse "sonnets"—stanzas of fourteen lines, some free-standing enough to be considered "poems," others clearly not. All were units of a larger project. At first he published them as *Notebook 1967–68* (1969; enlarged for a second printing the same year), then much enlarged, simply as *Notebook* (1970). The autobiographical sequence of sonnets ultimately published as *The Dolphin* was begun in 1970. In early 1972, the *Notebook* stanzas were split into two volumes: the sonnets about family became *For Lizzie and Harriet*, the others (with many new sonnets) *History*. *History, For Lizzie and Harriet*, and *The Dolphin* appeared together in 1973; Lowell never published another unrhymed sonnet.

In 1971, in the middle of this process, Lowell compared his new form with the Marvell stanza that he used in *Near the Ocean*:

> *Notebook* . . . is in unrhymed, loose blank-verse stanzas, a roomier stanza [than Marvell's], less a prosodist's darling. It can say almost anything conversation or correspondence can. . . . [It] allowed me rhetoric, formal construction, and quick breaks. Much of *Life Studies* is recollection; *Notebook* mixes the day-to-day with the history—the lamp by a tree out this window on Redcliffe Square . . . or maybe the rain, but always the instant, sometimes changing to the lost. A flash of haiku to lighten the distant. Has this something to do with a rhymeless sonnet? One poem must lead toward the next, but is fairly complete; it can stride on stilts, or talk. . . .

> I didn't find fourteen lines a handcuff. I gained more than I gave. It would have been a worry never to have known when a section must end; variation might have been monotony. Formlessness might have crowded me toward consecutive narrative. Sometimes I did want the traditional sonnet, an organism, split near the middle, and building to break with the last line. Often a poem didn't live until the last line cleared the lungs. . . .

> I wrote in end-stopped lines, and rewrote to keep a sense of line. I never wrote more, or used more ink in changes. Words came rapidly, almost four hundred sonnets in four years—a calendar of workdays. I did nothing but write; I was thinking lines even when teaching or playing tennis. Yet I had idleness, though drawn to spend more hours working than I ever had or perhaps will. Ideas sprang from the bushes, my head; five or

six sonnets started or reworked in a day. As I have said, I wished to describe the immediate instant. . . . Things I felt or saw, or read were drift in the whirlpool, the squeeze of the sonnet and the loose ravel of blank verse. I hoped in *Life Studies*—it was a limitation—that each poem might seem as open and single-surfaced as a photograph. *Notebook* is more jagged and imagined than was desirable in *Life Studies*. It's severe to be confined to rendering appearances. (*CPR*, 270–72)

This is Lowell's prefatory Note to *History*:

About 80 of the poems in *History* are new, the rest are taken from my last published poem, *Notebook* begun six years ago. All the poems have been changed, some heavily. I have plotted. My old title, *Notebook*, was more accurate than I wished, i.e., the composition was jumbled. I hope this jumble or jungle is cleared—that I have cut the waste marble from the figure.

Alex Calder writes of the principles underlying *History*: "In *History*, the sonnets—or sonnet titles since time is often stacked 'ply on ply' in an individual sonnet—are arranged in rough chronological order yet they do not constitute a chronological series. Unlike the *Notebooks* or *For Lizzie and Harriet*, *History* does not rely on an exterior line of events, such as a real or supposed time of writing, to cohere as a long poem. . . . [A] more positive parallel for the method and structure of *History* can be found in what Foucault, echoing Nietzsche, describes as genealogy (see Foucault, *Language, Counter-Memory, Practice*, 1977; 139–64). A genealogy, for Foucault, is a critical examination of patterns of descent and emergence. . . . First, as a study of descent, *History* is like a family tree in which a genealogy of 'the poet,' of the person of 'powerful vision,' traces tyrants as well as artists as ancestral types. As Foucault suggests, this form of genealogy might well parody the uses to which traditional history is put. . . . An author ought to be directing the lineup [of the powerful] but 'he' so often appears inside the procession, there can be no separating out of identities" (in Axelrod, *Essays*, 134–35).

Foucault's sentences describing Nietzschean "genealogy" describe the texture of discontinuities, refusals, surprises, reversals and retrievals that Lowell has given *History*: "[I]f the genealogist refuses to extend his faith in metaphysics, if he listens to history, he finds that there is 'something altogether different' behind things: not a timeless and essential secret, but the secret that they have no essence or that their essence was fabricated in a piecemeal fashion from alien forms. . . . The body is the inscribed surface of events (traced by language and dissolved by ideas), the locus of a dissociated Self (adopting the illusion of a substantial unity), and a volume in perpetual disintegration. . . . History becomes 'effective' to the degree that it introduces discontinuity into our very being—as it divides our emotions, dramatizes our instincts, multiplies our body and sets it against itself. . . . Knowledge is not made for understanding; it is made for cutting" (142, 148, 154). Foucault finally asserts, however, that genealogy possesses a healing function: "Its task is to become a curative science" (156). This Lowell's skepticism precludes; near the end of *History*, in "Reading Myself," he hopes not to cure, but to become food:

> the corpse of the insect lives embalmed in honey,
> prays that its perishable work live long
> enough for the sweet-tooth bear to desecrate—
> this open book . . . my open coffin.

The fact that in *History* there is, in Alex Calder's phrase, "no separating out of identities" follows the dictum of Emerson, in his essay "History": "Man is explicable by nothing less than all his history. Without hurry, without rest, the human spirit goes forth from the beginning to embody every faculty, every thought, every emotion which belongs to it, in appropriate events. . . . We, as we read, must become Greeks, Romans, Turks, priest and king, martyr and executioner; must fasten these images to some reality in our secret experience, or we shall learn nothing rightly. . . . The instinct of the mind, the purpose of nature, betrays itself in the use we make of the signal narrations of history. . . . [A]ll public facts are to be individualized, all private facts are to be generalized. Then at once History becomes fluid and true, and Biography deep and sublime" (*Essays, First Series*, 1841).

The copy-text is the second Farrar, Straus and Giroux printing. A list of corrections to the second printing prepared by Lowell in 1975 is incorporated here for the first time. Other changes derive from *SP* and the original galleys; corrections and changes are noted.

The sonnet-books include a number of shorter sonnet-sequences. Early versions of two sequences have been reproduced in Appendix IV: "Long Summer" and "Those Older." With regret, we do not reprint "Nineteen Thirties" (*SP*). Excerpted from the flow of *History*, starker and thereby clarified, the sequence nonetheless is too similar to the poems as they appear in *History* to reappear here as a separate unit. (For a list of poems in *History* that are not in *Notebook*, see Yenser, 325ff.)

[F.B.]

HISTORY

10 hunter's moon: Autumnal full moon (technically, the full moon following the harvest moon).
10–14 As the poet looks out, first at the moon, then at the landscape, what he sees is his own face.

MAN AND WOMAN

9 authentic Mother: The ideal Mary, the idea of Mary; as in Renaissance paintings.
10 Berenson: Bernard Berenson (1865–1959), American art historian and connoisseur of Italian art, especially Renaissance art; famous for his authentications and as advisor to great collections, he lived in Tuscany, near Florence.

BIRD?

2 *O mon avril*: O my April.
4 pileated: Having a crest.

DAWN

"New York is our cultural city and furthest from nature; Maine is nature, and Harvard may be somewhere in between, a university" (*CPR*, 268).

5 crimson: Harvard's color.

OUR FATHERS

13 agent provocateur: A secret agent sent to penetrate an organization and incite it to action that will incur punishment.

1 *casus belli*: An occasion that justifies war.
13 my old dog dies of joy: When Ulysses returns to Ithaca after twenty years his old dog recog-
   nizes him, and dies (*Odyssey*, XVII.326–27). Cf. "Returning" 1.4 in *FTUD*, 347.

KING DAVID OLD

3 Abishag: See note to "David and Bathsheba in the Public Garden" II.1.5 p. 1030.
13 Sion: See note to "The Quaker Graveyard in Nantucket" VI.1.8–10 p. 1010.

SOLOMON'S WISDOM

12–13 "This too is vanity" (Ecclesiastes 2:1). "Thy lips are like a thread of scarlet"; "I am a wall,
   and my breasts like towers" (Song of Solomon 4:3; 8:10).

SOLOMON, THE RICH MAN IN STATE

See "Those Older," stanzas 2 and 3, in Appendix IV, p. 941–42.

OLD WANDERER

The subject here is Israel Citkovitz, Caroline Blackwood's second husband. These lines were
written when he was alive; "In the Ward" (*DBD*, 748) is an elegy for him.
   The title refers to the legend of "the wandering Jew": see note to "91 Revere Street" 122
p. 1034.

JUDITH

10 Judith: As the Assyrian general Holofernes besieged a Jewish city, Judith (a widow of great
   beauty) entered the enemy camp and gained his confidence. As he lay in drunken sleep she
   then cut off his head. She returned to the city bearing the head, and the attackers were
   routed. Judith means "Jewess" in Hebrew.

ISRAEL 1

1 Alexander conquered the lands of present-day Israel in 332 B.C.
1 *romero*: pilgrim.
11 King Ahab ruled Israel (c. 874–c. 853 B.C.), married Jezebel, introduced the worship of Baal,
   and was killed fighting the Syrians.
14 The spots the leopard keeps were acquired, in Kipling's *Just So Stories* (1902), as camouflage.

ISRAEL 2

7 long march: An echo of Mao Tse-tung's "Long March" (1934–1935); from the mountain Pis-
   gah, after wandering in the desert for forty years, Moses saw (but was not allowed to enter)
   the land God had promised Israel (Deuteronomy 34).
14 *semper idem and ubique*: Always and everywhere the same.

HELEN

Based on Valéry's poem "Helen." See *IM*, 272.

ACHILLES TO THE DYING LYKAON

Based on the *Iliad*, XXI.122–35. See "The Killing of Lykaon" in *IM*, 197, and corresponding notes, p. 1047.

CASSANDRA 1

10–12 One legend (not in Homer) holds that Achilles was in love with Polyxena, daughter of Priam; Achilles' death at the hands of Paris is foretold in the *Iliad* (XXII.359–60).

CASSANDRA 2

Lines from this poem "steal distortedly from the Urdu poet, Ghalib, literally translated by Aijaz Ahmad" (Lowell's "Afterthought" to *Notebook*, p. 263). Aijaz Ahmad edited *Ghazals of Ghalib* (1971). Lowell uses Ahmad's version of Ghazals 4, 5, and 10.

CLYTEMNESTRA 1

Spoken by Lowell's mother; in *SP*, these lines become a section of the autobiographical sequence "Nineteen Thirties" (193). Their source is a notebook written by Charlotte Lowell in 1937 (see Hamilton, 385–86).

11–12 "Then Mother might smile and answer in a distant, though cosy and amused, voice, 'I usually manage to make myself pretty comfortable' " ("91 Revere Street" in *LS*, 139).

CLYTEMNESTRA 2

1 O Christmas tree, how green thy branches: From the song "O Tannenbaum."

WHITE GODDESS

White Goddess: The moon-goddess. The term was made famous by Robert Graves' *The White Goddess* (1948; revised, 1966). Graves writes: "[T]he language of poetic myth anciently current in the Mediterranean and Northern Europe was a magical language bound up with popular religious ceremonies in honor of the Moon-goddess, or Muse, some of them dating from the Old Stone Age. . . . Socrates, in turning his back on poetic myths, was really turning his back on the Moon-goddess who inspires them and who demanded that man should pay woman spiritual and sexual homage" (9–11).

7 götterdämmerung: The twilight of the gods.
9 The speaker of this poem has given a new title to Verdi's opera *Otello* (1887): *Desdemona*.

IKHNATON AND THE ONE GOD

Ikhnaton, Egyptian pharaoh (1379–1362 B.C.), briefly and against priestly opposition established monotheism in Egypt, the worship of the sun god Aton; Ikhnaton held that he was Aton's physical son.

1 Hera: queen of the Greek gods, wife of the often-unfaithful Zeus.

The Aswan High Dam was built from 1960 to 1970, the cornerstone of Egyptian President Gamal Abdel Nasser's economic plans.

2 Russian foremen: Soviet engineers supervised the project.

DOWN THE NILE

See "Long Summer," sections 10 and 11, in Appendix IV p. 947 and 948.

SAPPHO TO A GIRL

See "Three Letters to Anaktoria" in *IM*, 199.

14 Pleiades: The seven daughters of Atlas; Zeus helped them escape the hunter Orion by changing them into stars.

THE SPARTAN DEAD AT THERMOPYLAE

The narrow pass of Thermopylae (Greek for "hot gates") was on the boundary of Thessaly and Locris, the gate of eastern Greece. Here, in 480 B.C., relatively small Greek forces under the Spartan commander Leonidas for two days held back an immense Persian invading army under Xerxes. Leonidas' "Phocian allies fled before a Persian corps advancing by the mountain path of Anopaea and allowed Leonidas to be outflanked. The other Greek forces dispersed, but Leonidas and 300 companions remained to cover the retreat of the fleet from Artemisium and, after inflicting heavy losses, fell fighting" (*The Oxford Classical Dictionary*, 494). See "Pigeons" *IM*, 316, and "Epigram" *FTUD*, 339.

5–7 A pastiche of phrases from de Sélincourt's translation of Herodotus, *The Histories* (1972), pp. 512, 514, 518.
8 hoplites: Regular heavy-armed Greek infantry.
13–14 Simonides (c. 556–c. 468 B.C.) wrote this epitaph.

XERXES AND ALEXANDER

1–7 Xerxes: king of Persia 485 to 465 B.C.; see note to "The Vanity of Human Wishes" 12.8–16, p. 1071.
12 his fatal Babylon: Alexander died there.

ALEXANDER

3 Demosthenes: see "The Vanity of Human Wishes" 8.16–9.5 in *NTO*, 405–406. Demosthenes delivered the "Philippics" against Alexander's father, Philip of Macedon; Alexander, coming to power, demanded that Demosthenes be surrendered to him, then relented.
6 On his conquests, Alexander carried a copy of the *Iliad* annotated by Aristotle (who had been his teacher).
11 Medius: Medius of Larissa. Arrian writes that a few days before Alexander's death "[a]ccording to some accounts, when he wished to leave his friends at their drinking and retire to his bedroom, he happened to meet Medius, who at that time was the Companion [the Compan-

ions were Alexander's best cavalry] most closely in his confidence, and Medius asked him to come and continue drinking at his own table, adding that the party would be a merry one. The royal Diaries confirm the fact that he drank with Medius after his first carouse. Then (they continue) he left the table, bathed, and went to sleep, after which he supped with Medius and again set to drinking, continuing till late at night. Then, once more, he took a bath, ate a little, and went straight to sleep, with the fever [that killed him] already on him. . . . Next day he bathed again and offered sacrifice as usual, after which he . . . chatted to Medius" (*The Campaigns of Alexander*, trans. de Sélincourt [1971], 391–92).

DEATH OF ALEXANDER

"Lying speechless as the men filed by, [Alexander] yet struggled to raise his head, and in his eyes there was a look of recognition for each individual as he passed. . . . The Diaries say that [seven of his friends] spent the night in the temple of Serapis and asked the God if it would be better for Alexander to be carried to the Temple himself, in order to pray there and perhaps recover; but the God forbade it, and declared it would be better for him if he stayed where he was. The God's command was made public, and soon afterwards Alexander died—this, after all, being the 'better' thing" (Arrian, 393–94).

14 Perhaps Lowell is thinking of Alexander's response after murdering his friend Cleitus: "With a roar of pain and a groan, Cleitus fell, and immediately the king's anger left him. When he came to himself and saw his friends standing around him speechless, he snatched the weapon out of the dead body and would have plunged it into his own throat if the guards had not forestalled him by seizing his hands and carrying him by force into his chamber. There he spent the rest of the night and the whole of the following day sobbing in an agony of remorse" (Plutarch, *Alexander*, trans. Scott-Kilvert [1973], sec. 51–52, p. 309).

POOR ALEXANDER, POOR DIOGENES

Diogenes (4th cent. B.C.), founder of the Cynic school; famous for an extremely austere way of life. He despised worldly possessions, making his home in a tub. Often pictured carrying a lamp, looking for an honest man.

9 "Cynic" is from Greek *kunikos*, "like a dog"; Diogenes's nickname was *Kyon*, dog.
10 Diogenes growling at Alexander: See Plutarch, *Alexander*, sec. 14, p. 266.

THE REPUBLIC

1 Plato: In Plato's *Republic*, Socrates proposes banning poetry from the utopian State (X.607a).
8–14 In Chapter 96 of *Moby Dick*, Ishmael is at the helm facing the "try-works," scalding pots (where blubber is rendered) with a huge fire beneath. Staring into the fire, he sleeps briefly: "Convulsively my hands grasped the tiller, but with the crazy conceit that the tiller was, somehow, in some enchanted way, inverted. . . . Lo! in my brief sleep I had turned myself about, and was fronting the ship's stern, with my back to her prow and the compass. In an instant I faced back, just in time to prevent the vessel from flying up into the wind, and very probably capsizing her. . . . Look not too long in the face of the fire, O man! Never dream with thy hand on the helm! . . . Give not thyself up, then, to fire, lest it invert thee, deaden thee; as for the time it did me. There is a wisdom that is woe; but there is a woe that is madness."

2 proconsul: Governor of a province.

4 General Sulla: 138–78 B.C. Sulla "inaugurated the period of military dictatorships by marching on Rome with his legions. . . . The quasi-regal character of Sulla's dictatorship, unlimited in power and duration, set the model for the undisguised monarchies of Caesar and the second Triumvirate" (*The Oxford Classical Dictionary*, 866–67).

5 Marius, the people's soldier: Gaius Marius, c. 157–86 B.C. "Marius won . . . victories with a re-organized army, having converted the old citizen militia, recruited on a property basis, to a professional army of volunteers recruited from all classes. . . . After Sulla's departure for the East in 88, Marius returned to Italy, joined the democratic leader Cinna, occupied Rome, and was consul in 86 for the seventh time. . . . He now began to take vengeance on his enemies by cruel massacres" (*The Oxford Companion to Classical Literature*, 260–61).

HANNIBAL 1. ROMAN DISASTER AT THE TREBIA

Based on José-Maria de Heredia's "La Trebbia."

The scene (218 B.C.) is the river Trebia in northern Italy, not long after Hannibal crossed the Alps with his troops and elephants. Sempronius (Roman consul for this year, along with Scipio) has just won a skirmish against Hannibal; now he advances across the river Trebia and allows himself to be drawn into an ambush by Hannibal's hidden cavalry and infantry. (See Livy, *History*, XXI.51–56.)

10 Gallic villages: Cisalpine Gaul.

HANNIBAL 2. THE LIFE

Based on Juvenal's Tenth Satire (147–67). See "The Vanity of Human Wishes" 11 in *NTO*, 406–407.

MARCUS CATO 234–149 B.C.

Proverbial for fearless independence, honesty, and a hard-edged frugal practicality. "In 184 [Cato the Elder] held the censorship, the office that made him famous. He applied himself to the reformation of the lax morals of the Roman nobility, and to checking the luxury and extravagance of the wealthy. His ideal was a return to the primitive simplicity of a mainly agricultural State" (*The Oxford Companion to Classical Literature*, 94).

5 jumping her in thunderstorms: "For his own part, Cato declared, he never embraced his wife except when a loud peal of thunder occurred, and it was a favorite joke of his that he was a happy man whenever Jove took it into his head to thunder" (Plutarch, *Cato the Elder*, trans. Scott-Kilvert [1965], 139).

5 *Juppiter Tonans*: Jupiter the Thunderer.

10 Demosthenes: See "The Vanity of Human Wishes" 8.16–9.5 in *NTO*, 405–406, and corresponding note, p. 1071.

11 "Late in life he went as a commissioner to Carthage, and was so impressed by the danger to Rome from her reviving prosperity that he never ceased impressing on the Senate the necessity for her destruction: 'Carthago delenda est' [Carthage must die]" (*The Oxford Companion to Classical Literature*, 94).

MARCUS CATO 95–46 B.C.

Great-grandson of Cato the Elder (see above). "[A] man of unbending character, and absolute integrity, narrow, short-sighted, impervious to reason as to bribery. . . . He is one of the heroes of Lucan's *Pharsalia*. Dante devotes to him a great part of the first canto of his 'Purgatorio' " (*The Oxford Companion to Classical Literature*, 94).

1 For Sulla, see note to "Rome" 4 p. 1080.

5 wasn't invited back: "Sarpedon hearing [Cato's threat to kill Sulla], and at the same time seeing his countenance swelling with anger and determination, took care thenceforward to watch him strictly, lest he should hazard any desperate attempt" (Plutarch, *Cato the Younger*, trans. Dryden-Clough, [1924], 416–17).

7 stoned like Paul: St. Paul. After Cato persuaded the senate to order that those newly elected must account, in court under oath, for their actions to gain office, he was stoned by a crowd (Dryden-Clough, 462).

9 saved Caesar: "He was the chief political antagonist of Caesar and the triumvirate" (*The Oxford Companion to Classical Literature*, 94), in the name of saving the Republic.

HORACE: PARDON FOR A FRIEND

Based on Horace's *Ode* II.7, *O saepe mecum tempus in ultimum*. See "Serving Under Brutus" in *NTO*, 399, and corresponding notes, p. 1070.

CICERO, THE SACRIFICIAL KILLING

Text from *SP*.

A modern-dress version of the events just before the assassination of Cicero, or someone like Cicero; the poem begins with the poet trying to remember a "scarlet patch" from his reading.

2 Tacitus: Roman historian and statesman (A.D. c. 55–c. 117).

3 Pound, whose *Cantos* is an attempt to write a twentieth-century epic poem, said: "An epic is a poem including history" (*Social Credit: An Impact*, 1935). See "Ezra Pound," p. 537.

5 Cicero (106–43 B.C.), one of the most powerful men of his time (as orator, writer, politician), repeatedly attacked Mark Antony in the "Philippics," defending the Republic. Antony demanded the death of Cicero as the price of joining the second Triumvirate (with Lepidus and Octavian, who later became Augustus). Octavian, though he had earlier been helped by Cicero, reluctantly "sacrificed" Cicero. See "Dea Roma" 1.2 in *LWC*, 51, and corresponding note, p. 1040; "The Vanity of Human Wishes" 8 in *NTO*, 405.

5 Marius: See note to "Rome" 5 p. 1080. In 89 B.C. Marius fled Rome as Sulla's armies approached; he was captured alone hiding in a marsh, but escaped to Africa.

7–9 In *HIS* these lines read:

> Fascism is too much money for what we are,
> a republic keeping, freezing the high ranks,
> with heavy feet getting the baby enough milk.

10 Aware that he was on the list of those condemned to death, Cicero fled to one of his estates. As he was being carried from the house to the sea, assassins found him. "Cicero heard [Herennius] coming and ordered his servants to set the litter down where they were. He himself, in that characteristic posture of his, with his chin resting on his left hand, looked steadfastly at

his murderers. He was all covered in dust; his hair was long and disordered, and his face was pinched and wasted with his anxieties—so that most of those who stood by covered their faces while Herennius was killing him" (Plutarch, *Cicero*, trans. Rex Warner [1972], 360).

OVID AND CAESAR'S DAUGHTER

For the history of these lines, and annotation, see note to "Beyond the Alps" 3 p. 1063.

ANTONY AND CLEOPATRA

8 nausée: sensation of being sick, nausea.

NUNC EST BIBENDUM, CLEOPATRA'S DEATH

Based on Horace's *Ode* I.37; for another version, see "Cleopatra" in *NTO*, 400. For annotation, see corresponding notes, p. 1070.

1 *Nunc est bibendum, nunc pede liberum:* Line two translates this line. Lowell (in what probably is a memory slip) changes the final word of Horace's first line from "libero" to "liberum."

CALIGULA 1

This is Caligula waiting to become emperor; Tiberius Caesar, though "in senility" (12), is still alive. The text is adapted from Baudelaire's "Spleen" in *IM*, 236.

CALIGULA 2

See "Caligula" in *FTUD*, 360, and corresponding notes, p. 1062.

EMPRESS MESSALINA'S LAST BRIDEGROOM

Based on Juvenal's Tenth Satire (329–42). See "The Vanity of Human Wishes" 21. 2–18, in *NTO*, 411, and corresponding note, p. 1071–72.

WEEKLY JUVENAL, LATE-EMPIRE

The title refers as much to Karl Marx ("a Juvenal in apotheosis") as Juvenal himself. Each saw himself as issuing reports from, in effect, an empire in decline. Juvenal was not (literally) "Late-Empire"; he lived from A.D. c. 55 or 60 to c. 127. His corrosive sense of Rome's decadence nonetheless implies that it is late in the life of the Empire. Marx (who at times was a correspondent for the *New York Tribune*) wrote of an economic system that he felt must soon, because of inherent contradictions, break down. Lines 1–9 are about Juvenal; 10–12 about Marx.

1–2 Juvenal's Sixth Satire (1–2). For Romans, the age of Saturn (Latin god of agriculture, identified with the Greek god Cronus, the father of Jove) was the golden age: "when the world was young," women suckled "big strong babies," but "men's lives were different . . . they had no parents" (Satire VI, 9–13; trans. Green [1998]).
8 *Roma Meretrix*: Rome the Prostitute.
13–14 These lines parody the opening of Satire VI (arguably, itself a parody [Green, pp. xliv, 203]).

JUVENAL'S PRAYER

Based on Juvenal's Tenth Satire (346–66). See "The Vanity of Human Wishes" 22.1, p. 412; "Sound Mind, Sound Body" p. 597, and note p. 1127.

VITA BREVIS

A sonnet by Góngora, slightly changed from "The Ruins of Time" IV in *NTO*, 418. "*Vita brevis est, ars longa*": life is short, art long (Seneca, *De Brevitate Vitae* I, 1). Góngora's title echoes Seneca: "De la brevedad engañosa de la vida" (Of the Deceptive Brevity of Life).

9 Licio: Góngora's original is addressed to "Licio."

THE GOOD LIFE

This is Rome after the death of Commodus (A.D. 193), "Rome of the officers" (9), when army generals—warring among themselves, at times their allegiance for sale to the highest bidder— alone determined who became emperor. This period was prefigured by A.D. 69, when the dynasty founded by Julius Caesar fell with the death of Nero: in a single year, three successive emperors were either murdered or removed by competing army factions. In 193, "the Praetorian Guard . . . auctioned the Empire to Didius Julianus. Again, as in A.D. 69, provincial armies put forward their candidates for the throne. . . . Severus seized Rome, struck down his rivals, and established a new dynasty. His reign (193–211) was marked . . . above all by its military aspect: the civilian constitution of the Empire which Augustus had conceived was set aside. Abandoning all pretence of co-operation with the Senate, Severus openly showed that his authority rested on the support of the army. . . . [After the death of Alexander Severus in 235,] again the military element triumphed over the civil, and Alexander's murder was followed by half a century of military anarchy which nearly led to the final collapse of the Empire. Emperors followed one another thick and fast" (*The Oxford Classical Dictionary*, 777).

14 Cf. "Eternal vigilance is the price of liberty" (commonly quoted version of John Philpot Curran's "The condition upon which God hath given liberty to man is eternal vigilance"; also attributed to Jefferson).

ROME IN THE SIXTEENTH CENTURY

See "The Ruins of Time" II (after Quevedo) in *NTO*, 417, and corresponding notes, p. 1073.

ATTILA, HITLER

Attila the Hun, barbarian "Scourge of God," invaded the Roman Empire with perhaps half a million Huns and allies (A.D. 451–52).

9 in this coarsest, cruelest . . . : That is, in Hitler.

MOHAMMED

1 Henry VIII: Refused a divorce from Catherine of Aragon, Henry declared himself the ecclesi-
astical authority in England, dissolved the monasteries, and remarried.
6 *schrecklichkeit*: Frightfulness, horror.
8 jihad: Struggle; commonly understood as Holy War.

FAME

Lines from this poem borrow from Aijaz Ahmad's version of Ghazals 6, 7, and 9 in *Ghazals of
Ghalib* (1971). See note to "Cassandra 2" p. 1077.
7 Timur: Also known as Tamerlane ("Timur the Lame"), Timur (c. 1336–1405) extended the
Mongolian empire from India to the Mediterranean. His "reputation is that of a cruel con-
queror. After capturing certain cities he slaughtered thousands of the defenders (perhaps
80,000 at Delhi) and built pyramids of their skulls" (*The New Columbia Encyclopedia*, 2688).
9 Bosphorus: A narrow strait in Turkey, taken as the divide between Europe and Asia.

TIMUR OLD

See note to "Fame" 7, above.

7 Arc de Triomphe: A Parisian memorial built to commemorate Napoleon's victories.

NORTHMEN

Scandinavian Vikings (known as Danes in England) in the ninth and tenth centuries raided and
settled on the coasts of Europe; they plagued Charlemagne in the later part of his reign.

5 Skyfleets: U.S. bomber fleet armed with nuclear weapons, continuously airborne.
8 loved his three R's: Charlemagne established schools for children of all classes throughout his
empire; "although scarcely to be considered educated by later standards, [he] showed great
taste for learning and strove for purity in his Latin" (*The New Columbia Encyclopedia*, 507).
10 *we are begotten in sorrow to die in joy*: The death that is "joy" is a warrior's death, as exemplified
in the next poem; crystallizing the Vikings' ecstatic nihilism, the statement is "humor" (11)
partly because it reverses the usual sentiment. ("Die" also puns on sexual climax.)

END OF THE SAGA

3 Kriemhild: In the *Nibelungenlied* (Middle High German thirteenth-century epic), Kriemhild,
sister of the Burgundian king Gunther, exacts revenge on her brother and sister-in-law
for the death of her husband, Siegfried. (The *Nibelungenlied* draws from the same matrix of
narrative material as the Scandinavian and Icelandic "sagas," especially the prose "saga"
Volsungasaga.)
12 *Beines brichts, herzen nichts*: Broken bones, not hearts [our bones are broken, not our hearts].

DEATH OF COUNT ROLAND

Text from *SP*.
    Scenes from the *Chanson de Roland* (c. 1098–1100), which Lowell renders almost as Pre-
Raphaelite tableaux. Roland is a Frankish Christian hero, the nephew of Charlemagne; left to

guard the rear of Charlemagne's troops as they return to France after seven years fighting the Saracens in Spain, Roland and his friends are ambushed.

1 King Marsilius: Saracen leader, also called King Marsile. Saragossa: In the northeast Spanish Pyrenees.
6 it did to spark the Franco-Moorish War: The king's speech sparks the battles of the *Chanson de Roland*. In *HIS*, the line reads: "it did not spark the Franco-Moorish War. . . ."

ELOISE AND ABELARD

Peter Abelard (1079–1142): "his fame as a dialectician attracted great numbers of students to Paris; because of this fact Abelard is usually regarded as the founder of the Univ. of Paris [the Sorbonne]" (*The New Columbia Encyclopedia*, 5). Abelard and his student Eloise (died c. 1164) fell in love; she became pregnant and they married secretly. Abelard sent her to a convent; her uncle, thinking her abandoned, had Abelard castrated. He became a monk. His first theological work was burnt as heretical, and he was briefly imprisoned (1121). St. Bernard of Clairvaux had Abelard condemned by the Council of Sens (1141).

1 orthodox analysis: Freudian psychoanalysis.
14 *the dialectic*: "A Platonist in theology, Abelard emphasized the method of Aristotle's dialectic. His belief that the methods of logic could be applied to the truths of faith was in opposition to the mysticism of St. Bernard" (*The New Columbia Encyclopedia*, 5).

JOINVILLE AND LOUIS IX

Jean de Joinville (c. 1224–1317), governor of Champagne, accompanied Louis IX of France (St. Louis) on the Seventh Crusade (1248–1254); in old age (1304–1309) he dictated a memoir of Louis. The poem is based on paragraphs 122 and 422–37 of Natalis De Wailly's text (*The Life of St. Louis*, trans. Hague [1955]).

7 Acre: A coastal city in Palestine.
8 Sore of heart then: This follows a confrontation between Joinville and the other nobles. The King and nobles had been imprisoned by the Saracens; the King arranged their ransom. He then asked his council of nobles whether he should sail back to France. Joinville angered his elders, including Philip de Nemours (11), by saying that if the King leaves, the "meaner folk" (8) who are imprisoned never will be freed. The King then put off a decision. The scene at the "barred window" (9) follows.
14 Spoken by the King.

THE ARMY OF THE DUC DE NEMOURS

Charles Emmanuel, Duc de Nemours (1567–1595), supported the anti-Protestant politics of Henri, Duc de Guise; in 1588, when Henri and his brother, the cardinal of Lorraine, were assassinated with the complicity of King Henri III, Charles was arrested. He escaped, and was governor of Paris when Henri IV besieged it. Imprisoned in the chateau of Pierre-Encise by the archbishop of Lyons, he again escaped—then attacked Lyons, but was defeated.

1 In a letter to Henry James, Yeats sends the poem later published as "On Being Asked for a War Poem," then adds: "It is the only thing I have written of the war or will write. . . . I shall keep the neighborhood of the seven sleepers of Ephesus, hoping to catch their comfortable snores till bloody frivolity is over" (August 20, 1915).

5 Moses' anathemas: Acts banned by Mosaic Law.

7 *I am a Catholic because I am a wanton*: Cf. "A Frere ther was, a wantowne and a merye" (Chaucer, *The Canterbury Tales*, Prologue, 208).

DANTE 1

4 his poor souls eclipse the black and white of God: "The great sinners are imagined with such sympathy that Erich Auerbach believed that they almost crack Dante's theological system. . . . I find it hard to consider Dante as entirely orthodox" (Lowell, *CPR*, 216–17). Erich Auerbach: "The image of man eclipses the image of God. . . . The tremendous pattern was broken by the overwhelming power of the images it had to contain" (*Mimesis* [1953], 202).

6–9 From *Inferno*, XV.121–24. "Ser Brunetto": See headnote to "Brunetto Latini," Lowell's version of *Inferno* XV, on p. 1072. See also "For George Santayana" 2.3–5 in *LS*, 155.

10 All comes from a girl: *Beatrice* Portinari (see Glossary). "Beatrice? Saving Grace? She was born in Provence, in the heretical Toulouse of the troubadours—the lady, not one's wife, but the one the troubadour truly loves—chastely by necessity with Dante, but not always in the tradition. Where, where, in the whole *Commedia*, are Mrs. Dante and the Dante children? Dante's meeting with Beatrice in the *Purgatorio* burns with a fiercer love than Francesca's for Paolo. Without Beatrice, Dante's *Comedy* wouldn't exist but, as Pound said, would be 'a ladder leading to a balloon' " (Lowell, *CPR*, 218).

13–14 *Inferno*, XXIV.1–5. These are the "two Dante lines" that, in the "Afterthought" to *Notebook*, p. 263, Lowell says he owes to Philip Gambone. (Gambone was his student at Harvard.)

DANTE 2

13 Dante married Gemma Donati and had several children.

DANTE 3. BUONCONTE

The source is the *Purgatorio*, V.85–129. For annotation, see notes to "The Soldier" on p. 1017. Also see "Home" 9 in *DBD*, 825.

1 Giovanna: Buonconte's widow.

4 Casentino: The upper valley of the river Arno.

DANTE 4. PAOLO AND FRANCESCA

From *Inferno*, V.121–138. Dante in hell discovers a man and a woman whirling together in a ceaseless, violent wind; they were murdered by her husband. He asks how Love revealed itself to them.

6 Lancelot: The knight whose affair with Queen Guinevere foreshadowed the destruction of King Arthur's kingdom.

14 Galahalt: Gallehault, the intermediary between Lancelot and Guinevere (in the Old French *Lancelot du Lac*); his name came to symbolize pandering.

DANTE 5. WIND

13 They: Paolo and Francesca.

14 "To remember the present and the future is to have time and fate collapse on you in an eter-

nity of failed desire, the doom reserved for any hyper-imaginative mind" (Thomas R. Edwards, 34).

CANTERBURY

Canterbury: Canterbury Cathedral (constructed 1070–1180, 1379–1503) contains the tombs of the Black Prince and Henry IV, among others.

5 Edward the Black Prince (1330–1376), son of Edward III of England, father of Richard II. "It was apparently the French who called him the Black Prince, perhaps because he wore black armor; the name was not recorded in England until the 16th century. . . . [H]e established his reputation for valor at the Battle of Crécy (1346). . . . [T]he prince, though ill, directed the capture and burning of Limoges (1370) with needless massacre of the citizens" (*The New Columbia Encyclopedia*, 836).
6 *imprimatur*: Literally, "let it be imprinted" (New Latin); official sanction.
8 public school: An English private boarding school.

COLERIDGE AND RICHARD II

2–4 Coleridge on Shakespeare's *Richard II*: "[York's] species of accidental weakness is brought into parallel with Richard's continually increasing energy of thought, and as constantly diminishing power of acting. . . . It is clear that Shakespeare never meant to represent Richard II as a vulgar debauchee, but merely [as a man with] a wantonness in feminine shew, feminine *friendism*, intensely woman-like love of those immediately about him, mistaking the delight of being loved by him for a love for him. . . . Constant overflow of feelings; incapability of controlling them; waste of that energy which should be reserved for action in the passion and effort of resolves and menaces, and the consequent exhaustion. . . . Exhaustion counterfeiting quiet; and yet the habit of kingliness, the effect of flatteries from infancy, constantly producing a sort of *wordy* courage that betrays the inward impotence" (*Shakespearean Criticism*, ed. Raysor [1960], I, 136–40).
5 Richard unkinged saw shipwreck in the mirror: In *Richard II*, when Richard abdicates he asks for a mirror, "That it may show me what a face I have" (IV.i.256). Then he smashes it: "For there it is, cracked in an hundred shivers. / . . . How soon my sorrow hath destroyed my face."

DAMES DU TEMPS JADIS

See Villon's "Ballad for the Dead Ladies" in *IM*, 208, and headnote, p. 1048.

BOSWORTH FIELD

Text from *SP*.
Richard III (Dickon, the Duke of Gloucester) was defeated and killed at Bosworth Field (1485), ending the line of Yorkist kings.

8 we have dug him up past proof: The negative portrait of Richard III in Thomas More's biography is the basis for Shakespeare's *Richard III*; some recent historians have charged that his evil reputation is unjustified, the result of propagandists for Henry Tudor, who usurped Richard's crown.

3 Machiavelli in *The Prince* (ch. 12) writes that mercenaries "have no other love or other reason to hold them firm in the field except a bit of salary, which is not enough to make them want to die for you" (quoted in de Grazia, *Machiavelli in Hell* [1989], 156). As Florentine defense secretary he replaced mercenaries with a citizens' militia.

SIR THOMAS MORE

Text from *SP*.

Sir Thomas More (1478–1535) became Lord Chancellor in 1529, resigned in 1532. He refused to subscribe to the Act of Supremacy, which made Henry VIII the head of the English Church, and was beheaded in the Tower. The Roman Catholic Church canonized him in 1935. Anecdotes in the poem are versions of episodes in the biography by William Roper, his son-in-law.

1–4 These lines describe the celebrated portrait (1527) by Hans Holbein.
5 executioner: An accusation made by historians John Foxe (1563) and J. A. Froude (1856–1870); Anthony Hecht "believe[s] they have been convincingly refuted by R. W. Chambers (1935)" (Hecht, in Meyers, *Interviews*, 346).

ANNE BOLEYN

Despite its title, this poem is essentially about two kinds of painting and art: the art of Potter and Cuyp, naturalistically focused on landscape, farming, farm animals, the world that continues indifferent or untouched by the vicissitudes and fashions of court life, or the history of thought; and the art of Giorgione, focussed on the "great world," myth, literature, the court's fascination with a bucolic dreamworld, where the ostensible subject is a pretext for exploration and self-discovery, emphasizing human invention surpassing nature.

1 Potter . . . Cuyp: Paul Potter (1625–1654); Aelbert Cuyp (1620–1691). Helen Deese "associates Potter's famous and massive *Young Bull* with Henry VIII" (Deese, in Axelrod, *Essays*, 183).
3 Hegel: The German philosopher.
4 our rear-guard painters: Twentieth-century artists who rebel against departures from representation, "haters of abstraction"; their art nonetheless lacks Potter and Cuyp's "art of farming," their weight, mystery, inwardness ("tonnage and rumination of the sod," 8).
9 Henry VIII's second wife (1533–1536), Boleyn was tried on charges of adultery and incest, then beheaded. The rule-breaking abandon of her life, the whiteness of her throat, become emblems here of the Renaissance refusal to be bound by "nature" (12).
10 *raison d'état*: Reason of State; justification based on the needs of the State.
11 Giorgione: Renaissance Venetian painter (c. 1477–1510).
13 the Venetian: Giorgione.

DEATH OF ANNE BOLEYN

Text from *SP*. Anne Boleyn: see note to "Anne Boleyn" 9, above.

3 Wolsey: In order to marry Anne Boleyn, Henry VIII demanded a divorce from Catherine of Aragon; Archbishop Wolsey, Lord Chancellor, fell from power (1529) for failing quickly to procure Henry's divorce. (He had incurred Anne Boleyn's enmity by urging a French marriage on the King.)

3 J. A. Froude (1818–1894) wrote *The History of England from the Fall of Wolsey to the Defeat of the Spanish Armada* (1856–1870).

CRANACH'S MAN-HUNT

Lucas Cranach the Elder (1472–1553), German painter and engraver, whose etching *The Stag-Hunt of the Elector Frederick the Wise* (1529) also includes Maximilian I, Holy Roman Emperor and German king. (The Saxon dukes were among the seven "electors" who chose the Holy Roman Emperor.)

Helen Deese: "[Lowell associates] Lucas Cranach's *Stag Hunt* with a commemorative photograph of a group. . . . I believe that Lowell is looking at a real photograph of real people. . . . The details of the photograph merge into the details of Cranach's etching, suggesting that the first derives from the second, that the manhunt descends from the staghunt. The 'stream of the photograph' becomes the 'choppy, lavender stream' of the etching, where the stags are hunted from ambush by 'the Kaiser Maximilian' (of Austria), by his host Frederick, the 'wise Saxon elector.' . . . Frederick was called 'Wise' because he provided the political support for Luther's Reformation. Cranach was court painter for Frederick and unofficial court painter for Luther and the Reformation. Surely, the merging of photograph and etching, manhunt and staghunt, becomes a visualization of a truth: The Holocaust had a significant source in Luther's exhortations that Jews be hunted out from the German communities" (in Axelrod, *Essays*, 183).

CHARLES V BY TITIAN

Charles V (1500–1558), Holy Roman Emperor, King of Spain. Born at Ghent, raised in Flanders, he inherited a vast empire. The Venetian painter Titian's equestrian portrait is titled *Charles V at the Battle of Mühlberg* (he defeated John of Saxony there in 1547) or *Portrait of Charles V on Horseback*. In 1554 he began a series of abdications, giving countries and dominions to his brother and son; in 1558 he formally abdicated as emperor. His plans for a universal empire had been thwarted by the French, the Ottomans, the spread of Protestantism. Although he retired to the monastery of Yuste, he remained active in politics. See "Charles the Fifth and the Peasant" in *LWC*, 40.

10 Saturn was so fearful of usurpation that he attempted to eat each of his children.

EXECUTION 1

This poem and the next are fantasias or improvisations that begin with lines taken from (or modeled on) "Tichborne's elegy, written with his own hand in the Tower before his execution" (published 1586).

1 Tichborne, 2.4.
13 alba: Dawn. Gerontoi: Old men.

EXECUTION 2

See headnote to "Execution 1," above.

14 Cf. Tichborne, 3.4.

MARLOWE

Christopher Marlowe, author of *Tamburlaine the Great*, *Doctor Faustus*, *The Jew of Malta*, *Edward II*, accused by Thomas Kyd of holding and disseminating heretical, lewd religious and moral principles, suspected by others of being a government agent, at twenty-nine was stabbed by a drinking companion in Deptford.

5 "Marlowe's mighty line" (Ben Jonson, "To the Memory of My Beloved, the Author, Mr. William Shakespeare" [1623] 30).
7 hits: Hit plays.
10 Jesus spoke Aramaic, not Hebrew, Greek or Latin; the earliest form of the New Testament as we have it is in Greek.

DUC DE GUISE

Henri de Lorraine, 3rd Duc de Guise (1550–1588), formed the Catholic League after Henri III of France offered concessions to the Protestant Huguenots. He instigated the St. Bartholomew Day massacre of Huguenots and nearly seized the French throne. King Henri made him lieutenant general of France; then the king's guard murdered him.

8 Blois: The town in central France where the Duc de Guise was killed.

MARY STUART

Text from *SP*.
   Mary Queen of Scots was accused of complicity in the murder of her husband, Henry Stuart, Lord Darnley. The Earl of Bothwell was widely suspected of the murder; three months after the death of Darnley, Mary Stuart and Bothwell were married. Something like this situation becomes the premise of a modern-dress nightmare.

THE WIFE OF HENRI QUATRE 1

For annotation, see headnote to "The Banker's Daughter" p. 1033.

THE WIFE OF HENRI QUATRE 2

See note above.

MALHERBE, L'HOMME DE LETTRES

François de Malherbe (1555–1628), French poet and critic. L'Homme de Lettres: Man of letters.

GÓNGORA, THE TOMB OF CARDINAL SANDOVAL

See "The Ruins of Time" III in *NTO*, 418, and corresponding notes, p. 1073.

SPAIN LOST

See "The Ruins of Time" I in *NTO*, 417, and headnote, p. 1073.

Miré los muros de la patria mia: I saw the walls of my country.

REMBRANDT

Text from *SP*.

Rembrandt van Rijn (1606–1669), Dutch painter, etcher, draftsman.

1 "The first line reminds us of how old paint looks on a canvas, finely crackled" (Helen Deese, in Axelrod, *Essays*, 194).
2 *The Jewish Bridegroom* (painting, c. 1665), usually called *The Jewish Bride*.
4 flayed steer: *The Slaughtered Ox* (painting, 1655); a young woman, half in shadow, looks up at a hanging carcass.
8 The model for *Bathsheba with King David's Letter* (painting, 1654) was his housekeeper (and, for many years, lover) Hendrickje Stoffels. Kenneth Clark: "[T]his ample stomach, these heavy, practical hands and feet, achieve a nobility far greater than the ideal form of, shall we say, Titian's *Venus of Urbino*. Moreover, this Christian acceptance of the unfortunate body has permitted the Christian privilege of a soul" (*The Nude*, 439–41).
13 Lowell struggled to find the right word for the characteristic light in Rembrandt: in *Notebook*, "a red mist"; in *History*, "a brown mist"; in *Selected Poems* (rev.), "a copper mist".
14 idol: "Line fourteen derives from Francis Bacon's third class of idols. Bacon's 'Idols of the Marketplace' are not, as we moderns might assume, the ambitions of merchants. Rather they are words, abstract signifiers that create unsubstantial images or 'false notions,' words that 'wonderfully obstruct the understanding . . . throw all into confusion, and lead men away into numberless empty controversies and idle fancies' " (Deese, 195–96).

MILTON IN SEPARATION

Mary Powell, after a few weeks' marriage, left Milton (1642). He wrote four prose tracts defending divorce on grounds of incompatibility. Powell returned to him in 1645, bore him three daughters, then died in 1652. He married Catharine Woodcock in 1656; she died two years later. In 1663 he married Elizabeth Minshull, who survived him.

1 Christian Homer: Blind, Milton wrote an epic (*Paradise Lost*).
6 Eve: The subject of *Paradise Lost* is the expulsion from Eden.

MARRIAGE

1 stoneaxe surrendered its Celt soul: A pun on "celt," meaning "a prehistoric axlike tool" (Late Latin *celtis*, *celtes*, chisel), and "Celt," "one of the ancient people of western and central Europe, including the Britons and the Gauls" (with implications of uncompromising ferocity) (*American Heritage Dictionary*).

SAMUEL PEPYS

Samuel Pepys (1633–1703), English public official, wrote a diary in cipher (published after his death) giving a graphic portrait of daily life during the Restoration.

8 Charles II (1630–1685) had no legitimate offspring, but children by his many mistresses; the pleasure-loving tone of his court set the tone for the Restoration. He favored religious toleration, and died a Roman Catholic.
14 Hermetic: Pepys' diary was "sealed" in the sense that it was in cipher (lowercase "hermetic"), but his mind lacked an interest in the magical, the occult, in mystery sealed beneath a difficult surface, inaccessible to all but the initiate ("Hermetic").

JOHN GRAHAM AT KILLIECRANKIE

In 1688, James II of England was deposed by William of Orange, who had landed in England at the invitation of Protestant nobles. In 1689, Scottish soldier John Graham of Claverhouse, Viscount Dundee, in support of James, defeated William's army near Killiecrankie Pass in Scotland; Graham was killed in the battle. "The battle, disastrous as it was to the government forces, was in reality the end of the insurrection, for the controlling and commanding genius of the rebellion was no more" (*The Encyclopaedia Britannica*, 11th ed., VIII, 674).

12 opened a gap: Graham was pierced beneath his breastplate by the bullet that killed him.
14 *the King*: James II.

VERSAILLES

Louis XIV, the "Sun King" (reigned 1643–1715), is dying. Louis moved his court to the village of Versailles in 1682; an emblem of his reign, the palace and gardens that he built there are French classicism at its height.

PETER THE GREAT IN FRANCE

Peter the Great, czar of Russia, visited France in 1697–1698.

12 Louis Quinze: Louis XV (reigned 1715–1774).

BISHOP BERKELEY

George Berkeley (1685–1753), philosopher and divine. Berkeley "held that, when we affirm material things to be real, we mean no more than that they are perceived (*esse est percipi*). Material objects, on Berkeley's view, continue to exist when not perceived by us solely because they are objects of the thought of God" (*The Oxford Dictionary of the Christian Church*, 161).

3 From 1728 to 1731 Berkeley was in America.
4 Attila: See headnote to "Attila, Hitler" p. 1083. Rimbaud: French poet, who advocated derangement of the senses.
12 Whitman: see notes to "Shadow," p. 1147.

THE WORST SINNER, JONATHAN EDWARDS' GOD

See "Mr. Edwards and the Spider," 59, "After the Surprising Conversions," 61, in *LWC*; "Jonathan Edwards in Western Massachusetts" in *FTUD*, 353.

14 Cf. Voltaire, characterizing the philosophy of Leibnitz and his followers: "All is for the best in the best of all possible worlds" (*Candide*, ch. 1).

WATCHMAKER GOD

11 René Descartes (1596–1650), French philosopher and scientist. William Paley (1743–1805), English theologian.

3 See headnote to "David and Bathsheba in the Public Garden" p. 1030.
6 schoolmen: "The teachers of philosophy and theology at the medieval European universities, then usually called 'schools' " (*The Oxford Dictionary of the Christian Church*, 1247).

DIES IRAE

Lines 1–13 stitch together and vary phrases from Christian hymns and well-known religious texts. Dies Irae: Day of wrath, Judgment Day; see note to "The Day" on p. 1143.

POMPADOUR'S DAUGHTER

Madame de Pompadour (1721–1764): mistress of Louis XV for about five years after 1745, remaining his confidante until her death.

3 bell'Antonios: A "bell'Antonio" is a handsome "ladies' man" who is impotent; based on the title character in *Il bell'Antonio*, a novel by Vitaliano Brancati, then a film directed by Mauro Bolognini (co-scripted by Pier Paolo Pasolini) starring Marcello Mastroianni.
4 *les vieux*: The old ones.

LIFE AND CIVILIZATION

"Civilization" here is the Enlightenment, Locke and Voltaire, the conviction that life can be ordered on a rational basis; "Life" is "you."

8 John Locke (1632–1704), English empiricist philosopher, father of Liberalism; Voltaire (1694–1778), French Enlightenment poet, novelist, writer. The Liberal: "The final aim of liberalism [the development of liberty or freedom] . . . remains fixed, as does its characteristic belief not only in the essential goodness of man but also in his rationality" (*The New Columbia Encyclopedia*, 1572).

ROBESPIERRE AND MOZART AS STAGE

Text from *SP*.
  The poem contrasts revolution as theater with opera as theater. Robespierre was the dominant member of the Committee of Public Safety that began (1793) the Reign of Terror ("*la terreur*," 2) during the French Revolution. The National Convention in 1794 rose against him; he was summarily guillotined.

3 Saint Antoine: District of the poor in Paris.
5 *mort à Robespierre*: Death to Robespierre.
10 blue movie: pornographic movie.
11 Louis Seize: Louis XVI of France, executed in 1793. Living theater: in the 1960's, Julian Beck and Judith Malina's Living Theater performance group became fashionable; it emphasized improvisation, spontaneity, audience participation during performance.
13–14 Mozart's insolent slash: Mozart's opera *The Marriage of Figaro* (1786), libretto by Lorenzo Da Ponte, questions the practices and prerogatives of the aristocracy; its popularity has been seen as prefiguring the French Revolution. Figaro is a barber, about to be married. He is in

the service of a count who schemes to seduce his bride. Figaro in his first aria declares his militant will to defy the count.

13–14 The version in *HIS* reads:

> Mozart's barber *Figaro* could never
> cut the gold thread of the suffocating curtain.

SAINT-JUST 1767–93

Text from *SP*.

1 Missal: Book containing the prayers and responses needed to celebrate the Roman Catholic Mass.
6 Sparta: The militaristic city-state of ancient Greece.
14 Je sais où je vais: I know where I go.

VISION

7 Robespierre: See headnote to "Robespierre and Mozart as Stage," p. 1093.

NAPOLEON

Text from *SP*.

3 *Lives*: Biographies of Napoleon.
7 *sang-froid*: Literally, "cold blood"; composure, imperturbability.
10 The Jacobins grew increasingly radicalized as the Revolution proceeded; under their leader Robespierre, they instigated the Reign of Terror. With his fall (1794) they fell.
14 "And what was the result of this vast talent and power, of these immense armies, burned cities, squandered treasures, immolated millions of men, of this demoralized Europe? It came to no result. All passed away like the smoke of his artillery, and left no trace" (Emerson, "Napoleon; Or, the Man of the World").

BEFORE WATERLOO, THE LAST NIGHT

A version of Rilke's "Letzter Abend" ("The Last Evening"); for annotation and another version, see "The Shako" in *LWC*, 41, and corresponding notes, p. 1018.

WATERLOO

Text from *SP*.

14 *Glory* fading to *run for your life* and *shit*.

LEAVING HOME, MARSHAL NEY

Michel Ney (1769–1815), Marshal of France.

7 *Ancien Régime*: Old Order; originally, the French aristocracy before the Revolution of 1789. It is capable of reasserting its power, "locking in place," at any time ("at the tap of a glove").
8 scoopnets: The Power of the *Ancien Régime* that appears to be dead or nonexistent, but only lies hidden.

9 young voice: A cooper's son from Saarlouis, Marshal Ney rose to become one of Napoleon's greatest generals. Louis XVIII raised him to the peerage (1814); when Napoleon returned from Elba, Ney promised the King that he would stop Napoleon's march to Paris. Instead he joined Napoleon and served as one of his commanders at Waterloo. The house of peers condemned him for treason and he was shot.

14 This line was originally the last line of *DOL*; see note 2.1 on p. 1139. Before *DOL*, a version appeared in a prose statement about Lieutenant Calley; see final paragraph in note on "Women, Children, Babies, Cows, Cats," 1127.

BEETHOVEN

Text from *SP*.

1 *Leaves of Grass* is Whitman's lifework, endlessly revised throughout his lifetime.

7 Othello dies onstage; Lincoln was assassinated while president.

8 Beethoven dedicated his Third Symphony, the *Eroica* (composed 1803–1804), to Napoleon, but erased the dedication when Napoleon made himself emperor.

13 In Beethoven's opera *Fidelio* (begun 1805, completed 1814), a chorus of prisoners is released from their dungeon and briefly allowed light and open air ("Nur hier, nur hier ist Leben, / Der Kerker eine Gruft" [Only here, only here is life; / The prison is a tomb]; Act I).

14 As early as 1801, Beethoven realized he was going deaf.

WHILE HEARING THE ARCHDUKE TRIO

Beethoven's Trio for Pianoforte and Strings ("Archduke," Op. 97) was dedicated to his patron, Archduke Rudolph, youngest son of Holy Roman Emperor Leopold II and half-brother of Francis I, Emperor of Austria.

1 Archduke's War: Rudolph's brother Archduke Charles of Austria defeated Napoleon at Aspern in 1809, but was beaten at Wagram six weeks later.

13 Rudolph was childless; in 1819 he was made a cardinal, and became Archbishop of Olmütz.

GOETHE

Johann Wolfgang von Goethe (1749–1832), German poet, dramatist, novelist, statesman and scientist.

9 *Te Deum laudamus*: Literally, We praise Thee, O God; a traditional Latin hymn, with many musical settings.

10 *pauper amavi*: [As] a poor man I have loved; Ovid, *The Art of Love*, II.165. The entire line reads: "Pauperibus vates ego sum, quia pauper amavi" (I am a poet of poor men, for as a poor man I have loved).

13 daemon: The attendant god or spirit that drives one to follow or fulfill one's nature.

COLERIDGE

See "Coleridge and Richard II," 456, and corresponding notes, p. 1087.

9 positive negation: See the final lines of Coleridge's "Limbo":

A lurid thought is growthless, dull Privation,
Yet that is but a Purgatory curse;
Hell knows a fear far worse,
A fear—a future state;—'tis positive Negation!

LEOPARDI, THE INFINITE

See "The Infinite" in *IM*, 216.

THE LOST TUNE

Text from *SP*. The title echoes Sir Arthur Sullivan's once popular song, "The Lost Chord."

4 *vivace*: Lively, animated (a marking indicating speed and expression in music).
13 Franz Schubert wrote many songs, using poems as texts; see the two poems that follow.
14 greenroom: A waiting room or lounge where performers gather offstage.

DEATH AND THE MAIDEN

Franz Schubert's song "Death and the Maiden" ("Der Tod und das Mädchen") is a setting of a poem by Matthias Claudius. The poem is in two stanzas: in the first, a girl tells Death to pass her by because she is still young; in the second, Death tells her that he is her friend and she will sleep gently in his arms. See "Death and the Maiden" in *DOL*, 705.

1: Romantic painting, because it is not interested in or bound by naturalistic representation of the world, can make both "girl" and "Death" into emblems: the girl addressed by Death represents "Body" (having a body, the condition of being mortal) and Death can take on a body, a figural representation, in the scene. The conventions of realism or naturalism allow neither. Realistic conventions in opera are called "*verismo*" (4); in a *verismo* opera, Death cannot appear onstage as a tenor (or even baritone). Lowell may also be playing with the rhetorical elements of metaphor, the two parts of which are "tenor" (the actual substance or thing to which the image is compared) and "vehicle" (the image). Since *verismo* by definition is nonmetaphorical, its images have no "tenor."
6 Schubert's *Death and the Maiden*: Schubert wrote two works commonly called by this title: one is the setting of Matthias Claudius's poem discussed above; the other is his string quartet in D Minor (1824), which uses themes from the song. Here Lowell seems to be "hearing" (6) the string quartet; hearing the song (because the Girl and Death speak in separate stanzas) would not generate the question in line 8.
7 Schubert (1797–1828) died young.
8 *la femme fatale*: Literally, the fatal (deadly) woman; the common meaning is a woman whose seductive charms are dangerous.
14 *the madness of art*: " 'A second chance—*that's* the delusion. There never was to be but one. We work in the dark—we do what we can—we give what we have. Our doubt is our passion and our passion is our task. The rest is the madness of art' " (Henry James, "The Middle Years").

DIE FORELLE

Die Forelle: The trout. This poem translates the poem by C. F. D. Schubart made famous by Schubert's setting.

HEINE DYING IN PARIS 1

Based on Heine's "Der Scheidende." See "Heine Dying in Paris" II in *IM*, 227, and corresponding notes, p. 1049.

HEINE DYING IN PARIS 2

Based on Heine's "Mein Tag war heiter." See "Heine Dying in Paris" III in *IM*, 228, and corresponding notes, p. 1049.

OLD PRINTS: DECATUR, OLD HICKORY

3-6 Stephen Decatur, U.S. naval commander, in 1804 became famous by stealing with his men into Tripoli harbor and destroying the captured U.S. frigate *Philadelphia*; he later helped in the bombardment of Tripoli. "Our country! In her intercourse with foreign nations, may she always be in the right; but our country, right or wrong" (Decatur, *Toast given at Norfolk*, 1816).

8–14 Called "Old Hickory" by his admirers, Andrew Jackson (U.S. president, 1829–1837) was the one great military hero of the War of 1812. "The greatest popular hero of his time, a man of action, and an expansionist, he became associated with the movement toward increased popular participation in government. . . . His inauguration [as President] brought the 'rabble' into the White House, to the distaste of the established families. . . . [After retirement,] he lived out his life . . . still despised as a high-handed and capricious dictator by his enemies and revered as a forceful democratic leader by his followers" (*The New Columbia Encyclopedia*, 1388).

11 Simón Bolívar (1783–1830), "The Liberator," fought Spanish rule in South America, then with great controversy sought to unite the continent.

NORTHWEST SAVAGE

1 great silent majority: President Richard Nixon asked for the support of the "great silent majority" for his continuation of the war in Vietnam, against the "vocal minority" calling for withdrawal (November 3, 1969).

3 St. Paul, Minnesota.

4 W. H. Harrison (1773–1841), U.S. president (1841) who died in office after one month. After becoming secretary of the Northwest Territory in 1798, he helped open Ohio and Indiana to settlement. Indian opposition to white expansion resulted in the Battle of Tippecanoe, in which Harrison fought Shawnee forces (1811); the battle was indecisive, but Indian power was broken.

11 Jefferson provided the Choctaw Indians a small pension in return for 50 million acres of land along the banks of the Mississippi (1803).

HENRY AND WALDO

Henry David Thoreau (1817–1862); naturalist, author of *Walden* and "Civil Disobedience." Ralph Waldo Emerson (1803–1882); essayist, lecturer, poet, Thoreau's mentor and friend. For Lowell's essay on Thoreau and Emerson, see *CPR*, 186–88, 191–92.

1 Michel de Montaigne (1533–1592), essayist. Emerson: "Montaigne is the frankest and honestest of all writers. His French freedom runs into grossness; but he has anticipated all censure by the bounty of his own confessions" ("Montaigne; Or, the Skeptic").

5 Emerson on Thoreau: "[F]ew lives contain so many renunciations" ("Thoreau").
6 Mallarmé: See note to "Shifting Colors" 10.4, p. 1148.
8 " 'I love Henry,' said one of his friends, 'but I cannot like him; and as for taking his arm, I should as soon think of taking the arm of an elm-tree' " (Emerson, "Thoreau").

THOREAU I

See preceding poem's headnote.

9 Shiva, the killer and a third of God: Shiva is a Hindu deity; Brahma is the creator and Shiva the destroyer, while Vishnu mediates.

MARGARET FULLER DROWNED

Margaret Fuller (1810–1850), American writer and feminist. In Rome she married the Marchese Ossoli, a follower of Mazzini, and took part in the Revolution of 1848–1849. As she returned to the United States with husband and child, the ship went down.

1 Fuller: "It does not follow because many books are written by persons born in America that there exists an American literature" (*New York Tribune*, 1846).

HENRY ADAMS 1850

Henry Adams (1838–1918), historian and writer, author of *The Education of Henry Adams*. His father was U.S. minister to Great Britain; his grandfather and great-grandfather U.S. presidents. For Lowell on Adams, see *CPR*, 200–2.

11 Faneuil Hall: "The Cradle of Liberty," where Boston Town Meetings took place.
14 Napoleon's Old Guard: Imperial guard.

COLONEL CHARLES RUSSELL LOWELL 1835–64

Occasionem Cognosce: "Recognize the opportunity" (or "know your chance"), the Lowell family motto. For Colonel Charles Russell Lowell, see note to *For the Union Dead* 13.4 on p. 1066. "My renowned forebears. . . . The one I'd most like to have known myself is my military cousin, Charles Russell Lowell" (quoted in Meyers, *Interviews*, 96).

7 Cedar Creek: Civil War battle (October 18, 1864).
11 his general: General Philip H. Sheridan.

ABRAHAM LINCOLN

Text from *SP*. "One smiles, not without envy, at the ease and assured precocity with which these young men [Henry Adams and Charles Francis Adams], still in their twenties, could rip to shreds the policies of Lincoln and Secretary Seward" (*CPR*, 202). See *CPR*, 165–66, 192–93, for essays on Lincoln.

3 "War is not merely a political act, but also a political instrument, a continuation of political relations, a carrying out of the same by other means" (Carl von Clausewitz, *On War*).
9 *J'accuse*: I accuse; title and refrain of Emile Zola's famous letter to the President of the French Republic, defending Alfred Dreyfus (1898).

GEORGE ELIOT

Pseudonym of Mary Ann Evans (1819–1880), English novelist. In 1854 she began a relationship with writer and editor G. H. Lewes, which she considered a marriage; because Lewes's estranged wife was still living, this involved social ostracism. Their relationship lasted until his death in 1878; a brief marriage to John Cross followed (1880).

6 "Living? We'll leave that to the servants" (Villiers de L'Isle-Adam, *Axel*).
8 *Mormonage*: I.e., like the Mormons.

HUGO AT THÉOPHILE GAUTIER'S GRAVE

See "At Gautier's Grave," *IM*, 231, and corresponding notes, p. 1050.

BAUDELAIRE 1. THE ABYSS

See "The Abyss" in *IM*, 242, and corresponding note, p. 1051. For Lowell's remarks on translating Baudelaire, see note, p. 1050.

BAUDELAIRE 2. RECOLLECTION

See "Meditation" in *IM*, 240.

RIMBAUD 1. BOHEMIA

See "On the Road," part IV of "Eighteen-Seventy," in *IM*, 265.

7 at the Sign of the Great Bear: I.e., under the constellation Ursa Major.

RIMBAUD 2. A KNOWING GIRL

See "A Malicious Girl," part VI of "Eighteen-Seventy," in *IM*, 267.

RIMBAUD 3. SLEEPER IN THE VALLEY

See "The Sleeper in the Valley," part VII of "Eighteen-Seventy," in *IM*, 267.

RIMBAUD 4. THE EVIL

See "War" in *LWC*, 39, and "Evil," part VIII of "Eighteen-Seventy," in *IM*, 268.

3 Emperor: Napoleon III.

RIMBAUD 5. NAPOLEON AFTER SEDAN

See "Napoleon After Sedan," part II of "Eighteen-Seventy," in *IM*, 264, and corresponding notes, p. 1052.

La Lumière: the light; here, an honorific/ironic epithet Lowell confers on a contemporary woman.

11 Napoleon's Nephew: for Napoleon III, see notes to "Napoleon after Sedan" and "To the French of the Second Empire" p. 1052–53.

MALLARMÉ 1. SWAN

An imitation of Mallarmé's "Le vierge, le vivace et le bel aujourd'hui."

MALLARMÉ 2. GIFT OF A POEM

An imitation of Mallarmé's "Don du poëme."

1 Idumean: From Idumea, an ancient country south of the Dead Sea. Mallarmé has worked all night on the poem "Hérodiade"; Antipater, founder of the dynasty of Herod, was Idumean.

MAIN STREET

7 Sedan and Metz: Battles in which the French were defeated in the Franco-Prussian War (1870–1871).
13 In revolt against the national government, Parisians twice set up the Commune, a kind of proletarian dictatorship—during both the French Revolution (1792) and the Franco-Prussian War (1871). After the Reign of Terror, the power of the first Commune over the National Convention was broken (1794–1795); after a long siege in 1871, the second Commune was defeated and more than 17,000 Communards (partisans of the Commune) executed. In 1871, Communes were formed and suppressed in many other French cities.

LADY CYNTHIA ASQUITH, 1916

Cynthia Asquith (1887–1960); lines 1–7 quote from her *Diaries 1915–1918* (published 1968).

9 Judith: See note to "Judith," p. 1076.

VERDUN

Text from *SP.* After a combined loss of nearly 700,000 men, neither the French nor German armies gained strategic advantage from the eleven-month Battle of Verdun (1916).

CADET-PICTURE OF RILKE'S FATHER

See "The Cadet Picture of My Father" in *IM*, 275.

ANNENSKY: WHITE WINTER, BLACK SPRING

See "Black Spring" in *IM*, 299.

UNDER THE TSAR

8 sons of Belial: in *Paradise Lost*, Belial is a fallen angel, and the "sons of Belial" are homosexual (I.500–505; II.109). In Judges 19:22–25, the "sons of Belial" demand to "know" a visitor; he offers them his concubine instead.

ROMANOFFS

The Romanoffs were the ruling dynasty of Russia from 1613 to 1917.

4 Blacks: In the twentieth century, a term applied to various political or military groups (e.g., Black and Tans, Black Shirts, American Blacks or Afro-Americans).
4 The Reds (Bolsheviks, or Communists) and Whites (a collection of anti-Communist groups) fought the Russian Civil War of 1918–1920.
10 Tsar Nicholas II, the last Romanoff head of state, and his immediate family were executed in a cellar (1918). Nicholas's heir, Tzarevich Alexis (b. 1904), was a hemophiliac.
12 Vladimir Lenin (1870–1924), revolutionary Bolshevik leader.

RILKE SELF-PORTRAIT

See "Self-Portrait" in *IM*, 276.

MUSES OF GEORGE GROSZ

Grosz (1893–1959), the great visual satirist of post–World War I Weimar Germany.

6 Hindenburg: Paul von Hindenburg (1847–1934), German field marshal, president of the Weimar Republic. (Nearly senile, he reluctantly ceded power in 1933 by appointing Hitler chancellor, but remained a figurehead until his death.)
9 The Modern Language Association (of English and foreign-language academics) annually holds a convention.

THE POET

Thomas Hardy (1840–1928).

6 she lived, past sixty, then lived on in him: Hardy's great sequence "Poems of 1912–13" was written in response to the death of his first wife, Emma Gifford.

SCAR-FACE

Chicago mobster Al Capone, before his imprisonment for tax evasion (1931–1939), made a fortune by selling liquor during Prohibition, by controlling gambling and prostitution. His nickname was Scarface, from a knife wound on his left cheek.

3 our thing: "Cosa nostra" (Italian).
8 Little Caesar: Title of a film (1931) loosely based on Capone.

LITTLE MILLIONAIRE'S PAD, CHICAGO

3 *sans rigueur*: "Without rigor"; relaxed.
7 executive-Bronzino: In the style of Agnolo Bronzino (1503–1572), Florentine mannerist

painter. "Bronzino's sophisticated portraits are cold, unemotionally analytical and painted in a superbly controlled technique. The long, chilly faces and postures of his aristocratic subjects express an undisguised arrogance" (*The New Columbia Encyclopedia*).

11 Louis Quinze: A style that flourished under Louis XV of France (1710–1774), characterized by the use of free curves and rococo ornament, with rooms arranged for convenient use.

WOLVERINE, 1927

2 Ernest Seton Thompson: Writer and artist (1860–1946). "His stories and paintings of wildlife . . . were standard works on nature study and wood lore for boys and girls in the first quarter of the twentieth century" (*The New Columbia Encyclopedia*).

TWO FARMERS

See "Dunbarton" in *LS*, 168.

2 Velázquez': Spanish painter Diego Velázquez (1599–1660).

8 grandfather: Arthur Winslow; see "In Memory of Arthur Winslow" in *LWC*, 23, and corresponding notes, p. 1014.

13 Old Cato: See "Marcus Cato 234–149 B.C.," p. 440, and corresponding notes, p. 1080.

THE WELL

"Lowell's poetry gave one the sense of living in a well, the echoes were deep, and sound was finally lost in moss on stone" (Norman Mailer, *The Armies of the Night*) [1968], 125).

FIRST THINGS

Text from *SP*.

FIRST LOVE

Text from *SP*.

14 In *Notebook*: "The mania for phrases dried his heart" (p. 38). Jonathan Raban identifies the *Notebook* version as a quotation from Flaubert's mother (Hamilton, 431). Anthony Hecht comments: "[T]here is in this revision of the Flaubert poem an allegory of what Lowell must have felt about himself: if to others it appeared that his heart had dried, to the artist, to Lowell/Flaubert, it was clear that his heart was enlarged by the very act of finding words, by the very mania for phrases that so obsessed them both" (Meyers, *Interviews*, 340). An "enlarged" heart is also a medical term, a condition that can cause heart failure.

1930's I

The stanzas titled "1930's" for the most part adapt stanzas from the sequence "Long Summer" in *Notebook* (see Appendix IV, p. 943). In 1974 Lowell wrote to Robert Boyers that he now thought that this had been a mistake: "I put a section [of] 14 poems called 'Long Summer' in *Notebook*, into *History*. To do this I had to take immediate 1966 Maine experience and change it into recollections of boyhood. A symbolic solidity was lost. I intend to put this group in *Lizzie and Harriet* (with small changes from the original). It makes the whole book less delicate and more what I imagined" (January 22, 1974). But he never made these changes; for *Selected Poems* (1976), the majority of the stanzas remain titled "1930's" (though some sections return to *Notebook* texts). In *Selected Poems*, they are part of a separate sequence titled "Nineteen Thirties."

3 Dealer's Choice: A variation of poker, which allows the dealer to choose how the hand is played.

1930'S 3

10 Oskar Kokoschka (1886–1980), Austrian-born Expressionist painter.

1930'S 4

6 Custer: George Armstrong Custer (1839–1876), American army officer killed by the Sioux in the Battle of the Little Bighorn; Sitting Bull (8) led the Sioux forces.

BOBBY DELANO

2 St. Mark's: A private secondary school (as is Groton). See "St. Mark's, 1933" in *DBD*, 800.
9 Both title and refrain of a popular song.
14 Ajax: Perhaps the Ajax known as "the Greater Ajax," a warrior of great stature and prowess, the Son of Telamon, king of Salamis: "In the *Odyssey* (XI.543ff.) mention is made of his death in consequence of the arms of Achilles having been adjudged to Odysseus and not to him after the death of their owner. The story is probably that found in later authors, e.g. Sophocles (*Ajax*), that he went mad with anger and disappointment and finally killed himself" (*Oxford Classical Dictionary*, 26). Delano, however, shares characteristics with Ajax the Lesser, the Son of Oïleus or Ileus, the Locrian chieftain: "of hateful character and on occasion grossly rude (as in *Iliad* XXIII.473ff.)" (ibid.).

FOR FRANK PARKER 2

4 shipped oars: Put oars in place for rowing.
8 cottagers: Lowell stayed in Madaket on Nantucket with Parker, during the summer of 1935 (Mariani, 49).

1930'S 8

1 "Nature never did betray / The heart that loved her" (Wordsworth, "Tintern Abbey," 121–22).

1930'S 9

5 Great Mother: "She has the dual nature of creator and destroyer and is both nourisher, protector, provider of warmth and shelter, and the terrible forces of dissolution, devouring and death-dealing; she is the creator and nourisher of all life and its grave. . . . In Alchemy the Great Mother is dynamic as fire and heat, transforming, purifying, consuming and destroying; she is also the bearer of the embryo-ores in the earth-womb" (J. C. Cooper, *An Illustrated Encyclopaedia of Traditional Symbols*, 108).
6 Reichian prophets: Followers of psychiatrist and biophysicist Wilhelm Reich (1897–1957). "According to Reich's theories the universe is permeated by a primal, mass-free phenomenon that he called orgone energy; in the human organism the lack of repeated total discharge of

this energy through natural sexual release is considered the genesis not only of all individual neurosis but also of irrational social movements and collective neurotic disorder" (*The New Columbia Encyclopedia*, 2296).

ANNE DICK 1. 1936

See "Rebellion" in *LWC*, 32.

8 *Lycidas*: An elegy by Milton (1637).

ANNE DICK 2. 1936

2 *Anschluss*: The Nazi annexation of Austria (1938).
4 *Notebook* version: "I tasted first love gazing through your narrow" (p. 68).
7 Esplanade: A grassy park and promenade along the Charles River basin, Boston.
8 Claude: Claude Lorrain (c. 1600–1682), celebrated for not only his landscapes but also for scenes of harbors and seaports.
11 his unloved mother's death: Nero had his mother murdered. See note to "My Last Afternoon with Uncle Devereux Winslow" IV.3.8 on p. 1039.

FATHER

See "Rebellion" in *LWC*, 32.

8 Helios: The Sun-god. His son Phaethon "asked him a boon. The Sun granting him in advance anything he liked, he asked to guide the solar chariot for a day. But he was too weak to manage the solar horses, which bolted with him and were likely to set the world on fire till Zeus killed Phaethon with a thunderbolt" (*The Oxford Classical Dictionary*). This narrative, with "old Helios" as father and a son whose lack of control results in destruction, hangs in the shadows as threat or prophecy: "a parental sentence on each step misplaced" (10).

MOTHER AND FATHER 1

Text from *SP*.

2 Lowell's father died in 1950 and his mother in 1954.

MOTHER AND FATHER 2

10 *infantile*: Infantile paralysis, or polio; Dr. Jonas Salk developed the first vaccine that prevented it (1955).

MOTHER, 1972

11 See "Sailing Home from Rapallo" in *LS*, 179.

JOAN DICK AT EIGHTY

A letter received by Lowell from the mother of Anne Dick.

WILL NOT COME BACK

An imitation of the nineteenth-century Spanish poet Gustavo Adolfo Bécquer's "Volverán las os-curas golondrinas."

SECOND SHELLEY

6–8 Percy Bysshe Shelley (1792–1822), English Romantic poet, expelled from Oxford for his atheist polemics, throughout his life advocated radical social and political reform. Plagued briefly by financial difficulties, at the age of twenty-two he was left an income by his grand-father. He died sailing off the coast of Italy.

FORD MADOX FORD

For Lowell on Ford, see *CPR*, 3; "Ford Madox Ford" in *LS*, 153, and corresponding notes, p. 1035).

1 Samuel Butler: English novelist (1835–1902).
10 Joseph Conrad (1857–1924), Polish-born English novelist.
10 *mot juste*: right or exact word.
14 One relative (A. Lawrence Lowell) had been president of Harvard; another (James Russell Lowell), U.S. ambassador to England.

FORD MADOX FORD AND OTHERS

See headnote above.

1 "Writers walked through his mind and his life—young ones to be discovered, instructed, and en-tertained; contemporaries to be assembled, telegraphed, and celebrated; the dead friend to be resurrected in anecdote; the long, long dead to be freshly assaulted or defended. . . . He seemed to like nothing that was mediocre, and miss nothing that was good" (Lowell, *CPR*, 4).
13 "Two things fill the mind with ever-increasing wonder and awe . . . : the starry heavens above me and the moral law within me" (Immanuel Kant, *Critique of Pure Reason*, conclusion).

TO ALLEN TATE 1. 1937

For numerous details, see "Visiting the Tates" (*CPR*, 58).

4 Europe's last fling: Before World War II.
11 See note on Merrill Moore at "Unwanted" 5.1 on p. 1148.
12 Rexford G. Tugwell (1891–1979), Undersecretary of Agriculture, a member of Franklin Roo-sevelt's Brain Trust (his academic advisory group on the New Deal).

TO ALLEN TATE 2. 1960'S

10 Sourmash: Whiskey.
12–14 At Gettysburg, Major General George Pickett led a division of General James Long-street's Confederate troops. "His assault, famous as 'Pickett's charge,' on the Union center on Cemetery Hill (July 3, 1863) resulted in the virtual annihilation of his troops" (*The New Columbia Encyclopedia*, 2145).

TO ALLEN TATE 3. MICHAEL TATE AUGUST 1967–JULY 1968

1 muskellunge: A large species of pike, known as the "aristocrat of trophy fishes"; here, its elongate body is a falling star with its trail.

THREE POEMS 2. RIVER HARBOR

3 Aaron Burr (1756–1836), former U.S. vice-president, was arrested in 1807 leading a group of colonists, under suspicion that their aim was to establish an independent republic in the American Southwest or to seize territory in Spanish America. Burr was tried for treason, and acquitted.

THREE POEMS 3. SHIPWRECK PARTY

1 Luminism: A nineteenth-century American art movement, exploring the effects of diffused light, "majestic vistas bathed in the mystical light of a pristine sky" (*The New Columbia Encyclopedia*, 1628). In a letter to Elizabeth Bishop, Lowell praises her "enormous powers of realistic observation and of something seldom found with observation, luminism (meaning radiance and compression etc.)" (Mariani, 378). William Doreski, on Emerson (1) and luminism: "Historians of American art in recent years have found luminism the visual arts counterpart of transcendalism in literature. . . . Like luminism, Lowell's poem recognizes the ineffable in terms of silence, emptiness, and horizontality, and suggests that although these qualities have aesthetic merit, they stifle the individual voice, drowning Emerson in the very art that embodies his directives" (*Shifting Colors*, 152–53).
3 FitzHugh Lane: Luminist painter (1804–1865).

HUDSON RIVER DREAM

5 Lowell's Jewish ancestors are on his father's side.

LAST RESORT

1 *cri de coeur*: Cry from the heart.

DREAM OF FAIR LADIES

11 *Pace*: Peace.

RANDALL JARRELL 1. OCTOBER 1965

Text from *SP*. In October 1965 Jarrell died at the age of fifty-one. For Lowell on Jarrell, see *CPR*, 90–98.

RANDALL JARRELL 2

9–14 Jarrell's death. Lowell to Bishop: "He was undergoing treatment of an injured wrist at Chapel Hill, and 'lunged' in front of a car on a main highway near a bypass. He had a bottle of pain-killer in his pocket. It cannot be told for certain whether the death was suicide or an accident. I think suicide, but I'm not sure, and Mary [Jarrell]'s version, the official version, is accident. . . . Poor dear, he wanted to take care of himself!" (October 19, 1965).

13 "Child," used here as an epithet, implies a young hero; cf. Byron's "Childe Harold's Pilgrimage" or Browning's "Childe Roland to the Dark Tower Came." "In 13th and 14th centuries 'child' appears to have been applied to a young noble awaiting knighthood" (*OED*).

14 Jarrell "had the harsh luminosity of Shelley" (*CPR*, 91).

This is a stanza from a manuscript draft titled "Randall Jarrell 1913–1965" (Houghton bMS Am 1905 [2764]):

> Then to escape, and never to escape
> the eyes, lights piercing through the overpass,
> while, black-gloved, black-coated,
> you peer with harsh luminosity
> into the blank vacuity of the tunnel,
> and plod stubbornly out on the thruway,
> as if asleep, as if in the step with death,
> as if having met and approved—saying:
> "My life, what will you do with it?"

MUNICH 1938, JOHN CROWE RANSOM

1 In 1938, these leaders from Germany, Italy, France, and Great Britain signed the Munich Pact, conceding Nazi Germany's rights to annex the German-speaking area of Czechoslovakia. Despite this appeasement, World War II started in 1939.

8 African art: Lowell and Ransom saw this exhibition of African art at Kenyon College in 1963 (Mariani, 502, n.42).

11 hoplites: Ancient Greek foot soldiers.

PICTURE IN *THE LITERARY LIFE, A SCRAPBOOK*

This photograph, taken by a *Life* magazine photographer in April, 1947, shortly after Lowell won the Pulitzer Prize for *Lord Weary's Castle*, is reproduced on the cover of Mariani's biography. *The Literary Life* (subtitled "A Scrapbook Almanac of the Anglo-American Literary Scene from 1900 to 1950") is by Robert Phelps and Peter Deane (1968).

7 New Critic: The term "New Criticism" was coined by John Crowe Ransom in 1941; it called for the aesthetic evaluation and interpretation of literary works as self-sufficient objects, shifting attention from historical or biographical context. Verbal complexity and ambiguity were emphasized. Lowell's teachers—Ransom, Tate, Warren—were leaders of the movement.

FAMILY ALBUM

4 Roosevelt ran for president four times.

12 During World War II, more than 300,000 Allied troops cut off from land retreat by the invading German army were evacuated from Dunkirk (Dunkerque), France. "The retreat was carried out by all kinds of available British craft, some manned by civilian volunteers. . . . It is considered one of the epic actions of naval history" (*The New Columbia Encyclopedia*, 809).

DEUTSCHLAND ÜBER ALLES

"Germany over all": Nazi anthem.

3 the Duce's: Mussolini's.
4 reichsmark: The German monetary unit (until 1948); Hitler's government was the Third Reich.
9 In 1938 Hitler demanded *Lebensraum*, "living space," for all German peoples.

IN THE CAGE

See "In the Cage" in *LWC*, 55, and corresponding notes, p. 1021.

RATS

1 The "Israelites" were an African-American religious group imprisoned with Lowell. See Lowell, *CPR*, 362, and note to "In the Cage" 10, p. 1021).
5 "My friend stretched out his arm, and said, 'Only man is miserable.' I told my doctor that this summed up my morals and my aesthetics" (*CPR*, 362).

HELL

In the "Afterthought" to *Notebook*, Lowell writes: " 'Hell' is taken from two paragraphs of [J.] Glenn Gray's *The Warrior*[s], [1959, 59–60]."

9 *vecchi*: Old people.

SERPENT

In 1907 Hitler moved to Vienna, where twice he applied for admission to the Academy of Fine Arts, and twice was rejected.

WORDS

7 blind mouths: Milton, "Lycidas," 119.
8 Chicago: Here, gangster. Mussolini and Clara Petacci were gunned down and hanged from a street lamp; Hitler committed suicide with Eva Braun as enemies closed in.
11 Commune: See note to "Main Street" 13, p. 1100.
14 word: Here, Logos (Greek for "word"); "in Greek and Hebrew metaphysics, the unifying principle of the world" (*The New Columbia Encyclopedia*, 1604). In St. John's gospel, Jesus is the Word made flesh (John 1:14).

SUNRISE

In 1944, Vice Admiral Takijiro Onishi, commander of Japan's First Air Fleet in the Philippines, created the Special Attack Groups of suicide dive-bombing pilots, the kamikazes. He committed hara-kiri when Japan surrendered.

IN THE FORTIES I

The three sections titled "In the Forties" rewrite three stanzas from "The Mills of the Kavanaughs"; here they become memento and evocation of (as well as meditate) Lowell's marriage to Jean Stafford. For section 1, see stanza 15 on p. 79–80, and corresponding notes, p. 1027.

10 R.C.: Roman Catholic.

IN THE FORTIES 2

See "The Mills of the Kavanaughs," st. 34, p. 88.

IN THE FORTIES 3

See "The Mills of the Kavanaughs," st. 36, p. 88–89.

F. O. MATTHIESSEN 1902–50

Threatened with investigation by a committee of the Massachusetts Legislature pursuing Communists, Matthiessen—Harvard professor, homosexual, leftist—committed suicide. "Some recent scholars argue that Matthiessen's fears of the exposure of his left-wing activities and his homosexuality contributed to his suicide" (*Columbia Electronic Encyclopedia*, 6th ed. [2000]).

3 Czech-student human torches: Jan Palach set fire to himself in Prague's Wenceslas Square in January 1969, protesting the Warsaw Pact invasion after the Prague Spring of 1968.
9 Stonewall Jackson (1824–1863), Confederate general.
10 Matthiessen belonged to the Yale fraternity Skull and Bones.

SYLVIA PLATH

1 *A miniature mad talent*: English critic John Bayley's judgment of Plath ("The King as Commoner," *The Review*, 24, Dec. 1970, 3–7).

RANDALL JARRELL

11 In the months before his death, Jarrell's hand (cut smashing a window) would not, even after surgery, uncurl (Mariani, 339). *Kitten*: The name of Jarrell's cat.

THEODORE ROETHKE 1908–63

See "For Theodore Roethke" in *NTO*, 396, and corresponding note, p. 1069.

1 Yaddo: An estate in Saratoga Springs, New York, offering residencies to artists and academics.

IN DREAMS BEGIN RESPONSIBILITIES

This is the title of Delmore Schwartz's first book (1938), and of his greatest story. The words are probably William Butler Yeats's, though Yeats attributes them to an "Old Play" in the epigraph to *Responsibilities* (1914). (Schwartz changes Yeats's "responsibility" to "responsibilities.") See "To Delmore Schwartz" in *LS*, 157, and corresponding notes, p. 1036.

3 the problem is to keep the dream a movie: The protagonist of Schwartz's story goes to a movie theater at Coney Island; there, on the screen, he sees the courtship of his parents. Interrupting the movie, standing up, he yells at the figures on the screen that they must never marry.

7 Schwartz relentlessly revised his poems.

TABLETALK WITH NAMES 1970

1 he: Delmore Schwartz.

2 Schwartz, in a manic episode, was convinced that Nelson Rockefeller, governor of New York, was having an affair with his wife.

11 Elsa Morante: Italian novelist. Ezra: Ezra Pound.

OUR DEAD POETS

5 old Stalinist luminary: I.e., someone whose career thrived, while Stalin sent the recalcitrant to Siberia.

13 *nostalgie de la boue*: Love of mud; nostalgia for anonymity, for slime, for degradation; yearning for oblivion.

FOR ANN ADDEN 1. 1958

Hospitalized for manic-depression, Lowell "met a girl called Ann Adden, a 'psychiatric fieldworker' from Bennington College, and almost immediately began to announce plans for a 'new life.' . . . [S]he seems to have been thoroughly beguiled, and on more than one occasion helped Lowell play truant from the hospital" (Hamilton, 240).

See "1958" in *NTO*, 397, and corresponding notes, p. 1069.

FOR ANN ADDEN 2. HEIDEGGER STUDENT

3–4 The first atomic bomb used in warfare was dropped on Hiroshima, August 6, 1945, by order of President Harry S. Truman.

9 Martin Heidegger (1889–1976), German philosopher, author of *Being and Time*.

FOR ANN ADDEN 3. 1968

6 your Adden poem: "1958."

T. S. ELIOT

For Lowell on Eliot, see *CPR*, 48–52, 210–12.

EZRA POUND

Ezra Pound was committed to St. Elizabeth's Hospital for the criminally insane in Washington, D.C., after arrest for making radio broadcasts from Italy during World War II; Lowell visited him at St. Elizabeth's. Released after twelve years, he left America for Rapallo, Italy, where he lived with Olga Rudge. (Lowell first wrote Pound as a freshman at Harvard, in May 1936. For two letters and an early poem, see *The Yale Review*, January 1999, vol. 87#1, 54–62 [introductory note by Hannibal Hamlin]. After writing poetry for a year, he tells Pound: "If the 20th century is to realize a great art comparable to that of Chaucer and Shakespeare, the foundation will have to be your poems. . . . I would like to bring back momentum and movement in poetry on a grand scale" [58–59].)

3 Social Credit: An economic theory developed by C. H. Douglas, espoused by Pound.
4 I.e., Eliot was ". . . here with a black suit and black briefcase".
5 Possum: Eliot's nickname. In "Milton II" (1947), Eliot recanted many of his earlier strictures against Milton.
14 Oedipus means "swollen foot."

FEARS OF GOING BLIND

Wyndham Lewis (1882–1957), novelist, critic, artist, founder of Vorticism and a friend of Ezra Pound. "He went blind *c.* 1951 and refused an operation, which, though it might have restored his sight, could have damaged his brain" (William Cookson, *A Guide to the Cantos of Ezra Pound*, 163).

LOUIS MACNEICE 1907–63

Anglo-Irish poet and playwright. This poem was badly garbled in previous printings; lines 9 and 11 are corrected here according to an errata list for the second printing prepared by Lowell.

12 Epstein: British sculptor Sir Jacob Epstein (1880–1959).

WILLIAM CARLOS WILLIAMS

For Lowell on Williams, see *CPR*, 37–44.

ROBERT FROST

For Lowell on Frost, see *CPR*, 8–11, 206–8.

1 A pun on Coleridge's poem "Frost at Midnight."
7 Frost's son Carol committed suicide.
8 Merrill Moore: A psychiatrist, poet, and close friend of Lowell's mother; see note to "Unwanted" 5.1, p. 1148.

STALIN

Text from *SP*.
     See also Lowell's translation of Mandelstam's "Stalin," p. 915.

HARPO MARX

Harpo (Adolph Arthur Marx, 1888–1964) played the harp, and never spoke in the Marx Brothers films.

13 Siegfried Kracauer calls films "the 'glistening wheel of life' " (*Theory of Film* [1960], 170).

THE GOLDFISH

8 In earlier printings, line 11 was repeated here by mistake; the present line is from Lowell's errata list.

ACROSS CENTRAL PARK

Addressed to Jacqueline Kennedy (Hamilton, 340).

CHE GUEVARA

1 Ernesto "Che" Guevara (1928–1967), Argentinean medical doctor, guerrilla leader, revolutionary theorist; he fought with Castro in the 1950s and later led an insurgence in Bolivia. The Bolivian army captured and shot him.
5 Newpaper photo of the dead Guevara.

CARACAS 1

6 jerry skyscrapers: I.e., "jerry-built," flimsy.
7 El Presidente Leoni: Raúl Leoni was elected president of Venezuela in 1963. After a few years of political stability, in 1966 his government suppressed a military uprising; throughout the year, it fought guerrillas in the countryside and capital.

CARACAS 2

8 Drake: British explorer Sir Francis Drake (c. 1540–1596).

NORMAN MAILER

Novelist Norman Mailer joined Lowell in anti–Vietnam War marches in Washington; see Mailer's *The Armies of the Night* (1968).

8 Greenwich: In 1884, the prime meridian (or zero degree longitude) was defined as a line running through the Old Royal Observatory in Greenwich, England; each time zone is defined by its distance east or west of Greenwich.

LIBERTY AND REVOLUTION, BUENOS AIRES

See "Buenos Aires" in *FTUD*, 367, in Appendix III, p. 930, and notes, p. 1064.

6 Juan Perón (1895–1974), president of Argentina (1946–1955 and 1973–1974), deposed in 1955 by pro-democratic military officers.

CAN A PLUCKED BIRD LIVE?

7–8 The Anglo-American Thomas Paine (1737–1809) attacked British Edmund Burke's critique of the French Revolution: Burke (1729–1797) "is not affected by the reality of distress touching his heart, but by the showy resemblance of it striking his imagination. He pities the plumage but forgets the dying bird" (*The Rights of Man*, pt. I [1791]).
12 Rimbaud: The visionary French poet who wrote of the derangement of the senses; see *IM*, pp. 256–269, and "Rimbaud 1–5," pp. 488–490.

THE MARCH 1

The Pentagon March in Washington, D.C., against the Vietnam War on October 21, 1967. Dwight Macdonald: editor and writer.

10 The First Battle of Bull Run (1861) was the first important engagement of the Civil War; Union troops were routed, and their flight did not end until they reached Washington.
13 Martian: Of Mars, god of war; also, like a space-alien, a "Martian" in a science-fiction film.

THE MARCH 2

1 "For where two or three are gathered together in my name, there am I in the midst of them" (Jesus' words in Matthew 18:20).
4 Bastille: A fortress in Paris used as a prison until stormed by revolutionaries, July 14, 1789. The magazine version (*The New York Review of Books*, November 23, 1967): "their Bastille, their Pentagon".
8 MP: Military police.
14 Lowell's reaction to the March: "It was mainly the fragility of a person caught in this situation . . . as in that poem of Horace's where you throw away your little sword at the battle of Philippi and get out of the thing" (Meyers, *Interviews*, 144).

PACIFICATION OF COLUMBIA

Student strikes and rioting closed Columbia University in April 1968. Here is the magazine version (*The New York Review of Books*, June 20, 1968):

> A patch of tan, then blood-warm roof-tile, and tan
> patch and sky patch, as the jigsaw flung some mosque of Omar
> to vaultless consummation and blue consumption,
> exhalation of the sands of the desert to fire.
> I got the message, one the puzzle never sent . . .
> No destructive element emaciates
> Columbia this May Day afternoon;
> the thickened buildings look like buildings out
> of Raphael, colossal classic, dungeon feudal;
> horses, higher artistic types than their grooms,
> forage Broadway's median trees, as if
> nature were liberated . . . the police
> lean on the nervous, burnished hides, show they,
> at least, have learned to meet and reason together.
>
> *May 1, 1968*

[2 Omar: Omar Khayyám, Persian poet (1048?–1131?).]

7 May Day, the first day of May, celebrates spring; in Europe workers celebrate May Day as a labor holiday, as did Communist countries; said as "mayday," it is an airplane pilot's call for help.
9 Raphael (1483–1520), Renaissance painter; the background of his fresco *The School of Athens* depicts classical columns and arches.
14 "Come now, let us reason together": phrase often used by President Lyndon Johnson (Encarta Reference Library 2003). See Isaiah 1:18.

"The Restoration" commonly refers to the restoration of the monarchy in England (1660) after Oliver Cromwell's Commonwealth. Columbia University students staged a sit-in of President Grayson Kirk's office (April 1968). Lowell "saw Kirk not as some 'branch of the Scotch Church,' but merely 'some poor, odious, pitiful creature' " (Mariani, 361).

12 *White Goddess*: See headnote to "White Goddess," p. 1077.

THE NEW YORK INTELLECTUAL

Irving Howe's essay "The New York Intellectuals: A Chronicle & A Critique" appeared in *Commentary*, October 1968. The final paragraph: "Having been formed by, and through opposition to, the New York intellectual experience, I cannot look with joy at the prospect of its ending. But neither with dismay. Such breakups are inevitable, and out of them come new voices and energies. Yet, precisely at this moment of dispersion, might not some of the New York writers achieve renewed strength if they were to struggle once again for whatever has been salvaged from these last few decades? For the values of liberalism, for the politics of a democratic radicalism, for the norms of rationality and intelligence, for the standards of literary seriousness, for the life of the mind as a humane dedication—for all this it should again be worth finding themselves in a minority, even a beleaguered minority, and not with fantasies of martyrdom but with a quiet recognition that for the intellectual this is likely to be his usual condition" (51).

HISTORIAN'S DAUGHTER

6 I.e., if I photographed well.
8 wasp: White Anglo-Saxon Protestant.

WORSE TIMES

1–9 Plato's *Republic* argues against democratic rule; in *Statesman* (303b), he says that if the constitution is lawful and ordered, democracy is the least desirable form of government. Both Marx and Calvin (*Institutes of the Christian Religion* [1536–1559]) argue species of determinism (Marx, historical determinism; Calvin, predestination). Both Marxist governments and American Puritan communities (following Calvinist principles) suppressed some forms of artistic representation. The Scandinavian god Thor and the Hebrew King Saul (after Samuel withdrew religious sanctions from his monarchy) exerted power through physical force, elemental assertions of violence and military strength, not dialectical discussion.
14 Lowell wrote in *Commentary*, April 1969: "[T]he other morning, or some morning, I saw a newspaper photograph of students marching through Rome with banners showing a young Clark-Gable-style Stalin and a very fat old Mao—that was a salute to the glacier. No cause is pure enough to support these faces. We are fond of saying that our students have more generosity, idealism and freshness than any other group. Even granting this, still they are only us younger, and the violence that has betrayed our desires will also betray theirs if they trust to it" (Hamilton, 382).

STUDENT

1 Marshal Joffre: "By the end of 1914 the Western Front had settled into the heavily entrenched lines that existed until 1918. Throughout 1915 the French armies under Joffre attempted to

burst through the German positions at ruinous cost, and failed. . . . Joffre resigned on December 26, 1916" (*Encyclopædia Britannica* [2002]).

2 Roundhead: Radical Puritans during the English Civil War (1642–1651).

THE SPOCK SENTENCES IN BOSTON

Pediatrician and author Dr. Benjamin Spock "became a leading figure in demonstrations against U.S. participation in the Vietnam War. In 1968 he was sentenced to two years in prison for conspiring to aid resistance to the draft (military conscription), but a federal appeals court overruled his conviction" (*Encarta Encyclopedia* [2002]).

1 Parker House: Boston hotel, established 1856.

2–4 Taft (U.S. president, 1909–1913), British rulers Edward VII and (Edward's consort) Alexandra were emblems of pre–World War I conservative establishment power.

9 Tyre and Sidon: Wealthy mercantile trading cities in ancient Phoenicia.

10 *ab ovo*: From the egg, i.e., from the very beginning.

CHILD-PASTEL OF ADRIENNE RICH

Adrienne Rich (b. 1929), American poet and writer, emblematic figure whose concerns have moved from solitary artistic accomplishment, through bourgeois domesticity, antiwar and anti-nuclear-arms activism and racial politics, to feminism. This poem was first published in 1970, before her central engagement with feminism.

5 James Mill: Historian, economist and philosopher, father of precocious John Stuart Mill; a strict disciplinarian who directed his son's ambitious early academic training.

9 Montaigne: Here, emblem of skeptical privileged ego-driven thinking.

10 François Toussaint (Haitian leader), Frantz Fanon (author of *The Wretched of the Earth*), Malcolm X: revolutionary black thinkers and leaders.

11 *mutilés de guerre*: Those mutilated in the war.

13–14 disabled veteran: Rich has arthritis, which makes walking difficult; but given Lowell's skepticism about ideological passions, I suspect that "crutches" (14) is metaphoric as well. [F.B.]

THE REVOLUTION

6–14 Drawn from a letter to Lowell by poet and former student Richard Tillinghast, then teaching at the University of California, Berkeley. Lowell answered: "Your saying that I 'should be in on it' is as tho I were to offer you Castine by saying 'we seem likely to have a tidal wave and you should see the morale of a village in danger' " (Mariani, 374).

YOUTH

13–14 Cf. Michelangelo's *Pietà*, where the Virgin Mary holds the crucified Jesus.

TRUNKS

5–6 Cf. Aijaz Ahmad, *Ghazals of Ghalib* (1971), Ghazal 9 (line 7) and Ghazal 31 (line 6).

6 Diana: Virgin goddess, armed with bow and quiver.
13 eighty percent: "[Her] mind, as Hannah Arendt puts it, that wants to be ninety per cent right" (Lowell, letter to Elizabeth Bishop, 1968, quoted in Kiernan, *Seeing Mary Plain* [2000], 620).

4 a Dürer Saint Joan: Like an etching of Joan of Arc by Dürer (imagined; none exists).

1–5 See Hölderlin's "Hälfte des Lebens"; and "The Seasons" (Appendix VI, p. 984), and note, p. 1160.
7–10 Based on a letter from McCarthy to Lowell, 1969: "The real motive for the trip [to New York] is dentistry. A descending scale. I used long ago to come to New York to see a lover, then a psychoanalyst, then an editor or publisher, then a lawyer, and finally the dentist" (Kiernan, *Seeing Mary Plain*, 657).

13 Saturn: Planet, circled by seven main rings; the rings were first observed by Galileo in 1610. Saturn (or Cronus) was the head of the "old" gods, and deposed by his son Jupiter.

1–3 An evocation of Edouard Manet's painting *Boating* (1874), depicting two figures seated in the sun in a boat.
14 Cf. the game Rock, Paper, Scissors.

9 Nausicaa: The young girl who discovers Odysseus naked and shipwrecked, fearlessly greets him and shows him how to enter the palace of her father the king (*Odyssey*, VI–VII). She would marry him, and her father agrees, but Ulysses is already married.

The National Prohibition Act, designed to stop "the manufacture, sale, or transportation of intoxicating liquors" in the United States, went into effect on January 16, 1920; it was repealed in December 1933.

4 just married: In 1940.

12 Cf. the painting *Liberty Leading the People* (1830) by Eugène Delacroix.

FOR AUNT SARAH

Sarah Winslow Cotting, the sister of Lowell's mother. Sarah Payne Stuart describes Lowell reading this poem to Lowell family members, and a revision before publication (*My First Cousin Once Removed*, 9).

FLIGHT IN THE RAIN

14 *Deo gracias*: Thanks to God.

BLIZZARD IN CAMBRIDGE

Lowell in the sixties taught at Harvard (in Cambridge, Massachusetts) but lived in New York; this describes an attempt to return home.

THE HEAVENLY RAIN

3 Aseity: An independent power of being; capitalized, as here, God not subject to contingency or derivative from something outside itself.
9 skyward like the Firebird: In Russian legend, a mythological magical bird, akin to the Phoenix, reborn from its own ashes. In George Balanchine's choreography, "the Firebird refuses to be earth-bound and seems to resist nature by performing dashing movements that whip the very air about her" (*Balanchine's Complete Stories of the Great Ballets* [1977]).

MISANTHROPE AND PAINTER

4–5 In Shakespeare's *Othello*, the title character wrongly suspects his wife Desdemona of sleeping with his lieutenant Cassio.
13 Rothko: Mark Rothko (1903–1970), American abstract expressionist painter. Lowell's friend the painter Sidney Nolan describes the biographical genesis of this poem: "I was with Cal and this girlfriend of his in Boston, and at one point she said, 'When I'm in the room, the Rothko disappears' " (Hamilton, 387).

REDSKIN

13 wrath-break: Day of Wrath (*dies irae*), Day of Judgment.

NEW YORK

5 Port of Spain: The capital of Trinidad and Tobago.
12 In *HIS*, a comma follows "barricade".
13 categorical imperative: A moral law that is unconditional or absolute for all, the validity of which does not depend on motive or end (Kant's term).
13–14 Said by Frederick the Great, when the Guards hesitated at Kolin (June 18, 1757).

DREAM OF LEAK AND TERRA-COTTA

11 In *HIS*, "lift"; correction from original galleys.

FEVER

3 Pavlov's dogs: The Russian physiologist Ivan Pavlov did experiments on dogs (1898–1930), studying the conditional (or "conditioned") reflex.
14 "I woke up one morning and found myself famous" (Lord Byron, reported by Thomas Moore, *Letters and Journals of Lord Byron, with Notices of His Life* [1829] I, 258).

ACROSS THE YARD: LA IGNOTA

La Ignota: "The Unknown" (or, "The Unknown One").

2 Brunnhilde: The heroic soprano lead in Wagner's *Der Ring des Nibelungen*. Valkyrie daughter of the head of the gods (Wotan), she disobeys his orders.
5 I.e., since President Kennedy's death.

ELISABETH SCHWARZKOPF IN NEW YORK

This poem is a tribute to Schwarzkopf partly because it does *not* mention the controversy surrounding her Metropolitan Opera debut in New York (1964), delayed by many years because during World War II she sang for the Nazis. She made her New York debut in 1953 singing lieder, and by 1955 sang the Marschallin for the San Francisco Opera. New York was never a major venue for her.

7 *Was ist Sylvia* (Who Is Sylvia), the opening words of Schubert's setting ("An Sylvia") of a song from Shakespeare's *Two Gentlemen of Verona*; the song evokes feminine innocence and perfection. *Die alte Marschallin*: "The aging Marschallin" (Fieldmarshal's wife) in Richard Strauss's *Der Rosenkavalier* accepts with melancholy grace the encroachment of time and inevitable loss of a young lover; one of Schwarzkopf's most celebrated roles.

7 *Was*: In *HIS*, "*Wo*".

DIAMOND CUTTERS

3 47th Street: The diamond district of New York City.
4 Ur-kings: Ur, Mesopotamian city; clay tablets listing debts have been found there.
8 Melville, his years of success as a novelist over, spent nineteen years as a customs inspector on the docks of New York. For Lowell on Melville, see *CPR*, 197.

CANDLELIGHT LUNCHDATE

2 Table lamps shaped like stormlamps, with lightbulbs shaped like candles; therefore, the glass tubes ("chimneys") around the lightbulbs "don't smoke" (3).
3 *Chez Dreyfus*: Cambridge restaurant, now defunct.
6–7 Corrected according to Lowell's errata list.

TWO WALLS

8 The magazine version (*The New York Review of Books*, May 9, 1968) reads: "Don Giovanni must have drawn sword on such an avenger,". In the final scene of Mozart's opera, Don Giovanni meets the father of a woman he seduced; the father, now a statue made of stone, drags him to hell.

ABSTRACTION

2 Corrected according to Lowell's errata list.

9 In a 1969 letter to Elizabeth Hardwick, Lowell connects "almost unstopping composition with drinking. Nothing was written drunk, at least nothing was perfected and finished, but I have looked forward to whatever one gets from drinking, a stirring and a blurring?" (Mariani, 370).

DISSENTING ACADEMY

1 hack-moon: The crescent moon.

TAXI DRIVERS

1–3: Lowell in his workroom, or study.

GOITER TEST, UTOPIA FOR RACOONS

The lithium that Lowell took for manic-depression exacerbated a hyperthyroid condition: "all fall I've suffered from some sort of thyroid excess or deficiency, both at once in different 'areas,' I think" (Mariani, 370).

GOITER DELIRIUM, WERNER VON URSLINGEN

4 Leonardo's felons: Drawings of felons by Leonardo da Vinci, after autopsies.

11 memento mori: A reminder of death or mortality, such as a death's-head.

12 landsknecht: A mercenary.

12 Werner von Urslingen: also known as Guernieri, or simply Werner. Celebrated mercenary captain, who plundered Tuscany and Lombardy, and sacked Anagni (1358), after which he disappears.

14 *L'ennemi de Dieu et de merci*: The enemy of God and of mercy. The full inscription on his breastplate was "The enemy of God, of pity and of mercy."

UNDER THE DENTIST

9 Maria Callas: Soprano, diva (1923–1977); the Mad Scene from her 1955 live Berlin *Lucia* was played at Lowell's memorial service in New York (September 25, 1977).

WINDOW-LEDGE 1. THE BOURGEOIS

8 Louis-Philippe: King of the French 1830–1848. The revolution that brought him to power was a victory for the upper bourgeoisie over the aristocracy; after he had embittered the lower bourgeoisie by refusing them the franchise, faced with proletarian and middle-class insurrection, in 1848 he abdicated (*Encyclopædia Britannica* [2002]). Daumier liked to draw him as a large pear in a top hat; the king detested it.

WINDOW-LEDGE 2. GRAMSCI IN PRISON

Antonio Gramsci (1891–1937), Italian intellectual and politician, a founder of the Italian Communist Party, jailed by the Fascists (1926–1937).

4 Gramsci made this phrase into something like a programmatic slogan as early as 1919; he famously used it in *Letters from Prison* (1947). The phrase was coined by Romain Rolland (1866–1945).

FIVE HOUR POLITICAL RALLY

6 Goya balcony: As in Goya's painting *Majas on a Balcony* (c. 1808–1812) or fresco *A Miracle of St. Anthony of Padua* (1798).
7 Corrected according to Lowell's errata list.
11 This line added from Lowell's errata list.

FOR ROBERT KENNEDY 1925–68

Text from *SP*.
Here is the magazine version, from *The New Republic*, June 22, 1968:

R. F. K.
(1925–1968)

Here in my study, in its listlessness
of Vacancy, some old Victorian house,
air-tight and sheeted for old summers,
far from the hornet yatter of the bond—
is loneliness, a thin smoke thread of vital
air. What can I catch from you now?
Doom was woven in your nerves, your shirt,
woven in the great clan; they too were loyal,
you too were more than loyal to them . . . to death.
For them, like a prince, you daily left your tower
to walk through dirt in your best cloth. Here now,
alone, in my Plutarchan bubble, I miss
you, you out of Plutarch, made by hand—
forever approaching our maturity.

13 The Greek biographer and essayist Plutarch (A.D. 46?–120) is the source of much of what we know about the heroes and masters of the ancient world.
14 your maturity: In all earlier versions, including *HIS*, "our maturity." When the poem first appeared, poet and Kennedy supporter Donald Junkins criticized the phrase, suggesting "your" instead of "our." Lowell answered that "*Our* is not an editorial we," that "the secondary meaning[,] the only possible one, would give *our* the meaning of *man's* or *mankind's*, or the future of our country." Kennedy "may have been our hero; he was never mature; nor would anyone who knew him well and love[d] him, have thought so. To say that he was our maturity robs him of most of his true seriousness and pathos" (Mariani, 363).

FOR ROBERT KENNEDY 2

After winning the Democratic presidential primary in California on June 4, 1968, Kennedy spoke to his followers in Los Angeles' Ambassador Hotel. Shortly after midnight, leaving the hotel through a kitchen hallway, he was shot to death by Sirhan Sirhan.

ASSASSIN!

Les Enfants du Paradis (Children of Paradise) is a 1945 film directed by Marcel Carné and written by Jacques Prévert. The lines about the film (7–14) evoke the striking, severe stylistic decisions underlying Carné and Prévert's handling of the murder scene; but they are not "accurate" description.

FOR EUGENE MCCARTHY

Lowell was an informal advisor to Senator McCarthy during his campaign for the Democratic nomination for president, at times traveling with McCarthy's entourage.

14 In 1968 McCarthy challenged the sitting president, Lyndon Johnson, in early primaries for the presidential nomination of Johnson's own party; the central issue was Johnson's prosecution of the Vietnam War. McCarthy did so well that Johnson decided not to run for reelection.

OCEAN

10 Parnassus: A mountain consecrated to Apollo, the arts.

DREAM, THE REPUBLICAN CONVENTION

The Republican Party in 1968, which might have offered alternatives to pro–Vietnam War policies supported by the Democratic president, for the most part didn't; no liberal Democrat trusted Richard Nixon (who won the Republican nomination) to end the war, "with honor" (as he promised) or without.

FLAW

Chicago was the site of the Democratic Convention, where Eugene McCarthy was about to fight for the nomination against Vice President Hubert Humphrey, Johnson's choice.

1 eye-flaw: See note to "The Flaw," p. 1064.
12 Faust sells his soul to the Devil.

AFTER THE DEMOCRATIC CONVENTION

Days of antiwar demonstrations and violent Chicago police repression marked the 1968 Democratic presidential convention; Hubert Humphrey was nominated.

FROM PRAGUE 1968

In late August 1968, the Russian army invaded Czechoslovakia to halt the liberal "Prague Spring" movement.

ELECTION NIGHT

6 *New Statesman*: A liberal English weekly magazine.
7 Humphrey was the most liberal of the candidates, although the tactics by which he won the nomination left most liberals furious; George Wallace, the third party candidate, was the most conservative. Nixon won.

10 "McCarthy headquarters on the fifteenth floor of the Conrad-Hilton Hotel were broken into by the police, who began indiscriminately beating the students gathered there" (Mariani, 367).

AFTER THE ELECTION: FROM FRANK PARKER'S LOFT

1 Joffre: See note to "Student" 1, p. 1114. Marshal Ferdinand Foch, the commander of Allied forces during the closing months of World War I, was generally considered architect of the victory.

WEST SIDE SABBATH

6 *Entre autres*: Among others.
14 *Maypole*: In many cultures, dances around a garlanded pole are "part of spring rites to ensure fertility" (*Encyclopædia Britannica* [2002]).

EATING OUT ALONE

9 Paul Claudel: French diplomat and poet (1868–1955).
10 "Groton Academy, oh, it's a school of pigs." Groton is an exclusive private secondary school near Boston.
13 Racine: Classic French author (1639–1699), the range of whose vocabulary is famously chaste.

PAINTER

8 "*El sueño de la razon produce monstruos*" (legend in Goya's *Capricho* 43).
14 Constable: John Constable (1776–1837), English landscapist.

IN THE AMERICAN GRAIN

Title of a book on American character and history by William Carlos Williams (1925). For Lowell on Williams, see "William Carlos Williams," *HIS*, 539, and *CPR*, 29–44.

11 Williams, who lived in New Jersey, tried to make "a new art from itself—rooted in the locality which should give it fruit" (*The Autobiography of William Carlos Williams*, 174).

PUBLICATION DAY

Based on a letter to Lowell from the poet Marcia Nardi. In *Paterson*, Williams used her letters to him; she is "the 'Cress' of Williams's *Paterson*" (Mariani, 370).

12 In Mailer's *The Armies of the Night*.

LOSER

7 Simone de Beauvoir: Feminist French writer, author of *The Second Sex*.
8 *sagesse de crise*: Wisdom of crisis.

THE WINNER

Chess master Bobby Fischer.

3 In *HIS*, "muled".
4 mating: Checkmating.

THE JUST-FORTIES

11 From the 1920s.

MOON-LANDINGS

The first moon-landing was July 20, 1969.

3 white goddess: See note to "White Goddess," p. 1077.
4 On the lids of some Etruscan sarcophagi, there are terra-cotta statues of those entombed within.
11 The insane were thought to be under the influence of the moon, *luna*; therefore, "lunatic."

SHEIK WITHOUT SIX WIVES IN LONDON

7–9 A dangerous harem. Lilith: a child-killing demon, Adam's first wife. Goneril and Regan: King Lear's treacherous daughters. Hetaerae: Influential, cultivated courtesans of ancient Greece.

AFTER THE PLAY

10 Cromwell told his portrait painter to paint even his warts; commonly remembered as "warts and all."

ENGLISH-SPEAKING WORLD

2 Economist John Kenneth Galbraith's influential book (1958) proposed less emphasis on consumer goods and more on public services.
5 I.e., it's the end of.
8 *New Statesman*: A liberal English weekly magazine.

CHURCHILL 1970 RETROSPECTIVE

2 First names of Roosevelt; Stalin; and Churchill, who had died in 1965.
3 Iconic images of Churchill during World War II.
6 I.e., overruled plans of his war staff, in favor of bolder action.
7 Churchill's prose had a traditional English elevated eloquence; he wrote many books.
9 Rommel: The brilliant German general Erwin Rommel (1891–1944) was in charge of Hitler's North African campaign.
10 Churchill (PM, or Prime Minister) relieved British general Archibald Wavell from command of British forces in the Middle East in 1941, after defeats by Rommel's forces; because Churchill had earlier seriously reduced British strength in North Africa, many felt this was unjust.

11 An attempt to fool German forces about British strength.

12 Mufti: Ordinary or civilian clothes; Churchill was an amateur painter.

13 The German city of Dresden was firebombed and destroyed by the Allies (1945) against the advice of many, but at Churchill's insistence. Skeptics held that the city was of marginal military significance. Thousands of civilians died. This action has often been considered unjust; one of the reasons that Lowell gave for his refusal to be drafted was the saturation bombing of Hamburg, similar to that of Dresden (*CPR*, 280).

DE GAULLE'S CHIENLIT

Charles de Gaulle (1890–1970), French general and statesman, first president of the Fifth Republic. In May 1968 tumultuous student and worker demonstrations broke out in France. "De Gaulle referred to the students in the streets as 'chienlit,' which is a military term meaning 'bed-shitters.' The students responded with the slogan, 'Le chienlit, c'est lui.' This became one of the famous street cries of '68" (Arthur Goldhammer). "A broadcast [by de Gaulle] on May 30 brought a massive demonstration of support and a landslide Gaullist victory in the subsequent election" (*Encyclopædia Britannica* [2002]). The next year he was out of power.

DE GAULLE EST MORT

"De Gaulle is dead."

14 Gamal Abdel Nasser, nationalist and first president of Egypt, also died in 1970.

LÉVI-STRAUSS IN LONDON

Claude Lévi-Strauss (b. 1908), French anthropologist.

2 ammonites: Extinct marine mollusks; "they often link the rock layer in which they are found to specific geological time periods" (*Encarta Encyclopedia* [2002]).

10 *structuralism*: "In cultural anthropology, the school of thought developed by . . . Lévi-Strauss, in which cultures, viewed as systems, are analyzed in terms of the structural relations among their elements. According to Lévi-Strauss's theories, universal patterns in cultural systems are products of the invariant structure of the human mind" (*Encyclopædia Britannica* [2002]).

11–13 Here, Cézanne stands for the earnest artist whose work submits to the elemental nature of its subject and in embodying it becomes one with it; Picasso, the artist as virtuoso, whose work encounters and tames its subject.

14 "There is a crack in everything God has made" (Emerson, "Compensation").

HEDGEHOG

4 Sartre: French existentialist philosopher (1905–1980).

10 Giacometti: Alberto Giacometti (1901–1966), Swiss sculptor and painter.

VERLAINE, ETC.

1 Verlaine: French poet (like Shakespeare's Falstaff, a heavy drinker).

2–3 Punctuation corrected according to Lowell's errata list.

4 Valéry: French poet, writer, aesthetician.

13 *Fortuna*: The Roman goddess Fortune (not in the sense of "chance" or "luck," but "destiny"). "Trees have to be killed and cut down to make paper; Lowell needs paper to live in his poem; and out of these simple facts he springs a glittering, paradoxical final couplet" (Raban, *A Selection*, 180).

THE NIHILIST AS HERO

Text from *SP*.

3 Valéry: See note to "Verlaine, Etc." 4, above. "Valéry in paraphrase is speaking for the primacy of craft and 'intelligent labor' against mere inspiration, which is accidental. To the extent that discipline in craft serves the ends of 'la poésie pure,' the Satan here must be Valéry's Satan of 'Ébauche d'un serpent,' whom Alan Williamson quotes Lowell as calling 'the spirit that insists on perfection' " (Vereen Bell, 3–4).

13–14 The final couplet changed with each volume in which it appeared.
　　　　Notebook 1967–68:

> Only a nihilist desires the world
> to be as it is, or much more passable.

　　Notebook:

> A nihilist has to live in the world as is,
> gazing the impossible summit to rubble.

　　History:

> A nihilist has to live in the world as is,
> gazing the impassable summit to rubble.

IN THE BACK STACKS

4 studenten: Students.

READING MYSELF

6 Parnassus: See note to "Ocean" 10 on p. 1121.

LAST THINGS, BLACK PINES AT 4 A.M.

14 Trollope: Novelist.

PLAYING BALL WITH THE CRITIC

6–9 "The intelligent and not the stupid quote belongs to R. P. Blackmur" (Lowell, "Afterthought" in *Notebook*). The "intelligent quote" turns out to be the more negative one; see Blackmur's review of *LOU*, in Boyers and London, 3–4.

OUTLAWS, A GOODBYE TO SIDNEY NOLAN

Sidney Nolan (1917–1992), Australian artist, illustrated the first American edition of *NTO*.

3 *boules*: French outdoor bowling game. Pau: A city in France.
6 Nolan did many works based on the life of celebrated Australian outlaw Ned Kelly (1855–1880); there is an expression, "as game as Ned Kelly."

GRASSHOPPERS, FOR STANLEY KUNITZ 1970

Poet Stanley Kunitz grew up in Worcester.

FOR ELIZABETH BISHOP 1. WATER

See "Water" in *FTUD*, 321.

FOR ELIZABETH BISHOP 2. CASTINE MAINE

4–5 *North & South*: Bishop's first book. Yarmouth: town in Nova Scotia. Bishop was born in Worcester, Massachusetts, raised in Nova Scotia and Worcester, schooled in New England, lived in New York, Florida, Brazil, and finally New England.
7 Britain's Georges: In 1714, George I acceded to the British throne; his successors were George II, III and IV.
8 In the American Revolution, George III (1738–1820) lost the American colonies.

Some of the material in this sonnet Lowell tried to use earlier. A manuscript poem, "For Elizabeth Bishop: Flying to Rio de Janeiro 1956" (Houghton bMS Am 1905 [2238]), includes this stanza:

> You, with those Hanoverians' dreadnought force,
> the eyes of Argus, wish you were a horse,
> or some pater familias Sicilian
> in Greenwich Village, fixed to play the host,
> stand blood relations drinks, and never go outdoors,
> yet throw your weight about like Robert Frost.

[1 those Hanoverians: "Britain's Georges [who] rule your horoscope" (7) were members of the house of Hanover. 2 Argus: herdsman who had eyes all over his body.]

FOR ELIZABETH BISHOP 3. LETTER WITH POEMS FOR LETTER WITH POEMS

The letter this poem is based on is printed in Bishop's *One Art* (1994), 515–517.

FOR ELIZABETH BISHOP 4.

3 *plein air*: Painting "en plein air" is "in its strictest sense, the practice of painting landscape pictures out-of-doors; more loosely, the achievement of an intense impression of the open air (*plein air*) in a landscape painting" (*Encyclopædia Britannica* [2002]).
4 Albert Pinkham Ryder, American painter of seascapes and mystical allegorical scenes (1847–1917). His works are pervaded by thick, yellow light, usually moonlight; by rapidly

applying thick layers of pigment and then varnish, he created crackled surfaces. His lifework is about 150 paintings.

8 *A Catch or Key*, published in 1969, year of Ruth Berrien Fox's death.

WOMEN, CHILDREN, BABIES, COWS, CATS

Lieutenant William Calley testified that in March 1968 American soldiers massacred several hundred unarmed civilians at My Lai, Vietnam. Excerpts from his testimony at his court-martial:

"Well, I was ordered to go in there and destroy the enemy. That was my job on that day. That was the mission I was given. I did not sit down and think in terms of men, women, and children. They were all classified the same, and that was the classification that we dealt with, just as enemy soldiers. . . . You just make an estimate off the top of your head. There is no way to really figure out exact body count. At that time, everything went into a body count—VC [enemy soldiers], buffalo, pigs, cows."

In 1971, Calley was convicted of premeditated murder and sentenced to hard labor for the rest of his life. Public opinion polls disapproved of the verdict; President Nixon had Calley removed from the stockade and placed under house arrest. Under the title "Judgment Deferred on Lieutenant Calley," Lowell wrote in *The New York Review of Books* (May 6, 1971, p. 37): "A principle may kill more than an incident. I am sick with fresh impressions. Has no one the compassion to pass judgment on William Calley? His atrocity is cleared by the President, public, polls, rank and file of the right and left. He looks almost alive; like an old song, he stirs us with the gruff poignance of the professional young soldier. He too fought under television for our place in the sun. Why should the bait be eaten when the sharks swim free? I sense a coldness under the hysteria. Our nation looks up to heaven, and puts her armies above the law. No stumbling on the downward plunge from Hiroshima. Retribution is someone somewhere else and we are young. In a century perhaps no one will widen an eye at massacre, and only scattered corpses express a last histrionic concern for death. We are not hypocrites, we can learn to embrace people outside society—President Nixon, our own Huckleberry Finn who has to shoot everyone else on the raft." For Lowell's later use (and reversal) of "Why should the bait be eaten when the sharks swim free?" see "Leaving Home, Marshal Ney" p. 476, and note to "Dolphin" 2.1 on p. 1139.

IDENTIFICATION IN BELFAST

I.R.A.: Irish Republican Army, a.k.a. "the Provisionals" (3).

NON-VIOLENT

2 Code of the duel.
5 "Long live war, long live death!" (Falangist general Millán Astray's motto, Spanish Civil War). See "The Opposite House," 391.

SOUND MIND, SOUND BODY

In the spring of 1967, Lowell began taking lithium, which freed him for three years from his yearly manic-depressive breakdowns. This was written during that period.

1 "Mens sana in corpore sano": a sound mind in a sound body. The phrase has become proverbial, but is from Juvenal's Tenth Satire (1. 356). Lowell translates Juvenal's entire line as

"pray for / a healthy body and a healthy soul"; see "The Vanity of Human Wishes" 22.10–11, p. 412, and "Juvenal's Prayer" 6–7, p. 446.
3 "A sound mind in an unsound [insane] body."
9 Attila: The Hun general died the night after his wedding (453 A.D.).

I. A. RICHARDS 1. *GOODBYE EARTH*

Ivor Armstrong Richards (1893–1979), the English teacher and semanticist, became a poet late in life. First famous for *The Meaning of Meaning* (co-authored with C. K. Ogden, 1923; see "Waking in the Blue," 183) and books about how to read poetry, he published his first volume of poems, *Goodbye Earth*, in 1958. Lowell described him as "glistening with mountain-climbing and his first book of poems—replies to Wittgenstein and Oppenheimer and Coleridge and the obscurer Plato" (Mariani, 269).

I. A. RICHARDS 2. DEATH

12 Hob: Elf.

FOR JOHN BERRYMAN 1

See "For John Berryman" in *DBD*, 737. For Lowell on Berryman, see *CPR*, pp. 111–18.

4–5 In the "Afterthought" to *Notebook* (1970), Lowell writes about his own poems: "Accident threw up subjects, and the plot swallowed them—famished for human chances" (262).
11 Writers George Herbert, H. D. Thoreau, and Blaise Pascal all died near age forty.
13 Abraham was eighty-six when his first child was born (Genesis 16:15–16).

FOR JOHN BERRYMAN 2

2 Lowell was living in England when he heard of Berryman's death (January 7, 1972).
7 the Chelsea: Hotel in New York.
14 Berryman died by jumping from a bridge.

LAST NIGHT

11–14 Donald Hall, review of *Notebook* (in *The Review*, Spring–Summer, 1972).

RED AND BLACK BRICK BOSTON

13 "The things in Mr. Lowell's poems . . . keep to an extraordinary degree their stubborn, unmoved toughness, their senseless originality and contingency: no poet is more notable for what, I have read, Duns Scotus calls *haeccitas*—the contrary, persisting, and singular thinginess of every being in the world" (Randall Jarrell, "From the Kingdom of Necessity," review of *LWC*, first in *The Nation*, January 11, 1947, reprinted in *Poetry and the Age*, 216).

DEATH AND THE BRIDGE

Text from *SP*.

6 Isaiah 6:5–7.

11 Cro-Magnon: Early man; the first prehistoric people to produce art, they buried their dead.

8 The Rosetta Stone, found in Egypt by Napoleon's engineering corps (1799), displayed the same message in Greek, Egyptian demotic, and Egyptian hieroglyphic; by comparing the texts, for the first time scholars deciphered hieroglyphics.

9 annus mirabilis: Year of wonders. *Hero demens*: Mad hero, echoing the title of Seneca's play *Hercules Furens.*

14 carbon: Lowell's final image for the relation between writing and world has, since the demise of the typewriter, become unfamiliar. A "carbon" (or "carbons," line 6) is carbon paper: "A lightweight paper faced on one side with a dark waxy pigment that is transferred by the impact of typewriter keys or by writing pressure to any copying surface, as paper" (*American Heritage Dictionary*). In line 14, sunset abruptly becomes the night sky. Hard to decipher as a palimpsest, carbon-black and fragile, re-used carbon paper becomes the bright night sky: where a key struck, a gap shows light.

FOR LIZZIE AND HARRIET (1973)

The copy-text is the second Farrar, Straus and Giroux printing. All changes introduced into this text are from *Selected Poems* (rev.).

Lowell's introductory Note: "In another order, in other versions, all the poems in this book appeared in my last published poem, *Notebook*." For the genesis of *For Lizzie and Harriet*, see headnote to *History*, 1073.

1. HARRIET, BORN JANUARY 4, 1957
Lowell's daughter, Harriet Lowell.

1 Lowell writes in the "Afterthought" to *Notebook*: "My opening lines are as hermetic as any in the book. The 'fractions' mean that my daughter, born in January, is each July, a precision important to a child, something and a half years old. The 'Seaslug etc.' are her declining conceptions of God."

9–10 Diogenes Laertius on Thales (c. 625–c. 546 B.C.): "It is said that once, when he was taken out of doors by an old woman to observe the stars, he fell into a ditch. To his cry for help the old woman retorted, 'How can you expect to know all about the heavens, Thales, when you cannot even see what is just before your feet' " (*Lives of the Philosophers*, trans. Caponigri, 1969).

11–14 "The 'Harriet' poems were written a few months after the first production of Lowell's version of *Prometheus Bound*, and Lowell echoes Prometheus at the end of the first sonnet" (Raban, *Selection*, 182). From Lowell's *Prometheus Bound*: "Around some bend, under some moving stone, behind some thought, if it were ever the right thought, I will find my key. No, not just another of Nature's million petty clues, but a key, *my key*, *the* key, the one that must be there, because it can't be there—a face still friendly to chaos" (52–53).

2. HARRIET

6 "[T]he 'Arabs on the screen' were to be seen during the six-day war in June 1967 between Israel and Egypt" (Raban, *Selection*, 182).

3. ELIZABETH

Lowell's second wife, Elizabeth Hardwick ("Lizzie").

6 *Pace*: Peace.
7 Heart's-Ease: A name for several plants, such as the "wild pansy" and a mint plant also called Heal-all.

5. HARRIET

9 Shakespeare's Juliet was fourteen.

THROUGH THE NIGHT

1.10 *like the generation of leaves, the race of man: Iliad*, VI.146.
2.12 Alice Raveau recorded Gluck's *Orphée* in 1935. Gluck's *Orfeo ed Euridice* was first performed, in Italian, in 1762; Gluck supervised a French version in 1774.
2.13 "Where am I going without Eurydice?" Lowell has here translated into French, and conflated, the Italian version of the first two lines of Orpheus' most famous aria, "*Che farò senza Euridice*" (which literally translate, "What will I do without Eurydice? Where will I go without my love?"). The French version (recorded by Alice Raveau) begins, "*J'ai perdu mon Eurydice*" ("I have lost my Eurydice").

HARVARD

1.4 Place des Vosges: The oldest public square in Paris, with long arcades and sloping slate-roofed buildings surrounding a courtyard of lawn and trees.
2.11 "For all flesh is as grass, and all the glory of man as the flower of grass. The grass withereth, and the flower thereof falleth away: But the word of the Lord endureth for ever" (I Peter 1.24–25).
3.7 In "The Merchant's Tale" (*Canterbury Tales*), a sixty-year-old knight named January is betrayed by his young wife, May.

NEW YORK

4. DEAR SORROW I

4 E.g., Job 3:1ff, especially "My sighing cometh before I eat, and my roarings are poured out like the waters" (3:24).
6 Thomas (1795–1881) and Jane Baillie Welsh (1801–1866) Carlyle.

6. DEAR SORROW 3

Text is from *SP*. Lines 8–11 from second printing:

> Time that tinkers with objects lets man go,
> no doctor does the work of the carpenter.
> It's our nerve, the ideology, dies first—
> then you, so thumbed, worn out, used, got by heart.

See "New York 1962: Fragment" in *FTUD*, 372.

12. SAME PICTURE
See "New York 1962: Fragment" in *FTUD*, 372.

MEXICO
Text is from *SP*.

2 Text is from second printing; this section is omitted in *SP*.

2.5 depth-transference: On "transference": "[T]erm given to the relationship between patient and therapist. . . . The analyst is believed to become a symbolic representative of a person important in the patient's life, and the patient transfers his feelings about the person to the analyst" (*The New Columbia Encyclopedia*, 2775). "Depth-transference": a trendy neologism, characteristic of the "lay-neurotics."

2.7 analysis: I.e., psychoanalysis.

2.13 *Sigmund* Freud, *Karl* Marx.

3.11 The Aztec emperor Montezuma, seized by Hernán Cortés (1520) as a hostage, was forced to speak against resistance to Spanish rule. When the Aztecs drove the Spanish out, he was killed—whether by the Aztecs or Spanish is uncertain. Cortés reconquered them in 1521.

4.6 bull and cow: Cuernavaca means "cow horn."

5.3 "Large wall-bricks like loaves of risen bread—" (second printing).

5.10 "the sterile white salt of purity and blinding:" (second printing).

10.12 intercourse: "conversation" (second printing).

EIGHT MONTHS LATER

1. EIGHT MONTHS LATER

6 Lilith: Jewish female demon; in Jewish legend, Adam's first wife.

2. DIE GOLD ORANGEN
Based on Goethe's "Mignon: Kennst du das Land."

CIRCLES

2. DAS EWIG WEIBLICHE
"The eternal feminine" (Goethe, *Faust* II.12110); penultimate line of the "Chorus Mysticus" that ends *Faust*.

3. OUR TWENTIETH WEDDING ANNIVERSARY I (ELIZABETH)

6 Still lifes by Jean-Baptiste-Siméon Chardin (1699–1779).

5. THE HUMAN CONDITION

8 Charles Ives (1874–1954), American composer.

10 "And it came to pass, when the evil spirit from God was upon Saul, that David took an harp, and played with his hand: so Saul was refreshed, and was well, and the evil spirit departed from him" (I Samuel 16:23).

7. WORDS FOR MUFFIN, A GUINEA-PIG

9 Cromwell wanted to be painted with "all those roughnesses, pimples, warts, and everything as you see me, otherwise I will never pay a farthing for it" (quoted in Horace Walpole, *Anecdotes of Painting in England* [1762–1771]).

1. END OF CAMP ALAMOSOOK

8 Acadians: "In 1755 the British fell upon the peaceful Acadian farms and, seizing most of the Acadians, deported them to the more southerly British colonies, scattering them along the Atlantic coast from Maine to Georgia" (*The New Columbia Encyclopedia* [1975]).

2. FAMILIAR QUOTATIONS

This poem records Lowell's debt to Harriet's verbal inventions. *Bartlett's Familiar Quotations* (1968 edition) lists Harriet's contribution to "Fall 1961" (line 8 here) under her father's name.

3 See final two lines of "Child's Song," *FTUD*, 338.
4 Anton Webern: Austrian composer (1883–1945), who reduced Schoenberg's twelve-tone technique to minimalist essentials.
8 See stanza 4 of "Fall 1961," *FTUD*, 329.
14 See stanza 7 of "The Scream," *FTUD*, 327.

6. GROWTH

10 *Boris*: Mussorgsky's opera *Boris Godunov*.

7. THE GRADUATE

1 Transylvania University, in Lexington, Kentucky.

8. NO HEARING 1. THE DIALOGUE

The phrase "but no hearing" appears at the end of two consecutive stanzas of Herbert's "Deniall" (1633).

5 Samuel Johnson (1709–1784), literary critic, scholar, formidable conversationalist, poet.

9. NO HEARING 2. ALCOHOL

13 *Otello*: Verdi opera, based on Shakespeare's *Othello*.

10. NO HEARING 3.

4–5 Cf. Spenser's "Epithalamion" (1595): "So I unto my selfe alone will sing, / The woods shall to me answer and my Eccho ring" (17–18).
6 Penobscot River, Maine.
8–9 Dante was forced into exile at age thirty-seven.

11. NO HEARING 4.

8 The Maine Maritime Academy keeps this ship anchored at Castine.
13 Melville's "Bartleby, the Scrivener" (1856). Elizabeth Hardwick: "On the third day of copying, he is asked to collaborate in the matter of proof-reading. The laconic, implacable signature is at hand, the mysterious utterance that cannot be interpreted and cannot be misunderstood. Bartleby replies, 'I would prefer not to'" (*Herman Melville* [2000], 107).

13. MY HEAVENLY SHINER (ELIZABETH)

3 *entremets chinois et canadiens*: Chinese and Canadian sweets (desserts).
14 we were kind of religious, we thought in images: "[W]ise men . . . fasten words again to visible things; so that picturesque language is at once a commanding certificate that he who employs it is a man in alliance with truth and God. The moment our discourse rises above the

ground line of familiar facts and is inflamed with passion or exalted by thought, it clothes itself in images" (Emerson, "Nature," sec. IV).

OBIT

In the "Afterthought" to *Notebook* (1970), Lowell writes that "ideas and expressions in 'Obit' and another poem [come] from Herbert Marcuse" (263).

1.1 The *Notebook* version does not include this line, or the stanza break that follows.
2.3 During Lyndon Johnson's presidency, copper was added to silver coins.

THE DOLPHIN (1973)

The copy-text is the second Farrar, Straus and Giroux printing. A small number of changes are incorporated from *Selected Poems* (rev.); Lowell told Bidart that the large-scale rewriting in *Selected Poems* (cutting and joining parts of sonnets, etc.) was introduced to make a short selection of sonnets work, not intended as a revision of the whole.

The Dolphin fictionalizes the end of Lowell's marriage to Elizabeth Hardwick and his marriage to Caroline Blackwood. As in all his autobiographical poems (see *Afterword: On "Confessional" Poetry*, p. 995), fact and fiction are mixed. In the early spring of 1972, for the first time, he arrived at a version of the manuscript that he considered a whole: this he widely circulated among friends (Elizabeth Bishop, Stanley Kunitz, William Alfred, among others). Bishop responded to this "*Ur-Dolphin*" in a letter that has become famous: the book is "a great poem (I've never used the word 'great' before, that I remember)," "magnificent poetry," but must not be published as it stands (*One Art*, 561).

Bishop's central objection is to the book's use of Elizabeth Hardwick's letters:

There is a "mixture of fact & fiction," and you have *changed* her letters. That is "infinite mischief," I think. . . . *Art just isn't worth that much.* I keep remembering Hopkins's marvelous letter to Bridges about the idea of a "gentleman" being the highest thing ever conceived—higher than a "Christian," even, certainly than a poet. It's not being "gentle" to use personal, tragic, anguished letters that way—it's cruel. (562)

Lowell responded by fundamentally changing the book. Several of the poems in Hardwick's voice were muted by taking them out of direct quotation, placed in italics, their anger and anguish softened. Lowell wrote to Stanley Kunitz: "Most of the letter poems—E.B.'s [Elizabeth Bishop's] objection they were part fiction offered as truth—can go back to your old plan, a mixture of my voice, and another voice in my head, part me, part Lizzie [Elizabeth Hardwick], italicized, paraphrased, imperfectly, obsessively heard" (Kunitz, *The New York Review of Books*, October 16, 1977). In response to Bishop's objection that the chronology of the final part of the book was confusing, and to make "Lizzie more restful and gracious," Lowell placed Sheridan's birth before "Flight to New York" (reversing the actual chronology). Lowell wrote to Bidart:

I've read and long thought on Elizabeth [Bishop]'s letter. It's a kind of masterpiece of criticism, though her extreme paranoia (for God's sake don't repeat this) about revelations gives it a wildness. Most people will feel something of her doubts. The terrible thing isn't the mixing of fact and fiction, but the wife pleading with her husband to return—this backed by "documents." So far I've done this much: 1) most important—shift *Burden* [the section announcing Caroline's pregnancy and Sheridan's birth] before

Leaving America and *Flight to New York*. This strangely makes Lizzie more restful and gracious about the "departure." . . . 2) Several of the early letters, From My Wife, are now cut up into Voices (often using such title) (changing mostly pronouns) as if I were speaking and paraphrasing or repeating Lizzie. Most of the later letters I haven't been able to change much or at all. . . . Now the book must still be painful to Lizzie, and won't satisfy Elizabeth. As Caroline says, it can't be otherwise with the book's *donnée*. (Hamilton, 425–26)

These changes, along with much rewriting during the summer of 1972, significantly changed the book's dynamics—without (as Lowell predicted) satisfying its critics. For a description of some manuscript changes, see Gewanter, "Child of Collaboration: Robert Lowell's *Dolphin*," *Modern Philology* 93 (1995), 178–203. The *Ur-Dolphin* is catalogued at the Harry Ransom Research Center in Austin, Texas, as Box 5 folder 9 (*The Dolphin* Draft F); in the Elizabeth Bishop Papers at Vassar College, Box 82, Folder 82.5.

FISHNET

2 trouvailles: Finds, discoveries, strokes of inspiration.
4 This line was added in the second printing; the poem was originally thirteen lines.
13 the net will hang on the wall: Cf. Horace, *Odes*, I.5.13–16 ("*Quis multa gracilis te puer in rosa*"), "The votive tablet on the temple wall / Is witness that in tribute to the god / I have hung up my sea-soaked garment there" (Ferry, trans., *Odes of Horace* [1997]).
14 illegible bronze: Cf. Horace, *Odes*, III.30.1 ("*Exegi monumentum aere perennius*"), "Today I have finished a work outlasting bronze" (Ferry).

REDCLIFFE SQUARE

Caroline Blackwood's residence in West London.

3. AMERICA FROM OXFORD, MAY 1970

8 Brassman: Operation Brassman, the American military "incursion" into Cambodia during the Vietnam War.

5. THE SERPENT
Text is from *SP*.

11 "I see me—a green hunter who leaps from turn to turn" (second printing).
12–13 "hang my bugle in an invisible baldrick" (Shakespeare, *Much Ado About Nothing* I.i.241–42/1.1.197–98) refers to being a cuckold; "groping for trouts in a peculiar river" (Shakespeare, *Measure for Measure* I.ii.90/1.2.0.6) refers to illegal or forbidden sexual intercourse.

6. SYMPTOMS
Text is from *SP*.

1 This line was added in *SP*. In the second printing, the poem begins: "A dog seems to lap water from the pipes, / a wheeze of dogsmell and dog companionship—"
4 bag of waters: Bag of amniotic fluid.
7 my old infection: Manic-depression (bipolar illness). Until the advent of lithium treatment in 1967, Lowell for many years (each year, as fall became winter) had a manic breakdown. From spring 1967 until the time of this sonnet, early summer 1970, he was well.

HOSPITAL

2. JUVENILIA

11 proofs: Galley pages for an unpublished book.

5. WALTER RALEIGH
For Walter Raleigh (or Ralegh), see note to "Lady Ralegh's Lament," 1060.

6 Crimea and Waterloo: British victories, against Russia (1856) and France (1815).

14 Spanish Main: Mainland of Spanish America, particularly the coast of South America from the isthmus of Panama to the mouth of the Orinoco River; Spanish treasure fleets sailing from the Main were attacked by English buccaneers.

HOSPITAL II

2. LETTER

10 Harriet: Lowell's daughter.

3. OLD SNAPSHOT FROM VENICE 1952

4 Vittore Carpaccio (c. 1450–1522), narrative painter of Venetian pageantry and religious subjects, including *St. Jerome Leading the Tame Lion into the Monastery* (1502).

5 Jerome: St. Jerome (c. 347–420?), scholar, translator of the Bible, whose texts were the basis of the Vulgate. The lion is associated with Venice (the Lion of St. Mark), as well as Jerome: in a popular fable, Jerome pulled a thorn from the paw of a lion, which then became devoted to him.

6 Torcello: An island in the Lagoon of Venice.

7 *venti anni fa*: Twenty years ago.

CAROLINE

4. MARRIAGE?

6 *mais ça ira*: Literally, "but this will go"; but it will be all right.

11 The Roman emperor Hadrian built a wall across Cumberland (c. A.D. 122–126) as demarcation of the northern boundary and defense line of Roman Britain, protection from attacking Picts (Scots).

SUMMER BETWEEN TERMS

1.14 "Per aspera ad astra" (Latin proverb; literally, "through hard places to the stars").

FALL WEEKEND AT *MILGATE*

Milgate: Caroline Blackwood's country home in Kent, England, "early eighteenth-century Palladian and very old-South messy" (Lowell, quoted in Hamilton, 415). Once owned by mystical philosopher and Rosicrucian Robert Fludd (1574–1637), the house was rebuilt and enlarged in the eighteenth century.

1.6 the painter, your first husband: Lucien Freud.

2 Text is from *SP*.

7 "But in all Israel there was none to be so much praised as Absalom for his beauty: from the sole of his foot even to the crown of his head there was no blemish in him" (II Samuel 14:25); Absalom, son of King David, later rebelled against him.

12 Towton: Here in 1461, in a bloody and decisive battle, Lancastrians loyal to Henry VI were defeated by the Yorkist supporters of Edward IV.

MERMAID

2.3 Academicians: Members of the French Academy, founded in 1635 to maintain the purity of the French language and establish correct usage.

2.4 See "The Downlook" 7.2, p. 835, and corresponding note, p. 1148.

2.14 "Float like a butterfly, sting like a bee," Drew Bundini Brown's description of boxing champion Muhammad Ali (the words are often attributed to Ali himself).

3.3 *bel occhi grandi*: "Beautiful large eyes."

3.4 This photograph is reproduced in Hamilton following p. 404. See "Summer Tides" 11–14, p. 853.

4.8 Text from *SP*; "the Sunday ennui" (second printing).

4.9 Via Veneto: A fashionable street in Rome.

4.13 *inside-right*: Front-line position in British football (soccer).

THE MERMAID CHILDREN

1 Folkestone: Seaside town in southeast England.

IN THE MAIL

In the revised *Selected Poems* (1977), Lowell joined the final eight lines of this poem to six lines from "Summer Between Terms" 2. On the use of *Selected Poems* (1977) revisions in the text of *The Dolphin*, see headnote, p. 1133.

DOUBT

2. POINTING THE HORNS OF THE DILEMMA

3 Medea: The scorned, vengeful abandoned wife of Jason.

4 gorgon: Medusa (see Glossary).

WINTER AND LONDON

5. FREUD

2 After the Nazi occupation of Austria, Freud fled Vienna for England (1938).

7 *Moses and Monotheism* (1938).

6. HARRIET'S DONKEY

7 De Maupassant was "put away in a madhouse. There he crawled about on his hands and knees, devouring his own excrement. The last line in his hospital report read: *Monsieur de Maupassant va s'animaliser* [Monsieur de Maupassant is going to turn into an animal]" (Isaac Babel, *The Collected Stories*, trans. Walter Morison [1960], 338).

7–9 Hamlet is enjoined by his father's ghost to avenge his murder, stuck in a plot whose shape has become a convention (the Revenge Play); he becomes "scatological" in the "country matters" scene with Ophelia (III.ii.101–9) just before his play *The Mousetrap* is performed. Elizabethan theaters were open-air, under the "London sky."

14 Wittgenstein: "Death is not an event of life. Death is not lived through" (*Tractatus Logico-Philosophicus*, trans. Ogden [1922], 6.4311).

ARTIST'S MODEL

1.1 Hölderlin's poem "Hälfte des Lebens." See note to "The Seasons," p. 1160.

1.3 Edouard Manet's *The Bar at the Folies-Bergère* (1882).

2.2 Peke: Pekinese dog.

3.1 "If it were done when 'tis done, then 'twere well / It were done quickly" (Shakespeare, *Macbeth*, I.vii.1–2).

3.6 Text from *SP*; "We follow our plot obediently as actors" (second printing).

MARRIAGE

2. TIRED IRON

4 the war on reeds: The Vietnam War.

4 *noyades*: Wholesale execution by drowning during the French Reign of Terror (1793). Ricefields are flooded for planting.

3. GRUFF

11 Blake's "London" (1794) ends "How the youthful Harlot's curse / Blasts the new-born Infant's tear, / And blights with plagues the Marriage hearse."

5. KNOWING

2 Grandfather: For Arthur Winslow, see "In Memory of Arthur Winslow" *LWC*, 23, and corresponding notes, p. 1014.

6. GOLD LULL

4 *I feel tomorrow like I feel today:* W. C. Handy, "St. Louis Blues."

10. LATE SUMMER AT *MILGATE*
Text is from *SP*.

13. ROBERT SHERIDAN LOWELL
See "Sheridan" and "For Sheridan" in *DBD*, 779 and 793.

14. OVERHANGING CLOUD

2 Luxor Temples: Like the temple to Amon at Luxor, Egypt.

9 met Satan like Milton: Milton writing *Paradise Lost* (1667).

ANOTHER SUMMER

3. IVANA
Ivana: Daughter of Caroline Blackwood. Text is from *SP*.

4. ALIMONY

7 Santo Domingo: In October 1972, Lowell and Blackwood went "down to Santo Domingo for a double divorce (Cal from Lizzie, Caroline from Israel Citkovitz), and Cal's marriage to Caroline (all of this taking place within forty-eight hours, among the clack of typewriters in a shed and a ceremony conducted in Spanish)" (Mariani, 414).

LEAVING AMERICA FOR ENGLAND

3. TRUTH

3 voice of 1930 Oxford: A highly stylized, partly invented W. H. Auden, who "is permitted to voice his objections" (Hecht, 12). See also "The Spell" in *DBD*, 770.

5. SICK

12 over-limit: I.e., while fishing.

ON THE END OF THE PHONE

4 "When everything matters, ask and never know?" (second printing). Our text is from *Selected Poems* (1976), where the poem is mistakenly printed under the title "Plane Ticket." (In the 1977 *SP* [rev.], which has a changed selection from *DOL*, this sonnet is not included.)

CARS, WALKING, ETC., AN UNMAILED LETTER

8 warning like Hector's Ghost: For Hector, see note to "Bright Day in Boston" 9.5, p. 1145. At the beginning of Act II of Berlioz' *Les Troyens* (1858), Hector's Ghost warns Aeneas that he must flee Troy because the Greeks have overwhelmed it, then find Italy where his people will found a great empire and where "a hero's death awaits you"; near the beginning of Act V, he warns Aeneas that he must no longer delay leaving Carthage, must sail for Italy. (Hector's Ghost does not appear in the *Iliad*, *Aeneid*, or extant Greek drama.)

FLIGHT TO NEW YORK

1. PLANE-TICKET

6 I.e., Ford's novel *The Good Soldier* (1915), which begins, "This is the saddest story I have ever heard."
9 book of life: Psalms 69:28; Revelations 3:5; et al.

3. PURGATORY

1 portrait: The original portrait is a fresco in the Duomo of Florence by Domenico di Michelino (1417–1492), after Baldovinetti.
11–12 Cf. *Inferno*, I.116–17: "Ancient tormented spirits as they lament / In chorus the second death they must abide" (trans. Pinsky).

4. FLIGHT

11 American painter Lyonel Feininger (1871–1956), whose images of sailboats and skyscrapers are characterized by interlocking translucent planes and intersecting planes of color.

5. NEW YORK AGAIN

8 Keats on "Negative Capability": "when a man is capable of being in uncertainties, Mysteries, doubts, without any irritable reaching after fact & reason" (letter dated December 21–27, 1817).

6. NO MESSIAH

12 *Nolo*: "I refuse"; cf. "Noli me tangere," Christ's "Touch me not," said to Mary Magdalene after his resurrection (John 20:17). In Thomas Wyatt's sonnet "Whoso List to Hunt" (c. 1540), a hind's necklace reads *"Noli me tangere*, for Caesar's I am, / And wild for to hold, though I seem tame" (13–14).

7. DEATH AND THE MAIDEN

1 *Death and the Maiden*: In Matthias Claudius's poem (made famous by Franz Schubert's setting) a young girl asks Death to pass her by, not to touch her; then Death asks for her hand. See "Death and the Maiden" in *HIS*, 479, and corresponding notes, p. 1096.

11. CHRISTMAS

Text is from *SP*.

DOLPHIN

1.2 captive: "forgetful" (first printing); "a captive" (second printing); text is from *SP*.
1.2 In 1961, Lowell published a translation of Jean Racine's neoclassical tragedy *Phèdre* (1677). Racine's version of Euripides' *Hippolytus* (428 B.C.), written in alexandrines, respects the neoclassical ideal of the "unities" that dominated contemporary French drama; Racine is "the man of craft." There is a contrast in the play between this formal decorum, and the passion that drives the title character, the "wandering voice" (4) to which the decorum gives ferocious utterance. Phèdre loves her stepson; rejected by him, she tells her husband that he tried to seduce her; the husband kills his son; Phèdre then kills herself.
2.1 my eyes have seen what my hand did: Until the summer of 1972, the final line of the book was "Why should shark be eaten when the bait swim free?" (This later became the final line of "Leaving Home, Marshal Ney" in *HIS*, 476.) Late one night at Milgate, Lowell asserted that Shakespeare had been lucky in his first editors, Heminge and Condell. In the preface to the First Folio, they had said one of the best things ever said about Shakespeare: "His eyes saw what his hand did." He quoted this from memory. He then tried to find the preface in his library, and couldn't; his books were still in New York, and at Milgate he mostly had paperbacks. Next morning at breakfast, Lowell with sly, bemused pleasure showed everyone a revision of "Dolphin" with its present final line—a line which resonates throughout his work. When I returned to America, I looked up Heminge and Condell. Lowell's memory had invented the line. Heminge and Condell say something altogether more commonplace, that Shakespeare revised very little: "His mind and hand went together: And what he thought, he uttered with that easiness, that we have scarce received from him a blot in his papers." [F.B.]

DAY BY DAY (1977)

The copy-text is the first Farrar, Straus and Giroux printing.

Lowell writes of *Day by Day*: "I have been writing for the last three years in unrhymed free verse. At first I was so unused to this meter, it seemed like tree-climbing. It came back—gone now the sonnet's cramping and military beat" (from his final statement on his own work, "After Enjoying Six or Seven Essays on Me," p. 989). On March 4, 1976, he writes to Elizabeth Bishop: "I have been writing furiously in my doldrums, and always feel on the edge of being too raw . . . and more than on the edge." On March 31, 1976, to Robert Boyers: "It is all in a very personal[,] in a solitary sublime style—no public events, no embarrassing personal references to friends, I hope." On July 27, to Steven Axelrod: "I fear [*Day by Day*] comes close to tragic, though that's not clear either in the book or life."

Helen Vendler, reviewing *Day by Day* (*The New York Times Book Review*, August 14, 1977) says that the reader must "re-construct the scenario behind this book—Lowell's life in Kent, his hospitalization in England, his wife's sickness, their temporary stay in Boston, their separation, a reconciliation, a further rupture, a parting in Ireland, Lowell's return to America."

Francesco Rognoni, in the notes to his Italian translation (*Giorno per giorno*, Mondadori, 2001), offers the fullest annotation that these poems have received; our notes are indebted to his.

PART ONE
ULYSSES AND CIRCE

For Ulysses, Circe and Penelope, see under *Ulysses* in Glossary.

Lowell: "It's wonderful to write about a myth especially if what you write isn't wholly about yourself" (Hamilton, 459). "This Ulysses comes on as a man on the verge of being posthumous to himself, ventriloquizing (through the autobiographical voice of Robert Lowell) about his interlude with Circe, his sensual self-knowledge and his appeased curiosities. Ulysses begins the poem as a drowsy voluptuary and will end it as a killer about to strike, thus acting as a kind of correlative for the poet caught between his marriages and his manias. The poem is spoken in a middle voice, neither dramatic monologue exactly nor confessional lyric" (Seamus Heaney, *The Government of the Tongue*, 143). Cf. "Penelope" and "Ulysses" in *HIS*, 556.

I.5 Cf. *Aeneid* II.3.
IV.2.8 Dante, *Inferno*, XXVI.117.
V.1.1–4 See "Returning" in *FTUD*, 347.
VI "In that history and science of feeling which poetry (according to Wordsworth) takes on as its task, Lowell has made a certain trajectory his own: the curve which begins in possibility and ends grimly in necessity. . . . We have come to the finale of the long effort. First there was the naming of the world; then, in a search for new names, came the 'embarkation and carnival of glory,' complete with marital triumph; next the war and the exploration of the world, the folly of following the Circean moon, seeing 'the meanness and beacons of men'; finally, 'bleak-boned with survival,' the return, drawn by the myth of the unchanged home; what emotion is left to age but fury? Age finds in self the same prison that Ulysses found, at the beginning of the poem, in Circe's bed" (Helen Vendler, *Salmagundi*, Spring 1977, pp. 18, 21–22).
VI.2–4 Cf. Dante, *Inferno*, XXVI. 94–96.
VI.7 and VI.78 Cf. "Going to and fro" in *FTUD*, 343, and corresponding notes, p. 1060.

HOMECOMING

This poem is based on "Returning" in *FTUD*, 347, which in turn was based on Ungaretti's "Canzone."

SUICIDE

Cf. "The Ghost" in *LWC*, 52. Here the ghost is a suicide; her suicide is one of the things that the poet prophetically dreams, but "that have not happened yet" (1.5).

DEPARTURE

Spoken by a woman to her lover who waits to depart. *Intermissa, Venus, diu*: the first line of Horace's *Odes*, IV.I (the first sentence reads, "Long interrupted wars, Venus, you begin again"). Beginning with line 20, much of the poem is a set of variations on this ode.

PART TWO
OUR AFTERLIFE I

1.18 Ezra Pound died on November 1, 1972, Edmund Wilson June 12, 1972, W. H. Auden September 29, 1973. Mariani rightly points out that Lowell's comments on Wilson's *Patriotic Gore* illuminate Lowell's purposes in his own historical portraits: "I am braced by your portraits. I see now, I think, that all your life you have been writing a sort of *Plutarch's Lives*. . . . One might use the phrase: moral aristocrats for them. By this, I mean some queer tense twist of principle, changed to virtue by having been lived through the undefinable multiplicity of experience. No two persons are alike, all are glaringly imperfect, still there are heroes. You can see I've just come from your [Oliver Wendell] Holmes, whose principles mean nothing to me literally, but whose life seems so shining and cantless. Pardon this sprawl, and let me salute you, dear old fellow questioning Calvinist, on your triumphant book" (letter to Wilson, March 31, 1962, quoted in Mariani, 503).

OUR AFTERLIFE II

4.2 The Agrarians (see note to "Holy Matrimony" 2.10, p. 1045).
4.3 *schadenfreude*: Malicious joy; gloating.
7.4 Common Market: Britain joined the European Economic Community in 1973.

LOUISIANA STATE UNIVERSITY IN 1940

Robert Penn Warren taught Lowell there; "Red" (2.3) was his nickname.

4.16 Slightly misquoted final line of Warren's poem "Pursuit."

FOR JOHN BERRYMAN

See "For John Berryman 1" and "2" in *HIS*, 600, and "For John Berryman, 1914–1972" in *CPR*, 111.

1.12 *Les Maudits*: The damned; Verlaine titled his book about his fellow symbolists, including Mallarmé and Rimbaud, *Les Poètes maudits* (1884).
1.16 grands maîtres: Great masters.
3.3–6 Lowell writes of the young Berryman's visit to Maine: "We gossiped on the rocks of the millpond. . . . John could quote with vibrance to all lengths, even prose, even late Shakespeare, to show me what could be done with disrupted and mended syntax. This was the start of his real style" (*CPR*, 112).

3.10 this last *Dream Song*: That is, the final one written, beginning "I didn't. And I didn't" (printed as the penultimate poem in *Henry's Fate*, 1977).

3.13 Berryman died by leaping from a bridge.

4 "Except Love's fires the virtue have / To fright the frost out of the grave" (song from Ben Jonson's *The Sad Shepherd, or, A Tale of Robin Hood*, I.v.79–80).

JEAN STAFFORD, A LETTER

1.1 *Towmahss Mahnn*: Thomas Mann.

2.2 Stafford did postgraduate work for a year in Heidelberg, Paris and London; she had just returned to Colorado when she first met Lowell (1937).

SINCE 1939

2.1 Munich: The site of the British and French pact with Germany allowing Hitler to take over the Sudetenland of Czechoslovakia (1938); synonymous with "appeasement." See "Munich 1938, John Crowe Ransom" in *HIS*, 524.

6.5 Kitchener became an emblem of British military imperialism, retaking Khartoum (1898) after Gordon's death and ruthlessly securing Boer submission in South Africa (1902).

SQUARE OF BLACK

For Lowell on Lincoln, see *CPR*, 165–66, 192–93, and "Abraham Lincoln" in *HIS*, 485.

1.1 this book: *Poetry and Eloquence from the Blue and the Gray*, Part Nine of *The Photographic History of the Civil War* (1911; Castle Books reprint, 1957).

FETUS

"Lowell builds this poem from meditations on three types of photographic images—the news photo, the X ray, and the billboard" (Helen Deese, in Axelrod, *Essays*, 207).

The February 19, 1975, *Boston Globe* shows Dr. Kenneth C. Edelin and his lawyer William Homans leaving court. "Edelin and Homans are smiling broadly, even laughing, 'lost in the clouds,' because the 'friendly' court has just imposed a mere token sentence—one year of probation" (Deese).

IN THE WARD

For magazine version, see Appendix IV, p. 937.

Israel Citkovitz (1909–1974): composer; Caroline Blackwood's second husband. He was a protégé of Aaron Copland and studied with Nadia Boulanger. For an earlier poem on Citkovitz, see "Old Wanderer" in *HIS*, 426, and corresponding notes, p. 1076.

7.3 Citkovitz championed modernism, but was unconventional enough also to celebrate Rachmaninoff; see "Orpheus With His Lute," *Tempo*, Winter 1951–1952. The *Tempo* piece gives a good sense of the humane learning, irony, and regard for the past that characterized Citkovitz's aesthetics: "Beethoven having a prophetic sense of the deteriorating effects of Czerny's methods, warned that the increasing mechanizing of technique would kill the spirit. . . . In our time, the progress of the aesthetic hero is apt to be measured by the corpses of vanquished traditions strewn along his path. . . . In this day of pianists with or without

rubato—impossible to say which is worse—Rachmaninoff's rubato re-created the elo-
quence and sure musical instinct that must have characterized the rubato-practise of Mozart,
Beethoven or Chopin" (9–11).

8.8 Schoenberg's twelve-tone system was both strict (with rule-laden "precision," 8.6) and revo-
lutionary (its rejection of tonality was seen by many as "daimonic lawlessness," 8.7).

8.12–13 treacherous . . . to fecundity: Citkovitz stopped composing early in his career.

9 Die Sprache ist . . . : The language is not comprehended, but not incomprehensible? The Ger-
man is Lowell's—an attempt to reproduce a half-remembered riddling statement by Schoen-
berg asserting the essential comprehensibility of his innovations. The words apply, for
example, to *Sprechstimme* (halfway between speech and song) in Schoenberg's *Pierrot Lu-
naire* (1912), and the initial public response to it. An early version read, *Die sprache ist unver-
ständlich / und wahrnehmbar* (the language is incomprehensible / and perceptible). [F.B.]

BURIAL

4.1 Your father: Israel Citkovitz.

EAR OF CORN

1.2 wine baron: Baron Philippe de Rothschild (1902–1988), who owned Chateau Mouton. Low-
ell, in a letter to F.B., mentions *"Rothschild's Corn"* (October 24, 1974).

7.2 "Poetry makes nothing happen" (Auden, "In Memory of W. B. Yeats").

10.2 *hypnos kai hydor*: Sleep and water.

OFF CENTRAL PARK

For E.H.: Elizabeth Hardwick. The apartment Hardwick and Lowell shared when married is off
Central Park.

7.2 Eugénie: Wife of Napoleon III.

12.2 Harriet: Lowell's daughter.

13.3 Cézanne painted and drew Mont Sainte-Victoire repeatedly from the 1880s until his death
in 1906.

DEATH OF A CRITIC

II.7.1 Carlo Gesualdo (1566–1613), composer, Prince of Venosa, ordered the murder of his first
wife and her lover.

ENDINGS

3.6 From ages six to eight, Lowell attended the Potomac School near Washington.

PART THREE: DAY BY DAY
THE DAY

4.4 *dies illa*: "That day" (Latin), from the *Requiem*, where "that day" is the day of wrath (*"Dies
irae, dies illa"*), the day of tears (*"Lacrymosa dies illa"*), when all shall be judged; here, "in
the marriage with nothingness" (5.2), its meaning is reversed. See note to "St. Mark's, 1933"
6.1 on p. 1146.

William I, king of Normandy, defeated King Harold of England at the Battle of Hastings (1066); as William the Conqueror he ordered a detailed census of the economic resources of England, the Domesday Book (1085–1086), the better to tax. *Domesday* is a variant of *Doomsday*.

7.9 the Protector: Oliver Cromwell.
9 *Nulle terre sans seigneur*: No land without a ruler.
10.3 J. M. W. Turner, British painter.
11 kingfisher: See note to "Colloquy in Black Rock" 5.2, p. 1007; here, an emblem both of the aristocracy and of those who sought to destroy it. (John Peck notes in the last line "the pun on Cromwell's role in the bird's name, and the flight of landed gentry" [*Salmagundi*, Spring 1977, 35].)

LIVES

2.4 "Except ye be converted, and become as little children, ye shall not enter into the kingdom of heaven" (Matthew 18:3).
2.8 Great Cycle: "The Great Year represents a cycle of creation and destruction in the universe, or *aiones* of the Gnostics. It is a time of rebirth at which the world returns to its primordial state, an apocatastasis, the return of the Golden Age" (J. C. Cooper, *An Illustrated Encyclopaedia of Traditional Symbols* [1978]).

THE SPELL

The model is W. H. Auden (1907–1973). See also "Truth" in *DOL*, 697, and corresponding note, p. 1138.

36 *Comme le bon dieu le veut, le temps s'envole*: As the good lord wishes, time flies.

MILGATE

Milgate: See headnote to "Fall Weekend at *Milgate*," p. 1135.

6.6 Bearsted: The village nearest Milgate.
6.10 you: Caroline Blackwood.
6.14 Ulster: Blackwood was born in Ulster.

ANTS

1.2 make it new: Ezra Pound's famous injunction to the artist (*Make It New*, 1934).
4.10 *semper eadem*: Always the same.
6.12 See the "Brute Neighbors" chapter in Thoreau's *Walden*.

SHERIDAN

Lowell's son, Robert Sheridan Lowell. See "Robert Sheridan Lowell," 691, and "For Sheridan," 793.

MARRIAGE

I.2.13 he can choose both sides: See headnote to "George III," p. 1149.

II.1.1 Jan Van Eyck's *The Arnolfini Marriage* (1434). Deese (building on Panofsky) mounts an elaborate and convincing argument that Van Eyck's painting itself functioned as a marriage certificate, and that (because Lowell and Blackwood were not legally married at the time of the photograph in section I) "Lowell's poetic formalization of their marriage, his verbal interplay of painting and photograph, had to take the place of a more ordinary legalization that circumstances made difficult. The photographer's flash becomes a 'miracle of lighting,' creating the 'sacramental instant' of marriage" (in Axelrod, *Essays*, 203).

II.3.8 *sang de boeuf*: Dark red (literally, ox blood).

LOGAN AIRPORT, BOSTON

6.3–5 Cf. "Absence my presence is, strangeness my grace, / With them that walk against me is my sun" (Fulke Greville, "When all This All").

TO MOTHER

2.2 "Josephine Beauharnais, military wife." Beauharnais, whose first husband was a French general guillotined in the Reign of Terror, became Napoleon's first wife. Napoleon "was a 'sloven,' but Mother with her intense and extraordinary neatness could love this personage she wished to tidy, could imagine herself as a tidying, organizing hand to greatness. She began to bolt her food, and for a time slept on an Army cot and took cold dips in the morning. In all this she could be Napoleon made over in my Grandfather's Prussian image. It was always my grandfather she admired, even if she called him Napoleon" (*CPR*, 297).

ROBERT T. S. LOWELL

Lowell's father, Robert Traill Spence Lowell III. See "Commander Lowell" p. 172 and headnote p. 1039, "Rebellion" p. 32 and headnote p. 1016.

FOR SHERIDAN

See note to "Sheridan," p. 1144.

2.1 negative: Photographic negative.
3.4 Stamp on silver cutlery.

BRIGHT DAY IN BOSTON

4.6 Augustus Lowell: Lowell's ancestor; mill owner.
9.5 Hector: Son of Priam, head of the Trojan forces and Troy's greatest warrior—slain by Achilles, then dragged behind horses (*Iliad*, XXII.395ff).

PHILLIPS HOUSE REVISITED

See "In Memory of Arthur Winslow" I in *LWC*, 23, and corresponding notes, p. 1014.

9.3 "I came to mourn you, not to praise the craft / That netted you a million dollars, late / Hosing out gold in Colorado's waste" ("In Memory of Arthur Winslow" III, 1.2–4, p. 24).

See headnote to "91 Revere Street" on p. 1033; and "Bobby Delano" in *HIS*, 505.

1.1 form: "Grade" in most American schools; "fourth form" is the equivalent of sophomore.

6.1 *Huic ergo parce, Deus*: "Spare then this [one], God"; or, "Spare him then, God." Line 4 from the "Lacrymosa" of the *Requiem*. ("Lacrymosa" is immediately preceded by "*Dies irae, dies illa*," a poem sometimes attributed to Thomas of Celano. "Lacrymosa" is modelled on it; "*Huic ergo*" echoes line 36: "*supplicanti parce, Deus*.") See "The Day" in *DBD*, 763, and "Between the Porch and the Altar" IV in *LWC*, 47.

MORNING AFTER DINING WITH A FRIEND

William Meredith has given an account of this meeting; see *Poems Are Hard to Read* (1991), pp. 32–36, 223.

3.3 Combat Zone: An area of stripper-bars, crime and porn.

5.1 Metropolitan Opera, New York.

7.3 I.e., younger ideal form.

9.2 the language of the tribe: "Since our concern was speech, and speech impelled us / To purify the dialect of the tribe" (T. S. Eliot, "Little Gidding" II). Eliot's second line translates Mallarmé: "*Donner un sens plus pur aux mots de la tribu*" ("Le Tombeau d'Edgar Poe" 2.2).

RETURN IN MARCH

1.3 Harvard houses: Undergraduate residences, built in the Georgian style (deriving from the eighteenth century) in the 1930's. "The red brick house, with courses and cornices of white stone and trimmings of white painted woodwork, is what is popularly termed the Georgian style" (*The New Columbia Encyclopedia* 1975).

SUBURBAN SURF

8.1 *méchants*: Spiteful, nasty, wicked.

TURTLE

For this recurrent theme, see "The Neo-Classical Urn" in *FTUD*, 358, and "Bringing a Turtle Home" and "Returning Turtle" in *FLH*, 635.

SEVENTH YEAR

1.2 the place: Milgate Park. See "Fall Weekend at *Milgate*," 659, and corresponding headnote, p. 1135; "*Milgate*," p. 773.

6.2 In Cambridge, Massachusetts.

10.1 Hart Crane: See "Words For Hart Crane," 159, and corresponding notes, p. 1037.

RUNAWAY

19 your book: Blackwood's novel *Great Granny Webster* (1977).

1 In the style of British painter and decorator Edward Burne-Jones (1833–1898).
2 *The Priory*: A private hospital in a south London suburb.
21–24 Spoken by Blackwood.

HOME

1.12 Thorazine is a powerful antipsychotic.
9.4–5 Dante, *Purgatorio*, V.101–5. See "Dante 3. Buonconte" in *HIS*, 454, and "The Soldier" in *LWC*, 38.

SHADOW

1.1 I must borrow from Walt Whitman to praise this night: In "The Sleepers," Whitman praises the healing powers of sleep: "The swell'd and convuls'd and congested awake to themselves in condition. . . . / I know not how I came of you [addressing 'night'] and I know not where I go with you, but I know I came well and shall go well" (section 8).
1.4 Praise be to sleep and sleep's one god: In 1976 or 1977, Lowell and I discussed how bold, even shocking it was of Whitman in "When Lilacs Last in the Dooryard Bloom'd" to praise death:

> *Prais'd be the fathomless universe,*
> *For life and joy, and for objects and knowledge curious,*
> *And for love, sweet love—but praise! praise! praise!*
> *For the sure-enwinding arms of cool-enfolding death.*
>
> *Dark mother always gliding near with soft feet,*
> *Have none chanted for thee a chant of fullest welcome?*
> *Then I chant it for thee, I glorify thee above all,*
> *I bring thee a song that when thou must indeed come, come unfalteringly . . .*
>
> *The night in silence under many a star,*
> *The ocean shore and the husky whispering wave whose voice I know,*
> *And the soul turning to thee O vast and well-veil'd death,*
> *And the body gratefully nestling close to thee.*

(section 14)

I think that "sleep's one god" (1.4) is Death—Whitman's "dark mother," here "the Voyeur, the Mother" (1.5), the Creator of the Hebrew Bible who creates creatures who must die. ("Job's . . . I AM" [1.6] is the voice out of the whirlwind [Job 38:1] who essentially repeats God's I AM THAT I AM to Moses [Exodus 3:14].) God "soothes the doubtful murmurs of the heart" (1.7) with death; in the next line (2.1), Lowell describes the "Christian heaven" (2.4) that can be reached only after death. [F.B.]
4.1–2 Just before Cicero's death, "a flight of crows rose up into the air with a great noise and came flying towards Cicero's ship as it was being rowed to land. . . . [E]veryone regarded this as a bad omen" (Plutarch, *Cicero*, trans. Rex Warner, 359).

1.2 Hamilton points out that "enthusiasm is a word [Lowell] regularly uses to describe his manic episodes" (226).

2.7–8 "When the trees close . . . hard to find—": See "Suicide" 7.1–2, p. 725.

SHIFTING COLORS

10.1–2 This is not the directness: Cf. "I want words meat-hooked from the living steer" ("The Nihilist as Hero" in *HIS*, 590).

10.4 Mallarmé sought a "pure" poetry: "The pure work implies the disappearance of the poet as speaker, yielding his initiative to words, which are mobilized by the shock of their difference; they light up with reciprocal reflections like a virtual stream of fireworks over jewels, restoring perceptible breath to the former lyric impulse, or the enthusiastic personal directing of the sentence" (from "Crisis in Poetry" trans. May Ann Caws, *Selected Poetry and Prose*, [1982]). The result was an extremely dense, packed style, usually at a remove from representational surfaces; at his death, much work was left uncompleted. See "At Gautier's Grave" in *IM*, 231, and "Mallarmé 1. Swan" and "Mallarmé 2. Gift of a Poem" in *HIS*, 491.

UNWANTED

1.2 *Antabuse*: An antidrinking drug that causes a violent reaction to alcohol, even occasionally death; Lowell at times took it because alcohol could trigger a brief manic attack.

5.1 Merrill Moore was not only a psychiatrist but "a poet of some reputation. He had been a fringe member of the Southern 'Fugitive' group led by John Crowe Ransom and Allen Tate and was famous for writing only—but voluminously—in sonnet form" (Hamilton, 28).

7.1–11 For an earlier prose version of this episode, see *CPR*, 299–300.

8.2 *cri de coeur*: Cry of the heart.

10.5–12 See *CPR*, 301–2.

THE DOWNLOOK

5 Cf. Dante, *Inferno*, V. 120–23; and Lowell's version, "Dante 4. Paolo and Francesca" 1–2 in *HIS*, 455.

6.3–4 The semi-mythical poet Arion, surrounded by a murderous crew, sang to attract dolphins to his ship, then leapt into the sea. A dophin carried him safely to shore.

7.2 insupportable, trespassing tongue: In 1966 Pound said to Lowell, "Didn't Frost say you'd say anything once?" (Lowell, letter to James Laughlin, August 31, 1966). Cf. "Mermaid" 2.4, p. 665.

THANKS-OFFERING FOR RECOVERY

5 *homme sensuel*: Sensual man.

11 *ex voto*: Latin, "from a vow"; "the replica of the afflicted part of the body which Latin Catholics give to the saint believed responsible for the cure" (Alan Williamson, in Meyers, *Interviews*, 272). Elizabeth Bishop to Lowell: "Frank [Bidart] was also here for a drink just before he left for England his last visit—and at the very last moment I picked up that weird balsa-wood head & thrust it on him . . . I've been thinking I wanted to send you *something*, but hadn't been able to think of anything. I have—had, that is—two of those heads, picked up by Lota years ago—they are *ex-votos*—someone cured of a head injury or violent head-

aches, etc., gave one to his church or the shrine where he'd prayed for recovery. The remaining one is different wood, much heavier, and very neatly painted, with a pert little moustache, etc.—rather like a hairdresser's sign. It wasn't until Frank had taken off that I suddenly thought, 'Oh dear!—I was just looking around frantically for a souvenir for Cal— I hope to goodness he doesn't think I *meant* anything by it . . . !' (Because I certainly didn't— or certainly not consciously) Then last night Frank told me you've already written a poem about it—which of course I'm dying to see . . ." (April 16, 1976).

14 *Deo gratias*: Thanks to God.

EPILOGUE

"[I]n paintings, [we feel] the artist's mothering work of hand and mind. I once asked the master photographer Walker Evans how Vermeer's *View of Delft* (that perhaps first trompe l'oeil of landscape verisimilitude) differed from a photograph. He paused, staring, as if his eye could not give the answer. His answer was [John Crowe] Ransom's—art demands the intelligent pain or care behind each speck of brick, each spot of paint" (*CPR*, 27).

9 "with dim eyes and threadbare art" (*Salmagundi*, Spring 1977, 115).

15 Lowell, in 1963: "I started one of these poems [for *Life Studies*] in Marvell's four-foot couplet and showed it to my wife [Elizabeth Hardwick]. And she said 'Why not say what really happened?' (It wasn't the one about her.)" (Meyers, *Interviews*, 75).

17 "Among the Dutch painters, Jan Vermeer [1632–1675] was the most accurate in rendering the natural appearances of things and persons, in representing the effects of light passing from objects to retina, in recording compositionally what the eye has seen" (Helen Deese, in Axelrod, *Essays*, 185). Deese argues that the Vermeer painting embedded in Lowell's poem is *Woman in Blue Reading a Letter* (187). When Derek Walcott asked Lowell "what painter he imagined to be his complement," Lowell replied "Vermeer" (180).

APPENDIX *TRANSLATIONS*

RABBIT, WEASEL, AND CAT

Based on La Fontaine's "Le Chat, la Belette, et le petit Lapin" (VII.16).

5 Aurora: Dawn.
17 *casus belli*: An occasion that justifies war.

GEORGE III

Commissioned by *Newsweek* for its July 4, 1976, Bicentennial issue. Lowell wrote Peter Taylor of his son Sheridan, age four: "His bicentennial experiences in America have perhaps taught him[,] more than all his nursery schools, the ambivalence, which is really balance of power, of taking both sides. Here [England] people are a little bewildered when he stands up for King George" (September 11, 1975).

Axelrod lists the passages from Sherwin's *Uncorking Old Sherry* that Lowell adapts (*Essays*, 24–25).

17.2 Haldeman, Ehrlichman: President Richard M. Nixon's advisors H. R. "Bob" Haldeman and John Ehrlichman were both convicted of covering up the Watergate break-in.

23 Shelley's sonnet "England in 1819" begins with George III: "An old, mad, blind, despised, and dying king."

26.1 *Quand on s'amuse, que le temps fuit*: When one is amused, how time flies.

29.1–2 Unlike Nixon, who taped conversations in the Oval Office, providing the evidence that forced his resignation.

ARETHUSA TO LYCOTAS

4.3 Ocnus: In Hades he weaves a rope that a female donkey eats as fast as he can make it.

9.1 Hippolyta: Amazon warrior queen.

11.1 Kalends: The first of the month.

11.2 Lares: "*Lares Familiares*, the spirits who had the special care of the house and household, and were worshipped at the domestic hearth on the Kalends" (Harvey, *The Oxford Companion to Classical Literature*, 235); at Kalends their shrine was "open[ed]."

12.2 "The sputtering of a lamp was a good omen. The wine was dropped on the flame to ratify the omen" (*Propertius*, trans. Butler, Loeb Classical Library, 285).

15.2 "The headless spear was a kind of medal for meritorious service" (McCulloch, *The Poems of Sextus Propertius* [1972], 214).

LAST POEMS

EXECUTIONS

Completed after *Day by Day* had gone to press. In its early stages, titled "Princess," it appears in early manuscripts of *Day by Day*. Published in *The New York Review of Books*, July 14, 1977.

LONELINESS

Addressed to Elizabeth Hardwick, with whom he had spent the summer of 1977 in Castine, Maine.

SUMMER TIDES

Addressed to Caroline Blackwood. This is Lowell's final completed poem, finished August 31, 1977, thirteen days before his death. After "Summer Tides," he worked on a poem entitled "A Letter," but never brought it to coherence or clarity. For a stanza from "A Letter," see "Fragment," in Appendix VI, p. 988.

11 your portrait: See "Mermaid" 3.4–6 in *DOL*, 666, and corresponding note, p. 1136.

30 rotting the bulwark: "Literally, the front part of the lawn gave onto a precipice and there was a railing there and this was being eaten away and the whole thing was about to fall down" (Hamilton, 469).

NOTES TO APPENDICES

Notes to the Appendices are confined to publication information, variants, and translation of foreign phrases.

APPENDIX I: LAND OF UNLIKENESS (1944)

The copy text is the Cummington Press edition, a limited edition of 250 copies. Many of these poems appear revised in *Lord Weary's Castle*. Lowell never allowed *Land of Unlikeness* to be reprinted.

TITLE AND EPIGRAPH

"Such is the condition of those who live in the Land of Unlikeness. They are not happy there. Wandering, hopelessly revolving, in the 'circuit of the impious' those who tread this weary round suffer not only the loss of God but also the loss of themselves. They dare no longer look their own souls in the face; could they do it they would no longer recognize themselves. For when the soul has lost its likeness to God it is no longer like itself: *inde anima dissimilis Deo, inde dissimilis est et sibi* [from St. Bernard's sermons on the *Song of Songs*]; a likeness which is no longer like its original is like itself no more" (Etienne Gilson, *The Mystical Theology of Saint Bernard*, trans. A. H. Downes [1940] 58). "The title is taken from St. Bernard, but ultimately derives from St. Augustine's metaphor ('*regio dissimilitudinis*') ['land of unlikeness']" (Staples, 22).

THE PARK STREET CEMETERY

See "At the Indian Killer's Grave," *LWC*, 56, for revised portions of this poem.

2.4 *in saecula saeculorum*: forever and ever.

IN MEMORY OF ARTHUR WINSLOW

See "In Memory of Arthur Winslow," *LWC*, 23.

ON THE EVE OF THE FEAST OF THE IMMACULATE CONCEPTION, 1942

An earlier version was titled "To Our Lady on the Feast of the Immaculate Conception / (Variation on a poem by Vaughan)" (Houghton Library, bMS 1905 2051 F.100).

Here is the version of stanza 1 from *Sewanee Review* LI (1943) 393–94:

> Mother of God, whose burly love
> Rebuffed the sword, I must improve
> On the big wars
> And make a holiday with Mars
> Your Feast Day, while the pacifists' bluff
> Courage or call it what you please
> Plays blindman's buff
> Through virtue's knees.

THE BOSTON NATIVITY

In the magazine version, titled "Song of the Boston Nativity" (*Partisan Review* X [1943] 316–17), the first five stanzas are spoken by "*Our Lady of Freedom*" and the last stanza spoken by "*Chorus*."

6.3 magian: like the Magi.

A hurricane struck New England in 1938.

SALEM

See "Salem" in *LWC*, 29.

CONCORD

See "Concord" in *LWC*, 30.
    Here is the magazine version (*Partisan Review* X [1943] 316):

> Ford idles here in his inventor's search
> For history, for over the faked ricks,
> The Minute man, the Irish Catholics,
> The ruined Bridge and Walden's fished-out perch,
> The belfry of the Unitarian Church
> Clangs with preposterous torpor. Crucifix,
> On you the heirs of Caiaphas transfix
> Mammon's unbridled industry, the lurch
> For lines to harness Heraclitus' stream!
> This Church is Concord. Concord, where Thoreau
> And Emerson fleeced Heaven of Christ's robe,
> Concord, a place of peace, for hire or show,
> Renowned for its embattled farmers' scream,
> Whose echo girdled the imperfect globe.

NAPOLEON CROSSES THE BERESINA

See "Napoleon Crosses the Berezina" in *LWC*, 37.

SCENES FROM THE HISTORIC COMEDY

I. See "The Slough of Despond" in *LWC*, 63.
III.1.6. *Lignum Vitae*: "Tree or wood of life" (New Latin); a tropical American evergreen with
    durable, resinous wood. See "The Wood of Life," p. 882.

DEA ROMA

Dea Roma: The Goddess Rome. See "Dea Roma" in *LWC*, 51.

CHRIST FOR SALE

Jay Cantor suggests that in this poem—which attacks what the world has made of Christ—the
"auctioneers" of Christ ("four hog-fatted Jews," i.e., Jews who do not keep kosher) are the four
writers of the gospels: Matthew, Mark, Luke and John.

See "The Crucifix" *LWC*, 50.

THE WOOD OF LIFE (*GOOD FRIDAY*, 1942)

See note on "Scenes from the Historic Comedy" III.1.6 (above).

SATAN'S CONFESSION

For the very different magazine version, see *Kenyon Review* V (1943), 379–83.

CHRISTMAS EVE IN THE TIME OF WAR

See "Christmas Eve Under Hooker's Statue" in *LWC*, 21.

Here is an early version of extraordinary interest (*Partisan Review* X [1943], 314–15):

THE CAPITALIST'S MEDITATION BY THE CIVIL WAR MONUMENT, CHRISTMAS, 1942

Tonight the blackout. Twenty years ago
The playboys starred a neon tree; if Hell's
Inactive sting stuck in the stocking's toe,
A child could draw it. Union generals
Perching upon a pillar of dead snow,
Two cannon and a turdlike cairn of balls,
Livid in unfinished marble, know
Only the vulture's leavings of the warcloud:
Their dead-pans pray to the Wizard's Star for blood.

A blizzard soaps Christ's diapers, and all
The crowsfoot feathers mossing Mars' brass hat
Whiten to angels' wings, and the War's snowfall
Slogs down the philanthropic plutocrat
(Who swished his whited blossoms of goodwill,
Like the sunlight on the hot-beds of world debt)
And still the venery of Capital
Freezes the Puritan virtues into gold,
While Mars, pinched healer, taps their veins. I am cold,

War's coddling will not warm me up again.
Brazenly gracious Ares throws his arms
About his mother the mulct'd tycoon
(The pageantary understanding forms
Anonymous machinery from raw men,
Riding the whirlwind, it directs the drums);
I bawl for Santa Claus and Hamilton,

And slip the harness of war's vacant squeeze;
How can my funds for good and evil freeze?

This winter in Europe and America
The lights are out. Tonight Herodians lurch
Into the shuttered White House, manger or bar;
Blue lines of men and women are on the march,
And the unions' czars intrench for civil war:
The Union Generals tremble on their perch.
Tonight our rulers seek the Orient Star;
The gestapo dragoons the Magi's Star for blood.
I have no blood to suckle an infant God.

Mars is this winter's God. The Civil War
Barters the garish pathos of its bed—
Flaring poinsettia, sweet william, larkspur
And black-eyed Susan with her frizzled head—
For snows that blot indignity and honor;
But what is war to gold's eternal glimmer?
"I bring no peace-terms but the sword," Christ said,
"My nakedness was fingered and defiled,
And woe unto all those that are with child."

CISTERCIANS IN GERMANY

1.12 Unter den Linden: Perhaps the grandest thoroughfare in Berlin, originally a boulevard of
    linden trees.
3.11–14 See "At the Indian Killer's Grave" 5.8–11 in *LWC*, 58.

THE DRUNKEN FISHERMAN

See "The Drunken Fisherman" in *LWC*, 34.
    An earlier version was published in *Hika* (February 1939, 14–15), the undergraduate maga-
zine at Kenyon College, when Lowell was enrolled there:

FISHERMEN

We cast along the river, high
Up to its own nativity,
And found a fluid bow suspends
No pots of gold to weight its ends,
And only trammelled blood-mouthed trout,
That in straw-baskets thrashed about,
Converted wading into wealth:
We drew a currency of health.

A calendar to show the day,
A handkerchief to wave away
The flies, a chair depressed with storm,
Pouching a bottle in one arm,
A dusky bottle full of worms,

And slippers are our fishing terms:
The armchair in its anchorage
Contents the angles of old age.

Our labor once was well and just.
Our footsores and the roadside dust
Were not enduring pain or stain;
When absolution was the rain.
Wonder, our fluent and obscene
Misgivings kept the conscience clean.
A cinema of scenery stirred
Up sharpness that our memory blurred.

Our dashing river, pooling, drools
With heavy waters into holes;
A grain of sand inside the shoe
Mounts to a moon that can undo
Man and creation too; remorse
Stinking, has puddled in its course;
Tantrums take on a whalish rage:
This is the content of old age.

*   *   *

Is there no way to cast our line
Into mortality's decline?
The fisherman must cast about
When shallow waters peter out.
Might we progress by flaunting bait?
Will progress further us with fate?
No, death's enchanting process charms
The fisher, and the dozer storms.

CHILDREN OF LIGHT

See "Children of Light," *LWC*, 31.

LEVIATHAN

For an early version of this poem, see "Sublime Feriam Sidera Vertice" in Appendix V, p. 955.

APPENDIX II: AKHMATOVA AND MANDELSTAM

The copy text is *Poets on Street Corners*, edited by Olga Carlisle, 1968. Lowell worked from Carlisle's prose trots, with subsequent criticism and suggestions by Carlisle.

ANNA AKHMATOVA

REQUIEM

In *Poets on Street Corners*, the title is "The Requiem." Olga Carlisle's headnote for this poem: "Dedicated to the victims of the Stalinist repression in the late thirties, the Yezhovshchina, named after Yezhov, who was head of the secret police at the time. The *streltsi* were Peter the Great's musketeers whom he suspected of treason and had executed, with all sorts of refinements in cruelty, at the gates of the Kremlin in the presence of their families" (59).

Introduction 2.4.2 *Kyrie eleison*: Lord, have mercy.
Epilogue II.6.3 lie: In *Poets on Street Corners*, followed by a comma.

MANDELSTAM

In *Poets on Street Corners*, Olga Carlisle quotes a letter from Madame Osip Mandelstam (who Carlisle says knows English "very well"), to Robert Lowell in March 1967: "There are two different kinds of poetic translations. One kind is the rendering of verse with great skill but rather mechanically. It is pure translation and nothing else. . . . The other is a great moment, the meeting of two poets writing in two different languages. There is sudden recognition between them, as if the poet and his translator had struck up a close friendship. In such translations everything is unexpected, and only they belong to literature as such. Generally, they are quite free. . . . And that is why I greatly liked your translations of my husband's verse" (xiii).

The majority of the Mandelstam versions first appeared in *The New York Review of Books*, December 23, 1965, "translated by Robert Lowell and Olga Carlisle." The headnote is signed by both Lowell and Carlisle: "These poems, among the last by Osip Mandelstam, were written during the apocalyptic days of the great Stalinist purges in the Thirties. Our translations, while trying to be as faithful as possible to Mandelstam's images and meter, are not literal. Rather, they are adaptations attempting to recapture Mandelstam's tone and the atmosphere of his terrible last years." In *Poets on Street Corners* Carlisle calls these versions "Lowell's 'imitations,' " and lists them as simply "adapted by Robert Lowell." (Later, in regard to the many poems and translators who contributed to *Poets on Street Corners*, she writes that "In some instances I consider myself as co-translator of the poem" [xiv], without specifying in which instances.)

"PRESERVE MY WORDS FOREVER FOR THEIR AFTERTASTE OF MISFORTUNE AND SMOKE"

In *The New York Review of Books*, followed by a note: "According to the new edition of Mandelstam's collected poems, this poem is addressed to Anna Akhmatova."

FRAGMENTS

The final four stanzas are printed in *The New York Review of Books* as a separate poem, dated "Leningrad, January, 1931."

THE TURKISH WOMAN

In *The New York Review of Books*, followed by a note: "The title of this poem is Akhmatova's. In her opinion it is 'the best love poem of the century.' "

CHAPAYEV

Carlisle's headnote: "Vasily Chapayev was a famous partisan commander, a legendary figure of the Civil War, who drowned during a battle against the Whites. Chapayev's story was made into a memorable Soviet movie in 1934. In one scene, White officers, on foot, with cigarettes in their mouths, march into battle 'against the open loin of the steppes.' In Part 2, images out of *Chapayev* [the film] are mixed with Mandelstam's impressions as he was taken eastward into exile after his first arrest. On the train, the young soldiers who guarded him and Mm. Mandelstam were reading Pushkin" (151).

THE FUTURE

In *Poets on Street Corners*, without a title. In *The New York Review of Books* this poem is titled "The Future," with a note: "The title is Robert Lowell's."

APPENDIX III: MAGAZINE VERSIONS

BEYOND THE ALPS

Kenyon Review XV (1953) 398–401. See "Beyond the Alps" in *LS*, 113, and *FTUD*, 364; and "Ovid and Caesar's Daughter" in *HIS*, 442.

2.2 *l'Assunta*: The Assumed One (Mary, whose body was assumed into heaven). *Libertà*: Liberty, freedom.
2.9 Death to Americans.
5 Lines from this stanza became part of "For George Santayana" 2; see pp. 155–56.
6 This stanza was revised and printed as a separate poem in *Perspectives U.S.A.*, III (Spring, 1953), 67; and in Rolando Anzilotti's bilingual edition of Lowell's poems, *Poesie 1943–1952* (1955). Here is the new version, which Lowell did not again reprint:

SANTAYANA'S FAREWELL TO HIS NURSES

> The spirit giveth life; will letters kill
> The calm eccentric, if by heaven's will
> He found the Church too good to be believed?
> "You'll die," the Sisters answer, "as you lived."
> One wonders how they riddled what I wrote,
> Or if the nuns were too pragmatical
> To nurse illusion long. Believing Paul,
> Most miserable of men, had missed the boat
> By preaching truth was what his hand could reach,
> I gave the bottomless Evangel soul;
> Essence took heart and landscape from my speech.
> Dying, I fancied the Blue Sisters pressed
> Like geese-girls, hissing, "Rome must give her best,"
> Till Curtius in full armor filled the hole.

BUENOS AIRES

The New York Review of Books (February 1, 1963), 3. See "Buenos Aires" p. 367 and "Liberty and Revolution, Buenos Aires" (p. 544).

WASHINGTON

Included in *Lincoln and the Gettysburg Address,* ed. Allan Nevins (1964), 92. See "July in Washington" p. 366.

WAKING EARLY SUNDAY MORNING

The New York Review of Books (August 5, 1965). See "Waking Early Sunday Morning," p. 383, and Introduction, pp. ix–xiii.

IN THE WARD

Ploughshares 2.4 (1975), 45–47. See "In the Ward," p. 748.

APPENDIX IV: TWO SEQUENCES FROM *NOTEBOOK*

THOSE OLDER

Text is from *Notebook 1967–68* (1969). See "Those Older" 1 and 2 (p. 598) and "Solomon, the Rich Man in State" (p. 425).

LONG SUMMER

Text is from *Notebook* (1970). See numbered "1930's" stanzas in *HIS* (p. 502–509), "Down the Nile" (p. 434), "For Ann Adden 4. Coda" (p. 536), "Ice" (p. 604).

APPENDIX V: UNCOLLECTED POEMS

THE CITIES' SUMMER DEATH

Kenyon Review I (1939), 32.

THE DANDELION GIRLS

Kenyon Review I (1939), 33.

SUBLIME FERIAM SIDERA VERTICE

Hika (Feb. 1940), 17. Horace, Ode 1.1.36: "I shall strike the stars with my uplifted head." The first word in Horace's line is "sublimi," not "sublime."

PENTECOST, 1942

Common Sense XIV (December 1945), 30. This poem, along with "Monte Cassino" (below) and "The Soldier" (revised in *LWC*, 38), were published in *Common Sense* as "Three War Sonnets."

Common Sense XIV (December 1945), 30.

2 Emmanuel: "God with us" (Hebrew).

CARON, NON TI CRUCCIARE

A New Anthology of Modern Poetry (ed. Selden Rodman), 1946. "Lowell's title, from *Inferno*, Canto III, is spoken by Virgil, the master-poet and guide, who is responding to Charon's objections to taking a living being across the Styx. After exclaiming 'Charon, do not rage,' Virgil continues (in Charles Singleton's translation), 'Thus it is willed there where that can be done which is willed; and ask no more' " (Doreski, *Shifting Colors*, 22).

I.13 *lebensraum*: See note to "France" 13, p. 1018.
IV.7 An *Ave*: I.e., an *Ave Maria* or "Hail Mary" (a prayer).

THE PANTHER

Western Review XVII (1952–53), 256.

APPENDIX VI: POEMS IN MANUSCRIPT

THE TARTARS

Houghton Library, bMS Am 1905 2155.

This poem is translated by Arthur Waley as "Fighting South of the Ramparts" (*The Poetry and Career of Li Po*, 1950, 34–35), by Arthur Cooper as "We Fought South of the Walls . . ." (*Li Po and Tu Fu*, 1973, 152).

4 To the Han: I.e., down to the Han Dynasty (206 B.C.–220 A.D.).

THE BROOM

Houghton Library, bMS Am 1905 2778.

This version translates the first 37 lines of Leopardi's "La ginestra, o il fiore del deserto" (The Broom, or The Flower of the Desert).

EL DESDICHADO

Houghton Library, bMS Am 1905 2781.

CHRIST IN THE OLIVE GROVE

Houghton Library, bMS Am 1905 2781.

The New York Review of Books (October 22, 1981). "Bellosguardo" is only the first half of Montale's "Tempi di Bellosguardo." (Alan Williamson found and identified the texts.)

BEOWULF

Houghton Library, bMS Am 1905 2784.

THREE POEMS FOR *KADDISH*

Ploughshares 5.2 (1979), 70–73.
III.1.9 In *Ploughshares*, a comma followed "wilderness."

THE SEASONS

Houghton Library, bMS Am 1905 2784.

The genesis of this was an unfinished version of Hölderlin's "Hälfte des Lebens," which Lowell titled "Half of Life."

DIFFUGERE NIVES

Title: "The snows have fled."

VIVAMUS

Title: "Let us live."

BALLOON

Untitled in manuscript. The editors want to thank Grzegorz Kosc for bringing this poem to their attention.

[The provenance, even authorship of this poem is mysterious. It was found among Lowell's papers from his years in England, papers now at the Harry Ransom Center at the University of Texas. There are no drafts. As far as I know, he showed it to no one. It is an eerie transmutation of the penultimate stanza of "For the Union Dead" (p. 378). Or is it an imitation of an as-yet-unidentified original? Its texture is close to some of the poems in *Imitations*; it could have been triggered by rereading Saba's "Winter Noon" (p. 280). Its single-minded forward movement is unlike his late work. F. B.]

APPENDIX VII: AFTER ENJOYING SIX OR SEVEN ESSAYS ON ME

Salmagundi 37 (Spring 1977), 112–15.

GLOSSARY

Names of people, places, and works of art that recur in Lowell will be found here, or are cross-referenced in the Notes.

Acheron River of the Underworld that separates the realm of the dead from the realm of the living; also see **Styx**.

Aeneas Trojan hero, son of **Venus** and a mortal father. After escaping with his son and father and a band of followers from the ruins of Troy, he travels to Carthage where he becomes the lover of the queen, Dido. Then, commanded by the gods, he must leave her—sail to Italy, fight those who do not want to be conquered, and found there the Roman race.

Agamemnon See **Oresteia**.

Alexander the Great (356–323 B.C.), son of Philip of Macedon; he quickly conquered Asia Minor, Egypt, and western India, and ruled most of the Persian Empire.

Antony, Mark (82/81–30 B.C.), Roman general whose erotic and military alliance with **Cleopatra** precipitated civil war with Rome.

Aphrodite The Greek goddess of love; identified with the Roman goddess **Venus**.

Apollo The god of music and poetry; prophecy and reason; light and the sun. Often contrasted with **Dionysus**.

Beatrice Portinari (d. 1290), Dante's beloved, whom he met only briefly. She is his intercessor in the *Inferno*, goal in the *Purgatorio*, guide in the *Paradiso*.

Berryman, John (1914–1972), poet, author of *The Dream Songs*.

Bishop, Elizabeth (1911–1979), poet. Bishop's affections and art continued to be entangled with Lowell's from their first meeting (January, 1947).

Blackwood, Caroline (1931–1996), Anglo-Irish novelist and journalist; Lowell's third wife.

Caligula (A.D. 12–41), Roman emperor whose antic misanthropy and memorable inventions to humiliate the aristocracy led to his assassination.

Cassandra Princess of Troy who became **Agamemnon's** concubine after Troy's defeat; prophetess condemned to announce what no one comprehends; upon her arrival at Mycenae, murdered by **Clytemnestra**.

Charon The ferryman who conveys the dead in his boat across the **Styx** to the Underworld.

Cleopatra (69–30 B.C.), Queen of Egypt, whose political power was established by her consort Julius Caesar, then confirmed and destroyed by alliance with **Mark Antony**.

Clytemnestra See **Oresteia**.

Dionysus The god of wine; ecstasy; the dark powers; unreason; sexuality. Identified with the Roman wine-god Bacchus; contrasted with **Apollo**.

Don Giovanni Aristocratic charmer; seducer who cannot count his conquests; title character in Mozart's opera *Don Giovanni* (libretto by Da Ponte; 1787–1788). (Italian for "Don Juan.")

Edwards, Jonathan (1703–1758) American theologian and Calvinist minister; in 1942, Lowell planned to write Edwards biography.

Eurydice Wife of **Orpheus**; after she dies, Orpheus wins her release from the Underworld by singing for the gods there on condition that he not look back at her as they climb the path back to life.

Ford, Ford Madox (1873–1939), English novelist, editor, and critic; one of the seminal gures in the creation of Modernism.

Hannibal (247-c. 183–81 B.C.), commander of Carthaginian forces against Rome during the Second Punic War.

Hardwick, Elizabeth (Lizzie) (b. 1916), novelist, essayist; Lowell s second wife. Lowell returned to Hardwick in the nal months of his life.

Helen Daughter of Zeus and Leda; sister of **Clytemnestra**; the most beautiful of women. Married to Menelaus, she was carried away by Paris to Troy. The Greek princes, led by **Agamemnon**, lay siege to Troy for ten years to recover her.

Jarrell, Randall (1914–1965), poct, critic, novelist. Jarrell and Lowell were studying with John Crowe Ransom when they met at Kenyon College.

Lethe River in the Underworld; souls who drank from it forgot their previous existence.

Leviathan In Jewish mythology, a sea serpent in Psalms 74:14, killed by God; in Job 41, created by God, the emblem of God s power. Melville names whales Leviathan in *Moby Dick* (ch. 104; Extracts) (1851); Hobbes uses the term to describe the State in *Leviathan* (1651).

Lowell, Amy (1874–1925), poet, biographer; distant cousin to Lowell.

Lowell, Harriet (b. 1957), Lowell s daughter.

Lowell, James Russell (1819–1891), poet, essayist, American ambassador to England; Lowell s great-granduncle.

Lowell, Robert Sheridan (b. 1971), Lowell s son.

McLean s Private psychiatric hospital outside Boston.

Medusa One of the three Gorgons, who turned to stone anything that met its gaze. The head retained its power even in death. Perseus decapitated Medusa by gazing not directly at her but into a mirror, given him by Athena (**Minerva**).

Milgate Caroline Blackwood s country house (also known as Milgate Park), near Maidstone, Kent.

Minerva Roman goddess born not from the body of a woman but directly from the head of her father, Jove (Zeus). Patron and protector of the city, of the urban arts; often pictured in armor, with **Medusa** s head on her shield; identi ed with the Greek goddess Pallas Athena.

Orestes See **Oresteia**.

Oresteia One of the narratives to which Lowell returns again and again. When the father (King Agamemnon of Mycenae) returns triumphantly from war, he is murdered by his wife (Clytemnestra), with the help of her lover and ally (Aegisthus). The son (Orestes) must avenge the murder of his father but a child must not kill its mother. With the help of his sister (Electra), he succeeds in killing Clytemnestra and her lover, but the Furies pursue him.

Orpheus Legendary poet, the music of whose lyre left the wild beasts spellbound. After he was torn to pieces by Thracian maenads, his head oating down the Hebrus still sang. See **Eurydice**.

Parker, Frank (b. 1916), painter; Lowell s classmate at St. Mark s.

Schwartz, Delmore (1913–1966), poet, short-story writer, critic.

Stafford, Jean (1915–1979), novelist, short-story writer; Lowell s first wife.

Styx The principal river of the Underworld; the dead must pass either the **Styx** or **Acheron** to reach the realm of the dead.

Tate, Allen (1899–1979), poet, critic, novelist, editor; Lowell s teacher.

Taylor, Peter (1917–1994), short-story writer, novelist, sometime poet; for two years, Lowell s roommate at Kenyon College.

Ulysses Roman name for Odysseus, hero of *The Odyssey*; his ten-year return from Troy to his wife Penelope is perhaps the dominant myth of middle-aged love in Lowell. King of Ithaca, he leaves wife and son to ght for ten years at Troy; on the ten-year journey back he has a long absorbing dalliance with Circe, who bewitches his companions; returned to Ithaca at last, he nds Penelope surrounded by suitors.

Venus The Roman goddess of love; identi ed with the Greek goddess **Aphrodite**; the mother of **Aeneas**.

Winslow, Arthur (d. 1938) mining engineer; self-made millionaire; Lowell s maternal grand-father.

Winslow, Harriet (d. 1964), Lowell s cousin; she was more to me than my mother. Lowell and Elizabeth Hardwick rst spent summers in Castine, Maine, as her guests. Before her death, strokes con ned her for years to her home in Washington.

CHRONOLOGY

1917   Robert Traill Spence Lowell IV born March 1 in Boston, the only child of Robert Traill Spence Lowell III, USN, and Charlotte Winslow Lowell. Maternal ancestors include Pilgrim leader Edward Winslow (1595–1655), Plymouth colony governor Josiah Winslow (1629–1680), and Revolutionary War general John Stark (1728–1822); paternal ancestors include author Robert Traill Spence Lowell (1816–1891), poet James Russell Lowell (1819–1891), astronomer Percival Lowell (1855–1916), Harvard president A. Lawrence Lowell (1856–1943), and poet Amy Lowell (1874–1925).

1924   Lowell family settles permanently in Boston after periods in Philadelphia and Washington, D.C.

1924–30   Brimmer School in Boston.

1930–35   St. Mark's School in Southborough, Mass. Studies with Richard Eberhart, befriends Frank Parker.

1935–37   Harvard University. Meets Anne Dick. Fight with father.

1937   Spring and summer with Allen Tate at Clarksville, Tenn.

1937–40   Kenyon College. Studies with John Crowe Ransom, befriends Randall Jarrell and Peter Taylor. Graduates *summa cum laude* in Classics.

1940   Marries writer Jean Stafford on April 2.

1940–41   Converts to Roman Catholicism. Graduate study in English at Louisiana State University with Cleanth Brooks and Robert Penn Warren.

1941–42   Move to New York. Editorial assistant at Sheed & Ward.

1942–43   Writes poetry during year's stay with Allen Tate and Caroline Gordon at Monteagle, Tenn.

1943   Refuses military induction, sentenced in October to a year and a day for violating Selective Service Act. Serves five months in West Street detention center in New York and federal prison at Danbury, Conn. Parole in Black Rock, Conn.

1944   *Land of Unlikeness*. Jean Stafford's novel *Boston Adventure*. Move to Damariscotta Mills, Maine.

1946   *Lord Weary's Castle* (Pulitzer Prize). Befriends Delmore Schwartz and John Berryman. Separates from Stafford, moves to New York.

1947   Guggenheim Fellowship and American Academy grant. Befriends William Carlos Williams and Elizabeth Bishop.

1947–48   Poetry Consultant to the Library of Congress.

1948   Divorce from Jean Stafford. Leaves Roman Catholic Church.

1948–49   Yaddo Writers' Colony.

1949   Returns to New York. Member of committee awarding the Bollingen Prize to Ezra Pound for *Pisan Cantos*. Hospitalized for mental disturbance in March. Marries writer Elizabeth Hardwick, July 28.

1950   Teaches creative writing at the University of Iowa in spring and at Kenyon College in summer. Father dies in August.

1950–53   Lowell and Hardwick live in Europe.

1951   *The Mills of the Kavanaughs* (Harriet Monroe Prize).

1952   Teaches at the Seminar in American Studies at Salzburg.

1953   Teaches at the University of Iowa. Students include W. D. Snodgrass and Philip Levine. Teaches summer session at the University of Indiana.

1954   Lectures at the University of Cincinnati. Mother dies in Italy in February. Lowell and Hardwick relocate to Boston. Manic-depressive breakdown. Begins drafting autobiography.

1954–60   Lowell and Hardwick live on Marlborough St. in Boston.

1955–60   Teaches at Boston University. Students include Sylvia Plath, Anne Sexton, and George Starbuck.

1957   Daughter Harriet Winslow Lowell born, January 4. West Coast speaking tour in March–April. Drafts "Skunk Hour" at summer home in Castine, Maine. Bi-polar illness.

1958   Hospitalized in January. Meets Ann Adden. Continues work on *Life Studies*.

1959   *Life Studies* (National Book Award, Guinness Poetry Award).

1960   Reads "For the Union Dead" at Boston Arts Festival, June 5. Move to New York. Supports Kennedy for president.

1960–70   Residence on upper West Side in Manhattan.

1961   *Imitations* (Harriet Monroe Prize, Bollingen Prize). *Phaedra*.

1962   Summer in South America.

1963–77   Teaches at Harvard (on leave 1970–72, commutes from England for one semester yearly 1973–76).

1964   *For the Union Dead*. "My Kinsman, Major Molineux" and "Benito Cereno" premiere in New York. November 1 (Obie Award). Ford grant for drama.

1965   *The Old Glory*. Protests Vietnam War by publicly declining President Johnson's invitation to the White House Festival of the Arts. *Phaedra* premieres at Wesleyan University.

1966   Defeated for Oxford Chair of Poetry by English poet Edmund Blunden. Wins Sarah Josepha Hale Award.

1967   *Near the Ocean*. Joins Allen Ginsberg, Denise Levertov, Norman Mailer, and others in March on Pentagon. *Prometheus Bound* premieres at Yale University.

1968   *The Old Glory*, revised edition. "Endecott and the Red Cross" premieres in New York, April 18. Campaigns for Eugene McCarthy in primaries, refuses to vote for president in November.

1969   *Notebook 1967–68. Prometheus Bound*. Visits Israel.

1970   *Notebook*. Visiting Fellow, All Souls' College, Oxford.

1970–76   Residence in England with writer Caroline Blackwood.

1970–72   Teaches at Essex University. Befriends Seamus Heaney.

1971   Son Robert Sheridan Lowell born to Blackwood and Lowell.

1972   Divorce from Elizabeth Hardwick, marriage to Caroline Blackwood in October.

1973   *The Dolphin* (Pulitzer Prize). *For Lizzie and Harriet. History*.

1974   Copernicus Award for lifetime achievement in poetry.

1976   *Selected Poems*.

1977   *Day by Day* (National Book Critics Circle Award). *Selected Poems*, revised edition. American Academy Medal for Literature. Returns to Elizabeth Hardwick in the United

States. Dies of heart failure in New York, September 12. Episcopalian funeral service in Boston, September 16. Burial in family plot at Dunbarton, N.H.

1978   *The Oresteia of Aeschylus* published posthumously.

1987   *Collected Prose* published posthumously.

—STEVEN GOULD AXELROD
(adapted from *The Critical Response to Robert Lowell*, 1999).

SELECTED BIBLIOGRAPHY

Anzilotti, Rolando, ed. *Robert Lowell: A Tribute.* 1979.

Axelrod, Steven Gould. *Robert Lowell: Life and Art.* 1978.

Axelrod, Steven Gould, ed. *The Critical Response to Robert Lowell.* 1999.

Axelrod, Steven Gould, and Helen Deese, eds. *Robert Lowell: A Reference Guide,* 1982.

—————*Robert Lowell: Essays on the Poetry.* 1986.

Bell, Vereen. *Robert Lowell: Nihilist as Hero.* 1983.

Berryman, John. *The Freedom of the Poet.* 1976.

Bloom, Harold, ed. *Modern Critical Views: Robert Lowell.* 1987.

Boyers, Robert, and Michael London, eds. *Robert Lowell: A Portrait of the Artist in His Time.* 1970.

Breslin, James E. B. *From Modern to Contemporary.* 1984.

Breslin, Paul. *The Psycho-Political Muse.* 1987.

Brown, Ashley. "Robert Lowell." In *Dictionary of Literary Biography.* Vol. 5, *American Poets Since World War II,* ed. Donald J. Greiner. 1980.

Cooper, Phillip. *The Autobiographical Myth of Robert Lowell.* 1970.

Corbett, William. *Literary New England.* 1993.

Cosgrave, Patrick. *The Public Poetry of Robert Lowell.* 1970.

Crick, John F. *Robert Lowell.* 1974.

Doreski, William. *Robert Lowell's Shifting Colors.* 1999.

—————. *The Years of Our Friendship: Robert Lowell and Allen Tate.* 1990.

Edwards, Thomas R. *Imagination and Power: A Study of Poetry on Public Themes.* 1971.

Estrin, Barbara L. *The American Love Lyric After Auschwitz and Hiroshima.* 2001.

Fein, Richard J. *Robert Lowell.* 1979.

von Hallberg, Robert. *American Poetry and Culture: 1945–1980.* 1985.

Hamilton, Ian. *Robert Lowell: A Biography.* 1983.

Hammer, Langdon. *Hart Crane & Allen Tate: Janus-Faced Modernism.* 1993.

Hart, Henry. *Robert Lowell and the Sublime.* 1995.

Hass, Robert. *Twentieth Century Pleasures.* 1984.

Heaney, Seamus. *The Government of the Tongue.* 1988.

—————. *Preoccupations: Selected Prose 1968–1978.* 1980.

Hecht, Anthony. *Robert Lowell: A Lecture.* 1983.

Heymann, C. David. *American Aristocracy: The Lives and Times of James Russell, Amy, and Robert Lowell.* 1980.

Hobsbaum, P. *A Reader's Guide to Robert Lowell.* 1988.

Jarrell, Randall. *Poetry and the Age.* 1953.

Kalstone, David. *Becoming a Poet.* 1989.

Longenbach, James. *Modern Poetry After Modernism.* 1997.

Mackinnon, Lachlan. *Eliot, Auden, Lowell.* 1983.

Mariani, Paul. *Lost Puritan: A Life of Robert Lowell.* 1994.

Martin, Jay. *Robert Lowell.* 1970.

Martz, William J., ed. *The Achievement of Robert Lowell: A Comprehensive Selection of His Poems with a Critical Introduction.* 1966.

Mazzaro, Jerome. *The Achievement of Robert Lowell: 1939–1959.* 1960.

———. *The Poetic Themes of Robert Lowell.* 1965.

———. *Robert Lowell and Ovid.* 2000.

Mazzaro, Jerome, ed. *Profile of Robert Lowell.* 1971.

McClatchy, J. D. *White Paper.* 1989.

Meiners, R. K. *Everything to Be Endured: An Essay on Robert Lowell and Modern Poetry.* 1970.

Miehe, Patrick K. *The Robert Lowell Papers at the Houghton Library.* 1990.

Meyers, Jeffrey. *Manic Power: Robert Lowell and His Circle.* 1987.

Meyers, Jeffrey, ed. *Robert Lowell: Interviews and Memoirs.* 1988.

Ostroff, Anthony, ed. *The Contemporary Poet as Artist and Critic.* 1964.

Parkinson, Thomas, ed. *Robert Lowell: A Collection of Critical Essays.* 1968.

Perloff, Marjorie. *The Poetic Art of Robert Lowell.* 1973.

Pinsky, Robert. *The Situation of Poetry.* 1976.

Price, Jonathan, ed. *Critics on Robert Lowell.* 1972.

Procopiow, N. *Robert Lowell: The Poet and His Critics.* 1984.

Raban, Jonathan. *The Society of the Poem.* 1971.

Raban, Jonathan, ed. *Robert Lowell's Poems: A Selection.* 1974.

Raffel, Burton. *Robert Lowell.* 1981.

Ramazani, Jahan. *Poetry of Mourning.* 1994.

Rognoni, Francesco, ed. and trans. *Giorno per giorno.* 2001. [Italian edition of *Day by Day.*]

Rudman, Mark. *Robert Lowell: An Introduction to the Poetry.* 1983.

Sacks, Peter M. *The English Elegy.* 1985.

Smith, Vivian. *The Poetry of Robert Lowell.* 1974.

Staples, Hugh B. *Robert Lowell: The First Twenty Years.* 1962.

Stuart, Sarah Payne. *My First Cousin Once Removed: Money, Madness, and the Family of Robert Lowell.* 1998.

Tillinghast, Richard. *Robert Lowell's Life and Work: Damaged Grandeur.* 1995.

Travisano, Thomas. *Midcentury Quartet.* 1999.

Vendler, Helen. *The Given and the Made.* 1995.

———. *The Music of What Happens.* 1988.

———. *Part of Nature, Part of Us.* 1980.

Vendler, Helen, ed. *The Harper American Literature.* Vol. 2. 1987.

———. *Poems, Poets, Poetry.* 1997.

Wallingford, Katharine. *Robert Lowell's Language of the Self.* 1988.

Williamson, Alan. *Introspection and Contemporary Poetry.* 1984.

———. *Pity the Monsters: The Political Vision of Robert Lowell.* 1974.

Witek, Terri. *Robert Lowell and Life Studies: Revising the Self.* 1993.

Yenser, Stephen. *Circle to Circle: The Poetry of Robert Lowell.* 1975.

ACKNOWLEDGMENTS

This book is a collaboration, not only between the editors but between the editors and the many people who offered help. DeSales Harrison did the initial research collecting magazine and book versions of each Lowell poem, constructing a labyrinthine archive of Lowell's publication history. David Gewanter prepared the final texts for publication and did the initial draft of the Notes. Frank Bidart oversaw the whole.

Saskia Hamilton profoundly affected this book by the open hand with which she offered not-as-yet-published Lowell letters. Grzegorz Kosc made important suggestions about poems in manuscript. Steven Axelrod, Dan Chiasson, Louise Glück, Peter Sacks, Lloyd Schwartz, David Stang, and Helen Vendler read all the Notes and made innumerable valuable corrections and suggestions. From the beginning Vendler insisted that this edition must have Notes. When our research failed we turned to Peg Boyers, Robert Boyers, Lawrence Buell, Jay Cantor, Elizabeth Cornejo, David Ferry, Arthur Goldhammer, Robert von Hallberg, Meredith Hoppin, Jonathan Hufstader, Rachel Jacoff, Joshua Kellar, Gail Mazur, Hope Michelson, Anthony Moore, Robert Pinsky, Robert Polito, Joel Porte, Francesco Rognoni, Tom Sleigh, G. B. Tennyson, Roger M. Travis, Jr., and Arent van Wassenaer. James Longenbach's objections and advice were important at a crucial point. Louise Glück wrote one Note.

Robert Giroux, Lowell's exemplary editor and friend, many years ago helped make this edition possible.

Jonathan Galassi's editorial advice, care, and patience have been fundamental. We have relied on his impeccably generous assistant, James Wilson. Trent Duffy, the copy editor, saved us from many errors that familiarity had made invisible. Galassi's notes in his *Eugenio Montale: Collected Poems 1920–1954* (1998) were our model and our despair.

•

Rodney Dennis, who first constructed the Lowell archive at the Houghton Library at Harvard, from the beginning aided us. This has been carried on by his successor, Leslie Morris. At the Harry Ransom Center, John Kirkpatrick and Tara Wenger helped clarify recalcitrant puzzles. We thank the Houghton Library and the Harry Ransom Humanities Research Center, The University of Texas at Austin, for permission to print material from their archives.

—F.B.
—D.G.

INDEX OF TITLES